Notation

a = capital share in national income

a = fraction of defaulting borrowers in the credit market (Chapter 9)

b = productivity of labor in producing human capital

c = individual current consumption

d = depreciation rate

e = nominal exchange rate

f = per worker production function

g = function describing the relationship between current population and future population in the Malthusian growth model

h = time available to the consumer

i = inflation rate

i^e = anticipated inflation rate

k = capital per worker

l = leisure

l = land per worker (Chapter 6)

n = labor force growth rate

p = price of housing (Chapter 9)

p = fraction of the unemployed receiving wage offers each period (Chapter 17)

q = price of credit card balances

r = real interest rate

r^* = world real interest rate

r_1 = real interest rate at which consumers can lend

r_2 = real interest rate at which consumers can borrow

s = savings rate (Chapters 6 and 7)

s = separation rate (Chapter 17)

t = tax rate (Chapter 5)

t = current lump sum tax paid by the individual (Chapter 8)

t = fraction of early consumers (Chapter 16)

u = time spent producing consumption goods

w = real wage

w^* = reservation wage

we = lifetime wealth

x = money growth rate

y = individual current income

z = total factor productivity

B = bonds issued by the government

C = aggregate consumption

CA = current account surplus

D = government deficit

E = employment

G = government expenditures

GDP = gross domestic product

GNP = gross national product

H = human capital (Chapter 7)

H = quantity of housing held by consumer (Chapter 9)

I = investment

INT = interest paid to the government

K = capital stock

KA = capital account surplus
L = quantity of land (Chapter 6)
L = loan quantity chosen by a good borrower (Chapter 9)
L = real money demand function (Chapter 11)
M = money supply
$MC(I)$ = marginal cost of investment
$MB(I)$ = marginal benefit from investment
MPC = marginal propensity to consume
MP_K = marginal product of capital
MP_N = marginal product of labor
$MRS_{x,y}$ = marginal rate of substitution of x for y.
$MRT_{x,y}$ = marginal rate of transformation of x for y.
MU_c = marginal utility of consumption
N = employment
NFP = net factor payments
NL = number not in the labor force
NX = net exports
P = price level
P^* = foreign price level
PPF = production possibilities frontier
R = nominal interest rate
S = aggregate savings
S^p = private savings
S^g = government savings
T = total taxes
$TOT_{a,b}$ = terms of trade or world price of a in terms of b
TR = aggregate transfers from the government
U = utility function (Chapter 16)
U = unemployment (Chapter 17)
V = present value of profits
$V_e(w)$ = welfare of a worker with a job paying real wage w
V_u = welfare of an unemployed worker
W = nominal wage
X = credit card balances, in real terms
Y = aggregate real income
Y^d = disposable income
Y^T = trend level of output
π = profits

Notes

- Primes denote future variables—for example, C' denotes the future level of aggregate consumption.
- A superscript "-" denotes variables for the previous period—for example, B^- are bonds acquired in the previous period in Chapter 10.
- A superscript d denotes demand, for example N^d is labor demand.
- A superscript s denotes supply, for example N^s is labor supply.
- In Chapters 6 and 7, lowercase letters are variables in per-worker terms.

Macroeconomics

Fourth Edition

STEPHEN D. WILLIAMSON

Washington University in St. Louis

Addison-Wesley

Boston   Columbus   Indianapolis   New York   San Francisco   Upper Saddle River
Amsterdam   Cape Town   Dubai   London   Madrid   Milan   Munich   Paris   Montreal   Toronto
Delhi   Mexico City   Sao Paulo   Sydney   Hong Kong   Seoul   Singapore   Taipei   Tokyo

To

Cathy, Dave, and Andy

Editor in Chief: Donna Battista
AVP/Executive Editor: David Alexander
Editorial Project Managers: Gavin Broady
  and Emma Harper
Marketing Manager: Elizabeth Averbeck
Marketing Assistant: Ian Gold
Managing Editor: Nancy Fenton
Senior Manufacturing Buyer: Carol Melville
Art Director: Elena Sidorova
Cover Designer: Brenda Carmichael

Cover Art: Peter Carroll/Getty Images
Director of Media: Susan Schoenberg
Media Producer: Angela Lee
Supplements Editor: Alison Eusden
Full-Service Project Management/Composition:
  Laserwords
Printer/Binder: Edwards Brothers Malloy
Cover Printer: Lehigh Phoenix
Text Font: Berkeley Book

Credits and acknowledgments borrowed from other sources and reproduced, with permission, in this textbook appear on appropriate page within text.

Cataloging-in-Publication Data is on file at the Library of Congress

10 9 8 7 6 5 4

ISBN 10: 0-13-208845-2
ISBN 13: 978-0-13-208845-9

CONTENTS

PART III   Economic Growth   189

PREFACE

This book follows a modern approach to macroeconomics by building macroeconomic models from microeconomic principles. As such, it is consistent with the way that macroeconomic research is conducted today.

This approach has three advantages. First, it allows deeper insights into economic growth processes and business cycles, the key topics in macroeconomics. Second, an emphasis on microeconomic foundations better integrates the study of macroeconomics with approaches that students learn in courses in microeconomics and in field courses in economics. Learning in macroeconomics and microeconomics thus becomes mutually reinforcing, and students learn more. Third, in following an approach to macroeconomics that is consistent with current macroeconomic research, students will be better prepared for advanced study in economics.

What's New in the Fourth Edition

The first three editions of *Macroeconomics* had an excellent reception in the market. In the fourth edition, I build on the strengths of the first three editions, while producing a framework for students of macroeconomics that captures all of the latest developments in macroeconomic thinking, applied to recent economic events and developments in macroeconomic policy. The financial crisis in 2008–2009, the resulting worldwide recession, and the responses of monetary and fiscal policy to these events, has introduced a rich array of macroeconomic issues that are addressed in this revision. The book has been adapted to show how existing macroeconomic theory allows us to organize our thinking about the recent financial crisis and recession. As well, new material has been added to deepen the student's knowledge of the financial market factors that were important in recent events and to examine and critically evaluate some of the unusual recent policy interventions by the U.S. government and the Federal Reserve System.

In more detail, the key changes in the Fourth Edition are:

- A new running feature has been added, "Perspectives on the Financial Crisis." In each chapter, this feature is used to show how the economic model or models in each chapter can be used to understand key features of the financial crisis and the 2008–2009 recession. Examples are "Government Expenditures and the American Recovery and Investment Act of 2009," "Asymmetric Information and Interest Rate Spreads," "The Housing Market, Collateral, and Consumption," "The Total Government Spending Multiplier: Barro Versus Romer," and "The Effects of Monetary Policy When the Nominal Interest Rate Is Zero."

- A new chapter has been added, Chapter 9: "Credit Market Imperfections: Credit Frictions, Financial Crises, and Social Security." This chapter extends the material on credit market behavior in Chapter 8 to the study of the key credit market frictions that are important to the understanding of the causes of the financial crisis and the 2008–2009 recession. Data are used to illustrate the implications of credit market frictions for consumption behavior and interest rate spreads.

- Chapter 11 (Money, Banking, Prices, and Monetary Policy) has been revised to capture in a clear and accessible way the modern theory of money demand and money supply, which models the choices of consumers and firms between currency and alternative means of payment, while integrating the behavior of banks (the suppliers of these alternative means of payment) into the approach. This framework for money demand and supply is in line with the revised emphasis in this new edition on financial factors and the role of the banking sector.

- The approach to Keynesian price/wage stickiness has been changed entirely. Chapter 13 (New Keynesian Economics: Sticky Prices) is an essentially new chapter. The model used in Chapter 13 is in line with modern approaches to Keynesian Economics, which focus on sticky prices rather than sticky wages, and dispense with the "LM curve" of traditional Keynesian analysis. The approach in Chapter 13 allows a seamless treatment of Keynesian economics, without the heavy investment required in developing the IS/LM AD/AS apparatus, as the New Keynesian model is just a special case of the model developed in Chapter 11.

- New end-of-chapter problems have been added.

- "Working with the Data" sections at the end of each chapter allow students to work with our comprehensive online database. By working through these problems, students will learn more about economic data and how to use them and will deepen their knowledge of macroeconomic theory and issues.

Structure

The text begins in Part I with an introduction and study of measurement issues. Chapter 1 describes the approach taken in the book and the key ideas that students should take away. It previews the important issues that will be addressed throughout the book, along with some recent issues in macroeconomics, and the highlights of how these will be studied. Measurement is discussed in Chapters 2 and 3, first with regard to gross domestic product, prices, savings, and wealth, and then with regard to business cycles. In Chapter 3, we develop a set of key business cycle facts that will be used throughout the book, particularly in Chapters 12 and 13 where we investigate how alternative business cycle theories fit the facts.

Our study of macroeconomic theory begins in Part II. In Chapter 4, we study the behavior of consumers and firms in detail. In the one-period model developed in Chapter 5, we capture the behavior of all consumers and all firms in the economy with a single representative consumer and a single representative firm. The one-period model is used to show how changes in government spending and total factor productivity affect aggregate output, employment, consumption, and the real wage, and we analyze how proportional income taxation matters for aggregate activity and government tax revenue.

With a basic knowledge of static macroeconomic theory from Part II, we proceed in Part III to the study of the dynamic process of economic growth. In Chapter 6 we discuss a set of economic growth facts that are then used to organize our thinking in the context of models of economic growth. The first growth model we examine is a Malthusian growth model, consistent with the late-eighteenth-century ideas of Thomas Malthus. The Malthusian model predicts well the features of economic growth in the world before the Industrial Revolution, but it does not predict the sustained growth in per capita incomes that occurred in advanced countries after 1800. The Solow growth model, which we examine next, does a good job of explaining some important observations concerning modern economic growth. Finally, Chapter 6 explains growth accounting, which is an approach to disentangling the sources of growth. In Chapter 7 we discuss income disparities across countries in light of the predictions of the Solow model, and introduce a model of endogenous growth.

In Part IV, we first use the theory of consumer and firm behavior developed in Part II to construct (in Chapter 8) a two-period model that can be used to study consumption—savings decisions and the effects of government deficits on the economy. Chapter 9 extends the two-period model to include credit market imperfections, an approach that is important for understanding the recent world financial crisis, fiscal policy, and social security. The two-period model is then further extended to include investment behavior and to address a wide range of macroeconomic issues in the real intertemporal model of Chapter 10. This model will then serve as the basis for much of what is done in the remainder of the book.

In Part V, we include monetary phenomena in the real intertemporal model of Chapter 10, so as to construct a monetary intertemporal model. This model is used in Chapter 11 to study the role of money and alternative means of payment, to examine the effects of changes in the money supply on the economy, and to study the role of monetary policy. Then, in Chapters 12 and 13, we study equilibrium theories of the business cycles as well as New Keynesian business cycle theory. These theories are compared and contrasted, and we examine how alternative business cycle theories fit the data and how they help us to understand recent business cycle behavior in the United States.

Part VI is devoted to international macroeconomics. In Chapter 14, the models of Chapters 5 and 10 are used to show what benefits accrue from international trade, how changes in the relative prices of imports and exports affect the economy, and what determines the current account surplus. Then, in Chapter 15, we show how exchange rates are determined, and we investigate the roles of fiscal and monetary policy in an open economy that trades goods and assets with the rest of the world.

Finally, Part VII examines some important topics in macroeconomics. In Chapter 16, we study in more depth the role of money in the economy, and the effects of money growth on inflation and aggregate economic activity, banking, and deposit insurance. Then, in Chapter 17, we study the determinants of unemployment and two models of unemployment: the search model and the efficiency wage model. In Chapter 18, we see how central banks can cause inflation, either because they do not correctly understand the relationship between real macroeconomic activity and inflation, or because they cannot commit themselves to a low-inflation policy. We also study in this chapter how inflation has been reduced over the last twenty-five years in the United States, and how current monetary policy exposes the U.S. economy to the risk of future inflation.

Features

Several key features enhance the learning process and illuminate critical ideas for the student. The intent is to make macroeconomic theory transparent, accessible, and relevant.

Real-World Applications   Applications to current and historical problems are emphasized throughout in three running features. The first is a set of "Theory Confronts the Data" sections, which show how macroeconomic theory comes to life in matching (or sometimes falling short of matching) the characteristics of real-world economic data. A sampling of some of these sections includes a look at whether income per capita is converging across the countries of the world, consumption smoothing and the stock market, and how news affects the stock market and investment expenditures.

The second running feature is a series of "Macroeconomics in Action" boxes. These real-world applications relating directly to the theory encapsulate ideas from front-line research in macroeconomics and the history of economic thought, and they aid students in understanding the core material. For example, some of the subjects examined in these boxes are the pitfalls of macroeconomic forecasting, Henry Ford and technological change, business cycle models and Great Depression, and observed stickiness in nominal prices.

The third running feature, new to this edition, is a set of boxes on "Perspectives on the Financial Crisis." These boxes are aimed at using the theoretical frameworks in this book to organize our thinking about the recent world financial crisis and its implications for the 2008–2009 recession. Issues examined in these boxes include the financial causes of the 2008–2009 recession, working through credit market frictions, the housing market, and interest rate spreads. As well, we examine fiscal policy responses to the financial crisis and the 2008–2009 recession, by examining the role of the "multiplier" in policy discussions, and the implications for the government deficit and level of government debt. Further, we study aspects of recent monetary policy, including how monetary policy works when the nominal interest rate is close to zero and timing issues related to monetary policy versus fiscal policy.

Art Program   Graphs and charts are plentiful in this book, as visual representations of macroeconomic models that can be manipulated to derive important results and for showing the key features of important macro data in applications. To aid the student, graphs and charts use a consistent two-color system that encodes the meaning of particular elements in graphs and of shifts in curves.

End-of-Chapter Summary and List of Key Terms   Each chapter wraps up with a bullet-point summary of the key ideas contained in the chapter, followed by a glossary of the chapter's key terms. The key terms are listed in the order in which they appear in the chapter, and they are highlighted in bold typeface where they first appear.

Questions for Review   These questions are intended as self-tests for students after they have finished reading the chapter material. The questions relate directly to ideas and facts covered in the chapter, and answering them will be straightforward if the student has read and comprehended the chapter material.

Problems   The end-of-chapter problems will help the student in learning the material and applying the macroeconomic models developed in the chapter. These problems are intended to be challenging and thought-provoking.

"Working with the Data" Problems   These problems guide the student in making use of the database that can be accessed online from the website accompanying this text at www.aw-bc.com/williamson. The database is a comprehensive set of macroeconomic data, which can be used to understand the chapter material and to gain a deeper knowledge of macroeconomic data and phenomena.

Notation   For easy reference, definitions of all variables used in the text are contained on the end papers.

Mathematics and Mathematical Appendix   In the body of the text, the analysis is mainly graphical, with some knowledge of basic algebra required; calculus is not used. However, for students and instructors who desire a more rigorous treatment of the material in the text, a mathematical appendix develops the key models and results more formally, assuming a basic knowledge of calculus and the fundamentals of mathematical economics. The Mathematical Appendix also contains problems on this more advanced material.

Flexibility

This book was written to be user-friendly for instructors with different preferences and with different time allocations. The core material that is recommended for all instructors is the following:

Chapter 1. Introduction
Chapter 2. Measurement
Chapter 3. Business Cycle Measurement
Chapter 4. Consumer and Firm Behavior: The Work—Leisure Decision and Profit Maximization
Chapter 5. A Closed-Economy One-Period Macroeconomic Model
Chapter 8. A Two-Period Model: The Consumption–Savings Decision and Credit Markets
Chapter 10. A Real Intertemporal Model with Investment

Some instructors find measurement issues uninteresting and may choose to omit parts of Chapter 2, although at the minimum instructors should cover the key national income accounting identities. Parts of Chapter 3 can be omitted if the instructor chooses not to emphasize business cycles, but there are some important concepts introduced here that are generally useful in later chapters, such as the meaning of correlation and how to read scatter plots and time series plots.

Chapters 6 and 7 introduce economic growth at an early stage, in line with a modern role of growth theory in macroeconomics. However, Chapters 6 and 7 are essentially self-contained, and nothing is lost from leaving growth until later in the sequence—for example, after the business cycle material in Chapters 12 and 13. Although the text has an emphasis on microfoundations, Keynesian analysis receives a balanced treatment. For example, we study a Keynesian coordination failure model in Chapter 12, and examine a New Keynesian sticky price model in Chapter 13. Keynesian economics is fully integrated with equilibrium approaches to business cycle analysis, and the student does not need to learn a separate modeling framework; for example, the New Keynesian sticky price model is simply a special case of the general modeling framework developed in Chapter 11. Those instructors who choose to ignore Keynesian analysis can do so without any difficulty. Instructors can choose to emphasize economic growth or business cycle analysis, or they can give their course an international focus. As well, it is possible to deemphasize monetary factors. As a guide, the text can be adapted as follows:

Focus on Equilibrium Models. Omit Chapter 13 (New Keynesian Economics: Sticky Prices).
Focus on Economic Growth. Include Chapters 6 and 7, and consider dropping Chapters 12, 13, and 14, depending on time available.
Focus on Business Cycles. Drop Chapter 6 and 7, and include Chapters 11, 12, and 13.
International Focus. Chapters 14 and 15 can be moved up in the sequence. Chapter 14 can follow Chapter 10, and Chapter 15 can follow Chapter 11.
Advanced Mathematical Treatment. Add material as desired from the Mathematical Appendix.

Supplements

The following materials that accompany the main text will enrich the intermediate macroeconomics course for instructors and students alike.

Instructor's Manual/Test Item File   Written by Christian Zimmermann of the University of Connecticut, the Instructor's Manual/Test Item File provides strong instructor support. The

Instructor's Manual portion contains sections on Teaching Goals, which give an aerial view of the chapters; classroom discussion topics, which explore lecture-launching ideas and questions; chapter outlines; and solutions to all Questions for Review and Problems found in the text. The Test Item File portion contains multiple-choice questions and answers. The Test Item File is also available in Test Generator Software (TestGen-EQ with QuizMaster-EQ). Fully networkable, this software is available for Windows and Macintosh. TestGen-EQ's friendly graphical interface enables instructors to easily view, edit, and add questions; export questions to create tests; and print tests in a variety of fonts and forms. Search and sort features let the instructor quickly locate questions and arrange them in a preferred order. QuizMaster-EQ automatically grades the exams, stores results on a disk, and allows the instructor to view or print a variety of reports. The Instructor's Manual and Test Item File can be found on the instructor's portion of the website accompanying this book at www.pearsonhighered.com/williamson.

Study Guide   Prepared by John Stinespring of the University of Tampa, the Study Guide contains true/false questions, short-answer questions, and graphic/numerical questions, with complete answers—many presented as worked solutions.

PowerPoint Files   Prepared by Stephen Williamson, the PowerPoints highlight text learning objectives and key topics and serve as an excellent aid in classroom presentations and lectures.

Acknowledgments

Special thanks go to Donna Battista, David Alexander, Nancy Fenton, Elizabeth Averbeck and the extended team at Pearson Addison-Wesley who provided so much help and encouragement. I am also indebted to Dave Andolfatto, Scott Baier, Ken Beauchemin, Edward Kutsoati, Kuhong Kim, Young Sik Kim, Mike Loewy, B. Ravikumar, Ping Wang, and Bradley Wilson, who used early versions of the manuscript in their classes. Key critical input was also provided by the following reviewers, who helped immensely in improving the manuscript: Terry Alexander, Iowa State University; Alaa AlShawa, University of Western Ontario; David Aschauer, Bates College; Irasema Alonso, University of Rochester; David Andolfatto, Simon Fraser University; Scott Baier, Clemson University; Ken Beauchemin, State University of New York at Albany; Joydeep Bhattacharya, Iowa State University; Michael Binder, University of Maryland; Marco Cagetti, University of Virginia; Mustafa Caglayan, University of Liverpool; Gabriele Camera, Purdue University; Leo Chan, University of Kansas; Troy Davig, College of William and Mary; Matthias Doepke, UCLA; Ayse Y. Evrensel, Portland State University; Timothy Fuerst, Bowling Green State University; Lisa Geib-Gundersen, University of Maryland; John Graham, Rutgers University; Yu Hsing, Southeastern Louisiana University; Petur O. Jonsson, Fayetteville State University; Bryce Kanago, University of Northern Iowa; George Karras, University of Illinois; John Knowles, University of Pennsylvania; Hsien-Feng Lee, Taiwan University; Michael Loewy, University of South Florida; Kathryn Marshall, The Ohio State University; Steve McCafferty, The Ohio State University; Oliver Morand, University of Connecticut; Douglas Morgan, University of California, Santa Barbara; Giuseppe Moscarini, Yale University; Daniel Mulino, doctoral candidate, Yale University; Liwa Rachel Ngai, London School of Economics; Christopher Otrok, University of Virginia; Stephen Parente, University of Illinois at Urbana-Champaign; Prosper Raynold, Miami University; Kevin Reffett, Arizona State University; Robert J. Rossana, Wayne State University; Thomas Tallarini, Carnegie Mellon University; Paul Wachtel, Stern School of Business, New York University; Ping Wang, Vanderbilt University; Bradley Wilson, University of Alabama; Paul Zak, Claremont Graduate University; and Christian Zimmermann, University of Connecticut.

I also wish to thank the economists who worked on the supplements that accompany this text and who did such a fine job and John Stinespring of the University of Tampa (Study Guide author). Finally, I wish to thank those economists who specifically reviewed material on economic growth for this edition: Kenneth Beauchemin, State University of New York at Albany; William Blankenau, Kansas State University; Matthias Doepke, UCLA; Igor Livshits, University of Western Ontario; Christopher Otrok, University of Virginia; and Stephen Parente, University of Illinois at Urbana-Champaign.

About the Author

Stephen Williamson is the Robert S. Brookings Distinguished Professor in Arts and Sciences in the Department of Economics, Washington University in St. Louis and is a Visiting Scholar at the Federal Reserve Bank of Richmond and a Research Fellow at the Federal Reserve Bank of St. Louis. He received a B.Sc. in Mathematics and an M.A. in Economics from Queen's University in Kingston, Canada, and his Ph.D. from the University of Wisconsin–Madison. He has held academic positions at Queen's University, the University of Western Ontario, and the University of Iowa, and has worked as an economist at the Federal Reserve Bank of Minneapolis and the Bank of Canada. Professor Williamson has been an academic visitor at the Federal Reserve Banks of Atlanta, Cleveland, Kansas City, Minneapolis, New York, Philadelphia, the Bank of Canada, and the Board of Governors of the Federal Reserve System. He has also been a long-term visitor at the London School of Economics; the University of Edinburgh; Tilburg University, the Netherlands; Victoria University of Wellington, New Zealand; Seoul National University; Hong Kong University; and the University of Sydney. Professor Williamson has published scholarly articles in the *American Economic Review,* the *Journal of Political Economy,* the *Quarterly Journal of Economics,* the *Review of Economic Studies,* the *Journal of Economic Theory,* and the *Journal of Monetary Economics,* among other prestigious economics journals.

PART I

Introduction and Measurement Issues

Part I contains an introduction to macroeconomic analysis and a description of the approach in this text of building useful macroeconomic models based on microeconomic principles. We discuss the key ideas that are analyzed in the rest of this book as well as some current issues in macroeconomics. Then, to lay a foundation for what is done later, we explore how the key variables relating to macroeconomic theory are measured in practice. Finally, we analyze the key empirical facts concerning business cycles. The macroeconomic theory developed in Parts II to VII is aimed at understanding the key ideas and issues discussed in the introduction and in showing the successes and failures of theory in matching key empirical facts.

chapter 1

Introduction

This chapter frames the approach to macroeconomics that we take in this book, and it foreshadows the basic macroeconomic ideas and issues that we develop in later chapters. We first discuss what macroeconomics is, and we then go on to look at the two phenomena that are of primary interest to macroeconomists, economic growth and business cycles, in terms of post–1900 U.S. economic history. Then, we explain the approach this book takes—building macroeconomic models with microeconomic principles as a foundation—and discuss the issue of disagreement in macroeconomics. Finally, we explore the key lessons that we learn from macroeconomic theory, and we discuss how macroeconomics helps us understand recent and current issues.

What Is Macroeconomics?

Macroeconomists are motivated by large questions and by issues that affect many people and many nations of the world. Why are some countries exceedingly rich while others are exceedingly poor? Why are most Americans so much better off than their parents and grandparents? Why are there fluctuations in aggregate economic activity? What causes inflation? Why is there unemployment?

Macroeconomics is the study of the behavior of large collections of economic agents. It focuses on the aggregate behavior of consumers and firms, the behavior of governments, the overall level of economic activity in individual countries, the economic interactions among nations, and the effects of fiscal and monetary policy. Macroeconomics is distinct from microeconomics in that it deals with the overall effects on economies of the choices that all economic agents make, rather than on the choices of individual consumers or firms. Since the 1970s, however, the distinction between microeconomics and macroeconomics has blurred in that microeconomists and macroeconomists now use much the same kinds of tools. That is, the **economic models** that macroeconomists use, consisting of descriptions of consumers and firms, their objectives and constraints, and how they interact, are built up from microeconomic principles, and these models are typically analyzed and fit to data using methods similar to those used by microeconomists. What continues to make macroeconomics distinct, though, is the issues it focuses on, particularly **long-run growth** and **business cycles.** Long-run growth refers to the increase in a nation's productive capacity and average standard of living that occurs over a long period of time, whereas business cycles are the short-run ups and downs, or booms and recessions, in aggregate economic activity.

The approach in this book is consistently to build up macroeconomic analysis from microeconomic principles. There is some effort required in taking this type of approach, but the effort is well worth it. The result is that you will understand better how the economy works and how to improve it.

Gross Domestic Product, Economic Growth, and Business Cycles

To begin our study of macroeconomic phenomena, we must first understand what facts we are trying to explain. The most basic set of facts in macroeconomics has to do with the behavior of aggregate economic activity over time. One measure of aggregate economic activity is **gross domestic product (GDP)**, which is the quantity of goods and services produced within a country's borders during some specified period of time. GDP also represents the quantity of income earned by those contributing to domestic output. In Figure 1.1 we show real GDP per capita for the United States for the period 1900–2008. This is a measure of aggregate output that adjusts for inflation and population growth, and the unit of measure is thousands of 2000 dollars per person.

The first observation we can make concerning Figure 1.1 is that there has been sustained growth in per capita GDP during the period 1900–2008. In 1900, the average income for an American was $4,248 (2000 dollars), and this grew to $38,189 (2000 dollars) in 2008. Thus, the average American became about nine times richer in real terms over the course of 108 years, which is quite remarkable! The second important observation from Figure 1.1 is that, while growth in per capita real GDP was sustained over long periods of time in the United States during the period 1900–2008, this growth was certainly not steady. Growth was higher at some times than at others, and there were periods over which per capita real GDP declined. These fluctuations in economic growth are business cycles.

Two key, although unusual, business cycle events in U.S. economic history that show up in Figure 1.1 are the Great Depression and World War II, and these events dwarf any other twentieth-century business cycle events in the United States in terms of the magnitude of the short-run change in economic growth. During the Great Depression, real GDP per capita dropped from a peak of $7,105 (2000 dollars) per person in 1929 to a low of $5,056 (2000 dollars) per person in 1933, a decline of about 29%. At the peak of war production in 1944, GDP had risen to $13,053 (2000 dollars) per person, an increase of 158% from 1933. These wild gyrations in aggregate economic activity over a fifteen-year period are as phenomenal, and certainly every bit as interesting, as the long-run sustained growth in per capita GDP that occurred from 1900 to 2008. In addition to the Great Depression and World War II, Figure 1.1 shows other business cycle upturns and downturns in the growth of per capita real GDP in the United States that, although less dramatic than the Great Depression or World War II, represent important macroeconomic events in U.S. history.

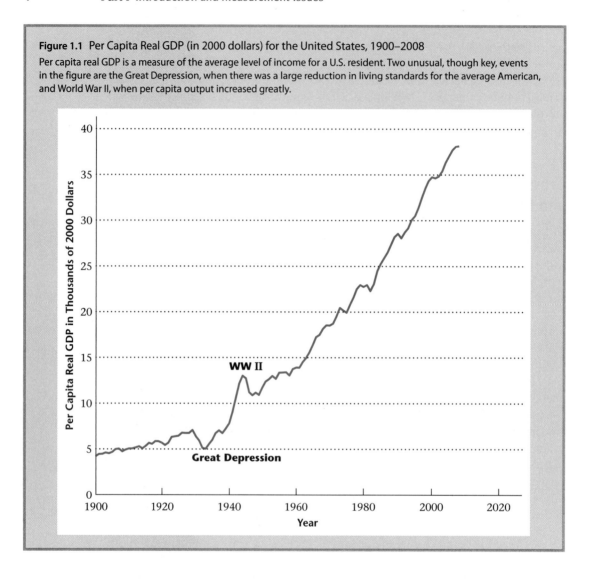

Figure 1.1 Per Capita Real GDP (in 2000 dollars) for the United States, 1900–2008

Per capita real GDP is a measure of the average level of income for a U.S. resident. Two unusual, though key, events in the figure are the Great Depression, when there was a large reduction in living standards for the average American, and World War II, when per capita output increased greatly.

Figure 1.1, thus, raises the following fundamental macroeconomic questions, which motivate much of the material in this book:

1. What causes sustained economic growth?
2. Could economic growth continue indefinitely, or is there some limit to growth?
3. Is there anything that governments can or should do to alter the rate of economic growth?
4. What causes business cycles?
5. Could the dramatic decreases and increases in economic growth that occurred during the Great Depression and World War II be repeated?
6. Should governments act to smooth business cycles?

In analyzing economic data to study economic growth and business cycles, it often proves useful to transform the data in various ways, so as to obtain sharper insights. For economic time series that exhibit growth, such as per capita real GDP in Figure 1.1, a useful transformation is to take the natural logarithm of the time series. To show why this is useful, suppose that y_t is an observation on an economic time series in period t; for example, y_t could represent per capita real GDP in year t, where $t = 1900, 1901, 1902$, etc. Then, the growth rate from period $t - 1$ to period t in y_t can be denoted by g_t, where

$$g_t = \frac{y_t}{y_{t-1}} - 1.$$

Now, if x is a small number, then $\ln(1 + x) \approx x$, that is, the natural logarithm of $1 + x$ is approximately equal to x. Therefore, if g_t is small,

$$\ln(1 + g_t) \approx g_t,$$

or

$$\ln\left(\frac{y_t}{y_{t-1}}\right) \approx g_t,$$

or

$$\ln y_t - \ln y_{t-1} \approx g_t.$$

Because $\ln y_t - \ln y_{t-1}$ is the slope of the graph of the natural logarithm of y_t between periods $t - 1$ and t, then the slope of the graph of the natural logarithm of a time series y_t is a good approximation to the growth rate of y_t when the growth rate is small.

In Figure 1.2 we graph the natural logarithm of real per capita GDP in the United States for the period 1900–2008. As explained above, the slope of the graph is a good approximation to the growth rate of real per capita GDP, so that changes in the slope (e.g., when there is a slight increase in the slope of the graph in the 1950s and 1960s) represent changes in the growth rate of real per capita GDP. It is striking that in Figure 1.2, except for the Great Depression and World War II, a straight line would fit the graph quite well. That is, over the period 1900–2008 (again, except for the Great Depression and World War II), growth in per capita real GDP has been "roughly" constant at about 2.1% per year.

A second useful transformation to carry out on an economic time series is to separate the series into two components: the growth or **trend** component and the business cycle component. For example, the business cycle component of real per capita GDP can be captured as the deviations of real per capita GDP from a smooth trend fit to the data. In Figure 1.3 we show the trend in the natural log of real per capita GDP as a colored line,[1] while the natural log of actual real per capita GDP is the black line. We then define the business cycle component of the natural log of real per capita

---

[1]Trend GDP was computed using a Hodrick-Prescott filter, as in E. Prescott, 1986. "Theory Ahead of Business Cycle Measurement," *Federal Reserve Bank of Minneapolis Quarterly Review,* Fall.

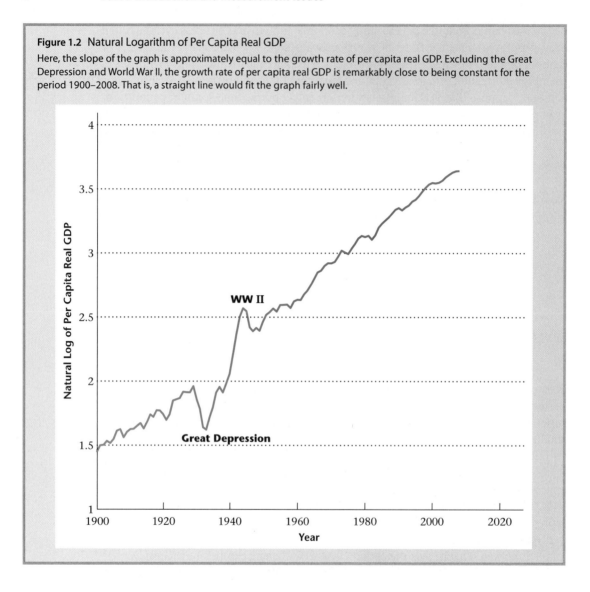

Figure 1.2 Natural Logarithm of Per Capita Real GDP

Here, the slope of the graph is approximately equal to the growth rate of per capita real GDP. Excluding the Great Depression and World War II, the growth rate of per capita real GDP is remarkably close to being constant for the period 1900–2008. That is, a straight line would fit the graph fairly well.

GDP to be the difference between the black line and the colored line in Figure 1.3. The logic behind this decomposition of real per capita GDP into trend and business cycle components is that it is often simpler and more productive to consider separately the theory that explains trend growth and the theory that explains business cycles, which are the deviations from trend.

In Figure 1.4 we show only the percentage deviations from trend in real per capita GDP. The Great Depression and World War II represent enormous deviations from trend in real per capita GDP relative to anything else during the time period in the figure. During the Great Depression the percentage deviation from trend in real per capita GDP was close to −20%, whereas the percentage deviation from trend was about 20% during World War II.

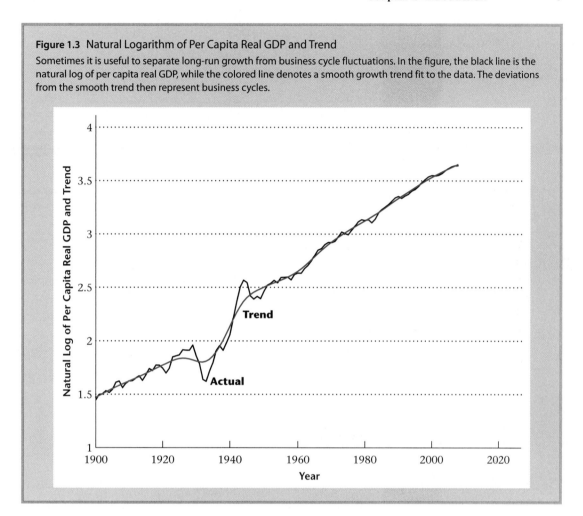

Figure 1.3 Natural Logarithm of Per Capita Real GDP and Trend

Sometimes it is useful to separate long-run growth from business cycle fluctuations. In the figure, the black line is the natural log of per capita real GDP, while the colored line denotes a smooth growth trend fit to the data. The deviations from the smooth trend then represent business cycles.

In the period after World War II, which is the focus of most business cycle analysis, the deviations from trend in real per capita GDP are at most about ±5%.[2]

Macroeconomic Models

Economics is a scientific pursuit involving the formulation and refinement of theories that can help us better understand how economies work and how they can be improved. In some sciences, such as chemistry and physics, theories are tested through laboratory experimentation. In economics, experimentation is a new and growing activity, but for

---

[2]The extremely large deviation from trend in real per capita GNP in the late 1920s is principally a statistical artifact of the particular detrending procedure used here, which is akin to drawing a smooth curve through the time series. The presence of the Great Depression forces the growth rate in the trend to decrease long before the Great Depression actually occurs.

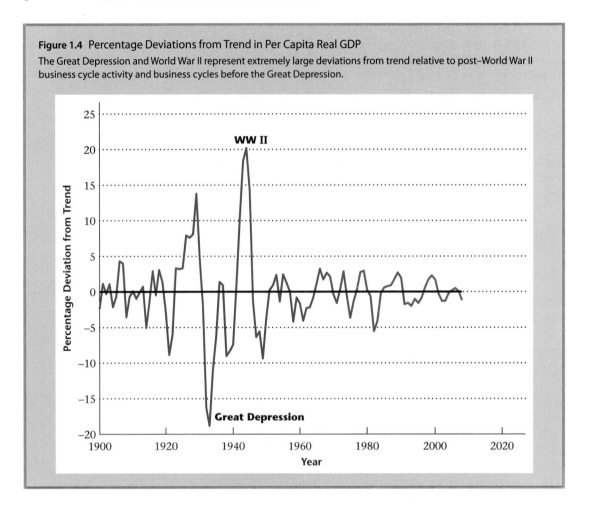

Figure 1.4 Percentage Deviations from Trend in Per Capita Real GDP

The Great Depression and World War II represent extremely large deviations from trend relative to post–World War II business cycle activity and business cycles before the Great Depression.

most economic theories experimental verification is simply impossible. For example, suppose an economist constructs a theory that implies that U.S. output would drop by half if there were no banks in the United States. To evaluate this theory, we could shut down all U.S. banks for a year to see what would happen. Of course, we know in advance that banks play a very important role in helping the U.S. economy function efficiently and that shutting them down for a year would likely cause significant irreparable damage. It is extremely unlikely, therefore, that the experiment would be carried out. In macroeconomics, most experiments that could be informative are simply too costly to carry out, and in this respect macroeconomics is much like meteorology or astronomy. In predicting the weather or how planets move in space, meteorologists and astronomers rely on **models**, which are artificial devices that can replicate the behavior of real weather systems or planetary systems, as the case may be.

Just like researchers in meteorology or astronomy, macroeconomists use models, which in our case are organized structures to explain long-run economic growth, why there are business cycles, and what role economic policy should play in the macroeconomy. All economic models are abstractions. They are not completely accurate descriptions of the world, nor are they intended to be. The purpose of an economic model is to capture the essential features of the world needed for analyzing a particular economic problem. To be useful then, a model must be simple, and simplicity requires that we leave out some "realistic" features of actual economies. For example, a roadmap is a model of a part of the earth's surface, and it is constructed with a particular purpose in mind, to help motorists guide themselves through the road system from one point to another. A roadmap is hardly a realistic depiction of the earth's surface, as it does not capture the curvature of the earth, and it does not typically include a great deal of information on topography, climate, and vegetation. However, this does not limit the map's usefulness; a roadmap serves the purpose for which it was constructed, and it does so without a lot of extraneous information.

To be specific, the basic structure of a macroeconomic model is a description of the following features:

1. The consumers and firms that interact in the economy.
2. The set of goods that consumers wish to consume.
3. Consumers' preferences over goods.
4. The technology available to firms for producing goods.
5. The resources available.

In this book, the descriptions of the above five features of any particular macroeconomic model are provided in mathematical and graphical terms.

Once we have a description of the main economic actors in a model economy (the consumers and firms), the goods consumers want, and the technology available to firms for producing goods from available resources, we want to then use the model to make predictions. This step requires that we specify two additional features of the model. First, we need to know what the goals of the consumers and firms in the model are. How do consumers and firms behave given the environment they live in? In all the models we use in this book, we assume that consumers and firms **optimize**, that is, they do the best they can given the constraints they face. Second, we must specify how consistency is achieved in terms of the actions of consumers and firms. In economic models, this means that the economy must be in **equilibrium**. Several different concepts of equilibrium are used in economic models, but the one that we use almost universally in this book is **competitive equilibrium**. In a competitive equilibrium, we assume that goods are bought and sold on markets in which consumers and firms are price-takers; they behave as if their actions have no effect on market prices. The economy is in equilibrium when market prices are such that the quantity of each good offered for sale (quantity supplied) is equal to the quantity that economic agents want to buy (quantity demanded) in each market.

Once we have a working economic model, with a specification of the economic environment, optimizing firms and consumers, and a notion of equilibrium, we can then begin to ask the model questions.[3] One way to think of this process is that the economic

---

[3]The following description of macroeconomic science is similar to that provided by Robert Lucas in "Methods and Problems in Business Cycle Theory," reprinted in *Studies in Business Cycle Theory,* 1981, MIT Press, pp. 271–296.

model is an experimental apparatus, and we want to attempt to run experiments using this apparatus. Typically, we begin by running experiments for which we know the answers. For example, suppose that we build an economic model so that we can study economic growth. The first experiment we might like to run is to determine, by working through the mathematics of the model, using graphical analysis, or running the model on a computer, whether in fact the model economy will grow. Further, will it grow in a manner that comes close to matching the data? If it does not, then we want to ask why and to determine whether it would be a good idea to refine the model in some way or to abandon it altogether and start over.

Ultimately, once we are satisfied that a model reasonably and accurately captures the economic phenomenon in which we are interested, we can start running experiments on the model for which we do not know the answers. An experiment we might want to conduct with the economic growth model is to ask, for example, how historical growth performance would have differed in the United States had the level of government spending been higher. Would aggregate economic activity have grown at a higher or a lower rate? How would this have affected the consumption of goods? Would economic welfare have been higher or lower?

In keeping with the principle that models should be simple and designed specifically for the problem at hand, we do not stick to a single all-purpose model in this book. Instead, we use an array of different models for different purposes, although these models share a common approach and some of the same principal building blocks. For example, sometimes it proves useful to build models that do not include international trade, macroeconomic growth, or the use of money in economic exchange, whereas at other times it is crucially important for the issue at hand that we explicitly model one, two, or perhaps all of these features.

Generally, macroeconomic research is a process whereby we continually attempt to develop better models, along with better methods for analyzing those models. Economic models continue to evolve in a way that helps us better understand the economic forces that shape the world in which we live, so that we can promote economic policies that make society better off.

Microeconomic Principles

This book emphasizes building macroeconomic models on sound microeconomic principles. Because the macroeconomy consists of many consumers and firms, each making decisions at the micro level, macroeconomic behavior is the sum of many microeconomic decisions. It is not immediately obvious, however, that the best way to construct a macroeconomic model is to work our way up from decision making at the microeconomic level. In physics, for example, there is often no loss in ignoring micro behavior. If I throw a brick from the top of a five-story building, and if I know the force that I exert on the brick and the force of gravity on the brick, then Newtonian physics does a very accurate job of predicting when and where the brick lands. However, Newtonian physics ignores micro behavior, which in this case is the behavior of the molecules in the brick.

Why is it that there may be no loss in ignoring the behavior of molecules in a brick, but that ignoring the microeconomic behavior of consumers and firms when doing macroeconomics could be devastating? Throwing a brick from a building does not affect the behavior of the molecules within the brick in any way that would significantly change the trajectory of the brick. Changes in government policy, however, generally alter the behavior of consumers and firms in ways that significantly affect the behavior of the economy as a whole. Any change in government policy effectively alters the features of the economic environment in which consumers and firms must make their decisions. To confidently predict the effects of a policy change on aggregate behavior, we must analyze how the change in policy affects individual consumers and firms. For example, if the federal government changes the income tax rate, and we are interested in the macroeconomic effects of this policy change, the most productive approach is first to use microeconomic principles to determine how a change in the tax rate affects an individual consumer's labor supply and consumption decisions, based on optimizing behavior. Then, we can aggregate these decisions to arrive at a conclusion that is consistent with how the individuals in the economy behave.

Macroeconomists were not always sympathetic to the notion that macro models should be microeconomically sound. Indeed, before the **rational expectations revolution** in the 1970s, which generally introduced more microeconomics into macroeconomics, most macroeconomists worked with models that did not have solid microeconomic foundations, although there were some exceptions.[4] The argument that macroeconomic policy analysis can be done in a sensible way only if microeconomic behavior is taken seriously was persuasively expressed by Robert E. Lucas, Jr. in a journal article published in 1976.[5] This argument is often referred to as the **Lucas critique**.

Disagreement in Macroeconomics

There is little disagreement in macroeconomics concerning the general approach to be taken to construct models of economic growth. The Solow growth model,[6] studied in Chapters 6 and 7, is a widely accepted framework for understanding the economic growth process, and **endogenous growth models**, which model the economic mechanism determining the rate of economic growth and are covered in Chapter 7, have been well received by most macroeconomists. This is not to say that disagreement has been absent from discussions of economic growth in macroeconomics, only that the disagreement has not generally been over basic approaches to modeling growth.

The study of business cycles in macroeconomics, however, is another story. As it turns out, there is much controversy among macroeconomists concerning business cycle theory and the role of the government in smoothing business cycles over time. In Chapters 12 and 13 we study four competing theories of the business cycle.

The first theory is **real business cycle theory**, initiated by Edward Prescott and Finn Kydland in the early 1980s.[7] Real business cycle theory implies that government policy

---

[4]See M. Friedman, 1968. "The Role of Monetary Policy," *American Economic Review* 58, 1–17.

[5]See R.E. Lucas, 1976. "Econometric Policy Evaluation: A Critique," *Carnegie-Rochester Conference Series on Public Policy* 1, 19–46.

[6]See R. Solow, 1956. "A Contribution to the Theory of Economic Growth," *Quarterly Journal of Economics* 70, 65–94.

[7]F. Kydland and E. Prescott, 1982. "Time to Build and Aggregate Fluctuations," *Econometrica* 50, 1345–1370.

aimed at smoothing business cycles is at best ineffective and at worst detrimental to the economy's performance. Real business cycle theorists argue that business cycles are caused primarily by shocks to the economy's technological ability to produce goods and services. The second approach is **market segmentation theory**. Early work on segmented markets models of money was done by Sanford Grossman and Laurence Weiss,[8] and by Julio Rotemberg,[9] with later important breakthroughs by Robert Lucas and Timothy Fuerst.[10] In market segmentation theory, shocks to the money supply have their first-round effects in financial markets, in part acting to relax financial constraints faced by firms, inducing them to hire more labor. Market segmentation theory implies that monetary policy can cause the aggregate economy to fluctuate in undesirable ways, but the theory also implies some potential benefits from active monetary policy. The third business cycle theory we study is the **Keynesian coordination failure theory**, which is one modern approach to **Keynesian** ideas. Keynesian macroeconomists are influenced by a line of work dating back to J. M. Keynes's *General Theory of Employment, Interest, and Money* published in 1936. Keynesians argue that the government can and should play an active role in smoothing out business cycles. In the coordination failure approach, business cycles can be caused by waves of self-fulfilling optimism and pessimism, and government policy may be effective in smoothing out business cycles.

All three of the aforementioned business cycle theories, covered in Chapter 12, are equilibrium models, that is, all prices and wages are perfectly flexible and move so that the quantity supplied equals the quantity demanded in each market. In the fourth theory we study, in Chapter 13, business cycles arise because prices are sufficiently inflexible that supply is not always equal to demand in all markets. This is a New Keynesian model, consistent with the ideas in Keynes General Theory, but incorporating recent developments in Keynesian economics.

This book seeks to take an objective view of all these competing theories of the business cycle. In Chapters 12 and 13, we study the key features of each of the above four theories of the business cycle, and we evaluate the theories in terms of how their predictions match the data.

What Do We Learn from Macroeconomic Analysis?

At this stage, it is useful to map out some of the basic insights that can be learned from macroeconomic analysis and that we develop in the remainder of this book. These are the following:

1. *What is produced and consumed in the economy is determined jointly by the economy's productive capacity and the preferences of consumers.*   In Chapters 4 and 5, we

[8]Grossman, S. and Weiss, L. 1983. "A Transactions-Based Model of the Monetary Transmission Mechanism," American Economic Review 73, 871–880.
[9]Rotemberg, J. 1984. "A Monetary Equilibrium Model with Transactions Costs," *Journal of Political Economy* 92, 40–58.
[10]See Lucas, R. 1990. "Liquidity and Interest Rates," *Journal of Economic Theory* 50, 237–264 and Fuerst, T. 1992. "Liquidity, Loanable Funds, and Real Activity," *Journal of Monetary Economics* 29, 3–24.

develop a one-period model of the economy, which specifies the technology for producing goods from available resources, the preferences of consumers over goods, and how optimizing consumers and firms come together in competitive markets to determine what is produced and consumed.

2. *In free market economies, there are strong forces that tend to produce socially efficient economic outcomes.* Social inefficiencies can arise, but they should be considered unusual. The notion that an unregulated economy peopled by selfish individuals could result in a socially efficient state of affairs is surprising, and this idea goes back at least as far as Adam Smith's *Wealth of Nations,* written in the eighteenth century. In Chapter 5, we show this result in our one-period model, and we explain the circumstances under which social inefficiencies can arise in practice.

3. *Improvements in a country's standard of living are brought about in the long run by technological progress.* In Chapters 6 and 7, we study the Solow growth model (along with the Malthusian model of economic growth and an endogenous growth model), which gives us a framework for understanding the forces that account for growth. This model shows that growth in aggregate output can be produced by growth in a country's capital stock, growth in the labor force, and technological progress. In the long run, however, growth in the standard of living of the average person comes to a stop unless there are continuous technological improvements. Thus, economic well-being ultimately cannot be improved simply by constructing more machines and buildings; economic progress depends on continuing advances in knowledge.

4. *A tax cut is not a free lunch.* When the government reduces taxes, this increases current incomes in the private sector, and it may seem that this implies that people are wealthier and may want to spend more. However, if the government reduces taxes and holds its spending constant, it must borrow more, and the government will have to increase taxes in the future to pay off this higher debt. Thus, future incomes in the private sector must fall. In Chapter 8, we show that there are circumstances under which a current tax cut has no effects whatsoever; the private sector is no wealthier, and there is no change in aggregate economic activity.

5. *Credit markets and banks play key roles in the macroeconomy.* The advocates of some mainstream economic theories—including theories of economic growth, real business cycle theory, and New Keynesian economics—have sometimes argued that consideration of credit markets, and the underlying frictions that make credit markets and banks work imperfectly, are safely ignored. Recent macroeconomic events, culminating in the world financial crisis in 2008–2009, have shown that this approach is hazardous. However, some standard economic tools can be used to make sense out of these recent macroeonomic events, and to analyze the appropriate fiscal and monetary policy responses to the financial crisis. In Chapter 9, we analyze credit market imperfections and show how they matter for the financial crisis, and we study some of the aggregate implications of the financial crisis in Chapters 10 through 13, along with some issues related to banking in Chapter 16.

6. *What consumers and firms anticipate for the future has an important bearing on current macroeconomic events.* In Chapters 8, 9, and 10, we consider two-period

models in which consumers and firms make dynamic decisions; consumers save for future consumption needs, and firms invest in plant and equipment so as to produce more in the future. If consumers anticipate, for example, that their future incomes will be high, they want to save less in the present and consume more, and this has important implications for current aggregate production, employment, and interest rates. If firms anticipate that a new technological innovation will come on line in the future, this makes them more inclined to invest today in new plant and equipment, and this in turn also affects aggregate production, employment, and interest rates. Consumers and firms are forward-looking in ways that matter for current aggregate economic activity and for government policy.

7. *Money takes many forms, and having it is much better than not having it. Once we have it, however, changing its quantity ultimately does not matter.* What differentiates money from other assets is its value as a medium of exchange, and having a medium of exchange makes economic transactions much easier in developed economies. Currently in the United States, there are several assets that act as a medium of exchange, including U.S. Federal Reserve notes, transactions deposits at banks, and travelers' checks. In Chapters 11 and 16, we explore the role of money and banking in the economy. One important result in Chapter 11 is that a one-time increase in the money supply, brought about by the central bank, has no long-run effect on any real economic magnitudes in the economy; it only increases all prices in the same proportion.

8. *Business cycles are similar, but they can have many causes.* In Chapter 3, we show that there are strong regularities in how aggregate macroeconomic variables fluctuate over the business cycle. In Chapters 12 and 13, we also study several theories that can potentially explain business cycles. The fact that there are several business cycle theories to choose from does not mean that only one can be right and all the others are wrong, although some may be more right than others. Potentially, all of these theories shed some light on why we have business cycles and what can be done about them.

9. *Countries gain from trading goods and assets with each other, but trade is also a source of shocks to the domestic economy.* Economists tend to support the lifting of trade restrictions, as free trade allows a country to exploit its comparative advantage in production and, thus, make its citizens better off. However, the integration of world financial and goods markets implies that events in other countries can cause domestic business cycles. In Chapters 14 and 15, we explore how changes in goods prices and interest rates on world markets affect the domestic economy.

10. *In the long run, inflation is caused by growth in the money supply.* **Inflation**, the rate of growth in the average level of prices, can vary over the short run for many reasons. Over the long run, however, the rate at which the central bank (the **Federal Reserve System** in the United States) causes the stock of money to grow determines what the inflation rate is. We study this process in Chapters 16 and 18.

11. *Unemployment is painful for individuals, but it is a necessary evil in modern economies.* There will always be unemployment in a well-functioning economy. Unemployment

is measured as the number of people who are not employed and are actively seeking work. Because all of these people are looking for something they do not have, unemployment might seem undesirable, but the time unemployed people spend searching for jobs is typically well spent from a social point of view. It is economically efficient for workers to be well matched with jobs, in terms of their skills, and if an individual spends a longer time searching for work, this increases the chances of a good match. In Chapter 17, we explore the determinants of the aggregate unemployment rate, in terms of two theories of unemployment, **search theory** and **efficiency wage theory**. Search theory explains unemployment in terms of the costs and benefits of searching for job offers, while efficiency wage theory posits that workers are unemployed because of an excess supply of labor brought about when firms pay high wages to induce their workers not to shirk.

12. *There may be a significant short-run trade-off between aggregate output and inflation, but aside from the inefficiencies caused by long-run inflation, there is no long-run trade-off.* In some countries and for some historical periods, a positive relationship appears to exist between the deviation of aggregate output from trend and the inflation rate. This relationship is called the **Phillips curve**, and in general the Phillips curve appears to be a quite unstable empirical relationship. The Friedman–Lucas money surprise model, discussed in Chapter 18, provides an explanation for the observed Phillips curve relationship. It also explains why the Phillips curve is unstable and does not represent a long-run trade-off between output and inflation that can be exploited by government policymakers. Also in Chapter 18, we explore the importance of commitment on the part of central bank policymakers in explaining inflation experience in the United States.

Understanding Recent and Current Macroeconomic Events

Part of the excitement of studying macroeconomics is that it can make sense of recent and currently unfolding economic events. In this section, we give an overview of some recent and current issues and how we can understand them better using macroeconomic tools.

Aggregate Productivity

A measure of productivity in the aggregate economy is **average labor productivity,** $\frac{Y}{N}$, where Y denotes aggregate output and N denotes employment. That is, we can measure aggregate productivity as the total quantity of output produced per worker. Aggregate productivity is important, as economic growth theory tells us that growth in aggregate productivity is what determines growth in living standards in the long run. In Figure 1.5 we plot the log of average labor productivity for the United States, measured as the log of real gross domestic product per worker. Here, we show the log of average labor productivity (the blue line), because then the slope of the graph denotes the growth rate in average labor productivity. The key features of Figure 1.5 are that average labor productivity grew at a high rate during the 1950s and most of the 1960s, growth slowed down from the late

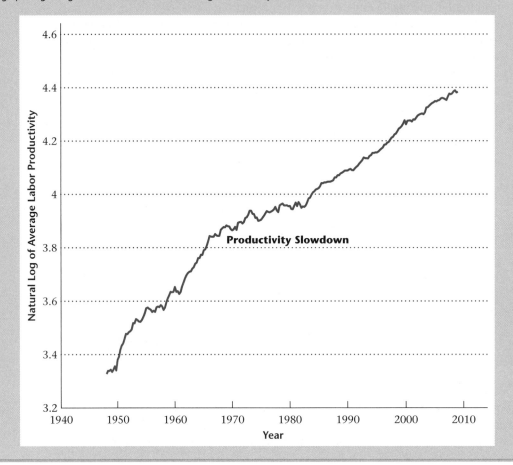

Figure 1.5 Natural Logarithm of Average Productivity

Average labor productivity is the quantity of aggregate output produced per worker. Because the graph is of the log of average labor productivity (the blue line), the slope of the graph is approximately the growth rate in average labor productivity. A key feature in the figure is the productivity slowdown, which we see as a decrease in the slope of the graph beginning in the late 1960s and continuing into the early 1980s.

1960s until the early 1980s, and then productivity growth increased beginning in the mid-1980s and remained high through the 1990s and into the early twenty-first century. The period from the late 1960s until the early 1980s is referred to as the **productivity slowdown.**

What caused the productivity slowdown, and what led to the resurgence in productivity growth after 1980? If we can understand this behavior of aggregate productivity, we might be able to avoid productivity slowdowns in the future and to bring about larger future increases in our standard of living. One potential explanation for the productivity slowdown is that it simply reflects a measurement problem. Estimates of economic growth during the productivity slowdown period could have been biased downward for various reasons, which would also cause productivity growth to be biased downward. This explanation seems quite unexciting, but economic measurement generally is imperfect. Economists have to be very careful in tempering their conclusions with a thorough knowledge of the data they are studying. A more exciting potential explanation for the productivity slowdown, and the subsequent increase in productivity growth, is that this is symptomatic of the adoption of new technology. Modern information technology began to be introduced in the late 1960s with the wide use of high-speed computers. In learning to use computer technology, there was a temporary adjustment period, which could have slowed down productivity growth from the late 1960s to the early 1980s. By the early 1980s, however, according to this story, people discovered how to embody new information technology in personal computers, and the 1990s saw further uses for computer technology via the Internet. Thus, the productivity slowdown could have been caused by the costs of adjusting to new technology, with productivity growth rebounding as information technology became widely diffused through the economy. We explore these issues further in Chapters 6 and 7.

Taxes, Government Spending, and the Government Deficit

In Figure 1.6 we show total taxes (the black line) and government spending (the colored line) by all levels of government (federal, state, and local) in the United States from 1947 to 2009, as percentages of total gross domestic product. Note the broad upward trend in both taxes and spending. Total taxes were almost 24% of GDP in 1947, and they increased to about 32% of GDP in 2000, while total spending rose from about 20% of GDP in 1960 to a high of more than 34% of GDP in the early 1990s. These trends generally reflect an increase in the size of government in the United States relative to the aggregate economy over this period.

What ramifications does a larger government have for the economy as a whole? How does higher government spending and taxation affect private economic activity? We show in Chapters 5 and 10 that increased government activity in general causes a **crowding out** of private economic activity. That is, the government competes for resources with the rest of the economy. If the size of the government increases, then through several economic mechanisms there is a reduction in the quantity of spending by private firms on new plant and equipment, and there is a reduction in private consumption expenditures.

An interesting feature of Figure 1.6 is that governments in the United States sometimes spent more than they received in the form of taxes, and sometimes the reverse was true. Just as is the case for private consumers, the government can in principle spend more than it earns by borrowing and accumulating debt, and it can earn more than it spends and save the difference, thus, reducing its debt. Figure 1.7 shows the total **government surplus** or total **government saving**, which is the difference between taxes and spending, for the period 1947–2009. From Figure 1.7, the government surplus was positive for most of the period from 1948 until 1970, but from 1970 until the late 1990s the surplus was usually negative. When there is a negative government surplus, we say that the government is running a deficit; the **government deficit** is the negative of the government surplus. The largest government deficits over this period were in 1975 and in early 2009, when the deficit exceeded 6% of GDP. There was only a

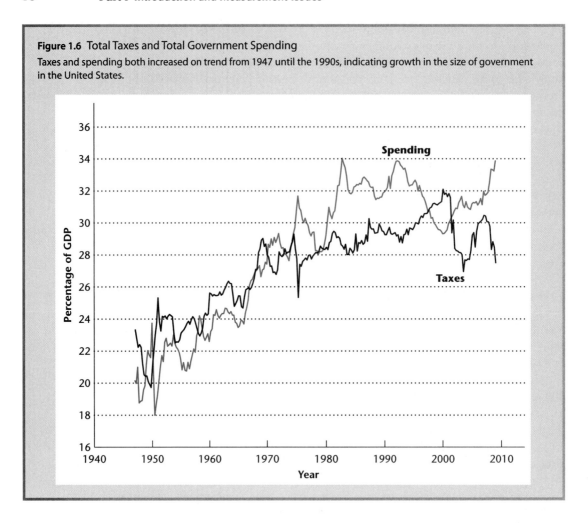

Figure 1.6 Total Taxes and Total Government Spending

Taxes and spending both increased on trend from 1947 until the 1990s, indicating growth in the size of government in the United States.

brief period after the late 1970s and governments in the United States ran a surplus; in 1999, the government surplus reached more than 2% of GDP. However, the surplus declined dramatically after 1999, reaching −4% of GDP in 2003 before increasing again and then dropping precipitously in the 2008–2009 recession.

What are the consequences of government deficits? We might think, in a manner similar to popular conceptions of household finance, that accumulating debt (running a deficit) is bad, whereas reducing debt (running a surplus) is good, but at the aggregate level the issue is not so simple. One principal difference between an individual and the government is that when the government accumulates debt by borrowing from its citizens, then this is debt that we as a nation owe to ourselves. Then, it turns out that the effects of a government deficit depend on what the source of the deficit is. Is the government running a deficit because taxes have decreased or because government spending has increased? If the deficit is the result of a decrease in taxes, then the government debt that is issued to finance the deficit will have to be paid off ultimately by higher future taxes.

Figure 1.7 The Total Government Surplus in the United States as a Percentage of GDP

The government surplus declines on trend until the early 1990s, increases, and then decreases again in 2000 before increasing somewhat and then decreasing precipitously. Except for a brief period in the late 1990s, the government surplus has been negative since 1980.

Thus, running a deficit in this case implies that there is a redistribution of the tax burden from one group to another; one group has its current taxes reduced while another has its future taxes increased. Under some circumstances, these two groups might essentially be the same, in which case there would be no consequences of having the government run a deficit. This idea, that government deficits do not matter under some conditions, is called the **Ricardian equivalence theorem**, and we study it in Chapter 8. In the case of a government deficit resulting from higher government spending, then there are always implications for aggregate economic activity, as discussed earlier in terms of the crowding out of private spending. We examine the effects of government spending in Chapters 5 and 10.

Interest Rates

Interest rates are important because they affect many private economic decisions, particularly the decisions of consumers as to how much they borrow and lend, and the decisions of firms concerning how much to invest in new plant and equipment. Further, movements in interest rates are an important element in the economic mechanism by which monetary policy affects real magnitudes in the short run. In Figure 1.8 we show the behavior of the short-term **nominal interest rate** (the blue line) in the United States over the period 1947–2009. This is the interest rate in money terms on 91-day U.S. Treasury bills, which are essentially riskless short-term government securities. The short-term nominal interest rate rose on trend through the 1950s, 1960s, and 1970s, reaching a high of more than 15% early in 1980. Since then, the nominal interest rate has declined on trend, and it was close to 0% in early 2009.

What explains the level of the nominal interest rate? In the figure we have plotted the inflation rate as the black line, which is measured here by the rate of increase in the consumer price index. The consumer price index is a measure of the price level, the average level of prices across goods in the economy. In the figure the inflation rate tracks the

Figure 1.8 The Nominal Interest Rate and the Inflation Rate
Macroeconomic theory tells us that the nominal interest rate and the inflation rate are positively related. In the figure, the nominal interest rate tends to track the ups and downs in the inflation rate.

nominal interest rate reasonably closely. Also, several of the peaks in inflation, around 1970, in the mid-1970s, around 1980, around 1990, and in 2001, are coupled with peaks in the nominal interest rate. Thus, the nominal interest rate tends to rise and fall with the inflation rate. Why is this? Economic decisions are based on real rather than nominal interest rates. The **real interest rate**, roughly speaking, is the nominal interest rate minus the expected rate of inflation. That is, the real interest rate is the rate that a borrower expects to have to repay, adjusting for the inflation that is expected to occur over the period of time until the borrower's debt is repaid. If Allen obtains a one-year car loan at an interest rate of 9%, and he expects the inflation rate to be 3% over the next year, then he faces a real interest rate on the car loan of 6%. Now, because economic decisions are based on real interest rates rather than nominal interest rates, market forces tend to determine the real interest rate. Therefore, as the inflation rate rises, the nominal interest rate tends to rise along with it. In Chapters 7 and 9, we study the determination of real and nominal interest rates in the long run, and the relationship between real and nominal rates.

In Figure 1.9 we plot an estimate of the real interest rate, which is the nominal interest rate minus the actual rate of inflation. Thus, this would be the actual real interest rate if consumers and firms could correctly anticipate inflation, so that actual inflation is equal to expected inflation. Consumers and firms cannot correctly anticipate the actual inflation rate. However, given that inflation does not change too much from quarter to quarter, their forecasts are fairly accurate, and our estimate of the real interest rate has a reasonably small measurement error. The real interest rate fluctuates a great deal over time. The real rate has sometimes been negative, falling to about −9% in the late 1940s, to −8% in the early 1950s, and to −7% in 1980. For most of the period since the early 1980s, the real interest rate has been positive, but it fell below zero early in the 1990s, in 2003, and in 2008.

In the short run, the real interest rate is affected by monetary policy, although there is some disagreement among macroeconomists concerning why the central bank can control the real interest rate, and for how long it can do so. We can give the following interpretation to the path of the real interest rate from the mid-1970s to 2008 in Figure 1.9. First, the real interest rate was low in the mid to late 1970s because the Federal Reserve (the Fed) was causing the money supply to grow at a high rate, that is, monetary policy was expansionary and accommodating. As a result of the high inflation caused by this high money growth, the Fed embarked on a contractionary course in the early 1980s, reducing money supply growth and causing the real interest rate to rise. Since the mid-1980s, the Fed has remained seriously concerned about the possibility that high inflation could reemerge, and it has for the most part maintained a nonaccommodating monetary policy stance, which has caused the real interest rate to be historically high. During the business cycle downturn in the early 1990s, the Fed temporarily relaxed, causing the real interest rate to dip to close to 0%. Then, in 2001, the Fed acted to reduce the real interest rate again, in response to a slowdown in aggregate economic activity. As there appeared to be no threat of serious inflation and economic activity had not picked up significantly, the real interest rate continued to fall through late 2003. Then, when the economy was growing at a high rate, and there was a greater threat from inflation, the real interest rate increased, through 2006. In 2008, the Fed

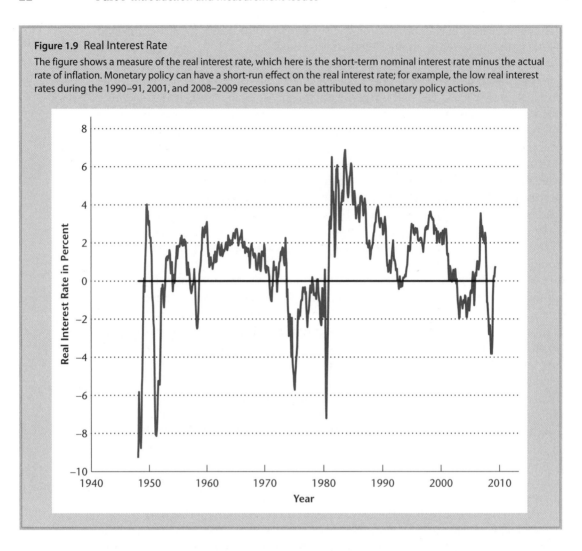

Figure 1.9 Real Interest Rate

The figure shows a measure of the real interest rate, which here is the short-term nominal interest rate minus the actual rate of inflation. Monetary policy can have a short-run effect on the real interest rate; for example, the low real interest rates during the 1990–91, 2001, and 2008–2009 recessions can be attributed to monetary policy actions.

aggressively reduced the real interest rate in response to the financial crisis and the developing recession. In Chapters 12 and 13, we study some theories of the business cycle that explain how the central bank can influence the real interest rate in the short run. While the rate of money growth may affect real interest rates in the long run, monetary policy is aimed not at setting the long-run real interest rate but at determining long-run inflation while staying in tune with the short-run effects of monetary policy.

Business Cycles in the United States

As was mentioned above, individual business cycle events may have many causes, and the causes that are important in one business cycle event may be very unimportant in others. For example, a particular recession might be attributed to monetary policy actions, while another recession may have been caused primarily by a downturn in aggregate productivity.

Figure 1.10 Percentage Deviation from Trend in Real GDP, 1947–2009

The key recessions occurring since 1970 are indicated in the figure by negative deviations of real GDP from trend in 1974–1975, 1981–1982, 1990–1991, 2001, and 2008–2009.

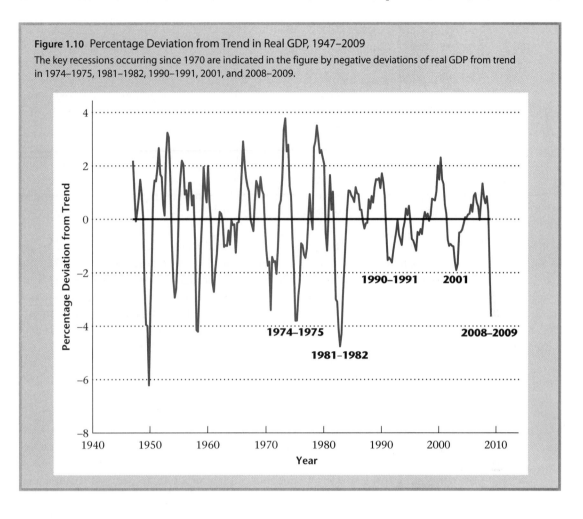

As above, we define business cycles to be the deviations from trend in aggregate economic activity. In Figure 1.10, we show the percentage deviations from trend in real GDP for the period 1947–2009. Recessions in the figure are negative deviations from trend, and the significant recent recessions in the United States were those of 1974–1975, 1981–1982, 1990–1991, 2001, and 2008–2009. What were the causes of these recessions?

Before the 1974–1975 recession, there was a particularly sharp rise in the price of energy on world markets, caused by a restriction of oil output by the Organization of Petroleum Exporting Countries (OPEC). In Chapters 4, 5, and 10, we explain how an increase in the price of energy acts to reduce productivity and leads to a decrease in aggregate output, which occurred in 1974–1975, as we see in Figure 1.10. Other features of the 1974–1975 recession, including a reduction in measured productivity, a fall in employment, and a decrease in consumption and investment expenditures, are all consistent with this recession having been caused by the increase in the price of energy.

The recession of 1981–1982, like the recession of 1974–1975, was preceded by a large increase in the price of energy, which in this case occurred in 1979–1980. For this second recession, the energy price increase perhaps happened too soon before the recession to have been its principal cause. As well, other evidence seems to point to monetary policy as the primary cause of the 1981–1982 recession. As we see later in this section, inflation had become relatively high in the 1970s in the United States, and by the early 1980s the Federal Reserve System (the Fed), under then-Chairman Paul Volcker, took dramatic steps to reduce inflation by restricting growth in the supply of money and driving up interest rates. This produced the side effect of a recession. While there is much controversy among macroeconomists concerning the short-run effects of monetary policy, and the role of money in the business cycle, most macroeconomists are inclined to view the 1981–1982 recession as being caused primarily by monetary policy.

The 1991–1992 recession was mild compared to the previous two major recessions (the negative deviation from trend in Figure 1.10 is smaller), and it was the only interruption in sustained economic growth over a roughly nineteen-year period from 1982 to 2001 in the United States. For this recession, it is difficult to pinpoint a single cause. Possibly an increase in energy prices during the Persian Gulf War was an important contributing factor, although this price increase was temporary.

The recession of 2001, although even milder than the 1991–1992 recession (see Figure 1.10), appears to have been the result of a collapse in optimism in the United States. During the 1990s, there was a boom in investment expenditures—spending on new plants, equipment, and housing—fed in part by great optimism concerning the revolution in information technology and its implications for future productivity. This optimism was also reflected in a large increase in the average price of stocks in the 1990s. In about 2000, optimism faded rapidly, investment expenditures and the stock market crashed, and the result was the recession of 2001. Also contributing to the 2001 recession were the terrorist attacks of September 2001, which directly disrupted financial activity in New York City and caused travelers to fear air travel and tourism.

The period after the 1981–1982 recession until 2008 is sometimes called the Great Moderation, as aggregate economic fluctuations became less volatile, relative to the 1947–1982 period. However, the 2008–2009 recession is anything but moderate. The deviation from trend in the first quarter of 2009 is close to −4%, and forecasters think that it is likely that the 2008–2009 recession will ultimately be more severe than the one in 1981–1982. Macroeconomists are only beginning to fully understand the causes of the 2008–2009 recession, rooted in the recent financial crisis originating in the United States, which began in 2007 and subsequently spread to the rest of the world. Regulatory failures in the U.S. financial system created profit opportunities for excessively risky mortgage lending, and a decline in the price of housing led to a wave of mortgage foreclosures and stress in financial markets. This recent recession illustrates the importance of financial market factors for aggregate economic activity.

Credit Markets and the Financial Crisis
The recent financial crisis and subsequent severe recession in 2008–2009 were essentially unanticipated events among professional macroeconomists. Although these events

have caused macroeconomists to revise their thinking concerning the importance of credit markets, banking, and financial relationships for aggregate economic activity, recent experience should not challenge our confidence in the use of mainstream macroeconomic theory to make sense of empirical observations and guide economic policy. One goal in the fourth edition of *Macroeconomics* is to show how received economic theory can be helpful in organizing our thinking about the financial crisis and the recent severe recession and in evaluating the fiscal and monetary policy responses to the crisis.

Issues related to the financial crisis and the recent recession are discussed in Chapters 9, 10, 12, 13, and 16, in particular. A critical aspect of economic theory that is very helpful for understanding the current crisis, is how credit market "frictions" or "imperfections" act to amplify shocks to the economy. Two imperfections that are analayzed, beginning in Chapter 9, are asymmetric information and limited commitment.

Asymmetric information refers to a situation where the economic actors on one side of a market have more information than the economic actors on the other side of the market. For example, financial institutions that extend loans in the credit market may have less information about the creditworthiness of would-be borrowers than do the borrowers themselves. In these circumstances, even borrowers who are very unlikely to default on a loan may be forced to pay a high interest rate on the loan, as lending institutions are unable to differentiate good borrowers from bad borrowers. That is, interest rates include a default premium, and this default premium tends to rise as lending institutions become increasingly pessimistic about the average creditworthiness of borrowers. Good borrowers suffer due to the asymmetric information problem.

One way to measure the size of the default premium in credit markets is to look at the difference between the long-term interest rate on relatively safe long-term corporate debt, and the interest rate on somewhat risky corporate debt. Figure 1.11 shows the difference (the interest rate "spread") between AAA-rated (safe) corporate bonds and BAA-rated (somewhat risky) corporate bonds for the period 1919–2009. First, note that there was a very large spike in this spread during the Great Depression in the 1930s and that each of the recessions since 1970 is associated with an increase in the spread (see Figure 1.10). Further, the size of the spread in the 2008–2009 recession was the largest observed since the Great Depression. This points to a large increase in the perceived average risk of default in credit markets. As we will show in Chapters 9 and 10, increases in perceived credit risk due to asymmetric information in consumer and corporate credit markets leads to decreases in aggregate consumption and investment expenditures, just as we have observed in 2008–2009.

The second credit market imperfection, limited commitment, refers to a borrower's lack of incentive to repay in the credit market. In general, lending institutions attempt to solve this incentive problem by requiring that a borrower post collateral when taking out a loan. For example, in taking out an auto loan, the borrower posts the car as collateral, and the borrower's house serves as collateral for a mortgage loan. In the event that the borrower does not repay the debt, the lender can seize the collateral. For a consumer, then, the value of assets held that are collateralizable, which consists mostly of

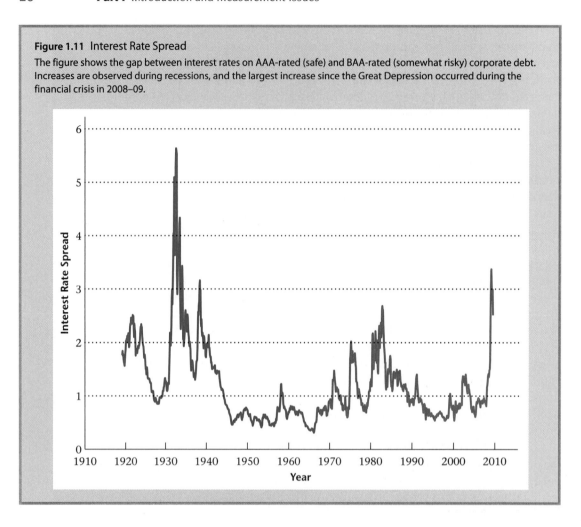

Figure 1.11 Interest Rate Spread

The figure shows the gap between interest rates on AAA-rated (safe) and BAA-rated (somewhat risky) corporate debt. Increases are observed during recessions, and the largest increase since the Great Depression occurred during the financial crisis in 2008–09.

housing in the U.S. economy, can matter for how much the consumer can borrow. For example, if the value of my house increases, this increases my ability to borrow in the form of a home equity loan, and I can use such a loan to finance consumption expenditures. For the economy as a whole, a decline in the price of housing can result in a significant drop in aggregate consumption, if a significant fraction of consumers is constrained in their ability to borrow by available collateral.

In Figure 1.12, we show the relative price of housing, captured here by the average price of houses in the United States divided by the consumer price index. This is a measure of the purchasing power of the housing stock, or the value of the aggregate stock of housing as collateral. Note in particular the drop in the relative price of housing of about 25% from its peak in 2005 to the beginning of 2009. This not only caused problems in the mortgage market, in that some mortgage borrowers then had the incentive to default on their mortgages, but it also caused a decrease in consumption expenditures, because of the decrease in collateralizable wealth.

Figure 1.12 Relative Price of Housing

The figures shows a drop of about 25% in the relative price of housing from the peak in 2005 to 2009. This represents a drop in the value of collateralizable wealth, which caused a decrease in consumption expenditures.

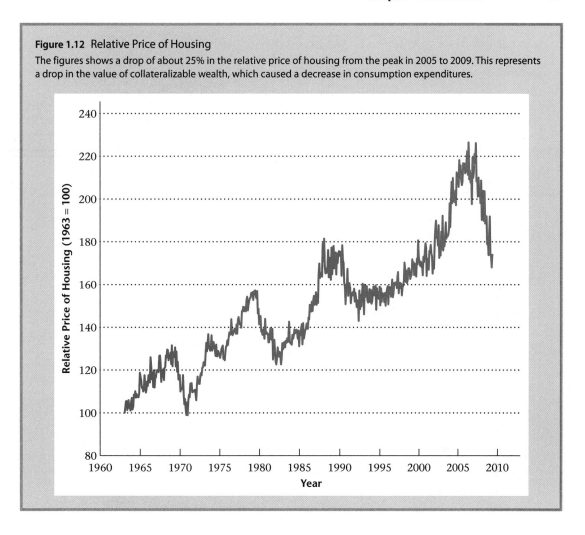

The Current Account Surplus and the Government Surplus

As the technology for transporting goods and information across countries has advanced and government-imposed impediments to trade have been reduced in the post–World War II period, the United States has become a more open economy. That is, trade in goods and in assets between the United States and the rest of the world has increased. The change in the flow of goods and services between the United States and the rest of the world is shown in Figure 1.13, where we plot U.S. exports (the black line) and imports (the colored line) as percentages of GDP from 1947 to 2009. U.S. exports increased from about 5% of GDP in 1947 to somewhat less than 12% of GDP in 2009, while imports increased from somewhat more than 3% in 1947 to about 14% in 2009. As mentioned previously, more trade has a positive effect on general economic welfare, as it allows countries to specialize in production and exploit their comparative advantages. However, more trade could also expose a given country to the transmission of business cycle

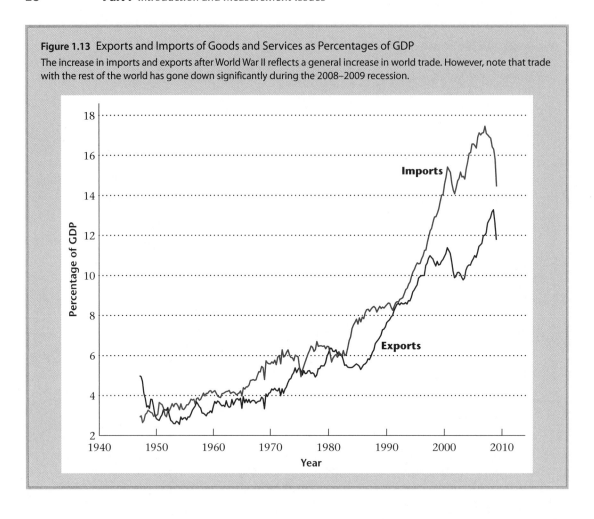

Figure 1.13 Exports and Imports of Goods and Services as Percentages of GDP

The increase in imports and exports after World War II reflects a general increase in world trade. However, note that trade with the rest of the world has gone down significantly during the 2008–2009 recession.

fluctuations from abroad, although this need not necessarily be the case. An interesting feature of the data in Figure 1.13 is the dramatic decrease in both imports and exports, as percentages of GDP, during the 2008–2009 recession.

While the level of trade with the outside world is important in terms of aggregate economic activity and how it fluctuates, the balance of trade also plays an important role in macroeconomic activity and macroeconomic policymaking. One measure of the balance of trade is the **current account surplus**, which is **net exports** of goods and services (exports minus imports) plus **net factor payments** (net income from abroad). In Figure 1.14 we have graphed the current account surplus for the period 1960–2008. In the figure the current account surplus was positive for most of the period 1960–1985, and it has been negative for most of the period 1985–2008.

Why is the current account surplus important? When the current account surplus in the United States is negative, there is a **current account deficit**, and the quantity of goods and services purchased abroad by domestic residents is larger than the quantity of domestic goods and services purchased by foreigners. To finance this current account

Figure 1.14 The Current Account Surplus and the Government Surplus

A decrease in the government surplus can cause a decrease in the current account surplus, as appears to have occurred in the 1980s. However, at other times, the current account surplus and government surplus move in opposite directions, more often than not.

deficit, residents of the United States and/or the U.S. government must be borrowing abroad. Is it a bad idea for a country to run a current account deficit? This need not be the case, for two reasons. First, just as it may make sense for an individual to borrow so as to smooth his or her flow of consumption over time, it may also be beneficial for a country to borrow in the short run by running a current account deficit so as to smooth aggregate consumption over time. Second, persistent current account deficits may make sense if the associated foreign borrowing is used to finance additions to the nation's productive capacity that will allow for higher future living standards.

What accounts for movements over time in the current account surplus? One important influence on the current account surplus is government spending. When the government increases its spending, holding taxes constant, this increases the government deficit, which needs to be financed by increased government borrowing. If the private sector does not save more, so as to increase its lending to the government, then the increased government borrowing is done abroad, and it shows up as an increase in the current account deficit. Thus, an increase in the government deficit can be coupled with an increase in the current account deficit. This is exactly what appears to have occurred in the United States in the mid-to-late 1980s. In Figure 1.14, we see a sharp decrease during this period in the current account surplus. As well, we have shown the government surplus in the figure, and this also decreases sharply in the 1980s (although the decline in the government surplus precedes the decline in the current account surplus). This phenomenon is referred to as the **twin deficits**.

The government surplus need not always be the primary influence on the current account surplus. For example, outside of the 1980s period mentioned above, the current account surplus and the government surplus moved in opposite directions more often than not. For example, from 2003–2008, the current account surplus and government surplus were essentially always moving in opposite directions.

We study international trade, the determinants of the current account surplus, and other issues associated with international business cycles and international financial relations in Chapters 14 and 15.

Inflation

Inflation, as mentioned earlier, is the rate of change in the average level of prices. The average level of prices is referred to as the price level. In Figure 1.15 we show the inflation rate, the black line in the figure, as the percentage rate of increase in the consumer price index over the period 1960–2009. The inflation rate was quite low in the early 1960s and then began climbing in the late 1960s, reaching peaks of about 12% per year in 1975 and about 14% per year in 1980. The inflation rate then declined steadily, reaching rates of 2% and even falling into the negative range in early 2009.

Inflation is economically costly, but the low recent rates of inflation we are experiencing are not viewed by the public or by policymakers as being worthy of much attention. However, it is certainly useful to understand the causes of inflation, its costs, and why and how inflation was reduced in the United States. There are good reasons to think that the inflation experience of the 1970s and early 1980s, or worse, could be repeated, especially given the 2008–2009 upheavals in financial markets and dramatic policy intervention by the U.S. Federal Reserve System. The inflation rate is explained in the long run by the rate of growth in the supply of money. Without money supply growth, prices cannot continue to increase, and higher money supply growth implies that there is more and more money chasing a given quantity of goods. This will ultimately cause prices to be bid up at a higher rate. In Figure 1.15 we show the rate of money growth (measured as the percentage rate of growth in M2, a broad monetary aggregate) as the colored line. Here, it is clear that the short-run relationship between the rate of inflation and the rate of money growth is very loose; there are many short-run ups and downs in the rate of money growth that are not reflected in similar movements in the inflation rate and vice versa. Thus, there must be other factors that explain short-run movements in the rate of inflation in addition to changes in the money growth rate.

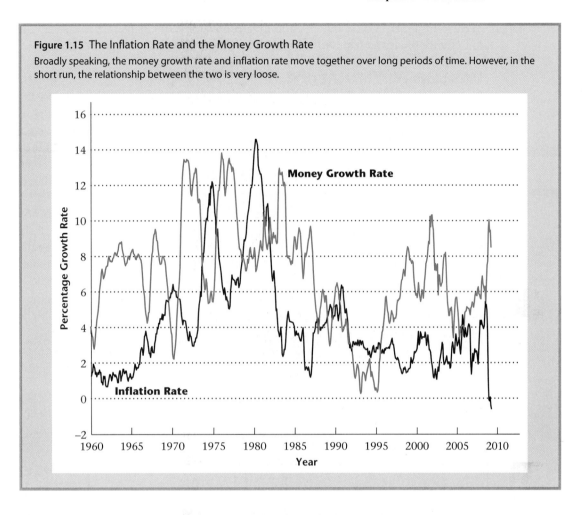

Figure 1.15 The Inflation Rate and the Money Growth Rate
Broadly speaking, the money growth rate and inflation rate move together over long periods of time. However, in the short run, the relationship between the two is very loose.

However, the broad trends in money growth in Figure 1.13 match the broad trends in the inflation rate. Money growth increases, on trend, until the 1980s, and then falls, as does the inflation rate, although money growth behavior is at times quite erratic. We study the short-run effects of nonmonetary factors on the price level in Chapters 11, 12, and 13, and in Chapter 16 the long-run effects of money growth on inflation are explored.

Long-run inflation is costly in that it tends to reduce employment, output, and consumption, as we show in Chapter 16. However, because inflation is caused in the long run by money growth, the central bank determines the long-run inflation rate through its control of the rate at which the money supply grows. Why would the central bank want to generate inflation if it is costly? In Chapter 18, we explore the answer to this question, with experience in the United States as a backdrop. Surprise increases in the rate of inflation can cause short-run increases in employment and output, and the central bank might be tempted to generate these short-run surprises, either because it has not learned the consequences of long-run inflation, or because there is a failure of the central bank to commit itself to long-run actions. In Chapter 18, we study the importance of central bank learning and commitment for the behavior of inflation.

Unemployment

Previously we explained how the phenomenon of unemployment need not represent a problem, because unemployment is in general a socially useful search activity that is necessary, although painful to the individuals involved. As macroeconomists, we are interested in what explains the level of unemployment and what the reasons are for fluctuations in unemployment over time. If we can understand these features, we can then go on to determine how macroeconomic policy can be formulated so that labor markets work as efficiently as possible.

In Figure 1.16 we show the unemployment rate in the United States for the period 1948–2009. There are three important features that can be observed in Figure 1.16. First, the average unemployment rate in the period after 1970 is much higher than the average unemployment rate before 1970. Second, the unemployment rate fluctuates

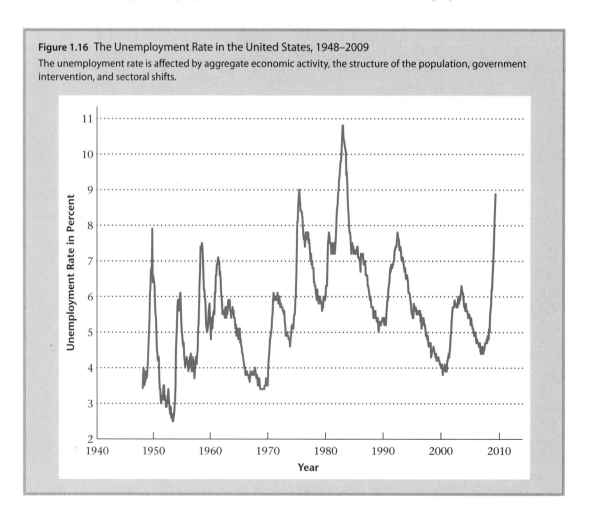

Figure 1.16 The Unemployment Rate in the United States, 1948–2009

The unemployment rate is affected by aggregate economic activity, the structure of the population, government intervention, and sectoral shifts.

significantly; it is not unusual for it to move up or down by four or five percentage points within a year or two. Third, since 1970 there was a trend increase in the unemployment rate until about the mid-1980s and then a trend decrease; in 1999 the unemployment rate was lower than it had been at any point since 1970. Following 1999, the unemployment increased in the 2001 recession before decreasing, and then increasing dramatically during the 2008–2009 recession. In early 2009, the unemployment rate was at its highest level since the 1981–1982 recession, and still rising. What explains these features of the data?

There are four factors affecting unemployment that can explain essentially all of the observed behavior of the unemployment rate in Figure 1.16. These four factors are aggregate economic activity, the structure of the population, government intervention, and sectoral shifts. First, in general the unemployment rate fluctuates inversely along with aggregate economic activity; when aggregate output is above trend, then the unemployment rate tends to be low. Second, the population structure affects the unemployment rate, as workers in different age cohorts tend to behave differently in the labor market. For example, younger workers have a weaker attachment to jobs than older workers, and they tend to experience more frequent episodes of unemployment as they change jobs early in their careers. Third, government intervention affects the unemployment rate, particularly through the unemployment insurance system. For example, more generous unemployment compensation implies that the cost of searching for a job is reduced, and unemployed workers then tend to search longer, increasing the unemployment rate. Fourth, sectoral shifts are long-run changes that occur in the sectoral structure of production. For example, in the United States there has been a shift from the manufacturing sector of the economy to the services sector. This kind of sectoral shift tends to displace workers from the declining sector, and they need to acquire new skills and to spend time searching to find jobs in the expanding sector of the economy. Therefore, the greater the extent of sectoral shifts occurring in the economy, the higher the unemployment rate is.

The fact that the unemployment rate is on average higher after 1970 than before, as observed in Figure 1.16, is probably mainly the result of changes in the population structure. The postwar baby boom generation entered the labor force mostly between the late 1960s and 1980, so that the working age population became more youthful through the 1970s, which would tend to push the unemployment rate up. Sectoral shifts may have also played a role in pushing up the unemployment rate after 1970. The unemployment rate fluctuated from 1948 to 2009 mainly because of fluctuations in aggregate economic activity. In Figure 1.17 we show deviations from trend in real GDP (in percentage terms) as the colored line and deviations from trend in the unemployment rate (in percentage points) as the black line. Clearly, when GDP is above (below) trend, the unemployment rate tends to be below (above) trend. Finally, the pattern in the unemployment rate since 1970 can be explained in part by the population structure and in part by the influence of aggregate economic activity. As the postwar baby boom generation began to age in the 1980s and 1990s, the unemployment rate fell as this large group of workers entered a phase in their careers when unemployment spells were less frequent. Also, the sustained growth in the U.S. economy from the early 1980s to 2008, interrupted only by the mild recessions in the early 1990s and 2001, contributed to a decrease in the unemployment rate. These recent long run factors make the increase in the unemployment rate in

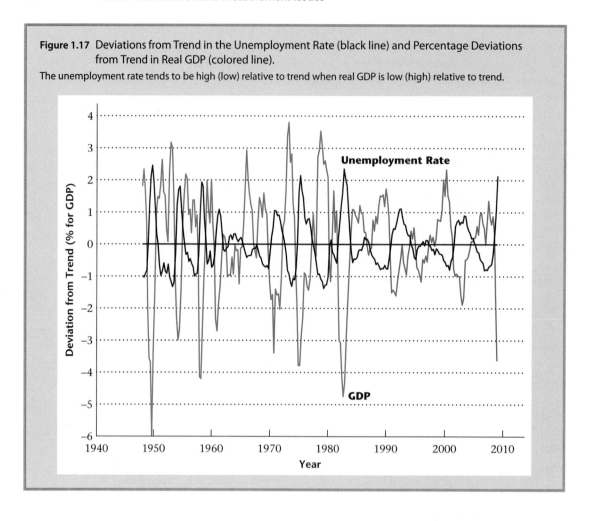

Figure 1.17 Deviations from Trend in the Unemployment Rate (black line) and Percentage Deviations from Trend in Real GDP (colored line).

The unemployment rate tends to be high (low) relative to trend when real GDP is low (high) relative to trend.

2008–2009 all the more dramatic. In some sense a 9% unemployment rate in 2009 represents a much higher degree of slack in the economy than an unemployment rate much higher than 9% would have in 1980.

We study determinants of the unemployment rate and theories of unemployment in Chapter 17.

Chapter Summary

- Modern macroeconomics analyzes issues associated with long-run growth and business cycles, using models that are built up from microeconomic principles.
- During the twentieth century, the United States experienced long-run sustained growth in per capita gross national product; we also observed that gross national product exhibits business cycle fluctuations about a smooth long-run trend.
- Two unusual but important events in twentieth-century U.S. economic history were the Great Depression and World War II.

- The primary questions of interest to macroeconomists involve the causes of long-run growth and business cycles and the appropriate role for government policy in influencing the performance of the economy.

- Macroeconomists rely mainly on abstract models to draw conclusions about how the world works, because it is usually very costly or impossible to experiment with the real economy. A good macroeconomic model is simple, while retaining all of the features essential for addressing the macroeconomic issue for which the model was intended.

- The models we construct and use in this book are ones in which price-taking consumers and firms optimize given the constraints they face and in which the actions of consumers and firms are consistent in a competitive equilibrium.

- Building models from microeconomic principles is important, because this will more often give us the correct answers to questions regarding the effects of changes in economic policy.

- There is relatively little disagreement among macroeconomists concerning approaches to modeling growth, but there are contentious issues in business cycle modeling, between Keynesian macroeconomists and those who argue for non-Keynesian alternative explanations for business cycles.

- The issues discussed in this chapter, to be addressed later in the book, are the productivity slowdown; taxes, government spending, and the government deficit; interest rates; business cycles in the United States; credit markets and the financial crisis; the current account surplus and the government surplus; inflation; and unemployment.

Key Terms

Average labor productivity The quantity of aggregate output produced per worker. (p. 15)

Business cycles Short-run ups and downs, or booms and recessions, in aggregate economic activity. (p. 2)

Competitive equilibrium Equilibrium in which firms and households are assumed to be price-takers, and market prices are such that the quantity supplied equals the quantity demanded in each market in the economy. (p. 9)

Crowding out The process by which government spending reduces private sector expenditures on investment and consumption. (p. 17)

Current account deficit Situation in which the current account surplus is negative. (p. 28)

Current account surplus Exports minus imports plus net factor payments to domestic residents from abroad. (p. 28)

Economic model A description of consumers and firms, their objectives and constraints, and how they interact. (p. 2)

Efficiency wage theory Theory positing that workers are unemployed because of an excess supply of

labor brought about when firms pay high wages to induce their workers not to shirk. (p. 15)

Endogenous growth models Models that describe the economic mechanism determining the rate of economic growth. (p. 11)

Equilibrium The situation in an economy when the actions of all the consumers and firms are consistent. (p. 9)

Federal Reserve System (Fed) The central bank of the United States. (p. 14)

Government deficit The negative of the government surplus. (p. 17)

Government saving Identical to the government surplus. (p. 17)

Government surplus The difference between taxes and government spending. (p. 17)

Gross domestic product (GDP) The quantity of goods and services produced within a country's borders during some specified period of time. (p. 3)

Inflation The rate of change in the average level of prices over time. (p. 14)

Keynesian Describes macroeconomists who are followers of J. M. Keynes and who see an active role for government in smoothing business cycles. (p. 12)

Keynesian coordination failure theory A modern incarnation of Keynesian business cycle theory positing that business cycles are caused by self-fulfilling waves of optimism and pessimism, which may be countered with government policy. (p. 12)

Long-run growth The increase in a nation's productive capacity and average standard of living that occurs over a long period of time. (p. 2)

Lucas critique The idea that macroeconomic policy analysis can be done in a sensible way only if microeconomic behavior is taken seriously. (p. 11)

Market segmentation theory A theory of how changes in the money supply can cause changes in real output and employment in the short run. The theory implies that monetary policy can contribute to undesirable fluctuations in the economy, but there is also potentially a role for active monetary policy. (p. 12)

Models Artificial devices that can replicate the behavior of real systems. (p. 8)

Net exports Exports of goods and services minus imports of goods and services. (p. 28)

Net factor payments These are the payments received by domestic factors of production from abroad minus the payments to foreign factors of production from domestic sources. (p. 28)

Nominal interest rate The interest rate in money terms. (p. 20)

Optimize The process by which economic agents (firms and consumers) do the best they can given the constraints they face. (p. 9)

Phillips curve A positive relationship between the deviation of aggregate output from trend and the inflation rate. (p. 15)

Productivity slowdown The period of low productivity growth occurring from the late 1960s until the early 1980s. (p. 16)

Rational expectations revolution Macroeconomics movement that occurred in the 1970s, introducing more microeconomics into macroeconomics. (p. 11)

Real business cycle theory Initiated by Finn Kydland and Edward Prescott, this theory implies that business cycles are caused primarily by shocks to technology and that the government should play a passive role over the business cycle. (p. 11)

Real interest rate Approximately equal to the nominal interest rate minus the expected rate of inflation. (p. 21)

Ricardian equivalence theorem Theory asserting that a change in taxation by the government has no effect. (p. 19)

Search theory Theory that explains unemployment in terms of the costs and benefits of searching for job offers. (p. 15)

Trend The smooth growth path around which an economic variable cycles. (p. 5)

Twin deficits The phenomenon during the late 1980s when the U.S. government was running a deficit at the same time that the United States was running a current account deficit. (p. 30)

Questions for Review

1. What are the primary defining characteristics of macroeconomics?

2. What makes macroeconomics different from microeconomics? What do they have in common?

3. How much richer was the average American in 2008 than in 1900?

4. What are two striking business cycle events in the United States during the last 108 years?

5. List six fundamental macroeconomic questions.

6. In a graph of the natural logarithm of an economic time series, what does the slope of the graph represent?

7. What is the difference between the trend and the business cycle component of an economic time series?

8. Explain why experimentation is difficult in macroeconomics.

9. Why should a macroeconomic model be simple?
10. Should a macroeconomic model be an exact description of the world? Explain why or why not.
11. What are the five elements that make up the basic structure of a macroeconomic model?
12. Why can macroeconomic models be useful? How do we determine whether they are useful?
13. Explain why a macroeconomic model should be built from microeconomic principles.
14. What are the four theories of the business cycle that we study?
15. What are two possible causes of the productivity slowdown?
16. What is the principal effect of an increase in government spending?
17. Why might a decrease in taxes have no effect?
18. What is the cause of inflation in the long run?
19. Explain the difference between the nominal interest rate and the real interest rate.
20. When did the five most recent recessions occur in the United States?
21. What role did credit market imperfections play in the recent financial crisis.
22. How are the government surplus and the current account surplus connected?
23. What causes inflation in the long run?
24. What are four factors that determine the quantity of unemployment?

Problems

1. Consider the following data on real GDP per capita in the United States:

Year	U.S. Real GDP Per Capita (2000 dollars)
1950	$11,745
1960	$13,951
1970	$18,561
1980	$22,784
1990	$28,598
1998	$33,544
1999	$34,367
2000	$34,785
2001	$34,677
2002	$34,876
2003	$35,423
2004	$36,357
2005	$37,063
2006	$37,725
2007	$38,116
2008	$38,189

   (a) Calculate the percentage growth rates in real GDP per capita in each of the years 1999 through 2008, from the previous year.
   (b) Now, instead of calculating the annual percentage growth rates in the years 1998 through 2008 directly, use as an approximation $100 \times (\ln y_t - \ln y_{t-1})$, where y_t is real per capita GDP in year t. How close does this approximation come to the actual growth rates you calculated in part (a)?
   (c) Repeat parts (a) and (b), but now calculate the percentage rates of growth in real per capita GDP from 1950 to 1960, from 1960 to 1970, from 1970 to 1980, 1980 to 1990, and 1990 to 2000. In this case, how large an error do you make by approximating the growth rate by the change in the natural log? Why is there a difference here relative to parts (a) and (b)?

2. Suppose that you had the special power to travel in time and to carry out any experiment you wanted on the economy. If you could turn back the clock to the time of the Great Depression, what experiment would you like to run on the U.S. economy? Why?

3. Give an example of a model that is used in some area other than economics, other than the roadmap

example explained in this chapter. What is unrealistic about this model? How well does the model perform its intended function?

4. Why do you think taxes would fall during a recession, as for example during the 2008–2009 recession (see Figure 1.6)?

5. Explain why the total government surplus became positive in the United States in the late 1990s, in terms of the behavior of taxes and government spending.

6. Does Figure 1.15 make you suspicious of the claim that a high rate of inflation is caused by a higher rate of money growth? Why or why not?

7. Why do you think the real interest rate was low during the three most recent recessions?

8. How do the behavior of imports and exports help to explain the decrease in the current account surplus beginning in the early 1990s?

9. Why do you think the unemployment rate in the United States was very low at the end of the 1960s?

Working with the Data

1. Graph gross domestic product (GDP) and gross national product (GNP) in 2000 dollars for 1947 and thereafter. Is there much difference in these two measures of aggregate economic activity for the United States?

2. Total government expenditures consist of expenditures by the federal government and by state and local governments. Calculate and graph the ratio of federal government expenditures to total government expenditures. Has the federal government become larger or smaller relative to state and local governments over time?

3. Using the consumer price index as a measure of the price level, calculate and graph the annual inflation rate for 1960 to 2008. Calculate this as the percentage increase in the CPI from December to December (the annual inflation rate for 1999 would be the percentage increase in the CPI from December 1998 to December 1999). In addition, calculate and graph on the same chart the percentage annual increase in M1 (a measure of the money supply) for the same years. How does your picture differ from Figure 1.15?

chapter 2

Measurement

Economics is built on the twin pillars of measurement and theory. Measurements of the performance of the economy motivate macroeconomists to build simple models that can organize our thinking about how the economy works. For example, surveys of consumer prices done every year can tell us something about how prices change over time and, coupled with observations on other economic variables, can help us to develop theories that explain why prices change over time. Meanwhile, economic theory can better inform us about the most efficient ways to carry out economic measurement. For example, theories of consumer behavior can tell us something about the appropriate way to use the prices of consumer goods to derive a price index that is a good measure of the price level.

Our goal in this chapter is to understand the basic issues concerning how key macroeconomic variables are measured. These key macroeconomic variables play important roles in the economic models that we construct and study in the remainder of this book. In particular, in the rest of this chapter we examine the measurement of GDP and its components, and the measurement of prices, savings, wealth, capital, and labor market variables.

Measuring GDP: The National Income and Product Accounts

The chief aim of national income accounting is to obtain a measure of the total quantity of goods and services produced for the market in a given country over a given period of time. For many issues in macroeconomics (although by no means for all), the measure of aggregate economic activity we are interested in is **gross domestic product (GDP)**, which is the dollar value of final output produced during a given period of time within the borders of the United States. GDP is published on a quarterly basis as part of the **National Income and Product Accounts (NIPA),** one source for which is the Survey of Current Business, published by the U.S. Department of Commerce.

There are three approaches to measuring GDP, each of which is incorporated in some way in NIPA. All three approaches give exactly the same measure of GDP, provided there are no errors of measurement in using any of these approaches. The three approaches are the **product approach,** the **expenditure approach,** and the **income approach.** We discuss each in turn, using an example.

In our running example, we consider a simple fictional economy that captures the essentials of national income accounting. This is an island economy where there is a coconut producer, a restaurant, consumers, and a government. The coconut producer owns all of the coconut trees on the island, harvests the coconuts that grow on the trees, and in the current year produces 10 million coconuts, which are sold for $2.00 each, yielding total revenue of $20 million. The coconut producer pays wages of $5 million to its workers (who are some of the consumers in this economy), $0.5 million in interest on a loan to some consumers, and $1.5 million in taxes to the government. The relevant data for the coconut producer are shown in Table 2.1.

Of the 10 million coconuts produced, 6 million go to the restaurant, which specializes in innovative ways of serving coconuts—for example "shredded coconut in its own milk," "coconut soup," and " coconut in the half-shell." The remaining 4 million coconuts are bought by the consumers. Again, all coconuts are $2 each. Coconuts serve two roles in this economy. First, a coconut is an **intermediate good,** a good that is produced and then used as an input to another production process—here, the production of restaurant food. Second, it is a final consumption good, in that coconuts are purchased by consumers. The restaurant sells $30 million in restaurant meals during the year (this is a rather large restaurant). The total cost of coconuts for the restaurant is $12 million, and the restaurant pays its workers $4 million in wages and the government $3 million in taxes. Data for the restaurant are provided in Table 2.2.

Next, we need to calculate after-tax profits for each of the producers (the coconut producer and the restaurant). After-tax profits in this example are simply

$$\text{After-tax profits} = \text{Total Revenue} - \text{Wages} - \text{Interest}$$
$$- \text{Cost of Intermediate Inputs} - \text{Taxes}.$$

Table 2.1   Coconut Producer

Total Revenue	$20 million
Wages	$5 million
Interest on Loan	$0.5 million
Taxes	$1.5 million

Table 2.2   Restaurant

Total Revenue	$30 million
Cost of Coconuts	$12 million
Wages	$4 million
Taxes	$3 million

Table 2.3	After-Tax Profits
Coconut Producer	$13 million
Restaurant	$11 million

Table 2.4	Government
Tax Revenue	$5.5 million
Wages	$5.5 million

Table 2.5	Consumers
Wage Income	$14.5 million
Interest Income	$0.5 million
Taxes	$1 million
Profits Distributed to Producers	$24 million

Therefore, from Tables 2.1 and 2.2 above, we calculate after-tax profits in Table 2.3.

The government's role in this economy is to provide protection from attacks from other islands. In the past, foreign invaders have destroyed coconut trees and made off with coconuts. The government collects taxes to provide national defense. That is, it uses all of its tax revenue to pay wages to the army. Total taxes collected are $5.5 million ($4.5 million from producers and $1 million from consumers), and so the data for the government are as shown in Table 2.4.

Consumers work for the producers and for the government, earning total wages of $14.5 million. They receive $0.5 million in interest from the coconut producer, pay $1 million in taxes to the government, and receive after-tax profits of $24 million from the producers, because some of the consumers own the coconut firm and the restaurant. Data for the consumers are shown in Table 2.5.

Now, given the abovementioned data for this simple economy, we examine how GDP would be calculated using the three different national income accounting approaches.

The Product Approach to Measuring GDP

The product approach to NIPA is also called the **value-added** approach. This is because the main principle in the product approach is that GDP is calculated as the sum of value added to goods and services across all productive units in the economy. To calculate GDP using the product approach, we add the value of all goods and services produced in the economy and then subtract the value of all intermediate goods used in production to obtain total value added. If we did not subtract the value of intermediate goods used in

Table 2.6 GDP Using the Product Approach	
Value added - coconuts	$20 million
Value added - restaurant food	$18 million
Value added - government	$5.5 million
GDP	$43.5 million

production, then we would be double-counting. In our example, we do not want to count the value of the coconuts used in the production of restaurant services as part of GDP.

In the example, the coconut producer does not use any intermediate goods in production, so value added in producing coconuts, which is the coconut producer's total revenue, is $20 million. For the restaurant, however, value added is total revenue minus the value of the coconuts used in production; thus, total value added for the restaurant is $18 million. For government production, we have a problem, because the national defense services provided by the government are not sold at market prices. Standard practice here is to value national defense services at the cost of the inputs to production. Here, the only input to production was labor, so the total value added for the government is $5.5 million. Total value added, or GDP, therefore, is $43.5 million. The GDP calculation using the product approach is summarized in Table 2.6.

The Expenditure Approach

In the expenditure approach, we calculate GDP as *total spending on all final goods and services production in the economy.* Note again that we do not count spending on intermediate goods. In the NIPA, total expenditure is calculated as

$$\text{Total expenditure} = C + I + G + NX,$$

where C denotes expenditures on consumption, I is investment expenditure, G is government expenditure, and NX is net exports—that is, total exports of U.S. goods and services minus total imports into the United States. We add exports because this includes goods and services produced within the United States. Imports are subtracted because, in general, each of $C, I,$ and G includes some goods and services that were produced abroad, and we do not want to include these in U.S. GDP.

In our example, there is no investment, no exports, and no imports, so that $I = NX = 0$. Consumers spend $8 million on coconuts and $30 million at the restaurant, so that $C = $38 million. For government expenditures, again we count the $5.5 million in wages spent by the government as if national defense services had been purchased as a final good at $5.5 million, and so $G = $5.5 million. Therefore, calculating GDP using the expenditure approach, we get

$$\text{GDP} = C + I + G + NX = \$43.5 \text{ million}.$$

The GDP calculation using the expenditure approach is shown in Table 2.7. Note that we obtain the same answer calculating GDP this way as using the product approach, as we should.

Table 2.7	GDP Using the Expenditure Approach
Consumption	$38 million
Investment	0
Government Expenditures	$5.5 million
Net Exports	0
GDP	$43.5 million

The Income Approach

To calculate GDP using the income approach, we *add up all income received by economic agents contributing to production.* Income includes the profits made by firms. In the NIPA, income includes compensation of employees (wages, salaries, and benefits), proprietors' income (self-employed firm owners), rental income, corporate profits, net interest, indirect business taxes (sales and excise taxes paid by businesses), and depreciation (consumption of fixed capital). Depreciation represents the value of productive capital (plant and equipment) that wears out during the period we are considering. Depreciation is taken out when we calculate profits, and so it needs to be added in again when we compute GDP.

In the example, we need to include the wage income of consumers, $14.5 million, as a component of GDP. In addition, we need to count the profits of producers. If we do this on an after-tax basis, total profits for the two producers are $24 million. Next, we add the interest income of consumers (this is net interest), which is $0.5 million. Finally, we need to add the taxes paid by producers to the government, which are essentially government income. This amount is $4.5 million. Total GDP is then $43.5 million, which of course is the same answer that we obtained for the other two approaches. The calculation of GDP using the income approach is summarized in Table 2.8.

Why do the product approach, the expenditure approach, and the income approach yield the same GDP measure? This is because the total quantity of output, or value added, in the economy is ultimately sold, thus showing up as expenditure, and what is spent on all output produced is income, in some form or other, for someone in the economy. If we let Y denote total GDP in the economy, then Y is total aggregate output,

Table 2.8	GDP Using the Income Approach
Wage Income	$14.5 million
After-tax profits	$24 million
Interest Income	$0.5 million
Taxes	$4.5 million
GDP	$43.5 million

and it is also aggregate income. Further, it is also true as an identity that aggregate income equals aggregate expenditure, or

$$Y = C + I + G + NX.$$

This relationship is sometimes referred to as the **income–expenditure identity,** as the quantity on the left-hand side of the identity is aggregate income, and the right-hand side is the sum of the components of aggregate expenditure.

An Example with Inventory Investment

One component of investment expenditures is inventory investment, which consists of any goods that are produced during the current period but are not consumed. Stocks of inventories consist of inventories of finished goods (for example, automobiles that are stored on the lot), goods in process (for example, automobiles still on the assembly line), and raw materials.

Suppose in our running example that everything is identical to the above, except that the coconut producer produces 13 million coconuts instead of 10 million, and that the extra 3 million coconuts are not sold but are stored as inventory. In terms of the value-added approach, GDP is the total value of coconuts produced, which is now $26 million, plus the value of restaurant food produced, $30 million, minus the value of intermediate goods used up in the production of restaurant food, $12 million, plus value added by the government, $5.5 million, for total GDP of $49.5 million. Note that we value the coconut inventory at the market price of coconuts in the example. In practice, this need not be the case; sometimes the book value of inventories carried by firms is not the same as market value, although sound economics says it should be.

Now, for the expenditure approach, $C = \$38$ million, $NX = 0$, and $G = \$5.5$ million as before, but now $I = \$6$ million, so GDP $= C + I + G + NX = \$49.5$ million. It may seem odd that the inventory investment of $6 million is counted as expenditure, because this does not appear to be expenditure on a final good or service. The convention, however, is to treat the inventory investment here as if the coconut producer bought $6 million in coconuts from itself.

Finally, in terms of the income approach, wage income to consumers is $14.5 million, interest income to consumers is $0.5 million, taxes are $4.5 million, as before, and total profits after taxes for the two producers are now $30 million, for total GDP of $49.5 million. Here, we add the $6 million in inventories to the coconut producer's profits, because this is an addition to the firm's assets.

An Example with International Trade

To show what can happen when international trade in goods comes into the picture, we take our original example and alter it slightly. Suppose that the restaurant imports 2 million coconuts from other islands at $2 each, in addition to the coconuts purchased from the domestic coconut producer, and that all of these coconuts are used in the restaurant. The restaurant still sells $30 million in restaurant food to domestic consumers.

Here, following the value-added approach, the value added by the domestic coconut producer is $20 million as before. For the restaurant, value added is the value of food produced, $30 million, minus the value of intermediate inputs, which is $16 million, including the cost of imported coconuts. As before, total value added for the government is $5.5 million. Therefore, GDP is total value added for the two producers and the government, or $39.5 million.

Next, using the expenditure approach, consumption of coconuts by consumers is $8 million and restaurant service consumption is $30 million, so that $C = $38 million. Government expenditures are the same as in the initial example, with $G = $5.5 million, and we have $I = 0$. Total exports are 0, while imports (of coconuts) are $4 million, so that net exports are $NX = -$4 million. We then have GDP $= C + I + G + NX = $39.5 million.

Finally, following the income approach, the wage income of consumers is $14.5 million, interest income of consumers is $0.5 million, and taxes are $4.5 million, as in the initial example. The after-tax profits of the coconut producer are $13 million, also as before. The change here is in the after-tax profits of the restaurant, which are reduced by $4 million, the value of the imported coconuts, so that after-tax restaurant profits are $7 million. Total GDP is then $39.5 million.

Gross National Product

Before 1991, **gross national product (GNP)** was used in the United States as the official measure of aggregate production. In line with international practice, however, the official measure became GDP in December of 1991. In practice, there is little difference between GDP and GNP in the United States, but in principle the difference could matter significantly. GNP measures the value of output produced by domestic factors of production, regardless of whether the production takes place (as is the case for GDP) inside U.S. borders. For example, if a Nike plant in Southeast Asia is owned and managed by U.S. residents, then the incomes accruing to U.S. factors of production include the managerial income and profits of this plant, and this is included in U.S. GNP, but not in U.S. GDP. Similarly, if a Honda plant in Ohio has Japanese owners, the profits of the plant would not be included in GNP, as these profits are not income for U.S. residents, but the profits would be included in GDP.

Gross national product is the sum of GDP and net factor payments (NFP) from abroad to domestic residents or

$$GNP = GDP + NFP,$$

where NFP denotes net factor payments from abroad. For 2008, GDP for the United States was $14,264.6 billion, and GNP was $14,397.8 billion, so NFP was $133.2 billion. Thus, for this typical year, the difference between GDP and GNP for the United States was 0.934% of GDP, which is small. For some countries, however, there is a significant difference between GDP and GNP, particularly for those countries where a large fraction of national productive capacity is foreign-owned, in which case NFP is significant.

What Does GDP Leave Out?

GDP is intended simply as a measure of the quantity of output produced and exchanged in the economy as a whole. Sometimes GDP, or GDP per person, however, is used as a measure of aggregate economic welfare. There are at least two problems with this approach. The first is that aggregate GDP does not take into account how income is distributed across the individuals in the population. At the extreme, if one person in the economy has all the income and the rest of the people have no income, the average level of economic welfare in the economy would be very low. Second, GDP leaves out all nonmarket activity, with work in the home being an example. If people eat restaurant meals rather than eating at home, then GDP rises, because there are now more services produced in the market than before. People should be better off as a result, because they had the option of eating at home but chose to go out. However, the increase in GDP exaggerates the increase in economic welfare, as GDP does not measure the value added when food is cooked at home.

GDP may be an inaccurate measure of welfare, but there are also some problems with GDP as a measure of aggregate output, and two of these problems are the following. First, economic activities in the so-called **underground economy** are, by definition, not counted in GDP. The underground economy includes any unreported economic activity. A high-profile example of underground activity is trade in illegal drugs; a low-profile example is the exchange of babysitting services for cash. Economic activity goes underground so as to avoid legal penalties and taxation, and underground activity often involves cash transactions. The size of the underground economy may indeed be significant in the United States, as evidenced by the fact that the quantity of U.S. currency held per U.S. resident was approximately \$2,776 in April 2009.[1] Clearly, most individuals engaged in standard market transactions do not hold this much currency. This large quantity of currency in circulation can in part be explained by the large amount of U.S. currency held outside the country, but it still reflects the fact that the underground economy matters for the measurement of GDP in the United States.

A second problem in measuring GDP, which we encountered in our example, involves how government expenditures are counted. Most of what the government produces is not sold at market prices. For example, how are we to value roads, bridges, and national defense services? The solution in the NIPA, as in our example, is to value government expenditures at cost, that is, the payments to all of the factors of production that went into producing the good or service. In some cases this could overvalue what is produced; for example, if the government produced something that nobody wanted, such as a bridge to nowhere. In other cases, government production could be undervalued; for example, we may be willing to pay much more for national defense than what it costs in terms of wages, salaries, materials, and so forth.

The Components of Aggregate Expenditure

Typically, particularly in constructing economic models to understand how the economy works, we are interested mainly in the expenditure side of the NIPA. Here, we consider each of the expenditure components in more detail. Table 2.9 gives the GDP components for 2008.

---

[1]*Source:* U.S. Department of Commerce and Board of Governors of the Federal Reserve System.

Table 2.9   Gross Domestic Product for 2008

Component of GDP	$Billions	% of GDP
GDP	14,264.6	100.0
Consumption	10,057.9	70.5
Durables	1023.2	7.2
Nondurables	2965.1	20.8
Services	6069.6	42.6
Investment	1993.5	14.0
Fixed Investment	2040.5	14.3
Nonresidential	1552.8	10.9
Residential	487.7	3.4
Inventory Investment	−47.0	−0.3
Net Exports	−669.2	−4.7
Exports	1859.4	13.0
Imports	2528.6	17.7
Government Expenditures	2882.4	20.2
Federal Defense	734.9	5.2
Federal Nondefense	337.0	2.4
State and Local	1810.4	12.7

Consumption   Consumption expenditures are the largest expenditure component of GDP, accounting for 70.5% of GDP in 2008 (see Table 2.9). **Consumption** is expenditure on consumer goods and services during the current period, and the components of consumption are durable goods, nondurable goods, and services. Durable goods include items like new automobiles, appliances, and furniture. Nondurables include food and clothing. Services are nontangible items like haircuts and hotel stays. Clearly, the division between durables and nondurables is somewhat imprecise because, for example, shoes (a nondurable) could be viewed as being as durable as washing machines (a durable). Further, some items included in consumption are clearly not consumed within the period. For example, if the period is one year, an automobile may provide services to the buyer for ten years or more, and is, therefore, not a consumption good but might economically be more appropriately considered an investment expenditure when it is bought. The purchase of a used car or other used durable good is not included in GDP, but the services provided (for example, by a dealer) in selling a used car would be included.

Investment   In Table 2.9, investment expenditures were 14.0% of GDP in 2008. **Investment** is expenditure on goods that are produced during the current period, but are not consumed during the current period. There are two types of investment. **Fixed investment** is production of capital, such as plant, equipment, and housing, and **inventory investment** consists of goods that are essentially put into storage. The components of fixed investment are nonresidential investment and residential investment. Nonresidential investment adds to the plant, equipment, and software that make up the capital stock for producing goods and services. Residential investment—housing—is also productive in that it produces housing services.

Although investment is a much smaller fraction of GDP than is consumption, investment plays a very important role in business cycles. Investment is much more variable than GDP or consumption, and some components of investment also tend to lead the business cycle. For example, an upward or downward blip in housing investment tends to precede an upward or downward blip in GDP. We study this phenomenon further in Chapter 3.

Net Exports   As exports were less than imports in 2008, the United States ran a trade deficit in goods and services with the rest of the world—that is, **net exports** were negative (see Table 2.9). Exports were 13.0% of GDP in 2008 while imports were 17.7% of GDP. Trade with the rest of the world in goods and services, therefore, is quite important to the U.S. economy, as we noted in Chapter 1.

Government Expenditures   **Government expenditures,** which consist of expenditures by federal, state, and local governments on final goods and services, were 20.2% of GDP in 2008, as seen in Table 2.9. The main components of government expenditures are federal defense spending (5.2% of GDP in 2008), federal nondefense spending (2.4% of GDP in 2008), and state and local spending (12.7% of GDP in 2008). The NIPA also makes the important distinction between government consumption and government gross investment, just as we distinguish between private consumption and private investment. An important point is that the government spending included in the NIPA is only the expenditures on final goods and services. This does not include **transfers,** which are very important in the government budget. These outlays essentially transfer purchasing power from one group of economic agents to another, and they include such items as Social Security payments and unemployment insurance payments. Transfers are not included in GDP, as they are simply money transfers from one group of people to another, or income redistribution rather than income creation.

Nominal and Real GDP and Price Indices

While the components of GDP for any specific time period give us the total dollar value of goods and services produced in the economy during that period, for many purposes we would like to make comparisons between GDP data in different time periods. This might tell us something about growth in the productive capacity of the economy over time and about growth in our standard of living. A problem, however, is that the average level of prices changes over time, so that generally part of the increase in GDP that we observe is the result of inflation. In this section, we show how to adjust for this effect of inflation on the growth in GDP and, in so doing, arrive at a measure of the price level and the inflation rate.

A **price index** is a weighted average of the prices of a set of the goods and services produced in the economy over a period of time. If the price index includes prices of all goods and services, then that price index is a measure of the general **price level,** or the average level of prices across goods and services. We use price indices to measure the **inflation rate,** which is the rate of change in the price level from one period of time to another. If we can measure the inflation rate, we can also determine how much of a change in GDP from one period to another is purely **nominal** and how much is **real**. A nominal change in GDP is a change in GDP that occurred only because the price level changed, whereas a real change in GDP is an increase in the actual quantity of goods and services (including, for example, the numbers of apples and oranges sold during a period of time), which is what ultimately matters for consumers.

Real GDP

To see how real GDP is calculated in the NIPA, it helps to consider an example. Imagine an economy in which the only goods produced are apples and oranges. In year 1, 50 apples and 100 oranges are produced, and the prices of apples and oranges are $1.00 and $0.80, respectively. In year 2, 80 apples and 120 oranges are produced, and the prices of apples and oranges are $1.25 and $1.60, respectively. These data are displayed in Table 2.10. For convenience in expressing the formulas for real GDP calculations, we let the quantities of apples and oranges, respectively, in year 1 be denoted by Q_1^a and Q_1^o with respective prices denoted by P_1^a and P_1^o. Quantities and prices in year 2 are represented similarly (see Table 2.10).

The calculation of nominal GDP in each year is straightforward here, as there are no intermediate goods. Year 1 nominal GDP is

$$GDP_1 = P_1^a Q_1^a + P_1^o Q_1^o = (\$1.00 \times 50) + (\$0.80 \times 100) = \$130.$$

Similarly, year 2 nominal GDP is

$$GDP_2 = P_2^a Q_2^a + P_2^o Q_2^o = (\$1.25 \times 80) + (\$1.60 \times 120) = \$292,$$

so the percentage increase in nominal GDP from year 1 to year 2 is equal to

$$\left(\frac{GDP_2}{GDP_1} - 1 \right) \times 100\% = \left(\frac{292}{130} - 1 \right) \times 100\% = 125\%.$$

That is, nominal GDP more than doubled from year 1 to year 2.

Now, the question is, how much of this increase in nominal GDP is accounted for by inflation and how much by an increase in the real quantity of aggregate output produced? Until 1996, the practice in the U.S. NIPA was first to choose a base year and then to calculate real GDP using these base year prices. That is, rather than multiplying the quantities produced in a given year by current year prices (which is what we do when calculating

Table 2.10   Data for Real GDP Example

	Apples	Oranges
Quantity in Year 1	$Q_1^a = 50$	$Q_1^o = 100$
Price in Year 1	$P_1^a = \$1.00$	$P_1^o = \$0.80$
Quantity in Year 2	$Q_2^a = 80$	$Q_2^o = 120$
Price in Year 2	$P_2^a = \$1.25$	$P_2^o = \$1.60$

nominal GDP), we multiply by base year prices to obtain real GDP. In the example, suppose that we use year 1 as the base year, and let $RGDP_1^1$ and $RGDP_2^1$ denote real GDP in years 1 and 2, respectively, calculated using year 1 as the base year. Then, real GDP in year 1 is the same as nominal GDP for that year, because year 1 is the base year, so we have

$$RGDP_1^1 = GDP_1 = \$130.$$

Now, for year 2 real GDP, we use year 2 quantities and year 1 prices to obtain

$$RGDP_2^1 = P_1^a Q_2^a + P_1^o Q_2^o = (\$1.00 \times 80) + (\$0.80 \times 120) = \$176.$$

Therefore, the ratio of real GDP in year 2 to real GDP in year 1, using year 1 as the base year is

$$g_1 = \frac{RGDP_2^1}{RGDP_1^1} = \frac{176}{130} = 1.354,$$

so the percentage increase in real GDP using this approach is $(1.354 - 1) \times 100\% = 35.4\%$. Alternatively, suppose that we use year 2 as the base year and let $RGDP_1^2$ and $RGDP_2^2$ denote real GDP in years 1 and 2, respectively, calculated using this approach. Then, year 2 real GDP is the same as year 2 nominal GDP, that is

$$RGDP_2^2 = GDP_2 = \$292.$$

Year 1 GDP, using year 1 quantities and year 2 prices, is

$$RGDP_1^2 = P_2^a Q_1^a + P_2^o Q_1^o = (\$1.25 \times 50) + (\$1.60 \times 100) = \$222.50.$$

Then, the ratio of real GDP in year 2 to real GDP in year 1, using year 2 as the base year, is

$$g_2 = \frac{RGDP_2^2}{RGDP_1^2} = \frac{292}{222.5} = 1.312,$$

and the percentage increase in GDP from year 1 to year 2 is $(1.312 - 1) \times 100\% = 31.2\%$.

A key message from the example is that the choice of the base year matters for the calculation of GDP. If year 1 is used as the base year, then the increase in real GDP is 35.4%, and if year 2 is the base year, real GDP is calculated to increase by 31.2%. The reason the choice of the base year matters in the example, and in reality, is that the relative prices of goods change over time. That is, the relative price of apples to oranges is $\frac{\$1.00}{\$0.80} = 1.25$ in year 1, and this relative price is $\frac{\$1.25}{\$1.60} = 0.78$ in year 2. Therefore, apples became cheaper relative to oranges from year 1 to year 2. If relative prices had remained the same between year 1 and year 2, then the choice of the base year would not matter. In calculating real GDP, the problem of changing relative prices would not be too great in calculating GDP close to the base year (say, 2008 or 2009 relative to a base year in 2007), because relative prices would typically not change much over a short period of time. Over many years, however, the problem could be severe, for example, in calculating real GDP in 2009 relative to a base year in 1982. The solution to this problem, adopted in the NIPA, is to use a **chain-weighting** scheme for calculating real GDP.

With the chain-weighting approach, a *Fisher index* is used, and the approach is essentially like using a rolling base period. The chain-weighted ratio of real GDP in year 2 to real GDP in year 1 is

$$g_c = \sqrt{g_1 \times g_2} = \sqrt{1.354 \times 1.312} = 1.333,$$

so that the chain-weighted ratio of real GDP in the two years is a geometric average of the ratios calculated using each of years 1 and 2 as base years.[2] In the example, we calculate the percentage growth rate in real GDP from year 1 to year 2 using the chain-weighting method to be $(1.333 - 1) \times 100\% = 33.3\%$. The growth rate in this case falls between the growth rates we calculated using the other two approaches, which is of course what we should get given that chain-weighting effectively averages (geometrically) the growth rates calculated using years 1 and 2 as base years.

Now, once we have the chain-weighted ratio of real GDP in one year relative to another (g_c in this case), we can calculate real GDP in terms of the dollars of any year we choose. For example, in our example, if we want real GDP in year 1 dollars, then real GDP in year 1 is the same as nominal GDP or $GDP_1 = \$130$, and real GDP in year 2 is equal to $GDP_1 \times g_c = \$130 \times 1.333 = \$173.29$. Alternatively, if we want real GDP in year 2 dollars, then real GDP in year 2 is $GDP_2 = \$292$, and real GDP in year 1 is $\frac{GDP_2}{g_c} = \frac{\$292}{1.333} = \$219.05$.

In practice, the growth rates in real GDP in adjacent years are calculated just as we have done it here, and then real GDP is "chained" together from one year to the next. Chain-weighting should in principle give a more accurate measure of the year-to-year, or quarter-to-quarter, changes in real GDP. In Figure 2.1 we show nominal GDP and real GDP, calculated using the chain-weighting approach, for the United States over the period 1947–2009. Real GDP is measured here in 2000 dollars, so that real GDP is equal to nominal GDP in 2000. Because the inflation rate was generally positive over the period 1947–2009, and was particularly high in the 1970s, real GDP grows in Figure 2.1 at a lower rate than does nominal GDP.

Measures of the Price Level

There are two commonly used measures of the price level. The first is the **implicit GDP price deflator,** and the second is the **consumer price index (CPI).** The implicit GDP price deflator is measured as

$$\text{Implicit GDP Price deflator} = \frac{\text{Nominal GDP}}{\text{Real GDP}} \times 100.$$

Here, multiplying by 100 just normalizes the price deflator to 100 in the year we are choosing nominal GDP to be equal to real GDP. For the example above, the price deflator we calculate would depend on whether we use year 1 or year 2 as a base year,

---

[2]For more detail on the calculation of real GDP using the chain-weighting method, see *A Guide to the NIPA's,* available from the Bureau of Economic Analysis at http://www.bea.doc.gov/bea/an/nipaguid.htm.

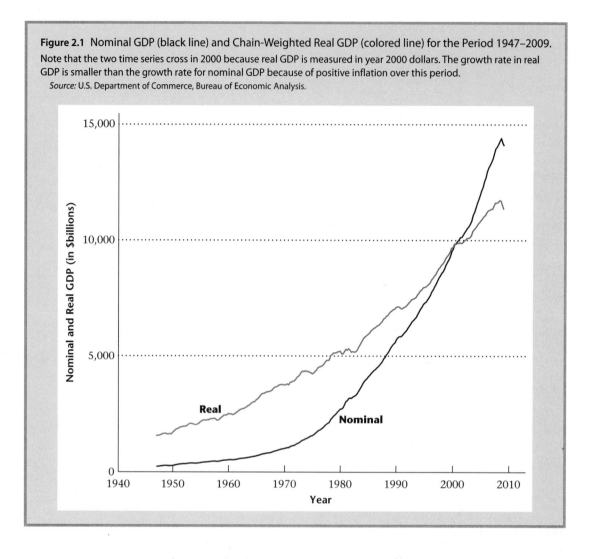

Figure 2.1 Nominal GDP (black line) and Chain-Weighted Real GDP (colored line) for the Period 1947–2009.
Note that the two time series cross in 2000 because real GDP is measured in year 2000 dollars. The growth rate in real GDP is smaller than the growth rate for nominal GDP because of positive inflation over this period.
Source: U.S. Department of Commerce, Bureau of Economic Analysis.

or compute chain-weighted real GDP. We give the results in Table 2.11, and arbitrarily choose chain-weighted real GDP to be in year 1 dollars. Note in Table 2.11 that the answers we get for the percentage rate of inflation between year 1 and year 2 depend critically on how we measure real GDP.

The alternative measure of the price level, the CPI, is not as broadly based as the implicit GDP price deflator, because it includes only goods and services that are purchased by consumers. Further, the CPI is a fixed-weight price index, which takes the quantities in some base year as being the typical goods bought by the average consumer during that base year, and then uses those quantities as weights to calculate the index in each year. Thus, the CPI in the current year would be

$$\text{Current year CPI} = \frac{\text{Cost of base year quantities at current prices}}{\text{Cost of base year quantities at base year prices}} \times 100.$$

Table 2.11   Implicit GDP Price Deflators, Example

	Year 1	Year 2	% Increase
Year 1 = base year	100	165.9	65.9
Year 2 = base year	58.4	100	71.2
Chain-weighting	100	168.5	68.5

In the example, if we take year 1 as the base year, then the year 1 (base year) CPI is 100, and the year 2 CPI is $\frac{222.5}{130} \times 100 = 171.2$, so that the percentage increase in the CPI from year 1 to year 2 is 71.2%.

In practice, there can be substantial differences between the inflation rates calculated using the implicit GDP price deflator and those calculated using the CPI. Figure 2.2 shows the GDP deflator inflation rate (the black line) and CPI inflation rate (the blue line), calculated quarter by quarter, for the United States over the period 1947–2009. The two measures of the inflation rate track each other broadly, but the CPI inflation rate tends to be more volatile than the GDP deflator inflation rate. At times, there can be large differences between the two measures. For example, in late 1979, the CPI inflation rate exceeded 14%, while the GDP deflator inflation rate was about a bit more than 10%. These differences in inflation rate measures could matter greatly for contracts (for example, labor contracts) that are geared to the inflation rate or for the formulation of monetary policy, where close attention is paid to inflation performance.

Figure 2.2 shows the differences we can observe in measured inflation rates, depending on whether we use the CPI or the implicit GDP price deflator as a measure of the price level. As well, over long periods of time there can be very large differences in the rates of inflation calculated using the two alternative price level measures. To see this, in Figure 2.3 we show the CPI and GDP price deflator in levels for the period 1947–2009, normalizing by setting each measure equal to 100 in the first quarter of 1947. What the picture tells us is that, if we accept the CPI as a good measure of the price level, then the cost of living increased by a factor of 9.85 over 62 years. However, the GDP price deflator indicates an increase in the cost of living by a factor of only 8.22. Put another way, the average annual inflation rate between 1947 and 2006 was 3.76% as measured by the CPI, and 3.46% as measured by the implicit GDP price deflator. These differences reflect a well-known upward bias in the CPI measure of inflation.

The GDP price deflator tends to yield a better measure of the inflation rate than does the CPI. However, in some cases there are alternatives to either the GDP price deflator or the CPI, which serve the purpose better. For example, if we are interested only in measuring the cost of living for consumers living in the United States, then it may be preferable to use the implicit consumption deflator rather than the implicit GDP price deflator as a measure of the price level. The implicit consumption deflator is a price index including only the goods and services that are included in consumption

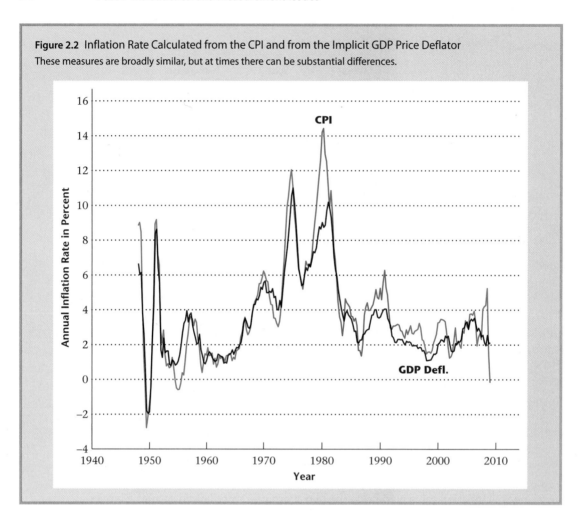

Figure 2.2 Inflation Rate Calculated from the CPI and from the Implicit GDP Price Deflator
These measures are broadly similar, but at times there can be substantial differences.

expenditures. The GDP price deflator includes the prices of investment goods, exports, and goods and services sold to the government, none of which would matter directly for consumers. However, if we are looking for a price index reflecting the price of aggregate output produced in the United States, then the GDP price deflator is the appropriate measure.

Problems with Measuring Real GDP and the Price Level

As we saw above, particularly in how the implicit GDP price deflator is derived, the measurement of real GDP and the measurement of the price level are intimately related. If a particular measure of real GDP underestimates growth in real GDP, then the rate of inflation is overestimated. In practice, there are three important problems with measuring real GDP and the price level.

Figure 2.3 The Price Level as Measured by the CPI and the Implicit GDP Price Deflator, 1947–2009

In the figure, each price level measure is set to 100 in the first quarter of 1947. The CPI increases by a factor of 9.85 over the whole period, while the implicit GDP price deflator increases by a factor of 8.22.

Source: The U.S. Department of Commerce and the Bureau of Labor Statistics.

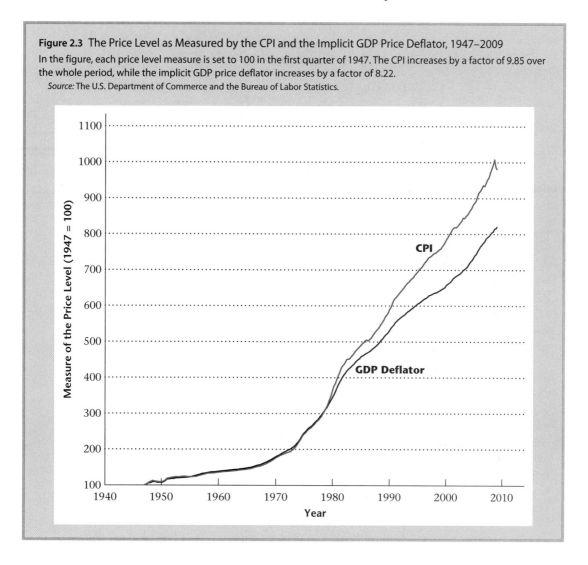

The first problem was mentioned above, which is that relative prices change over time. We showed how chain-weighting corrects for this problem in the measurement of real GDP and, therefore, corrects for the bias that relative price changes would introduce in the measurement of inflation using the implicit GDP price deflator. Changes in relative prices can also introduce severe bias in how the CPI measures inflation. When there is a relative price change, consumers typically purchase less of the goods that have become more expensive and more of those that have become relatively cheap. In the previous example, apples became cheaper relative to oranges in year 2, and the ratio of apples consumed to oranges consumed increased. In computing the CPI, the implicit assumption is that consumers do not change their buying habits when relative price changes occur, which is clearly false. As a result, goods that become relatively

MACROECONOMICS IN ACTION
Comparing Real GDP Across Countries and the Penn Effect

Just as it is useful to obtain a measure of real GDP for a given country so that we can study the growth of output over time in that country, it is also important to be able to make comparisons between real GDPs, or GDPs per person, in different countries. For example, if we can compare real GDP across all countries in the world, we can potentially learn the reasons for differences in the standard of living across countries. This is one of the issues that will concern us when we study economic growth, particularly in Chapter 7.

Coming up with comparable measures of GDP is potentially a daunting task. First, although international organizations have worked to standardize the national income and product accounts across countries, there can still be significant differences in how key data are collected in different countries. For example, poor countries may have limited resources available to devote to data collection. However, even if the prices and quantities of final goods and services were measured without error in all countries, there would still be a problem in making international real GDP comparisons. This is because the prices of identical goods sold in different countries are typically significantly different, even after we express prices in units of the same currency.

To understand the measurement problem, suppose that P denotes the price of goods and services in the United States (in U.S. dollars), and P^* the price of goods and services in Mexico (in Mexican pesos). Also, suppose that e is the exchange rate of U.S. dollars for Mexican pesos, that is e is the price of a peso in dollars. Then, eP^* would be the cost of Mexican goods and services for an American, or the price in dollars of Mexican goods and services. If we observed that $P = eP^*$ then we would say that we observed the *law of one price* or *purchasing power parity*, in that prices of goods and services would be the same in the United States and Mexico, correcting for exchange rates. In fact, what we tend to observe is that $P > eP^*$ for the United States and Mexico, that is goods and services prices in United States dollars tend to be higher in the United States than in Mexico. This difference is particularly large for services, such as auto repairs, which are difficult to trade across international borders.

The *Penn effect* refers to the regularity in data on prices and exchange rates across countries, that prices tend to be higher, correcting for currency exchange rates, in high-income countries than in low-income countries. The problem is that, if we made real GDP comparisons across countries by just expressing all prices in the same currencies, then we would exaggerate the differences in income between rich and poor countries. For example, for the United States and Mexico, if the same quantity of a given good were produced in each country, we would tend to measure this as a smaller contribution to real GDP in Mexico than in the United States if we expressed the quantity produced in terms of its value in U.S. dollars.

An approach to correcting for the Penn effect is to make international real GDP comparisons based on purchasing power parity. For example, for the United States and Mexico, if P is the U.S. price level (in U.S. dollars), and P^* is the Mexican price level (in Mexican pesos), then to compare GDP in the United States with GDP in Mexico, we would multiply nominal quantities for Mexico by P/P^* rather than by e. This is the approach taken in the *Penn World Tables,* a comprehensive set of international data developed by Alan Heston, Robert Summers, and Bettina

Aten at the University of Pennsylvania.[3] We will make use of the Penn World Tables when we study economic growth in Chapters 6 and 7.

---

[3]Alan Heston, Robert Summers, and Bettina Aten, Penn World Table Version 6.2, Center For International Comparisons of Production, Income, and Prices at the University of Pennsylvania, September 2006.

more expensive receive a higher weight than they should in the CPI, and, therefore, the CPI-based measure of the rate of inflation is biased upward. This is a serious policy issue, because some federal transfer payments, including Social Security, are indexed to the CPI, and, therefore, an upward bias in CPI inflation would also commit the federal government to higher transfer payments, which in turn would increase the size of the federal government budget deficit. Also, federal income tax brackets are geared to CPI inflation. Upward bias in CPI inflation causes tax revenues to fall, increasing the government deficit. Rather than the rate of increase in the CPI, a more accurate measure of the rate of inflation in consumer goods is the implicit consumption price deflator, which is the price deflator associated with chain-weighted real consumption expenditures.

A second problem in measuring real GDP is changes in the quality of goods over time. Consider the case of 2009 vintage cars versus 1950 vintage cars. Clearly, the price of a new car in 2009 was much higher than the price of a new car in 1950, but the 2009 car is very different from the 1950 car. In 2009, most cars sold in the United States had computerized devices to monitor engine performance, automatic transmissions, power windows, air bags, seat belts, and CD players, none of which were standard equipment (or in some cases even invented) in 1950. In a sense, the 2009 car is "more car," because its quality is higher; therefore, some of the increase in price from 1950–2009 simply represents the fact that the buyer is receiving more in exchange for his or her money. To the extent that NIPA does not compensate for changes in quality over time, growth in real GDP is biased downward and inflation is biased upward.

A third problem is how measured GDP takes account of new goods. For example, personal computers were introduced in the early 1980s, and they did not exist in the NIPA before then. Clearly, we cannot make a straightforward calculation of real GDP growth from the 1970s to the 1980s, as there were no prices existing for personal computers in the 1970s. If the NIPA does not correctly take account of the fact that the new personal computers that were introduced (initially at very high prices) were a huge quality advance over old-fashioned calculators and slide rules, then this could bias downward the measure of real GDP growth and bias upward the measure of the inflation rate.

Perspectives on the Financial Crisis

House Prices and GDP Measurement

A key feature of the financial market crisis that began in the United States in 2008 and spread worldwide was the dramatic fall in the price of housing in the United States. Figure 2.4 shows the relative price of housing in the United States, measured as the average national price of a single-detached house, divided by the consumer price index. This relative price is normalized to be equal to 100 in 1963. From 1963 to 2006, the price of housing in the United States grew at a higher rate than the rate of inflation, as measured by the consumer price index, as indicated by the fact that the relative price of housing increases in the figure. There was a high rate of increase after 1995 in the relative price of housing, with a particularly pronounced increase from 2000 to 2006.

Figure 2.4 The Relative Price of Housing in the United States

The figure shows the relative price of housing, measured as the price of housing in dollars divided by the consumer price index. Of particular note is the sharp decline beginning in 2006.

This latter rapid increase in the relative price of housing can be attributed to the high demand for housing generated by innovations in the mortgage market. During this period, there was a dramatic increase in the quantity of mortgage loans made in the so-called "subprime" mortgage market. Subprime mortgages are mortgage loans granted to typically low-income borrowers with a higher-than-average risk of default. Some of these subprime mortgages were made with little screening of borrowers and with very generous terms (at least in the short run), including low interest rates and low down payments.

An unforseen development was the dramatic decrease in the relative price of housing beginning in 2006. In Figure 2.4, from the peak in the relative price of housing until early 2009, the relative price of housing fell about 25%. Exactly why the price of housing decreased over this latter period in the figure is a subject of some debate among economists. Some economists argue that the rapid increase in the price of housing up to 2006 was an asset price "bubble." According to proponents of what we could call the *bubble view,* leading up to 2006 the price of housing became detached from its fundamental economic determinants—incomes, the prices of other goods and services, interest rates, construction costs, scarcity of land—and was propelled by speculation that prices would continue to increase. According to the bubble view, bubbles inevitably pop, which is consistent with the large decrease in house prices beginning in 2006. Alternatively, according to the *fundamental view,* market prices of assets can always be explained (maybe through some hard thinking and research) by factors affecting supply and demand,

in this case the supply and demand for housing. A potential explanation for the 2006–2009 decrease in the price of housing is that housing market participants came to realize that much of the subprime mortgage lending that had occurred was to borrowers that could really not afford to live in the houses that they had acquired. Subprime borrowers began to default on their loans and vacate their houses, and new subprime lending was cut off. All this served to reduce the demand for housing and lower the price of houses.

Whether the bubble view or the fundamental view is correct, there is a case to be made that the price of housing at the beginning of 2009 more correctly reflects the value of housing to residents of the United States than did the price of housing at the peak of the housing boom in 2006. What implications does this have for the measurement of GDP? In 2006, real GDP was 11,294.8 billion (2000) dollars, while real residential construction was 552.9 billion (2000) dollars.[4] Thus, residential construction accounted for about 4.9% of GDP. When residential construction is measured, the output of new housing is measured at the prices at which the houses sell. Thus, if the relative price of housing had been 25% lower in 2006, residential construction would have been 25% lower, or 414.7 billion (2000) dollars instead of 552.9 billion (2000) dollars. This amounts to a reduction in real GDP of 1.2%, which is a significant quantity. Potentially, this is a mismeasurement in GDP of about $460 per U.S. resident, or about half the reduction in real GDP experienced in a mild recession.

---

[4]Source: Department of Commerce, Bureau of Economic Analysis.

Savings, Wealth, and Capital

While the components of GDP in the NIPA measure aggregate activity that takes place within the current period, another key aspect of the economy that is of interest to macroeconomists is aggregate productive capacity and how aggregate savings adds to this productive capacity. In this section we explore, by way of several accounting identities, the relationships among savings, wealth, and capital.

An important distinction in economics is between **flows** and **stocks**. A flow is a rate per unit time, while a stock is the quantity in existence of some object at a point in time. In the NIPA, GDP, consumption, investment, government spending, and net exports are all flows. For example, GDP is measured in dollars spent per period. In contrast, the quantity of housing in existence in the United States at the end of a given year is a stock. In the following, we see that national saving is a flow, while the nation's wealth is a stock. In this case, national saving is the flow that is added to the stock of the nation's wealth in each year. A classic analogy is the example of water flowing into a bathtub, where the quantity of water coming out of the faucet per minute is a flow, while the quantity of water in the bathtub at any point in time is a stock.

Savings can mean very different things, depending on whether we are referring to the private (nongovernment) sector, the government, or the nation as a whole. For the private sector, to determine savings we first need to start with what the private sector has available to spend, which is **private disposable income**, denoted Y^d. We have

$$Y^d = Y + NFP + TR + INT - T,$$

where Y is GDP, NFP is net factor payments from abroad to U.S. residents, TR is transfers from the government to the private sector, INT is interest on the government debt, and T is taxes. Recall that GNP is $Y + NFP$. What the private sector saves is simply what it has available to spend minus what it consumes, and so letting S^p denote **private sector saving**, we have

$$S^p = Y^d - C = Y + NFP + TR + INT - T - C.$$

What the government has available to spend is its tax revenue, T, minus TR, minus INT, and what it consumes is government expenditures, G. Thus, **government saving** S^g is given by

$$S^g = T - TR - INT - G.$$

Government saving is simply the **government surplus,** and the government surplus is the negative of the **government deficit,** denoted D, or

$$D = -S^g = -T + TR + INT + G,$$

which is just government outlays minus government receipts. If we add private saving and government saving, we obtain **national saving,**

$$S = S^p + S^g = Y + NFP - C - G,$$

which is GNP minus private consumption, minus government consumption. Because the income—expenditure identity gives $Y = C + I + G + NX$, we can substitute for Y in the previous equation to obtain

$$\begin{aligned} S &= Y + NFP - C - G \\ &= C + I + G + NX + NFP - C - G \\ &= I + NX + NFP. \end{aligned}$$

Thus, national saving must equal investment plus net exports plus net factor payments from abroad. The quantity $NX + NFP$ is the **current account surplus** with the rest of the world, which we denote CA; thus, we have

$$S = I + CA.$$

The current account surplus is a measure of the balance of trade in goods with the rest of the world. The above identity reflects the fact that any domestic savings not absorbed by domestic investment must be shipped outside the country in the form of goods and services.

As a flow, national saving represents additions to the nation's wealth. Because $S = I + CA$, wealth is accumulated in two ways. First, wealth is accumulated through investment, I, which is additions to the nation's **capital stock.** The capital stock is the quantity of plants, equipment, housing, and inventories in existence in an economy at a point in time. Second, wealth is accumulated through current account surpluses, CA, because a current account surplus implies that U.S. residents are accumulating claims on foreigners. The current account surplus, CA, represents increases in claims on foreigners because if goods are flowing from the United States to other countries, then these goods must be paid for with a transfer of wealth from outside the United States to U.S. residents. The current account surplus is then a flow, while the quantity of claims on foreigners in existence in the United States is a stock.

Labor Market Measurement

The labor market variables we focus on here are those measured in the monthly household survey, carried out by the Bureau of Labor Statistics. In this survey, people are divided into three groups: the **employed**—those who worked part-time or full-time during the past week; the **unemployed**—those who were not employed during the past week but actively searched for work at some time during the last four weeks; and **not in the labor force**—those who are neither employed or unemployed. Thus, the labor force is the employed plus the unemployed.

Of key interest in analyzing the results of the household survey are the **unemployment rate,** measured as

$$\text{Unemployment rate} = \frac{\text{Number unemployed}}{\text{Labor force}},$$

the **participation rate,** measured as

$$\text{Participation rate} = \frac{\text{Labor force}}{\text{Total working age population}},$$

and the **employment/population ratio,** measured as

$$\text{Employment/Population Ratio} = \frac{\text{Total employment}}{\text{Total working age population}}.$$

The unemployment rate is potentially useful as a measure of **labor market tightness,** which is the degree of difficulty firms face in hiring workers.[5] However, there are two ways in which the unemployment rate might mismeasure labor market tightness (see Macroeconomics in Action: Measuring Unemployment and Labor Force Attachment). First, some people, referred to as **discouraged workers,** are not counted in the labor force and have stopped searching for work but actually wish to be employed. Thus, during a long recession, when the level of aggregate economic activity is depressed for an extended duration, the unemployment rate possibly might fall only because some unemployed people have become discouraged and stopped looking for work. In this circumstance, labor market tightness would not really have increased with the decrease in the unemployment rate, but we might be fooled into thinking so.

The second factor that could cause the unemployment rate to be a bad measure of labor market tightness is that the unemployment rate does not adjust for how intensively the unemployed are searching for work. When the unemployment rate is high, the unemployed might not search very hard for work—for example, each worker might spend one or two hours per day trying to find work. When the unemployment rate is low, however, the unemployed might all be searching very hard—for example, they might each search eight or ten hours per day. If this were the case, then the unemployment rate would be a biased measure of labor market tightness, since it would actually be easier for a firm to hire a worker in a recession and harder for a firm to hire a worker during a boom in economic activity than what the unemployment rate reflects on its own.

Partly because of problems in interpreting what movements in the unemployment rate mean, macroeconomists often focus attention on the level and growth rate of employment when they analyze the implications of labor market activity. Empirically, sometimes we have a greater interest in the behavior of the participation rate or the employment/population ratio than in the unemployment rate. Theoretically, many of the models we analyze in this book do not explain the behavior of unemployment; however, we study some explanations for unemployment in Chapters 13 and 16.

So far, we have learned how aggregate economic activity is measured in the NIPA, how nominal GDP can be decomposed to obtain measures of real GDP and the price level, what the relationships are among savings, wealth, and capital, and what the key measurement issues in the labor market are. Before we begin our study of macroeconomic theory in Chapter 4, in Chapter 3 we deal with business cycle measurement, deriving a set of key business cycle facts that focus our theoretical discussion in the following chapters.

---

[5] Another measure of labor market tightness is the the number of unemployed divided by the number of job vacancies, where vacancies are the number of job openings in the economy that firms are trying to fill. Unfortunately, the measures that exist of vacanies in the U.S. economy are notoriously poor, at least going back more than a few years from the present.

MACROECONOMICS IN ACTION
Measuring Unemployment and Labor Force Attachment

The traditional approach to labor market measurement is to divide the working age population into three groups, the employed (E), the unemployed (U), and those not in the labor force (N). This approach is useful, as the economic behavior of the three groups is in principle distinct. Those in group E are engaged in the production of goods and services for the market, those in group U are engaged in search activity with the goal of joining group E, and those in group N are engaged in home production (child care and home maintenance, for example) and leisure. Once labor market measurement is done in this way, we can then use the data in conjunction with economic theory to understand better why people choose to be in each of the three groups and to understand the implications for government policy.

Some recent research casts doubt on the traditional approach to labor market measurement. Leaving aside the issue of who should be counted as employed (rules about how many hours of work constitute employment are clearly arbitrary), there are varying degrees of search activity and separation from the labor force in the groups U and N, respectively. Stephen Jones and Craig Riddell[6] find that these differences among people in groups U and N appear to matter sufficiently that we should change how people are categorized in the labor force survey.

The first issue addressed by Jones and Riddell is related to the behavior of discouraged workers, or what they call the "marginally attached." This group of people expresses a desire to be employed, but they are not engaged in any of the activities constituting search behavior. A possibility is that the marginally attached are just engaged in wishful thinking and that they are appropriately included in N. However, Jones and Riddell's statistical analysis shows that the behavior of the marginally attached is distinct from the remainder of the people in group N, as well as from those included in U. Further, the marginally attached constitute a significant fraction of the population. This finding points to the need for distinguishing the marginally attached from U and N in the labor force survey.

A second issue studied by Jones and Riddell is the behavior of the subgroup of marginally attached people who are "waiting." This group is not actively searching for work but is waiting for a recall from a layoff period, waiting for replies from potential employers, or other such activities. Jones and Riddell find that it would be appropriate to categorize the waiting as U rather than N. In fact, the waiting are more likely to be employed in the future than are those in group U.

Finally, Jones and Riddell examine the differing behavior of those who are currently classified as U. There is some question as to whether those who simply look at job postings in newspapers, for example, should be classified as U rather than N, as such persons may be uninterested in actually contacting potential employers. However, the general behavior of those engaged in low-level search activity shares more with the remainder of the U group than with the N group.

Ultimately, the primary recommendation coming from the work of Jones and Riddell is that labor market measurement and research should be conducted based on the notion of four distinct groups. Adding a group of discouraged workers (the marginally attached) to the three traditional labor market groups appears to be a sound approach.

---

[6]See S.R.G. Jones and W.C. Riddell, 1999. "The Measurement of Unemployment: An Empirical Approach," *Econometrica* 67, 147–162.

Chapter Summary

- Gross domestic product (GDP) is measured in the National Income and Product Accounts (NIPA) of the United States. GDP can be measured via the product approach, the expenditure approach, or the income approach, which each yield the same quantity of GDP in a given period if there is no measurement error.

- GDP must be used carefully as a measure of aggregate welfare, because it leaves out home production. Further, there are problems with GDP as a measure of aggregate output, because of the existence of the underground economy and because government output is difficult to measure.

- It is useful to take account of how much of nominal GDP growth is accounted for by inflation and how much is growth in real GDP. Two approaches to measuring real GDP are choosing a base year and chain-weighting. The latter is the current method used in the NIPA. Chain-weighting corrects for the bias that arises in real GDP calculations when a base year is used and there are changes in relative prices over time. Problems with real GDP measurement arise because it is difficult to account for changes in the quality of goods over time and because new goods are introduced and others become obsolete.

- Private saving is private disposable income minus consumption, while government saving is government receipts minus government spending and transfers. The government surplus is equal to government saving. National saving is the sum of private and government saving and is equal to investment expenditures plus the current account surplus. National saving is just the accumulation of national wealth, which comes in the form of additions to the capital stock (investment) and additions to domestic claims on foreigners (the current account surplus).

- The labor market variables we focus on are those measured in the household survey of the Bureau of Labor Statistics. The working age population consists of the employed, the unemployed (those searching for work), and those not in the labor force. Three key labor market variables are the unemployment rate, the participation rate, and the employment/population ratio. The unemployment rate is sometimes used as a measure of labor market tightness, but care must be taken in how the unemployment rate is interpreted in this respect.

Key Terms

Capital stock The quantity of plant, equipment, housing, and inventories in existence in an economy at a point in time. (p. 61)

Chain-weighting An approach to calculating real GDP that uses a rolling base year. (p. 50)

Consumer price index (CPI) Expenditures on base year quantities at current year prices divided by total expenditures on base year quantities at base year prices, all multiplied by 100. (p. 51)

Consumption Goods and services produced and consumed during the current period. (p. 47)

Current account surplus Net exports plus net factor payments from abroad. (p. 61)

Discouraged workers Those who are not counted in the labor force and have stopped searching for work but actually wish to be employed. (p. 62)

Employed In the Bureau of Labor Statistics household survey, those who worked part-time or full-time during the past week. (p. 61)

Employment/population ratio The ratio of total employment to total working age population. (p. 62)

Expenditure approach The approach to GDP measurement that determines GDP as total spending on all final goods and services production in the economy. (p. 40)

Fixed Investment Investment in plant, equipment, and housing. (p. 47)

Flow A rate per unit time. (p. 60)

Government deficit The negative of the government surplus. (p. 60)

Government expenditures Expenditures by federal, state, and local governments on final goods and services. (p. 48)

Government saving Taxes minus transfers, minus interest on the government debt, minus government expenditures. (p. 60)

Government surplus Identical to government saving. (p. 60)

Gross domestic product (GDP) The dollar value of final output produced during a given period of time within a country's borders. (p. 39)

Gross national product (GNP) $GNP = GDP$ plus net factor payments to U.S. residents from abroad. (p. 45)

Implicit GDP price deflator Nominal GDP divided by real GDP, all multiplied by 100. (p. 51)

Income approach The approach to GDP measurement that determines GDP as the sum of all incomes received by economic agents contributing to production. (p. 40)

Income–expenditure identity $Y = C + I + G + NX$, where Y is aggregate income (output), C is consumption expenditures, I is investment expenditures, G is government expenditures, and NX is net exports. (p. 44)

Inflation rate The rate of change in the price level from one period to another. (p. 48)

Intermediate good A good that is produced and then used as an input in another production process. (p. 40)

Inventory investment Goods produced in the current period that are set aside for future periods. (p. 47)

Investment Goods produced in the current period but not consumed in the current period. (p. 47)

Labor market tightness The degree of difficulty firms face in hiring workers. (p. 62)

National Income and Product Accounts (NIPA) The official U.S. accounts of aggregate economic activity, which include GDP measurements. (p. 39)

National saving Private sector saving plus government saving. (p. 60)

Net exports Expenditures on domestically produced goods and services by foreigners (exports) minus expenditures on foreign-produced goods and services by domestic residents (imports). (p. 48)

Nominal change The change in the dollar value of a good, service, or asset. (p. 49)

Not in the labor force In the Bureau of Labor Statistics household survey, those who are neither employed or unemployed. (p. 61)

Participation rate The number in the labor force divided by the working age population. (p. 61)

Price index A weighted average of prices of some set of goods produced in the economy during a particular period. (p. 48)

Price level The average level of prices across all goods and services in the economy. (p. 48)

Private disposable income GDP plus net factor payments, plus transfers from the government, plus interest on the government debt, minus taxes. (p. 60)

Private sector saving Private disposable income minus consumption expenditures. (p. 60)

Product approach The approach to GDP measurement that determines GDP as the sum of value added to goods and services in production across all productive units in the economy. (p. 40)

Real change The change in the quantity of a good, service, or asset. (p. 49)

Stock Quantity in existence of some object at a point in time. (p. 60)

Transfers Government outlays that are transfers of purchasing power from one group of private economic agents to another. (p. 48)

Underground economy All unreported economic activity. (p. 46)

Unemployed In the Bureau of Labor Statistics household survey, those who were not employed during the past week but actively searched for work at some time during the last four weeks. (p. 61)

Unemployment rate The number of unemployed divided by the number in the labor force. (p. 61)

Value added The value of goods produced minus the value of intermediate goods used in production. (p. 41)

Questions for Review

1. What are the three approaches to measuring GDP?
2. Explain the concept of value added.
3. Why is the income—expenditure identity important?
4. What is the difference between GDP and GNP?

5. Is GDP a good measure of economic welfare? Why or why not?

6. What are two difficulties in the measurement of aggregate output using GDP?

7. What is the largest expenditure component of GDP?

8. What is investment?

9. Is national defense a large fraction of government spending?

10. Why does the base year matter in calculating real GDP?

11. Explain what chain-weighting is.

12. Explain three problems in the measurement of real GDP.

13. What are the differences and similarities among private sector saving, government saving, and national saving?

14. What are the two ways in which national wealth is accumulated?

15. Give two reasons that the unemployment rate may mismeasure the degree of labor market tightness.

Problems

1. Assume an economy where there are two producers: a wheat producer and a bread producer. In a given year, the wheat producer grows 30 million bushels of wheat of which 25 million bushels are sold to the bread producer at $3 per bushel, and 5 million bushels are stored by the wheat producer to use as seed for next year's crop. The bread producer produces and sells 100 million loaves of bread to consumers for $3.50 per loaf. Determine GDP in this economy during this year using the product and expenditure approaches.

2. Assume an economy with a coal producer, a steel producer, and some consumers (there is no government). In a given year, the coal producer produces 15 million tons of coal and sells it for $5 per ton. The coal producer pays $50 million in wages to consumers. The steel producer uses 25 million tons of coal as an input into steel production, all purchased at $5 per ton. Of this, 15 million tons of coal comes from the domestic coal producer and 10 million tons is imported. The steel producer produces 10 million tons of steel and sells it for $20 per ton. Domestic consumers buy 8 million tons of steel, and 2 million tons are exported. The steel producer pays consumers $40 million in wages. All profits made by domestic producers are distributed to domestic consumers.
   (a) Determine GDP using (i) the product approach, (ii) the expenditure approach, and (iii) the income approach.

   (b) Determine the current account surplus.

   (c) What is GNP in this economy? Determine GNP and GDP in the case where the coal producer is owned by foreigners, so that the profits of the domestic coal producer go to foreigners and are not distributed to domestic consumers.

3. Assume an economy with two firms. Firm A produces wheat and firm B produces bread. In a given year, firm A produces 50,000 bushels of wheat, sells 20,000 bushels of wheat to firm B at $3 per bushel, exports 25,000 bushels of wheat at $3 per bushel, and stores 5,000 bushels as inventory. Firm A pays $50,000 in wages to consumers. Firm B produces 50,000 loaves of bread, and sells all of it to domestic consumers at $2 per loaf. Firm B pays consumers $20,000 in wages. In addition to the 50,000 loaves of bread consumers buy from firm B, consumers import and consume 15,000 loaves of bread, and they pay $1 per loaf for this imported bread. Calculate gross domestic product for the year using (a) the product approach, (b) the expenditure approach, and (c) the income approach.

4. In year 1 and year 2, there are two products produced in a given economy, computers and bread. Suppose that there are no intermediate goods. In year 1, 20 computers are produced and sold at $1,000 each, and in year 2, 25 computers are sold at $1,500 each. In year 1, 10,000 loaves of bread

are sold for $1.00 each, and in year 2, 12,000 loaves of bread are sold for $1.10 each.

(a) Calculate nominal GDP in each year.

(b) Calculate real GDP in each year, and the percentage increase in real GDP from year 1 to year 2 using year 1 as the base year. Next, do the same calculations using the chain-weighting method.

(c) Calculate the implicit GDP price deflator and the percentage inflation rate from year 1 to year 2 using year 1 as the base year. Next, do the same calculations using the chain-weighting method.

(d) Suppose that computers in year 2 are twice as productive as computers in year 1. That is, computers are of higher quality in year 2 in the sense that one computer in year 2 is equivalent to two computers in year 1. How does this change your calculations in parts (a) to (c)? Explain any differences.

5. Assume an economy in which only broccoli and cauliflower are produced. In year 1, 500 million pounds of broccoli are produced and consumed and its price is $0.50 per pound, while 300 million pounds of cauliflower are produced and consumed and its price is $0.80 per pound. In year 2, 400 million pounds of broccoli are produced and consumed and its price is $0.60 per pound, while 350 million pounds of cauliflower are produced and its price is $0.85 per pound.

(a) Using year 1 as the base year, calculate the GDP price deflator in years 1 and 2, and calculate the rate of inflation between years 1 and 2 from the GDP price deflator.

(b) Using year 1 as the base year, calculate the CPI in years 1 and 2, and calculate the CPI rate of inflation. Explain any differences in your results between parts (a) and (b).

6. Consider an economy with a corn producer, some consumers, and a government. In a given year, the corn producer grows 30 million bushels of corn and the market price for corn is $5 per bushel. Of the 30 million bushels produced, 20 million bushels are sold to consumers, 5 million are stored in inventory, and 5 million are sold to the government to feed the army. The corn producer pays $60 million in wages to consumers and $20 million in taxes to the government. Consumers pay $10 million in taxes to the government, receive

$10 million in interest on the government debt, and receive $5 million in Social Security payments from the government. The profits of the corn producer are distributed to consumers.

(a) Calculate GDP using (i) the product approach, (ii) the expenditure approach, and (iii) the income approach.

(b) Calculate private disposable income, private sector saving, government saving, national saving, and the government deficit. Is the government budget in deficit or surplus?

7. In some countries, price controls exist on some goods, which set maximum prices at which these goods can be sold. Indeed, the United States experienced a period of wage and price controls when the Nixon administration introduced wage and price controls in 1971. Sometimes the existence of price controls leads to the growth of black markets, where goods are exchanged at prices above the legal maximums. Carefully explain how price controls present a problem for measuring GDP and for measuring the price level and inflation.

8. In this chapter, we learned that the quantity of U.S. currency outstanding per resident was $2,776 in April 2009. Suppose that we were to try to use this number to estimate the amount of output produced in the underground economy in the United States during 2009. Discuss how we would use this information on the quantity of currency in circulation, and what additional information you would want to have to come up with a good estimate. In your answer, you will need to consider how underground transactions might take place by other means in the United States than through the use of U.S. currency, and how some of U.S. currency is not being used for underground transactions in the United States.

9. Part of Gross Domestic Product consists of production in the so-called FIRE sector (finance, insurance, and real estate). Value-added is notoriously difficult to measure in the FIRE sector, as it is hard to determine exactly what the inputs and outputs are. For example, banks are included in the FIRE sector, and we know that they contribute to our well-being by making borrowing and lending more efficient and by providing transactions services. However, as most of the inputs and outputs associated with a bank are not actual physical quantities, it is much more difficult to measure

value-added in banking than in the production of apples, for example. Recently, there have been several high-profile financial scandals—for example, the Enron affair, and the Madoff scandal in New York—where financial firms and individuals earned large incomes but actually provided little or no financial services. Discuss the implications that such criminal financial activity has for the measurement of GDP.

10. In the United States, a large fraction of transactions among banks takes place over Fedwire, which is an electronic payments system operated by the Federal Reserve System.[7] During 2008, on an average day, 521,000 payments were made over Fedwire, with a total value of $2.7 trillion. The median value of such transactions was $24,000, and the average value was $5.8 million. To put this in context, annual GDP in 2008 was $14.3 trillion, so average total *daily* transactions over Fedwire were about 19% of total *annual* GDP. Do these statistics indicate that there might be some large measurement error in the official US national income accounts, or is this entirely consistent with official GDP numbers being accurate measures of aggregate economic activity? Explain, and discuss your answer.

11. Consider the identity
$$S^p - I = CA + D,$$
where S^p is private sector saving, I is investment, CA is the current account surplus, and D is the government deficit.
(a) Show that the above identity holds.
(b) Explain what the above identity means.

12. Let K_t denote the quantity of capital a country has at the beginning of period t. Also, suppose that

capital depreciates at a constant rate d, so that dK_t of the capital stock wears out during period t. If investment during period t is denoted by I_t, and the country does not trade with the rest of the world (the current account surplus is always zero), then we can say that the quantity of capital at the beginning of period $t + 1$ is given by
$$K_{t+1} = (1 - d)K_t + I_t$$
Suppose at the beginning of year 0 that this country has 80 units of capital. Investment expenditures are 10 units in each of years 0, 1, 2, 3, 4, ..., 10. The capital stock depreciates by 10% per year.
(a) Calculate the quantity of capital at the beginning of years 0, 1, 2, 3, 4, ..., 10.
(b) Repeat part (a), except assume now that the country begins year 0 with 100 units of capital. Explain what happens now, and discuss your results in parts (a) and (b).

13. Suppose that the government deficit is 10, interest on the government debt is 5, taxes are 40, government expenditures are 30, consumption expenditures are 80, net factor payments are 10, the current account surplus is −5, and national saving is 20. Calculate the following (not necessarily in the order given):
(a) Private disposable income
(b) Transfers from the government to the private sector
(c) Gross national product
(d) Gross domestic product
(e) The government surplus
(f) Net exports
(g) Investment expenditures

14. Suppose that the unemployment rate is 5%, the total working age population is 100 million, and the number of unemployed is 2.5 million. Determine: (a) the participation rate; (b) the labor force; (c) the number of employed workers; (d) the employment/population ratio.

---

[7]See http://www.federalreserve.gov/paymentsystems/coreprinciples/default.htm

Working with the Data

1. Calculate consumption of durables, consumption of nondurables, and consumption of services as percentages of total consumption, and plot these time series. Comment on the changes that have taken place over time in the consumption of services relative to durables and nondurables.

2. Macroeconomists sometimes study the behavior of the consumer price index, leaving out food and energy prices. Calculate the year-to-year inflation rate (December to December),

in percentage terms, using the consumer price index (all items) and using the consumer price index less food and energy. Plot the two inflation rates, and comment on the differences. Why would we want to neglect food and energy in our calculation of the CPI? Why would we not want to neglect these items?

3. Plot the stocks of capital, private nonresidential capital, private residential capital, government capital, and consumer durable goods over time. Comment on the movements in these time series and the proportion that each component of capital takes up in the total.

chapter 3

Business Cycle Measurement

Before we go on to build models of aggregate economic activity that can explain why business cycles exist and what, if anything, should be done about them, we must understand the key features that we observe in economic data that define a business cycle. In this chapter, we move beyond the study of the measurement of gross domestic product (GDP), the price level, savings, and wealth, which we covered in Chapter 2, to an examination of the regularities in the relationships among aggregate economic variables as they fluctuate over time.

We show that business cycles are quite irregular, in that the changes in real GDP are unpredictable; macroeconomic forecasters often have a difficult time predicting the timing of a business cycle upturn or downturn. Business cycles are quite regular, however, in terms of co-movements, which is to say that macroeconomic variables move together in highly predictable ways. We focus separately on the components of real GDP, nominal variables, and labor market variables.

This chapter describes a set of key business cycle facts concerning co-movements in U.S. macroeconomic data. In Chapters 4, 5, 8 and 9, we use these facts to show how our models can make sense of what we observe in the data. Then, in Chapters 12 and 13, we use the key business cycle facts to help us evaluate alternative theories of the business cycle.

Regularities in GDP Fluctuations

The primary defining feature of **business cycles** is that they are *fluctuations about trend in real GDP*. Recall from Chapter 1 that we represent the trend in real GDP with a smooth curve that closely fits actual real GDP, with the trend representing that part of real GDP that can be explained by long-run growth factors. What is left over, the deviations from trend, we take to represent business cycle activity.

In Figure 3.1 we show idealized business cycle activity in real GDP, with fluctuations about a long-run trend. In the figure, real GDP is represented by the black line, while the trend is represented by the colored line. There are **peaks** and **troughs** in real GDP, a peak being a relatively large positive deviation from trend, and a trough a relatively large negative deviation from trend. Peaks and troughs in the deviations from trend in real GDP are referred to as **turning points**. In a manner analogous to wave

Figure 3.1 Idealized Business Cycles

The black curve is an idealized path for real GDP over time, while the colored line is the growth trend in real GDP. Real GDP cycles around the trend over time, with the maximum negative deviation from trend being a trough and the maximum positive deviation from trend being a peak. The amplitude is the size of the maximum deviation from trend, and the frequency is the number of peaks that occur within a year's time.

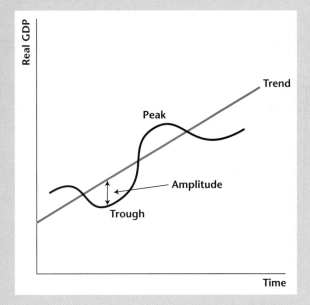

motion in the physical sciences, we can think of the maximum deviation from trend in Figure 3.1 as the **amplitude** of the business cycle, and the number of peaks in real GDP that occur per year as the **frequency** of the business cycle.

Next, in Figure 3.2 we show the actual percentage deviations from trend in real GDP for the United States over the period 1947–2009. A series of positive deviations from trend culminating in a peak represents a **boom**, whereas a series of negative deviations from trend culminating in a trough represents a **recession**. In Figure 3.2, we have marked five important recessions, occurring in 1973–1975, 1981–1982, 1990–1991, 2001, and 2008–2009. The first two of these recessions were quite significant, with the deviation from trend in real GDP exceeding 4%, whereas the middle two were relatively mild, with deviations from trend of between 1% and 2%. The most recent recession, which is currently underway, is predicted to be at least as severe as the 1981–1982 recession.

An examination of Figure 3.2 indicates a striking regularity, which is that the deviations from trend in real GDP are **persistent**. That is, when real GDP is above trend, it tends to stay above trend, and when it is below trend, it tends to stay below trend. This feature is quite important in terms of economic forecasting over the short run; persistence implies that we can fairly confidently predict that if real GDP is currently below

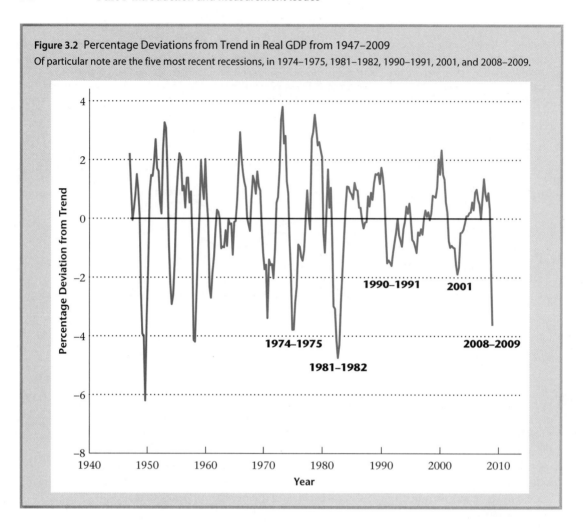

Figure 3.2 Percentage Deviations from Trend in Real GDP from 1947–2009

Of particular note are the five most recent recessions, in 1974–1975, 1981–1982, 1990–1991, 2001, and 2008–2009.

(above) trend, then it will be below (above) trend several months from now. Other than being persistent, however, the deviations from trend in real GDP are actually quite irregular. There are three other features to note in Figure 3.2:

1. The time series of deviations from trend in real GDP is quite choppy.

2. There is no regularity in the amplitude of fluctuations in real GDP about trend. Some of the peaks and troughs represent large deviations from trend, whereas other peaks and troughs represent small deviations from trend.

3. There is no regularity in the frequency of fluctuations in real GDP about trend. The length of time between peaks and troughs in real GDP varies considerably.

Although deviations from trend in real GDP are persistent, which makes short-term forecasting relatively easy, the above three features imply that longer-term forecasting is difficult. The choppiness of fluctuations in real GDP make these fluctuations difficult to predict, while the lack of regularity in the amplitude and frequency of fluctuations implies that it is difficult to predict the severity and length of recessions and booms. Therefore, predicting future fluctuations in real GDP by looking only at past real GDP is much like attempting to forecast the weather by looking out the window. If it is sunny today, it is likely that it will be sunny tomorrow (weather is persistent), but the fact that it is sunny today may give us very little information on whether it will be sunny one week from today.

MACROECONOMICS IN ACTION
The Pitfalls of Macroeconomic Forecasting

In the United States, macroeconomic forecasting is done by government agencies such as the Congressional Budget Office and the Federal Reserve System and by private firms such as the Conference Board that sell forecasts to government and businesses. There are essentially three approaches to macroeconomic forecasting: judgmental forecasting, model forecasting, and statistical forecasting.

Judgmental forecasters gather various kinds of information and data from official and unofficial sources, and then they forecast future macroeconomic activity based on their own informal judgment about how the economy works. A judgmental forecaster does not use sophisticated statistical methods or macroeconomic theory in a rigorous way but instead relies on his or her "gut feelings" about where the economy is headed.

Model forecasting is done using an explicit macroeconomic model that is constructed using macroeconomic theory. The types of models used vary considerably, but those developed in the 1960s and 1970s,

some of which are still in use at central banks, in governments, and at private forecasting firms, consist of several hundred equations that capture the relationships among several hundred macroeconomic variables. A forecast using one of these models can involve work by a team of people who fine-tune the model before the forecast, then generate a forecast that is a computer simulation of the model's predictions for future macroeconomic activity.

Statistical forecasting is a reaction to model forecasting, in that some macroeconomists argue that forecasting models had simply got out of hand. These macroeconomists argue that typical macroeconomic forecasting models are so large and complicated that no one actually understands how they work. Further, as they argue, a forecasting exercise with a large team of forecasters typically degenerates into an exercise where members of the team supply "add factors" to the model to make the forecast results conform to their own judgment concerning how the forecast should look. At worst then, the model is not

(Continued)

allowed to make predictions but is simply a device for enforcing national income accounting identities (like the income—expenditure identity). As critics argued, the forecast is then judgmental and not a model forecast at all.

An example of a statistical model is the Bayesian Vector Autoregression (or BVAR) model developed at the Federal Reserve Bank of Minneapolis in the 1970s and 1980s. This is a model that is quite small and simple, and, once up and running, it can generate a forecast using the time of one person who need not be a trained economist.

No matter what the forecasting method used, macroeconomic forecasters can often be wrong, particularly in predicting turning points and in making predictions over a long horizon. A case in point occurred during the 2001 recession. In January 2001, the Congressional Budget Office (CBO) forecast that there would be a mild slowdown in real GDP growth from 3.8% in 2000 to 2.4% in 2001, with a recovery to robust growth of 3.4% in real GDP in 2002.[1] This forecast turned out to be exceedingly optimistic, particularly for 2001, as real GDP ultimately grew by 0.3% in

2001 and 2.4% in 2002. The CBO failed to predict the 2001 recession, which included negative growth in real GDP in the first, second, and third quarters of 2001. Perhaps surprisingly, the events of September 11, 2001, cannot receive much of the blame for the large forecast error for 2001, as real GDP actually grew by 2.7% in the fourth quarter of 2001 at a time when the airlines and the travel industry were suffering from the negative effects of the terrorist attacks.

Were the economists at the CBO in January 2001 an especially bad group of forecasters? Apparently not, as the Blue Chip consensus forecast (an average of 50 private-sector forecasts) in January 2001 was if anything slightly more optimistic than the CBO forecast, predicting growth in real GDP of 2.6% and 3.4% for 2001 and 2002, respectively.[2] The evidence would seem to indicate that the large error in the CBO forecast was not because of incompetence. This is simply an example illustrating that macroeconomic forecasters are often wrong because forecasting the course of the macroeconomy can be extremely difficult.

---

[1]See "The Budget and Economic Outlook: Fiscal Years 2002–2011, January 2001," at http://www.cbo.gov/showdoc.cfm?index=2727\&sequence=3.

[2]See "The Budget and Economic Outlook: Fiscal Years 2002–2011, January 2001," at http://www.cbo.gov/showdoc.cfm?index=2727/&sequence=3.

Co-movement

While real GDP fluctuates in irregular patterns, macroeconomic variables fluctuate together in patterns that exhibit strong regularities. We refer to these patterns in fluctuations as **co-movement**. Robert Lucas once remarked that "with respect to qualitative behavior of co-movements among [economic time] series, business cycles are all alike."[3]

Macroeconomic variables are measured as **time series**; for example, real GDP is measured in a series of quarterly observations over time. When we examine co-movements in macroeconomic time series, typically we look at these time series two at a time, and

---

[3]See R. Lucas, "Understanding Business Cycles," in *Studies in Business Cycle Theory*, MIT Press, p. 218.

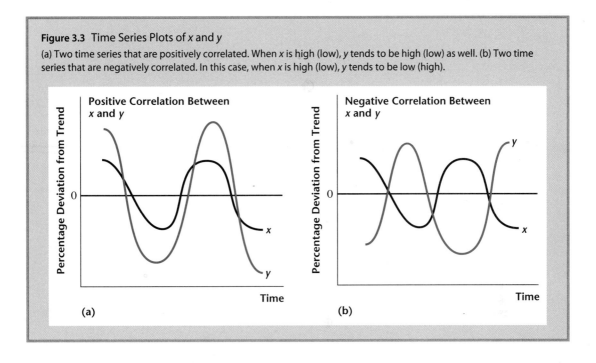

Figure 3.3 Time Series Plots of *x* and *y*

(a) Two time series that are positively correlated. When *x* is high (low), *y* tends to be high (low) as well. (b) Two time series that are negatively correlated. In this case, when *x* is high (low), *y* tends to be low (high).

a good starting point is to plot the data. Suppose, for example, that we have two macroeconomic time series and we would like to study their co-movement. We first transform these two time series by removing trends, and we let *x* and *y* denote the percentage deviations from trend in the two time series. One way to plot *x* and *y* is in time series form, as in Figure 3.3. What we want to look for first in the time series plot is a pattern of **positive correlation** or **negative correlation** in *x* and *y*. In Figure 3.3(a), there is positive correlation between *x* and *y*: *x* is high when *y* is high, and *x* is low when *y* is low. That is, one economic time series tends to be above (below) trend when the other economic time series is above (below) trend. In Figure 3.3(b) *x* and *y* are negatively correlated: *x* is high (low) when *y* is low (high).

Another way to plot the data is as a **scatter plot**, with *x* on the horizontal axis and *y* on the vertical axis. In Figure 3.4, each point in the scatter plot is an observation on *x* and *y* for a particular time period. Here, whether *x* and *y* are positively or negatively correlated is determined by the slope of a straight line that best fits the points in the scatter plot. The top panel of Figure 3.4 shows a positive correlation between *x* and *y*, the middle panel a negative correlation, and the bottom panel a zero correlation. For example, if we had data on aggregate consumption and aggregate income over time and constructed a scatter plot of consumption (on the *y* axis) against income (on the *x* axis), we would observe a positive correlation; a positively sloped straight line would provide a good fit to the points in the scatter plot.

Macroeconomists are often primarily interested in how an individual macroeconomic variable comoves with real GDP. An economic variable is said to be **procyclical**

Figure 3.4 Correlations Between Variables *y* and *x*

(a) A scatter plot of two variables, *x* and *y*, that are positively correlated. (b) *x* and *y* are negatively correlated. (c) *x* and *y* are uncorrelated.

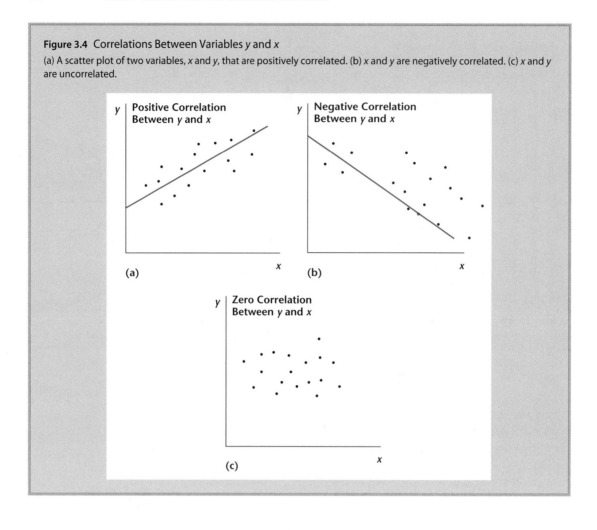

if its deviations from trend are positively correlated with the deviations from trend in real GDP, **countercyclical** if its deviations from trend are negatively correlated with the deviations from trend in real GDP, and **acyclical** if it is neither procyclical nor countercyclical. As an example of co-movement between two macroeconomic time series, we consider real GDP and real imports for the United States over the period 1947–2009. In Figure 3.5 we plot the percentage deviations from trend in real GDP (the colored line) and real imports (the black line) in time series form. There is a distinct pattern of positive correlation in Figure 3.5; when GDP is high (low) relative to trend, imports tend to be high (low) relative to trend. This positive correlation also shows up in the scatter plot in Figure 3.6, where we show a graph of observations of percentage deviations from trend in imports versus percentage deviations from trend in GDP. Note that a straight line fit to the points in Figure 3.6 would have a positive slope.

Figure 3.5 Imports and GDP

The figure, as an example, shows the time series of percentage deviations from trend in real imports (black line) and real GDP (colored line) for the United States for the period 1947–2009. Imports and GDP are clearly positively correlated, so imports are procyclical.

Source: U.S. Department of Commerce, Bureau of Economic Analysis.

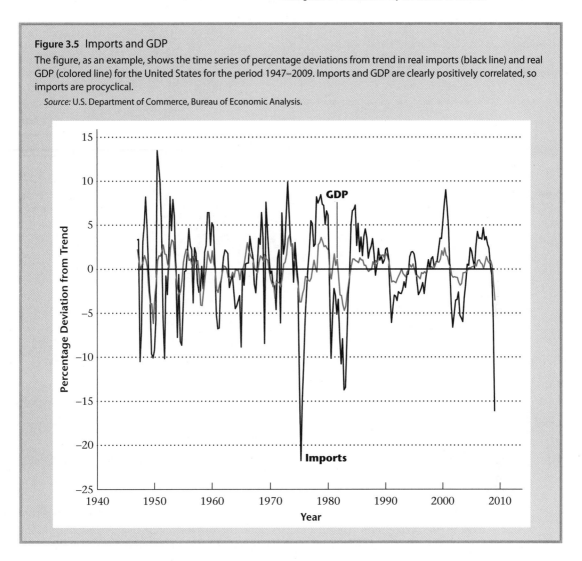

A measure of the degree of correlation between two variables is the **correlation coefficient**. The correlation coefficient between two variables, x and y, takes on values between -1 and 1. If the correlation coefficient is 1, then x and y are **perfectly positively correlated** and a scatter plot of observations on x and y falls on a positively sloped straight line. If the correlation coefficient is -1, then x and y are **perfectly negatively correlated** and a scatter plot would consist of points on a negatively sloped straight line. If the correlation coefficient is 0, then x and y are uncorrelated. In the example above, the percentage deviations from trend in real GDP and real imports have a correlation coefficient of 0.69, indicating positive correlation.

Figure 3.6 Scatter Plot of Imports and GDP

The figure shows the same data as in Figure 3.5 but in a scatter plot rather than in time series form. Here, we again observe the positive correlation between imports and GDP, as a positively sloped straight line would best fit the scatter plot. Again, imports are procyclical.

Source: U.S. Department of Commerce, Bureau of Economic Analysis.

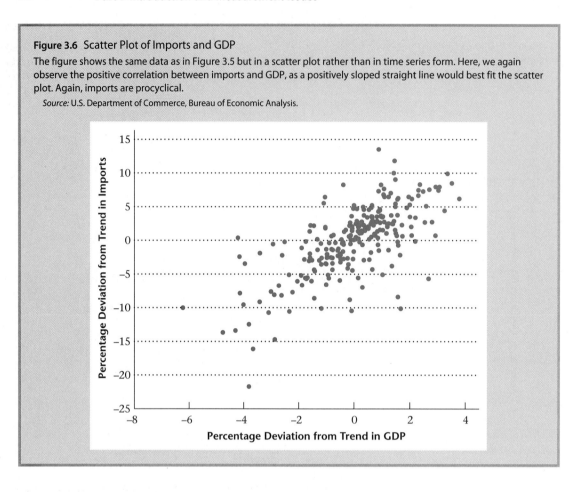

An important element of co-movement is the leading and lagging relationships that exist in macroeconomic data. If a macroeconomic variable tends to aid in predicting the future path of real GDP, we say that it is a **leading variable**, whereas if real GDP helps to predict the future path of a particular macroeconomic variable, then that variable is said to be a **lagging variable**. In Figure 3.7 we show idealized time series plots of the percentage deviations from trend in real GDP and two variables, x and y. In Figure 3.7(a), variable x is a leading variable, whereas variable y is a lagging variable in Figure 3.7(b). A **coincident variable** is one which neither leads nor lags real GDP.

A knowledge of the regularities in leading relationships among economic variables can be very useful in macroeconomic forecasting and policymaking. Typically, macroeconomic variables that somehow efficiently summarize available information about future macroeconomic activity are potentially useful in predicting the future path of real GDP. For example, the stock market is a candidate as a useful leading economic variable. Finance theory tells us that stock market prices summarize information about the future profitability of firms in the economy, so movements in stock market prices potentially are important signals about future movements in real GDP. However, the

Figure 3.7 Leading and Lagging Variables

In (a), *x* is a leading variable, as its peaks and troughs tend to precede those of real GDP. In (b), *y* is a lagging variable, as the peaks and troughs in real GDP tend to lead those in *y*.

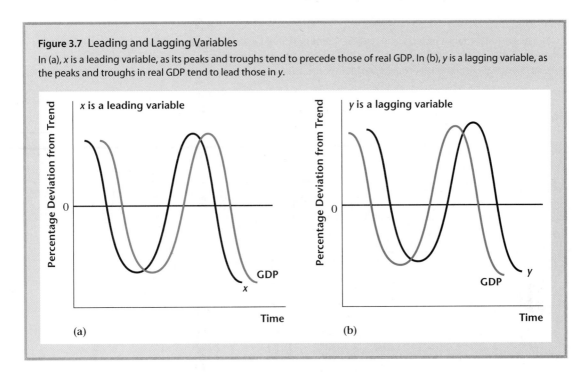

stock market is notoriously volatile—stock market prices can move by large amounts on a given day, for no reason that appears related to any useful new information. Paul Samuelson, a Nobel-prize-winning economist, is famously quoted as saying, "the stock market has forecast nine out of the last five recessions."

Another key leading macroeconomic variable is the number of housing starts in the United States, which is measured on a monthly basis. A housing start occurs when the construction project is started for a private dwelling. This dwelling could be a single detached house, or a unit in a multi-household building. A housing start therefore represents a commitment to a quantity of residential investment that will take place over the next few months (or possibly a couple of years, for a large apartment building, for example). To undertake such a commitment, the builder should have some confidence that economic conditions will be sufficiently good that the dwelling can be sold quickly once the project is completed. Thus, housing starts will increase and decrease with information that causes economic decision makers to become more optimistic or pessimistic, respectively, about the future. Residential investment is not a large fraction of GDP, accounting for only 3.4% of GDP in 2008, but it is highly volatile, and it is the highly volatile components of GDP that will contribute most to the decline in GDP during a recession. Indeed, there is wide agreement that the 2008–2009 recession was triggered by problems in the housing sector and mortgage market.

In Figure 3.8, we show the percentage deviations from trend in real GDP and in housing starts for the period 1959–2009. In the figure, the percentage deviations from

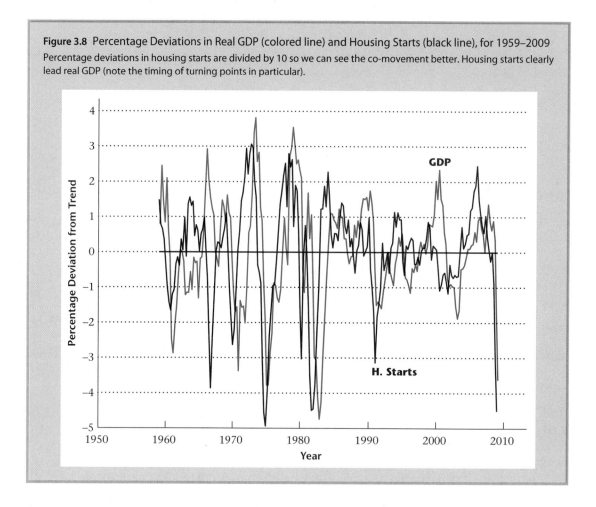

Figure 3.8 Percentage Deviations in Real GDP (colored line) and Housing Starts (black line), for 1959–2009

Percentage deviations in housing starts are divided by 10 so we can see the co-movement better. Housing starts clearly lead real GDP (note the timing of turning points in particular).

trend in housing starts are divided by 10, so that one can see the co-movements more clearly. Thus, a 4% deviation from trend in housing starts in the figure represents a 40% deviation from trend in housing starts. The figure shows a clear leading relationship between housing starts and GDP. Note in particular that turning points in housing starts tend to lead turning points in real GDP. An additional interesting feature is what it tells us about the recent collapse in the housing market. Housing starts fell from a peak of about 25% above trend in 2006 (about 2.5% in the figure) to well less than 40% below trend (4% in the figure) in 2009. Such a drop is not unprecedented, as we see in the figure, but nevertheless very large.

A final important feature of co-movements among economic variables is the key regularities in the variability of economic variables over the business cycle. As we will see, some macroeconomic variables are highly volatile, while others behave in a very smooth way relative to trend. These patterns in variability are an important part of business cycle behavior that we would like to understand. A measure of cyclical variability is the **standard deviation** of the percentage deviations from trend. For example, in Figure 3.5, imports are much more variable than GDP. The standard deviation of the percentage deviations from trend in imports is more than twice that for GDP.

Next we examine some key macroeconomic variables, and we evaluate for each whether they are (1) procyclical or countercyclical, (2) leading or lagging, and (3) more or less variable relative to real GDP. These facts then make up the set of important business cycle regularities that we explain using macroeconomic theory.

The Components of GDP

In Figure 3.9 we show the percentage deviations from trend in real aggregate consumption (the black line) and real GDP (the colored line). Clearly, the deviations from

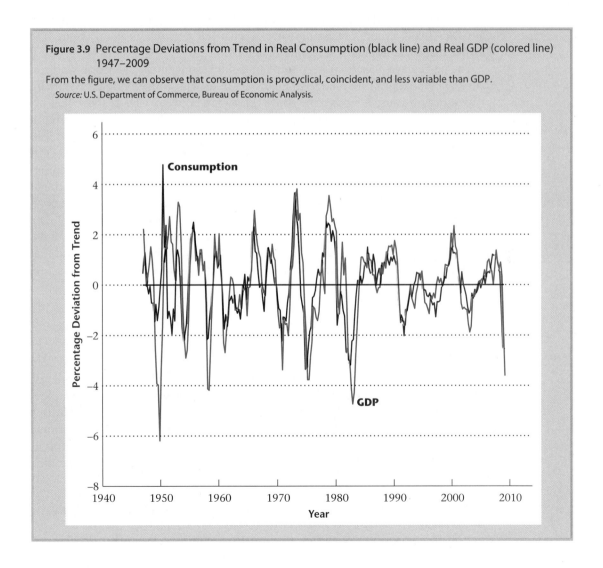

Figure 3.9 Percentage Deviations from Trend in Real Consumption (black line) and Real GDP (colored line) 1947–2009

From the figure, we can observe that consumption is procyclical, coincident, and less variable than GDP.

Source: U.S. Department of Commerce, Bureau of Economic Analysis.

trend in consumption and in GDP are highly positively correlated, in that consumption tends to be above (below) trend when GDP is above (below) trend; these two time series move very closely together. The correlation coefficient between the percentage deviation from trend in real consumption and the percentage deviation from trend in real GDP is 0.76, which is greater than zero, so consumption is procyclical. There appears to be no discernible lead/lag relationship between real consumption and real GDP in Figure 3.9—the turning points in consumption do not appear to lead or lag the turning points in real GDP. Consumption, therefore, is a coincident variable.

From Figure 3.9, note that consumption is less variable than GDP, in that the deviations from trend in consumption tend to be smaller than those in GDP. In Chapter 8 we study the theory of consumption decisions over time, and this theory explains why consumption tends to be smoother than GDP. For the data displayed in Figure 3.9, the standard deviation of the percentage deviations in real consumption is 75.9% of that for real GDP. This is a more precise measure of what our eyes tell us about Figure 3.9, which is that consumption is smoother than GDP.

The percentage deviations from trend in real investment (the black line) and real GDP (the colored line) are plotted in Figure 3.10. As with consumption, investment is procyclical, because it tends to be above (below) trend when GDP is above (below) trend. The correlation coefficient between the percentage deviations from trend in investment and those in GDP is 0.84. There is no tendency for investment to lead or lag GDP from Figure 3.10, and so investment is a coincident variable. However, some components of investment, in particular residential investment and inventory investment, tend to lead the business cycle. In contrast to consumption, investment is much more volatile than is GDP. This is indicated in Figure 3.10, where the deviations from trend in investment tend to be much larger than those for GDP. The standard deviation of the percentage deviations from trend in investment is 478.9% of what it is for GDP. Given that some components of investment lead GDP and that it is highly volatile, investment can play a very important role over the business cycle.

Nominal Variables

The correlation between money prices and aggregate economic activity has long been of interest to macroeconomists. In the 1950s, A. W. Phillips observed that there was a negative relationship between the rate of change in money wages and the unemployment rate in the United Kingdom, a relationship that came to be known as the **Phillips curve**.[4] If we take the unemployment rate to be a measure of aggregate economic activity (as we see in Chapter 16, the unemployment rate is a strongly countercyclical variable; when real GDP is above trend, the unemployment rate is low), then the

---

[4]See A. Phillips, 1958, "The Relationship Between Unemployment and the Rate of Change of Money Wages in the United Kingdom, 1861–1957," *Econometrica* 25, 283–299.

Figure 3.10 Percentage Deviations from Trend in Real Investment (black line) and Real GDP (colored line)

We can observe from the figure that investment is procyclical, coincident, and more variable than GDP.

Source: U.S. Department of Commerce, Bureau of Economic Analysis.

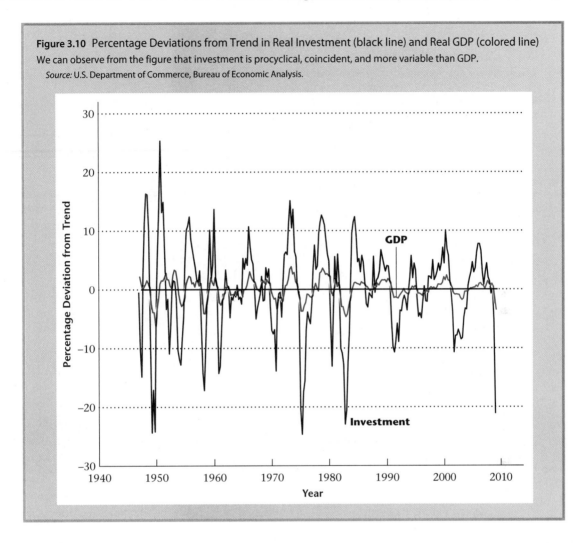

Phillips curve captures a positive relationship between the rate of change in a money price (the money wage) and the level of aggregate economic activity. Since Phillips made his initial observation, "Phillips curve" has come to be applied to any positive relationship between the rate of change in money prices or wages, or the deviation from trend in money prices or wages, and the deviation from trend in aggregate economic activity. As we see in Chapter 17, observed Phillips curves are notoriously unstable—that is, they tend to shift over time—and there are sound theories to explain this instability. However, a regularity in the 1947–2009 period in the United States is the negative correlation between deviations of the price level from trend and deviations of GDP from trend, observed in the scatter plot in Figure 3.11. We might think of this as a **reverse Phillips curve**, as there is a negative rather than a positive correlation between the price level and real GDP, with the correlation coefficient for the

Figure 3.11 Scatter Plot for the Percentage Deviations from Trend in the Price Level (the Implicit GDP Price Deflator) and Real GDP

The figure shows a negative correlation between the two for 1947–2009; therefore, the price level is countercyclical for this period. The figure captures a reverse Phillips curve relationship.

Source: U.S. Department of Commerce, Bureau of Economic Analysis.

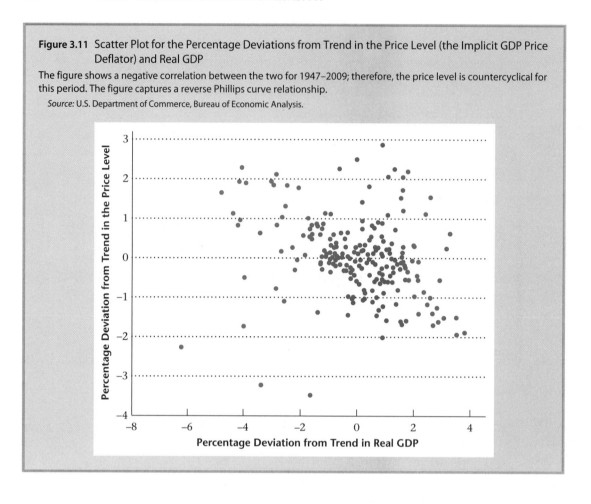

data in Figure 3.11 being −0.23. Over the period 1947–2009, therefore, the price level is a countercyclical variable.

In Figure 3.12 the price level (black line) is quite smooth relative to real GDP (colored line); the standard deviation of the percentage deviations from trend in the price level is 57.4% of that for GDP. The price level tends to be much smoother than most asset prices. For example, the average price of shares traded on the stock market is highly variable relative to the money prices of goods and services. In Figure 3.12 there appears to be no tendency for the price level to lead or lag real GDP, so that the price level appears to be coincident.

Whether the price level is procyclical or countercyclical and whether it is a leading or a lagging variable can play an important role in resolving debates concerning the causes of business cycles, as we see in Chapters 12 and 13. In contrast to the 1947–2009 U.S. data examined previously, it appears that the price level was a procyclical variable over some periods of history in some countries, for example, during the period between the World Wars in the United States. An alternative interpretation of Figure 3.12 is that the price level is a procyclical and lagging variable. That is, when

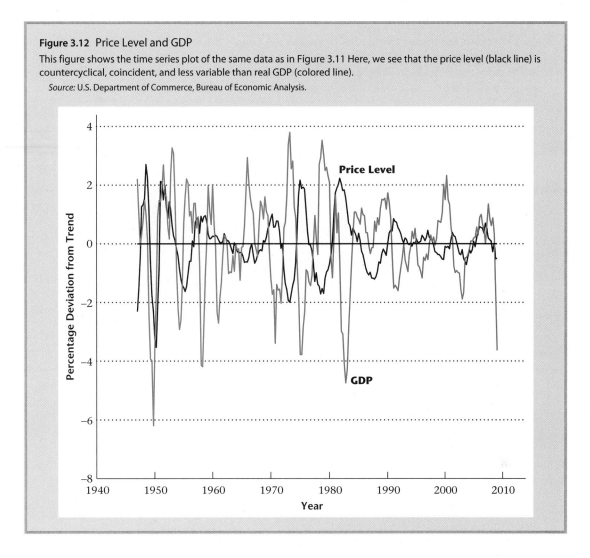

Figure 3.12 Price Level and GDP

This figure shows the time series plot of the same data as in Figure 3.11 Here, we see that the price level (black line) is countercyclical, coincident, and less variable than real GDP (colored line).

Source: U.S. Department of Commerce, Bureau of Economic Analysis.

real GDP is above (below) trend, the price level tends to be above (below) trend about two years later. Without other evidence to guide us, however, we stick to the interpretation that the price level is a countercyclical coincident variable in the post—World War II U.S. data.

In addition to Phillips curve relationships and reverse Phillips curve relationships, a key element of the co-movement between nominal variables and aggregate economic activity is the positive correlation between deviations from trend in the nominal money supply and deviations from trend in real GDP. The money supply is a measure of the nominal quantity of assets used in making transactions in the economy. In the United States, the money supply includes U.S. currency and checking accounts at banks and other depository institutions. In Figure 3.13 we show the percentage deviations from trend in a measure of the money supply (black line) and in real GDP (colored line) over

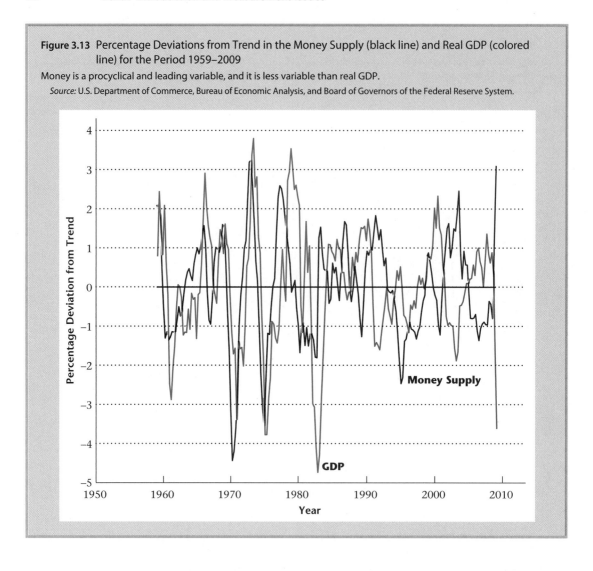

Figure 3.13 Percentage Deviations from Trend in the Money Supply (black line) and Real GDP (colored line) for the Period 1959–2009

Money is a procyclical and leading variable, and it is less variable than real GDP.

Source: U.S. Department of Commerce, Bureau of Economic Analysis, and Board of Governors of the Federal Reserve System.

the period 1959–2009.[5] The procyclical nature of the money supply is quite pronounced until about 1980, after which the link between the money supply and real GDP weakens. The correlation coefficient for the data in Figure 3.13 is 0.26. Another important observation concerning the nominal money supply and real GDP is that money tends to be a leading variable, which we observe as a tendency for turning points in the money supply to lead turning points in GDP in Figure 3.13. This observation was emphasized by Milton Friedman and Anna Schwartz,[6] who studied the

---

[5]The money supply measure used here is M2. In Chapters 10 and 16, we discuss the measurement of the money supply in more detail.

[6]See M. Friedman and A. Schwartz, 1963, *A Monetary History of the United States: 1867–1960*, Princeton University Press, Princeton, NJ.

behavior of the money supply and real GDP in the United States over the period 1867–1960.

The money supply is somewhat smoother than GDP, with the standard deviation of the percentage deviations from trend in the money supply being 80.4% of what it is for GDP. This can also be observed in Figure 3.13.

Labor Market Variables

The last business cycle regularities we examine are those in labor markets, relating to the variables we determine in the business cycle models in Chapters 10 through 13.

MACROECONOMICS IN ACTION
The Correlation Between the Price Level and Aggregate Output Across Countries and Over Time

In Chapters 9 through 12 we will study how the co-movements among macroeconomic variables can be affected by the types of shocks that are hitting the economy, the relative severity of those shocks, and the manner in which macroeconomic policy reacts to these shocks. One interesting way in which this is reflected in the data is in the correlation we see between the price level and aggregate output. For example, in the United States an increase in the price of oil on world markets will tend to increase the price level and reduce aggregate output, producing a negative correlation between these two variables, or a countercyclical price level. However, an increase in the money supply, engineered by the Federal Reserve System, will tend to increase the price level and increase aggregate output, producing a procyclical price level. Whether the price level is countercyclical or procyclical in the data might then be determined by which is more important, shocks to the world price of oil or money supply shocks.

David Backus and Patrick Kehoe have studied the properties of business cycles across countries and over long periods of time[7]. A finding of theirs is that the correlations among real variables are remarkably similar across countries and over time. However the correlation between the price level and aggregate output is not. After World War II, the price level was countercyclical in most of the countries that Backus and Kehoe study,[8] just as we saw for the United States in the data from 1947–2009. However, before World War I, and between the World Wars, the price level was procyclical in most of the countries in this set. This is an important piece of information that will be useful for us in evaluating theories of the business cycle in Chapters 12 and 13.

---

[7]See D. Backus and P. Kehoe, 1992. "International Evidence on the Historical Properties of Business Cycles," American Economic Review 82, 864–888.

[8]Australia, Canada, Denmark, Germany, Italy, Japan, Norway, Sweden, the U.K., and the United States.

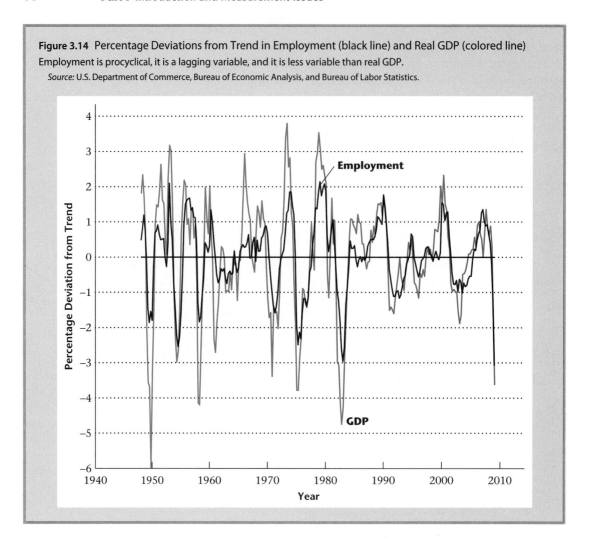

Figure 3.14 Percentage Deviations from Trend in Employment (black line) and Real GDP (colored line)
Employment is procyclical, it is a lagging variable, and it is less variable than real GDP.
Source: U.S. Department of Commerce, Bureau of Economic Analysis, and Bureau of Labor Statistics.

First, in Figure 3.14 we show percentage deviations from trend in employment (black line) and in real GDP (colored line) for the period 1948–2009. Clearly, the deviations from trend in employment closely track those in real GDP, so employment is a procyclical variable. The correlation coefficient for the data in Figure 3.14 is 0.80. In terms of lead/lag relationships, we can observe a tendency in Figure 3.14 for turning points in employment to lag turning points in GDP, so employment is a lagging variable. Employment is less variable than GDP, with the standard deviation of the percentage deviation from trend for employment being 61.5% of that for real GDP in Figure 3.14.

In the macroeconomic models we analyze, a key variable is the market **real wage**, which is the purchasing power of the wage earned per hour worked. This is measured from the data as the average money wage for all workers, divided by the price level.

The cyclical behavior of the real wage proves to be crucial in helping us discriminate among different theories of the business cycle in Chapters 12 and 13. The weight of empirical evidence indicates that the real wage is procyclical.[9] We do not show data on the aggregate real wage, as it is difficult to measure the relationship between real wages and real GDP by examining aggregate data. The key problem is that the composition of the labor force tends to change over the business cycle, which tends to bias the correlation between the real wage and real GDP. There is no strong evidence on whether the real wage is a leading or a lagging variable.

Productivity plays a key role in the economy, as was mentioned in Chapter 1, and in later chapters productivity is an important element in our study of business cycles and economic growth. One measure of productivity is **average labor productivity**, $\frac{Y}{N}$, where Y is aggregate output and N is total labor input. For our purposes, Y is GDP and N is total employment, so we are measuring average labor productivity as output per worker. In Figure 3.15 we show the percentage deviations from trend in real GDP (colored line) and average labor productivity (black line). From the figure, average labor productivity is clearly a procyclical variable. The correlation coefficient for percentage deviations from trend in real GDP and average labor productivity is 0.81. Average labor productivity is less volatile than GDP; the standard deviation of the percentage deviations from trend in average labor productivity is 62.4% of that for real GDP. Further, there is no apparent tendency for average labor productivity to lead or lag real GDP in Figure 3.15, so average labor productivity is a coincident variable. In Chapters 12 and 13, the predictions of different business cycle theories for the co-movements between average labor productivity and real GDP are important in helping us to evaluate and compare these theories.

Seasonal Adjustment

The economic data we are studying in this chapter, and most data that is used in macroeconomic research and in formulating macroeconomic policy, is **seasonally adjusted**. That is, in most macroeconomic time series, there exists a predictable seasonal component. For example, GDP tends to be low during the summer months when workers are on vacation, investment expenditure tends to be low in the winter months when building roads, bridges, and some types of structures is more difficult, and the money supply tends to be high during the December holiday season, when the quantity of retail transactions is high.

There are various methods for seasonally adjusting data, but the basic idea is to observe historical seasonal patterns and then take out the extra amount that we tend to see on average during a particular week, month, or quarter, simply because of the time of year. For example, to seasonally adjust the money supply, we would want to subtract some quantity in December which is just due to the extra spending over the

---

[9]See G. Solon, R. Barsky, and J. Parker, 1994, "Measuring the Cyclicality of Real Wages: How Important Is Composition Bias?" *Quarterly Journal of Economics*, February, 1–25.

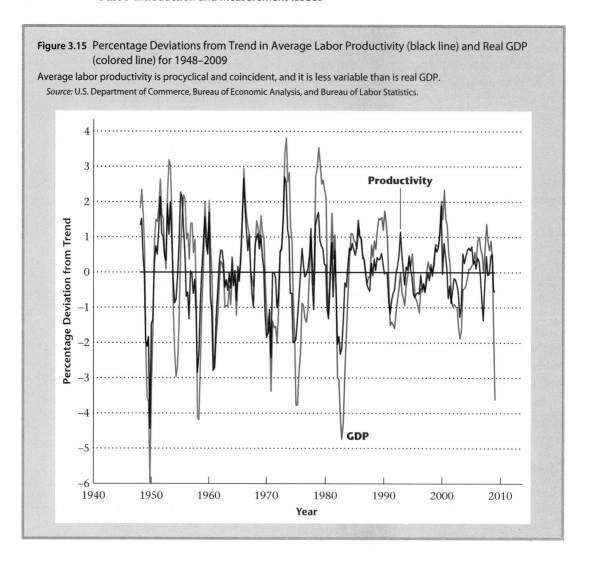

Figure 3.15 Percentage Deviations from Trend in Average Labor Productivity (black line) and Real GDP (colored line) for 1948–2009

Average labor productivity is procyclical and coincident, and it is less variable than is real GDP.

Source: U.S. Department of Commerce, Bureau of Economic Analysis, and Bureau of Labor Statistics.

holiday season. To see what seasonal adjustment can do, in Figure 3.16 we show the seasonally adjusted money supply (M1 in this case) and seasonally unadjusted money supply. As can be seen in the figure, seasonal adjustment tends to smooth out a time series that has a seasonal component.

Working with seasonally adjusted data can often be the appropriate thing to do, but one has to be careful that the process of seasonal adjustment is not masking important phenomena that might interest us. For example, there may be economic factors that cause the nature of seasonality to change over time. For example, technological developments may make it less costly to do road construction in the winter, and thus reduce the seasonal fluctuations we see in investment expenditure. If we confine our attention to only seasonally adjusted data, we might not be aware that this process was occurring.

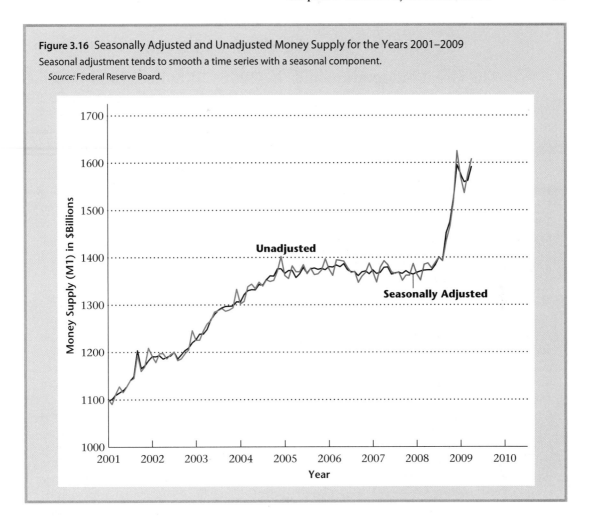

Figure 3.16 Seasonally Adjusted and Unadjusted Money Supply for the Years 2001–2009
Seasonal adjustment tends to smooth a time series with a seasonal component.
Source: Federal Reserve Board.

Co-movement Summary

To summarize the business cycle facts discussed above, we present Tables 3.1 and 3.2. These two tables, particularly Table 3.2, prove very useful, particularly when we discuss the predictions of different theories of the business cycle in Chapters 12 and 13. A first test of the usefulness of macroeconomic theories is their ability to match what we see in macroeconomic data.

We have concluded our study of measurement issues in that we now know the basics of national income accounting, basic macroeconomic accounting identities, price measurement, labor market facts, and business cycle facts. In the next chapters, we proceed to build useful macroeconomic models, starting with some basic microeconomic principles concerning the behavior of consumers and firms.

Perspectives on the Financial Crisis

The Great Moderation and the 2008–2009 Recession

After the 1981–1982 recession, there was a long period, until 2008, sometimes called the Great Moderation, which featured relatively mild fluctuations in real GDP and a relatively low and stable rate of inflation. Here, we will focus exclusively on the first feature, which we can see in Figure 3.2. From 1947 until the end of the 1981–1982 recession, deviations from trend in real GDP in Figure 3.2 were as much or more than ±4%, but after 1982 and before 2008, deviations from trend were typically no more than ±2%. An instructive view of the Great Moderation, written while it was underway, is in a speech by Ben Bernanke, the current Chair of the Board of Governors of the Federal Reserve System, delivered in 2004 when he was a Governor on the Board.[10] Bernanke takes note of the Great Moderation, and lists three possible reasons for it. First, there may have been structural changes in the economy that made it more resilient over this period and less susceptible to external shocks. Second, economic policy may have been better in countering the effects of these external shocks. Third, we may just have been lucky, in the sense that there were fewer shocks to the economy, and these shocks were smaller.

In his speech, Bernanke argues that the Great Moderation was not just good luck, but could be attributed in good part to wiser monetary policy. He also suggests, in part, that structural changes, including "the increased depth and sophistication of financial markets ...," made the economy more resilient. However, our experience in the financial crisis, beginning in 2008, and in the 2008–2009 recession, which will likely prove to be worse than the 1981–1982 recession (see Figure 3.2), is anything but moderate. Financial markets once thought to be deep and sophisticated are now considered deeply flawed, in part due to poor regulation. If monetary policymakers were so good at reducing fluctuations in aggregate GDP in the Great Moderation, why could they not prevent or substantially reduce the large economic downturn in 2008–2009?

The Great Moderation episode provides a good lesson for economic policy. With the benefit of hindsight, monetary policymakers, including Ben Bernanke, were too complacent, and too inclined to attribute good economic performance to their own skill. From the point of view of 2009, the Great Moderation now seems most likely to be the product of good luck.

---

[10]See http://www.federalreserve.gov/BOARDDOCS/SPEECHES/2004/20040220/default.htm

Table 3.1 Correlation Coefficients and Variability of Percentage Deviations from Trend

	Correlation Coefficient	Standard Deviation (% of S.D. of GDP)
Consumption	0.76	75.9
Investment	0.84	478.9
Price Level	−0.23	57.4
Money Supply	0.26	80.4
Employment	0.80	61.5
Average Labor Productivity	0.81	62.4

Table 3.2 Summary of Business Cycle Facts

	Cyclicality	Lead/Lag	Variation Relative to GDP
Consumption	Procyclical	Coincident	Smaller
Investment	Procyclical	Coincident	Larger
Price Level	Countercyclical	Coincident	Smaller
Money Supply	Procyclical	Leading	Smaller
Employment	Procyclical	Lagging	Smaller
Real Wage	Procyclical	?	?
Average Labor Productivity	Procyclical	Coincident	Smaller

Chapter Summary

- The key business cycle facts relate to the deviations of important macroeconomic variables from their trends and the co-movements in these deviations from trend.

- The most important business cycle fact is that real GDP fluctuates about trend in an irregular fashion. Although deviations from trend in real GDP are persistent, there is no observed regularity in the amplitude or frequency of fluctuations in real GDP about trend.

- Business cycles are similar mainly in terms of the co-movements among macroeconomic time series. Co-movement can be discerned by plotting the percentage deviations from trend in two economic variables in a time series or in a scatter plot or by calculating the correlation coefficient between the percentage deviations from trend.

- We are interested principally in how a particular variable moves about trend relative to real GDP (whether it is procyclical, countercyclical, or acyclical), whether it is a leading, lagging, or coincident variable (relative to real GDP), and how variable it is relative to real GDP.

- Consumption is procyclical, coincident, and less variable than real GDP.
- Investment is procyclical, coincident, and more variable than real GDP.
- In the data set we examined here, the price level is a countercyclical variable (there is a reverse Phillips curve), it is coincident, and it is less variable than GDP.
- The money supply is procyclical, leading, and about as variable as real GDP. The fact that the money supply tends to lead real GDP was assigned much importance by Milton Friedman.
- In the labor market, employment is procyclical, lagging, and less variable than real GDP. The real wage, too, is procyclical. There is, however, no consensus among macroeconomists on whether the real wage is a leading or lagging variable. Average labor productivity is procyclical, coincident, and less variable than real GDP.
- Many macreconomic time series used in economic analysis are seasonally adjusted. Seasonal adjustment takes out the predictable seasonal component, for example the effect of extra spending over the December holiday season on the money supply.

Key Terms

Acyclical Describes an economic variable that is neither procyclical nor countercyclical. (p. 76)

Amplitude The maximum deviation from trend in an economic time series. (p. 71)

Average labor productivity Equal to Y/N where Y is aggregate output and N is total labor input. (p. 89)

Boom A series of positive deviations from trend in real GDP, culminating in a peak. (p. 71)

Business cycles Fluctuations about trend in real GDP. (p. 70)

Coincident variable An economic variable that neither leads nor lags real GDP. (p. 78)

Co-movement How aggregate economic variables move together over the business cycle. (p. 74)

Correlation coefficient A measure of the degree of correlation between two variables. (p. 77)

Countercyclical Describes an economic variable that tends to be below (above) trend when real GDP is above (below) trend. (p. 76)

Frequency The number of peaks in an economic time series that occur per year. (p. 71)

Lagging variable An economic variable that past real GDP helps to predict. (p. 78)

Leading variable An economic variable that helps to predict future real GDP. (p. 78)

Negative correlation Relationship between two economic time series when a straight line fit to a scatter plot of the two variables has a negative slope. (p. 75)

Peak A relatively large positive deviation from trend in real GDP. (p. 70)

Perfectly negatively correlated Describes two variables that have a correlation coefficient of -1. (p. 77)

Perfectly positively correlated Describes two variables that have a correlation coefficient of 1. (p. 77)

Persistent Describes an economic time series that tends to stay above (below) trend when it has been above (below) trend during the recent past. (p. 71)

Phillips curve A positive correlation between a money price or the rate of change in a money price and a measure of aggregate economic activity. (p. 82)

Positive correlation Relationship between two economic time series when a straight line fit to a scatter plot of the two variables has a positive slope. (p. 75)

Procyclical Describes an economic variable that tends to be above (below) trend when real GDP is above (below) trend. (p. 75)

Real wage The purchasing power of the wage earned per hour worked. (p. 88)

Recession A series of negative deviations from trend in real GDP, culminating in a trough. (p. 71)

Reverse Phillips curve A negative correlation between a money price or the rate of change in a money price and a measure of aggregate economic activity. (p. 83)

Scatter plot A plot of two variables, x and y, with x measured on the horizontal axis and y measured on the vertical axis. (p. 75)

Seasonal adjustment The statistical process of removing the predictable seasonal component from an economic time series. (p. 89)

Standard deviation A measure of variability. The cyclical variability in an economic time series can be measured by the standard deviation of the percentage deviations from trend. (p. 80)

Time series Sequential measurements of an economic variable over time. (p. 74)

Trough A relatively large negative deviation from trend in real GDP. (p. 70)

Turning points Peaks and troughs in real GDP. (p. 70)

Questions for Review

1. What is the primary defining feature of business cycles?
2. Besides persistence, what are three important features of the deviations from trend in GDP?
3. Explain why forecasting GDP over the long term is difficult.
4. Why are the co-movements in aggregate economic variables important?
5. What did Robert Lucas say about the co-movements among economic variables?
6. How can we discern positive and negative correlation in a time series plot? In a scatter plot?
7. Give a noneconomic example of two variables that are positively correlated and an example of two variables that are negatively correlated.
8. Why is the index of leading economic indicators useful for forecasting GDP?
9. What are the three features of co-movement that macroeconomists are interested in?
10. Describe the key business cycle regularities in consumption and investment expenditures.
11. What are the key business cycle regularities with respect to the price level and the money supply?
12. Does a Phillips curve relationship exist in the data set that was studied in this chapter?
13. What are the key business cycle regularities in the labor market?

Problems

1. In Figure 3.2, what do "typical" patterns of deviations from trend in real GDP tell us about the potential length and severity of the 2008–2009 recession? Figure 3.2 includes data only up to the first quarter of 2009. How does your forecast of GDP beyond the first quarter of 2009, using only the information in Figure 3.2, compare to what actually happened? Discuss.

2. In Figure 3.17 the percentage deviations from trend in GDP (Y) and government expenditures (G) for the period 1947–2009 are plotted. Figure 3.18 is a scatter plot of the same data.
   (a) Which is more variable, Y or G?
   (b) Is G procyclical, countercylical, or acyclical, and how can you tell? What do you think explains this?

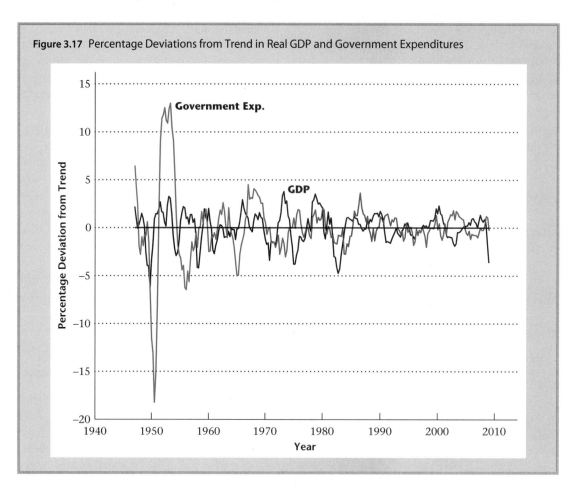

Figure 3.17 Percentage Deviations from Trend in Real GDP and Government Expenditures

(c) Is there any tendency for *G* to lead or lag *Y*, or is *G* coincident?

3. Figure 3.19 shows the percentage deviations from trend in GDP (*Y*) and exports, and Figure 3.20 shows the same data in a scatter plot. Repeat parts (a), (b), and (c) of question 1, but for exports instead of *G*.

4. Figure 3.21 shows time series for two economic variables, *X* and *Z*. Does *X* lead *Z*, or does *Z* lead *X*? Explain.

5. We have measured average labor productivity in this chapter as *Y/N*, where *Y* is real GDP and *N* is employment. The business cycle facts concerning employment relate to how the denominator *N* co-moves with the numerator *Y*, and those concerning average labor productivity relate to how *Y/N* co-moves with *Y*. Explain how the business cycle facts concerning employment and average labor productivity in Tables 3.1 and 3.2 are consistent.

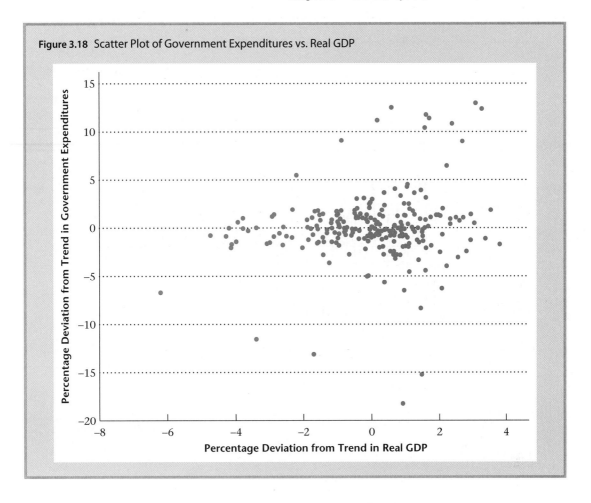

Figure 3.18 Scatter Plot of Government Expenditures vs. Real GDP

6. Consumption of durables is more variable relative to trend than is consumption of nondurables, and consumption of nondurables is more variable relative to trend than is consumption of services. Speculate on why we observe these phenomena and relate this to the key business cycle facts in Tables 3.1 and 3.2.

7. The Great Moderation in part refers to the moderate variability in real GDP that occurred after the 1981–1982 recession and before the 2008–2009 recession. In Figure 3.12, what do you observe about the behavior of the deviations from trend in the price level over the period 1947–2009? Relate this to the Great Moderation experience and discuss.

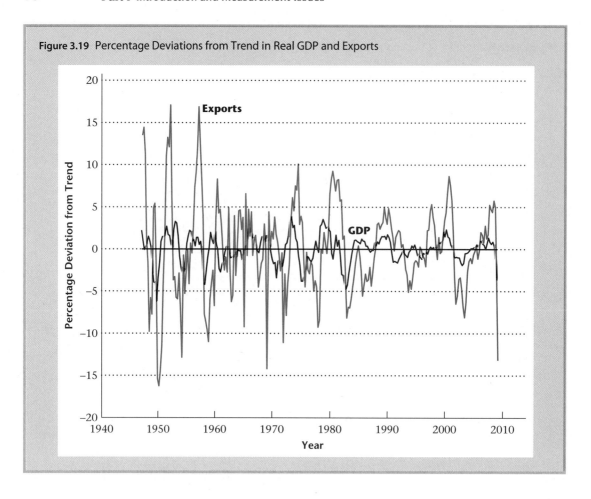

Figure 3.19 Percentage Deviations from Trend in Real GDP and Exports

Working with the Data

1. Calculate the year-to-year (December-to-December) percentage increase in the consumer price index (CPI), and then do a scatter plot of this against the unemployment rate (match the December 1996 unemployment rate with the percentage change in the CPI from December 1995 to December 1996, for example). Do you observe a positive correlation, a negative correlation, or a correlation that is essentially zero? Is there a Phillips curve relationship here or a reverse Phillips curve?

2. The index of industrial production is an output measure that is not as comprehensive as GDP, but it is available on a more timely basis (monthly rather than quarterly). Calculate the percentage year-to-year (December-to-December) growth rates in the index of industrial production and the percentage year-to-year growth rates in the money supply (M2). Graph the growth in industrial production and in the money supply using a time series plot and using a scatter plot.

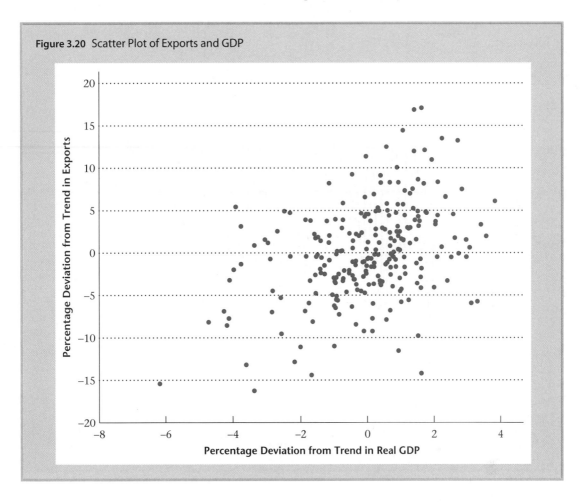

Figure 3.20 Scatter Plot of Exports and GDP

(a) Are growth in industrial production and in the money supply positively correlated or negatively correlated?

(b) Does one time series lead the other, or are they coincident?

(c) Are your answers to (a) and (b) consistent with what we observed in Figure 3.13? Explain.

3. Plot: (i) detrended GDP and detrended consumption of durables; (ii) detrended GDP and detrended consumption of nondurables; (iii) detrended GDP and detrended consumption of services.

(a) What do you notice in these plots compared to Figure 3.9 for GDP and total consumption and Figure 3.10 for GDP and investment?

(b) Provide an explanation for your observations in part (a).

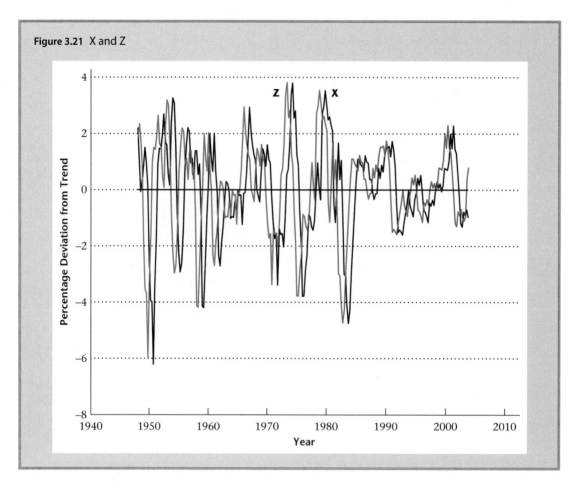

Figure 3.21 X and Z

4. Plot detrended GDP along with each of detrended residential investment, detrended non-residential investment, and inventory investment.
   (a) Which of the components of investment shows the most (least) variability relative to GDP?
   (b) What lead/lag patterns do you detect in the plots?
   (c) Provide possible explanations for the patterns you detected in parts (a) and (b).

PART II

A One-Period Model of the Macroeconomy

The goal of Part II is to construct a working model of the macroeconomy that can be used to analyze some key macroeconomic issues. The basic building blocks of this model are the microeconomic behavior of consumers and firms. We start in Chapter 4 by analyzing the behavior of a representative consumer and a representative firm, with each making decisions over one period. The representative consumer's fundamental choice in this environment concerns how to allocate time between work and leisure, making himself or herself as well off as possible while obeying his or her budget constraint. The representative firm chooses how much labor it should hire so as to maximize profits. In Chapter 5, we build consumer behavior and firm behavior into a one-period macroeconomic model, in which there is a government that can spend and tax. This model is then used to show that, under ideal conditions, free market outcomes can be socially efficient, government spending crowds out private consumption while increasing aggregate output, and increases in productivity increase welfare, consumption, and aggregate output.

chapter 4

Consumer and Firm Behavior: The Work–Leisure Decision and Profit Maximization

Chapters 2 and 3 focused on how we measure variables of macroeconomic interest. We now turn to the construction and analysis of a particular macroeconomic model. Recall that, in Chapter 1, we saw how a macroeconomic model is built from a description of consumers and their preferences over goods and of firms and the technology available to produce goods from available resources. In this chapter, we focus on the behavior of consumers and firms in a simple model environment with only one time period. One-period decision making for consumers and firms limits the kinds of macroeconomic issues we can address with the resulting model. This simplification, however, makes it easier to understand the basic microeconomic principles of consumer and firm optimization on which we build in the rest of this book. Given that there is only one time period, consumers and firms make **static**, as opposed to **dynamic**, decisions. Dynamic decision making involves planning over more than one period, as, for example, when individuals make decisions concerning how much to spend today and how much to save for the future. Dynamic decisions are analyzed in Parts III and IV.

With regard to consumer behavior, we focus on how a consumer makes choices concerning the tradeoff between consuming and working. For the consumer, consuming more goods comes at a cost: The consumer must work harder and will enjoy less leisure time. Primarily, we are interested in how a consumer's work—leisure choice is affected by his or her preferences and by the constraints he or she faces. For example, we want to know how a change in the market wage rate and in the consumer's nonwage income affects his or her choices concerning how much to work, how much to consume, and how much leisure time to take. For the firm, we focus on how the available technology for producing goods, and the market environment influence the firm's decision concerning how much labor to hire during the period.

As we discussed in Chapter 1, a fundamental principle that we adhere to here is that consumers and firms optimize. That is, a consumer wishes to make himself or herself as well off as possible given the constraints he or she faces. Likewise, a firm acts to maximize profits, given market prices and the available technology. The optimization principle is a very powerful and useful tool in economics, and it helps in sharpening the predictions of economic models. Given optimizing behavior by consumers and firms, we can then analyze how these economic agents respond to changes in the environment in which they live. For example, we show how consumers and firms change the quantity of labor supplied and the quantity of labor demanded, respectively, in response to a change in the market wage rate, and how consumers respond to a change in taxes. The knowledge we build up in this chapter concerning these optimal responses is critical in the next chapter, where we study what happens in the economy as a whole when there is an important shock to the system, for example, a large increase in government spending or a major new invention.

The Representative Consumer

To begin, we consider the behavior of a single representative consumer, who acts as a stand-in for all of the consumers in the economy. We show how to represent a consumer's preferences over the available goods in the economy and how to represent the consumer's budget constraint, which tells us what goods it is feasible for the consumer to purchase given market prices. We then put preferences together with the budget constraint to determine how the consumer behaves given market prices, and how he or she responds to a change in nonwage income and to a change in the market wage rate.

The Representative Consumer's Preferences

It proves simplest to analyze consumer choice, and is just right for the issues we want to address in this chapter and the next to suppose that there are two goods that consumers desire. The first is a physical good, which we can think of as an aggregation of all consumer goods in the economy, or measured aggregate consumption. We call this the **consumption good.** The second good is **leisure**, which is any time spent not working in the market. In terms of our definition, therefore, leisure could include recreational activities, sleep, and work at home (cooking, yardwork, housecleaning).

For macroeconomic purposes, it proves convenient to suppose that all consumers in the economy are identical. In reality, of course, consumers are not identical, but for many macroeconomic issues diversity among consumers is not essential to addressing the economics of the problem at hand, and considering it only clouds our thinking. Identical consumers, in general, behave in identical ways, and so we need only analyze the behavior of one of these consumers. Further, if all consumers are identical, the economy behaves as if there were only one consumer, and it is, therefore, convenient to write down the model as having only a single **representative consumer.** We must recognize, however, that the representative consumer in our macroeconomic model plays the role of a stand-in for all consumers in the economy.

A key step in determining how the representative consumer makes choices is to show how we can capture the preferences of the representative consumer over leisure and consumption goods by a **utility function**, written as

$$U(C,l),$$

where U is the utility function, C is the quantity of consumption, and l is the quantity of leisure. We refer to a particular combination of consumption and leisure—for example,

(C_1, l_1), where C_1 is a particular consumption quantity and l_1 is a particular quantity of leisure—as a **consumption bundle**. The utility function represents how the consumer ranks different consumption bundles. That is, suppose that there are two different consumption bundles, representing different quantities of consumption and leisure, denoted (C_1, l_1) and (C_2, l_2). We say that (C_1, l_1) is strictly preferred by the consumer to (C_2, l_2) if

$$U(C_1, l_1) > U(C_2, l_2);$$

(C_2, l_2) is strictly preferred to (C_1, l_1) if

$$U(C_1, l_1) < U(C_2, l_2);$$

and the consumer is indifferent between the two consumption bundles if

$$U(C_1, l_1) = U(C_2, l_2).$$

It is useful to think of $U(C, l)$ as giving the level of happiness, or utility, that the consumer receives from consuming the bundle (C, l). The actual level of utility, however, is irrelevant; all that matters for the consumer is what the level of utility is from a given consumption bundle *relative* to another one.

To use our representation of the consumer's preferences for analyzing macroeconomic issues, we must make some assumptions concerning the form that preferences take. These assumptions are useful for making the analysis work, and they are also consistent with how consumers actually behave. We assume that the representative consumer's preferences have three properties: More is preferred to less; the consumer likes diversity in his or her consumption bundle; and consumption and leisure are normal goods. We discuss each of these in turn.

1. *More is always preferred to less.*   A consumer always prefers a consumption bundle that contains more consumption, more leisure, or both. This may appear unnatural, because it seems that we can get too much of a good thing. For example, consuming too much of one good may sometimes make one worse off, as when we overeat. In terms of general consumption goods, however, the average consumer in the United States today consumes far more than the average consumer 200 years ago would have dreamed possible, and it certainly seems that the average consumer today in the United States would like to consume more if it were feasible. Indeed, even the extremely wealthy appear to desire more than they have.

2. *The consumer likes diversity in his or her consumption bundle.*   To see that this is a natural property of consumer preferences, consider a consumer who, instead of consuming consumption goods and leisure, is making a decision about where to eat lunch during the week. Lynn can go to one of two restaurants to eat lunch, one of which serves only hamburgers, while the other serves only tuna sandwiches. One choice open to Lynn is to eat a hamburger for lunch on each day of the week, and another choice is to eat tuna sandwiches all week. Suppose that Lynn is indifferent between these two choices. If she has a preference for diversity, Lynn would prefer to alternate between restaurants during the week rather than eat at one place every day. In the case of our representative consumer, who is choosing

among consumption bundles with different combinations of consumption goods and leisure, a preference for diversity means that, if the consumer is indifferent between two consumption bundles, then some mixture of the two consumption bundles is preferable to either one. At the extreme, suppose that the consumer is indifferent between a consumption bundle that has 6 units of consumption and no leisure and another bundle that has no consumption goods and 8 units of leisure. Then, a preference for diversity implies that the consumer would prefer a third consumption bundle, consisting of half of each of the other bundles, to having either of the other consumption bundles. This preferable third consumption bundle would have 3 units of consumption goods and 4 units of leisure.

3. *Consumption and leisure are normal goods.* A good is **normal** for a consumer if the quantity of the good that he or she purchases increases when income increases. For example, meals at high-quality restaurants are a normal good for most people; if our income increases, we tend to eat out more in good places. In contrast, a good is **inferior** for a consumer if he or she purchases less of that good when income increases. An example of an inferior good is food from Bob Evans; most people would tend to eat less at Bob Evans as their income increases. In our model, then, given that consumption and leisure are normal goods, the representative consumer purchases more consumption goods and increases his or her leisure time when income increases. This seems intuitively appealing; if, for example, you received a windfall increase in your income, perhaps through an inheritance, you would probably want to consume more goods as well as taking more vacation time (leisure). In practice, the behavior of consumers is consistent with consumption and leisure being normal goods.

While we postpone discussion of property (3) of the representative consumer's preferences until we have more machinery to analyze how the consumer behaves, our next step is to show how we represent properties (1) and (2) graphically. It is helpful to consider the representative consumer's preferences using a graphical representation of the utility function, called the **indifference map.** The indifference map is a family of **indifference curves.**

> DEFINITION 1 An *indifference curve* connects a set of points, with these points representing consumption bundles among which the consumer is indifferent.

Figure 4.1 shows two indifference curves. In the figure, I_1 is an indifference curve, and two points on the indifference curve are (C_1, l_1) (point B) and (C_2, l_2) (point D). Because these two consumption bundles lie on the same indifference curve, we must have $U(C_1, l_1) = U(C_2, l_2)$. That is, being indifferent implies that the consumer receives the same level of happiness from each consumption bundle. Another indifference curve is I_2. Because indifference curve I_2 lies above indifference curve I_1, and we know more is preferred to less, consumption bundles on I_2 are strictly preferred

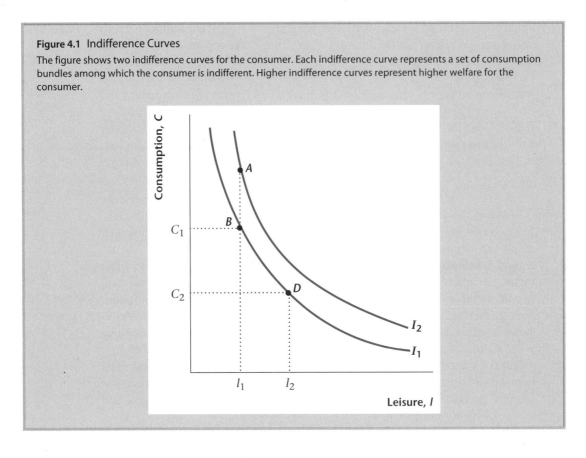

Figure 4.1 Indifference Curves

The figure shows two indifference curves for the consumer. Each indifference curve represents a set of consumption bundles among which the consumer is indifferent. Higher indifference curves represent higher welfare for the consumer.

to consumption bundles on I_1. For example, consider point A, which represents a consumption bundle with the same quantity of leisure as at point B, but with a higher quantity of the consumption good. Because more is preferred to less, A is strictly preferred to B.

An indifference curve has two key properties:

1. An indifference curve slopes downward.
2. An indifference curve is convex, that is bowed-in toward the origin.

Because the indifference map is just the graphical representation of preferences, it should not be surprising that the properties of the indifference curve are related to the properties of preferences, (1) and (2), described above. In fact, property (1) of an indifference curve follows from property (1) of preferences (more is always preferred to less), and property (2) of an indifference curve follows from property (2) of preferences (the consumer likes diversity in his or her consumption bundle).

To see why the fact that indifference curves slope downward follows from the fact that more is preferred to less, consider Figure 4.2. At point A, consumption is C_1 and leisure is l_1. Suppose that we now consider holding the quantity of leisure

Figure 4.2 Properties of Indifference Curves

Indifference curves are downward-sloping because more is preferred to less. A preference for diversity implies that indifference curves are convex (bowed-in toward the origin). The slope of an indifference curve is the negative of the marginal rate of substitution.

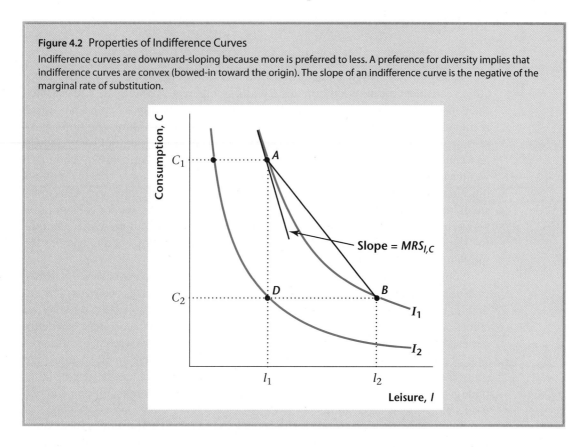

constant for the consumer at l_1 and reduce the consumer's quantity of consumption to C_2, so that the consumer now has the consumption bundle represented by point D. Because more is preferred to less, point D must be on a lower indifference curve (indifference curve I_2) than is point A (on indifference curve I_1). Now we can ask how much leisure we would have to add to l_1, holding consumption constant at C_2, to obtain a consumption bundle B such that the consumer is indifferent between A and B. Point B must lie below and to the right of point A because, if we are taking consumption goods away from the consumer, we need to give him or her more leisure. Thus, the indifference curve I_1 is downward-sloping because more is preferred to less.

To understand why the convexity of the indifference curve follows from the preference of the representative consumer for diversity, we introduce the following concept.

DEFINITION 2   *The **marginal rate of substitution** of leisure for consumption, denoted* $MRS_{l,C}$, *is the rate at which the consumer is just willing to substitute leisure for consumption goods.*

We have

$$MRS_{l,C} = -[\text{the slope of the indifference curve passing through } (C, l)].$$

To see why the marginal rate of substitution is minus the slope of the indifference curve, consider consumption bundles A and B in Figure 4.2. There, the rate at which the consumer is willing to substitute leisure for consumption in moving from A to B is the ratio $\frac{C_1 - C_2}{l_2 - l_1}$, or minus the slope of the line segment AB. Minus the slope of AB tells us how much consumption we need to take away for each unit of leisure added as we move from A to B, with the consumer being just indifferent between A and B. If we imagine choosing a point like point B on the indifference curve I_1 below point A but closer and closer to A, then as the distance between that point and A becomes small, the rate at which the consumer is willing to substitute leisure for consumption between A and the chosen point is the marginal rate of substitution, which is minus the slope of the indifference curve at point A (or minus the slope of a tangent to the indifference curve at A).

Suppose, for example, that Krystyna can choose how many weeks of vacation to take each year and that she currently works 50 weeks in the year and takes two weeks of vacation, so that her leisure time is two weeks. To keep things simple, suppose Krystyna consumes only coconuts, so that we can measure her consumption in coconuts. Currently, she eats 500 coconuts per year. If Krystyna were to take one more week of vacation per year, she would be just as happy as she is now if she were to give up 50 coconuts per year. This implies that Krystyna's marginal rate of substitution of leisure for consumption, given her current consumption bundle of 500 coconuts of consumption and two weeks of leisure, is 50 coconuts per week.

Stating that an indifference curve is convex [property (2) of the indifference curve] is identical to stating that the marginal rate of substitution is diminishing. That is, note that the indifference curve in Figure 4.2 becomes flatter as we move down the indifference curve from left to right, that is, as the consumer receives more leisure and less of the consumption good. Thus, minus the slope of the indifference curve becomes smaller as leisure increases and consumption decreases. In other words, the marginal rate of substitution is diminishing. This is because, as we increase the quantity of leisure and reduce the quantity of consumption, the consumer needs to be compensated more and more in terms of leisure time to give up another unit of consumption. The consumer requires this extra compensation because of a preference for diversity.

To give a concrete example of a preference for diversity in terms of a consumption-leisure choice, suppose that Allen sleeps 8 hours in every 24-hour period. He therefore has 112 hours per week to split between work and leisure. Consider two situations. In the first, Allen takes 10 hours of leisure per week and works 102 hours, and in the second he takes 102 hours of leisure per week and works 10 hours. In the first circumstance, Allen is willing to give up much more consumption expenditure in exchange for one extra hour of leisure than in the second case.

The Representative Consumer's Budget Constraint

Now that we know something about the representative consumer's preferences, we must also specify his or her constraints and objectives to predict what he or she will do. We assume that the representative consumer behaves competitively. Here, **competitive behavior** means that the consumer is a price-taker; that is, he or she treats market prices as being given and acts as if his or her actions have no effect on those prices. This is certainly an accurate description of reality if the consumer is small relative to the market, but of course this is not literally true if there is only one consumer. Recall, however, that the single representative consumer is a stand-in for all the consumers in the economy. Even though it is obvious that real economies do not have only one consumer, a real economy can still behave as if there were a single representative consumer.

An important assumption that we make at this stage is that there is no money in this economy. That is, there is no government-supplied currency to be used in exchange, and no banks through which people can conduct transactions, for example, through transactions accounts that can be used in conjunction with debit cards and checks. For some macroeconomic issues, the complication of introducing money does not add anything to our analysis and is best left out. Later, however, in Chapters 10 to 13, we begin to analyze the role that money plays in the macroeconomy, so that we can address issues such as the effects of inflation and the conduct of monetary policy.

An economy without monetary exchange is a **barter** economy. In a barter economy, all trade involves exchanges of goods for goods. There are only two goods here: consumption goods and time. When time is used at home, we call it leisure time, and when time is exchanged in the market, we call it work—more explicitly, labor time. Any trades in this economy must involve exchanges of labor time for consumption goods, or vice versa. The consumer is assumed to have h hours of time available, which can be allocated between leisure time, l, and time spent working (or labor supply), denoted by N^s. The **time constraint** for the consumer is then

$$l + N^s = h, \tag{4-1}$$

which states that leisure time plus time spent working must sum to total time available.

The Consumer's Real Disposable Income   Having specified how the representative consumer allocates time between work and leisure, we can describe the consumer's real disposable income, which is wage income plus dividend income minus taxes.

Labor time is sold by the consumer in the labor market at a price w in terms of consumption goods. That is, one unit of labor time exchanges for w units of consumption goods. Therefore, w is the **real wage**, or the wage rate of the consumer in units of purchasing power. Throughout, the consumption good plays the role of **numeraire**, or the good in which all prices and quantities are denominated. In actual economies, money is the numeraire, but in our barter economy model, the choice of numeraire is arbitrary. We choose the consumption good as numeraire, as this is a common convention.

If the consumer works N^s hours, then his or her real wage income is wN^s, which is expressed in units of the consumption good. The second source of income for the consumer is profits distributed as dividends from firms. We let π be the quantity of profits, in real terms, that the consumer receives. In our model, firms have to be owned by someone, and this someone must be the representative consumer. Any profits earned by firms, therefore, must be distributed to the representative consumer as income, which we can think of as dividends. We refer to π as real **dividend income**.

Finally, the consumer pays taxes to the government. We assume that the real quantity of taxes is a lump-sum amount T. A **lump-sum tax** is a tax that does not depend in any way on the actions of the economic agent who is being taxed. In practice, no taxes are lump sum; for example, the quantity of sales taxes we pay depends on the quantity of taxable goods that we buy, and our income taxes depend on how much we work. Taxes that are not lump sum have important effects on the effective prices that consumers face in the market. For example, an increase in the sales tax on gasoline increases the effective price of gasoline for consumers relative to other goods. This change in the effective relative price of gasoline in turn affects the demand for gasoline and for other goods. These distorting effects of taxation are important, but we confine attention to lump-sum taxation for now, as this is simpler, from a modeling perspective.

Real wage income plus real dividend income minus taxes is the consumer's real disposable income, and this is what the consumer has available to spend on consumption goods.

The Budget Constraint   Now that we know how the representative consumer can allocate time between work and leisure and what his or her real disposable income is, we can derive the consumer's budget constraint algebraically and show it graphically.

We can view the representative consumer as receiving his or her real disposable income and spending it in the market for consumption goods. What actually happens, however, is that the consumer receives income and pays taxes in terms of consumption goods, and then he or she decides how much to consume out of this disposable income. Because this is a one-period economy, which implies that the consumer has no motive to save, and because the consumer prefers more to less, all disposable income is consumed, so that we have

$$C = wN^s + \pi - T, \tag{4-2}$$

or, total real consumption equals real disposable income. Equation (4-2) is the consumer's **budget constraint.** Now, substituting for N^s in (4-2) using Equation (4-1), we get

$$C = w(h - l) + \pi - T. \tag{4-3}$$

The interpretation of Equation (4-3) is that the right-hand side is real disposable income, while the left-hand side is expenditure on consumption goods, so that total market expenditure is equal to disposable income.

Alternatively, if we add wl to both sides of (4-3), we get

$$C + wl = wh + \pi - T. \tag{4-4}$$

An interpretation of Equation (4-4) is that the right-hand side is the implicit quantity of real disposable income the consumer has, and the left-hand side is implicit expenditure on the two goods, consumption and leisure. On the right-hand side of (4-4), because the consumer has h units of time, with each unit of time valued in real terms according to the market real wage w, and $\pi - T$ is real dividend income minus taxes,

Figure 4.3 Representative Consumer's Budget Constraint when $T > \pi$

The figure shows the consumer's budget constraint for the case in which taxes are greater than the consumer's dividend income. The slope of the budget constraint is $-w$, and the constraint shifts with the quantity of nonwage real disposable income, $\pi - T$. All points in the shaded area and on the budget constraint can be purchased by the consumer.

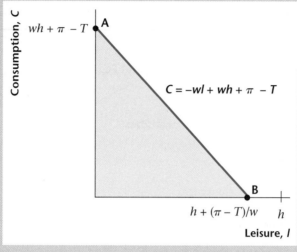

the total quantity of implicit real disposable income is $wh + \pi - T$. On the left-hand side of (4-4), C is what is spent on consumption goods, while wl is what is implicitly "spent" on leisure. That is, w is the market price of leisure time, because each unit of leisure is forgone labor, and labor time is priced at the real wage w. Thus, $C + wl$ is implicit real expenditure on consumption goods and leisure.

To graph the consumer's budget constraint, it is convenient to write Equation (4-4), in slope—intercept form, with C as the dependent variable, to get

$$C = -wl + wh + \pi - T, \tag{4-5}$$

so that the slope of the budget constraint is $-w$, and the vertical intercept is $wh + \pi - T$. In Figure 4.3 we graph the budget constraint, Equation (4-5), as the line AB. Here, we have drawn the budget constraint for the case where $T > \pi$, so that dividend income minus taxes, $\pi - T$, is negative. Further, by setting $C = 0$ in Equation (4-5) and solving for l, we can get the horizontal intercept, $h + \frac{\pi - T}{w}$. The vertical intercept is the maximum quantity of consumption attainable for the consumer, which is what is achieved if the consumer works h hours and consumes no leisure. The horizontal intercept is the maximum number of hours of leisure that the consumer can take and still be able to pay the lump-sum tax.

Figure 4.4 shows what the consumer's budget constraint looks like in the case where $T < \pi$, in which case dividend income minus taxes, $\pi - T$, is positive. Here,

Figure 4.4 Representative Consumer's Budget Constraint when $T < \pi$

The figure shows the consumer's budget constraint when taxes are less than dividend income. This implies that the budget constraint is kinked. The examples we study always deal with this case, rather than the one in which taxes are greater than dividend income. Consumption bundles in the shaded region and on the budget constraint are feasible for the consumer; all other consumption bundles are not feasible.

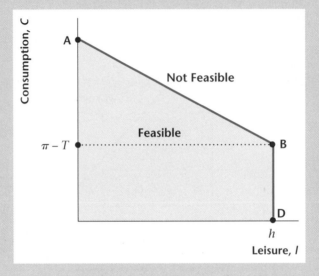

the budget constraint is somewhat unusual, as it is kinked; the slope of the budget constraint is $-w$ over its upper portion, and the constraint is vertical over its lower portion. There is a kink in the budget constraint because the consumer cannot consume more than h hours of leisure. Thus, at point B we have $l = h$, which implies that the number of hours worked by the consumer is zero. Points along BD all involve the consumer working zero hours and consuming some amount $C \leq \pi - T$—that is, the consumer always has the option of throwing away some of his or her dividend income. Even though the consumer does not work at point B, we have $C = \pi - T > 0$, as dividend income exceeds taxes. In what follows, we always consider the case where $\pi - T > 0$, as this is the more complicated case (because of the kink in the consumer's budget constraint), and because ultimately it does not make any difference for our analysis whether we look only at the case $\pi - T > 0$ or $\pi - T < 0$.

The representative consumer's budget constraint tells us what consumption bundles are feasible for him or her to consume given the market real wage, dividend income, and taxes. In Figure 4.4, consumption bundles in the shaded region inside and on the budget constraint are feasible; all other consumption bundles are infeasible.

Consumer Optimization

We have now described the representative consumer's preferences over consumption and leisure and determined the budget constraint that tells us what combinations of consumption and leisure are feasible. Our next step is to put preferences together with the budget constraint so as to analyze how the representative consumer behaves.

To determine what choice of consumption and leisure the consumer makes, we assume that the consumer is **rational.** Rationality in this context means that the representative consumer knows his or her own preferences and budget constraint and can evaluate which feasible consumption bundle is best for him or her. Basically, we are assuming that the consumer can make an informed optimization decision.

> DEFINITION 3 *The **optimal consumption bundle** is the point representing a consumption-leisure pair that is on the highest possible indifference curve and is on or inside the consumer's budget constraint.*

Consider Figure 4.5, and note that we are considering only the case where $T < \pi$, because ignoring the case where $T > \pi$ does not matter. We want to demonstrate why point H, where indifference curve I_1 is just tangent to the budget constraint ABD, is the optimal consumption bundle for the consumer. First, the consumer would never choose a consumption bundle inside the budget constraint. This is because the consumer prefers more to less. For example, consider a point like J in Figure 4.5, which lies inside the budget constraint. Clearly, point F, which is on the budget constraint, is strictly preferred by the consumer to J because the consumer gets more consumption at point F than at J, while receiving the same quantity of leisure. Further, the consumer would not choose any points along BD other than B; B is preferred to any point on BD because more consumption goods are preferred to less consumption goods.

In considering the consumer's optimization problem, given our reasoning thus far we can restrict attention solely to points on the line segment AB in Figure 4.5. Which of these points does the consumer choose? Given the assumptions we have made about the representative consumer's preferences, we are guaranteed that there is a single consumption bundle on AB that is optimal for the consumer: the point at which an indifference curve is tangent to AB. Why is this the best the consumer can do? Again, consider Figure 4.5. At a point like F, minus the slope of the indifference curve passing through F, or $MRS_{l,C}$, is greater than minus the slope of the budget constraint at F, which is equal to w. Alternatively, at F the rate at which the consumer is willing to trade leisure for consumption is greater than the rate at which the consumer can trade leisure for consumption in the market, or $MRS_{l,C} > w$. The consumer would be better off, therefore, if he or she sacrificed consumption for more leisure by moving from point F in the direction of H. In so doing, the consumer moves to successively higher indifference curves, which is another indication that he or she is becoming better off. Similarly, at point E in Figure 4.5, the indifference curve is flatter than the budget constraint, so that $MRS_{l,C} < w$. Thus, moving from point E toward point H implies that the consumer substitutes consumption for leisure

Figure 4.5 Consumer Optimization

The consumption bundle represented by point *H*, where an indifference curve is tangent to the budget constraint, is the optimal consumption bundle for the consumer. Points inside the budget constraint, such as *J*, cannot be optimal (more is preferred to less), and points such as *E* and *F*, where an indifference curve cuts the budget constraint, also cannot be optimal.

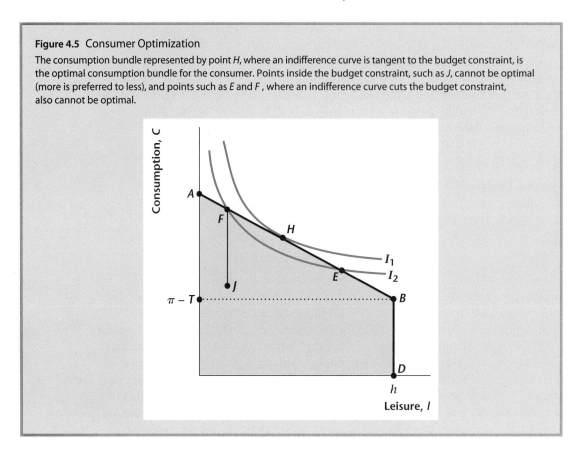

and moves to higher indifference curves, becoming better off as a result. At point *H*, where an indifference curve is just tangent to the budget constraint, the rate at which the consumer is willing to trade leisure for consumption is equal to the rate at which leisure trades for consumption in the market, and, thus, the consumer is at his or her optimum. In other words, when the representative consumer is optimizing, we have

$$MRS_{l,C} = w, \tag{4-6}$$

or the marginal rate of substitution of leisure for consumption is equal to the real wage. In Equation (4-6), this optimizing, or marginal, condition, takes the following form: marginal rate of substitution of leisure for consumption equals the **relative price** of leisure in terms of consumption goods. In general, the relative price of a good *x* in terms of a good *y* is the number of units of *y* that trade for a unit of *x*. It is generally true that consumer optimization in competitive markets implies that the consumer sets the marginal rate of substitution of any good *x* for any other good *y* equal to the relative price of *x* in terms of *y*. We use this fact in later chapters.

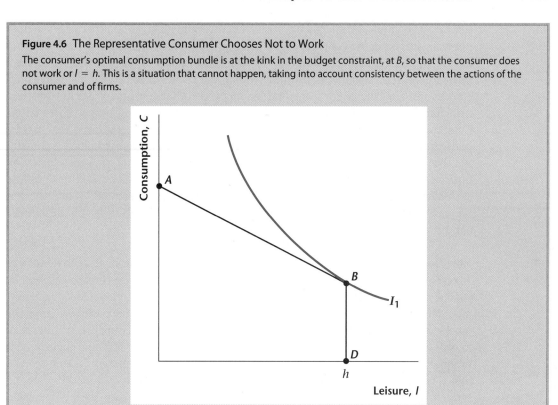

Figure 4.6 The Representative Consumer Chooses Not to Work

The consumer's optimal consumption bundle is at the kink in the budget constraint, at B, so that the consumer does not work or $l = h$. This is a situation that cannot happen, taking into account consistency between the actions of the consumer and of firms.

Given the way we have drawn the budget constraint in Figure 4.5, there seems no obvious reason that the highest indifference curve could not be reached at point B, in which case the consumer would choose to consume all of his or her time as leisure, as in Figure 4.6. However, this could not happen when we take account of the interaction of consumers and firms—it would imply that the representative consumer would not work, in which case nothing would be produced, and, therefore, the consumer would not have anything to consume. The assumption that the consumer always wishes to consume some of both goods (the consumption good and leisure) prevents the consumer from choosing either point A or point B in Figure 4.5.

The assumption that the representative consumer behaves optimally subject to his or her constraints is very powerful in giving us predictions about what the consumer does when his or her budget constraint changes, or when his or her preferences change. Is it plausible to assume that a consumer makes optimizing decisions? In our own lives, we can generally think of many occasions on which we did not make optimal decisions. For example, suppose Jennifer is self-employed and can choose how much vacation to take every year. Suppose that, for ten years, Jennifer takes two weeks of vacation every summer. One year, by chance, she takes three weeks of vacation and finds that she is much happier than before. We might imagine this happening not because Jennifer's preferences or budget constraint changed, but because she does not really know her own preferences without experimenting with different consumption-leisure combinations. This would violate the assumption of rationality that we have made for the representative consumer, who always knows exactly what his or her preferences are. The defense for using optimizing behavior for consumers as a fundamental principle in our models is that mistakes by consumers are not likely to persist for a long time. Eventually, people learn how to behave optimally. Also, what is important, particularly in terms of macroeconomic models, is that people on average behave optimally, not that each individual in the economy always does so. Further, if we were to abandon optimization behavior, there would be many possible alternatives, and it would be extremely difficult to get our models to make any predictions at all. While there is typically only one way to behave optimally, there are many ways in which individuals can be stupid!

How Does the Representative Consumer Respond to a Change in Real Dividends or Taxes?   Recall from Chapter 1 that a macroeconomic model, once constructed, can be used to conduct "experiments," somewhat like the experiments conducted by a chemist or a physicist using a laboratory apparatus. Now that we have shown how the representative consumer makes choices about consumption and leisure, we are interested as economists in how the consumer responds to changes in the economic environment he or she faces. We carry out two experiments on the representative consumer. The first is to change his or her real dividend income minus taxes, $\pi - T$, and the second is to change the market real wage w that he or she faces. In each case, we are interested in how these experiments affect the quantities of consumption and leisure chosen by the representative consumer.

We first look at a change in real dividend income minus taxes, or $\pi - T$, which is the component of real disposable income that does not depend on the real wage w. In changing $\pi - T$, we hold w constant. A change in $\pi - T$ could be caused either by a change in π or a change in T, or both. For example, an increase in π could be caused by an increase in the productivity of firms, which in turn results in an increase in the dividends that are paid to the consumer. Similarly, if T decreases, this represents a tax cut for the consumer, and disposable income increases. In any case, we think of the increase in $\pi - T$ as producing a **pure income effect** on the consumer's choices, because prices remain the same (w remains constant) while disposable income increases.

For the case where $\pi > T$, we consider an increase in $\pi - T$ (recall that the $\pi < T$ case is not fundamentally different). In Figure 4.7 suppose that initially $\pi = \pi_1$ and $T = T_1$, and then there are changes in π and T so that $\pi = \pi_2$ and $T = T_2$ with $\pi_2 - T_2 > \pi_1 - T_1$. Recall that the vertical intercept of the budget constraint is $wh + \pi - T$, so that initially the budget constraint of the consumer is ABD and, with the increase in $\pi - T$, the constraint shifts out to FJD. FJ is parallel to AB, because the real wage has not changed, leaving the slope of the budget constraint ($-w$) identical to what it was initially. Now suppose that initially the consumer chooses point H, where the highest indifference curve I_1 is reached on the initial budget constraint, and we have $l = l_1$ and $C = C_1$. When $\pi - T$ increases, which consumption bundle does

Figure 4.7 An Increase in $\pi - T$ for the Consumer

Initially the consumer chooses H, and when $\pi - T$ rises this shifts the budget constraint out in a parallel fashion (the real wage, which determines the slope of the budget constraint, stays constant). Consumption and leisure both increase, as both are normal goods.

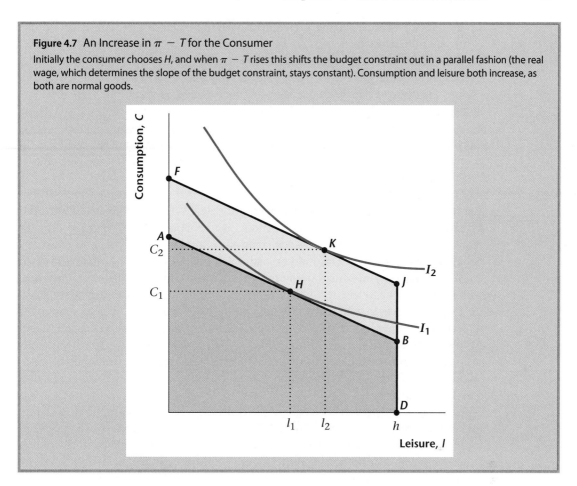

the consumer choose? We have the consumer choosing point K, where the indifference curve I_2 is tangent to the new budget constraint. At point K, we have $l = l_2$ and $C = C_2$, so that consumption and leisure are both higher. Why would this necessarily be the case? Indeed, we could draw indifference curves that are consistent with more being preferred to less and a preference for diversity and have the consumer choose either less consumption or less leisure when income increases. Recall, however, that we assumed earlier in this chapter that consumption and leisure are normal goods. This means that, if we hold the real wage constant, then an increase in income implies that the representative consumer chooses more consumption and more leisure, as is the case in Figure 4.7.

To see why it is natural to assume that consumption and leisure are both normal goods, consider a consumer, Gillian, who receives a windfall increase in her income from winning a lottery. It seems likely that, as a result, Gillian spends more on consumption goods and takes more vacation time, thus working less and increasing leisure time. This would happen only if Gillian's preferences have the property that consumption and leisure are normal goods.

The assumption that consumption and leisure are both normal implies that higher nonwage disposable income increases consumption and reduces labor supply. Thus, for example, given lower real taxes, consumers spend more and work less. The increase in income is given in Figure 4.7 by the distance AF, but the increase in consumption, $C_2 - C_1$, is less than AF. This is because, although nonwage income increases, wage income falls because the consumer is working less. The reduction in income from the decrease in wage income does not completely offset the increase in nonwage income, as consumption has to increase because it is a normal good.

The Representative Consumer and Changes in the Real Wage: Income and Substitution Effects   The second experiment we conduct is to change the real wage faced by the representative consumer, holding everything else constant. In studying how consumer behavior changes when the market real wage changes, we care about how the consumer's quantity of consumption is affected, but we are perhaps most concerned with what happens to leisure and labor supply. In elementary economics, we typically treat supply curves as being upward-sloping, in that the quantity of a good supplied increases with the market price of the good, holding everything else constant. Labor supply, however, is different. Although it is straightforward to show that the quantity of consumption goods chosen by the consumer increases when the real wage increases, labor supply, N^s, may rise or fall when the real wage rises. Part of this section focuses on why this is the case.

In considering how the behavior of the consumer changes in response to a change in the real wage w, we hold constant real dividends π and real taxes T. We do the experiment in this way to remove the pure income effect on consumer behavior that we studied in the previous subsection. Consider Figure 4.8, where initially the budget constraint is ABD, and an increase in the real wage w causes the budget constraint to shift out to EBD. Here, EB is steeper than AB because the real wage has increased, but the kink in the budget constraint remains fixed at B, as nonwage disposable income, $\pi - T$, is unchanged. Initially, the consumer chooses point F, where indifference curve I_1 is tangent to the initial budget constraint. Here, $l = l_1$ and $C = C_1$. When the real wage increases, the consumer might choose a point like H, where indifference curve I_2 is tangent to the new budget constraint. As Figure 4.8 is drawn, leisure remains unchanged at l_1, and consumption increases from C_1 to C_2. What we want to show is that, given that consumption and leisure are normal goods, consumption must increase but leisure may increase or decrease in response to an increase in the real wage. To understand why this is the case, we need to introduce the concepts of *substitution effect* and *income effect*.

The effects of an increase in the real wage on the consumer's optimal choice of consumption and leisure can be broken down into an income effect and a substitution effect as follows. First, given the new higher real wage, suppose that we take away dividend income from the consumer or increase taxes until he or she chooses a consumption bundle O that is on the initial indifference curve I_1. Thus, given the increase in the

Figure 4.8 Increase in the Real Wage Rate–Income and Substitution Effects

An increase in the real wage shifts the budget constraint from *ABD* to *EBD*. The kink in the constraint remains fixed, and the budget constraint becomes steeper. Consumption must increase, but leisure may rise or fall, because of opposing substitution and income effects. The substitution effect is the movement from *F* to *O*; the income effect is the movement from *O* to *H*.

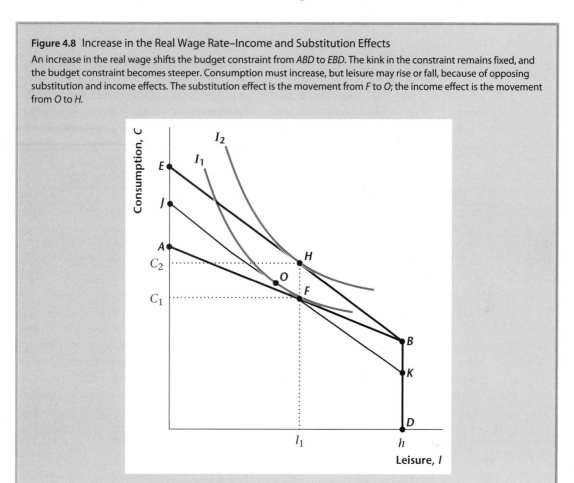

real wage, we have taken real disposable income away from the consumer so that he or she is just indifferent between the consumption bundle chosen (point *O*) and the initial consumption bundle (*F*). It is as if the consumer now faces the budget constraint *JKD*. The movement from *F* to *O* is a pure **substitution effect** in that it just captures the movement along the indifference curve in response to the increase in the real wage. The real wage increases, so that leisure has become more expensive relative to consumption goods, and the consumer substitutes away from the good that has become more expensive (leisure) to the one that has become relatively cheaper (consumption). Therefore, the substitution effect of the real wage increase is for consumption to increase and for leisure to decrease, and so the substitution effect is for labor supply, $N^s = h - l$, to increase.

Now, the movement from *O* to *H* is then a pure **income effect**, as the real wage stays the same as the budget constraint shifts out from *JKD* to *EBD*, and nonwage income increases. Because both goods are normal, consumption increases and leisure increases in moving from O to H. Thus, when the real wage increases, the consumer can consume more consumption goods and more leisure, because the budget constraint has shifted out. On net, then, consumption must increase, because the substitution and income effects both act to increase consumption. There are opposing substitution and income effects on leisure, however, so that it is ultimately unclear whether leisure rises or falls. Therefore, an increase in the real wage could lead to an increase or a decrease in labor supply N^s.

To understand the intuition behind this result, assume Alex is working 40 hours per week and earning $15.00 per hour, so that his weekly wage income is $600.00. Now suppose that Alex's wage rate increases to $20.00 per hour and that he is free to set his hours of work. On the one hand, because his wage rate is now higher, the cost of taking leisure has increased, and Alex may choose to work more (the substitution effect). On the other hand, he could now work 30 hours per week, still receive $600.00 in wage income per week, and enjoy 10 more hours of free time (the income effect), so that Alex may choose to reduce his hours of work.

While some of the analysis we do, particularly in Chapter 5, involves work with indifference curves, it is sometimes useful to summarize consumer behavior with supply and demand relationships. In Chapter 9 and in later chapters, it often proves useful to work at the level of supply and demand curves in different markets. Then, an important relationship is the **labor supply curve**, which tells us how much labor the representative consumer wishes to supply given any real wage. To construct the labor supply curve, one could imagine presenting the representative consumer with different real wage rates and asking what quantity of labor the consumer would choose to supply at each wage rate. That is, suppose $l(w)$ is a function that tells us how much leisure the consumer wishes to consume, given the real wage w. Then, the labor supply curve is given by

$$N^s(w) = h - l(w).$$

Now, because the effect of a wage increase on the consumer's leisure choice is ambiguous, we do not know whether labor supply is increasing or decreasing in the real wage. Assuming that the substitution effect is larger than the income effect of a change in the real wage, labor supply increases with an increase in the real wage, and the labor supply schedule is upward-sloping as in Figure 4.9. Furthermore, we know that, because the quantity of leisure increases when nonwage disposable income increases, an increase in nonwage disposable income shifts the labor supply curve to the left, that is, from N^s to N_1^s as shown in Figure 4.10. In analysis where we work with supply and demand relationships, we typically assume that the substitution effect of an increase in the real wage dominates the income effect, so that the labor supply curve is upward-sloping, as in Figure 4.9.

An Example: Consumption and Leisure Are Perfect Complements   An example of consumer optimization that we can work out in a straightforward way, both algebraically and graphically, is the case in which the representative consumer's preferences have the **perfect complements** property. Goods are perfect complements

Figure 4.9 Labor Supply Curve

The labor supply curve tells us how much labor the consumer wishes to supply for each possible value for the real wage. Here, the labor supply curve is upward-sloping, which implies that the substitution effect of an increase in the real wage is larger than the income effect for the consumer.

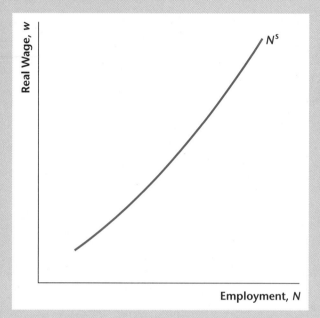

for the consumer if he or she always wishes to consume these goods in fixed proportions. In practice, there are many cases of goods that are perfect complements. For example, right shoes are almost always consumed one-to-one with left shoes, in that a right shoe is typically not much good without the left shoe. Also, cars and tires are usually consumed in fixed proportions of one to four (ignoring the spare tire, of course).

If consumption and leisure are perfect complements, then the consumer always wishes to have $\frac{C}{l}$ equal to some constant, or

$$C = al, \tag{4-7}$$

where $a > 0$ is a constant. With perfect complements, the indifference curves of the consumer are L-shaped, as in Figure 4.11, with the right angles of the indifference curves falling along the line $C = al$. At a point such as E on indifference curve I_2, adding more consumption while holding leisure constant simply makes the consumer indifferent, as does adding more leisure while holding consumption constant. The consumer can be better off only if he or she receives more of both goods. Note that perfect complements preferences do not satisfy all the properties for preferences that we assumed in general. More is not always preferred to less, as the consumer is not better off with more of one

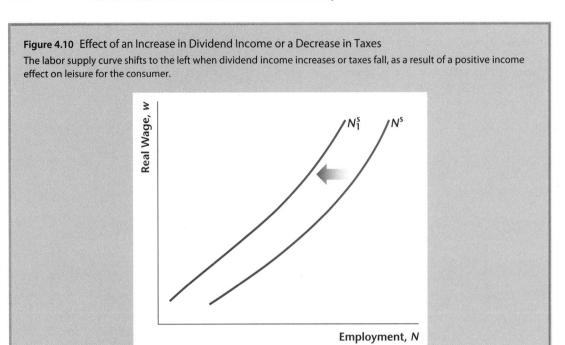

Figure 4.10 Effect of an Increase in Dividend Income or a Decrease in Taxes
The labor supply curve shifts to the left when dividend income increases or taxes fall, as a result of a positive income effect on leisure for the consumer.

good unless he or she has more of the other good as well. However, the consumer does have a preference for diversity, but of a very dramatic sort. That is, as we move downward along the indifference curve, the slope does not become flatter in a smooth way but goes instantly from vertical to horizontal.

The optimal consumption bundle for the consumer is always along the line $C = al$, as in Figure 4.11, where the budget constraint is ABD and the consumer optimizes by choosing a point that is on the budget constraint and on the highest indifference curve, which is point F. Algebraically, the quantities of consumption and leisure must solve (4-7) and must also satisfy the budget constraint

$$C = w(h - l) + \pi - T. \tag{4-8}$$

Now, Equations (4-7) and (4-8) are two equations in the two unknowns, C and l, with a, w, h, π, and T given. We can solve these two equations for the two unknowns by substitution to get

$$l = \frac{wh + \pi - T}{a + w},$$

$$C = \frac{a(wh + \pi - T)}{a + w}.$$

From the above solution, note that leisure and consumption increase with nonwage disposable income $\pi - T$, and we can also show that consumption and leisure both

Figure 4.11 Perfect Complements

When consumption and leisure are perfect complements for the consumer, indifference curves are L-shaped with right angles along the line $C = al.$, where a is a constant. The budget constraint is *ABD*, and the optimal consumption bundle is always on the line $C = al.$

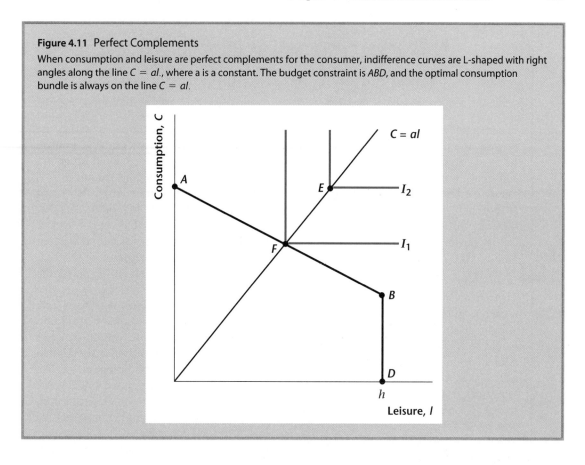

increase when the real wage *w* increases. With perfect complements there are no substitution effects. Further, if *a* increases, so that the consumer prefers more consumption relative to leisure, then it is obvious that the consumer chooses more of *C* and less of *l* at the optimum.

We use perfect complements preferences in examples in Chapter 8. Another simple example that is dealt with in the problems at the end of this chapter is the case where preferences have the **perfect substitutes** property. In that case, the marginal rate of substitution is constant and the indifference curves are downward-sloping straight lines.

The Representative Firm

In our model economy, consumers and firms come together to exchange labor for consumption goods. While the representative consumer supplies labor and demands consumption goods, we turn now to the behavior of firms, which demand labor and supply consumption goods. The choices of the firms are determined by the available

MACROECONOMICS IN ACTION
Labor Supply and Taxes in the G-7 Countries

In our simple model of consumer behavior, an easy way to study the effects of income taxation on the consumer would be to assume that the consumer's wage income is taxed at a constant rate, t. Then, supposing that the lump sum tax is zero, or $T = 0$, the consumer would pay total taxes of $tw(h - l)$, and the consumer's budget constraint would be

$$C = w(1 - t)(h - l) + \pi.$$

Then, if we wanted to analyze the effects of a change in the income tax rate t on labor supply, given the market real wage w, this would be the same as analyzing the effects of a change in the real wage, since now $w(1 - t)$ is the effective real wage for the consumer, and an increase in t is equivalent to a decrease in the consumer's effective real wage. From our analysis in this chapter, we know that theory tells us that an increase in the income tax rate t may cause an increase or a decrease in the quantity of labor supplied, depending on the relative strengths of opposing income and substitution effects. For example, an increase in t will reduce labor supply only if the substitution effect is large relative to the income effect. That is, if the substitution effect is relatively large, then there can be a large disincentive effect on hours of work as the result of an income tax rate increase.

One approach to determining whether the disincentive effect of income taxation on labor supply is important is to study the behavior of workers in different countries with different income tax systems, and see what we observe. In an article in the Minneapolis Federal Reserve Bank *Quarterly Review*, Edward

Prescott does just that.[1] Prescott studies the G-7 countries, which are Canada, France, Germany, Italy, Japan, the United Kingdom, and the United States, and examines two periods of time, which are 1970–1974 and 1993–1996. One key feature of the data that Prescott focuses on is that, in the earlier period, labor supplied per person was about the same in France, Germany, and Italy as it was in the United States. However, by the 1990s, Americans were working about twice as hard (in hours worked per person) as their counterparts in France, Germany, and Italy.

What could account for this difference in labor supply behavior between the United States and Europe? Possibly Europeans just like vacations more than Americans do (indifference curves are different in the United States from Europe) or market wages (before taxes) are higher in the United States than in Europe. Prescott argues that the major reason for this difference in labor supply behavior is differences in marginal tax rates. That is, in real-world income tax systems, typically the tax rate varies with the level of income. For example, in the United States the poor are taxed at a lower rate than are the rich. The marginal tax rate is the tax rate paid on the last dollar of income that a person earns, and this is the tax rate that matters for that person's behavior. In France, Germany, and Italy, in the period 1993–1996, the marginal tax rate for the average person was about 60%, compared to 40% in the United States. For this to matter for labor

---

[1]Prescott, E. 2004. "Why Do Americans Work More Than Europeans?" *Minneapolis Federal Reserve Bank Quarterly Review* 28, No. 1, 2–13.

supply behavior, it would have to be the case that there is a very large substitution effect of a change in the real wage on the quantity of labor supplied, relative to the income effect. Prescott measures these effects and finds that, indeed, the measured substitution effect is very large.

How could Prescott's findings matter to us as economists? One example that he uses relates to social security systems. Later, in Chapter 8, we will study different types of social security systems and how they work to

provide income for people in retirement. The type of social security system in place in the United States is a "pay-as-you-go" system, which funds payments to retirees from taxes collected from the working age population. If Prescott's results are correct, economic efficiency could be improved greatly by moving from pay-as-you-go to an alternative social security system that does not tax workers at such high rates, thus increasing the quantity of labor supplied.

technology and by profit maximization. As with consumer behavior, we ultimately focus here on the choices of a single, representative firm.

The firms in this economy own productive capital (plant and equipment), and they hire labor to produce consumption goods. We can describe the production technology available to each firm by a **production function,** which describes the technological possibilities for converting factor inputs into outputs. We can express this relationship in algebraic terms as

$$Y = zF(K, N^d), \tag{4-9}$$

where z is total factor productivity, Y is output of consumption goods, K is the quantity of capital input in the production process, N^d is the quantity of labor input measured as total hours worked by employees of the firm, and F is a function. Because this is a one-period or static (as opposed to dynamic) model, we treat K as being a fixed input to production, and N^d as a variable factor of production. That is, in the short run, firms cannot vary the quantity of plant and equipment (K) they have, but they have flexibility in hiring and laying off workers (N^d). **Total factor productivity** z captures the degree of sophistication of the production process. That is, an increase in z makes both factors of production, K and N^d, more productive, in that, given factor inputs, higher z implies that more output can be produced.

For example, suppose that the above production function represents the technology available to a bakery. The quantity of capital, K, includes the building in which the bakery operates, ovens for baking bread, a computer for doing the bakery accounts, and other miscellaneous equipment. The quantity of labor, N^d, is total hours worked by all the bakery employees, including the manager, the bakers who operate the ovens, and the employees who work selling the bakery's products to customers. The variable z, total factor productivity, can be affected by the techniques used for organizing production. For example, bread could be produced either by having each baker operate an individual oven, using this oven to produce different kinds of bread, or each baker could specialize in making a particular kind of bread and use the oven that happens to be available when an oven is needed. If the latter production method produces more bread per day using the same inputs of capital and labor, then that production process implies a higher value of z than does the first process.

For our analysis, we need to discuss several important properties of the production function. Before doing this, we need the following definition.

> DEFINITION 4   *The **marginal product** of a factor of production is the additional output that can be produced with one additional unit of that factor input, holding constant the quantities of the other factor inputs.*

In the production function of Equation (4-9), there are two factor inputs, labor and capital. Figure 4.12 shows a graph of the production function, fixing the quantity of capital at some arbitrary value, K^*, and allowing the labor input, N^d, to vary. Some of the properties of this graph require further explanation. In the figure, the marginal product of labor, given the quantity of labor N^*, is the slope of the production function at point A; this is because the slope of the production function is the additional output produced from an additional unit of the labor input when the quantity of labor is N^* and the quantity of capital is K^*. We let MP_N denote the marginal product of labor.

Next, in Figure 4.13 we graph the production function again, but this time we fix the quantity of labor at N^* and allow the quantity of capital to vary. In Figure 4.13, the marginal product of capital, denoted MP_K, given the quantity of capital K^*, is the slope of the production function at point A.

The production function has five key properties, which we will discuss in turn.

1. *The production function exhibits constant returns to scale.*   **Constant returns to scale** means that, given any constant $x > 0$, the following relationship holds:

$$zF(xK, xN^d) = xzF(K, N^d).$$

That is, if all factor inputs are changed by a factor x, then output changes by the same factor x. For example, if all factor inputs double ($x = 2$), then output also doubles. The alternatives to constant returns to scale in production are **increasing returns to scale** and **decreasing returns to scale.** Increasing returns to scale implies that large firms (firms producing a large quantity of output) are more efficient than small firms, whereas decreasing returns to scale implies that small firms are more efficient than large firms. With constant returns to scale, a small firm is just as efficient as a large firm. Indeed, constant returns to scale means that a very large firm simply replicates how a very small firm produces many times over. Given a constant-returns-to-scale production function, the

Figure 4.12 Production Function, Fixing the Quantity of Capital and Varying the Quantity of Labor

The marginal product of labor is the slope of the production function at a given point. Note that the marginal product of labor declines with the quantity of labor.

economy behaves in exactly the same way if there were many small firms producing consumption goods as it would if there were a few large firms, provided that all firms behave competitively (they are price-takers in product and factor markets). Given this, it is most convenient to suppose that there is only one firm in the economy, the **representative firm.** Just as with the representative consumer, it is helpful to think of the representative firm as a convenient stand-in for many firms, which all have the same constant-returns-to-scale production function. In practice, it is clear that in some industries decreasing returns to scale are important. For example, high-quality restaurant food seems to be produced most efficiently on a small scale. Alternatively, increasing returns to scale are important in the automobile industry, where essentially all production occurs in very large scale firms, such as General Motors (which of course is not as large-scale as it once was). This does not mean, however, that it is harmful to assume that there exists constant returns to scale in production at the aggregate level, as is the case in our model. This is because even the largest firm in the U.S. economy produces a small amount of output relative to U.S. GDP, and the aggregate economy can exhibit constant returns to scale in aggregate production, even if this is not literally true for each firm in the economy.

Figure 4.13 Production Function, Fixing the Quantity of Labor and Varying the Quantity of Capital
The slope of the production function is the marginal product of capital, and the marginal product of capital declines with the quantity of capital.

2. *The production function has the property that output increases when either the capital input or the labor input increases.* In other words, the marginal products of labor and capital are both positive: $MP_N > 0$ and $MP_K > 0$. In Figures 4.12 and 4.13, these properties of the production function are exhibited by the upward slope of the production function. Recall that the slope of the production function in Figure 4.12 is the marginal product of labor and the slope in Figure 4.13 is the marginal product of capital. Positive marginal products are quite natural properties of the production function, as this states simply that more inputs yield more output. In the bakery example discussed previously, if the bakery hires more workers given the same capital equipment, it will produce more bread, and if it installs more ovens given the same quantity of workers, it will also produce more bread.

3. *The marginal product of labor decreases as the quantity of labor increases.* In Figure 4.12 the declining marginal product of labor is reflected in the concavity of the production function. That is, the slope of the production function in Figure 4.12, which is equal to MP_N, decreases as N^d increases. The following example helps to illustrate why the marginal product of labor should fall as the quantity of labor input increases: Suppose accountants work in an office

building that has one photocopy machine, and suppose that they work with pencils and paper but at random intervals need to use the photocopy machine. The first accountant added to the production process, Sara, is very productive— that is, she has a high marginal product—as she can use the photocopy machine whenever she wants. However, when the second accountant, Paul, is added, Sara on occasion wants to use the machine and she gets up from her desk, walks to the machine, and finds that Paul is using it. Thus, some time is wasted that could otherwise be spent working. Paul and Sara produce more than Sara alone, but what Paul adds to production (his marginal product) is lower than the marginal product of Sara. Similarly, adding a third accountant, Julia, makes for even more congestion around the photocopy machine, and Julia's marginal product is lower than Paul's marginal product, which is lower than Sara's. Figure 4.14 shows the representative firm's marginal product of labor schedule. This is a graph of the firm's marginal product, given a fixed quantity of capital, as a function of the labor input. That is, this is the graph of the slope of the production function in Figure 4.12. The marginal product schedule is always positive, and it slopes downward.

4. *The marginal product of capital decreases as the quantity of capital increases.* This property of the production function is very similar to the previous one, and it is illustrated in Figure 4.13 by the decreasing slope, or concavity, of the production

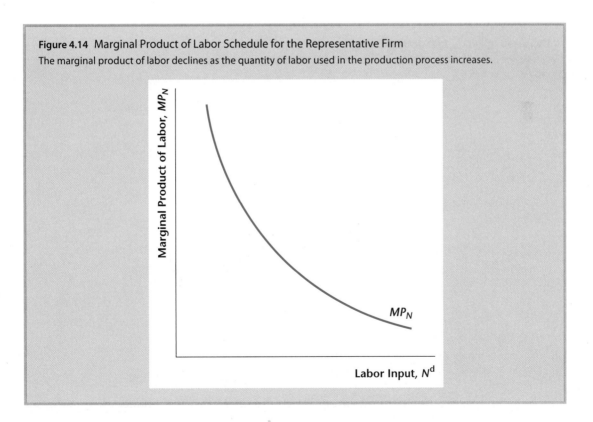

Figure 4.14 Marginal Product of Labor Schedule for the Representative Firm
The marginal product of labor declines as the quantity of labor used in the production process increases.

function. In terms of the example above, if we suppose that Sara, Paul, and Julia are the accountants working in the office and imagine what happens as we add photocopy machines, we can gain some intuition as to why the decreasing-marginal-product-of-capital property is natural. Adding the first photocopy machine adds a great deal to total output, as Sara, Paul, and Julia now can duplicate documents that formerly had to be copied by hand. With three accountants in the office, however, there is congestion around the machine. This congestion is relieved with the addition of a second machine, so that the second machine increases output, but the marginal product of the second machine is smaller than the marginal product of the first machine, and so on.

5. *The marginal product of labor increases as the quantity of the capital input increases.* To provide some intuition for this property of the production function, return to the example of the accounting firm. Suppose that Sara, Paul, and Julia initially have one photocopy machine to work with. Adding another photocopy machine amounts to adding capital equipment, and this relieves congestion around the copy machine and makes each of Sara, Paul, and Julia more productive, including Julia, who was the last accountant added to the workforce at the firm. Therefore, adding more capital increases the marginal product of labor, for each quantity of labor. In Figure 4.15 an increase in the quantity of capital from K_1 to K_2 shifts the marginal product of labor schedule to the right, from MP_N^1 to MP_N^2.

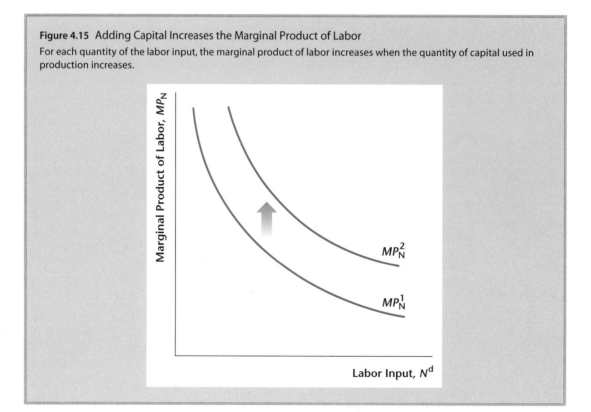

Figure 4.15 Adding Capital Increases the Marginal Product of Labor

For each quantity of the labor input, the marginal product of labor increases when the quantity of capital used in production increases.

The Effect of a Change in Total Factor Productivity on the Production Function

Changes in total factor productivity, z, are critical to our understanding of the causes of economic growth and business cycles, so we must understand how a change in z alters the production technology. An increase in total factor productivity z has two important effects. First, because more output can be produced given capital and labor inputs when z increases, this shifts the production function up. In Figure 4.16, with the quantity of capital fixed at K^*, there is an upward shift in the production function when z increases from z_1 to z_2. Second, the marginal product of labor increases when z increases. This is reflected in the fact that the slope of the production function when $z = z_2$ in Figure 4.16 is higher than the slope given $z = z_1$, for any given quantity of the labor input, N^d. In Figure 4.17 the marginal product of labor schedule shifts to the right from MP_N^1 to MP_N^2 when z increases. An increase in z has a similar effect on the marginal product of labor schedule to an increase in the capital stock (see Figure 4.15).

What could cause a change in total factor productivity? In general, an increase in z arises from anything that permits more output to be produced for given inputs. In the macroeconomy, there are many factors that can cause z to increase. One of these factors is technological innovation. The best examples of technological innovations that increase total factor productivity are changes in the organization of production or in management

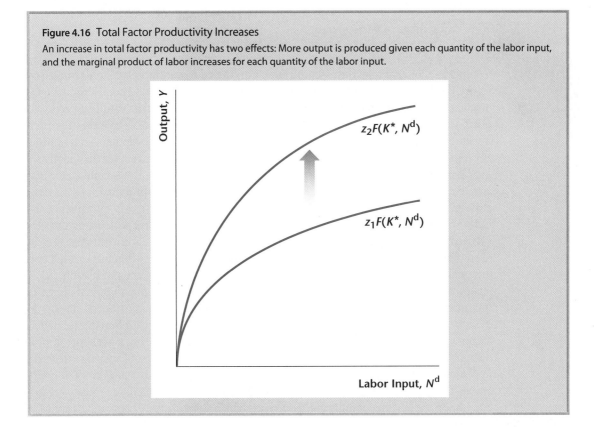

Figure 4.16 Total Factor Productivity Increases

An increase in total factor productivity has two effects: More output is produced given each quantity of the labor input, and the marginal product of labor increases for each quantity of the labor input.

Figure 4.17 Effect of an Increase in Total Factor Productivity on the Marginal Product of Labor
When total factor productivity increases, the marginal product of labor schedule shifts to the right.

techniques. For example, the assembly line, introduced to automobile manufacturing by Henry Ford (see Macroeconomics in Action: Henry Ford and Total Factor Productivity) brought about a huge increase in the quantity of Model T Fords that could be produced using the same quantities of capital equipment and workers. Some of the most important inventions of the twentieth century—for example, the personal computer—might more appropriately be considered to involve increases in the capital stock rather than increases in z, because the new technology is embodied in capital equipment. A second factor that acts to increase z is good weather. Weather is very important for production in the agricultural and construction sectors, in particular. For example, crop yields are higher, given factor inputs, if rainfall is higher (as long as it is not too high), and construction projects proceed more quickly if rainfall is lower. A third factor affecting z is government regulations. For example, if the government imposes regulations requiring that firms install pollution abatement equipment, this may be good for the welfare of the population, but it results in a decrease in z. This happens because pollution abatement equipment increases the quantity of the capital input in the production process but contributes nothing to measured output. Finally, an increase in the relative price of energy is often interpreted as a decrease in z. When the relative price of energy increases, firms use less energy in production, and this reduces the productivity of both capital and labor, thus causing a decrease in z. Major increases in the price of energy occurred in the United States in 1973–1974 and in 1979, 1990, 2000, and then in 2002 through 2008. These energy price increases had important macroeconomic consequences, which we study in Chapters 5, 9, and 11.

MACROECONOMICS IN ACTION
Henry Ford and Total Factor Productivity

The Ford Motor Company was founded in 1903 by Henry Ford and a financial backer, but Ford achieved only modest success until the introduction to the market of the Model T Ford in 1908. This car proved to be extremely popular, because it was light, strong, simple, and relatively easy to drive. Given the high demand for Model T cars, Henry Ford decided to increase output, but he did this not by simply replicating his existing production process through the construction of identical plants; rather, he increased total factor productivity, while also augmenting the capital and labor inputs in production. A key element of the total factor productivity increase was the introduction of the assembly line to automobile manufacturing. Henry Ford borrowed this idea from assembly lines used in the Chicago meat-packing industry. However, the general principle at work in the assembly line was known much earlier, for example by Adam Smith, the father of modern economics. In the *Wealth of Nations*, Smith discusses how production was organized in a pin factory, as an illustration of what he called the "division of labor":

> One man draws out the wire, another straightens it, a third cuts it ... the important business of making a pin is, in this manner, divided into about eighteen distinct operations ...[2]

Smith was impressed by how the specialization of tasks led to increased productivity in the manufacture of pins. More than a century later, Henry Ford's assembly line replaced an arrangement where automobiles were assembled by teams that each accumulated parts and completed a single automobile in a single location in the plant. Just as in the pin factory, Ford was able to exploit the gains from specialization that the assembly line permitted, where each worker performed only one specialized task, and, therefore, automobiles could be completed at a much higher rate. The increase in total factor productivity at the Ford Motor Company was reflected in the fact that, in 1914, 13,000 workers produced 260,720 cars at Ford, while in the rest of the U.S. automobile industry 66,350 workers produced 286,770 cars. Thus, output per worker at Ford was almost five times that in the rest of the U.S. auto industry! We do not have measures of the size of the capital stock at Ford and elsewhere in the auto industry, so that there is a slim chance that the higher quantity of output per worker at Ford could have been due simply to higher capital per worker. However, it seems safe to say that total factor productivity at Ford Motor Company increased by a remarkable amount because of the innovations of Henry Ford, and these innovations were quickly imitated in the rest of the auto industry.[3]

---

[2]See Adam Smith, *An Enquiry into the Nature and Causes of the Wealth of Nations*, Liberty Fund, Indianapolis, reprinted 1981, p. 15.

[3]See H. Ford, 1926, *My Life and Work*, Doubleday, Page and Co., New York; A. Nevins, 1954, *Ford: The Times, the Man, the Company*, Charles Scribner's and Sons, New York.

Total Factor Productivity and the U.S. Aggregate Production Function

So far we have assumed that the production function for the representative firm takes the form $Y = zF(K, N^d)$, where the function F has some very general properties (constant returns to scale, diminishing marginal products, etc.). When macroeconomists work with data to test theories, or when they want to simulate a macroeconomic model on the computer to study some quantitative aspects of a theory, they need to be much more specific about the form the production function takes. A very common production function used in theory and empirical work is the **Cobb–Douglas production function.** This function takes the form

$$Y = zK^a(N^d)^{1-a},$$

where a is a parameter, with $0 < a < 1$. The exponents on K and N^d in the function sum to 1 ($a + 1 - a = 1$), which reflects constant returns to scale. If there are profit-maximizing, price-taking firms and constant returns to scale, then a Cobb–Douglas production function implies that a will be the share that capital receives of national income (in our model, the profits of firms), and $1 - a$ the share that labor receives (wage income before taxes) in equilibrium. What is remarkable is that, from the National Income and Product Accounts (NIPA) of the United States, the capital and labor shares of national income have been roughly constant in the United States, which is consistent with the Cobb–Douglas production function. Given this, an empirical estimate

of a is the average share of capital in national income, which from the data is about 0.36,[4] or 36%, so a good approximation to the actual U.S. aggregate production function is

$$Y = zK^{0.36}(N^d)^{0.64}. \qquad (4\text{-}10)$$

In Equation (4-10), the quantities Y, K, and N^d can all be measured. For example, Y can be measured as real GDP from the NIPA, K can be measured as the total quantity of capital in existence, built up from expenditures on capital goods in the NIPA, and N^d can be measured as total employment, in the Current Population Survey done by the Bureau of Labor Statistics. But how is total factor productivity z measured? Total factor productivity cannot be measured directly, but it can be measured indirectly, as a residual. That is, from Equation (4-10), if we can measure Y, K, and N^d, then a measure of z is the **Solow residual,** which is calculated as

$$z = \frac{Y}{K^{0.36}(N^d)^{0.64}}. \qquad (4\text{-}11)$$

This measure of total factor productivity is named after Robert Solow.[5] In Figure 4.18 we graph the Solow residual for the United States for the period 1948–2006, calculated using Equation (4-11) and measurements of Y, K, and N^d as described above. Measured total factor productivity grows over time, and it fluctuates about trend. In Chapters 6, 7, and 11, we see how growth and fluctuations in total factor productivity can cause growth and fluctuations in real GDP.

[4]See E. Prescott, 1986, "Theory Ahead of Business Cycle Measurement," *Federal Reserve Bank of Minneapolis Quarterly Review,* Fall, 9–22.

[5]See R. Solow, 1957, "Technical Change and the Aggregate Production Function," *Review of Economic Statistics* 39, 312–320.

Figure 4.18 The Solow Residual for the United States

The Solow residual is a measure of total factor productivity, and it is calculated here using a Cobb Douglas production function. Measured total factor productivity has increased over time, and it also fluctuates about trend, as shown for the period 1948–2009.

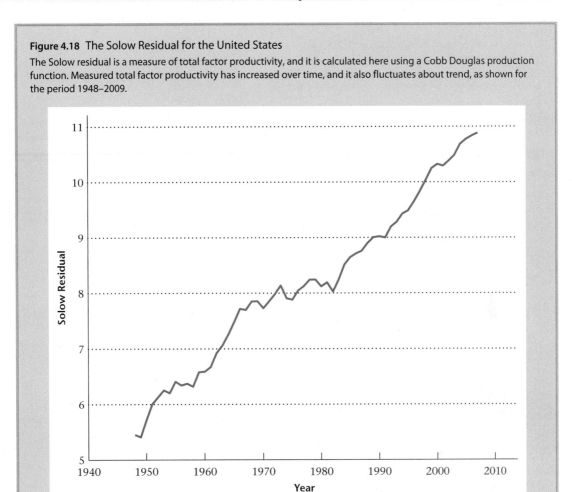

The Profit Maximization Problem of the Representative Firm

Now that we have studied the properties of the representative firm's production technology, we can examine the determinants of the firm's demand for labor. Like the representative consumer, the representative firm behaves competitively in that it takes as given the real wage, which is the price at which labor trades for consumption goods. The goal of the firm is to maximize its profits, given by $Y - wN^d$, where Y is the total revenue that the firm receives from selling its output, in units of the consumption good, and wN^d is the total real cost of the labor input, or total real variable costs. Then, substituting for Y using the production function $Y = zF(K, N^d)$, the firm's problem is to choose N^d to maximize

$$\pi = zF(K, N^d) - wN^d,$$

where K is fixed. Here, π is real profit. In Figure 4.19 we graph the revenue function, $zF(K, N^d)$, and the variable cost function, wN^d. Profit is then the difference between

Figure 4.19 Revenue, Variable Costs, and Profit Maximization

$Y = zF(K,N^d)$ is the firm's revenue, while wN^d is the firm's variable cost. Profits are the difference between the former and the latter. The firm maximizes profits at the point where marginal revenue equals marginal cost, or $MP_N = w$. Maximized profits are the distance AB, or the distance ED.

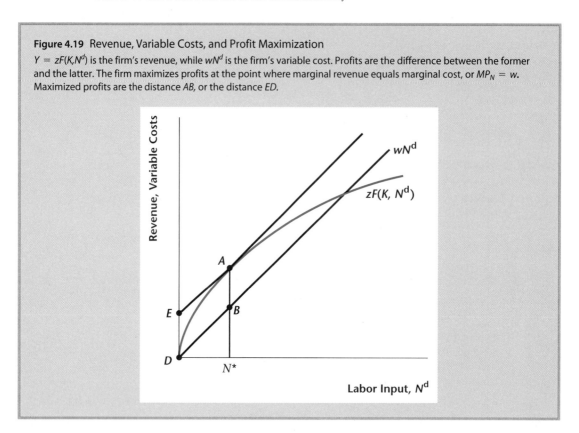

total revenue and total variable cost. Here, to maximize profits, the firm chooses $N^d = N^*$ in Figure 4.19. The maximized quantity of profits, π^*, is the distance AB in Figure 4.19. For future reference, π^* is the distance ED, where AE is a line drawn parallel to the variable cost function. Thus, AE has slope w. At the profit-maximizing quantity of labor, N^*, the slope of the total revenue function is equal to the slope of the total variable cost function. The slope of the total revenue function, however, is just the slope of the production function, or the marginal product of labor, and the slope of the total variable cost function is the real wage w. Thus, the firm maximizes profits by setting

$$MP_N = w. \tag{4-12}$$

To understand the intuition behind Equation (4-12), note that the contribution to the firm's profits of having employees work an extra hour is the extra output produced minus what the extra input costs—that is, $MP_N - w$. Given a fixed quantity of capital, the marginal product of labor is very high for the first hour worked by employees, and the way we have drawn the production function in Figure 4.12, MP_N is very large for $N^d = 0$, so that $MP_N - w > 0$ for $N^d = 0$, and it is worthwhile for the firm to hire the first unit of labor, as this implies positive profits. As the firm hires more labor, MP_N falls, so that each additional unit of labor is contributing less to revenue, but contributing the same amount, w, to costs. Eventually, at $N^d = N^*$, the firm has hired enough labor so that hiring an additional unit implies $MP_N - w < 0$, which in turn means that hiring an additional unit of labor only causes profits to go down, and this cannot be optimal. Therefore, the profit-maximizing firm chooses its labor input according to Equation (4-12).

In our earlier example of the accounting firm, suppose that there is one photocopy machine at the firm, and output for the firm can be measured in terms of the clients the firm has. Each client pays $20,000 per year to the firm, and the wage rate for an accountant is $50,000 per year. Therefore, the real wage is $\frac{50,000}{20,000} = 2.5$ clients. If the firm has 1 accountant, it can handle 5 clients per year, if it has 2 accountants it can handle 9 clients per year, and if it has 3 accountants it can handle 11 clients per year. What is the profit-maximizing number of accountants for the firm to hire? If the firm hires Sara, her marginal product is 5 clients per year, which exceeds the real wage of 2.5 clients, and so it would be worthwhile for the firm to hire Sara. If the firm hires Sara and Paul, then Paul's marginal product is 4 clients per year, which also exceeds the market real wage, and so it would also be worthwhile to hire Paul. If the firm hires Sara, Paul, and Julia, then Julia's marginal product is 2 clients per year, which is less than the market real wage of 2.5 clients. Therefore, it would be optimal in this case for the firm to hire 2 accountants, Sara and Paul.

Our analysis tells us that the representative firm's marginal product of labor schedule, as shown in Figure 4.20, is the firm's demand curve for labor. This is

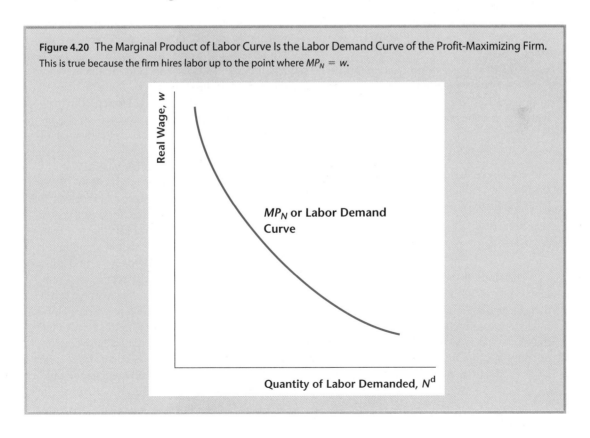

Figure 4.20 The Marginal Product of Labor Curve Is the Labor Demand Curve of the Profit-Maximizing Firm. This is true because the firm hires labor up to the point where $MP_N = w$.

because the firm maximizes profits for the quantity of labor input that implies $MP_N = w$. Therefore, given a real wage w, the marginal product of labor schedule tells us how much labor the firm needs to hire such that $MP_N = w$, and so the marginal product of labor schedule and the firm's demand curve for labor are the same thing.

Perspectives on the Financial Crisis

Productivity and the 2008–2009 Recession

Recall from the discussion in Chapters 1 and 3 that average labor productivity is an alternative measure to total factor productivity of the efficiency with which output can be produced from inputs at the aggregate level. As discussed in those earlier chapters, average labor productivity is defined as $\frac{Y}{N}$, where Y is aggregate output and N is the aggregate labor input. In Chapter 3, the measure we used for average labor productivity was total real GDP divided by total employment.

If the U.S. aggregate production function is a Cobb–Douglas production function, as discussed in the previous Theory Confronts the Data box, with capital share parameter .36, then

$$Y = zK^{.36}N^{.64},$$

and dividing both sides of this equation by N and simplifying implies that we can write average labor productivity as

$$\frac{Y}{N} = z\left(\frac{K}{N}\right)^{.36}.$$

Therefore, if the U.S. aggregate production function is Cobb–Douglas (which fits the data well), then average labor productivity is proportional to total factor productivity, but average labor productivity also is an increasing function of the quantity of capital-per-worker $\frac{K}{N}$. Thus, average labor productivity and total factor productivity

are mathematically closely related, but they are not the same thing.

For our purposes here, average labor productivity is a relatively more useful measure of productivity, as it is available on a more timely basis than is total factor productivity. At the time of this writing, total factor productivity can be measured only up to the end of 2007 (because capital is not measured in a timely fashion), whereas average labor productivity measures are available up to the first quarter of 2009. Figure 4.21 shows average labor productivity for the period 1948–2009. Note the similarity to Figure 4.18, although average labor productivity is more choppy, since it is measured on a quarterly basis, rather than annual, as for total factor productivity.

Figure 4.22 shows percentage deviations from trend in average labor productivity. Recall from Chapter 3 that two key business cycle facts are that average labor productivity is procyclical and coincident. Note in particular the decreases in average labor productivity below trend in the 1974–1975, 1981–1982, 1990–1991, and 2001 recessions. However, note also that there is only a slight decline below trend in average labor productivity in the 2008–2009 recession. Thus, the behavior of average labor productivity in the 2008–2009 recession does not fit these two key business cycle facts. This has occurred in spite of the fact that the 2008–2009 recession could well be more severe than any of the previous four recessions, in terms of the negative percentage deviation from trend in real GDP.

Thus, the 2008–2009 recession appears to be quite different from any of the last four recessions in the United States in terms of the co-movements in aggregate variables. Potentially, this difference can be explained by the fact that the 2008–2009 recession was caused by problems originating in the housing sector and financial markets, quite unlike anything that had occurred in any other contractionary episode

after World War II in the United States. As we will discuss in later chapters, the previous four recessions in the United States can be attributed mainly to some combination of shocks to productivity itself, tight monetary policy, and pessimism about the future payoffs to current investment expenditures. In future chapters, we will explore how the unique features of the 2008–2009 recession and the financial crisis require hard work on the part of economists to determine the correct macroeconomic policy responses.

Figure 4.21 Average Labor Productivity

Average labor productivity behaves much like total factor productivity, although it is not the same quantity. Compare this figure to Figure 4.18.

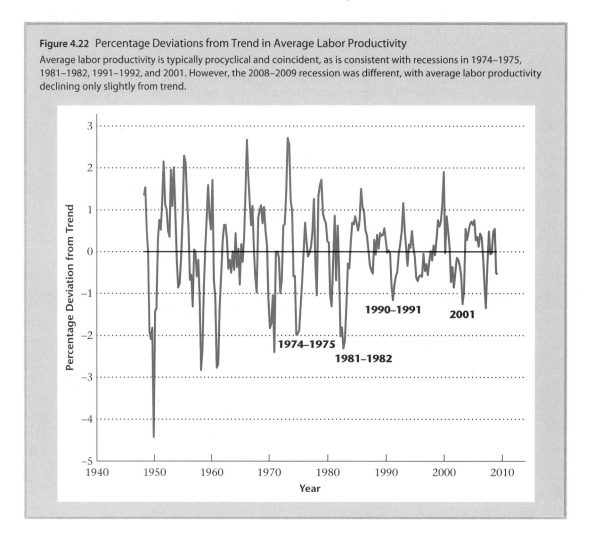

Figure 4.22 Percentage Deviations from Trend in Average Labor Productivity

Average labor productivity is typically procyclical and coincident, as is consistent with recessions in 1974–1975, 1981–1982, 1991–1992, and 2001. However, the 2008–2009 recession was different, with average labor productivity declining only slightly from trend.

In this chapter, we have determined the important elements of the microeconomic behavior of a representative consumer and a representative firm. In the next chapter, we put this behavior together in a macroeconomic model that can be used to address some important macroeconomic issues. In this model, the consumer and the firm interact in markets, where the consumer supplies labor and demands consumption goods, and the firm demands labor and supplies consumption goods.

Chapter Summary

- In this chapter, we studied the behavior of the representative consumer and the representative firm in a one-period, or static, environment. This behavior is the basis for constructing a macroeconomic model that we can work with in Chapter 5.
- The representative consumer stands in for the large number of consumers that exist in the economy as a whole, and the representative firm stands in for a large number of firms.

- The representative consumer's goal is to choose consumption and leisure to make himself or herself as well off as possible while respecting his or her budget constraint.

- The consumer's preferences have the properties that more is always preferred to less and that there is preference for diversity in consumption and leisure. The consumer is a price-taker in that he or she treats the market real wage as given, and his or her real disposable income is real wage income plus real dividend income, minus real taxes.

- Graphically, the representative consumer optimizes by choosing the consumption bundle where an indifference curve is tangent to the budget constraint or, what is the same thing, the marginal rate of substitution of leisure for consumption is equal to the real wage.

- Under the assumption that consumption and leisure are normal goods, an increase in the representative consumer's income leads to an increase in consumption and an increase in leisure, implying that labor supply goes down.

- An increase in the real wage leads to an increase in consumption, but it may cause leisure to rise or fall, because there are opposing income and substitution effects. The consumer's labor supply, therefore, may increase or decrease when the real wage increases.

- The representative firm chooses the quantity of labor to hire so as to maximize profits, with the quantity of capital fixed in this one-period environment.

- The firm's production technology is captured by the production function, which has constant returns to scale, a diminishing marginal product of labor, and a diminishing marginal product of capital. Further, the marginal products of labor and capital are positive, and the marginal product of labor increases with the quantity of capital.

- An increase in total factor productivity increases the quantity of output that can be produced with any quantities of labor and capital, and it increases the marginal product of labor.

- When the firm optimizes, it sets the marginal product of labor equal to the real wage. This implies that the firm's marginal product of labor schedule is its demand curve for labor.

Key Terms

Barter An exchange of goods for goods. (p. 109)

Budget constraint Condition that consumption equals wage income plus nonwage income minus taxes. (p. 110)

Cobb–Douglas production function A particular mathematical form for the production function that fits U.S. aggregate data well. (p. 134)

Competitive behavior Actions taken by a consumer or firm if market prices are outside its control. (p. 109)

Constant returns to scale A property of the production technology whereby if the firm increases all inputs by a factor x this increases output by the same factor x. (p. 126)

Consumption bundle A given consumption–leisure combination. (p. 104)

Consumption good A single good that represents an aggregation of all consumer goods in the economy. (p. 103)

Decreasing returns to scale A property of the production technology whereby if the firm increases all inputs by a factor x this increases output by less than the factor x. (p. 126)

Dividend income Profits of firms that are distributed to the consumer, who owns the firms. (p. 109)

Dynamic decision A decision made by a consumer or firm for more than one time period. (p. 102)

Income effect The effect on the quantity consumed of a good of a price change, as a result of having an effectively different income. (p. 119)

Increasing returns to scale A property of the production technology whereby if the firm increases all inputs by a factor x this increases output by more than the factor x. (p. 126)

Indifference curve A set of points that represents consumption bundles among which a consumer is indifferent. (p. 105)

Indifference map A set of indifference curves representing a consumer's preferences over goods; has the same information as the utility function. (p. 105)

Inferior good A good for which consumption decreases as income increases. (p. 105)

Labor supply curve A relationship describing the quantity of labor supplied for each level of the real wage. (p. 120)

Leisure Time spent not working in the market. (p. 103)

Lump-sum tax A tax that is unaffected by the actions of the consumer or firm being taxed. (p. 110)

Marginal product The additional output produced when another unit of a factor of production is added to the production process. (p. 126)

Marginal rate of substitution Minus the slope of an indifference curve, or the rate at which the consumer is just willing to trade one good for another. (p. 107)

Normal good A good for which consumption increases as income increases. (p. 105)

Numeraire The good in which prices are denominated. (p. 109)

Optimal consumption bundle The consumption bundle for which the consumer is as well off as possible while satisfying the budget constraint. (p. 113)

Perfect complements Two goods that are always consumed in fixed proportions. (p. 120)

Perfect substitutes Two goods with a constant marginal rate of substitution between them. (p. 123)

Production function A function describing the technological possibilities for converting factor inputs into output. (p. 125)

Pure income effect The effect on the consumer's optimal consumption bundle due to a change in real disposable income, holding prices constant. (p. 116)

Rational Describes a consumer who can make an informed optimizing decision. (p. 113)

Real wage The wage rate in units of the consumption good. (p. 109)

Relative price The price of a good in units of another good. (p. 114)

Representative consumer A stand-in for all consumers in the economy. (p. 103)

Representative firm A stand-in for all firms in the economy. (p. 127)

Solow residual A measure of total factor productivity obtained as a residual from the production function, given measures of aggregate output, labor input, and capital input. (p. 134)

Static decision A decision made by a consumer or firm for only one time period. (p. 102)

Substitution effect The effect on the quantity consumed of a good of a price change, holding the consumer's welfare constant. (p. 119)

Time constraint Condition that hours worked plus leisure time sum to total time available to the consumer. (p. 109)

Total factor productivity A variable in the production function that makes all factors of production more productive if it increases. (p. 125)

Utility function A function that captures a consumer's preferences over goods. (p. 103)

Questions for Review

All questions refer to the elements of the macroeconomic model developed in this chapter.

1. What goods do consumers consume in this model?
2. How are a consumer's preferences over goods represented?
3. What three properties do the preferences of the representative consumer have? Explain the importance of each.
4. What two properties do indifference curves have? How are these properties associated with the properties of the consumer's preferences?

5. What is the representative consumer's goal?

6. When the consumer chooses his or her optimal consumption bundle while respecting his or her budget constraint, what condition is satisfied?

7. How is the representative consumer's behavior affected by an increase in real dividend income?

8. How is the representative consumer's behavior affected by an increase in real taxes?

9. Why might hours worked by the representative consumer decrease when the real wage increases?

10. What is the representative firm's goal?

11. Why is the marginal product of labor diminishing?

12. What are the effects on the production function of an increase in total factor productivity?

13. Explain why the marginal product of labor curve is the firm's labor demand curve.

Problems

1. Using a diagram, show that, if the consumer prefers more to less, then indifference curves cannot cross.

2. In this chapter, we showed an example in which the consumer has preferences for consumption with the perfect complements property. Suppose, alternatively, that leisure and consumption goods are perfect substitutes. In this case, an indifference curve is described by the equation

$$u = al + bC,$$

where a and b are positive constants, and u is the level of utility. That is, a given indifference curve has a particular value for u, with higher indifference curves having higher values u.

(a) Show what the consumer's indifference curves look like when consumption and leisure are perfect substitutes and determine graphically and algebraically what consumption bundle the consumer chooses. Show that the consumption bundle the consumer chooses depends on the relationship between a/b and w, and explain why.

(b) Do you think it likely that any consumer would treat consumption goods and leisure as perfect substitutes?

(c) Given perfect substitutes, is more preferred to less? Do preferences satisfy the diminishing marginal rate of substitution property?

3. Consider the consumer choice example in this chapter, where consumption and leisure are perfect

complements. Assume that the consumer always desires a consumption bundle where the quantities of consumption and leisure are equal, that is $a = 1$.

(a) Suppose that $w = .75, \pi = .8, h = 16$, and $T = 6$. Determine the consumer's optimal choice of consumption and leisure, and show this in a diagram.

(b) Now suppose that $w = 1.5, \pi = .8, h = 16$, and $T = 6$. Again, determine the consumer's optimal choice of consumption and leisure, and show this in your diagram. Explain how and why the consumer's optimal consumption bundle changes, with reference to income and substitution effects.

4. Suppose that the government imposes a proportional income tax on the representative consumer's wage income. That is, the consumer's wage income is $w(1 - t)(h - l)$ where t is the tax rate. What effect does the income tax have on consumption and labor supply? Explain your results in terms of income and substitution effects.

5. Suppose, as in the federal income tax code for the United States, that the representative consumer faces a wage income tax with a standard deduction. That is, the representative consumer pays no tax on wage income for the first x units of real wage income, and then pays a proportional tax t on each unit of real wage income greater than x. Therefore, the consumer's budget constraint is given by $C = w(h - l) + \pi$ if $w(h - l) \le x$, or $C = (1 - t)w(h - l) + tx + \pi$ if $w(h - l) \ge x$.

Now, suppose that the government reduces the tax deduction x. Using diagrams, determine the effects of this tax change on the consumer and explain your results in terms of income and substitution effects. Make sure that you consider two cases. In the first case the consumer does not pay any tax before is x reduced, and in the second case the consumer pays a positive tax before x is reduced.

6. Suppose that the representative consumer's dividend income increases, and his or her wage rate falls at the same time. Determine the effects on consumption and labor supply and explain your results in terms of income and substitution effects.

7. Suppose that a consumer can earn a higher wage rate for working overtime. That is, for the first q hours the consumer works, he or she receives a real wage rate of w_1, and for hours worked more than q he or she receives w_2, where $w_2 > w_1$. Suppose that the consumer pays no taxes and receives no nonwage income, and he or she is free to choose hours of work.
   (a) Draw the consumer's budget constraint and show his or her optimal choice of consumption and leisure.
   (b) Show that the consumer would never work q hours or anything very close to q hours. Explain the intuition behind this.
   (c) Determine what happens if the overtime wage rate w_2 increases. Explain your results in terms of income and substitution effects. You must consider the case of a worker who initially works overtime, and a worker who initially does not work overtime.

8. Show that the consumer is better off with a lump-sum tax rather than a proportional tax on wage income (as in question 4) given that either tax yields the same revenue for the government. You must use a diagram to show this. (Hint: The consumption bundle the consumer chooses under the proportional tax must be just affordable given the lump-sum tax.)

9. Recall that leisure time in our model of the representative consumer is intended to capture any time spent not working in the market, including production at home such as yard work and caring for children. Suppose that the government were to provide free day care for children and, for the purpose of analyzing the effects of this, assume that this has no effect on the market real wage w, taxes T, and dividend income π. Determine the effects of the day care program on consumption, leisure, and hours worked for the consumer.

10. Suppose that the government imposes a producer tax. That is, the firm pays t units of consumption goods to the government for each unit of output it produces. Determine the effect of this tax on the firm's demand for labor.

11. Suppose that the government subsidizes employment. That is, the government pays the firm s units of consumption goods for each unit of labor that the firm hires. Determine the effect of the subsidy on the firm's demand for labor.

12. Suppose that the firm has a minimum quantity of employment, N^*, that is, the firm can produce no output unless the labor input is greater than or equal to N^*. Otherwise, the firm produces output according to the same production function as specified in this chapter. Given these circumstances, determine the effects of an increase in the real wage on the firm's choice of labor input. Construct the firm's demand curve for labor.

13. Supposing that a single consumer works for a firm, the quantity of labor input for the firm, N, is identical to the quantity of hours worked by the consumer, $h - l$. Graph the relationship between output produced, Y on the vertical axis and leisure hours of the consumer, l, on the horizontal axis, which is implied by the production function of the firm. (In Chapter 5, we refer to this relationship as the production possibilities frontier.) What is the slope of the curve you have graphed?

14. In the course of producing its output, a firm causes pollution. The government passes a law that requires the firm to stop polluting, and the firm discovers that it can prevent the pollution by hiring x workers for every worker that is producing output. That is, if the firm hires N workers, then xN workers are required to clean up the pollution caused by the N workers who are actually producing output. Determine the effect of the pollution regulation on the firm's profit-maximizing choice of labor input and on the firm's labor demand curve.

15. Suppose a firm has a production function given by $Y = zK^{0.3}N^{0.7}$.
    (a) If $z = 1$ and $K = 1$, graph the production function. Is the marginal product of labor positive and diminishing?
    (b) Now, graph the production function when $z = 1$ and $K = 1$. Explain how the production function changed from part (a).
    (c) Next, graph the production function when $z = 1$ and $K = 2$. What happened now?
    (d) Given this production function, the marginal product of labor is given by $MP_N = 0.7K^{0.3}N^{-0.3}$. Graph the marginal product of labor for $(z, K) = (1, 1), (2, 1), (1, 2)$, and explain what you get.

Working with the Data

1. The ratio of employment to total labor force might be taken to be a measure of the fraction of time spent working by the average working age person in the population. This measure might correspond to the concept of employment, N, in our model.
    (a) Calculate and plot the ratio of employment to the total labor force for the years 1980 through 2009.
    (b) Given that the real wage in the United States was increasing from 1980 to 2009, comment on what you observe in your plot.
    (c) How would you tell a story about the income and substitution effects in labor supply decisions that would be consistent with this data?
    (d) Do you think that the ratio of employment to the total labor force is a good measure of average hours worked per person in the economy? Explain why or why not.

2. Using annual data on real gross domestic product, employment, and the total capital stock, calculate the Solow residual using a Cobb–Douglas production function for the years 1948 through 2007.
    (a) Calculate the percentage growth rate in the Solow residual for each of the years 1949 through 2007.
    (b) Calculate the percentage growth rate in real GDP for the years 1949 through 2007.
    (c) Plot the percentage growth rates in parts (a) and (b), and comment on the relationship between the two. What might explain this relationship?

chapter 5

A Closed-Economy One-Period Macroeconomic Model

In Chapter 4, we studied the microeconomic behavior of a representative consumer and a representative firm. In this chapter, our first goal is to take this microeconomic behavior and build it into a working model of the macroeconomy. Then, we use this model to illustrate how unconstrained markets can produce economic outcomes that are socially efficient. This social efficiency proves to be useful in how we use our model to analyze some important macroeconomic issues. We show how increases in government spending increase aggregate output and crowd out private consumption expenditures and how increases in productivity lead to increases in aggregate output and the standard of living. Finally, we will consider a version of the model where the economic outcome in an economy with unconstrained private markets is not socially efficient, because government tax collection distorts private decisions. This allows us to explore how the incentive effects of the income tax matter for aggregate economic activity.

We start our approach to macroeconomic modeling in this chapter by analyzing how consumers and firms interact in markets in a **closed economy**. This is a model of a single country that has no interaction with the rest of the world—it does not trade with other countries. It is easier to first understand how a closed economy works, and much of the economic intuition we build up for the closed-economy case carries over to an **open economy**, where international trade is allowed. Further, for many economic questions, particularly the ones addressed in this chapter, the answers are not fundamentally different if we allow the economy to be open.

There are three different actors in this economy, the representative consumer who stands in for the many consumers in the economy that sell labor and buy goods, the representative firm that stands in for the many firms in the economy that buy labor and sell goods, and the government. We have already described the behavior of the representative consumer and representative firm in detail in Chapter 4, and we only need to explain what the government does.

Government

The behavior of the government is quite simple in our model. It wishes to purchase a given quantity of consumption goods, G, and finances these purchases by taxing the representative consumer. In practice, governments provide many different goods and services, including roads and bridges, national defense, air traffic control, and education. Which goods and services the government should provide is the subject of much political and economic debate, but economists generally agree that the government has a special role to play in providing **public goods**, such as national defense, which are difficult or impossible for the private sector to provide. National defense is a good example of a public good, because it is difficult or impossible to get individuals to pay for national defense in a private market according to how much national defense services each one receives and how much each individual values national defense.

To keep things as simple as possible, for now we are not specific about the public goods nature of government expenditure. What we want to capture here is that government spending uses up resources, and we model this by assuming that government spending simply involves taking goods from the private sector. Output is produced in the private sector, and the government purchases an **exogenous** amount G of this output, with the remainder consumed by the representative consumer. An exogenous variable is determined outside the model, while an **endogenous** variable is determined by the model itself. Government spending is exogenous in our model, as we are assuming that government spending is independent of what happens in the rest of the economy. The government must abide by the **government budget constraint**, which we write as

$$G = T,$$

or government purchases equal taxes, in real terms.

Introducing the government in this way allows us to study some basic effects of **fiscal policy**. In general, fiscal policy refers to the government's choices over its expenditures, taxes, transfers, and borrowing. Recall from Chapter 2 that government expenditures are purchases of final goods and services, while transfers are simply reallocations of purchasing power from one set of individuals to another. Because this is a one-period economic environment, the government's choices are very limited, as described by the above government budget constraint. The government cannot borrow to finance government expenditures because there is no future in which to repay its debt, and the government does not tax more than it spends, as this would imply that the government would foolishly throw goods away. The government budget deficit, which is $G - T$ here, is always zero. Thus, the only elements of fiscal policy we study in this chapter are the setting of government purchases, G, and the macroeconomic effects of changing G. In Chapter 8, we explore what happens when the government can run deficits and surpluses.

Competitive Equilibrium

Now that we have looked at the behavior of the representative consumer, the representative firm, and the government, what remains in constructing our model is to show how consistency is obtained in the actions of all these economic agents. Once we have done this, we can use this model to make predictions about how the whole economy behaves in response to changes in the economic environment.

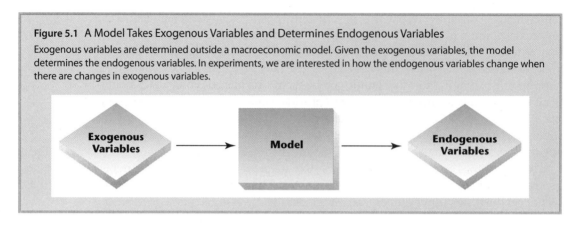

Figure 5.1 A Model Takes Exogenous Variables and Determines Endogenous Variables
Exogenous variables are determined outside a macroeconomic model. Given the exogenous variables, the model determines the endogenous variables. In experiments, we are interested in how the endogenous variables change when there are changes in exogenous variables.

Mathematically, a macroeconomic model takes the exogenous variables, which for the purposes of the problem at hand are determined outside the system we are modeling and determines values for the endogenous variables, as outlined in Figure 5.1. In the model we are working with here, the exogenous variables are G, z, and K—that is, government spending, total factor productivity, and the economy's capital stock, respectively. The endogenous variables are C, N^s, N^d, T, Y, and w—that is, consumption, labor supply, labor demand, taxes, aggregate output, and the market real wage; respectively. Making use of the model is a process of running experiments to determine how changes in the exogenous variables change the endogenous variables. By running these experiments, we hope to understand real-world macroeconomic events and to say something about macroeconomic policy. For example, one of the experiments we run on our model in this chapter is to change exogenous government spending and then determine the effects on consumption, employment, aggregate output, and the real wage. This helps us to understand, for example, the events that occurred in the U.S. economy during World War II, when there was a large increase in government spending.

By consistency we mean that, given market prices, demand is equal to supply in each market in the economy. Such a state of affairs is called a **competitive equilibrium**. Here, competitive refers to the fact that all consumers and firms are price-takers, and the economy is in equilibrium when the actions of all consumers and firms are consistent. When demand equals supply in all markets, we say that markets **clear**. In our model economy, there is only one price, which is the real wage w. We can also think of the economy as having only one market, on which labor time is exchanged for consumption goods. In this labor market, the representative consumer supplies labor and the representative firm demands labor. A competitive equilibrium is achieved when, given the exogenous variables G, z, and K, the real wage w is such that, at that wage, *the quantity of labor the consumer wishes to supply is equal to the quantity of labor the firm wishes to hire.* The consumer's supply of labor is in part determined by taxes T and dividend income π. In a competitive equilibrium, T must satisfy the government budget constraint, and π must be equal to the profits generated by the firm.

A competitive equilibrium is a set of endogenous quantities, C (consumption), N^s (labor supply), N^d (labor demand), T (taxes), and Y (aggregate output), and an endogenous real wage w, such that, given the exogenous variables G (government spending), z (total factor productivity), and K (capital stock), the following are satisfied:

1. The representative consumer chooses C (consumption) and N^s (labor supply) to make himself or herself as well off as possible subject to his or her budget constraint, given w (the real wage), T (taxes), and π (dividend income). That is, the representative consumer optimizes given his or her budget constraint, which is determined by the real wage, taxes, and the profits that the consumer receives from the firm as dividend income.

2. The representative firm chooses N^d (quantity of labor demand) to maximize profits, with maximized output $Y = zF(K, N^d)$ and maximized profits $\pi = Y - wN^d$. The firm treats z (total factor productivity), K (the capital stock), and w (the real wage) as given. That is, the representative firm optimizes given total factor productivity, its capital stock, and the market real wage. In equilibrium, the profits that the representative firm earns must be equal to the dividend income that is received by the consumer.

3. The market for labor clears, that is, $N^d = N^s$. The quantity of labor that the representative firm wants to hire is equal to the quantity of labor the representative consumer wants to supply.

4. The government budget constraint is satisfied, that is, $G = T$. The taxes paid by consumers are equal to the exogenous quantity of government spending.

An important property of a competitive equilibrium is that

$$Y = C + G, \tag{5-1}$$

which is the income-expenditure identity. Recall from Chapter 2 that we generally state the income-expenditure identity as $Y = C + I + G + NX$, where I is investment and NX is net exports. In this economy, there is no investment expenditure, as there is only one period, and net exports are zero, as the economy is closed, so that $I = 0$ and $NX = 0$.

To show why the income-expenditure identity holds in equilibrium, we start with the representative consumer's budget constraint,

$$C = wN^s + \pi - T, \tag{5-2}$$

or consumption expenditures equal real wage income plus real dividend income minus taxes. In equilibrium, dividend income is equal to the firm's maximized profits, or $\pi = Y - wN^d$, and the government budget constraint is satisfied, so that $T = G$. If we then substitute in Equation (5-2) for π and T, we get

$$C = wN^s + Y - wN^d - G. \tag{5-3}$$

In equilibrium, labor supply is equal to labor demand, or $N^s = N^d$, which then gives us, substituting for N^s in Equation (5-3) and rearranging, the identity in Equation (5-1).

There are many ways to work with macroeconomic models. Modern macroeconomic researchers sometimes work with an algebraic representation of a model, sometimes with a formulation of a model that can be put on a computer and simulated, and sometimes with a model in graphical form. We use the last approach most often in this book. In doing graphical analysis, sometimes the simplest approach is to work with a model in the form of supply and demand curves, with one supply curve and one demand curve for each market under consideration. As the number of markets in the model increases, this approach becomes most practical, and in Chapters 10 to 13 and some later chapters, we work mainly with models in the form of supply and demand curves. These supply and demand curves are derived from the microeconomic behavior of consumers and firms, as was the case when we examined labor supply and labor demand curves in Chapter 4, but the underlying microeconomic behavior is not explicit. For our analysis here, however, where exchange takes place between the representative consumer and the representative firm in only one market, it is relatively straightforward to be entirely explicit about microeconomic principles. The approach we follow in this chapter is to study competitive equilibrium in our model by examining the consumer's and the firm's decisions in the same diagram, so that we can determine how aggregate consistency is achieved in competitive equilibrium.

We want to start first with the production technology operated by the representative firm. In a competitive equilibrium, $N^d = N^s = N$—that is, labor demand equals labor supply—and we refer to N as employment. Then, as in Chapter 4, from the production function, output is given by

$$Y = zF(K, N), \tag{5-4}$$

and we graph the production function in Figure 5.2(a), for a given capital stock K. Because the representative consumer has a maximum of h hours to spend working, N can be no larger than h, which implies that the most output that could be produced in this economy is Y^* in Figure 5.2(a).

Another way to graph the production function, which proves very useful for integrating the firm's production behavior with the consumer's behavior, is to use the fact that, in equilibrium, we have $N = h - l$. Substituting for N in the production function (5-4), we get

$$Y = zF(K, h - l), \tag{5-5}$$

which is a relationship between output Y and leisure l, given the exogenous variables z and K. If we graph this relationship, as Figure 5.2(b), with leisure on the horizontal axis and Y on the vertical axis, then we get a mirror image of the production function in Figure 5.2(a). That is, the point $(l, Y) = (h, 0)$ in panel (b) of the figure corresponds to the point $(N, Y) = (0, 0)$ in panel (a). When the consumer takes all of his or her time as leisure, then employment is zero and nothing gets produced. As leisure falls in (b) from h, employment increases in (a) from zero, and output increases. In (b), when $l = 0$, the consumer is using all of his or her time for work and consuming no leisure and the maximum quantity of output, Y^*, is produced. Because the slope of the production function in panel (a) of the figure is MP_N, the marginal product of labor, the slope of the relationship in panel (b) is $-MP_N$, because this relationship is just the mirror image of the production function.

Figure 5.2 The Production Function and the Production Possibilities Frontier

Panel (a) shows the equilibrium relationship between the quantity of leisure consumed by the representative consumer and aggregate output. The relationship in (b) is the mirror image of the production function in (a). In (c), we show the production possibilities frontier (PPF), which is the technological relationship between C and l, determined by shifting the relationship in (b) down by the amount G. The shaded region in (c) represents consumption bundles that are technologically feasible to produce in this economy.

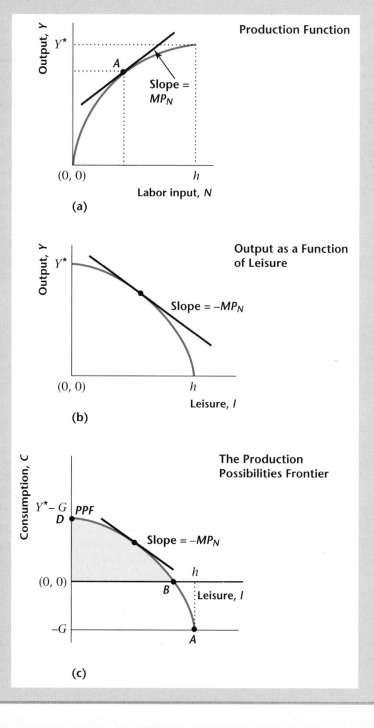

Now, because in equilibrium $C = Y - G$, from the income-expenditure identity, given (5-5) we get

$$C = zF(K, h - l) - G,$$

which is a relationship between C and l, given the exogenous variables z, K, and G. This relationship is graphed in Figure 5.2(c), and it is just the relationship in (b) shifted down by the amount G, because consumption is output minus government spending in equilibrium. The relationship in Figure 5.2(c) is called a **production possibilities frontier** (PPF), and it describes what the technological possibilities are for the economy as a whole, in terms of the production of consumption goods and leisure. Although leisure is not literally produced, all of the points in the shaded area inside the PPF and on the PPF in Figure 5.2(c) are technologically possible in this economy. The PPF captures the trade-off between leisure and consumption that the available production technology makes available to the representative consumer in the economy. The points on the PPF on AB are not feasible for this economy, as consumption is negative. Only the points on the PPF on DB are feasible, because here enough consumption goods are produced so that the government can take some of these goods and still leave something for private consumption.

As in Figure 5.2(b), the slope of the PPF in (c) is $-MP_N$. Another name for the negative of the slope of the PPF is the **marginal rate of transformation**. The marginal rate of transformation is the rate at which one good can be converted technologically into another; in this case, the marginal rate of transformation is the rate at which leisure can be converted in the economy into consumption goods through work. We let $MRT_{l,C}$ denote the marginal rate of transformation of leisure into consumption. Then, we have

$$MRT_{l,C} = MP_N = -(\text{the slope of the PPF}).$$

Our next step is to put the PPF together with the consumer's indifference curves, and to show how we can analyze a competitive equilibrium in a single diagram in Figure 5.3. In the figure, the PPF is given by the curve HF. From the relationship between the production function and the PPF in Figure 5.2, and given what we know about the profit-maximizing decision of the firm from Chapter 4, we can determine the production point on the PPF chosen by the firm, given the equilibrium real wage w. That is, the representative firm chooses the labor input to maximize profits in equilibrium by setting $MP_N = w$, and so in equilibrium minus the slope of the PPF must be equal to w, because $MRT_{l,C} = MP_N = w$ in equilibrium. Therefore, if w is an equilibrium real wage rate, we can draw a line AD in Figure 5.3 that has slope $-w$ and that is tangent to the PPF at point J, where $MP_N = w$. Then, the firm chooses labor demand equal to $h - l^*$ and produces $Y^* = zF(K, h - l^*)$, from the production function. Maximized profits for the firm are $\pi^* = zF(K, h - l^*) - w(h - l^*)$ (total revenue minus the cost of hiring labor), or the distance DH in Figure 5.3 (recall this from Chapter 4). Now, DB in Figure 5.3 is equal to $\pi^* - G = \pi^* - T$, from the government budget constraint $G = T$.

Now, an interesting feature of the figure is that ADB in the figure is the budget constraint that the consumer faces in equilibrium, because the slope of AD is $-w$ and the length of DB is the consumer's dividend income minus taxes, where dividend income is the profits that the firm earns and distributes to the consumer. Because J represents the

Figure 5.3 Competitive Equilibrium

This figure brings together the representative consumer's preferences and the representative firm's production technology to determine a competitive equilibrium. Point J represents the equilibrium consumption bundle. ADB is the budget constraint faced by the consumer in equilibrium, with the slope of AD equal to minus the real wage and the distance DB equal to dividend income minus taxes.

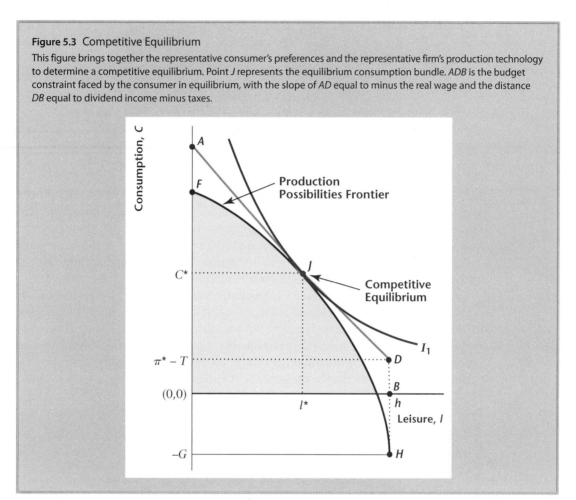

competitive equilibrium production point, where C^* is the quantity of consumption goods produced by the firm and $h - l^*$ is the quantity of labor hired by the firm, then it must be the case (as is required for aggregate consistency) that C^* is also the quantity of consumption goods that the representative consumer desires and l^* is the quantity of leisure the consumer desires. This implies that an indifference curve (curve I_1 in Figure 5.3) must be tangent to AD (the budget constraint) at point J in Figure 5.3. Given this, in equilibrium at point J we have $MRS_{l,C} = w$—that is, the marginal rate of substitution of leisure for consumption for the consumer is equal to the real wage. Because $MRT_{l,C} = MP_N = w$ in equilibrium, we have, at point J in Figure 5.3,

$$MRS_{l,C} = MRT_{l,C} = MP_N, \qquad (5\text{-}6)$$

or the marginal rate of substitution of leisure for consumption is equal to the marginal rate of transformation, which is equal to the marginal product of labor. That is, because the consumer and the firm face the same market real wage in equilibrium, the rate at which the consumer is just willing to trade leisure for consumption is the same as the rate at which leisure can be converted into consumption goods using the production technology.

The condition expressed in Equation (5-6) is important in the next subsection in establishing the economic efficiency of a competitive equilibrium. The connection between market outcomes and economic efficiency is critical in making the analysis of macroeconomic issues with this model simple.

Optimality

Now that we know what the characteristics of a competitive equilibrium are from Figure 5.3, we can analyze the connection between a competitive equilibrium and economic efficiency. This connection is important for two reasons. First, this illustrates how free markets can produce socially optimal outcomes. Second, it proves to be much easier to analyze a social optimum than a competitive equilibrium in this model, so our analysis in this section allows us to use our model efficiently.

An important part of economics is analyzing how markets act to arrange production and consumption activities and asking how this arrangement compares with some ideal or efficient arrangement. Typically, the efficiency criterion that economists use in evaluating market outcomes is **Pareto optimality**. (Pareto, a nineteenth-century Italian economist, is famous for, among other things, his application of mathematics to economic analysis and introducing the concept of indifference curves.)

DEFINITION 1   *A competitive equilibrium is **Pareto optimal** if there is no way to rearrange production or to reallocate goods so that someone is made better off without making someone else worse off.*

For this model, we would like to ask whether the competitive equilibrium is Pareto optimal, but our job is relatively easy because there is only one representative consumer, so we do not have to consider how goods are allocated across people. In our model, we can focus solely on how production is arranged to make the representative consumer as well off as possible. To construct the Pareto optimum here, we introduce the device of a fictitious social planner. This device is commonly used to determine efficiency in economic models. The social planner does not have to deal with markets, and he or she can simply order the representative firm to hire a given quantity of labor and produce a given quantity of consumption goods. The planner also has the power to coerce the consumer into supplying the required amount of labor. Produced consumption goods are taken by the planner, G is given to the government, and the remainder is allocated to the consumer. The social planner is benevolent, and he or she chooses quantities so as to make the representative consumer as well off as possible. In this way, the choices of the social planner tell us what, in the best possible circumstances, could be achieved in our model economy.

The social planner's problem is to choose C and l, given the technology for converting l into C, to make the representative consumer as well off as possible. That is, the social planner chooses a consumption bundle that is on or within the production possibilities frontier (PPF), and that is on the highest possible indifference curve for the consumer. In Figure 5.4 the Pareto optimum is located at point B, where an indifference curve is just tangent to the PPF—curve AH. The social planner's problem is very similar to the representative consumer's problem of making himself or herself as well off as possible given his or her budget constraint. The only difference is that the budget constraint of the consumer is a straight line, while the PPF is bowed-out from the origin (i.e., it is concave).

From Figure 5.4, because the slope of the indifference curve is minus the marginal rate of substitution, $-MRS_{l,C}$, and the slope of the PPF is minus the marginal rate of transformation, $-MRT_{l,C}$, or minus the marginal product of labor, $-MP_N$, the Pareto optimum has the property that

$$MRS_{l,C} = MRT_{l,C} = MP_N.$$

Figure 5.4 Pareto Optimality

The Pareto optimum is the point that a social planner would choose where the representative consumer is as well off as possible given the technology for producing consumption goods using labor as an input. Here the Pareto optimum is B, where an indifference curve is tangent to the PPF.

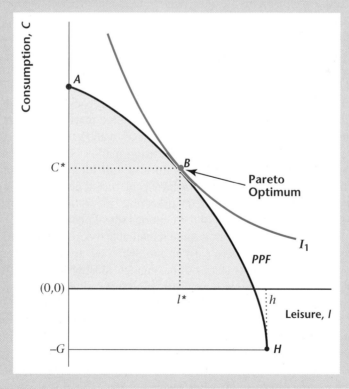

This is the same property that a competitive equilibrium has, or Equation (5-6). Comparing Figures 5.3 and 5.4, we easily see that the Pareto optimum and the competitive equilibrium are the same thing, because a competitive equilibrium is the point where an indifference curve is tangent to the *PPF* in Figure 5.3, and the same is true of the Pareto optimum in Figure 5.4. A key result of this chapter is that, for this model, the competitive equilibrium is identical to the Pareto optimum.

There are two fundamental principles in economics that apply here, and these are the following:

DEFINITION 2   *The* **first fundamental theorem of welfare economics** *states that, under certain conditions, a competitive equilibrium is Pareto optimal.*

DEFINITION 3   *The* **second fundamental theorem of welfare economics** *states that, under certain conditions, a Pareto optimum is a competitive equilibrium.*

These two theorems are often referred to as the "first welfare theorem" and the "second welfare theorem." In our model, one can clearly see, from Figures 5.3 and 5.4, that the first and second welfare theorems hold, because there is one competitive equilibrium and one Pareto optimum, and they are clearly the same thing. In other kinds of economic models, however, showing whether the first and second welfare theorems hold can be hard work.

The idea behind the first welfare theorem goes back at least as far as Adam Smith's *Wealth of Nations*. Smith argued that an unfettered market economy composed of self-interested consumers and firms could achieve an allocation of resources and goods that was socially efficient, in that an unrestricted market economy would behave as if an "invisible hand" were guiding the actions of individuals toward a state of affairs that was beneficial for all. The model we have constructed here has the property that a competitive equilibrium, or unfettered market outcome, is the same outcome that would be chosen by the invisible hand of the fictitious social planner.

The first welfare theorem is quite remarkable, because it appears to be inconsistent with the training we receive early in life, when we are typically encouraged to have empathy for others and to share our belongings. Most people value generosity and compassion, and so it certainly seems surprising that individuals motivated only by greed and profit maximization could achieve some kind of social utopia. If we consider, however, economies with many consumers instead of a single representative consumer, then a Pareto optimum might have the property that some people are very poor and some are very rich. That is, we may not be able to make the poor better off without making the rich worse off. At the extreme, a state of affairs where one person has all of society's wealth may be Pareto optimal, but few would argue that this is a sensible way to arrange an economy. Pareto optimality is a very narrow concept of social optimality. In some instances, society is interested in equity as well as efficiency, and there may be a trade-off between the two.

Sources of Social Inefficiencies

What could cause a competitive equilibrium to fail to be Pareto optimal? In practice, many factors can result in inefficiency in a market economy.

First, a competitive equilibrium may not be Pareto optimal because of **externalities**. An externality is any activity for which an individual firm or consumer does not take account of all associated costs and benefits; externalities can be positive or negative. For example, pollution is a common example of a negative externality. Suppose that Disgusting Chemical Corporation (DCC) produces and sells chemicals, and in the production process generates a by-product that is released as a gas into the atmosphere. This by-product stinks and is hazardous, and there are people who live close to DCC who are worse off as the result of the air pollution that DCC produces; however, the negative externality that is produced in the form of pollution costs to the neighbors of DCC is not reflected in any way in DCC's profits. DCC, therefore, does not take the pollution externality into account in deciding how much labor to hire and the quantity of chemicals to produce. As a result, DCC tends to produce more of these pollution-causing chemicals than is socially optimal. The key problem is that there is not a market on which pollution (or the rights to pollute) is traded. If such a market existed, then private markets would not fail to produce a socially optimal outcome. This is because the people who bear the costs of pollution could sell the rights to pollute to DCC, and there would then be a cost to DCC for polluting, which DCC would take into account in making production decisions. In practice, there do not exist markets in pollution rights for all types of pollution that exist, although there have been some experiments with such markets. Typically, governments take other kinds of approaches to try to correct the negative externalities generated by pollution, such as regulation and taxation.

A positive externality is a benefit that other people receive for which an individual is not compensated. For example, suppose that DCC has an attractive head office designed by a high-profile architect in a major city. This building yields a benefit to people who can walk by the building on a public street and admire the fine architecture. These people do not compensate the firm for this positive externality, as it would be very costly or impossible to set up a fee structure for the public viewing of the building. As a result, DCC tends to underinvest in its head office. Likely, the building that DCC would construct would be less attractive than if the firm took account of the positive externality. Positive externalities, therefore, lead to social inefficiencies, just as negative externalities do, and the root cause of an externality is a market failure; it is too costly or impossible to set up a market to buy and sell the benefits or costs associated with the externality.

A second reason that a competitive equilibrium may not be Pareto optimal is that there are **distorting taxes**. In Chapter 4 we discussed the difference between a lump-sum tax, which does not depend on the actions of the person being taxed, and a distorting tax, which does. An example of a distorting tax in our model would be if government purchases were financed by a proportional wage income tax rather than by a lump-sum tax. That is, for each unit of real wage income earned, the representative consumer pays t units of consumption goods to the government, so that t is the tax rate. Then, wage income is $w(1 - t)(h - l)$, and the effective wage for the consumer is $w(1 - t)$. Then, when the consumer optimizes, he or she sets $MRS_{l,C} = w(1 - t)$, while the firm optimizes by setting $MP_N = w$. Therefore, in a competitive equilibrium

$$MRS_{l,C} < MP_N = MRT_{l,C},$$

so that the tax drives a "wedge" between the marginal rate of substitution and the marginal product of labor. Equation (5-6), therefore, does not hold, as required for a Pareto optimum, so that the competitive equilibrium is not Pareto optimal and the first welfare theorem does not hold. In a competitive equilibrium, a proportional wage income tax tends to discourage work (so long as the substitution effect of a change in the wage is larger than the income effect), and there tends to be too much leisure consumed relative to consumption goods. We will explore the aggregate effects of distorting taxes on labor income later in this chapter. In practice, all taxes, including sales taxes, the income tax, and property taxes, cause distortions. Lump-sum taxes are, in fact, infeasible to implement in practice,[1] although this does not mean that having lump-sum taxes in our model is nonsense. The assumption of lump-sum taxation in our model is a convenient simplification, in that for most of the macroeconomic issues we address with this model, the effects of more realistic distorting taxation are unimportant.

A third reason market economies do not achieve efficiency is that firms may not be price-takers. If a firm is large relative to the market, then we say it has monopoly power (monopoly power need not imply only one firm in an industry), and it can use its monopoly power to act strategically to restrict output, raise prices, and increase profits. Monopoly power tends to lead to underproduction relative to what is socially optimal. There are many examples of monopoly power in the United States. For example, the market in computer operating systems is dominated by a few producers (Microsoft is a very large producer relative to the market), as is automobile manufacturing.

Because there are good reasons to believe that the three inefficiencies discussed above—externalities, tax distortions, and monopoly power—are important in modern economies, two questions arise. First, why should we analyze an economy that is efficient in the sense that a competitive equilibrium for this economy is Pareto optimal? The reason is that in studying most macroeconomic issues, an economic model with inefficiencies behaves much like an economic model without inefficiencies. However, actually modeling all of these inefficiencies would add clutter to our model and make it more difficult to work with, and it is often best to leave out these extraneous details. The equivalence of the competitive equilibrium and the Pareto optimum in our model proves to be quite powerful in terms of analyzing a competitive equilibrium. This is because determining the competitive equilibrium need only involve solving the social planner's problem and not the more complicated problem of determining prices and quantities in a competitive equilibrium.

---

[1]This is because any lump-sum tax is large enough that someone cannot pay it. Therefore, some people must be exempt from the tax; but, if this is so, then people will alter their behavior so as to be exempt from the tax, so that the tax will, therefore, distort private decisions.

A second question that arises concerning real-world social inefficiencies is whether Adam Smith was completely off track in emphasizing the tendency of unrestricted markets to produce socially efficient outcomes. It might appear that the existence of externalities, tax distortions, and monopoly power should lead us to press for various government regulations to offset the negative effects of these inefficiencies. However, the tendency of unregulated markets to produce efficient outcomes is a powerful one, and sometimes the cost of government regulations, in terms of added waste, outweighs the gains, in terms of correcting private market failures. The cure can be worse than the disease.

How to Use the Model

The key to using our model is the equivalence between the competitive equilibrium and the Pareto optimum. We need only draw a picture as in Figure 5.5, where we are essentially considering the solution to the social planner's problem. Here, the PPF is curve AH, and the competitive equilibrium (or Pareto optimum) is at point B, where an indifference curve, I_1, is tangent to the PPF. The equilibrium quantity of consumption

Figure 5.5 Using the Second Welfare Theorem to Determine a Competitive Equilibrium

Because the competitive equilibrium and the Pareto optimum are the same thing, we can analyze a competitive equilibrium by working out the Pareto optimum, which is point B in the figure. At the Pareto optimum, an indifference curve is tangent to the PPF, and the equilibrium real wage is equal to minus the slope of the PPF and minus the slope of the indifference curve at B.

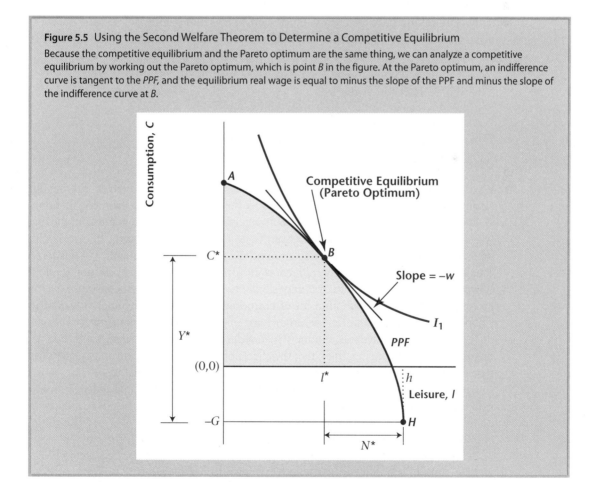

is then C^*, and the equilibrium quantity of leisure is l^*. The quantity of employment is $N^* = h - l^*$, as shown in Figure 5.5, and the quantity of output is $Y^* = C^* + G$, as also shown in the figure. The real wage w is determined by minus the slope of the *PPF*, or minus the slope of the indifference curve I_1 at point B. The real wage is determined in this way because we know that, in equilibrium, the firm optimizes by setting the marginal product of labor equal to the real wage, and the consumer optimizes by setting the marginal rate of substitution equal to the real wage.

What we are primarily interested in now is how a change in an exogenous variable affects the key endogenous variables $C, Y, N,$ and w. The exogenous variables $G, z,$ and K, which are government spending, total factor productivity, and the capital stock, respectively, all alter the endogenous variables by shifting the *PPF* in particular ways. We examine these effects and their interpretation in the next sections.

Figure 5.5 illustrates a key concept of this chapter in the clearest possible way. What is produced and consumed in the economy is determined entirely by the interaction of consumer preferences with the technology available to firms. Although economic activity involves a complicated array of transactions among many economic actors, fundamentally aggregate economic activity boils down to the preferences of consumers, as captured by the representative consumer's indifference curves, and the technology of firms, as captured by the *PPF*. Both consumer preferences and the firm's technology are important for determining aggregate output, aggregate consumption, employment, and the real wage. A change either in indifference curves or the *PPF* affects what is produced and consumed.

Working with the Model: The Effects of a Change in Government Purchases

Recall from Chapter 1 that working with a macroeconomic model involves carrying out experiments. The first experiment we conduct here is to change government spending G, and ask what this does to aggregate output, consumption, employment, and the real wage. In Figure 5.6 an increase in G from G_1 to G_2 shifts the *PPF* from PPF_1 to PPF_2, where the shift down is by the same amount, $G_2 - G_1$, for each quantity of leisure, l. This shift leaves the slope of the *PPF* constant for each l. The effect of shifting the *PPF* downward by a constant amount is very similar to shifting the budget constraint for the consumer through a reduction in his or her nonwage disposable income, as we did in Chapter 4. Indeed, because $G = T$, an increase in government spending must necessarily increase taxes by the same amount, which reduces the consumer's disposable income. It should not be surprising, then, that the effects of an increase in government spending essentially involve a negative income effect on consumption and leisure.

In Figure 5.6 the initial equilibrium is at point A, where indifference curve I_1 is tangent to PPF_1, the initial *PPF*. Here, equilibrium consumption is C_1, while the equilibrium quantity of leisure is l_1, and so equilibrium employment is $N_1 = h - l_1$. The initial equilibrium real wage is minus the slope of the indifference curve (or minus the slope of PPF_1) at point A. Now, when government spending increases, the *PPF* shifts to PPF_2, and the equilibrium point is at B, where consumption and leisure are both lower, at C_2

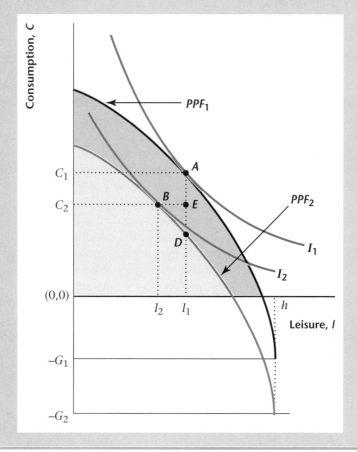

Figure 5.6 Equilibrium Effects of an Increase in Government Spending

An increase in government spending shifts the *PPF* down by the amount of the increase in G. There are negative income effects on consumption and leisure, so that both *C* and *l* fall, and employment rises, while output (equal to *C* + *G*) increases.

and l_2, respectively. Why do consumption and leisure decrease? This is because consumption and leisure are normal goods.[2] Given the normal goods assumption, a negative income effect from the downward shift in the *PPF* must reduce consumption and leisure. Because leisure falls, then employment, which is $N_2 = h - l_2$, must rise. Further, because employment increases, the quantity of output must rise. We know this because the quantity of capital is fixed in the experiment, while employment has increased. With the same quantity of one factor of production (capital), and more of the other (labor), and with total factor productivity held constant, output must increase.

---

[2]Alert readers will notice that the definition of what a normal good is needs to be altered here from how we defined it in Chapter 4, because we are dealing with a shift in the nonlinear PPF rather than a shift in a linear budget constraint. The spirit of the approach remains the same, however. For more details, see the Mathematical Appendix.

Now, the income–expenditure identity tells us that $Y = C + G$; therefore, $C = Y - G$, and so

$$\Delta C = \Delta Y - \Delta G,$$

where Δ denotes "the change in." Thus, because $\Delta Y > 0$, we have that $\Delta C > -\Delta G$, so that private consumption is **crowded out** by government purchases, but it is not completely crowded out as a result of the increase in output. In Figure 5.6 ΔG is the distance AD, and ΔC is the distance AE. A larger government, reflected in increased government spending, results in more output being produced, because there is a negative income effect on leisure and, therefore, a positive effect on labor supply. However, a larger government reduces private consumption, through a negative income effect produced by the higher taxes required to finance higher government spending. As the representative consumer pays higher taxes, his or her disposable income falls, and in equilibrium he or she spends less on consumption goods and works harder to support a larger government.

What happens to the real wage when G increases? In Figure 5.6 the slope of PPF_2 is identical to the slope of PPF_1 for each quantity of leisure, l. Therefore, because the PPF becomes steeper as l increases (the marginal product of labor increases as employment decreases), PPF_2 at point B is less steep than is PPF_1 at point A. Thus, because minus the slope of the PPF at the equilibrium point is equal to the equilibrium real wage, the real wage falls as a result of the increase in government spending. The real wage must fall, as we know that equilibrium employment rises, and the representative firm would hire more labor only in response to a reduction in the market real wage.

Now, a question we might like to ask is whether fluctuations in government spending are a likely cause of business cycles. Recall that in Chapter 3 we developed a set of key business cycle facts. If fluctuations in government spending are important in causing

Government Spending in World War II

THEORY confronts the DATA

Wars typically involve huge increases in government expenditure, and they therefore represent interesting "natural experiments" that we can examine as an informal empirical test of the predictions of our model. An interesting example involves the effects of increased government spending in the United States during World War II. Shortly after the beginning of U.S. involvement in World War II in late 1941, aggregate output was channeled from private consumption to military uses, and there was a sharp increase in total real GDP. Figure 5.7 shows the natural logarithms of real GDP, real consumption expenditures, and real government expenditures for the period 1929–2008. Of particular note is the extremely large increase in government expenditures that occurred during World War II, which clearly swamps the small fluctuations in G about trend that happened before and after World War II. Clearly, GDP also increases above trend in the figure during World War II, and consumption dips somewhat below trend. Thus, these observations on the behavior of consumption and output during World War II are consistent with our model, in that private consumption is crowded out somewhat and output increases.

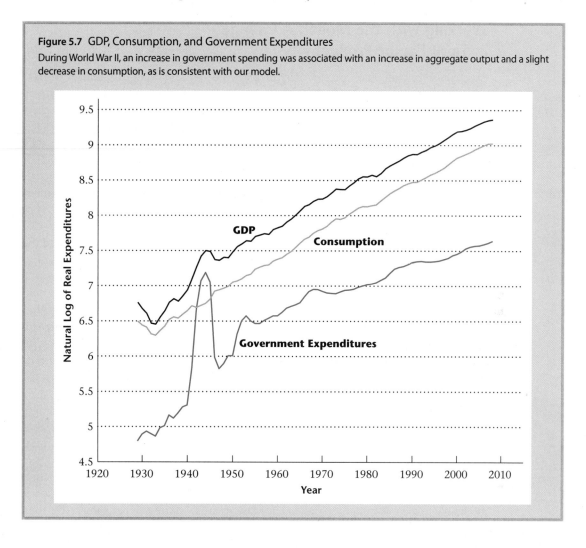

Figure 5.7 GDP, Consumption, and Government Expenditures

During World War II, an increase in government spending was associated with an increase in aggregate output and a slight decrease in consumption, as is consistent with our model.

business cycles, then it should be the case that our model can replicate these key business cycle facts in response to a change in G. The model predicts that, when government spending increases, aggregate output and employment increase, and consumption and the real wage decrease. One of our key business cycle facts is that employment is procyclical. This fact is consistent with government spending shocks causing business cycles, because employment always moves in the same direction as aggregate output in response to a change in G. Additional business cycle facts are that consumption and the real wage are procyclical, but the model predicts that consumption and the real wage are countercyclical in response to government spending shocks. This is because, when G changes, consumption and the real wage always move in the direction opposite to the resulting change in Y. Therefore, government spending shocks do not appear to be a good candidate as a cause of business cycles. Whatever the primary cause of business cycles, it is unlikely to be the fact that governments change their spending plans from time to time. We explore this idea further in Chapters 12 and 13.

Working with the Model: A Change in Total Factor Productivity

An increase in total factor productivity involves a better technology for converting factor inputs into aggregate output. As we see in this section, increases in total factor productivity increase consumption and aggregate output, but there is an ambiguous effect on employment. This ambiguity is the result of opposing income and substitution effects on labor supply. While an increase in government spending essentially produces only an income effect on consumer behavior, an increase in total factor productivity generates both an income effect and a substitution effect.

Suppose that total factor productivity z increases. As mentioned previously, the interpretation of an increase in z is as a technological innovation (a new invention or an advance in management techniques), a spell of good weather, a relaxation in government regulations, or a decrease in the price of energy. The interpretation of the increase in z and the resulting effects depend on what we take one period in the model to represent relative to time in the real world. One period could be many years—in which case, we interpret the results from the model as capturing what happens over the long run—or one period could be a month, a quarter, or a year—in which case, we are studying short-run effects. After we examine what the model tells us, we provide interpretations in terms of the **short-run** and **long-run** economic implications. In general, the short run in macroeconomics typically refers to effects that occur within a year's time, whereas the long run refers to effects occurring beyond a year's time. However, what is taken to be the boundary between the short run and the long run can vary considerably in different contexts.

The effect of an increase in z is to shift the production function up, as in Figure 5.8. An increase in z not only permits more output to be produced given the quantity of labor input, but it increases the marginal product of labor for each quantity of labor input; that is, the slope of the production function increases for each N. In Figure 5.8, z increases from z_1 to z_2. We can show exactly the same shift in the production function as a shift outward in the PPF in Figure 5.9 from AB to AD. Here, more consumption is attainable given the better technology, for any quantity of leisure consumed. Further, the trade-off between consumption and leisure has improved, in that the new PPF is steeper for any given quantity of leisure. That is, because MP_N increases and the slope of the PPF is $-MP_N$, the PPF is steeper when z increases.

Figure 5.9 allows us to determine all the equilibrium effects of an increase in z. Here, indifference curve I_1 is tangent to the initial PPF at point F. After the shift in the PPF, the economy is at a point such as H, where there is a tangency between the new PPF and indifference curve I_2. What must be the case is that consumption increases in moving from F to H, in this case increasing from C_1 to C_2. Leisure, however, may increase or decrease, and here we have shown the case where it remains the same at l_1. Because $Y = C + G$ in equilibrium and because G remains constant and C increases, there is an increase in aggregate output, and because $N = h - l$, employment is unchanged (but employment could have increased or decreased). The equilibrium real wage is minus the slope of the PPF at point H (i.e., $w = MP_N$). When we separate the income and substitution effects of the increase in z, in the next stage of our analysis, we show that the real wage must increase in equilibrium. In Figure 5.9 the PPF clearly is

Figure 5.8 Increase in Total Factor Productivity

An increase in total factor productivity shifts the production function up and increases the marginal product of labor for each quantity of the labor input.

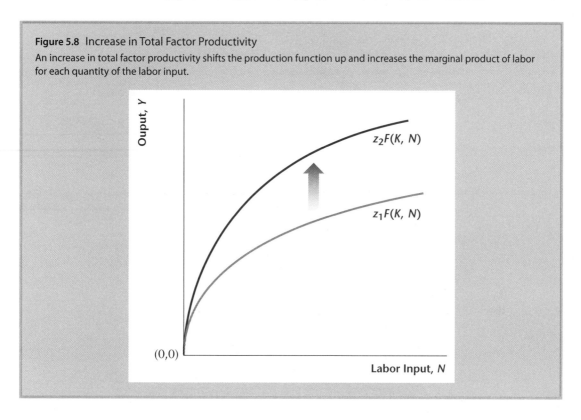

steeper at H than at F, so that the real wage is higher in equilibrium, but we show how this must be true in general, even when the quantities of leisure and employment change.

To see why consumption has to increase and why the change in leisure is ambiguous, we separate the shift in the PPF into an income effect and a substitution effect. In Figure 5.10, PPF_1 is the original PPF, and it shifts to PPF_2 when z increases from z_1 to z_2. The initial equilibrium is at point A, and the final equilibrium is at point B after z increases. The equation for PPF_2 is given by

$$C = z_2 F(K, h - l) - G.$$

Now, consider constructing an artificial PPF, called PPF_3, which is obtained by shifting PPF_2 downward by a constant amount. That is, the equation for PPF_3 is given by

$$C = z_2 F(K, h - l) - G - C_0.$$

Here C_0 is a constant that is large enough so that PPF_3 is just tangent to the initial indifference curve I_1. What we are doing here is taking consumption (i.e., "income") away from the representative consumer to obtain the pure substitution effect of an increase in z. In Figure 5.10 the substitution effect is then the movement from A to D, and the income effect is the movement from D to B. Much the same as when we considered income and substitution effects for a consumer facing an increase in his or her wage rate, here the substitution effect is for consumption to increase and leisure to

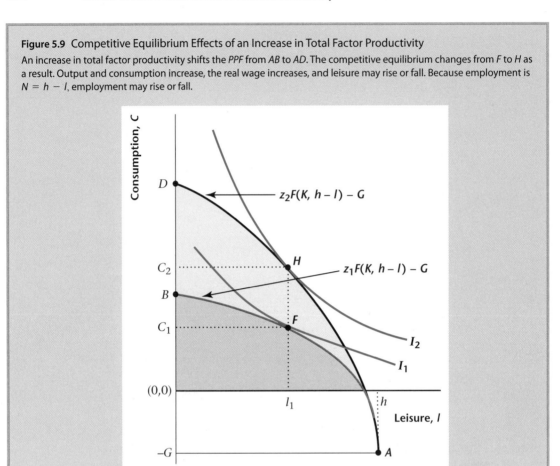

Figure 5.9 Competitive Equilibrium Effects of an Increase in Total Factor Productivity

An increase in total factor productivity shifts the *PPF* from *AB* to *AD*. The competitive equilibrium changes from *F* to *H* as a result. Output and consumption increase, the real wage increases, and leisure may rise or fall. Because employment is $N = h - l$, employment may rise or fall.

decrease, so that hours worked increase. Also, the income effect is for both consumption and leisure to increase. As before, consumption must increase as both goods are normal, but leisure may increase or decrease because of opposing income and substitution effects.

Now, why must the real wage increase in moving from *A* to *B*, even if the quantities of leisure and employment rise or fall? First, the substitution effect involves an increase in $MRS_{l,C}$ (the indifference curve gets steeper) in moving along the indifference curve from *A* to *D*. Second, because PPF_2 is just PPF_3 shifted up by a fixed amount, the slope of PPF_2 is the same as the slope of PPF_3 for each quantity of leisure. As the quantity of leisure is higher at point *B* than at point *D*, the *PPF* is steeper at *B* than at *D*, and so $MRS_{l,C}$ also increases in moving from *D* to *B*. Thus, the real wage, which is equal to the marginal rate of substitution in equilibrium, must be higher in equilibrium when *z* is higher.

The increase in total factor productivity causes an increase in the marginal productivity of labor, which increases the demand for labor by firms, driving up the real wage.

Figure 5.10 Income and Substitution Effects of an Increase in Total Factor Productivity

Here, the effects of an increase in total factor productivity are separated into substitution and income effects. The increase in total factor productivity involves a shift from PPF_1 to PPF_2. The curve PPF_3 is an artificial PPF, and it is PPF_2 with the income effect of the increase in z taken out. The substitution effect is the movement from A to D, and the income effect is the movement from D to B.

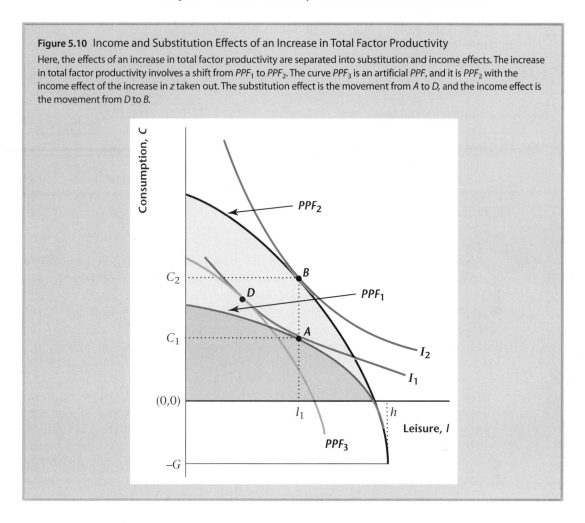

Workers now have more income given the number of hours worked, and they spend the increased income on consumption goods. Because there are offsetting income and substitution effects on the quantity of labor supplied, however, hours worked may increase or decrease. An important feature of the increase in total factor productivity is that the welfare of the representative consumer must increase. That is, the representative consumer must consume on a higher indifference curve when z increases. Therefore, increases in total factor productivity unambiguously increase the aggregate standard of living.

Interpretation of the Model's Predictions

Figure 5.9 tells a story about the long-term economic effects of long-run improvements in technology, such as those that have occurred in the United States since World War II. There have been many important technological innovations since World War II, particularly in electronics and information technology. Also, some key observations from post–World War II U.S. data are that aggregate output has increased steadily, consumption has increased, the real wage has increased, and hours worked per employed person have remained roughly constant. Figure 5.9 matches these observations in that it predicts that a technological advance leads to increased output, increased consumption, a higher real wage, and ambiguous effects on hours worked. Thus, if income and substitution effects roughly cancel over the long run, then the model is consistent with the fact that hours worked per person have remained roughly constant over the post–World War II period in the United States. There may have been many other factors in addition to technological change affecting output, consumption, the real wage, and hours worked over this period in U.S. history. Our model, however, tells us that empirical observations for this period are consistent with technological innovations having been an important contributing factor to changes in these key macroeconomic variables.

A second interpretation of Figure 5.9 is in terms of short-run aggregate fluctuations in macroeconomic variables. Could fluctuations in total factor productivity be an important cause of business cycles? Recall from Chapter 3 that three key business cycle facts are that consumption is procyclical, employment is procyclical, and the real wage is procyclical. From Figure 5.9, our model predicts that, in response to an increase in z, aggregate output increases, consumption increases, employment may increase or decrease, and the real wage increases. Therefore, the model is consistent with procyclical consumption and real wages, as consumption and the real wage always move in the same direction as output when z changes. Employment, however, may be procyclical or countercyclical, depending on the strength of opposing income and substitution effects. For the model to be consistent with the data requires that the substitution effect dominate the income effect, so that the consumer wants to increase labor supply in response to an increase in the market real wage. Thus, it is certainly possible that total factor productivity shocks could be a primary cause of business cycles, but to be consistent with the data requires that workers increase and decrease labor supply in response to increases and decreases in total factor productivity over the business cycle.

Some macroeconomists, the advocates of **real business cycle theory,** view total factor productivity shocks as the most important cause of business cycles. This view may seem to be contradicted by the long-run evidence that the income and substitution effects on labor supply of real wage increases appear to roughly cancel in the post–World War II period. Real business cycle theorists, however, argue that much of the short-run variation in labor supply is the result of **intertemporal substitution of labor,** which is the substitution of labor over time in response to real wage movements. For example, a worker may choose to work harder in the present if he or she views his or her wage as being temporarily high, while planning to take more vacation in the future. The worker basically "makes hay while the sun shines." In this way, even though income and substitution effects may cancel in the long run, in the short run the substitution effect of an increase in the real wage could outweigh the income effect. We explore intertemporal substitution further in Chapters 8 to 12.

Total Factor Productivity, Real GDP, and Energy Prices

Shocks to total factor productivity appear to play a key role in business cycles. As evidence of this, Figure 5.11 shows the percentage deviations from trend in real GDP and in the Solow residual for the period 1948–2007. Recall from Chapter 4 that the Solow residual is a measure of total factor productivity, calculated as the quantity of real output that cannot be accounted for by capital and labor inputs. Clearly, the figure shows that the Solow residual and real GDP move together closely. This observation is part of the motivation for real business cycle theory, which we study in detail in Chapter 12. Real

Figure 5.11 Deviations from Trend in GDP and the Solow Residual

Deviations from trend in the Solow residual closely track deviations from trend in real GDP, as is consistent with real business cycle theory.

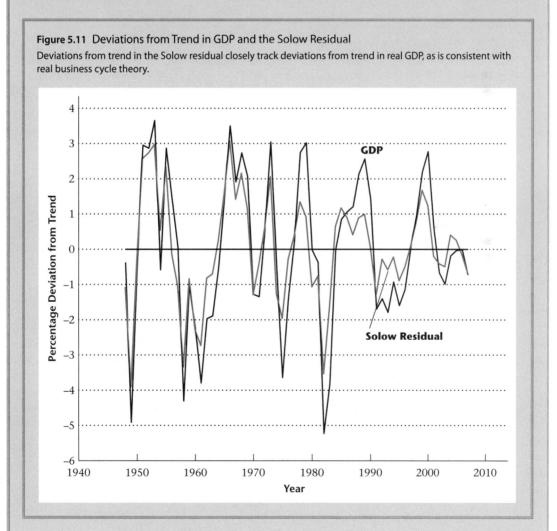

(Continued)

business cycle theorists argue that shocks to total factor productivity are the primary source of business cycles, and that seems hard to deny given Figure 5.11, if we accept that the Solow residual is a good measure of total factor productivity (there are some doubts about this, as we discuss in Chapter 12). Other data fit the predictions of our model closely. In particular, the fluctuations in real GDP and the Solow residual in Figure 5.11 are tracked closely by fluctuations about trend in consumption and employment (see Chapter 3), as the theory predicts (so long

as the substitution effect on labor supply of an increase in total factor productivity outweighs the income effect).

Although Figure 5.11 shows a strong link between fluctuations about trend in total factor productivity and real GDP, the figure is not informative about the underlying shocks that are causing total factor productivity to fluctuate. In Chapter 4, we discussed how changes in total factor productivity can arise because of technological innovation, changes in the weather, changes in government regulations, and changes in the

Figure 5.12 The Relative Price of Energy

The relative price of energy is measured by the ratio of the producer price index for fuels, related products, and power, to the producer price index for all commodities, normalized to 100 in 1948. Each of the last five recessions, in 1974–1975, 1981–1982, 1991–1992, 2001, and 2008–2009, was preceded by a spike in the relative price of energy.

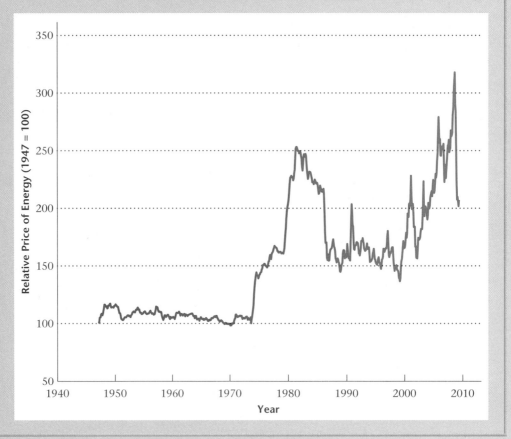

relative price of energy, among other things. Since the 1970s, large changes in the relative price of energy appear to have been a key influence on total factor productivity and have played an important role in post-1970 recessions.

In Figure 5.12, we show the relative price of energy in the United States, for the period 1948–2009, measured as the ratio of the producer price index for fuels, related products, and power, to the producer price index for all commodities. As can be seen in Figures 5.11 and 5.12, several large increases in the relative price of energy were followed closely by sharp decreases below trend in the Solow residual and real GDP. In particular, the Organization of Petroleum Exporting Countries (OPEC) sharply reduced output of crude oil in 1973 and in 1979, leading to large increases in the relative price of energy in 1973–1974 and 1979–1980 (see Figure 5.12). These two events were followed closely by recessions in 1974–1975 and 1981–1982. Similarly, the increases in the relative price of energy during the Persian Gulf War (1990) and in 2000 were followed, respectively, by the recessions of

1990–1991 and 2001. In Figure 5.11, we have data for the Solow residual only up to 2007, so there is no evidence on measured total factor productivity leading up to the 2008–2009 recession. However, it is notable that the relative price of energy reached its peak during the entire period 1948–2009 in mid-2008, just before real GDP started to decrease in the United States, with the relative price of energy at more than three times its level in 1948.

Increases in the relative price of energy were certainly not the only factor contributing to post-1970 recessions. In particular, monetary policy appears to have contributed significantly to the 1981–1982 recession, the events of 9/11/01 and an investment collapse driven by pessimism were important causes of the 2001 recession, and financial factors clearly played a key role in the 2008–2009 recession. It seems clear, however, that large movements in the relative price of energy were of significant importance in post-1970 U.S. business cycles and will continue to be important for macroeconomic events in the United States in the future.

Perspectives on the Financial Crisis

Government Expenditures and the American Recovery and Reinvestment Act of 2009

The American Recovery and Reinvestment Act (ARRA) was signed into law by President Obama on February 17, 2009.[3] This act of Congress was motivated by the belief that the government has an obligation to pursue economic policies that will increase aggregate economic activity when real GDP falls below trend, as occurred in 2008–2009 (see Figure 3.2). Keynesian macroeconomics, which we will study and evaluate in

Chapters 12 and 13, provides the foundation (a weak foundation in the eyes of some economists) for the belief that the government has an important role to play in smoothing business cycles.

The ARRA authorizes a total of $787 billion in changes in items in the budget of the U.S. government. Since $787 billion represents 5.5% of annual GDP for 2008 in the United States, this appears to be a very large number. However, to understand the implications of the ARRA for the

---

[3]See http://en.wikipedia.org/wiki/Recovery_bill

aggregate economy, we need to determine the economic importance of the different items included in the Act. First, about $288 billion of the $787 billion consists of tax cuts, for individuals and corporations. Next, about $209 billion is accounted for by government transfers. Neither of these two items is part of G, government spending, as we have represented it in our one-period model. A tax cut is just a reduction in government revenue or receipts, and recall from Chapter 2 that a government transfer (for example for unemployment insurance) is not part of GDP, since it is not expenditure on a final good or service, and is therefore not included in G. This

leaves about $290 billion in government expenditures on goods and services in the ARRA. If this were all spent in one year (which is unlikely to be the case—the extra expenditure authorized may continue into 2010 and 2011), then this would account for a 10.1% increase in government expenditures over annual government expenditures in 2008, or an amount equal to 2.0% of 2008 GDP. Thus, even if we take out the parts of the ARRA that are not included in measured GDP, the increase in expenditure is large.

Next, to get a perspective on government expenditures authorized in the ARRA, consider Figure 5.13, where we show government

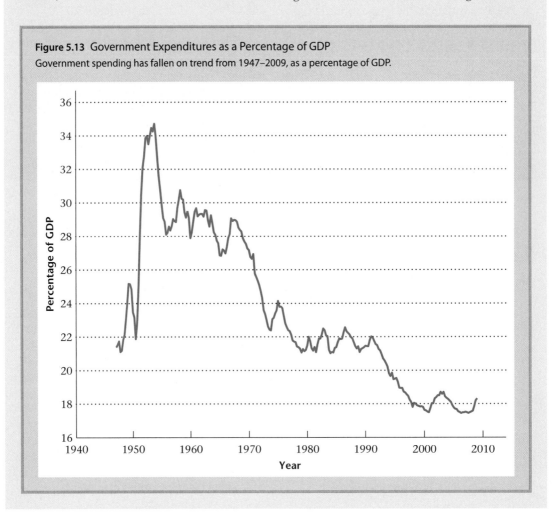

Figure 5.13 Government Expenditures as a Percentage of GDP
Government spending has fallen on trend from 1947–2009, as a percentage of GDP.

expenditures as a percentage of GDP for 1947–2009. An interesting feature of the figure is that government expenditures as a fraction of GDP have been falling on trend since the mid-1950s. Another interesting feature is that this quantity held roughly steady at about 22% during the Republican administrations of Ronald Reagan and George H.W. Bush, from 1980–1992, but declined during the Democratic Clinton administration from 1992–2000. Note that, even if government spending as a fraction of GDP were to increase from 18% (the value in the first quarter of 2009) to 20%, in line with our calculations

above, then this fraction would be no larger than what it was in the mid-1990s. Thus, in historical terms, the level of spending authorized in the ARRA does not seem to be a big deal.

To understand the broader spending implications of the ARRA, in Figure 5.14 we show total government outlays as a percentage of GDP for 1947–2009. Government outlays include government expenditures on goods and services as well as transfers and interest on the government debt (recall the discussion from Chapter 2). While Figure 5.13 appears to indicate a declining role for government in the economy since

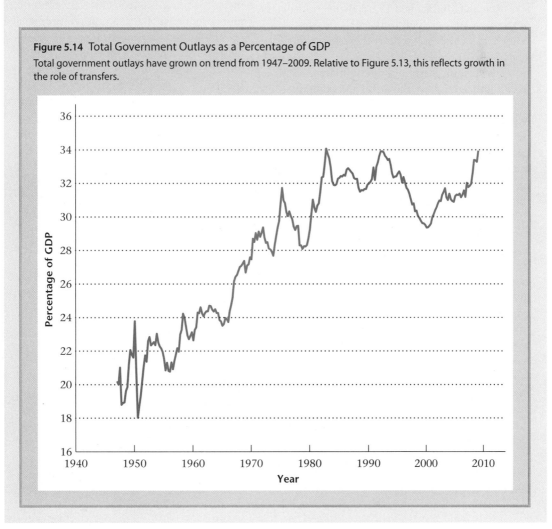

Figure 5.14 Total Government Outlays as a Percentage of GDP

Total government outlays have grown on trend from 1947–2009. Relative to Figure 5.13, this reflects growth in the role of transfers.

World War II, Figure 5.14 indicates an increasing role. The difference is due to growth in transfers. While all levels of government are spending less on goods and services as a fraction of GDP, government transfer programs have grown enormously. These transfer programs include Social Security and Medicare (at the federal level), and Medicaid and unemployment insurance (at the state level). Thus, in terms of the total budget of all levels of government, the additional spending on goods and services and government transfers in the ARRA adds a large amount to an already large quantity of total government outlays. Note that, in Figure 5.13, total government outlays, at 34% of GDP in the first quarter of 2009, is at its highest level over the whole period since 1947.

The taxation and transfer items in the ARRA have implications for the government budget deficit and for deficit financing, which we will explore in later chapters. For now we will focus on what an additional 2% of GDP in spending by the government on goods and services might mean for aggregate economic activity, using our one-period model as a vehicle for organizing our thinking.

First, in the context of our one-period model, what could cause GDP to fall, as it did in 2008–2009? One possibility is that there was a decline in total factor productivity, which would cause the production possibilities frontier to shift inward. In response to such a shock to the economy the government could engineer an increase in G, government spending on goods, which would act to increase real GDP, increase employment, and reduce consumption, as in Figure 5.6. However, our model certainly does not tell us that this government policy response makes any sense, as the initial reduction in real GDP was just the result of the economy's optimal response to bad circumstances. Increasing G to offset the reduction in GDP caused by the negative shock to productivity will just serve to reduce leisure and consumption and make the representative

consumer worse off. Is our model missing something here? Consider some alternatives:

1. In the one-period model as we have constructed it, government spending is a deadweight loss to the economy. That is, when the government spends in the model, it buys goods and throws them away. Some types of government expenditures work exactly like this in practice. For example, military expenditure, while it protects us, economically is a pure loss of resources for the economy as a whole. However, some types of government spending act to make the economy more productive. For example, government spending on roads and bridges effectively increases the nation's capital stock and shifts out the production possibilities frontier. Indeed, it is straightforward to extend the one-period model to the analysis of productive government spending, as you are asked to do in the end-of-chapter problems. In the ARRA, much of the spending increases might be classified as productive government spending, including $90.9 billion of spending on education, $80.9 billion on infrastructure, $61.3 billion on energy projects, and $8.9 billion on science. Why spend this money now? One argument is that a recession is an ideal time for productive government expenditures, such as bridge and road improvements, that will have to be done anyway. Why not undertake these projects when the materials and labor can be had at a low price? On the negative side, some of these projects may have been ill-considered and introduced in a hasty way, and therefore not likely to be productive at all.

2. Prominent supporters of the ARRA, for example the Nobel-prize-winning economist Paul Krugman, who writes for the *New York Times,* typically use Keynesian arguments to argue in favor of the spending program. Keynesian thought, which we will address in

Chapters 12 and 13, holds that there are short run inefficiencies in the economy, which effectively imply that the aggregate economy can operate inside the production possibilities frontier. Government "stimulus"—short run increases in government expenditure—can, according to Keynesians, push the economy from inside the production possibilities frontier to the frontier, thus correcting the inefficiency. There is plenty to find fault with in Keynesian economics. For example, Keynesians sometimes neglect the costs of moving unemployed resources to the government sector, or the awkward timing issues in implementing fiscal policy. As an example of the latter, in spite of the fact that the ARRA was passed quickly, much of the appropriated money may not actually be spent until late in 2009, in 2010, or in 2011. It is quite possible that the current recession will be over by late 2009, at which time a growing private economy may just be hampered (i.e., crowded out) by the additional resources being absorbed in the public sector.

3. The one-period model does not account for financial factors, which appear to be at the heart of the causes of the 2008–2009 recession. This is certainly a valid criticism. How can we make recommendations about government policy in a model that does not incorporate features that appear to be important for the problem at hand? The counterargument is that we need to start somewhere. The one-period model gives us some insight into how the economy works and a solid base on which to build. Further, it is not clear that financial factors are the only reason that GDP fell below trend in 2008–2009. For example, in the "Theory Confronts Data: Total Factor Productivity, Real GDP, and Energy Prices" box, we showed the large runup in energy prices to mid-2008, and we know that high energy prices essentially work like a negative shock to aggregate total factor productivity. This type of shock is something that we can analyze in our one-period model. To the extent that high energy prices are responsible for the 2008–2009 recession, there is less reason to think that an increase in government spending in response to the recession is appropriate.

A Distorting Tax on Wage Income, Tax Rate Changes, and the Laffer Curve

We are now ready to consider a version of the model in which there is a distorting tax. As was discussed earlier in this chapter, distorting taxes imply in general that a competitive equilibrium is not Pareto optimal, and so we will not be able to use the same approach to analyzing the model as previously. The distorting tax we will consider is a proportional tax on wage income. This will capture, in a simple way, some features of income taxation in the United States and other countries and will allow us to discuss some fiscal policy issues, including the incentive effects of income taxation. We will show that, surprisingly, it is possible for tax revenue collected by the government to increase when the income tax rate goes down, a feature illustrated in what has come to be known as the "Laffer curve." The form that the Laffer curve takes in the U.S. economy is of key importance for the effects of tax rate changes on labor supply and on tax revenue for the government.

A Simplified One–Period Model with Proportional Income Taxation

To keep the analysis simple and transparent for the purpose at hand, assume that output is produced only with labor as an input, with production by the representative firm according to the relationship

$$Y = zN^d, \tag{5-7}$$

with Y denoting aggregate output, N^d the firm's labor input, and z total factor productivity. Here, with labor the only factor of production, we have continued to assume that there is constant returns to scale in production, so that increasing N^d by a factor x increases output Y by the same factor x.

Now, in a competitive equilibrium, since labor demand equals labor supply, or $N^d = h - l$ and consumption plus government spending equals output, or $C + G = Y$, therefore from (5-7) we can write the production possibilities frontier (PPF) as

$$C = z(h - l) - G, \tag{5-8}$$

and we have graphed the PPF as AB in Figure 5.15. Note that the PPF is now linear. At point A, the representative consumer takes zero units of leisure and consumes the

Figure 5.15 The Production Possibilities Frontier in the Simplified Model

The production possibilities frontier is linear. The maximum quantity of consumption (when the quantity of leisure is zero) is $zh - G$.

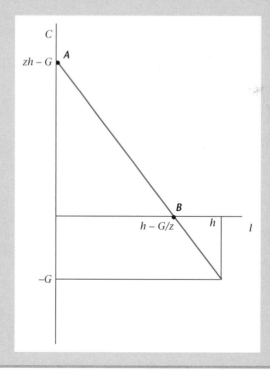

maximum amount of consumption possible, $zh - G$, while at point B the consumer consumes zero and works $\frac{G}{z}$ units of time (with $l = h - \frac{G}{z}$) so as to supply the government with G units of goods.

To purchase G units of goods, the government imposes a proportional tax on the consumer's wage income. Assume that this is the only tax in this economy. In particular, there are no lump-sum taxes, or $T = 0$. Letting t denote the tax rate, the consumer will pay $tw(h - l)$ in taxes to the government, so that we can write the consumer's budget constraint as

$$C = w(1 - t)(h - l) + \pi, \tag{5-9}$$

or consumption is equal to after-tax wage income plus dividend income. Note that $w(1 - t)$ is the effective wage rate for the consumer, or the after-tax real wage.

Next, consider the profit maximization problem for the representative firm. Profits for the firm are given by

$$\pi = Y - wN^d = (z - w)N^d, \tag{5-10}$$

from (5-7). The firm chooses N^d to make π as large as possible, given z and w. Here, $z - w$ is the profit that the firm makes for each unit of labor input, and this is the same no matter how much labor the firm hires. Thus, if $z > w$, then the firm earns positive profits for each unit of labor hired, and it would want to hire an infinite quantity of labor. If $z < w$, then profits are negative for any quantity of labor hired, so the firm would hire no labor. However, if $z = w$, then profits are zero for the firm no matter what it does, so the firm is indifferent concerning how much labor to hire. As a result, the firm's demand curve for labor, denoted by $N^d(w)$ is infinitely elastic at the wage $w = z$, as shown in Figure 5.16.

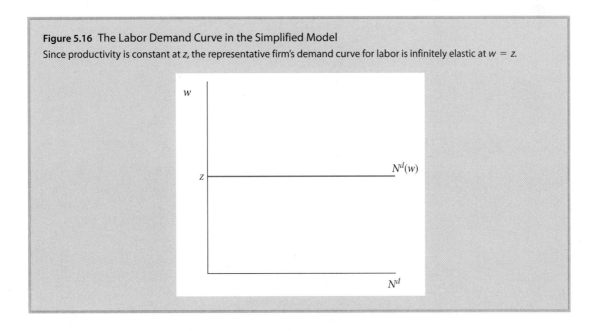

Figure 5.16 The Labor Demand Curve in the Simplified Model
Since productivity is constant at z, the representative firm's demand curve for labor is infinitely elastic at $w = z$.

Therefore, in equilibrium, no matter what the supply curve for labor $N^s(w)$ is (as determined by the representative consumer's behavior), the equilibrium wage must be $w = z$. This simplifies our work dramatically. Further, since $w = z$ in equilibrium, therefore from (5-10) the firm must earn zero profits in equilibrium, or $\pi = 0$, so dividend income for the representative consumer must also be zero in equilibrium. Therefore, setting $w = z$ and $\pi = 0$ in equation (5-9), in equilibrium the consumer's budget constraint is

$$C = z(1 - t)(h - l). \tag{5-11}$$

In equilibrium, the consumer chooses consumption C and leisure l to satisfy his or her budget constraint (equation (5-11)), and markets clear, which is summarized by equation (5-8). Note that (5-8) and (5-11) in turn imply that the government's budget constraint is satisfied, since if we substitute for C in equation (5-8) using (5-11), we get $G = zt(h - l)$, or total government spending equals total tax revenue. We can depict a competitive equilibrium as in Figure 5.17. Here, AB is the PPF, or the combinations of C and l which satisfy equation (5-8). As well, the budget constraint faced by the consumer in equilibrium is DF, or the combinations of C and l that satisfy equation (5-11). In equilibrium the tax rate t adjusts so that the point on DF that the consumer chooses

Figure 5.17 Competitive Equilibrium in the Simplified Model with a Proportional Tax on Labor Income
The competitive equilibrium is point H, and the Pareto optimum is point E.

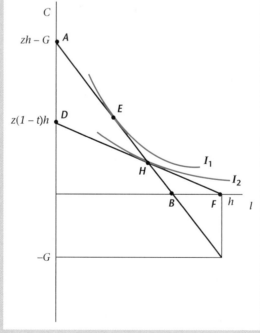

is at point H, where DF intersects AB, which is what is required for market clearing. Therefore, in equilibrium, an indifference curve is tangent to DF at point H. This indifference curve necessarily cuts the PPF as shown, since AB is steeper than $DF(z > z(1 - t))$.

One conclusion is that the Pareto optimum, at E, is different from the competitive equilibrium, at H. That is, because the income tax distorts private decisions, the competitive equilibrium is not socially efficient. The welfare loss due to the distorting tax can be measured by how much better off the consumer is at point E than at point H (note that H is on a lower indifference curve than E). A second conclusion is that consumption and output must be higher and leisure lower at point E than at point H. This is due to the fact that indifference curves cannot cross, a property of indifference curves illustrated in a problem in Chapter 4. That is, the distorting income tax gives consumers a disincentive to work, and tends to lower aggregate consumption and aggregate output. Of course, if the government needs to collect taxes, and all taxes distort private decisions, it may be necessary to put up with these negative incentive effects of income taxation.

Income Tax Revenue and the Laffer Curve   To get another perspective on a competitive equilibrium with an income tax, we will take the following approach. First, we can ask how much income tax revenue the government could generate for each tax rate t, taking into account the quantity of labor that the consumer will want to supply at each of those tax rates. Then, we can determine the equilibrium tax rate (or tax rates) that will finance government expenditures G. This approach will be informative about the potential effects of changing the tax rate.

To start, we know that in equilibrium the consumer faces his or her budget constraint (5-11), and chooses C and l to satisfy (5-11) given the tax rate t, and the equilibrium real wage $w = z$. If we ask what quantity of leisure the consumer would choose given each tax rate t, we can derive a function $l(t)$, which describes the quantity of leisure the consumer chooses if the after-tax real wage is $z(1 - t)$, taking z as given. This would then tell us that the tax revenue that the government can collect if the income tax rate is t is

$$REV = tz[h - l(t)], \tag{5-12}$$

where REV is total revenue from the income tax. In equation (5-12), t is the tax rate, and $z[h - l(t)]$ is the **tax base**, which is the value of the quantity traded in the market of the object being taxed, which in this case is the quantity of labor, valued in terms of consumption goods by multiplying by the real wage rate z. It is important to recognize in equation (5-12) that total tax revenue depends not only on the tax rate, but on the size of the tax base, which in turn depends on the tax rate. If the tax base does not change when t increases, then tax revenue will increase when the tax rate increases. However, it is possible for tax revenue to go *down* when t increases. This would occur if $l(t)$ increases sufficiently when t increases, that a declining tax base offsets the effect of an increase in the tax rate on REV in equation (5-12) so that REV falls when t increases. For this to occur, the substitution effect of a change in the after-tax real wage would have to be large relative to the income effect. That is, since an increase in t implies a decrease in the equilibrium real wage $z(1 - t)$, for REV to decline when t increases there would have to be a large decrease in the quantity of labor supplied, $h - l(t)$, or in other words a large disincentive to work due to a higher income tax rate.

Figure 5.18 A Laffer Curve

The Laffer curve is the relationship between income tax revenue and the income tax rate. Tax revenue must be zero when $t = 0$ (the tax rate is zero) and $t = 1$ (because no one will work if all income is taxed away). The government can maximize tax revenue by setting $t = t^*$. If the government wishes to finance government spending equal to G, it can set a tax rate of t_1 (on the good side of the Laffer curve) or t_2 (on the bad side of the Laffer curve).

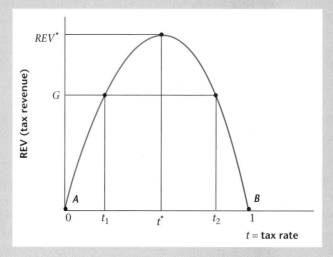

In Figure 5.18, we show a typical graph for equation (5-12), where we plot total tax revenue against the tax rate, taking into account the effects of the consumer's choice concerning the quantity of labor supplied in response to the tax rate. The curve AB in the figure is called a **Laffer curve**. The Laffer curve gets its name from the economist Arthur Laffer, and "Laffer curve" typically denotes any curve that shows the quantity of tax revenue generated by the government as a function of a tax rate. Theoretically, we cannot say a lot about the shape of the curve between the points A and B in Figure 5.18. In practice, the shape of the curve between A and B depends on the details of labor supply behavior for all possible after-tax real wage rates. However, points A and B will always be on the curve, since if the tax rate t is zero, then tax revenue must be zero ($t = 0$ implies $REV = 0$ in equation (5-12)), which gives us point A, and the consumer will not work and the tax base is zero if $t = 1$ ($t = 1$ implies $l(1) = h$ and $REV = 0$ in equation (5-12)), which gives us point B. In the figure, there is a maximum amount of tax revenue that the government can generate. That is, if the tax rate is t^*, then the maximum tax revenue REV^* accrues to the government.

Now, given the quantity of government spending G, in our model the government will have to choose the tax rate t to generate enough revenue to finance this quantity of spending, or from (5-12), in equilibrium,

$$G = tz[h - l(t)],$$

which is another version of the government's budget constraint. In Figure 5.18, note first that if $G > REV^*$ then it is impossible for the government to collect enough tax revenue to finance its spending. However, if $G < REV^*$ (the case we want to consider) then given the quantity of government spending G, there are two possible equilibrium tax rates. What is true in general is that there will be *at least* two tax rates that can generate enough tax revenue to finance any quantity of government expenditure $G < REV^*$. We have shown a simple Laffer curve, where if $G < REV^*$ in the figure, then there are two possible equilibrium tax rates, shown here as t_1 and t_2, where $t_2 > t_1$. It is possible that the Laffer curve could have a more complicated shape, with the potential for *more* than two equilibrium tax rates.

Now, given that there are two equilibrium tax rates, t_1 and t_2, for any quantity of government expenditure G, consider what a competitive equilibrium will look like in the context of the diagram we used earlier in this section. In Figure 5.19, the competitive equilibrium with the low tax rate t_1 is given by point F, while the one with the high tax rate t_2 is given by point H. Recall that a competitive equilibrium will always lie on the PPF given by curve AB, and on the budget constraint faced by the consumer in equilibrium. When the tax rate is t_2, the consumer's budget constraint is less steep, and lies below the budget constraint in the equilibrium where the tax rate is t_1. Therefore, we can say that the quantity of consumption, C, is higher, the quantity of labor supplied,

Figure 5.19 There Can Be Two Competitive Equilibria

Given government spending equal to G, as in Figure 5.16, there are two equilibrium tax rates. The low-tax-rate (high-tax-rate) equilibrium is at point $F(H)$. In the low-tax-rate equilibrium consumption and output are higher, and leisure is lower, than in the high-tax-rate equilibrium.

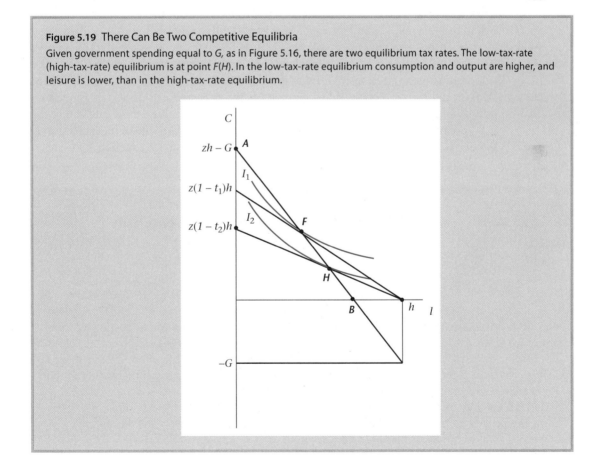

$h - l$, is higher, leisure, l, is lower, and aggregate output ($Y = C + G$) is higher in the low-tax-rate equilibrium than in the high-tax-rate equilibrium. Further, since point F must be on a higher indifference curve than point H, the consumer is better off in the equilibrium with a low tax rate than in the one with a higher tax rate.

A sensible government would never choose the high tax rate t_2 since it could collect the same quantity of tax revenue with the low tax rate t_1 and make the representative consumer better off. However, we might imagine that a less-than-sensible government could get stuck in a bad equilibrium with the high tax rate t_2, and thus be on the wrong side of the Laffer curve in Figure 5.18, that is the side of the Laffer curve where an increase in the tax rate will reduce tax revenue, rather than on the side where an increase in the tax rate will increase tax revenue. During the 1980 Presidential election, Ronald Reagan, supported by the reasoning of so-called **supply-side economists**, put forward an economic program including reductions in income tax rates. Supply-side economists believed that there are large incentive effects of income taxes on labor supply and that tax rate reductions will increase the quantity of labor supplied by a large amount. Reagan's arguments can be interpreted as being that the U.S. economy in 1980 was at a point corresponding to the equilibrium in Figures 5.18 and 5.19 with the high tax rate t_2. That is, Reagan argued that tax rates could be reduced without sacrificing any tax revenue, everyone would work harder as a result, GDP would be higher, and everyone would be better off. Reagan's views are consistent with theory, but the empirical question is whether the U.S. economy was operating in 1980 on the good side of the Laffer curve (the upward-sloping portion) or the bad side (the downward-sloping portion). Supply-side arguments surfaced again during the second Bush administration, although George W. Bush did not use supply-side arguments as the primary focus of his tax-rate reduction plan. The general consensus among economists concerning this debate is that the U.S. economy is typically on the good side, rather than the bad side of the Laffer curve. We discuss this further in the following Theory Confronts the Data section.

THEORY confronts the DATA

Is the U.S. Economy on the Bad Side of the Laffer Curve?

Being on the "bad side" of the Laffer curve means, as we have discussed in this subsection, that a decrease in income tax rates will lead to a large enough increase in the quantity of labor supplied that tax revenue increases. In his campaign for the presidency prior to the 1980 U.S. election, Ronald Reagan proposed an economic program that included reductions in income tax rates, and part of his argument for the program was that this would increase the quantity of labor supplied and also increase income tax revenue. This argument was derided by Reagan's opponent in the Republican primaries, George H.W. Bush, as "voodoo economics." As we have shown, Reagan's arguments for his proposals were consistent with economic theory, but only if the U.S. economy in 1980 was on the bad side of the Laffer curve.

Ultimately, Reagan's economic proposals were enacted in the Economic Recovery Act of

1981 (August 1981), often referred to as the Kemp–Roth Tax Cut.[4] To understand how the tax cuts were implemented, it is important to understand the structure of the federal income tax in the United States. At the federal level, income is taxed at different rates for different individuals. That is, an individual with a low level of income faces a lower tax rate than does a person with a high level of income—this type of income tax system is called a *progressive tax system*. For an individual, the incentive effects of the income tax depend on their marginal tax rate, which is the tax rate on the last dollar of income earned. This is because a change in the marginal tax rate is what will change an individual's labor supply decision at the margin. In 1980 the top marginal tax rate was 70%, and the lowest marginal tax rate for an individual paying any income tax was 14%. The Kemp–Roth tax cuts reduced all marginal tax rates, with the top tax rate falling from 70% to 50%, and the bottom tax rate falling from 14% to 11%.

Tax cut proposals were also a centerpiece of George W. Bush's campaign for President leading up to the 2000 federal election, twenty years after Ronald Reagan was first elected president. However, Bush did not frame his argument for tax cuts in the same way as Reagan. He did not typically speak about the incentive effects of tax rate cuts on labor supply and the resulting increases in tax revenue that were possible, although it appeared he was unconcerned about the implications for federal government tax revenue. In June 2001, the Economic Growth and Tax Relief Reconciliation Act of 2001 was passed, which provided for, among other things, reduction of the 39.6%, 36%, 31%, and 28% marginal tax rates to 35%, 33%, 28%, and 25%, respectively.

Now, if the U.S. economy were indeed operating on the inefficient downward-sloping portion of the Laffer curve in both 1981 and 2001, then we should be able to find evidence in the data that

federal income tax revenues increased following the enactment of each of the tax cut bills discussed above. Figure 5.20 shows the ratio of federal personal tax revenue (including income tax revenue) to GDP from 1947 to 2009, in percentage terms. There are two important factors that will have a bearing on our explanation of what we see in the figure, in addition to changes in income tax rates. First, total income tax revenue as a percentage of GDP will tend to increase in booms and decrease in recessions, because as average income increases the average tax rate increases due to the progressive income tax. Second, federal personal tax revenue includes capital gains taxes along with income tax revenue. Therefore, when stock prices increase at a high rate, the quantity in Figure 5.20 will tend to increase as stockholders realize higher capital gains.

In Figure 5.20, note first that there is a temporary reduction in federal personal taxes relative to GDP during the 1973–1974 recession. Tax revenues then rise, and fall again during the 1981–1982 recession, but in spite of the recovery from the recession and robust economic growth during the 1980s, tax revenue remains low, falling during the 1990–1991 recession. Then, after the 1991–1992 recession, the rapid growth in GDP and unusually high rate of growth in stock market prices in the United States cause an increase in tax revenues until the decline in the stock prices in 2000 and the recession of 2001. After 2000, personal taxes fall from over 10% of GDP to about 6.5% of GDP and subsequently recover only to the levels seen in the 1980s. This evidence appears to be consistent with the U.S. economy being on the good side of the Laffer curve, where a decrease in income tax rates will cause a decrease in tax revenue. The fact that tax revenues did not recover after either the 1981–1982 recession, or after the 2001 recession, is consistent with the reductions in tax rates in 1981 and 2001 causing substantial decreases in tax revenues for the federal government.

---

[4]See http://en.wikipedia.org/wiki/Kemp-Roth_Tax_Cut

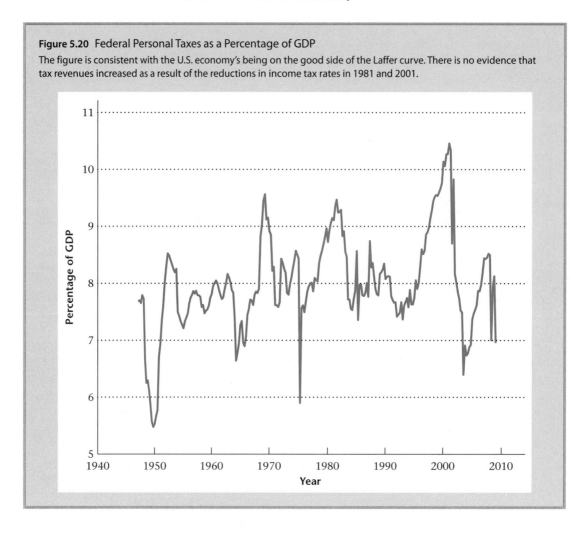

Figure 5.20 Federal Personal Taxes as a Percentage of GDP

The figure is consistent with the U.S. economy's being on the good side of the Laffer curve. There is no evidence that tax revenues increased as a result of the reductions in income tax rates in 1981 and 2001.

Now that we have gained some knowledge from a one-period model concerning how the macroeconomy functions, we can move on in Part III to study the causes and consequences of economic growth.

Chapter Summary

- In this chapter, we took the consumer behavior and firm behavior developed in Chapter 4, added government behavior, and constructed a complete one-period macroeconomic model.
- In a competitive equilibrium, the actions of the representative consumer, the representative firm, and the government must be mutually consistent, which implies that the market on which labor is exchanged for goods must clear, and the government budget constraint must hold.

- In a competitive equilibrium, aggregate output, consumption, employment, taxes, and the real wage (the endogenous variables) are determined given the capital stock, total factor productivity, and government spending (the exogenous variables).

- A competitive equilibrium can be represented in a single diagram, and this diagram was used to illustrate the equivalence between the competitive equilibrium and the Pareto optimum, which is an economically efficient state of affairs.

- The model shows how an increase in government spending has a pure negative income effect on the representative consumer, so that employment increases and consumption decreases. Government spending thus crowds out private consumption, but not completely, as there is an increase in aggregate output.

- An increase in total factor productivity, which may arise from improved technology, leads to an increase in output, consumption, and the real wage, but employment may increase or decrease due to opposing income and substitution effects.

- With a distorting tax on wage income, the incentive effects of tax rate changes have important incentive effects on labor supply. These incentive effects produce a Laffer curve, and it is possible that, for high tax rates, increases in the tax rate cause a reduction in tax revenue for the government.

Key Terms

Closed economy An economy that does not trade with the rest of the world.(p. 146)

Competitive equilibrium A state of the economy where prices and quantities are such that the behavior of price-taking consumers and firms is consistent. (p. 148)

Crowding out The displacement of private expenditures by government purchases.(p. 162)

Distorting tax A tax, such as an income tax, that creates a difference between the effective prices faced by buyers and sellers of some good.(p. 157)

Endogenous variable A variable that the model determines.(p. 147)

Exogenous variable A variable determined outside the model.(p. 147)

Externality The effect an action taken by an economic agent has on another economic agent or agents, where the agent performing the action does not take into account this effect on others.(p. 157)

First fundamental theorem of welfare economics (or first welfare theorem) Result stating that, under certain conditions, a competitive equilibrium is Pareto optimal.(p. 156)

Fiscal policy The government's choices over government expenditures, taxes, transfers, and government borrowing.(p. 147)

Government budget constraint An equation describing the sources and uses of government revenues. (p. 147)

Intertemporal substitution of labor The substitution of labor over time by a worker in response to movements in real wages.(p. 168)

Laffer curve The relationship between the tax revenue collected by the government and the tax rate.(p. 180)

Long run Typically describes macroeconomic effects that occur beyond a year's time.(p. 164)

Marginal rate of transformation Minus the slope of the *PPF*, or the rate at which one good in the economy can be technologically exchanged for another.(p. 152)

Market clearing When supply equals demand in a particular market or markets.

Open economy An economy that engages in trade with the rest of the world.(p. 146)

Pareto optimality A state of the economy that cannot be improved on by making one consumer better off without making another worse off.(p. 154)

Production possibilities frontier (*PPF*) The boundary of a set that describes what consumption bundles are technologically feasible to produce.(p. 152)

Public goods Goods that are difficult or impossible for the private sector to provide, for example, national defense.(p. 147)

Real business cycle theory A theory postulating that the primary cause of aggregate fluctuations is fluctuations in total factor productivity. (p. 168)

Second fundamental theorem of welfare economics (or second welfare theorem) Result stating that, under certain conditions, a Pareto optimum is a competitive equilibrium.(p. 156)

Short run Typically describes macroeconomic effects that occur within a year's time.(p. 164)

Supply-side economists Economists who argue that there are large incentive effects from income taxation, so that a decrease in the income tax rate will cause a very large increase in the quantity of labor supplied.(p. 182)

Tax base The quantity that is subject to a particular tax. For example, the tax base for the tax on labor income is the quantity of labor supplied.(p. 179)

Questions for Review

1. Why is it useful to study a closed-economy model?
2. What is the role of the government in the one-period, closed-economy model?
3. Can the government run a deficit in the one-period model? Why or why not?
4. What are the endogenous variables in the model?
5. What are the exogenous variables in the model?
6. What are the four conditions that a competitive equilibrium must satisfy for this model?
7. What is the economic significance of the slope of the production possibilities frontier?
8. Why is the competitive equilibrium in this model Pareto optimal?
9. Explain the difference between the first and second welfare theorems. Why is each useful?
10. Give three reasons that an equilibrium might not be Pareto optimal.
11. What are the effects of an increase in government purchases?
12. Why does government spending crowd out government purchases?
13. What are the equilibrium effects of an increase in total factor productivity?
14. Explain why employment may rise or fall in response to an increase in total factor productivity.
15. Why does a distorting tax on labor income lead to an inefficient economic outcome?
16. How are the incentive effects of income taxation important for the Laffer curve?
17. Explain what happens when the economy is on the bad side of the Laffer curve and the income tax rate falls.

Problems

All questions refer to the macroeconomic model developed in this chapter.

1. Many negative externalities exist in cities. For example, a high concentration of automobile traffic in cities generates pollution and causes congestion, and both pollution and congestion are negative externalities. When a particular person decides to drive a car in a city on a given day, he or she does not take into account the negative effects that driving his or her car has in terms of pollution and deterring other drivers from reaching their destinations (congestion). Although negative externalities (including pollution and congestion) appear to abound in cities, people still prefer to live in cities (otherwise, they would not exist). In economic terms, discuss the forces that cause people to prefer life in the city. How do these forces relate to whether or not market outcomes are economically efficient?

2. Suppose that the government decides to reduce taxes. In the model used in this chapter, determine the effects this has on aggregate output, consumption, employment, and the real wage and explain your results.

3. Suppose that there is a natural disaster that destroys part of the nation's capital stock.
   (a) Determine the effects on aggregate output, consumption, employment, and the real wage, with reference to income and substitution effects, and explain your results.
   (b) Do you think that changes in the capital stock are a likely cause of business cycles? Explain, with reference to your answer to part (a) and the key business cycle facts described in Chapter 3.

4. Suppose that total factor productivity, z, affects the productivity of government production just as it affects private production. That is, suppose that when the government collects taxes, that it acquires goods that are then turned into government-produced goods according to $G = zT$ so that z units of government goods are produced for each unit of taxes collected. With the government setting G, an increase in z implies that a smaller quantity of taxes are required to finance the given quantity of government purchases G. Under these circumstances, using a diagram determine the effects of an increase in z on output, consumption, employment, and the real wage, treating G as given. Explain your results.

5. Suppose that the representative consumer's preferences change, in that his or her marginal rate of substitution of leisure for consumption increases for any quantities of consumption and leisure.
   (a) Explain what this change in preferences means in more intuitive language.
   (b) What effects does this have on the equilibrium real wage, hours worked, output, and consumption?
   (c) Do you think that preference shifts like this might explain why economies experience recessions (periods when output is low)? Explain why or why not, with reference to the key business cycle facts in Chapter 3.

6. Since 1973, military service in the United States has been voluntary. In this question, use the one-period model in this chapter to evaluate the macroeconomic effects of conscription relative to a voluntary military service. Assume that the government needs a hours of the representative consumer's time in order to run the armed services, where $a < h$.
   (a) Suppose that the government chooses conscription. That is, the government forces the representative consumer to supply a units of time to the government as military service, in exchange for $\bar{c}$ units of goods. The government finances the payment for military service $\bar{c}$ with a lump-sum tax. Use a diagram to show the effects of conscription on aggregate consumption, the real wage, leisure, employment, and aggregate output.
   (b) Now, suppose alternatively that the government chooses to make military service voluntary. As in part (a), the government needs a units of the representative consumer's time to run the military, but must now purchase this time at the going market real wage. Assume that the government uses lump-sum taxation to fund the wage payments for military service. Again, use a diagram to show the effects on aggregate consumption, the real wage, leisure, employment, and aggregate output.
   (c) Compare your results in parts (a) and (b). Is the representative consumer better off with conscription or voluntary military service? Explain your results.
   (d) Are there factors that you think are left out of our one-period model that you think are important for the problem at hand? If so, what, and how might including these factors change your answer?

7. Suppose that government spending makes private firms more productive; for example, government spending on roads and bridges lowers the cost of transportation. This means that there are now two effects of government spending, the first being the effects discussed in this chapter of an increase in G and the second being similar to the effects of an increase in the nation's capital stock K.
   (a) Show that an increase in government spending that is productive in this fashion could increase welfare for the representative consumer.

(b) Show that the equilibrium effects on consumption and hours worked of an increase in government spending of this type are ambiguous but that output increases. You must consider income and substitution effects to show this.

8. In the one-period model, education can be represented as time spent by the representative consumer that is neither leisure time applied to producing output. What the economy gains in the future is that the representative consumer then has more time available, as measured in terms of effective units of labor time (adjusted for skill level, or what economists call human capital).

   (a) Using the one-period model, show what effects additional education has in the present on consumption, leisure, employment, aggregate output, and the real wage.

   (b) Similarly, show the effects the additional education that people acquire today will have in the future on consumption, leisure, employment, aggregate output, and the real wage.

(c) What does your analysis in parts (a) and (b) have to say about the trade-offs society makes between the present and the future in investing in education?

9. In the simplified model with proportional taxation there can be two equilibria, one with a high tax rate and one with a low tax rate. Now, suppose that government spending increases. Determine the effects of an increase in G on consumption, leisure, labor supply, real output, and the tax rate in a high-tax-rate equilibrium and in a low-tax-rate equilibrium. How do your results differ? Explain why.

10. Suppose that the substitution effect of an increase in the real wage is always larger than the income effect for the representative consumer. Also assume that the economy is always in the low-tax-rate equilibrium on the good side of the Laffer curve. Determine the effects of an increase in total factor productivity, z, on the Laffer curve, on the equilibrium tax rate, and on consumption, leisure, the quantity of labor supplied, and output.

Working with the Data

1. Calculate and plot the annual percentage growth rates in real GDP and in total real government purchases from 1948 to 2009. Calculate these growth rates from quarterly data, as percentage growth rates from four quarters previous.

   (a) Does there appear to be any relationship between the growth rates in GDP and in government purchases?

   (b) What does your answer to part (a) tell you about the role in business cycles of fluctuations in government purchases?

2. Calculate the real wage as the employment cost index divided by the consumer price index. With reference to Figure 5.11, do fluctuations in the real wage about trend appear to be consistent with the notion that shocks to total factor productivity are the primary cause of business cycles?

PART III

Economic Growth

In this part, we study the primary facts of economic growth and the key macroeconomic models that economists have used to understand these facts. In Chapter 6, we first examine the Malthusian model of economic growth, in which population growth increases with the standard of living. Any improvement in the technology for producing goods leads to more population growth, and in the long run there is no improvement in the standard of living. The Malthusian model does a good job of explaining economic growth in the world prior to the Industrial Revolution in the nineteenth century, but it cannot explain growth experience after 1800. What Malthus did not envision was the role of capital accumulation in economic growth. Capital accumulation plays an important role in the Solow model of economic growth, which is the preeminent framework used in modern economic growth theory. The Solow growth model predicts that long-run improvements in the standard of living are generated by technological progress, that countries with high (low) savings rates tend to have high (low) levels of per-capita income, and that countries with high (low) rates of population growth tend to have low (high) levels of per capita income. The Solow growth model gives much more optimistic implications than does the Malthusian model concerning the prospects for improvements in the standard of living. Finally, in Chapter 6 we study growth accounting, an approach to attributing economic growth to growth in factors of production and in productivity.

In Chapter 7, we first study the predictions of the Solow growth model for convergence in standards of living across countries. In the data, there is a tendency for convergence in per-capita incomes among the richest countries in the world, but apparently no tendency for convergence among all countries. The Solow model is consistent with this if we allow for differences in the adoption of technology across countries, or differences in the efficiency with which factors of production are allocated across firms in individual economies. Next in Chapter 7, we examine an endogenous growth model, which allows us to analyze the determinants of the rate of economic growth. This endogenous growth model has the property that differences in standards of living persist across countries and that education is an important factor in determining the rate of economic growth.

chapter 6

Economic Growth: Malthus and Solow

The two primary phenomena that macroeconomists study are business cycles and economic growth. Although much macroeconomic research focuses on business cycles, the study of economic growth has also received a good deal of attention, especially since the late 1980s. Robert Lucas[1] has argued that the potential social gains from a greater understanding of business cycles are dwarfed by the gains from understanding growth. This is because, even if (most optimistically) business cycles could be completely eliminated, the worst events we would be able to avoid would be reductions of real GDP below trend on the order of 5%, based on post–World War II U.S. data. However, if changes in economic policy could cause the growth rate of real GDP to increase by 1% per year for 100 years, then GDP would be 2.7 times higher after 100 years than it would otherwise have been.

The effects of economic growth have been phenomenal. Per-capita U.S. income in 2008 was $46,178,[2] but before the Industrial Revolution in the early nineteenth century, per-capita U.S. income was only several hundred 2008 dollars. In fact, before 1800 the standard of living differed little over time and across countries. Since the Industrial Revolution, however, economic growth has not been uniform across countries, and there are currently wide disparities in standards of living among the countries of the world. In 2000, income per capita in Mexico was 23.5% of what it was in the United States, in Egypt it was 13.2% of that in the United States, and in Burundi it was about 2.0% of the U.S. figure. Currently, there also exist large differences in rates of growth across countries. Between 1960 and 2000, while real income per capita was growing at an average rate of 2.48% in the United States, the comparable figure for Madagascar was −1.07%, for Nicaragua it was −0.03%, for Hong Kong it was 5.40%, and for Taiwan it was 6.68%.[3]

---

[1]See R. Lucas, 1987, *Models of Business Cycles,* Basil Blackwell, Oxford, UK.

[2]Source: Bureau of Economic Analysis, Department of Commerce.

[3]The income-per-capita statistics come for A. Heston, R. Summers, and B. Aten, *Penn World Table Version 6.2,* Center for International Comparisons at the University of Pennsylvania (CICUP), September 2006, available at pwt.econ.upenn.edu.

In this chapter we first discuss some basic economic growth facts, and this provides a useful context in which to organize our thinking using some standard models of growth. The first model we study formalizes the ideas of Thomas Malthus, who wrote in the late eighteenth century. This Malthusian model has the property that any improvement in the technology for producing goods leads to increased population growth, so that in the long run there is no improvement in the standard of living. The population is sufficiently higher that there is no increase in per-capita consumption and per-capita output. Consistent with the conclusions of Malthus, the model predicts that the only means for improving the standard of living is population control.

The Malthusian model yields quite pessimistic predictions concerning the prospects for long-run growth in per-capita incomes. Of course, the predictions of Malthus were wrong, as he did not foresee the Industrial Revolution. After the Industrial Revolution, economic growth was in part driven by growth in the stock of capital over time and was not limited by fixed factors of production (such as land), as in the Malthusian model.

Next, we study the Solow growth model, which is the most widely used model of economic growth, developed by Robert Solow in the 1950s.[4] The Solow growth model makes important predictions concerning the effects of savings rates, population growth, and changes in total factor productivity on a nation's standard of living and growth rate of GDP. We show that these predictions match economic data quite well.

A key implication of the Solow growth model is that a country's standard of living cannot continue to improve in the long run in the absence of continuing increases in total factor productivity. In the short run, the standard of living can improve if a country's residents save and invest more, thus accumulating more capital. However, the Solow growth model tells us that building more productive capacity will not improve long-run living standards unless the production technology becomes more efficient. The Solow model therefore implies more optimistic prospects for long-run improvement in the standard of living than is the case for the Malthusian model, but only to a point. The Solow model tells us that improvements in knowledge and technical ability are necessary to sustain growth.

The Solow growth model is an **exogenous growth model,** in that growth is caused in the model by forces that are not explained by the model itself. To gain a deeper understanding of economic growth, it is useful to examine the economic factors that cause growth, and this is done in **endogenous growth models,** one of which we examine in Chapter 7.

Finally, in this chapter we study growth accounting, which is an approach to attributing the growth in GDP to growth in factor inputs and in total factor productivity. Growth accounting can highlight interesting features of the data, such as the slowdown in productivity growth that occurred in the United States from the late 1960s to the early 1980s and the rebound in productivity growth in the 1980s and 1990s.

---

[4]See R. Solow, 1956, "A Contribution to the Theory of Economic Growth," *Quarterly Journal of Economics* 70, 65–94.

Economic Growth Facts

Before proceeding to construct and analyze models of economic growth, we summarize the key empirical regularities relating to growth within and across countries. This gives us a framework for evaluating our models and helps in organizing our thinking about growth. The important growth facts are the following:

1. *Before the Industrial Revolution in about 1800, standards of living differed little over time and across countries.*   There appeared to have been essentially no improvement in standards of living for a long period of time prior to 1800. Although population and aggregate income grew, with growth sometimes interrupted by disease and wars, population growth kept up with growth in aggregate income, so that there was little change in per capita real income. Living standards did not vary much across the countries of the world. In particular, Western Europe and Asia had similar standards of living.

2. *Since the Industrial Revolution, per capita income growth has been sustained in the richest countries. In the United States, average annual growth in per capita income has been about 2% since 1900.*   The Industrial Revolution began about 1800 in the United Kingdom, and the United States eventually surpassed the United Kingdom as the world industrial leader. Figure 6.1 shows the natural logarithm of per capita income in the United States for the years 1900–2008. Recall from Chapter 1 that the slope of the natural log of a time series is approximately equal to the growth rate. What is remarkable about the figure is that a straight line would be a fairly good fit to the natural log of per capita income in the United States over this period of 108 years. That is, average per capita income growth in the United States has not strayed far from an average growth rate of about 2% per year for the whole period, except for major interruptions like the Great Depression (1929–1939) and World War II (1941–1945) and the minor variability introduced by business cycles.

3. *There is a positive correlation between the rate of investment and output per worker across countries.*   In Figure 6.2 we show a scatter plot of output per worker (as a percentage of output per worker in the United States) versus the rate of investment (as a percentage of aggregate output) in the countries of the world in 2000. Clearly, a straight line fit to these points would have a positive slope, so the two variables are positively correlated. Thus, countries in which a relatively large (small) fraction of output is channeled into investment tend to have a relatively high (low) standard of living. This fact is particularly important in checking the predictions of the Solow growth model against the data.

4. *There is a negative correlation between the population growth rate and output per worker across countries.*   Figure 6.3 shows a scatter plot of output per worker (as a percentage of output per worker in the United States) versus the average annual population growth rate for 1960–2000 for the countries of the world. Here, a straight line fit to the points in the figure would have a negative slope, so the two variables are negatively correlated. Countries with high (low) population growth rates tend to have low (high) standards of living. As with the previous fact, this one is important in matching the predictions of the Solow growth model with the data.

5. *Differences in per capita incomes increased dramatically among countries of the world between 1800 and 1950, with the gap widening between the countries of Western Europe,*

Figure 6.1 Natural Logarithm of Per Capita Real GDP

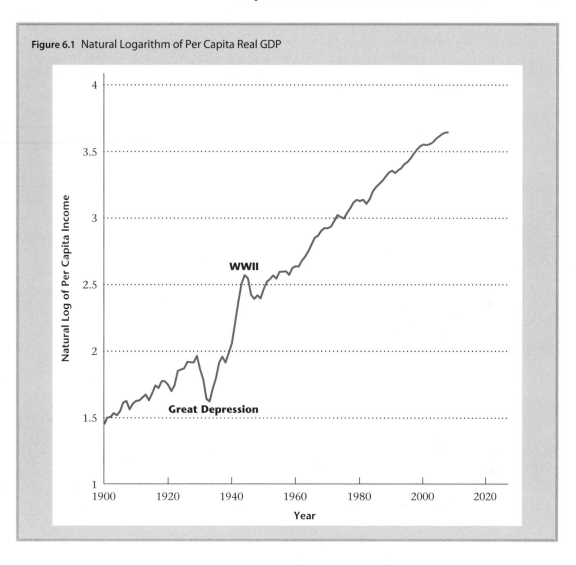

the United States, Canada, Australia, and New Zealand, as a group, and the rest of the world. A question that interests us in this chapter and the next is whether standards of living are converging across countries of the world. The Industrial Revolution spread in the early nineteenth century from the United Kingdom to Western Europe and the United States, then to the new countries of Canada, Australia, and New Zealand. The countries of Africa, Asia, and South America were mainly left behind, with some Asian (and to some extent South American) countries closing the gap with the rich countries later in the twentieth century. Between 1800 and 1950, there was a divergence between living standards in the richest and poorest countries of the world.[5]

---

[5]See S. Parente and E. Prescott, 2000. *Barriers to Riches*, MIT Press, Cambridge, MA.

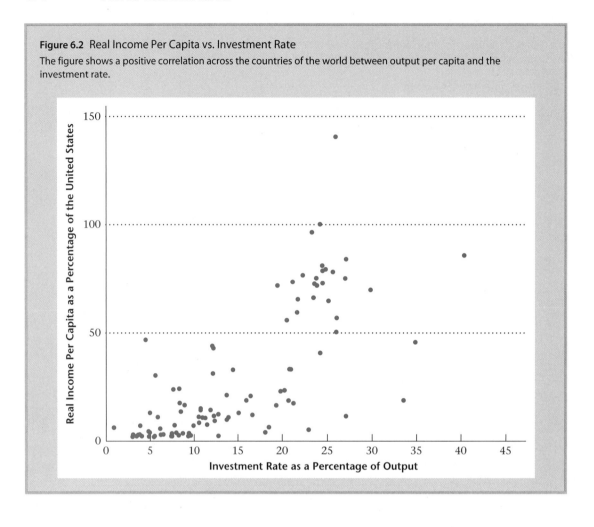

Figure 6.2 Real Income Per Capita vs. Investment Rate

The figure shows a positive correlation across the countries of the world between output per capita and the investment rate.

6. *There is essentially no correlation across countries between the level of output per worker in 1960 and the average rate of growth in output per worker for the years 1960–2000.* Standards of living would be converging across countries if income (output) per worker were converging to a common value. For this to happen, it would have to be the case that poor countries (those with low levels of income per worker) are growing at a higher rate than are rich countries (those with high levels of income per worker). Thus, if convergence in incomes per worker is occurring, we should observe a negative correlation between the growth rate in income per worker and the level of income per worker across countries. Figure 6.4 looks at data for 1960–2000, the period for which good data exists for most of the countries in the world. The figure shows the average rate of growth in output per worker for the period 1960 to 2000, versus the level of output per worker (as a percentage of output per worker in the United States) in 1960 for a set of 99 countries. There is essentially no correlation shown in the figure, which indicates that, for all countries of the world, convergence is not detectable for this period.

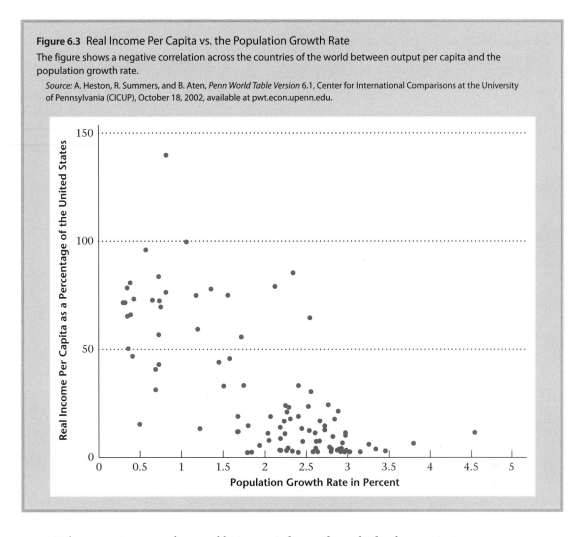

Figure 6.3 Real Income Per Capita vs. the Population Growth Rate

The figure shows a negative correlation across the countries of the world between output per capita and the population growth rate.

Source: A. Heston, R. Summers, and B. Aten, *Penn World Table Version* 6.1, Center for International Comparisons at the University of Pennsylvania (CICUP), October 18, 2002, available at pwt.econ.upenn.edu.

7. *Richer countries are much more alike in terms of rates of growth of real per capita income than are poor countries.*   In Figure 6.4, we observe that there is a much wider vertical scatter in the points on the left-hand part of the scatter plot than on the right-hand side. That is, the variability in the real income growth rates is much smaller for rich countries than for poor countries.

In this chapter and Chapter 7, we use growth facts 1 to 7 to motivate the structure of our models and as checks on the predictions of those models.

The Malthusian Model of Economic Growth

In 1798, Thomas Malthus, a political economist in England, wrote the highly influential *An Essay on the Principle of Population*.[6] Malthus did not construct a formal economic

---

[6]See Malthus, T. 1798. "An Essay on the Principle of Population," St. Paul's Church-Yard, London, available at http://www.ac.wwu.edu/~stephan/malthus/malthus.0.html.

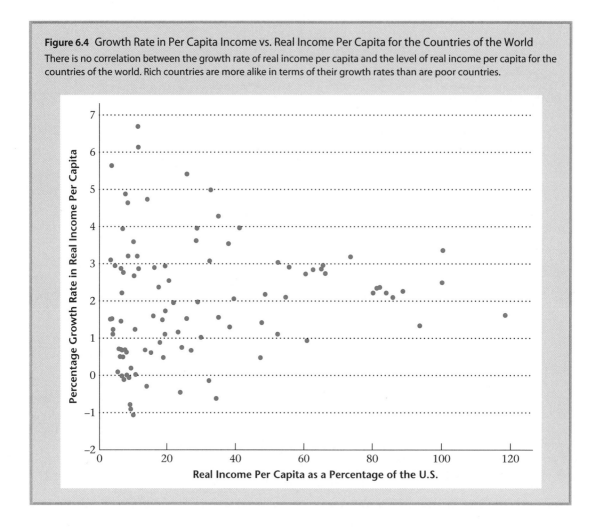

Figure 6.4 Growth Rate in Per Capita Income vs. Real Income Per Capita for the Countries of the World

There is no correlation between the growth rate of real income per capita and the level of real income per capita for the countries of the world. Rich countries are more alike in terms of their growth rates than are poor countries.

model of the type that we would use in modern economic arguments, but his ideas are clearly stated and coherent and can be easily translated into a structure that is easy to understand.

Malthus argued that any advances in the technology for producing food would inevitably lead to further population growth, with the higher population ultimately reducing the average person to the subsistence level of consumption he or she had before the advance in technology. The population and level of aggregate consumption could grow over time, but in the long run there would be no increase in the standard of living unless there were some limits on population growth. Malthusian theory is, therefore, very pessimistic about the prospects for increases in the standard of living, with collective intervention in the form of forced family planning required to bring about gains in per capita income.

The following model formalizes Malthusian theory. The model is a dynamic one with many periods, although for most of the analysis we confine attention to what happens in the *current period* and the *future period* (the period following the current period). We start with an aggregate production function that specifies how current aggregate output, Y, is produced using current inputs of land, L, and current labor, N, that is

$$Y = zF(L, N), \tag{6-1}$$

where z is total factor productivity, and F is a function having the same properties, including constant returns to scale, that we specified in Chapter 4, except here land replaces capital in the production function. It helps to think of Y as being food, which is perishable from period to period. In this economy there is no investment (and, therefore, no saving—recall from Chapter 2 that savings equals investment in a closed economy) as we assume there is no way to store food from one period to the next and no technology for converting food into capital. For simplicity, there is assumed to be no government spending. Land, L, is in fixed supply. That is, as was the case in Western Europe in 1798, essentially all of the land that could potentially be used for agriculture is under cultivation. Assume that each person in this economy is willing to work at any wage and has one unit of labor to supply (a normalization), so that N in Equation (6-1) is both the population and the labor input.

If we let N' denote the population next period, then

$$N' = N + \text{Births} - \text{Deaths}.$$

or

$$N' = N + N(\text{birth rate} - \text{death rate}), \tag{6-2}$$

where the birth rate is the ratio of births to population, and the death rate is the ratio of deaths to population. Now, particularly before the Industrial Revolution, it is natural that the birth rate would be an increasing function of consumption per capita, $\frac{C}{N}$, which is a measure of nutrition, with C denoting aggregate consumption. As consumption per person rises, and nutrition improves, people will have more children by choice, as they are then better able to provide for children, and better nutrition also increases fertility. Similarly, the death rate is a decreasing function of $\frac{C}{N}$, because better nutrition decreases infant mortality, and generally makes the population more healthy, thus increasing the average lifespan. This implies that we can write equation (6-2) (after dividing both sides by N) as

$$\frac{N'}{N} = g\left(\frac{C}{N}\right), \tag{6-3}$$

where g is an increasing function. Note that $\frac{N'}{N}$ in equation (6-3) is one plus the population growth rate. We show the relationship described by Equation (6-3) in Figure 6.5.

In equilibrium, all goods produced are consumed, so $C = Y$, which is the income-expenditure identity for this economy (because $I = G = NX = 0$ here; see Chapter 2). Therefore, substituting C for Y in Equation (6-3), in equilibrium we have

$$C = zF(L, N). \tag{6-4}$$

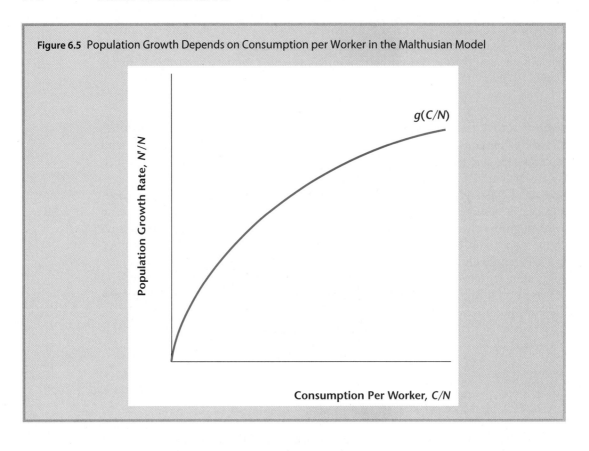

Figure 6.5 Population Growth Depends on Consumption per Worker in the Malthusian Model

(Vertical axis: Population Growth Rate, N'/N; *horizontal axis:* Consumption Per Worker, C/N; *curve labeled* $g(C/N)$*.)*

We can then use Equation (6-4) to substitute for C in Equation (6-3) to get

$$\frac{N'}{N} = g\left(\frac{zF(L, N)}{N}\right). \tag{6-5}$$

Now, recall from Chapter 4 that the constant-returns-to-scale property of the production function implies that

$$xzF(L, N) = zF(xL, xN)$$

for any $x > 0$, so if $x = \frac{1}{N}$ in the above equation, then

$$\frac{zF(L, N)}{N} = zF\left(\frac{L}{N}, 1\right).$$

As a result, we can rewrite Equation (6-5), after multiplying each side by N, as

$$N' = g\left[zF\left(\frac{L}{N}, 1\right)\right]N. \tag{6-6}$$

Here, Equation (6-6) tells us how the population evolves over time in equilibrium, as it gives the future population as a function of the current population. We assume that the relationship described in Equation (6-6) can be depicted as in Figure 6.6.[7] In the figure N^* is a rest point or **steady state** for the population, determined by the point where the curve intersects the 45° line. If the current population is N^*, then the future population is N^*, and the population is N^* forever after. In the figure, if $N < N^*$ then $N' > N$ and the population increases, whereas if $N > N^*$, then $N' < N$ and the population decreases. Thus, whatever the population is currently, it eventually comes to rest at N^* in the long run. That is, the steady state N^* is the long-run equilibrium for the population.

The reason that population converges to a steady state is the following. Suppose, on the one hand, that the population is currently below its steady state value. Then there will be a relatively large quantity of consumption per worker, and this will imply that the population growth rate is relatively large and positive, and the population will

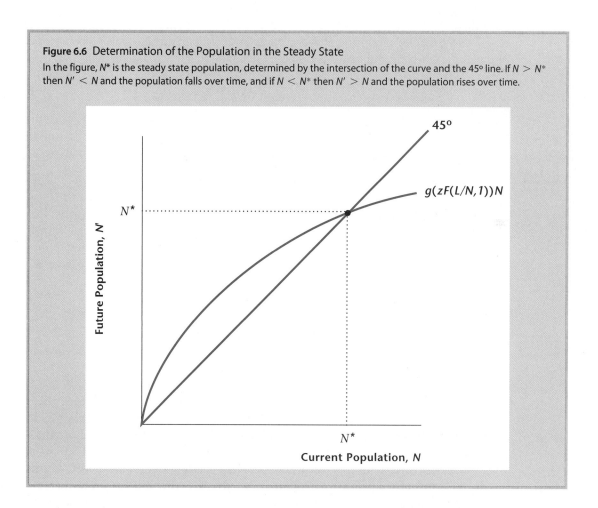

Figure 6.6 Determination of the Population in the Steady State

In the figure, N^* is the steady state population, determined by the intersection of the curve and the 45° line. If $N > N^*$ then $N' < N$ and the population falls over time, and if $N < N^*$ then $N' > N$ and the population rises over time.

[7]For example, if $F(L, N) = L^\alpha N^{1-\alpha}$ and $g\left(\frac{C}{N}\right) = \left(\frac{C}{N}\right)^\gamma$, with $0 < \alpha < 1$ and $0 < \gamma < 1$, we get these properties.

increase. On the other hand, suppose that the population is above its steady state value. Then there will be a small quantity of consumption per worker, and the population growth rate will be relatively low and negative, so that the population will decrease.

Because the quantity of land is fixed, when the population converges to the long-run equilibrium N^*, aggregate consumption (equal to aggregate output here) converges, from Equation (6-4), to

$$C^* = zF(L, N^*).$$

Analysis of the Steady State in the Malthusian Model

Because the Malthusian economy converges to a long-run steady state equilibrium with constant population and constant aggregate consumption, it is useful to analyze this steady state to determine what features of the environment affect steady state variables. In this subsection, we show how this type of analysis is done.

Given that the production function F has the constant returns to scale property, if we divide the left-hand and right-hand sides of Equation (6-1) by N and rearrange, we get

$$\frac{Y}{N} = zF\left(\frac{L}{N}, 1\right).$$

Then letting lower-case letters denote per-worker quantities, that is $y \equiv \frac{Y}{N}$ (output per worker), $l \equiv \frac{L}{N}$ (land per worker), and $c \equiv \frac{C}{N}$ (consumption per worker), we have

$$y = zf(l), \tag{6-7}$$

where $zf(l)$ is the **per-worker production function**, which describes the quantity of output per worker y that can be produced for each quantity of land per worker l, with the function f defined by $f(l) \equiv F(l, 1)$. The per-worker production function is displayed in Figure 6.7. Then, as $c = y$ in equilibrium, from Equation (6-7) we have

$$c = zf(l) \tag{6-8}$$

We can also rewrite Equation (6-3) as

$$\frac{N'}{N} = g(c). \tag{6-9}$$

Now, we can display Equations (6-8) and (6-9) in Figure 6.8. In the steady state, $N' = N = N^*$, so $\frac{N'}{N} = 1$, and in panel (b) of the figure this determines c^*, the steady state quantity of consumption per worker. Then, in panel (a) of the figure, c^* determines the steady state quantity of land per worker, l^*. Because the quantity of land is fixed at L, we can then determine the steady state population as $N^* = \frac{L}{l^*}$. In the model, we can take the standard of living as being given by steady state consumption per worker, c^*. Therefore, the long-run standard of living is determined entirely by the function g,

Figure 6.7 The Per-Worker Production Function

This describes the relationship between output per worker and land per worker in the Malthusian model, assuming constant returns to scale.

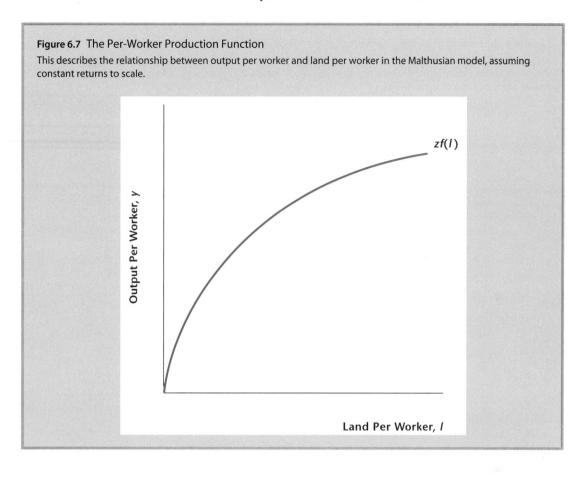

which captures the effect of the standard of living on population growth. The key property of the model is that nothing in panel (a) of Figure 6.8 affects c^*, so that improvements in the production technology or increases in the quantity of land have no effect on the long-run standard of living.

The Effects of an Increase in z on the Steady State   We now consider an experiment in which total factor productivity increases, which we can interpret as an improvement in agricultural techniques. That is, suppose that the economy is initially in a steady state, with a given level of total factor productivity z_1, which then increases once and for all time to z_2. The steady state effects are shown in Figure 6.9. In panel (a) of the figure, the per-worker production function shifts up from $z_1 f(l)$ to $z_2 f(l)$. This has no effect on steady state consumption per worker c^*, which is determined in panel (b) of the figure. In the new steady state, in panel (a) the quantity of land per worker falls from l_1^* to l_2^*. This implies that the steady state population increases from $N_1^* = \frac{L}{l_1^*}$ to $N_2^* = \frac{L}{l_2^*}$.

Figure 6.8 Determination of the Steady State in the Malthusian Model

In panel (b), steady state consumption per worker c^* is determined as the level of consumption per worker that implies no population growth. Given c^*, the quantity of land per worker in the steady state l^* is determined from the per-worker production function in panel (a).

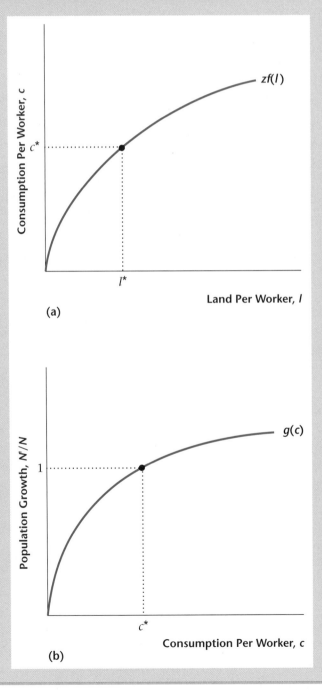

Figure 6.9 The Effect of an Increase in z in the Malthusian Model

When z increases, land per worker decreases in the steady state (so the population increases) and consumption per worker remains the same.

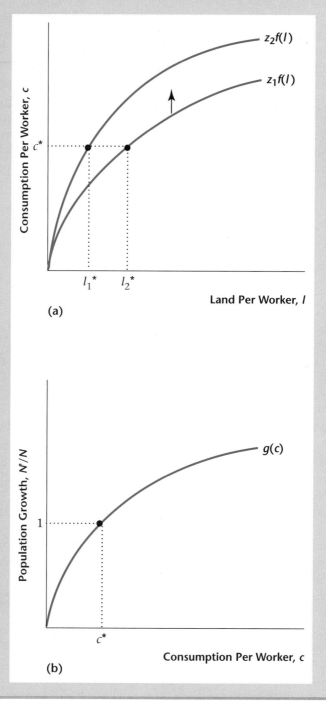

The economy does not move to the new steady state instantaneously, as it takes time for the population and consumption to adjust. Figure 6.10 shows how the adjustment takes place in terms of the paths of consumption per worker and population. The economy is in a steady state before time T, at which time there is an increase in total factor productivity. Initially, the effect of this is to increase output, consumption, and consumption per worker, as there is no effect on the current population at time T. However, because consumption per worker has increased, there is an increase in population growth. As the population grows after period T, in panel (b) of the figure, consumption per worker falls (given the fixed quantity of land), until consumption per worker converges to c^*, its initial level, and the population converges to its new higher level N_2^*.

This then gives the pessimistic Malthusian result that improvements in the technology for producing food do not improve the standard of living in the long run. A better technology generates better nutrition and more population growth, and the extra population ultimately consumes all of the extra food produced, so that each person is no better off than before the technological improvement.

Population Control   How can society be better off in a Malthusian world? The prescription Malthus proposed was state-mandated population control. If the government were to institute something like the "one child only" policy introduced in China, this would have the effect of reducing the rate of population growth for each level of consumption per worker. In panel (b) of Figure 6.11, the function $g_1(c)$ shifts down to $g_2(c)$ as the result of the population control policy. In the steady state, consumption per worker increases from c_1^* to c_2^* in panel (b) of the figure, and this implies that the quantity of land per worker rises in the steady state in panel (a) from l_1^* to l_2^*. Because the quantity of land is fixed, the population falls in the steady state from $N_1^* = L/l_1^*$ to $N_2^* = L/l_2^*$. Here, a reduction in the size of the population increases output per worker and consumption per worker, and everyone is better off in the long run.

How Useful is the Malthusian Model of Economic Growth?

Given what was known in 1798, when Malthus wrote his essay, the Malthusian model could be judged to be quite successful. Our first economic growth fact, discussed at the beginning of this chapter, was that before the Industrial Revolution in about 1800, standards of living differed little over time and across countries. The Malthusian model predicts this, if population growth depends in the same way on consumption per worker across countries. Before the Industrial Revolution, production in the world was mainly agricultural; the population grew over time, as did aggregate production, but there appeared to have been no significant improvements in the average standard of living. This is all consistent with the Malthusian model.

As is well-known from the perspective of the early twenty-first century however, Malthus was far too pessimistic. There was sustained growth in standards of living in the richest countries of the world after 1800 without any significant government population control in place in the countries with the strongest performance. As well, the richest countries of the world have experienced a large drop in birth rates. Currently, in spite of advances in health care that have increased life expectancy dramatically in the richer countries, population in most of these richer countries would be declining without

Figure 6.10 Adjustment to the Steady State in the Malthusian Model When z Increases

In the figure, z increases at time T, which causes consumption per worker to increase and then decline to its steady state value over time, with the population increasing over time to its steady state value.

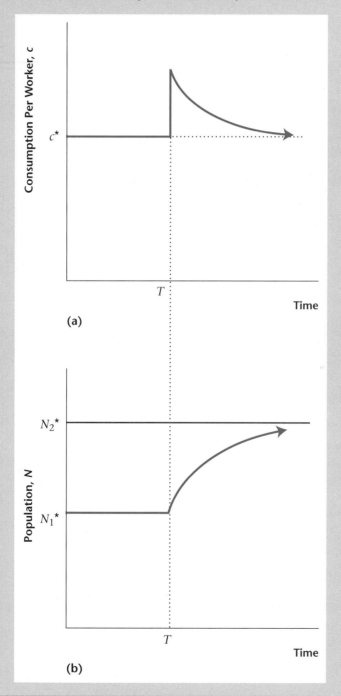

Figure 6.11 Population Control in the Malthusian Model

In the figure, population control policy shifts the function $g_1(c)$ to $g_2(c)$. In the steady state, consumption per worker increases and land per worker decreases (the population falls).

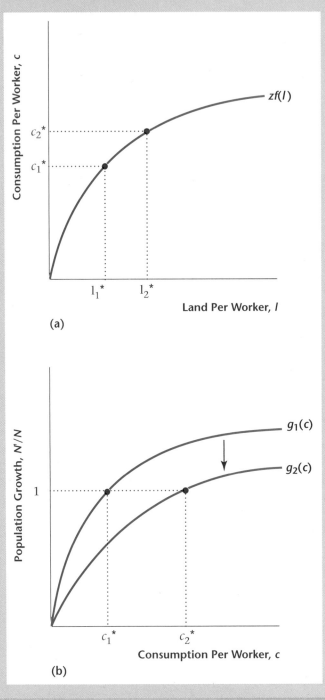

(a)

(b)

immigration. Thus, Malthus was ultimately wrong, both concerning the ability of economies to produce long-run improvements in the standard of living and the effect of the standard of living on population growth.

Why was Malthus wrong? First, he did not allow for the effect of increases in the capital stock on production. In contrast to land, which is limited in supply, there is no limit to the size of the capital stock, and having more capital implies that there is more productive capacity to produce additional capital. That is, capital can reproduce itself. The Solow growth model, which we develop later in this chapter, allows us to explore the role of capital accumulation in growth.

Second, Malthus did not account for all of the effects of economic forces on population growth. While it is clear that a higher standard of living reduces death rates through better nutrition and health care, there has also proved to be a reduction in birth rates. As the economy develops, there are better opportunities for working outside the home. In terms of family decisions, the opportunity cost of raising a large family becomes large in the face of high market wages, and more time is spent working in the market rather than raising children at home.

The Solow Model: Exogenous Growth

The Solow growth model is very simple, yet it makes sharp predictions concerning the sources of economic growth, what causes living standards to increase over time, what happens to the level and growth rate of aggregate income when the savings rate or the population growth rate rises, and what we should observe happening to relative living standards across countries over time. This model is much more optimistic about the prospects for long-run improvements in the standard of living than is the Malthusian model. Sustained increases in the standard of living can occur in the model, but sustained technological advances are necessary for this. As well, the Solow model does a good job of explaining the economic growth facts discussed early in this chapter.

In constructing this model, we begin with a description of the consumers who live in this environment and of the production technology. As with the Malthusian model, we treat dynamics seriously here. We study how this economy evolves over time in a competitive equilibrium, and a good part of our analysis concerns the steady state of the model which we know, from our analysis of the Malthusian model, is the long-run equilibrium or rest point.

Consumers

As in the Malthusian model, there are many periods, but we will analyze the economy in terms of the "current" and the "future" period. In contrast to the Malthusian model we suppose that the population grows exogenously. That is, there is a growing population of consumers, with N denoting the population in the current period. As in the Malthusian model, N also is the labor force, or the quantity of employment. The population grows over time, with

$$N' = (1 + n)N, \qquad (6\text{-}10)$$

where N' is the population in the future period and $n > -1$. Here, n is the rate of growth in the population, which is assumed to be constant over time. We are allowing for the possibility that $n < 0$, in which case the population would be shrinking over time.

In each period, a given consumer has one unit of time available, and we assume that consumers do not value leisure, so that they supply their one unit of time as labor in each period. In this model, the population is identical to the labor force, because we have assumed that all members of the population work. We then refer to N as the number of workers or the labor force and to n as the growth rate in the labor force.

Consumers collectively receive all current real output Y as income (through wage income and dividend income from firms), because there is no government sector and no taxes. In contrast to all of the models we have considered to this point, consumers here face a decision concerning how much of their current income to consume and how much to save. For simplicity, we assume that consumers consume a constant fraction of income in each period; that is,

$$C = (1 - s)Y, \tag{6-11}$$

where C is current consumption. For consumers, $C + S = Y$, where S is aggregate savings, so from Equation (6-11) we have $S = sY$ and s is then the aggregate savings rate. In Chapter 8 we discuss in more depth how consumers make their consumption–savings decisions.

The Representative Firm
Output is produced by a representative firm, according to the production function

$$Y = zF(K, N), \tag{6-12}$$

where Y is current output, z is current total factor productivity, K is the current capital stock, and N is the current labor input. The production function F has all of the properties that we studied in Chapter 4. As in the Malthusian model, constant returns to scale implies that, dividing both sides of equation (6-12) by N and rearranging, we get

$$\frac{Y}{N} = zF\left(\frac{K}{N}, 1\right). \tag{6-13}$$

In Equation (6-13), $\frac{Y}{N}$ is output per worker, and $\frac{K}{N}$ is capital per worker, and so (6-13) tells us that if the production function has constant returns to scale, then output per worker [on the left-hand side of (6-13)] depends only on the quantity of capital per worker [on the right-hand side of (6-13)]. For simplicity, as in the Malthusian model we can rewrite Equation (6-13) as

$$y = zf(k),$$

where y is output per worker, k is capital per worker, and $f(k)$ is the per-worker production function, which is defined by $f(k) \equiv F(k, 1)$. We use lowercase letters in what follows to refer to per-worker quantities. The per-worker production function is graphed in Figure 6.12. A key property of the per-worker production function is that its slope is the marginal product of capital, MP_K. This is because adding one unit to k, the quantity of capital per worker, increases y, output per worker, by the marginal product of capital, because $f(k) = F(k, 1)$. As the slope of the per-worker production function is MP_K, and because MP_K is diminishing with K, the per-worker production function in the figure is concave—that is, its slope decreases as k increases.

We suppose that some of the capital stock wears out through use each period. That is, there is depreciation, and we assume that the depreciation rate is a constant d, where $0 < d < 1$. Then, the capital stock changes over time according to

$$K' = (1 - d)K + I, \qquad (6\text{-}14)$$

where K' is the future capital stock, K is the current capital stock, and I is investment.

Competitive Equilibrium

Now that we have described the behavior of consumers and firms in the Solow growth model, we can put this behavior together and determine how consistency is achieved in a competitive equilibrium. In this economy, there are two markets in the current period. In the first market, current consumption goods are traded for current labor; in the second market, current consumption goods are traded for capital. That is, capital is the asset in this model, and consumers save by accumulating it. The labor market and

Figure 6.12 The Per-Worker Production Function

This function is the relationship between aggregate output per worker and capital per worker determined by the constant-returns-to-scale production function. The slope of the per-worker production function is the marginal product of capital, MP_K.

the capital market must clear in each period. In the labor market, the quantity of labor is always determined by the inelastic supply of labor, which is N. That is, because the supply of labor is N no matter what the real wage, the real wage adjusts in the current period so that the representative firm wishes to hire N workers. Letting S denote the aggregate quantity of saving in the current period, the capital market is in equilibrium in the current period if $S = I$, that is, if what consumers wish to save equals the quantity of investment. However, because $S = Y - C$ in this economy—that is, national savings is aggregate income minus consumption as there is no government—we can write the equilibrium condition as

$$Y = C + I, \tag{6-15}$$

or current output is equal to aggregate consumption plus aggregate investment. From equation (6-14) we have that $I = K' - (1 - d)K$, and so using this and equation (6-11) to substitute for C and I in equation (6-15), we get

$$Y = (1 - s)Y + K' - (1 - d)K,$$

or, rearranging terms and simplifying,

$$K' = sY + (1 - d)K; \tag{6-16}$$

that is, the capital stock in the future period is the quantity of aggregate savings in the current period ($S = Y - C = sY$) plus the capital stock left over from the current period that has not depreciated. Then if we substitute for Y in equation (6-16) using the production function from equation (6-12), we get

$$K' = szF(K, N) + (1 - d)K. \tag{6-17}$$

Equation (6-17) states that the stock of capital in the future period is equal to the quantity of savings in the current period (identical to the quantity of investment) plus the quantity of current capital that remains in the future after depreciation.

Now, it is convenient to express equation (6-17) in per-worker terms, by dividing each term on the right-hand and left-hand sides of (6-17) by N, the number of workers, to get

$$\frac{K'}{N} = sz\frac{F(K, N)}{N} + (1 - d)\frac{K}{N},$$

and then multiplying the left-hand side by $1 = \frac{N'}{N'}$, which gives

$$\frac{K'}{N}\frac{N'}{N'} = sz\frac{F(K, N)}{N} + (1 - d)\frac{K}{N}.$$

Then we can rewrite this as

$$k'(1 + n) = szf(k) + (1 - d)k. \tag{6-18}$$

In equation (6-18), $k' = \frac{K'}{N'}$ is the future quantity of capital per worker, $\frac{N'}{N} = 1 + n$ from equation (6-10), and the first term on the right-hand side of (6-18) comes from the fact that $\frac{F(K,N)}{N} = F\left(\frac{K}{N}, 1\right)$ because the production function has constant returns to scale, and at $F\left(\frac{K}{N}, 1\right) = f(k)$ by definition. We can then divide the right-hand and left-hand sides of Equation (18) by $1 + n$ to obtain

$$k' = \frac{szf(k)}{1 + n} + \frac{(1 - d)k}{1 + n}. \tag{6-19}$$

Equation (6-19) is a key equation that summarizes most of what we need to know about competitive equilibrium in the Solow growth model, and we use this equation to derive the important implications of the model. This equation determines the future stock of capital per worker, k' on the left-hand side of the equation, as a function of the current stock of capital per worker, k, on the right-hand side.

In Figure 6.13 we graph the relationship given by equation (6-19). In the figure, the curve has a decreasing slope because of the decreasing slope of the per-worker production function $f(k)$ in Figure 6.12. In the figure, the 45° line is the line along which $k' = k$, and the point at which the 45° line intersects the curve given by equation (6-19) is the steady state. Once the economy reaches the steady state, where current capital per worker $k = k^*$, then future capital per worker $k' = k^*$, and the economy has k^* units of capital per worker forever after. If the current stock of capital per worker, k, is less than the steady state value, so $k < k^*$, then from the figure $k' > k$, and the capital stock per worker increases from the current period to the future period. In this situation, current investment is sufficiently large, relative to depreciation and growth in the labor force, that the per-worker quantity

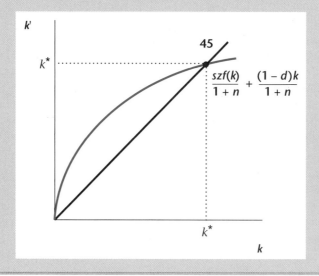

Figure 6.13 Determination of the Steady State Quantity of Capital per Worker

The colored curve is the relationship between current capital per worker, k, and future capital per worker, k', determined in a competitive equilibrium in the Solow growth model. The steady state quantity of capital per worker is k^*, given by the intersection of the 45° line (the black line) with the colored curve.

of capital increases. However, if $k > k^*$, then we have $k' < k$, and the capital stock per worker decreases from the current period to the future period. In this situation, investment is sufficiently small that it cannot keep up with depreciation and labor force growth, and the per-worker quantity of capital declines from the current period to the future period. Therefore, if the quantity of capital per worker is smaller than its steady state value, it increases until it reaches the steady state, and if the quantity of capital per worker is larger than its steady state value, it decreases until it reaches the steady state.

Because the Solow growth model predicts that the quantity of capital per worker converges to a constant, k^*, in the long run, it also predicts that the quantity of output per worker converges to a constant, which is $y^* = zf(k^*)$ from the per-worker production function. The Solow model then tells us that, if the savings rate s, the labor force growth rate n, and total factor productivity z are constant, then real income per worker cannot grow in the long run. Thus, since real income per worker is also real income per capita in the model, we can take y as a measure of the standard of living. The model then concludes that there can be no long-run betterment in living standards under these circumstances. Why does this happen? The reason is that the marginal product of capital is diminishing. Output per worker can grow only as long as capital per worker continues to grow. However, the marginal return to investment, which is determined by the marginal product of capital, declines as the per-worker capital stock grows. That is, as the capital stock per worker grows, it takes more and more investment per worker in the current period to produce one unit of additional capital per worker for the future period. Therefore, as the economy grows, new investment ultimately only just keeps up with depreciation and the growth of the labor force, and growth in per-worker output ceases.

In the long run, when the economy converges to the steady state quantity of capital per worker, k^*, all real aggregate quantities grow at the rate n, which is the growth rate in the labor force. That is, the aggregate quantity of capital in the steady state is $K = k^*N$, and because k^* is a constant and N grows at the rate n, K must also grow at the rate n. Similarly, aggregate real output is $Y = y^*N = zf(k^*)N$, and so Y also grows at the rate n. Further, the quantity of investment is equal to savings, so that investment in the steady state is $I = sY = szf(k^*)N$, and because $szf(k^*)$ is a constant, I also grows at the rate n in the steady state. As well, aggregate consumption is $C = (1 - s)zf(k^*)N$, so that consumption also grows at the rate n in the steady state. In the long run, therefore, if the savings rate, the labor force growth rate, and total factor productivity are constant, then growth rates in aggregate quantities are determined by the growth rate in the labor force. This is one sense in which the Solow growth model is an exogenous growth model. In the long run, the Solow model tells us that growth in key macroeconomic aggregates is determined by exogenous labor force growth when the savings rate, the labor force growth rate, and total factor productivity are constant.

Analysis of the Steady State

In this section, we put the Solow growth model to work. We perform some experiments with the model, analyzing how the steady state or long-run equilibrium is affected by changes in the savings rate, the population growth rate, and total factor productivity. We then show how the response of the model to these experiments is consistent with what we see in the data.

To analyze the steady state, we start with equation (6-19), which determines the future capital stock per worker, k' given the current capital stock per worker, k. In the steady state, we have $k = k' = k^*$, and so substituting k^* in equation (6-19) for k and k' we get

$$k^* = \frac{szf(k^*)}{1 + n} + \frac{(1 - d)k^*}{1 + n},$$

multiplying both sides of this equation by $1 + n$ and rearranging, we get

$$szf(k^*) = (n + d)k^*. \qquad (6\text{-}20)$$

Equation (6-20) solves for the steady state capital stock per worker, k^*. It is this equation we wish to analyze to determine the effects of changes in the savings rate s, in the population growth rate n, and in total factor productivity z on the steady state quantity of capital per worker, k^*.

We graph the left-hand and right-hand sides of Equation (6-20) in Figure 6.14, where the intersection of the two curves determines the steady state quantity of capital per worker, which we denote by k_1^* in the figure. The curve $szf(k^*)$ is the per-worker production function multiplied by the savings rate s, and so this function inherits the

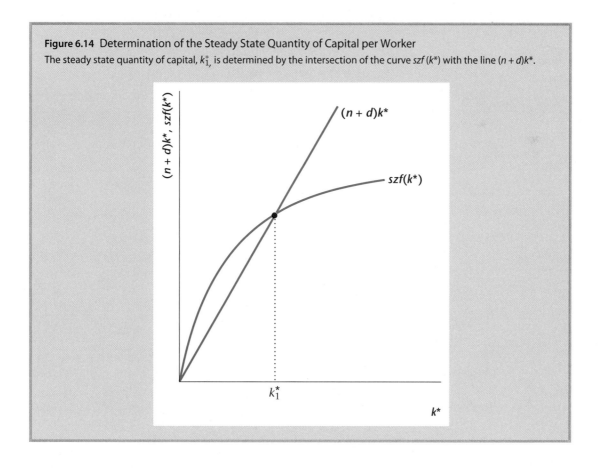

Figure 6.14 Determination of the Steady State Quantity of Capital per Worker
The steady state quantity of capital, k_1^*, is determined by the intersection of the curve $szf(k^*)$ with the line $(n + d)k^*$.

properties of the per-worker production function in Figure 6.12. The curve $(n + d)k^*$ in Figure 6.14 is a straight line with slope $n + d$.

The Steady State Effects of an Increase in the Savings Rate A key experiment to consider in the Solow growth model is a change in the savings rate s. We can interpret a change in s as occurring due to a change in the preferences of consumers. For example, if consumers care more about the future, they save more, and s increases. A change in s could also be brought about through government policy, for example, if the government were to subsidize savings (although in Chapter 8, we show that this has opposing income and substitution effects on savings). With regard to government policy, we need to be careful about interpreting our results, because to be completely rigorous we should build a description of government behavior into the model.

In Figure 6.15 we show the effect of an increase in the savings rate, from s_1 to s_2, on the steady state quantity of capital per worker. The increase in s shifts the curve $szf(k^*)$ up, and k^* increases from k_1^* to k_2^*. Therefore, in the new steady state, the quantity of capital per worker is higher, which implies that output per worker is also higher, given the per-worker production function $y = zf(k^*)$. Although the levels of capital per

Figure 6.15 Effect of an Increase in the Savings Rate on the Steady State Quantity of Capital per Worker
An increase in the savings rate shifts the curve $szf(k^*)$ up, resulting in an increase in the quantity of capital per worker from k_1^* to k_2^*.

worker and output per worker are higher in the new steady state, the increase in the savings rate has no effect on the growth rates of aggregate variables. Before and after the increase in the savings rate, the aggregate capital stock K, aggregate output Y, aggregate investment I, and aggregate consumption C grow at the rate of growth in the labor force, n. This is perhaps surprising, as we might think that a country that invests and saves more, thus accumulating capital at a higher rate, would grow faster.

Although the growth rates of aggregate variables are unaffected by the increase in the savings rate in the steady state, it may take some time for the adjustment from one steady state to another to take place. In Figure 6.16 we show the path that the natural logarithm of output follows when there is an increase in the savings rate, with time measured along the horizontal axis. Before time T, aggregate output is growing at the constant rate n (recall that if the growth rate is constant, then the time path of the natural logarithm is a straight line), and then the savings rate increases at time T. Aggregate output then adjusts to its higher growth path after period T, but in the transition to the new growth path, the rate of growth in Y is higher than n. The temporarily high growth rate in transition results from a higher rate of capital accumulation when the savings rate increases, which translates into a higher growth rate in aggregate output. As capital is accumulated at a higher rate, however, the marginal product of capital diminishes, and growth slows down, ultimately converging to the steady state growth rate n.

Consumption per Worker and Golden Rule Capital Accumulation We know from Chapter 2 that GDP, or GDP per person, is often used as a measure of aggregate welfare. However, what consumers ultimately care about is their lifetime consumption. In this model, given our focus on steady states, an aggregate welfare measure we might want

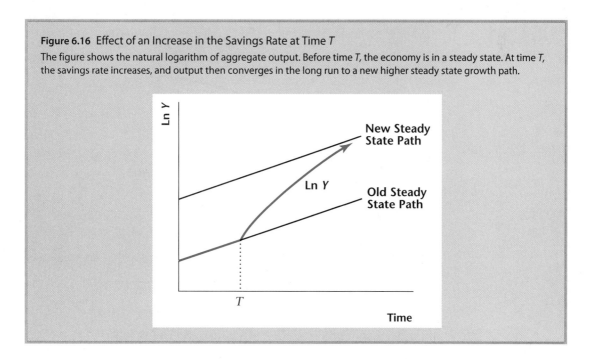

Figure 6.16 Effect of an Increase in the Savings Rate at Time T
The figure shows the natural logarithm of aggregate output. Before time T, the economy is in a steady state. At time T, the savings rate increases, and output then converges in the long run to a new higher steady state growth path.

to consider is the steady state level of consumption per worker. In this subsection, we show how to determine steady state consumption per worker from a diagram similar to Figure 6.15. Then, we show that there is a given quantity of capital per worker that maximizes consumption per worker in the steady state. This implies that an increase in the savings rate could cause a decrease in steady state consumption per worker, even though an increase in the savings rate always increases output per worker.

Consumption per worker in the steady state is $c = (1 - s)zf(k^*)$, which is the difference between steady state income per worker, $y^* = zf(k^*)$, and steady state savings per worker, which is $szf(k^*)$. If we add the per-worker production function to Figure 6.15, as we have done in Figure 6.17, then the steady state quantity of capital per worker in the figure is k_1^*, and steady state consumption per worker is the distance AB, which is the difference between output per worker and savings per worker. Consumption per worker in the steady state is also the difference between output per worker, $y^* = zf(k^*)$, and $(n + d)k^*$.

Next, because consumption per worker in the steady state is

$$c^* = zf(k^*) - (n + d)k^*$$

in Figure 6.18(a), we have in Figure 6.18(b) plotted c^* against the steady state quantity of capital per worker, k^*. There is a quantity of capital per worker for which

Figure 6.17 Steady State Consumption per Worker

Consumption per worker in the steady state is shown as the distance AB, given the steady state quantity of capital per worker, k_1^*.

Figure 6.18 The Golden Rule Quantity of Capital per Worker

This quantity, which maximizes consumption per worker in the steady state, is k_{gr}^*, and the maximized quantity of consumption per worker is c^{**}. The golden rule savings rate sgr achieves the golden rule quantity of capital per worker in a competitive equilibrium steady state.

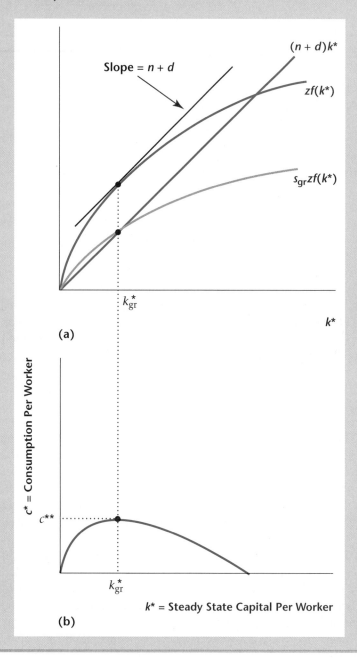

consumption per worker is maximized, which we denote by k_{gr}^* in the figure. If the steady state quantity of capital is k_{gr}^*, then maximum consumption per worker is c^{**}. Here, k_{gr}^* is called the **golden rule quantity of capital per worker.** The golden rule has the property, from Figure 6.18(a), that the slope of the per-worker production function where $k^* = k_{gr}^*$ is equal to the slope of the function $(n + d)k^*$. That is, because the slope of the per-worker production function is the marginal product of capital, MP_K, at the golden rule steady state we have

$$MP_K = n + d.$$

Therefore, when capital is accumulated at a rate that maximizes consumption per worker in the steady state, the marginal product of capital equals the population growth rate plus the depreciation rate.

How can the golden rule be achieved in the steady state? In Figure 6.18(a), we show that if the savings rate is s_{gr}, then the curve $s_{gr}zf(k^*)$ intersects the line $(n + d)k^*$ where $k^* = k_{gr}^*$. Thus, s_{gr} is the **golden rule savings rate.** If savings takes place at the golden rule savings rate, then in the steady state the current population consumes and saves the appropriate amount so that, in each succeeding period, the population can continue to consume this maximum amount per person. The golden rule is a biblical reference, which comes from the dictum that we should treat others as we would like ourselves to be treated.

From Figure 6.18(b), if the steady state capital stock per worker is less than k_{gr}^*, then an increase in the savings rate s increases the steady state capital stock per worker and increases consumption per worker. However, if $k^* > k_{gr}^*$, then an increase in the savings rate increases k^* and causes a decrease in consumption per worker.

Suppose that we calculated the golden rule savings rate for the United States and found that the actual U.S. savings rate was different from the golden rule rate. For example, suppose we found that the actual savings rate was lower than the golden rule savings rate. Would this necessarily imply that the government should implement a change in policy that would increase the savings rate? The answer is no, for two reasons. First, any increase in the savings rate would come at a cost in current consumption. It would take time to build up a higher stock of capital to support higher consumption per worker in the new steady state, and the current generation may be unwilling to bear this short-term cost. Second, in practice, savings behavior is the result of optimizing decisions by individual consumers. In general, we should presume that private market outcomes achieve the correct trade-off between current consumption and savings, unless we have good reasons to believe that there exists some market failure that the government can efficiently correct.

The Steady State Effects of an Increase in Labor Force Growth   The next experiment we carry out with the Solow model is to ask what happens in the long run if the labor force growth rate increases. As labor is a factor of production, it is clear that higher labor force growth ultimately causes aggregate output to grow at a higher rate. But what is the effect on output per worker in the steady state? With aggregate output growing at a higher rate, there is a larger and larger "income pie" to split up, but with more and more workers to share this pie. As we show, the Solow growth model predicts that capital per worker and output per worker will decrease in the steady state when the labor force growth rate increases, but aggregate output will grow at a higher rate, which is the new rate of labor force growth.

In Figure 6.19 we show the steady state effects of an increase in the labor force growth rate, from n_1 to n_2. Initially, the quantity of capital per worker is k_1^*, determined by the intersection of the curves $szf(k^*)$ and $(n_1 + d)k^*$. When the population growth rate increases, this results in a decrease in the quantity of capital per worker to k_2^* in the figure. Because capital per worker falls, output per worker also falls, from the per-worker production function. That is, output per worker falls from $zf(k_1^*)$ to $zf(k_2^*)$. The reason for this result is that, when the labor force grows at a higher rate, the current labor force faces a tougher task in building capital for next period's consumers, who are a proportionately larger group. Thus, output per worker and capital per worker are ultimately lower in the steady state.

We have already determined that aggregate output, aggregate consumption, and aggregate investment grow at the labor force growth rate n in the steady state. Therefore, when the labor force growth rate increases, growth in all of these variables must also increase. This is an example that shows that higher growth in aggregate income need not be associated, in the long run, with higher income per worker.

Figure 6.19 Steady State Effects of an Increase in the Labor Force Growth Rate
An increase in the labor force growth rate from n_1 to n_2 causes a decrease in the steady state quantity of capital per worker.

The Solow Growth Model, Investment Rates, and Population Growth

Now that we know something about the predictions that the Solow growth model makes, we can evaluate the model by matching its predictions with the data. It has only been relatively recently that economists have had access to comprehensive national income accounts data for essentially all countries in the world. The Penn World Tables, which are the work of Alan Heston, Robert Summers, and Bettina Aten at the University of Pennsylvania,[8] allow for comparisons of GDP, among other macroeconomic variables, across countries. Making these comparisons is a complicated measurement exercise, as GDP in different countries at a given point in time is measured in different currencies, and simply making adjustments using foreign exchange rates does not give the right answers. A limitation of the Penn World Tables is that they only extend back to 1950. A few decades of data may not tell us all we need to know, in terms of matching the long-run predictions of the Solow growth model. Can the steady state be achieved within a few decades? As we will see, however, two of the predictions of the Solow model appear to match the data in the Penn World Tables quite well.

Two key predictions of the Solow growth model are that, in the long run, an increase in the savings rate causes an increase in the quantity of income per worker, and an increase in the labor force growth rate causes a decrease in the quantity of income per worker. We examine in turn the fit of each of these predictions with the data.

The savings rate in the Solow growth model is the ratio of investment expenditures to GDP, and since the population is identical to the labor force in the model, income per worker is the same thing as income per capita. The Solow model thus predicts that, if we look at data from a set of countries in the world, we should see a positive correlation between GDP per capita and the ratio of investment to GDP. This is the correlation that we discussed in the Economic Growth Facts section earlier in this chapter. In Figure 6.2 we observe that a positively sloped line would provide the best fit for the points in the figure, so that the investment rate and income per worker are positively correlated across the countries of the world. Clearly, as the Solow model predicts, countries with high (low) ratios of investment to GDP also have high (low) quantities of income per worker.

Next, the Solow model predicts that, in data for a set of countries, we should observe the labor force growth rate to be negatively correlated with output per worker. Since the labor force growth rate in the model is the same thing as the population growth rate, and output per worker is the same thing as income per worker, the prediction is that the population growth rate and the level of income per worker should be negatively correlated, which is the fourth economic growth fact we discussed early in this chapter. In Figure 6.3, we observe a negative correlation between the population growth rate and income per worker across countries, as the Solow model predicts.

---

[8]The income-per-worker statistics come from A. Heston, R. Summers, and B. Aten, *Penn World Table Version 6.2*, Center for International Comparisons at the University of Pennsylvania (CICUP), November 2006, available at pwt .econ.upenn.edu.

The Steady State Effects of an Increase in Total Factor Productivity   If we take real income per worker to be a measure of the standard of living in a country, what we have shown thus far is that, in the Solow model, an increase in the savings rate or a decrease in the labor force growth rate can increase the standard of living in the long run. However, increases in the savings rate and reductions in the labor force growth rate cannot bring about an ever-increasing standard of living in a country. This is because the savings rate must always be below 1 (no country would have a savings rate equal to 1, as this would imply zero consumption), and the labor force growth rate cannot fall indefinitely. The Solow model predicts that a country's standard of living can continue to increase in the long run only if there are continuing increases in total factor productivity, as we show here.

In Figure 6.20 we show the effect of increases in total factor productivity. First, an increase in total factor productivity from z_1 to z_2 results in an increase in capital per worker from k_1^* to k_2^* and an increase in output per worker as a result. A further increase in total factor productivity to z_3 causes an additional increase in capital per worker to k_3^* and an additional increase in output per worker. These increases in capital per worker and output per worker can continue indefinitely, as long as the increases in total factor productivity continue.

This is a key insight that comes from the Solow growth model. An increase in a country's propensity to save or a decrease in the labor force growth rate imply one-time

Figure 6.20 Increases in Total Factor Productivity in the Solow Growth Model

Increases in total factor productivity from z_1 to z_2 and from z_2 to z_3 cause increases in the quantity of capital per worker from k_1^* to k_2^* and from k_2^* to k_3^*. Thus, increases in total factor productivity lead to increases in output per worker.

increases in a country's standard of living, but there can be unbounded growth in the standard of living only if total factor productivity continues to grow. The source of continual long-run betterment in a country's standard of living, therefore, can only be the process of devising better methods for putting factor inputs together to produce output, thus generating increases in total factor productivity.

In contrast to the Malthusian model, where the gains from technological advance are dissipated by a higher population, the Solow model gives a more optimistic outlook for increases in the standard of living over time. If we accept the Solow model, it tells us that the steady increase in per-capita income that occurred since 1900 in the United States (see Figure 6.1) was caused by sustained increases in total factor productivity over a period of 108 years. If technological advances can be sustained for such a long period, there appears to be no reason why these advances cannot occur indefinitely into the future.

Perspectives on the Financial Crisis
The Solow Growth Model and the 2008–2009 Recession

Much discussion of the 2008–2009 financial crisis and the associated decline in aggregate economic activity focuses on the role of credit markets, the banking system, and other financial factors, in explaining the behavior of aggregate economic variables. However, a case can be made that we can understand at least the broad outlines of the 2008–2009 recession in terms of the effects of a decline in total factor productivity in the Solow growth model, which leaves out details such as the workings of credit and the banking system. As we discussed in Chapter 5, the large increase in the relative price of energy to mid-2008 could have contributed in part to a decline in aggregate total factor productivity in the United States. Further, it is possible to think of disruption in credit markets as being reflected in a decrease in aggregate productivity. This is because, if credit markets are temporarily not functioning to properly allocate resources, then there can be a misallocation of factors of production (labor and capital) across productive units in the economy. Then, even if there has been no change in the technology available to individual firms for producing output from capital and labor inputs, there can be a reduction in aggregate total

factor productivity because labor and capital are being used inefficiently in the economy as a whole.

Suppose that we accept as given that total factor productivity declined in 2008, causing the 2008–2009 recession. An approach to modeling this in the Solow growth model is to "calibrate" the model and run it on the computer. In calibrating a model, we fit it to available empirical facts. To do this, first assume, as in Chapter 4, that the production function is Cobb–Douglas, with capital share parameter .36, which gives $F(K, N) = K^{.36}N^{.64}$, and the per-worker production function is then $zf(k) = zk^{.36}$. Recall from Chapter 4 that the Cobb–Douglas production function provides a close fit to U.S. aggregate data, and capital's share of national income in the United States does not stray too far from 36%. For annual data, reasonable values for the annual depreciation rate of capital and population growth rate are $d = .1$ and $n = .01$, respectively.[9] If we set the savings rate equal to the ratio of investment expenditures to GDP in the U.S.

[9]See E. Prescott, 1986. "Theory Ahead of Business Cycle Measurement," *Federal Reserve Bank of Minneapolis Quarterly Review,* Fall.

economy for 2008, we get $s = .14$ (aggregate savings is equal to aggregate investment in equilibrium in the Solow growth model). This then tells us that, from equation (6-19), we can determine the steady state quantity of capital as the solution to

$$sz(k^*)^{.36} = (n + d)k^*,$$

so solving for k^* from this equation, we get

$$k^* = \left(\frac{sz}{n + d}\right)^{\frac{1}{.64}} = 1.4576z^{1.5625}, \quad (6\text{-}21)$$

and since $y = zk^{.36}$ (from the per-worker production function), the steady state quantity of output per worker is

$$y^* = z(k^*)^{.36} = 1.1453z^{1.5625}. \quad (6\text{-}22)$$

Now, we can use equation (6-18) to determine what capital and output per worker are outside of the steady state. Given $f(k) = k^{.36}$, $d = .1, n = .01$, and $s = .14$, equation (6-18) takes the form

$$k' = .1386zk^{.36} + .8911k, \quad (6\text{-}23)$$

and from the per-worker production function,

$$y = zk^{.36}. \quad (6\text{-}24)$$

Now, we will consider cases where the economy does not grow in the steady state, and think of this as giving predictions concerning the deviations of capital and output from trend. Then, to roughly replicate the time leading up to the 2008–2009 recession, suppose that total factor productivity was constant for a long period of time at its initial value $z = 1$ (here $z = 1$ is just a normalization). Then, from equations (6-21) and (6-22), the steady state values of capital per worker and output per worker would then be $k^* = 1.4576$ and $y^* = 1.1453$. Recall from Chapter 3 that the deviation from trend in real GDP reached almost −4% in the first quarter of 2009 and will probably go lower before the recession is over.

To roughly replicate a comparable drop in real GDP in the Solow growth model, suppose first that z drops temporarily, for one period, by 5%. In Figure 6.21, we show the resulting quantities of output per worker as the path "temporary (1)," with output per worker at the steady state level for $z = 1$ in the first 10 periods, where we want to think of one period as one year. Then, z drops during period 11 to .95, a 5% decrease in total factor productivity. This drop in productivity is only temporary, with $z = 1$ for periods 12, 13, 14, . . . , 40. In Figure 6.21, capital per worker and output per worker in periods 12, 13, 14, . . . , 40, are calculated using equations (6-23) and (6-24). Then, output was scaled so that output per worker would be equal to 100 in periods 1 through 10, and then we can clearly see the resulting percentage drop in output. Note that the temporary drop in total factor productivity produces a recession—a temporary drop in output per worker in period 11. In period 12, productivity returns to its initial level, but note that output per worker does not immediately return to its steady state level. This is because there has been less investment in period 11 than would otherwise be the case. When the economy recovers in period 12 in Figure 6.21 on the path temporary (1), there is less capital per worker, and therefore less output, than if the temporary decrease in total factory productivity had not occurred.

Now, suppose that the decline in productivity is more long-lived, lasting two years instead of one. The results are also pictured in Figure 6.21, as the path "temporary (2)" where we see that output is even lower (although not by much) in year 12 (the second year of the productivity decline) than in year 11. Further, the reduction in output per worker in years 13, 14, 15, . . . , 40 is larger than for "temporary (1)," because more capital accumulation was foregone in the longer recession. In Figure 6.21, we show what happens over a thirty-year period if the drop in productivity is permanent. Output per worker will continue to fall to its steady state level. In this case, $z = .95$ implies a steady state level of output per worker, from equation (6-22) of 1.0571, which is 7.7% lower

(Continued)

Figure 6.21 Simulation of a Calibrated Solow Growth Model: Temporary and Permanent Declines in TFP

The figure shows the paths of output per capita. Until period 11, total factor productivity is constant and output per capita is at its steady state level. Productivity falls by 5% in period 11. "Temporary (1)" denotes output per capita when productivity drops for only one period, and "temporary (2)" is output per capita when productivity drops for two consecutive periods. The path denoted "permanent" is output per capita when total factor productivity decreases permanently. In each case, output per capita is scaled to be equal to 100 before the productivity decrease occurs.

than in the steady state with $z = 1$. Note that, in period 20 (10 years after the initial decrease in z) output per worker has declined by 6.4% from period 10 on its path to the steady state.

These computer simulations indicate some of the potential costs of a recession. If the recession is caused by a temporary reduction in total factor productivity, output can be signficantly below its steady state value, even after total factor productivity has recovered. This is because investment expenditures are lower during a recession, which lowers the capital stock, yielding a lingering effect on aggregate output. As well, a long-lived decline in total factor productivity can cause a long period of decline in aggregate output below trend, as for instance in the "lost decade" of the 1990s in Japan.

Growth Accounting

If aggregate real output is to grow over time, it is necessary for a factor or factors of production to be increasing over time or for there to be increases in total factor productivity. Typically, growing economies are experiencing growth in factors of production and in total factor productivity. A useful exercise is to measure how much of the growth in aggregate output over a given period of time is accounted for by growth in each of the inputs to production and by increases in total factor productivity. This exercise is called **growth accounting**, and it can be helpful in developing theories of economic growth and for discriminating among different theories. Growth accounting was introduced in the 1950s by Robert Solow, who also developed the growth model we have just studied in the previous section.[10]

Growth accounting starts by considering the aggregate production function from the Solow growth model,

$$Y = zF(K, N),$$

where Y is aggregate output, z is total factor productivity, F is the production function, K is the capital input, and N is the labor input. To use the aggregate production function in conjunction with data on output and factor inputs, we need a specific form for the function F. The widely used Cobb–Douglas production function, as discussed in Chapter 4, provides a good fit to U.S. aggregate data, and it is also a good analytical tool for growth accounting. For the production function to be Cobb–Douglas, the function F takes the form

$$F(K, N) = K^a N^{1-a}, \tag{6-25}$$

where a is a number between 0 and 1. Recall from Chapter 4 that, in a competitive equilibrium, a is the fraction of national income that goes to the capital input, and $1 - a$ is the fraction that goes to the labor input. In postwar U.S. data, the labor share in national income has been roughly constant at 64%,[11] so we can set $a = 0.36$, and our production function is then

$$Y = zK^{0.36}N^{0.64}. \tag{6-26}$$

If we have measures of aggregate output, the capital input, and the labor input, denoted $\hat{Y}$, $\hat{K}$, and $\hat{N}$, respectively, then total factor productivity z can be measured as a residual, as discussed in Chapter 4. The Solow residual, denoted $\hat{z}$, is measured from the production function, equation (6-26), as

$$\hat{z} = \frac{\hat{Y}}{\hat{K}^{0.36}\hat{N}^{0.64}}. \tag{6-27}$$

The Solow residual is of course named after Robert Solow. This measure of total factor productivity is a residual, because it is the output that remains to be accounted for after we measure the direct contribution of the capital and labor inputs to output, as

---

[10]See R. Solow, 1957, "Technical Change and the Aggregate Production Function," *Review of Economic Statistics* 39, 312–320.

[11]See E. Prescott, 1986, "Theory Ahead of Business Cycle Measurement," *Federal Reserve Bank of Minneapolis Quarterly Review*, Fall, 9–22.

discussed in Chapter 4. Total factor productivity has many interpretations, as we studied in Chapters 4 and 5, and, hence, so does the Solow residual. Increases in measured total factor productivity could be the result of new inventions, good weather, new management techniques, favorable changes in government regulations, decreases in the relative price of energy, or any other factor that causes more aggregate output to be produced given the same quantities of aggregate factor inputs.

Solow Residuals, the Productivity Slowdown, and the Productivity Recovery

A first exercise we work through is to calculate and graph Solow residuals from post–World War II U.S. data and then explain what is interesting in the resulting figure. Using GDP for $\hat{Y}$, measured aggregate output, total employment for $\hat{N}$, and a measure of the capital stock for $\hat{K}$, we calculated the Solow residual $\hat{z}$ using Equation (6-27) and plotted its natural logarithm in Figure 6.22, for the period 1948–2007. We can see that growth in total factor productivity was very high throughout most of the 1950s and 1960s, as evidenced

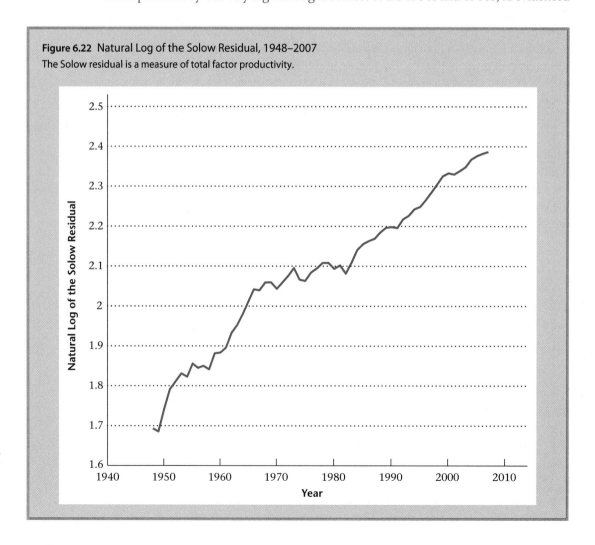

Figure 6.22 Natural Log of the Solow Residual, 1948–2007
The Solow residual is a measure of total factor productivity.

Table 6.1	Average Annual Growth Rates in the Solow Residual
Years	**Average Annual Growth Rate**
1950–1960	1.42
1960–1970	1.61
1970–1980	0.50
1980–1990	1.05
1990–2000	1.36
2000–2007	0.76

by the steep slope in the graph during those periods. However, there was a dramatic decrease in total factor productivity growth beginning in the late 1960s and continuing into the 1980s, which is referred to as the **productivity slowdown.** The productivity slowdown is also seen in Table 6.1, where we show the average percentage growth in the Solow residual from 1950–1960, 1960–1970, 1970–1980, 1980–1990, 1990–2000, and 2000–2007. Note in the table that total factor productivity growth, as measured by growth in the Solow residual, was high in the 1950s and very high in the 1960s. The growth rate fell considerably in the 1970s, picked up in the 1980s, and then was quite high again in the 1990s, with weak productivity growth from 2000–2008.

There are at least three reasons given by economists for the productivity slowdown:

1. The measured productivity slowdown might have been a measurement problem. Over this period, there was a shift in the United States from the production of manufactured goods to the production of services. Earlier, in Chapter 2, we discussed the problems associated with measuring real growth in GDP due to changes in the quality of goods and services over time. This measurement problem is especially severe in the service sector. Thus, if production is shifting from goods to services, then there tends to be an increase in the downward bias in measuring growth in GDP. GDP growth and total factor productivity growth can appear to be low, when they actually are not.

2. The productivity slowdown could have resulted from increases in the relative price of energy. There were two large increases in the price of oil imported to the United States in the 1970s: one in 1973–1974 and one in 1979–1980. An effect of the increase in oil prices was that old capital equipment that was not energy efficient—for example, buildings in cold climates with poor insulation—became obsolete. It was possible that obsolete plant and equipment were scrapped or fell out of use, and that this scenario was not adequately captured in the capital stock measure. That is, some of the measured capital stock was not actually productive. Essentially then, this is another type of measurement problem, but it is a problem in measuring inputs, whereas the measurement issue discussed in the first point is a problem in measuring output.

3. The productivity slowdown could have been caused by the costs of adopting new technology. Some economists—for example, Jeremy Greenwood and Mehmet Yorukoglu[12]—mark the early 1970s as the beginning of the information revolution, when computer and other information technology began to be widely adopted in the United States. With any dramatically new technology, time is required for workers to learn how to use the new technology, which is embodied in new capital equipment like computers. During this learning period, productivity growth can be low, because workers are spending some of their time investing in learning on the job, and they are, therefore, contributing less to measured output.

Productivity growth recovered in the 1980s and 1990s, as we can see from Figure 6.22 and Table 6.1. However, productivity growth then decreased in 2000–2007 from what it had been during the 1990s, although the productivity growth rate was lower in the 1970s than from 2000–2007. These later observations are certainly consistent with (3) above, in that we could argue that, by the mid-1980s, American workers had learned how to use new information technology and were then able to reap the rewards of this technology, as reflected in higher productivity. By the end of the 1990s, the U.S. economy may have realized most of the efficiency advantages from advanced information technology, and so productivity growth was not as great from 2000–2007. Low productivity growth in 2000–2007 could also have resulted from rapid increases in energy prices over that period, as is consistent with (2) above.

The Cyclical Properties of Solow Residuals   From Figure 6.23, it is clear that there are cyclical fluctuations in Solow residuals about trend growth. In Figure 6.23 we plot percentage deviations from trend in Solow residuals for the years 1948–2007, along with percentage deviations from trend in GDP. Note that the fluctuations in Solow residuals about trend are highly positively correlated with the fluctuations in GDP about trend (recall our discussion of correlations and comovements from Chapter 3). In fact, the Solow residual moves very closely with GDP, so that fluctuations in total factor productivity could be an important explanation for why GDP fluctuates. This is the key idea in real business cycle theory, which we will study in Chapter 12.

A Growth Accounting Exercise

Now that we know how the Solow residual is constructed and what some of its empirical properties are, we can do a full growth accounting exercise. By way of example, we show here how we can use the Cobb–Douglas production function (6-26) and observations on GDP, the capital stock, and employment to obtain measures of the contributions to growth in real output of growth in the capital stock, in employment, and in total factor productivity.

---

[12]See J. Greenwood and M. Yorukoglu, "1974," University of Rochester working paper.

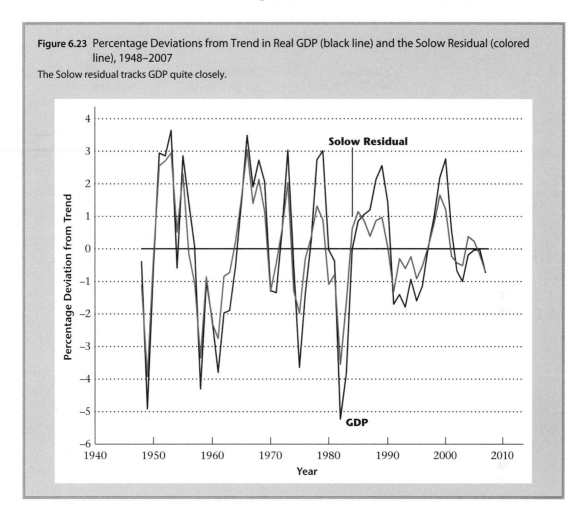

Figure 6.23 Percentage Deviations from Trend in Real GDP (black line) and the Solow Residual (colored line), 1948–2007

The Solow residual tracks GDP quite closely.

To do growth accounting, we use equation (6-27) to calculate the Solow residual $\hat{z}$. In Table 6.2 we show data on real GDP, the capital stock, and employment at 10-year intervals from 1950 to 2000, and for 2005. This is the data we use to carry out our growth accounting exercise. The Solow residual $\hat{z}$ in the table was calculated using equation (6-27).

Now, taking the data from Table 6.2, we calculate the average annual growth rates for measured output, capital, employment, and the Solow residual for the periods 1950–1960, 1960–1970, 1970–1980, 1980–1990, 1990–2000, and 2000–2005. If X_n is the value of a variable in year n, and X_m is the value of that variable in year m, where $n > m$, then the average annual growth rate in X between year m and year n, denoted by g_{mn}, is given by

$$g_{mn} = \left(\frac{X_n}{X_m}\right)^{\frac{1}{n-m}} - 1.$$

Table 6.2   Measured GDP, Capital Stock, Employment, and Solow Residual

Year	$\hat{Y}$ (billions of 2000 dollars)	$\hat{K}$ (billions of 2000 dollars)	$\hat{N}$ (millions)	$\hat{z}$
1950	1777.3	5991.8	58.89	5.715
1960	2501.8	8602.1	65.78	6.580
1970	3771.9	12557.1	78.69	7.721
1980	5161.7	17273.8	99.30	8.115
1990	7112.5	22877.9	118.80	9.011
2000	9817.0	29917.1	136.90	10.312
2007	11523.9	35910.4	146.05	10.875

For example, in Table 6.2, GDP in 1950 is 1,777.3 billion 2000 dollars, or $Y_{1950} = 1,777.3$. Further, $Y_{1960} = 2,501.8$ from Table 6.2. Then, we have $n - m = 10$, and the average annual growth rate in GDP from 1950 to 1960 in Table 6.3 is $\left(\frac{2501.8}{1777.3}\right)^{\frac{1}{10}} - 1 = 0.0348$, or 3.48%.

Table 6.3 shows that average annual growth in real GDP was very high during the 1960s, and somewhat lower in the 1950s, 1970s, 1980s, and 1990s. The growth rate of real GDP was considerably lower, at 2.32%, in 2000–2007. The very high growth in the 1960s came from all sources, as growth in capital was very high, growth in employment was somewhat high, and growth in total factor productivity (as measured by growth in $\hat{z}$) was high. Note that, in spite of the productivity slowdown in the 1970s, output still grew at a reasonably high rate, due to high growth in factors of production. During the 1970s, capital was accumulated at a high rate. Further, employment growth was unusually high, in part because of rapid increases in the female labor force

Table 6.3   Average Annual Growth Rates

Years	$\hat{Y}$	$\hat{K}$	$\hat{N}$	$\hat{z}$
1950–1960	3.48	3.68	1.11	1.42
1960–1970	4.19	3.86	1.80	1.61
1970–1980	3.19	3.24	2.36	0.50
1980–1990	3.26	2.85	1.81	1.05
1990–2000	3.28	2.72	1.43	1.36
2000–2007	2.32	2.64	0.93	0.76

MACROECONOMICS IN ACTION

East Asian Miracles and Total Factor Productivity Growth

If we examine the recent history of world growth, some countries stand out as growth miracles and others are growth disasters. A careful study of the causes of growth miracles and growth disasters is instructive, because we would like to know how a growth miracle could be replicated or how a disaster could be avoided. Four countries that stand out as growth miracles are the so-called "East Asian Tigers," Hong Kong, Singapore, South Korea, and Taiwan. From the data in Table 6.4, between 1966 and 1991, real GDP grew at an average annual rate of 7.3% in Hong Kong, and between 1966 and 1990 the average annual growth rates of real GDP in Singapore, South Korea, and Taiwan were 8.7%, 10.3%, and 9.4%, respectively. In the table, annual average growth in real GDP in the United States over the period 1966 to 1990 was 3.0%. Thus, it seems extraordinary that such high growth rates could be sustained for about a quarter of a century in East Asia.

A prediction of the Solow growth model is that a country's standard of living can continue to increase over the long run only if there are sustained increases in total factor productivity. Thus, most economists (who are trained to view the world through the lens of the Solow growth model) would tend to think that the very high sustained rates of GDP growth experienced in East Asia had been driven primarily by very high total factor productivity growth.

Alwyn Young, in an article in the *Quarterly Journal of Economics*,[13] did a growth accounting exercise for each of Hong Kong, Singapore, South Korea, and Taiwan to evaluate whether it was high growth in total factor

---

[13]A. Young, 1995, "The Tyranny of Numbers: Confronting the Statistical Realities of the East Asian Growth Experience," *Quarterly Journal of Economics 110*, 641–680.

Table 6.4 East Asian Growth Miracles (Average Annual Growth Rates)

	Output	Capital	Labor	Total Factor Productivity
Hong Kong (1966–1991)	7.3%	7.7%	2.6%	2.3%
Singapore (1966–1990)	8.7%	10.8%	4.5%	0.2%
South Korea (1966–1990)	10.3%	12.9%	5.4%	1.7%
Taiwan (1966–1990)	9.4%	11.8%	4.6%	2.6%
United States (1966–1990)	3.0%	3.2%	2.0%	0.6%

(Continued)

productivity that explained the high growth in real GDP in these countries. Surprisingly, Young found that total factor productivity growth in Hong Kong, Singapore, South Korea, and Taiwan was anything but miraculous. The high rates of GDP growth in these countries were mainly due to high growth rates in factor inputs.

From Table 6.4, the average growth rates in capital were extremely high in these East Asian countries, ranging from 7.7% per year in Hong Kong to 12.9% per year in South Korea. These growth rates compare with an average growth rate in capital in the United States of 3.2% over the period 1966–1990. High rates of growth in the capital stocks of the East Asian countries were caused by high rates of investment. Also, average rates of growth in the labor force range from 2.6% per year in Hong Kong to 5.4% per year in South Korea, as compared with 2.0% in the United States over the period 1966–1990. The large increases in the labor force in East Asia were driven partly by population growth and partly by increases in labor force participation, particularly among women. For example, in Singapore the labor force participation rate for all workers increased from 27% to 51% from 1966 to 1990, and population grew at an average rate of 1.9% per year.

Ultimately, Young concluded that total factor productivity growth during this period in Hong Kong, Singapore, South Korea, and Taiwan was far short of miraculous, ranging from an average growth rate of 0.2% in Singapore to 2.6% in Taiwan. In the United States over the period 1966–1990, total factor productivity grew at an average annual rate of 0.6%. While total factor productivity growth

exceeded that in the United States for three of these four countries, the difference is not as impressive as the difference in GDP growth rates. Therefore, while GDP growth in these four East Asian countries was extremely impressive, this high growth was mainly the result of unusually high growth rates in capital and labor.

There are two important implications of Young's analysis. The first is that the high growth in East Asia over the period from the mid-1960s to the early 1990s is probably not sustainable over a longer period. There is a limit to how much labor force participation rates can grow and thus contribute to growth in the labor force; namely, once the labor force participation rate reaches 100%, it cannot increase further. Also, consumers in these countries may not want to continue to forgo large quantities of current consumption to support the high rates of investment required to make the capital stock grow quickly. Second, Young's analysis makes it clear that the East Asian experience would be extremely difficult to replicate in the United States. The labor force participation rate is close to 70% in the United States, which is much higher than in East Asia, and so there is little scope in the United States for rapid growth in the labor force due to increased labor force participation. To mimic the East Asian experience would require that a very large fraction of U.S. GDP be devoted to investment, and this is not consistent with recent U.S. history. Note that growth in the U.S. capital stock averaged 3.2% per year over 1966–1990 and has slowed since then, while average growth in capital stocks ranged from 7.7% in Hong Kong to 12.9% in South Korea during the period of East Asian miracle growth.

participation rate. While growth in capital and employment declined in the 1980s and 1990s, there was a pickup in total factor productivity growth. This increase in total factor productivity growth was the driving force behind the high growth rate in aggregate output in the 1990s. From 2000–2007, the low growth rate in output relative to the 1990s is explained by weak growth in employment and in total factor productivity.

In the next chapter, we study the persistence in disparities in standards of living across countries of the world and how the Solow growth model addresses these facts. As well, we introduce an endogenous growth model, which is used to discuss convergence in incomes across countries and the role of education in growth, among other issues.

Chapter Summary

- We discussed seven economic growth facts. These were:
    1. Before the Industrial Revolution in about 1800, standards of living differed little over time and across countries.
    2. Since the Industrial Revolution, per-capita income growth has been sustained in the richest countries. In the United States, average annual growth in per-capita income has been about 2% since 1869.
    3. There is a positive correlation between the rate of investment and output per worker across countries.
    4. There is a negative correlation between the population growth rate and output per worker across countries.
    5. Differences in per capita incomes increased dramatically among countries of the world between 1800 and 1950, with the gap widening between the countries of Western Europe, the United States, Canada, Australia, and New Zealand, as a group, and the rest of the world.
    6. There is essentially no correlation across countries between the level of output per worker in 1960 and the average rate of growth in output per worker for the years 1960–2000.
    7. Richer countries are much more alike in terms of rates of growth of real per capita income than are poor countries.

- The first model was the Malthusian growth model, in which population growth depends positively on consumption per worker, and output is produced from the labor input and a fixed quantity of land.

- The Malthusian model predicts that an increase in total factor productivity has no effect on consumption per worker in the long run, but the population increases. The standard of living can only increase in the long run if population growth is reduced, perhaps by governmental population control.

- The Solow growth model is a model of exogenous growth in that, in the long-run steady state of this model, growth in aggregate output, aggregate consumption, and aggregate investment is explained by exogenous growth in the labor force.

- In the Solow growth model, output per worker converges in the long run to a steady state level, in the absence of a change in total factor productivity. The model predicts that output per worker increases in the long run when the savings rate increases or when the population growth rate decreases. Both of these predictions are consistent with the data.

- An increase in the savings rate could cause consumption per worker to increase or decrease in the Solow growth model. The golden rule savings rate maximizes consumption per worker in the steady state. The Solow growth model also predicts that a country's standard of living, as measured by income per worker, cannot increase in the long run unless there is ever-increasing total factor productivity.

- Growth accounting is an approach to measuring the contributions to growth in aggregate output from growth in the capital stock, in employment, and in total factor productivity. The latter is measured by the Solow residual.

- Measured Solow residuals for the United States using a Cobb–Douglas production function show a productivity slowdown occurring in the late 1960s and continuing into the 1980s. Suggested reasons for the productivity slowdown are (1) errors in measuring aggregate output; (2) errors in measuring the inputs to production, particularly capital; and (3) learning costs due to the adoption of new information technology.

- There is a recovery in productivity growth in the 1980s and 1990s, with lower productivity growth from 2000–2007 than in the 1990s. These observations are consistent with the fact that most of the learning costs of new information technology were bygones by the mid-1980s, and with the fact that energy prices increased rapidly after 2000.

- Cyclically, deviations from trend in the Solow residual track closely the deviations from trend in aggregate output. This empirical observation is important for real business cycle theory, discussed in Chapter 12.

Key Terms

Endogenous growth model A model in which growth is caused by forces determined by the model. (p. 191)

Exogenous growth model A model in which growth is not caused by forces determined by the model. (p. 191)

Golden rule quantity of capital per worker The quantity of capital per worker that maximizes consumption per worker in the steady state. (p. 218)

Golden rule savings rate The savings rate that implies consumption per worker is maximized in the steady state of a competitive equilibrium. (p. 218)

Growth accounting Uses the production function and data on aggregate output, the capital input, and the labor input, to measure the contributions of growth in capital, the labor force, and total factor productivity to growth in aggregate output. (p. 225)

Per-worker production function In the Malthusian model, $y = zf(l)$, where y is output per worker, z is total factor productivity, l is the quantity of land per worker, and f is a function. This describes the relationship between output per worker and land per worker, given constant returns to scale. In the Solow growth model, the per-worker production function is $y = zf(k)$, where y is output per worker, z is total factor productivity, k is the quantity of capital per worker, and f is a function. The per-worker production function in this case describes the relationship between output per worker and capital per worker, given constant returns to scale. (p. 200)

Productivity slowdown A decrease in the rate of measured total factor productivity growth beginning in the late 1960s and continuing into the 1980s. (p. 227)

Steady state A long run equilibrium or rest point. The Malthusian model and Solow model both have the property that the economy converges to a single steady state. (p. 199)

Questions For Review

1. What is the difference between exogenous growth and endogenous growth?
2. What are the seven economic growth facts?
3. What is the effect of an increase in total factor productivity on steady state population and consumption per worker in the Malthusian model?
4. What can increase the standard of living in the Malthusian model?
5. Was Malthus right? Why or why not?
6. What are the characteristics of a steady state in the Solow growth model?
7. In the Solow growth model, what are the steady state effects of an increase in the savings rate, of an increase in the population growth rate, and of an increase in total factor productivity?
8. Explain what determines the golden rule quantity of capital per worker and the golden rule savings rate.
9. In what sense does the Solow growth model give optimistic conclusions about the prospects for improvement in the standard of living, relative to the Malthusian model?
10. Why is a Cobb–Douglas production function useful for analyzing economic growth?
11. What is the parameter a in the production function in equation (6-25)?
12. What does the Solow residual measure, and what are its empirical properties?
13. What are three possible causes for the productivity slowdown?
14. What explains the recovery in productivity growth in the 1980s and 1990s and the reduction in productivity growth beginning in 2000?
15. What are the three factors that account for growth in GDP?
16. What was miraculous about growth in East Asian countries over the period 1966–1991? What was not miraculous about growth in these countries at this time?

Problems

1. In the Malthusian model, suppose that the quantity of land increases. Using diagrams, determine what effects this has in the long-run steady state and explain your results.
2. In the Malthusian model, suppose that there is a technological advance that reduces death rates. Using diagrams, determine the effects of this in the long-run steady state and explain your results.
3. In the Solow growth model, suppose that the marginal product of capital increases for each quantity of the capital input, given the labor input.
   (a) Show the effects of this on the aggregate production function.
   (b) Using a diagram, determine the effects on the quantity of capital per worker and on output per worker in the steady state.
   (c) Explain your results.

4. Suppose that the depreciation rate increases. In the Solow growth model, determine the effects of this on the quantity of capital per worker and on output per worker in the steady state. Explain the economic intuition behind your results.
5. Suppose that the economy is initially in a steady state and that some of the nation's capital stock is destroyed because of a natural disaster or a war.
   (a) Determine the long-run effects of this on the quantity of capital per worker and on output per worker.
   (b) In the short run, does aggregate output grow at a rate higher or lower than the growth rate of the labor force?
   (c) After World War II, growth in real GDP in Germany and Japan was very high. How do your

results in parts (a) and (b) shed light on this historical experience?

6. If total factor productivity decreases, determine using diagrams how this affects the golden rule quantity of capital per worker and the golden rule savings rate. Explain your results.

7. Modify the Solow growth model by including government spending, as follows. The government purchases G units of consumption goods in the current period, where $G = gN$ and g is a positive constant. The government finances its purchases through lump-sum taxes on consumers, where T denotes total taxes, and the government budget is balanced each period, so that $G = T$. Consumers consume a constant fraction of disposable income—that is, $C = (1 - s)(Y - T)$, where s is the savings rate, with $0 < s < 1$.
   (a) Derive equations similar to (6-18), (6-19), and (6-20), and show in a diagram how the quantity of capital per worker, k^*, is determined.
   (b) Show that there can be two steady states, one with high k^* and one with low k^*.
   (c) Ignore the steady state with low k^* (it can be shown that this steady state is "unstable"). Determine the effects of an increase in g on capital per worker and on output per worker in the steady state. What are the effects on the growth rates of aggregate output, aggregate consumption, and aggregate investment?
   (d) Explain your results.

8. Determine the effects of a decrease in the population growth rate on the golden rule quantity of capital per worker and on the golden rule savings rate. Explain your results.

9. Suppose that we modify the Solow growth model by allowing long-run technological progress. That is, suppose that $z = 1$ for convenience, and that there is labor-augmenting technological progress, with a production function
$$Y = F(K, bN),$$
where b denotes the number of units of "human capital" per worker, and bN is "efficiency units" of labor. Letting b' denote future human capital per

worker, assume that $b' = (1 + f)b$, where f is the growth rate in human capital.
   (a) Show that the long run equilibrium has the property that $k^{**} = \frac{K}{bN}$ is a constant. At what rate does aggregate output, aggregate consumption, aggregate investment, and per-capita income grow in this steady state? Explain.
   (b) What is the effect of an increase in f on the growth in per-capita income? Discuss relative to how the standard Solow growth model behaves.

10. Suppose in the Solow growth model that $s = .25, n = .02, d = .08$, and $f(k) = k^{.3}$.
   (a) Suppose that $z = 2$. What is the steady state level of capital per worker and consumption per worker?
   (b) Now, suppose that initially $z = 2$ and the economy is in the steady state you calculated in part (a). Then suppose that z falls to 1.8 permanently. What is the new steady state? Determine capital per worker and output per worker in each of the first 10 periods after z falls, and show this in a figure.
   (c) Now, suppose alternatively that $z = 2$ initially, the economy is in the steady state, and then z falls to 1.8, but now for only 10 periods. Then, $z = 2$ forever. Determine the path followed by capital per worker and output per worker in the first 10 periods after z falls. Again, show this in a figure.
   (d) What conclusions can you draw from your results in parts (a) through (c)? Discuss.

11. Alter the Solow growth model so that the production technology is given by $Y = zK$, where Y is output, K is capital, and z is total factor productivity. Thus, output is produced only with capital.
   (a) Show that it is possible for income per person to grow indefinitely.
   (b) Also show that an increase in the savings rate increases the growth rate in per capita income.
   (c) From parts (a) and (b), what are the differences between this model and the basic Solow growth model? Account for these differences and discuss.

12. Consider the following data:
    (a) Calculate the Solow residual for each year from 1995 to 2007.
    (b) Calculate percentage rates of growth in output, capital, employment, and total factor

productivity for the years 1996 to 2007. In each year, what contributes the most to growth in aggregate output? What contributes the least? Are there any surprises here? If so, explain.

Year	Y (billions of 2000 dollars)	K (billions of 2000 dollars	N (millions)
1995	8031.7	25487.3	124.9
1996	8328.9	26222.3	126.7
1997	8703.5	27018.1	129.6
1998	9066.9	27915.9	131.5
1999	9470.3	28899.9	133.5
2000	9817.0	29917.1	136.9
2001	9890.7	30793.4	136.9
2002	10048.8	31599.6	136.5
2003	10301.0	32426.2	137.7
2004	10703.5	33304.9	139.2
2005	11048.6	34191.7	141.7
2006	11294.8	35079.9	144.4
2007	11523.9	35910.4	146.0

Working with the Data

1. The total capital stock consists of private equipment capital, private structures capital, private residential capital, and government capital. Determine the growth rates of each of these components of the capital stock for each decade from 1930 until 2000. Which component of capital was the most important, and which was the least important, as a contributor to growth in the total capital stock in each decade? Comment on your results.

2. For the periods 1950–1960, 1960–1970, 1970–1980, 1980–1990, and 1990–2000, determine the growth rates in the total population, in the labor force, and in employment. What explains the differences among these three growth rates for each period?

3. Determine the quantity of capital per worker for the years 1950, 1960, 1970, 1980, 1990, and 2000, and calculate the growth rates of capital per worker for the periods 1950–1960, 1960–1970, 1970–1980, 1980–1990, and 1990–2000. Relate these growth rates to the data on total factor productivity growth in Table 6.3.

chapter 7

Income Disparity Among Countries and Endogenous Growth

This chapter extends the material in Chapter 6 to some additional issues related to the predictions of the Solow growth model and to the study of endogenous growth theory. Here, we are particularly interested in learning more about the reasons for the large income disparities that continue to exist among the countries of the world.

The Solow growth model makes strong predictions concerning the ability of poor countries to catch up with rich countries. That is, in this model income per capita converges among countries that are initially rich and poor but otherwise identical. The model tells us that countries that are initially poor in terms of income per capita grow at a faster rate than countries that are initially rich. In the context of the Solow growth model, the richest countries of the world look roughly as if they have converged. That is, among the countries that were relatively rich in 1960, subsequent average annual growth rates of per capita income did not differ that much. However, among the poorer countries of the world, income per capita does not appear to be converging, and the poorest countries of the world seem to be falling behind the richest ones, rather than catching up. Therefore, if we suppose that all countries are identical, particularly with regard to the technology that they have access to, then the Solow model is not entirely consistent with the way in which the distribution of income is evolving in the world.

However, what if different countries do not have access to the same technology? This can arise if groups who might lose from technological change in particular countries have the power to prevent new technologies from being adopted. For example, if the legal structure in a country gives power to labor unions, then these unions might prevent firms from introducing technologies that make the skills of union members obsolete. As well, political barriers to international trade (tariffs, import quotas, and subsidies) shield firms from international competition and block the incentives to develop new technologies. Then, if different countries have different barriers to technology adoption, this can explain the differences in standards of living across countries, in a manner consistent with the Solow growth model.

We might also observe different aggregate technological capacities across countries if there are differences in the efficiency with which factors of production are allocated across firms in different economies. For example, in sub-Saharan Africa, political corruption and poor financial arrangements may increase profit opportunities for firms that are politically well-connected or happen to know the right bankers, but do not actually possess efficient technologies for producing goods. This is less likely to happen in countries such as the United States, Sweden, Canada, or Australia, where there is less political corruption and highly developed financial systems, which tend to direct factors of production to their most efficient uses.

An alternative set of models that can explain persistent differences in standards of living across countries is the set of endogenous growth models. In this chapter, we consider a simple model of endogenous growth, and we show how some of the predictions of this model differ from those of the Solow growth model. The endogenous growth model we study shows how the accumulation of skills and education is important to economic growth. We use the model to evaluate how economic policy might affect the quantity of resources allocated to skills and education and how this affects growth.

In contrast to the Solow growth model, the endogenous growth model we study does not predict convergence in levels of per capita income across countries when countries are identical except for being initially rich and initially poor. In fact, the endogenous growth model predicts that differences in per capita income persist forever. The model indicates some of the factors that can be important in explaining the continuing disparities in living standards between the richest and poorest countries of the world.

Convergence

In Chapter 6, we discussed large disparities that exist in levels of per capita income and in growth rates of per capita income across the countries of the world. While these statistics tell us something about the wide variation in standards of living and in growth experience in the world, we would also like to know whether these disparities are increasing or decreasing over time and why. Is there a tendency for poor countries to catch up with rich countries with respect to standards of living? If the poor countries are not catching up, why is this so, and what could the poor countries do about it?

The Solow growth model makes strong predictions about the ability of poor countries to catch up with rich ones. For example, suppose two countries are identical with respect to total factor productivities (they share the same technology), labor force growth rates, and savings rates. However, the rich country initially has a higher level of capital per worker than does the poor country. Given the per-worker production function, the rich country also has a higher quantity of output per worker than the poor country. The Solow growth model predicts that both countries will converge to the same level of capital per worker and output per worker. Ultimately, the poor country will catch up to the rich country with regard to living standards.

In Figure 7.1, we show the relationship between current capital per worker, k, and future capital per worker, k' from the Solow growth model. The poor country initially has quantity k_p of capital per worker, while the rich country initially has quantity k_r of capital per worker. Capital per worker and output per worker grow in both countries, but in the long run, both countries have k^* units of capital per worker and the same quantity of output per worker. In Figure 7.2 we show the paths

Figure 7.1 Rich and Poor Countries and the Steady State

Two otherwise identical countries have initial capital stocks per worker of k_p (the poor country) and k_r (the rich country). Both countries converge in the long-run steady state to the quantity k^* of capital per worker.

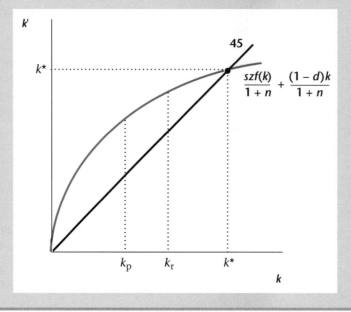

Figure 7.2 Convergence in Income per Worker Across Countries in the Solow Growth Model

Two otherwise identical countries, one with lower income per worker (the poor country) than the other (the rich country), both converge in the long-run steady state to the same level of income per worker, y_1^*.

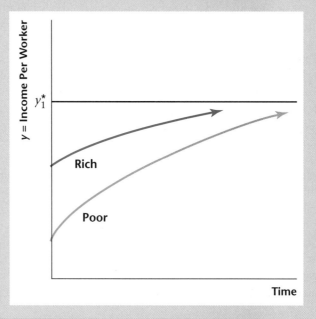

followed over time by real income per worker in the rich country and poor country. The initial gap between the rich and poor countries narrows over time and disappears in the long run.

The rich country and poor country in the example above also have identical growth rates of aggregate output (equal to their identical labor force growth rates) in the long run. Recall that the Solow growth model predicts aggregate output will grow at the rate of labor force growth in the long run, thus, if the rich and poor countries have the same labor force growth rate, their long-run growth rates in aggregate output will be identical. Supposing that the rich and poor countries also have the same initial labor force levels, the growth paths of aggregate output, as predicted by the Solow growth model, will be the same in the long run. In Figure 7.3 the black line denotes the long-run growth path of the natural logarithm of aggregate output in the rich and poor countries. As predicted by the Solow growth model, if aggregate output is initially lower in the poor country, its growth rate in aggregate output will be larger than that for the rich country, and this will cause the level of aggregate output in the poor country to catch up to the level in the rich country. In the long run, growth in aggregate output in the rich and poor countries converges to the same rate.

Therefore, given no differences among countries in terms of access to technology, the Solow model is quite optimistic about the prospects for countries of the world that

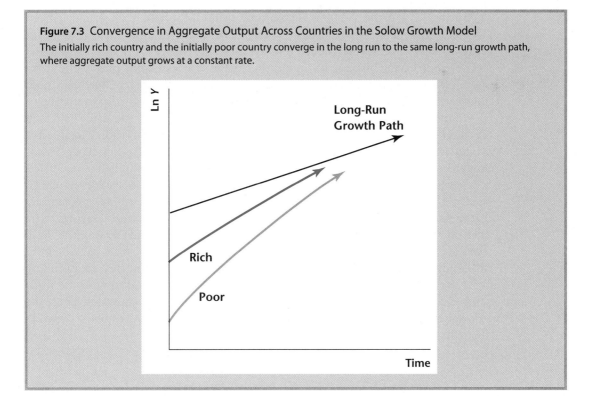

Figure 7.3 Convergence in Aggregate Output Across Countries in the Solow Growth Model
The initially rich country and the initially poor country converge in the long run to the same long-run growth path, where aggregate output grows at a constant rate.

are currently poor. Under these conditions the model predicts that, left alone, the countries of the world will converge to similar standards of living, with some differences across countries explained by differences in savings rates and population growth rates.

However, suppose that countries do not have access to the same technology. This could happen for at least two reasons. First, there exist barriers to the adoption of new technology, and these barriers can differ across countries.[1] Barriers to technology adoption can arise if the government introduces laws that make it easy for labor unions to organize and gives them greater power in bargaining with firms. This then makes it easier for unions to block the introduction of new technologies. Powerful unions are able to negotiate high wages and benefits for their members, and they also try to prevent their members from being displaced from their jobs by new technologies that make union members' skills obsolete. For example, automobile industry unions would typically resist the use of robots that would displace labor in auto assembly plants. Also, barriers to entry can arise when governments introduce trade restrictions that shield domestic industries from foreign competition. This can have the effect of taking away the incentives for firms in those industries to develop more efficient technologies. For example, the United States currently imposes tariffs on imports of lumber from foreign countries, and grants large subsidies to U.S. farmers. These government interventions act to reduce technological innovation by U.S. lumber companies and U.S. farmers, and this has a negative effect on total factor productivity in the United States.

A second reason that the level of aggregate technology can differ across different countries is that economies may differ in how efficiently factors of production are allocated across firms in the economy. For example, political corruption can result in advantages for inefficient firms—for instance, if a politician's relatives are awarded government contracts or if subsidies are granted to industries in exchange for bribes. As well, the less developed is the financial sector of the economy, the less ill-equipped is the economy to allocate resources to their best uses. For example, in an economy with poor financial markets, an innovative new firm may find it difficult to borrow to start up.

To the extent that barriers to the adoption of new technology and inefficiencies in the allocation of factors of production differ across countries, this causes total factor productivity to differ, and convergence in standards of living does not occur. To see how this works, consider Figure 7.4. Suppose that there are three different countries, which we call poor, middle income, and rich, and that these countries have levels of total factor productivity z_p, z_m, and z_r, respectively, where $z_p < z_m < z_r$. We also suppose that these countries have identical population growth rates and identical savings rates. Then, in Figure 7.4, in the steady state the poor, middle income, and rich countries have levels of capital per worker of k_p^*, k_m^*, and k_r^*, respectively, so that output per worker in the steady state is ranked according to poor, middle income, and rich, in ascending order. In the steady state, standards of living are permanently different in the three countries, but aggregate output grows at the same rate in these countries. Thus, the Solow model can explain disparities across countries in income per capita, if there are differences in aggregate technology across countries.

---

[1]See S. Parente and E. Prescott, 2000. *Barriers to Riches,* MIT Press, Cambridge, MA.

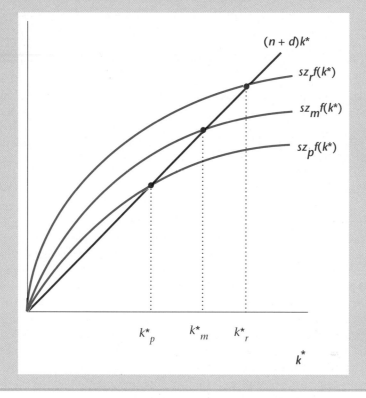

Figure 7.4 Differences in Total Factor Productivity Can Explain Disparity in Income per Worker Across Countries

If countries have different levels of total factor productivity due to differing barriers to technology adoption, then capital per worker and income per worker differ across countries in the steady state.

If the large disparity in income per capita across countries of the world is in part due to barriers to the adoption of technology and allocative inefficiencies, what can poor countries do to catch up to the rich countries?[2] First, governments can promote greater competition among firms. If monopoly power is not protected by governments, then firms have to develop and implement new technologies to remain competitive, so that productivity will be higher. Second, governments can promote free trade. Just as with greater domestic competition, greater competition between countries promotes innovation and the adoption of the best technologies. Third, governments should privatize production where there is no good economic case for government ownership. Government ownership where it is unnecessary often leads to protection of employment at the expense of efficiency, and this tends to lower total factor productivity. Fourth, governments can promote the enforcement of laws, so as to mitigate political corruption.

---

[2]For an elaboration on these arguments, see S. Parente and E. Prescott, 2000. *Barriers to Riches*, MIT Press, Cambridge, MA.

Is Income Per Worker Converging in the World?

THEORY confronts the DATA

If income per worker is converging among countries of the world, we would observe over time that the dispersion in income per worker was falling. As well, if we observed the countries of the world at a given point in time, we would see that income per worker was growing at a higher rate in poor countries than in rich countries. That is, we should see a negative correlation between the rate of growth in income per worker and the level of income per worker across countries.

In this section we look at the evidence for convergence in the world economy. From fact (6) in the Economic Growth Facts section in Chapter 6, recall that, when we look at all countries in the world, there is essentially no correlation between the level of output per worker in 1960 and the average growth rate of output per worker between 1960 and 2000. Fact (7) is that richer countries are much more alike in terms of rates of growth of real per capita income than are poor countries. Therefore, between 1960 and 2000 there appeared to be no convergence among all the countries in the world. However, there is evidence for convergence among the richest countries of the world for the same period, since these countries behave roughly like a group of countries that has achieved convergence, since their growth rates of per capita income do not differ much (at least relative to what we see for poor countries).

The following story makes these observations on convergence from the data consistent with the predictions of the Solow growth model. First, we can think of the richest countries of the world in 1960 (the Western European countries, the United States, Canada, Australia, and New Zealand) as having access to roughly the same technology. The Solow growth model then tells us that we should

expect convergence in standards of living among these countries, with some minor differences accounted for by differences in population growth and savings rates. Second, the tendency for differences in standards of living to persist among the poor countries of the world can be explained in the Solow model by different levels of total factor productivity in those countries brought about by differing barriers to technology adoption, and differing degrees of inefficiency in the allocation of factors of production among firms in the economy.

To support the idea that persistent disparity in income per capita across countries could be caused by barriers to technology adoption, we need additional evidence for the existence of such barriers and evidence that the barriers differ significantly among countries. In their book *Barriers to Riches,* Stephen Parente and Edward Prescott provide considerable evidence of both types in examining experience in particular industries and countries.[3] They argue that evidence of resistance to the adoption of new technology can be found in the textiles industry and in the mining industry in the United States. Further, if we look at particular industries and measure productivities in those industries across countries, the evidence supports the idea that barriers to technology adoption are important for explaining productivity differences.

A key feature of the data that supports the idea that there are barriers preventing poor countries from adopting the technologies used by the richest countries of the world is that growth miracles have not occurred for the very rich. In the United States, as we observed in Chapter 6, the growth rate of income per

---

[3]See S. Parente and E. Prescott, 2000. *Barriers to Riches,* MIT Press, Cambridge, MA.

capita has not strayed far from 2% per annum since 1900. The important growth miracles after World War II occurred in Japan, South Korea, Taiwan, Singapore, and Hong Kong. At the time when growth took off in these countries, they were all well behind the standard of living in the United States. The growth miracles in these countries are consistent with barriers to technology adoption being removed, which then allowed income per capita to quickly approach that of the United States. However, perhaps we need to be somewhat skeptical of this explanation, as our study of the East Asian growth miracles in Chapter 6 indicated that these growth miracles were due primarily to high growth in factors of production, not to high growth in total factor productivity.

Some economists have studied the extent of the effect of the misallocation of factors of production across firms in explaining cross-country differences in standards of living. For example, Chang-Tai Hsieh and Peter Klenow estimate that, if capital and labor were allocated as efficiently across firms in China and India as in the United States, then total factor productivity would by 30% to 50% higher in China, and 40% to 60% higher in India.[4] This evidence suggests that the elimination of government corruption, inefficiencies in the financial sector, and inefficient taxes and subsidies could go a long way toward making the countries of the world look more alike in terms of their standards of living.

[4]C. Hsieh and P. Klenow, 2008. "Misallocation and Manufacturing TFP in China and India," forthcoming, *Quarterly Journal of Economics.*

Endogenous Growth: A Model of Human Capital Accumulation

Perhaps the primary deficiency of the Solow growth model is that it does not explain a key observation, which is growth itself. The Solow model relies on increases in total factor productivity coming from outside the model to generate long-run increases in per capita output, and this seems unsatisfactory, as we would like to understand the economic forces behind increases in total factor productivity. Total factor productivity growth involves research and development by firms, education, and training on the job, and all of these activities are responsive to the economic environment. We might like an economic growth model to answer the following questions: How does total factor productivity growth respond to the quantity of public funds spent on public education? How is total factor productivity growth affected by subsidies to research and development? Does it make sense to have the government intervene to promote economic growth? While the Solow growth model cannot answer these questions, a model of endogenous growth, where growth rates are explained by the model, potentially can.

The endogenous growth model that we work with here is a simplification of a model developed by Robert Lucas.[5] Another important earlier contributor to research on endogenous growth was Paul Romer.[6] In the model, the representative consumer allocates his or her time between supplying labor to produce output and accumulating

[5]R. Lucas, 1988, "On the Mechanics of Economic Development," *Journal of Monetary Economics* 22, July, 3–42.

[6]See P. Romer, 1986, "Increasing Returns and Long-Run Growth," *Journal of Political Economy* 94, 500–521.

human capital, where human capital is the accumulated stock of skills and education that a worker has at a point in time. The higher the human capital that workers have, the more they can produce, and the more new human capital they can produce. Thus, a higher level of human capital means that the economy can grow at a faster rate.

If we think in terms of real-world economies, at any given time some of the working age population is employed and producing goods and services, some are in school, and some are unemployed or not in the labor force. There is a social opportunity cost associated with people of working age who are in school, as these people could otherwise be producing goods and services. By acquiring schooling, however, people accumulate skills (human capital), and a more highly skilled labor force in the future permits more future output to be produced. Also, a more highly skilled population can better pass on skills to others, and so human capital accumulation is more efficient if the level of human capital is higher.

Human capital accumulation, therefore, is an investment, just like investment in plant and equipment, as there are associated current costs and future benefits. However, there are good reasons to think that physical investment is fundamentally different from human capital investment, in addition to the obvious difference that physical investment is embodied in machines and buildings, and human capital investment is embodied in people. Recall that in the Solow growth model there are diminishing marginal returns to the accumulation of physical capital, because adding more capital to a fixed labor force should eventually yield lower increases in output at the margin. Human capital accumulation differs in that there appears to be no limit to human knowledge or to how productive individuals can become given increases in knowledge and skills. Paul Romer has argued that a key feature of knowledge is **nonrivalry**.[7] That is, a particular person's acquisition of knowledge does not reduce the ability of someone else to acquire the same knowledge. Most goods are rivalrous; for example, my consumption of hotel services limits the ability of others to benefit from hotel services, as only a fixed number of hotel rooms is available in a given city at a given time. Physical capital accumulation also involves rivalry, as the acquisition of plant and equipment by a firm uses up resources that could be used by other firms to acquire plant and equipment. Diminishing marginal returns to human capital investment seems unnatural. The lack of diminishing returns to human capital investment leads to unbounded growth in the model we study here, even though there are no exogenous forces propelling economic growth.

The Representative Consumer

Our endogenous growth model has a representative consumer, who starts the current period with H^s units of human capital. In each period, the consumer has one unit of time (as in the Malthusian model and the Solow model, the fact that there is one unit of time is simply a normalization), which can be allocated between work and accumulating human capital. For simplicity, we assume the consumer does not use time for leisure. Let u denote the fraction of time devoted to working in each period, so that the number of **efficiency units of labor** devoted to work is uH^s. That is, the number of units of labor that the consumer effectively supplies is the number of units of time spent working multiplied by the consumer's quantity of human capital. The consumer's

---

[7]See P. Romer, 1990, "Endogenous Technological Change," *Journal of Political Economy* 98, S71–S102.

quantity of human capital is the measure of the productivity of the consumer's time when he or she is working. For each efficiency unit of labor supplied, the consumer receives the current real wage w. For simplicity, we assume the consumer cannot save, and so the consumer's budget constraint in the current period is

$$C = wuH^s, \qquad (7\text{-}1)$$

or consumption is equal to total labor earnings.

Although the consumer cannot save, he or she can trade off current consumption for future consumption by accumulating human capital. Because u units of time are used for work, the remainder, $1 - u$, is used for human capital accumulation. The technology for accumulating human capital is given by

$$H^{s'} = b(1 - u)H^s; \qquad (7\text{-}2)$$

that is, the stock of human capital in the future period, denoted by $H^{s'}$, varies in proportion to the number of current efficiency units of labor devoted to human capital accumulation, which is $(1 - u)H^s$. Here, b is a parameter that captures the efficiency of the human capital accumulation technology, with $b > 0$. Thus, equation (7-2) represents the idea that accumulating skills and education is easier, the more skills and education an individual (or society) has.

The Representative Firm

For simplicity there is no physical capital in this model, and the representative firm produces output using only efficiency units of labor. The production function is given by

$$Y = zuH^d, \qquad (7\text{-}3)$$

where Y is current output, $z > 0$ is the marginal product of efficiency units of labor, and uH^d is the current input of efficiency units of labor into production. That is, uH^d is the demand for efficiency units of labor by the representative firm. The production function in equation (7-3) has constant returns to scale, because there is only one input into production, efficiency units of labor, and increasing the quantity of efficiency units of labor increases output in the same proportion. For example, increasing efficiency units of labor uH^d by 1% increases current output by 1%.

The representative firm hires the quantity of efficiency units of labor, uH^d, that maximizes current profits, where profits are

$$\pi = Y - wuH^d,$$

which is the quantity of output produced minus the wages paid to workers. Substituting for Y from equation (7-3), we get

$$\pi = zuH^d - wuH^d = (z - w)uH^d. \qquad (7\text{-}4)$$

Now, if $z - w < 0$, then in equation (7-4) profits are negative if the firm hires a positive quantity of efficiency units of labor, so that the firm maximizes profits by setting $uH^d = 0$. If $z - w > 0$, then profits are $z - w$ for each efficiency unit hired, so that

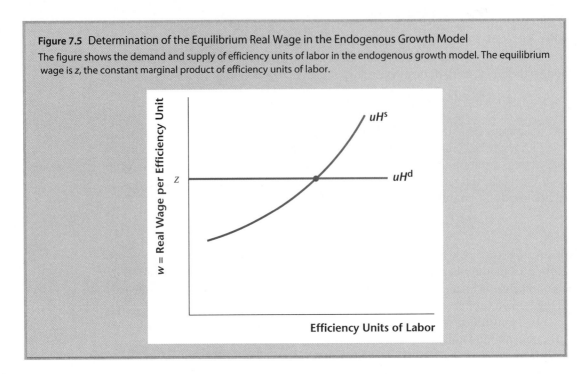

Figure 7.5 Determination of the Equilibrium Real Wage in the Endogenous Growth Model

The figure shows the demand and supply of efficiency units of labor in the endogenous growth model. The equilibrium wage is z, the constant marginal product of efficiency units of labor.

the firm wants to hire an infinite quantity of workers to maximize profits. If $z = w$, then the firm's profits are zero for any quantity of workers hired, so that the firm is indifferent about the quantity of efficiency units of labor hired. We conclude that the firm's demand curve for efficiency units of labor is infinitely elastic at $w = z$. In Figure 7.5 we show the firm's demand curve for efficiency units of labor, which is just a special case of the demand curve being identical to the marginal product schedule for efficiency units of labor. Here, the marginal product of efficiency units of labor is a constant, z. What this implies is that no matter what the supply curve for efficiency units of labor, the intersection between demand and supply always occurs, as in Figure 7.5, at a real wage of $w = z$. That is, the equilibrium real wage per efficiency unit of labor is always $w = z$. This then implies that the real wage per hour of work is $wH^d = zH^d$, and so the real wage as we would measure it empirically changes in proportion to the quantity of human capital of the representative consumer.

Competitive Equilibrium

Working out the competitive equilibrium here is quite straightforward. There is only one market each period, on which consumption goods are traded for efficiency units of labor, and we know already that this market always clears at a real wage of $w = z$. Market clearing gives $uH^s = uH^d$ (the supply of efficiency units of labor is equal to the demand), and so $H^s = H^d = H$. Therefore, substituting in equations (7-1) and (7-2) for w and H^s, we get

$$C = zuH, \tag{7-5}$$

and

$$H' = b(1 - u)H. \qquad (7\text{-}6)$$

Therefore, equation (7-6) determines future human capital H' given current human capital H, and we show this relationship in Figure 7.6. The slope of the colored line in the figure is $b(1 - u)$, and if $b(1 - u) > 1$, then we have $H' > H$, so that future human capital is always greater than current human capital, and, therefore, human capital grows over time without bound. From equation (7-6), the growth rate of human capital is

$$\frac{H'}{H} - 1 = b(1 - u) - 1, \qquad (7\text{-}7)$$

which is a constant. What is important here is that the growth rate of human capital increases if b increases or if u decreases. Recall that b determines the efficiency of the human capital accumulation technology, which could be interpreted as the efficiency of the educational sector. Thus, the model predicts that countries with more efficient education systems should experience higher rates of growth in human capital. If u decreases, then more time is devoted to human capital accumulation and less to producing output in each period. As seems natural, this causes the growth rate in human capital to increase.

Now, equation (7-5) will also hold in the future period, so that $C' = zuH'$ where C' is future consumption, and, therefore, from equation (7-5) we can determine the growth rate of consumption, which is

$$\frac{C'}{C} - 1 = \frac{zuH'}{zuH} - 1 = \frac{H'}{H} - 1 = b(1 - u) - 1,$$

Figure 7.6 Human Capital Accumulation in the Endogenous Growth Model

The colored line shows the quantity of future human capital H' as a function of current human capital H. As drawn $H' > H$ for any H, so human capital continues to increase forever.

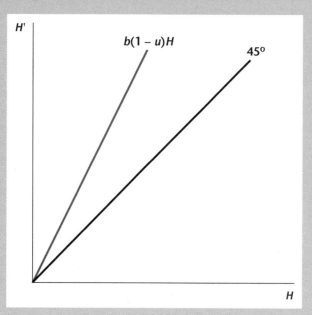

that is, the growth rate of consumption is identical to the growth rate of human capital. Further, from equations (7-3) and (7-5), $C = Y$, which we also know must hold in equilibrium, given the income–expenditure identity from Chapter 2 (our model has no investment, no government, and no net exports). Therefore, human capital, consumption, and output all grow at the same rate, $b(1 - u) - 1$, in equilibrium.

This model economy does not grow because of any exogenous forces. There is no population growth (there is a single representative consumer), and the production technology does not change over time (b and z remain fixed). Growth occurs, therefore, because of endogenous forces, with the growth rate determined by b and u. The key element in the model that leads to unbounded growth is the fact that the production function, given by equation (7-3), does not exhibit decreasing returns to scale in human capital. That is, the production function has constant returns to scale in human capital, because output increases in proportion to human capital, given u. For example, if human capital increases by 10%, then, holding u constant, output increases by 10%. In the Solow growth model, growth is limited because of the decreasing marginal product of physical capital, but here the marginal product of human capital does not decrease as the quantity of human capital used in production increases. The marginal product of human capital does not fall as human capital increases, because knowledge and skills are nonrivalrous; additional education and skills do not reduce the extra output that can be achieved through the acquisition of more education and skills.

Economic Policy and Growth

Our endogenous growth model suggests that government policies can affect the growth rates of aggregate output and consumption. Because the common growth rate of human capital, consumption, and output depends on b and u, it is useful to think about how government policy might affect b and u. As b is the efficiency of the human capital accumulation technology, b could be affected by government policies that make the educational system more efficient. For example, this might be accomplished through the implementation of better incentives for performance in the school system, or possibly by changing the mix of public and private education. Exactly what policies the government would have to pursue to increase b we cannot say here without being much more specific in modeling the education system. However, it certainly seems feasible for governments to affect the efficiency of education, and politicians seem to believe this, too.

Government policy could also change the rate of economic growth by changing u. For example, this could be done through taxes or subsidies to education. If the government subsidizes education, then such a policy would make human capital accumulation more desirable relative to current production, and so u would decrease, and the growth rate of output and consumption would increase.

Now, suppose that the government had the power to decrease u or to increase b, thus increasing the growth rate of consumption and output. Would this be a good idea or not? To answer this question, we would have to ask how the representative consumer's welfare would change as a result. Now, clearly a decrease in u increases the growth rate of consumption, which is $b(1 - u) - 1$, but there is also a second effect, in that the level of consumption goes down. That is, current consumption is $C = zuH$, and so in the very first period if u decreases, then C must also fall, because initial human capital H is given. Recall from Chapter 1 that if we graph the natural logarithm of a variable against time, then the slope of the graph is approximately the growth rate. Because consumption grows at the constant rate $b(1 - u) - 1$ in equilibrium, if we graph the natural log of consumption against time, this is a straight line. The slope of the graph of consumption increases as u decreases and the growth rate of consumption increases, and the vertical intercept of the graph decreases as u decreases, as this reduces consumption in the very first period. There is, therefore, a trade-off for the representative consumer when u decreases: consumption is sacrificed early on, but consumption grows at a higher rate, so that consumption ultimately is higher than it was with a higher level of u. Thus, the path for consumption shifts as in Figure 7.7. In the figure, consumption is lower after the change in u until period T, and after period T consumption is higher than it would otherwise have been.

It is not clear that the consumer would prefer the new consumption path with the higher growth rate of consumption, even though consumption is higher in the long run. There is a cost to higher growth, which is that consumption in the near term must be forgone. Which consumption path the consumer prefers depends on how patient he or she is. Preferences could be such that the consumer is very impatient, in which case he or she

Figure 7.7 Effect of a Decrease in u on the Consumption Path in the Endogenous Growth Model
The figure shows the effect of a decrease in u, which increases the fraction of time spent accumulating human capital each period. The growth path for consumption (consumption is equal to income) pivots; thus, there is a short-run decrease in consumption, but consumption is higher in the long run.

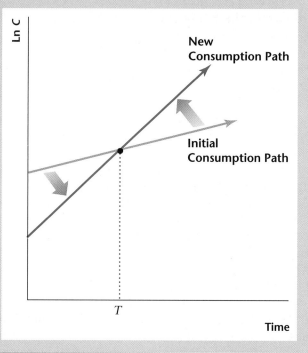

would tend to prefer the initial consumption path with a low growth rate of consumption. Alternatively, the consumer might be very patient, tending to prefer the new consumption path with a high growth rate of consumption. The conclusion is that, even if the government could engineer a higher rate of growth by causing u to fall—say through education subsidies—this may not be desirable because of the near-term costs involved.

We could do a similar analysis for the case in which the government causes the growth rate of consumption to increase through an increase in b, the parameter governing the efficiency of human capital accumulation. In this case, the model is not explicit about the near-term costs of increasing the growth rate of consumption by increasing b. That is, current consumption is given by $C = zuH$, so consumption in the very first period does not depend on b. However, if the government were to increase b through education policy, for example, this would entail some real resource costs. Suppose that the government chose to make public education more efficient by increasing monitoring of teacher and student performance. Clearly, there would be a cost to this monitoring in terms of labor time. We might represent this cost in our model as a reduction in the level of consumption, as labor is diverted from goods production to government monitoring activities. Therefore, b would increase, which would increase the growth rate of consumption, but as in the case in which we examined the effects of a decrease in u, there would be a decrease in consumption in the very first period. Thus, the relationship between the new consumption path after the increase in b and the initial consumption path would be just as in Figure 7.7. As in the case where u falls, it is not clear whether the representative consumer is better off when the growth rate of consumption is higher, because there are short-term costs in terms of lost consumption.

Convergence in the Endogenous Growth Model

In the Solow growth model, with exogenous growth, countries that are in all respects identical, except for their initial quantities of capital per worker, have in the long run the same level and growth rate of income per worker. We showed in the previous section that this prediction of the Solow growth model is consistent with data on the evolution of income per capita in the richest countries of the world but not with data for poorer countries. To explain disparities among the poor countries, and disparities between the rich and poor, with the Solow model, we must appeal to significant differences among countries in something exogenous in the Solow growth model, which could be total factor productivity.

In the endogenous growth model we have constructed here, convergence does not occur even if countries are identical in all respects except that there are differences in the initial level of human capital. To see this, note first that in the endogenous growth model, consumption is equal to income, and there is only one consumer, so that per capita income is identical to aggregate income. Accordingly, current consumption is given by $C = zuH$, and consumption grows at a constant rate $b(1 - u) - 1$, so that the natural log of consumption graphed against time is a straight line, as we showed in Figure 7.7. Now, suppose that we consider two countries that have the same technology and allocate labor in the same way between goods production and human capital accumulation. That is, b, z, and u are the same in the two countries. However, suppose that these countries differ according to their initial human capital levels. The rich country has a high level of initial human capital, denoted H_r, and the poor country has a low level of human capital, denoted H_p, which implies that consumption in the rich country is initially $C = zuH_r$, which is greater than initial consumption in the poor country, $C = zuH_p$. Now, because b and u are identical in the two countries, $b(1 - u) - 1$, the growth rate of consumption, is also identical for the rich and poor countries. Therefore, the growth paths of consumption for the rich country and the poor country are as in Figure 7.8. That is, initial differences in income and consumption across rich and poor countries persist forever, and there is no convergence.

How do we reconcile the predictions of the endogenous growth model concerning convergence with the facts? The model appears consistent with the fact that there are persistent differences in income per capita among poorer countries and persistent differences in income per capita between the poorer countries of the world and the richer countries. However, the model appears inconsistent with the fact that incomes per capita seem to have converged among the richer nations of the world. Perhaps an explanation for this is that, in regions of the world where labor and capital are mobile, and where skills are more easily transferred, there are important **human capital externalities,** as discussed by Robert Lucas.[8] A human capital externality exists when contact with others with high levels of human capital increases our human capital or makes us more productive. Human capital externalities can explain the existence of cities and the specialized activities that take place there. Why, for

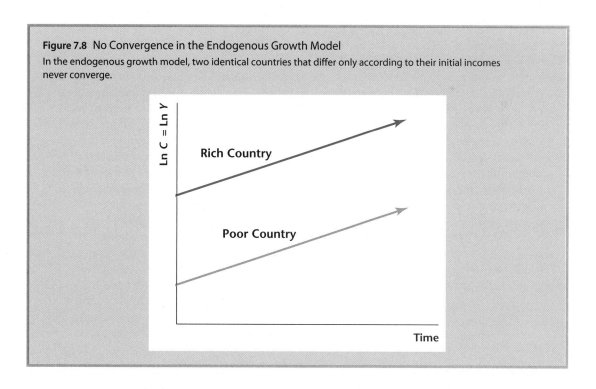

Figure 7.8 No Convergence in the Endogenous Growth Model

In the endogenous growth model, two identical countries that differ only according to their initial incomes never converge.

[8]R. Lucas, 1988, "On the Mechanics of Economic Development," *Journal of Monetary Economics* 22, July, 3–42.

MACROECONOMICS IN ACTION
Education and Growth

In cross-country economic data, economists have observed that there is a positive correlation between the level of education of a country's population (as measured for example by average years of schooling across the population) and the rate of growth in real GDP.[9] Mark Bils and Peter Klenow estimate that, in terms of average educational attainment of a country in 1960, one more year of schooling on average is associated with 0.30 more percentage points in average annual growth in GDP per capita from 1960 to 1990.[10] One might be tempted to conclude, given this observation, that a more highly educated population *causes* the economic growth rate to rise. Then, some might argue that, since economic growth is a good thing, it would then be a good idea for the government to take steps to increase schooling and boost growth. However, this argument would be sloppy economics.

A correlation observed in economic data need not reflect causation, just as correlations observed in other kinds of scientific data need not tell us what causes what. For example, one could conclude from observing a positive correlation in the incidence of lung cancer and smoking across the population that lung cancer causes people to smoke. There are at least two other possible explanations for the lung cancer/smoking correlation. One is that there is some third factor that is correlated with both the incidence of lung cancer and with smoking, and that is actually the root explanation

for the correlation. For example, it could be that poor people tend to have lung cancer, and poor people tend to smoke, and that there is something about being poor (bad living conditions, for example) that causes lung cancer. A second alternative explanation—the one backed by a large body of scientific evidence—is that smoking causes lung cancer.

Now, in terms of the correlation between average educational attainment and economic growth, we have an analogous empirical problem to the one of interpreting the correlation between lung cancer and smoking. That is, the correlation between education and growth could mean that: (i) higher education causes the growth rate of GDP to be higher; (ii) some third factor causes educational attainment and the growth rate of GDP to be positively correlated; or (iii) higher economic growth causes more education. In fact, all of (i)–(iii) could be at work, and as economists we are interested in how each of (i)–(iii) contributes to the correlation, in part because this will be informative about the potential effects of government policies toward education. This is the type of exercise carried out by Mark Bils and Peter Klenow in an article in the *American Economic Review*.[11]

What are the particular economic mechanisms at work in cases (i)–(iii) above? For (i), the model of endogenous we growth we studied in the previous section of this chapter provides some insight into how more education can cause the economic growth rate to be higher. In the model, if the average individual in society devotes more time to accumulating human capital, which we can interpret as

[9]See, for example, Barro, R. 1990. "Economic Growth in a Cross Section of Countries," *Quarterly Journal of Economics* 106, 407–443.

[10]Bils, M. and Klenow, P. 2000. "Does Schooling Cause Growth?" *American Economic Review* 90, 1160–1183.

[11]Bils, M. and Klenow, P. 2000. "Does Schooling Cause Growth?" *American Economic Review* 90, 1160–1183.

education, then aggregate output will grow at a higher rate. With regard to (ii) above, how might factors other than education and economic growth cause educational attainment and the economic growth rate to move together? As Bils and Klenow argue, in countries with sound legal systems that adequately enforce property rights, educational attainment is high because people know that investing in education will have large future payoffs. In such societies, the growth rate of GDP is also high, in part because the enforcement of property rights leads to greater innovation, research, and development. Thus, we will see a positive correlation across countries between education and growth, but not because of a direct causal relationship between the two.

Finally, for (iii) above, educational attainment could be high because people anticipate high future economic growth. A high rate of future economic growth will imply a high rate of return to education, since a high rate of growth should increase the gap between the wages of high-skill and low-skill workers.

Bils and Klenow essentially find that causation running from education to growth accounts for only about 30% of the relationship between education and growth. This suggests that, if we are interested in government policies that promote growth, then perhaps improvements in patent policy or in the role of government in research and development are more important than improvements in education policy.

Perspectives on the Financial Crisis
Human Capital and Recessions

In Chapter 6, we showed how the Solow growth model helps us to organize our thinking about what is lost in a recession. In particular a recession, whatever its cause, represents not only lost current output and consumption, but lost future output and consumption. A decrease in future output and consumption occurs because investment falls during a recession, reducing the capital stock below what it would otherwise be, and therefore reducing the economy's future capacity to produce output. However, the Solow growth model captures only the role of physical capital in production, and not the role of human capital.

Human capital is important in analyzing the effects of recessions, as human capital accumulation (the acquisition of skills and education) may actually by countercyclical, in contrast to physical capital accumulation, which is procyclical. A positive aspect of a recession is that it represents an opportunity for unemployed workers, or those not in the labor force who would otherwise choose to work, to acquire more human capital. This human capital accumulation takes the form of college education, continuing education, and other activities that increase the level of skill.

Although the opportunity cost of time is low during a recession, which would tend to encourage more human capital acquisition, it is also true that human capital accumulation requires financial resources, and that the average consumer is more financially constrained during a recession. Thus economic theory tells us that human capital accumulation could increase or decrease during a recession; theory does not predict that human capital acquisition is unambiguously countercyclical. However, evidence indicates that human capital accumulation is in fact countercyclical in the United States. College enrollments are countercyclical, and some econometric

(Continued)

evidence indicates that all forms of human capital accumulation are countercyclical.[12]

Now, suppose that we use our endogenous growth model to obtain some measure of the effects of the 2008–2009 recession. A measure of u that we could use is the employment/population ratio, discussed in Chapter 1, and later in Chapter 17, which is the ratio of the number of employed people in the U.S. economy to total working age population. Using this ratio as a measure of u assumes that all of the working age population not employed was accumulating human capital, which is certainly not true, but for our purposes this will not do much harm. In December 2006, the employment/population ratio reached .634, and then it declined to .597 by May 2009. Since $b(1 - u) - 1$ is the growth rate of output in our economy, if the model is to capture an average annual growth rate in aggregate output for the United States of 3%, then we will have

$$b(1 - u) - 1 = .03,$$

so

$$b = \frac{1.03}{1 - u} = \frac{1.03}{.366} = 2.814,$$

if $u = .634$.

Now, suppose that the economy had been growing at 3% per year, with $b = 2.814$, and $u = .634$. This is not exactly what has been happening in the U.S. economy, for example, over the period since World War II. Over that period u

[12]See D. DeJong and B. Ingram, 2001. "The Cyclical Behavior of Skill Acquistion," *Review of Economic Dynamics* 4, 536–561.

increased significantly, as measured by the employment/population ratio. Again, for the purposes of our argument, this is not a big deal. Now, suppose that u falls temporarily, for one year, to .597, just as happened in early 2009. This will have a direct effect on output and consumption, from equation (7-5), and we can think of there being an additional negative temporary effect on output and consumption due to a decrease in z. However, we are primarily interested in the effect on human capital. From equation (7-6), the ratio of human capital at the beginning of the year after the recession, to what it would have been if u had remained at .634 is $\frac{1 - .597}{1 - .634} = 1.1011$. Thus, human capital would be more than 10% higher as a result of the recession occurring. Although consumption and output were lost in the recession, after the recession is over, consumption and output resume growing at 3% when u returns to a level of .634. Further, since human capital begins the post-recession period more than 10% higher than previously, output and consumption will be more than 10% higher in the future than if the recession had not occurred. As well, in our endogenous growth model this effect is permanent.

An estimate of a 10% permanent increase in output in the future as a result of a recession is certainly very optimistic. This is because we have to recognize that not all of the non-employed are accumulating human capital, and that there is a decrease in physical capital that results from the recession. Still the fact that more human capital is accumulated during a recession is something of a silver lining, and our endogenous growth model gives us some insight into how this process works.

example, would people specializing in financial activities want to bear the congestion and pollution of New York City unless there were significant positive externalities involved in working there? In highly developed regions of the world where there are greater opportunities through business contacts and education in other countries and regions for taking advantage of human capital externalities, large differences in the levels of human capital across regions cannot persist, and there is convergence in income per worker. However, less developed countries interact to a low degree with highly developed countries, and people with high levels of human capital tend to move to the highly developed countries from the less developed countries (the "brain drain"). Thus, differences in human capital can persist across very rich and very poor countries.

We have now completed our study of economic growth in this part. In Part IV, we move on to a detailed examination of savings behavior and government deficits, and we begin building a model that is the basis for our study of business cycles.

Chapter Summary

- If all countries are identical, except for initial differences in capital per worker, the Solow growth model predicts that there will be convergence among countries. That is, in the long run, all countries will have the same level of income per worker, and aggregate income will be growing at the same rate in all countries.
- In the data, there is evidence for convergence among the richest countries of the world, but convergence does not appear to be occurring among all countries or among the poorest countries.
- The Solow growth model is consistent with the data if there are significant barriers to technology adoption, and these barriers differ among countries. This implies long-run differences in the level of total factor productivity and standards of living across countries.
- We constructed an endogenous growth model with human capital accumulation. This model has the property that, even with no increases in total factor productivity and no population growth, there can be unlimited growth in aggregate output and aggregate consumption, fueled by growth in the stock of human capital (i.e., skills and education).
- In the endogenous growth model, the rate of growth of output and consumption is determined by the efficiency of human capital accumulation and the allocation of labor time between goods production and human capital accumulation.
- If the government could introduce policies that altered the efficiency of human capital accumulation or the allocation of labor time, it could alter the rate of economic growth in the endogenous growth model.
- Increasing the rate of economic growth may or may not improve economic welfare, because an increase in the growth rate of aggregate consumption is always associated with lower consumption in the short run.
- In the endogenous growth model, per capita incomes do not converge across rich and poor countries, even if countries are identical except for initial levels of human capital.

Key Terms

Efficiency units of labor The effective number of units of labor input after adjusting for the quantity of human capital possessed by workers. (p. 246)

Human capital The accumulated stock of skills and education that a worker has at a point in time. (p. 246)

Human capital externalities Effects that exist if the human capital of others affects one's productivity. (p. 253)

Nonrivalry A feature of knowledge, in that acquisition of knowledge does not reduce the ability of others to acquire it. (p. 246)

Questions For Review

1. If countries are initially identical, except with respect to levels of capital per worker, what does the Solow model predict will happen to these countries in the long run? Is this consistent with the data?
2. How is the Solow model consistent with evidence on convergence across countries?
3. What can cause barriers to the adoption of technology?
4. How can a country overcome barriers to technology adoption?
5. What causes economic growth in the endogenous growth model?
6. Why is knowledge nonrivalrous?
7. What two factors affect the growth rate of income and consumption in the endogenous growth model?
8. If the government could increase the rate of growth of consumption, should it? Why or why not?
9. Is there convergence in the levels and rates of growth of per capita income in the endogenous growth model? Why or why not?

Problems

1. Could differences across countries in population growth account for the persistence in income disparity across countries? Use the Solow growth model to address this question and discuss.

2. In the Solow growth model, suppose that the per-worker production function is given by $y = zk^{.3}$, with $s = .25, d = 0.1$, and $n = 0.02$.
   (a) Suppose in country A that $z = 1$. Calculate income per capita and capital per worker in country A.
   (b) Suppose in country B that $z = 2$. Now calculate income per capita and capital per worker in country B.
   (c) As measured by GDP per capita, how much richer is country B than country A? What does this tell us about the potential for differences in total factor productivity to explain differences in standards of living across countries?

3. Suppose that z, the marginal product of efficiency units of labor, increases in the endogenous growth model. What effects does this have on the rates of growth and the levels of human capital, consumption, and output? Explain your results.

4. Introduce government activity in the endogenous growth model as follows. In addition to working u units of time in producing goods, the representative consumer works v units of time for the government and produces gvH goods for government use in the current period, where $g > 0$. The consumer now spends $1 - u - v$ units of time each period accumulating human capital.
   (a) Suppose that v increases with u decreasing by an equal amount. Determine the effects on the level and the rate of growth of consumption. Draw a diagram showing the initial path followed by the natural logarithm of consumption and the corresponding path after v increases.
   (b) Suppose that v increases with u held constant. Determine the effects on the level and the rate of growth of consumption. Draw a diagram showing the initial path followed by the natural logarithm of consumption and the corresponding path after v increases.
   (c) Explain your results and any differences between parts (a) and (b).

5. Suppose that the government makes a one-time investment in new public school buildings, which results in a one-time reduction in consumption. The new public school buildings increase the efficiency with which human capital is accumulated. Determine the effects of this on the paths of

aggregate consumption and aggregate output over time. Is it clear that this investment in new schools is a good idea? Explain.

6. Reinterpret the endogenous growth model in this chapter as follows. Suppose that there are two groups of people in a country, the low-skilled and the high-skilled. The low-skilled have less human capital per person initially than do the high-skilled. In the economy as a whole, output is produced using efficiency units of labor, and total factor productivity is z, just as in the endogenous growth model in this chapter. Each individual in this economy accumulates human capital on their own, and each has one unit of time to split between human capital accumulation and work. However, now $b = b_h$ for the high-skilled, $b = b_l$ for the low-skilled, $u = u_h$ for the high-skilled, and $u = u_l$ for the low-skilled. In the United States, there has been an increase in the gap between the wages of high-skilled workers and low-skilled workers, that has occurred over the last 30 years or so. Determine how this model can explain this observation, and discuss.

7. Suppose there are two countries. In the rich country the representative consumer has H_r units of human capital, and total factor productivity is z_r. In the poor country, the representative consumer has H_p units of human capital, and total factor productivity is z_p. Assume that b and u are the same in the rich and poor countries, that $H_r > H_p$ and $z_r > z_p$.
   (a) How do the levels of income per capita, the growth rates of income per capita, and real wages compare between the rich and poor countries?
   (b) If consumers could choose their country of residence, where would they want to live?

   (c) If each country could determine immigration policy, what should they do to maximize the welfare of the current residents?
   (d) What is the immigration policy that maximizes the welfare of the citizens of both countries?
   (e) Explain your results. Do you think this is a good model for analyzing the effects of immigration? Why or why not?

8. In the endogenous growth model, suppose that there are now three possible uses of time. Let u denote the fraction of time spent working, s the fraction of time spent neither working nor accumulating human capital (call this *unemployment*), with $1 - u - s$ the fraction of time spent accumulating human capital. Assume that $z = 1$ and $b = 4.2$. Assume that the economy begins period 1 with 100 units of human capital.
   (a) Suppose that for periods 1, 2, 3, ..., 10, that $u = .7$ and $s = .05$. Calculate aggregate consumption, output, and the quantity of human capital in each of these periods.
   (b) Suppose that, in period 11, $u = .6$ and $s = .15$. Then, in periods 12, 13, 14, ..., $u = .7$ and $s = .05$. Calculate aggregate consumption, output, and the quantity of human capital in periods 11, 12, 13, ..., 20.
   (c) Suppose alternatively that, in period 11, $u = .6$ and $s = .05$. Again, calculate aggregate consumption, output, and the quantity of human capital in periods 11, 12, 13, ..., 20.
   (d) Now, suppose that, in period 11, $u = .6$ and $s = .10$. Again, calculate aggregate consumption, output, and the quantity of human capital in periods 11, 12, 13, ..., 20.
   (e) What do you conclude from your results in parts (a)–(d)? Discuss.

Working with the Data

1. Calculate the standard deviation of income per worker for the countries of the world for 1960 and 2000. Does this indicate that convergence is occurring or not? For the same years, calculate the standard deviation of income per worker for the poor countries (less than 20% of income per worker in the United States in 1960) and for the rich countries (greater than 20% of income per worker in the United States in 1960). What does this tell you about convergence among the rich and the poor?

2. Suppose that we divide the countries of the world into three groups: low income per worker in 1960 (less than 33% of income per worker in the United States), middle income per worker in 1960 (between 33% and 67% of income per worker in the United States), and high income (greater than 67% of income per worker in the United States).

   (a) Calculate average income per worker for the low income, middle income, and high income countries, respectively, for 1960 and 2000, and calculate the rates of growth of average income for the low, middle, and high income countries between 1960 and 2000.

   (b) Do the statistics you calculated in part (a) indicate any tendency for convergence among these three groups of countries?

PART IV

Savings, Investment, and Government Deficits

In this part, we explore further the macroeconomics of intertemporal decisions and dynamic issues. We start in Chapter 8 by considering the consumption–savings decisions of consumers, building on our knowledge of consumer behavior from Chapter 4. We then study the Ricardian equivalence theorem, which states that, under certain conditions, a change in the timing of taxes by the government has no effects on real macroeconomic variables or on the welfare of consumers. A key implication of the Ricardian equivalence theorem is that a cut in taxes by the government is not a free lunch.

The Ricardian equivalence theorem provides a foundation on which to build our understanding of some key credit market "frictions," which matter a great deal for macroeconomic policy. We explore the issues related to these key frictions in Chapter 9. The first frictions relate to credit market imperfections—asymmetric information and limited commitment—that cause the interest rates at which credit market participants borrow to exceed the rates at which they lend and result in situations where borrowers are required to post collateral to get loans. Credit market imperfections played an important role in the recent financial crisis, and we will explore this in Chapter 9. Another credit market friction relates to the fact that people only live for finite periods of time, which potentially provides a role for social security programs. Pay-as-you-go and fully funded social security systems are studied in the latter sections of Chapter 9.

In Chapter 10, we use what was learned about the microeconomics of consumption–savings behavior in Chapters 8 and 9, along with an analysis of the intertemporal labor supply behavior of consumers and the investment decisions of firms, to construct a complete intertemporal macroeconomic model. This model is the basis for most of what we do in the rest of this book. The model is used in Chapter 10 to show the effects of macroeconomic shocks on output, employment, consumption, investment, the real wage, and the real interest rate. As well, we focus on the effects of expectations about the future on current events.

chapter *8*

A Two-Period Model: The Consumption–Savings Decision and Credit Markets

This chapter focuses on **intertemporal decisions** and the implications of intertemporal decision making for how government deficits affect macroeconomic activity. Intertemporal decisions involve economic trade-offs across periods of time. In Chapters 6 and 7, we studied the Solow growth model, where consumers made arbitrary intertemporal decisions about consumption and savings, consuming a constant fraction of income. In this chapter, we analyze these decisions at a deeper level, studying the microeconomic behavior of a consumer who must make a dynamic **consumption–savings decision.** In doing so, we apply what we learned in Chapter 4 concerning how a consumer optimizes subject to his or her budget constraint. We then study a model with many consumers and with a government that need not balance its budget and can issue debt to finance a government budget deficit. An important implication of this model is that the **Ricardian equivalence theorem** holds. This theorem states that there are conditions under which the size of the government's deficit is irrelevant, in that it does not affect any macroeconomic variables of importance or the economic welfare of any individual.

The consumption–savings decision involves intertemporal choice, as this is fundamentally a decision involving a tradeoff between current and future consumption. Similarly, the government's decision concerning the financing of government expenditures is an intertemporal choice, involving a trade-off between current and future taxes. If the government decreases taxes in the present, it must borrow from the private sector to do so, which implies that future taxes must increase to pay off the higher government debt. Essentially, the government's financing decision is a decision about the quantity of government saving or the size of the government deficit, making it closely related to the consumption–savings decisions of private consumers.

To study the consumption–savings decisions of consumers and the government's intertemporal choices, we work in this chapter with a **two-period model,** which is the simplest framework for understanding intertemporal choice and dynamic issues. We treat the first period in the model as the current period and the second period as the future period. In intertemporal choice, a key variable of interest is the **real interest rate,** which in the model is the interest rate at which consumers and the government can borrow and lend. The real interest rate determines the relative price of consumption in the future in terms of consumption in the present. With respect to consumer choice, we are interested in how savings and consumption in the present and in the future are affected by changes in the market real interest rate and in the consumer's present and future incomes. With respect to the effects of real interest rate changes, income and substitution effects are important, and we can apply here what was learned in Chapters 4 and 5 about how to isolate income and substitution effects in a consumer's choice problem.

An important principle in the response of consumption to changes in income is **consumption smoothing.** That is, there are natural forces that cause consumers to wish to have a smooth consumption path over time, as opposed to a choppy one. Consumption-smoothing behavior is implied by particular properties of indifference curves that we have already studied in Chapter 4. Consumption-smoothing behavior also has important implications for how consumers respond in the aggregate to changes in government policies or other features of their external environment that affect their income streams.

While it remains true here, as in the one-period model studied in Chapter 5, that an increase in government spending has real effects on macroeconomic activity, the Ricardian equivalence theorem establishes conditions under which the timing of taxation does not matter for aggregate economic activity. David Ricardo, for whom the Ricardian equivalence theorem is named, is best known for his work in the early nineteenth century on the theory of comparative advantage and international trade. Ricardian equivalence runs counter to much of public debate, which attaches importance to the size of the government deficit. We explain why Ricardian equivalence is important in economic analysis and why the Ricardian equivalence theorem is a useful starting point for thinking about how the burden of the government debt is shared. A key implication of the Ricardian equivalence theorem is that a tax cut is not a free lunch. A tax cut may not matter at all, or it may involve a redistribution of wealth within the current population or across generations.

Some interesting issues arise due to "frictions" in credit markets that cause departures from Ricardian equivalence. These frictions are important in analyzing the current financial crisis, and in understanding how social security systems work. These issues will be addressed in Chapter 9.

To maintain simplicity and to retain focus on the important ideas in this chapter, our two-period model leaves out production and investment. In Chapter 10, we reintroduce production and add investment decisions by firms so that we can understand more completely the aggregate determination of output, employment, consumption, investment, the real wage rate, and the interest rate.

A Two-Period Model of the Economy

A consumer's consumption–savings decision is fundamentally a decision involving a tradeoff between current and future consumption. By saving, a consumer gives up consumption in exchange for assets in the present to consume more in the future. Alternatively, a consumer can dissave by borrowing in the present to gain more current consumption, thus sacrificing future consumption when the loan is repaid. Borrowing (or dissaving) is thus negative savings.

A consumer's consumption–savings decision is a dynamic decision in that it has implications over more than one period of time, as opposed to the consumer's static work–leisure decision considered in Chapters 4 and 5. We model the consumer's dynamic problem here in the simplest possible way, namely, in a two-period model. In this model, we denote the first period as the current period and the second period as the future period. For some economic problems, assuming that decision making by consumers takes place over two periods is obviously unrealistic. For example, if a period is a quarter, and because the working life of a typical individual is about 200 quarters, then a 200-period model might seem more appropriate. However, the results we consider in this chapter all generalize to more elaborate models with many periods or an infinite number of periods. The reason for studying models with two periods is that they are simple to analyze, while capturing the essentials of dynamic decision making by consumers and firms.

Consumers

There are no difficulties, in terms of what we want to accomplish with this model, in supposing that there are many different consumers rather than a single representative consumer. Therefore, we assume that there are N consumers, and we can think of N being a large number. We assume that each consumer lives for two periods, the current period and the future period. We further suppose that consumers do not make a work–leisure decision in either period but simply receive exogenous income. Assuming that incomes are exogenous allows us to focus attention on what we are interested in here, which is the consumer's consumption–savings decision. Let y be a consumer's real income in the current period, and y' be real income in the future period. Throughout, we use lowercase letters to refer to variables at the individual level and uppercase letters for aggregate variables. Primes denote variables in the future period (for example, y' denotes the consumer's future income). Each consumer pays lump-sum taxes t in the current period and t' in the future period. Suppose that incomes can be different for different consumers, but that all consumers pay the same taxes. If we let a consumer's savings in the current period be s, then the consumer's budget constraint in the current period is

$$c + s = y - t, \tag{8-1}$$

where c is current period consumption. Here, equation (8-1) states that consumption plus savings in the current period must equal disposable income in the current period. We assume that the consumer starts the current period with no assets. This does not matter in any important way for our analysis.

In equation (8-1), if $s > 0$, then the consumer is a lender on the credit market, and if $s < 0$, the consumer is a borrower. We suppose that the financial asset that is traded in the credit market is a bond. In the model, bonds can be issued by consumers as well as by the government. If a consumer lends, he or she buys bonds; if he or she borrows, there is a sale of bonds. There are two important assumptions here. The first is that all bonds are indistinguishable, because consumers never default on their debts, so that there is no risk associated with holding a bond. In practice, different credit instruments are associated with different levels of risk. Interest-bearing securities issued by the U.S. government are essentially riskless, while corporate bonds may be risky if investors feel that the corporate issuer might default, and a loan made by a bank to a consumer may also be quite risky. The second important assumption is that bonds are traded directly in the credit market. In practice, much of the economy's credit activity is channeled through financial intermediaries, an example of which is a commercial bank. For example, when a consumer borrows to purchase a car, the loan is usually taken out at a commercial bank or other depository institution; a consumer typically does not borrow directly from the ultimate lender (in the case of a commercial bank, the ultimate lenders include the depositors at the bank). For the problems we address with this model, we simplify matters considerably, without any key loss in the insights we get, to assume away credit risk and financial institutions like commercial banks. Credit risk and financial intermediation are discussed in detail in Chapters 9 and 16.

In our model, one bond issued in the current period is a promise to pay $1 + r$ units of the consumption good in the future period, so that the real interest rate on each bond is r. Because this implies that one unit of current consumption can be exchanged in the credit market for $1 + r$ units of the future consumption good, the relative price of future consumption in terms of current consumption is $\frac{1}{1 + r}$. Recall from Chapter 1 that in practice the real interest rate is approximately the nominal interest rate (the interest rate in money terms) minus the inflation rate. We study the relationship between real and nominal interest rates in Chapter 11.

A key assumption here is that the real rate of interest at which a consumer can lend is the same as the real rate of interest at which a consumer can borrow. In practice, consumers typically borrow at higher rates of interest than they can lend at. For example, the interest rates on consumer loans are usually several percentage points higher than the interest rates on bank deposits, reflecting the costs for the bank of taking deposits and making loans. The assumption that borrowing and lending rates of interest are the same matters for some of what we do here, and we ultimately show what difference this makes to our analysis.

In the future period, the consumer has disposable income $y' - t'$ and receives the interest and principal on his or her savings, which totals $(1 + r)s$. Because the future period is the final period, the consumer chooses to finish this period with no assets, consuming all disposable income and the interest and principal on savings (we assume there are no bequests to descendants). We then have

$$c' = y' - t' + (1 + r)s, \tag{8-2}$$

where c' is consumption in the future period. In equation (8-2), if $s < 0$, the consumer pays the interest and principal on his or her loan (retires the bonds he or she issued in the current period) and then consumes what remains of his or her future period disposable income.

The consumer chooses current consumption and future consumption, c and c', respectively, and savings s to make himself or herself as well off as possible while satisfying the budget constraints (8-1) and (8-2).

The Consumer's Lifetime Budget Constraint   We can work with diagrams similar to those used in Chapter 4 to analyze the consumer's work–leisure decision, if we take the two budget constraints expressed in equations (8-1) and (8-2) and write them as a single lifetime budget constraint. To do this, we first use equation (8-2) to solve for s to get

$$s = \frac{c' - y' + t'}{1 + r}. \tag{8-3}$$

Then, substitute for s from (8-3) in (8-1) to get

$$c + \frac{c' - y' + t'}{1 + r} = y - t,$$

or rearranging,

$$c + \frac{c'}{1 + r} = y + \frac{y'}{1 + r} - t - \frac{t'}{1 + r}. \tag{8-4}$$

Equation (8-4) is the consumer's **lifetime budget constraint,** and it states that the **present value** of lifetime consumption $c + \frac{c'}{1+r}$ equals the present value of lifetime income $y + \frac{y'}{1+r}$ minus the present value of lifetime taxes $t + \frac{t'}{1+r}$. The present value here is the value in terms of period 1 consumption goods. That is, $\frac{1}{1+r}$ is the relative price of future consumption goods in terms of current consumption goods, because a consumer can give up 1 unit of current consumption goods and obtain $1 + r$ units of future consumption goods by saving for one period. The problem of the consumer is now simplified, in that he or she chooses c and c' to make himself or herself as well off as possible, while satisfying the budget constraint (8-4) and given $r, y, y', t,$ and t'. Once we have determined what the consumer's optimal consumption is in the current and future periods, we can determine savings, s, from the current period budget constraint (8-1).

For a numerical example to illustrate present values, suppose that current income is $y = 110$ while future income is $y' = 120$. Taxes in the current period are $t = 20$, and taxes in the future period are $t' = 10$. Also suppose that the real interest rate is 10%, so that $r = 0.1$. In this example, the relative price of future consumption goods in terms of current consumption goods is $\frac{1}{1+r} = 0.909$. Here, when we discount future income and future taxes to obtain these quantities in units of current consumption goods, we multiply by the discount factor 0.909. The fact that the discount factor is less than 1 indicates that having a given amount of income in the future is worth less to the consumer than having the same amount of income in the current period. The present discounted value of lifetime income is

$$y + \frac{y'}{1 + r} = 110 + (120 \times 0.909) = 219.1,$$

and the present value of lifetime taxes is

$$t + \frac{t'}{1 + r} = 20 + (10 \times 0.909) = 29.1.$$

Then, in this example, we can write the consumer's lifetime budget constraint from equation (8-4) as

$$c + 0.909c' = 190.$$

We label the present value of lifetime disposable income, the quantity on the right-hand side of equation (8-4), as **lifetime wealth**, *we*, because this is the quantity of resources that the consumer has available to spend on consumption, in present-value terms, over his or her lifetime. We then have

$$we = y + \frac{y'}{1 + r} - t - \frac{t'}{1 + r}, \tag{8-5}$$

and we can rewrite equation (8-4) as

$$c + \frac{c'}{1 + r} = we. \tag{8-6}$$

In Figure 8.1 we graph the consumer's lifetime budget constraint as expressed in equation (8-6). Writing this equation in slope-intercept form, we have

$$c' = -(1 + r)c + we(1 + r). \tag{8-7}$$

Figure 8.1 Consumer's Lifetime Budget Constraint

The lifetime budget constraint defines the quantities of current and future consumption the consumer can acquire, given current and future income and taxes, through borrowing and lending on the credit market. To the northwest of the endowment point E, the consumer is a lender with positive savings; to the southeast of E, he or she is a borrower with negative savings.

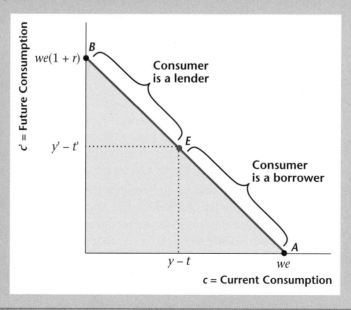

Therefore, in equation (8-7) and in Figure 8.1, the vertical intercept, $we(1 + r)$, is what could be consumed in the future period if the consumer saved all of his or her current-period disposable income and consumed lifetime wealth (after earning the real interest rate r on savings) in the future period. The horizontal intercept in equation (8-7) and Figure 8.1, we, is what could be consumed if the consumer borrowed the maximum amount possible against future period disposable income and consumed all of lifetime wealth in the current period. The slope of the lifetime budget constraint is $-(1 + r)$, which is determined by the real interest rate. Point E in Figure 8.1 is the **endowment point**, which is the consumption bundle the consumer gets if he or she simply consumes disposable income in the current period and in the future period—that is, $c = y - t$ and $c' = y' - t'$—with zero savings in the current period. You can verify by substituting $c = y - t$ and $c' = y' - t'$ in equation (8-4) that the endowment point satisfies the lifetime budget constraint. Now, any point along BE in Figure 8.1 implies that $s \geq 0$, so that the consumer is a lender, because $c \leq y - t$. Also, a consumption bundle along AE in Figure 8.1 implies that the consumer is a borrower with $s \leq 0$.

Any point on or inside AB in the shaded area in Figure 8.1 represents a feasible consumption bundle, that is, a combination of current-period and future-period consumptions that satisfies the consumer's lifetime budget constraint. As may be clear by now, the way we approach the consumer's problem here is very similar to our analysis of the consumer's work–leisure decision in Chapter 4. Once we describe the consumer's preferences and add indifference curves to the budget constraint as depicted in Figure 8.1, we can determine the consumer's optimal consumption bundle.

The Consumer's Preferences   As with the consumer's work–leisure decision in Chapter 4, the consumption bundle that is chosen by the consumer, which here is a combination of current-period and future-period consumptions, is determined jointly by the consumer's budget constraint and his or her preferences. Just as in Chapter 4, we assume that preferences have three properties, which are the following:

1. More is always preferred to less. Here, this means that more current consumption or more future consumption always makes the consumer better off.

2. The consumer likes diversity in his or her consumption bundle. Here, a preference for diversity has a specific meaning in terms of the consumer's desire to smooth consumption over time. Namely, the consumer has a dislike for having large differences in consumption between the current period and the future period. Note that this does not mean that the consumer would always choose to have equal consumption in the current and future periods.

3. Current consumption and future consumption are normal goods. This implies that if there is a parallel shift to the right in the consumer's budget constraint, then current consumption and future consumption both increase. This is related to the consumer's desire to smooth consumption over time. If there is a parallel shift to the right in the consumer's budget constraint, this is because lifetime wealth we has increased. Given the consumer's desire to smooth consumption over time, any increase in lifetime wealth implies that the consumer chooses more consumption in the present and in the future.

As in Chapter 4, we represent preferences with an indifference map, which is a family of indifference curves. A typical indifference map is shown in Figure 8.2, where the marginal rate of substitution of consumption in the current period for consumption in the future period, or $MRS_{c,c'}$, is minus the slope of an indifference curve. For example, $MRS_{c,c'}$ at point A in Figure 8.2 is minus the slope of a tangent to the indifference curve at point A. Recall that a preference for diversity, or diminishing marginal rate of substitution, is captured by the convexity in an indifference curve, which here also represents a consumer's desire to smooth consumption over time. On indifference curve I_1, at point A the consumer has a large quantity of current consumption and a small quantity of future consumption, and he or she needs to be given a large quantity of current consumption to willingly give up a small quantity of future consumption (minus the slope of the indifference curve at A is small). Conversely, at point B the consumer has a small quantity of current consumption and a large quantity of future consumption, and he or she needs to be given a large quantity of future consumption to give up a small quantity of current consumption (minus the slope of the indifference curve is large). Thus, the consumer does not like large differences in consumption between the two periods.

Figure 8.2 A Consumer's Indifference Curves

The figure shows the indifference map of a consumer. Indifference curves are convex and downward-sloping. Minus the slope of an indifference curve is the marginal rate of substitution of current consumption for future consumption.

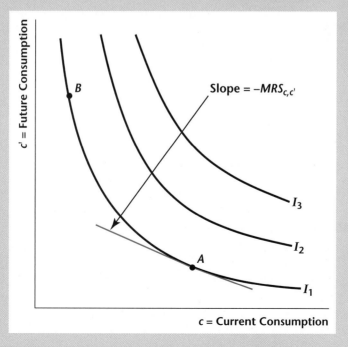

As an example to show why consumption smoothing is a natural property for preferences to have, suppose that Sara is a consumer living on a desert island and that she eats only coconuts. Suppose that coconuts can be stored for two weeks without spoiling and that Sara has 20 coconuts to last for this week (the current period) and next week (the future period). One option that Sara has is to eat 5 coconuts this week and 15 coconuts next week. Suppose that Sara is just indifferent between this first consumption bundle and a second bundle that involves eating 17 coconuts this week and 3 coconuts next week. However, eating only 5 coconuts in the first week or only 3 coconuts in the second week leaves Sara rather hungry. She would, in fact, prefer to eat 11 coconuts in the first week and 9 coconuts in the second week, rather than either of the other two consumption bundles. This third consumption bundle combines half of the first consumption bundle with half of the second consumption bundle. That is, $\frac{5 + 17}{2} = 11$ and $\frac{15 + 3}{2} = 9$. Sara's preferences reflect a desire for consumption smoothing or a preference for diversity in her consumption bundle, that seems natural. In Table 8.1 we show the consumption bundles amongst which Sara chooses.

Consumer Optimization   As with the work–leisure decision we considered in Chapter 4, the consumer's optimal consumption bundle here is determined by where an indifference curve is tangent to the budget constraint. In Figure 8.3 we show the optimal consumption choice for a consumer who decides to be a lender. The endowment point is at E, while the consumer chooses the consumption bundle at point A, where $(c, c') = (c^*, c'^*)$. At point A, it is then the case that

$$MRS_{c,c'} = 1 + r; \tag{8-8}$$

that is, the marginal rate of substitution of current consumption for future consumption (minus the slope of the indifference curve) is equal to the relative price of current consumption in terms of future consumption ($1 + r$, which is minus the slope of the consumer's lifetime budget constraint). Recall from Chapter 4 that equation (8-8) is a particular case of a standard marginal condition that is implied by consumer optimization (at the optimum, the marginal rate of substitution of good 1 for good 2 is equal to the relative price of good 1 in terms of good 2). Here, the consumer optimizes by choosing the consumption bundle on his or her lifetime budget constraint where the rate at which he or she is willing to trade off current consumption for future consumption is the same as the rate at which he or she can trade current consumption for future

Table 8.1   Sara's Desire for Consumption Smoothing

	Week 1 Coconuts	Week 2 Coconuts	Total Consumption
Bundle 1	5	15	20
Bundle 2	17	3	20
Preferred Bundle	11	9	20

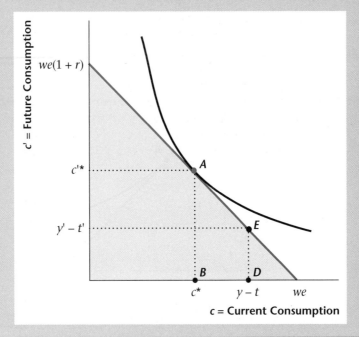

Figure 8.3 A Consumer Who Is a Lender

The optimal consumption bundle for the consumer is at point A, where the marginal rate of substitution (minus the slope of an indifference curve) is equal to 1 + r (minus the slope of the lifetime budget constraint). The consumer is a lender, as the consumption bundle chosen implies positive savings, with E being the endowment point.

consumption in the market (by saving). At point A in Figure 8.3, the quantity of savings is $s = y - t - c^*$, or the distance BD. Similarly, Figure 8.4 shows the case of a consumer who chooses to be a borrower. That is, the endowment point is E and the consumer chooses point A, where $(c, c') = (c^*, c'^*)$. Here, the quantity the consumer borrows in the first period is $-s = c^* - y + t$, or the distance DB.

In the next stage in our analysis, we consider some experiments that tell us how the consumer responds to changes in current income, future income, and interest rates.

An Increase in Current-Period Income From Chapter 4, we know that an increase in a consumer's dividend income or a reduction in taxes amounts to a pure income effect, which increases consumption and reduces labor supply. Here, we want to focus on how an increase in the consumer's current income affects intertemporal decisions. In particular, we want to know the effects of an increase in current income on current consumption, future consumption, and savings. As we show, these effects reflect the consumer's desire for consumption smoothing.

Suppose that, holding the interest rate, taxes in the current and future periods, and future income constant, a consumer receives an increase in period 1 income. Asking the consumer's response to this change in income is much like asking how an individual

Figure 8.4 A Consumer Who Is a Borrower

The optimal consumption bundle is at point A. Because current consumption exceeds current disposable income, saving is negative, and so the consumer is a borrower.

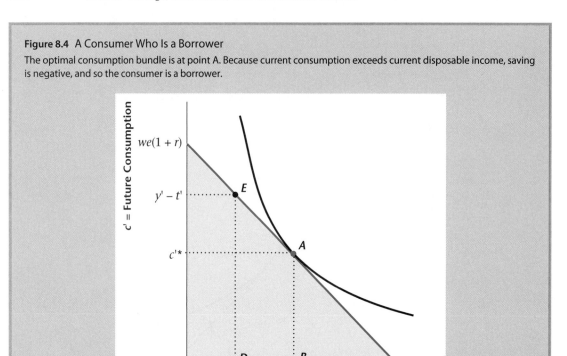

would react to winning a lottery. In Figure 8.5 the initial endowment point is at E_1, and the consumer initially chooses the consumption bundle represented by point A. In this figure we have shown the case of a consumer who is initially a lender, but it does not make a difference for what we want to show if the consumer is a borrower. We suppose that current-period income increases from y_1 to y_2. The result is that lifetime wealth increases from

$$we_1 = y_1 + \frac{y'}{1+r} - t - \frac{t'}{1+r}$$

to

$$we_2 = y_2 + \frac{y'}{1+r} - t - \frac{t'}{1+r},$$

and the change in lifetime wealth is

$$\Delta we = we_2 - we_1 = y_2 - y_1.$$

The effect is that the budget constraint shifts to the right by the amount $y_2 - y_1$, which is the distance E_1E_2, where E_2 is the new endowment point. The slope of the budget constraint remains unchanged, as the real interest rate is the same.

Figure 8.5 The Effects of an Increase in Current Income for a Lender

When current income increases, lifetime wealth increases from we_1 to we_2. The lifetime budget constraint shifts out, and the slope of the constraint remains unchanged, because the real interest rate does not change. Initially, the consumer chooses A, and he or she chooses B after current income increases. Current and future consumption both increase (both goods are normal), and current consumption increases by less than the increase in current income.

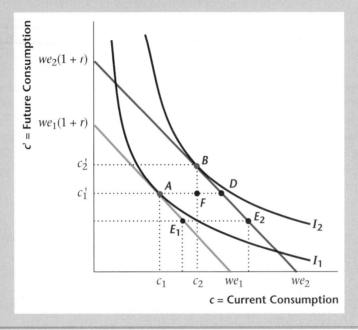

Because current-period consumption and future consumption are normal goods, the consumer now chooses a consumption bundle represented by a point like B, where consumption in both periods has risen from the previous values. Current consumption increases from c_1 to c_2, and future consumption increases from c_1' to c_2'. Thus, if current income increases, the consumer wishes to spread this additional income over both periods and not consume it all in the current period. In Figure 8.5 the increase in current income is the distance AD, while the increase in current consumption is the distance AF, which is less than the distance AD. The change in the consumer's savings is given by

$$\Delta s = \Delta y - \Delta t - \Delta c, \qquad (8\text{-}9)$$

and because $\Delta t = 0$, and $\Delta y > \Delta c > 0$, we have $\Delta s > 0$. Thus, an increase in current income causes an increase in consumption in both periods and an increase in savings.

Our analysis tells us that any one consumer who receives an increase in his or her current income consumes more during the current period but also saves some of the increase in income so as to consume more in the future. This behavior arises because of the consumer's desire to smooth consumption over time. This behavior is intuitively reasonable. For example, consider a consumer, Paul, who is currently 25 years of age and wins $1 million in a lottery. Paul could certainly spend all of his lottery winnings on consumption goods within the current year and save nothing, but it would seem more sensible if he consumed a small part of his winnings in the current year and saved a substantial fraction to consume more for the rest of his life.

If all consumers act to smooth their consumption relative to their income, then aggregate consumption should likewise be smooth relative to aggregate income. Indeed, this prediction of our theory is consistent with what we see in the data. Recall from Chapter 3 that real aggregate consumption is less variable than is real GDP. The difference in variability between aggregate consumption and GDP is even larger if we take account of the fact that some of what is included in aggregate consumption is not consumption in the economic sense. For example, purchases of new automobiles are included in the NIPA as consumption of durables, but the purchase of a car might more appropriately be included in investment, because the car yields a flow of consumption services over its entire lifetime. In the data, expenditures on consumer durables are much more variable than actual consumption, measured as the flow of consumption services that consumers receive from goods. In Figure 8.6 we show the percentage deviations from trend in the consumption of durables, and in GDP for the period 1947–2009. Clearly, the consumption of durables is much more variable than aggregate income, and if we compare Figure 8.6 to Figure 3.10 in Chapter 3, it is clear that durables consumption behaves much like aggregate investment. However, Figure 8.7 depicts the percentage deviations from trend in the consumption of nondurables and services and in real GDP. Here, clearly there is much less variability in the consumption of nondurables and services—which comes fairly close to measuring a flow of consumption services—than in real GDP. What we observe in Figure 8.7 accurately reflects the tendency of consumers to smooth consumption over time relative to income.

Although aggregate data on consumption and income is clearly qualitatively consistent with consumption-smoothing behavior on the part of consumers, macroeconomists have been interested in the quantitative match between consumption theory and the data. The question is whether measured consumption is smooth enough relative to measured income to be consistent with theory. Generally, the conclusion from empirical work is that, while the theory points in the right direction, there is some **excess variability** of aggregate consumption relative to aggregate income. That is, while consumption is smoother than income, as the theory predicts, consumption is not quite smooth enough to tightly match the theory.[1] Thus, the theory needs some more work if it is to fit the facts. Two possible explanations for the excess variability in consumption are the following:

1. There are imperfections in the credit market. Our theory assumes that a consumer can smooth consumption by borrowing or lending at the market real interest rate r. In reality, consumers cannot borrow all they would like at the market interest rate, and market loan interest rates are typically higher than the interest rates at which consumers lend. As a result, in reality consumers may have less ability to

[1]See, for example, O.P. Attanasio, 1999. "Consumption," in *Handbook of Macroeconomics*, J. Taylor and M. Woodford, eds., 741–812, Elsevier.

Figure 8.6 Percentage Deviations from Trend in Consumption of Durables and Real GDP

The consumption of durables is economically similar to investment expenditures, which is why consumer durables expenditure is much more volatile than real GDP, as shown in the figure.

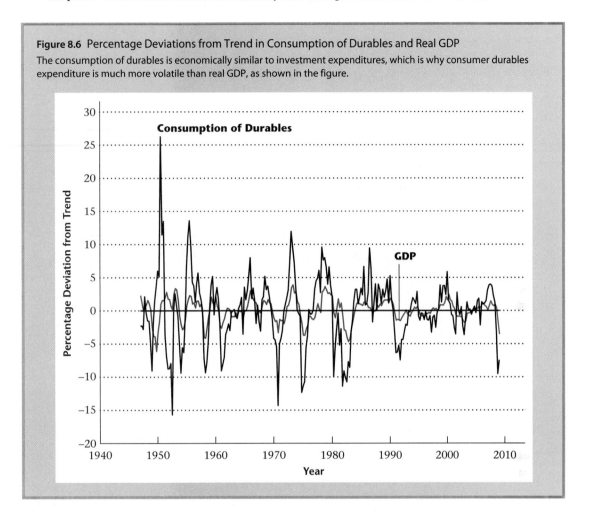

smooth consumption than they do in the theory. We could complicate the model by introducing credit market imperfections, and this might help to explain the data better. However, this would make the model considerably more complicated. We further discuss credit market imperfections in Chapter 9.

2. When all consumers are trying to smooth consumption in the same way simultaneously, this changes market prices. The consumption-smoothing theory we have studied thus far does not take into account the interaction of consumers with each other and with other sectors of the economy. All consumers may wish to smooth consumption over time, but aggregate consumption must fall during a recession because aggregate income is lower then. Similarly, aggregate consumption must rise in a boom. The way that consumers are reconciled to having high consumption when output is high, and low consumption when output is low, is through movements in market prices, including the market interest rate. Shortly, we will study how individual consumers react to changes in the real interest rate.

Figure 8.7 Percentage Deviations from Trend in Consumption of Nondurables and Services and Real GDP

The consumption of nondurables and services is fairly close to a pure flow of consumption services, so it is not surprising that consumption of nondurables and services is much smoother than real GDP, reflecting the motive of consumers to smooth consumption relative to income.

An Increase in Future Income   While a consumer's response to a change in his or her current income is informative about consumption-smoothing behavior, we are also interested in the effects on consumer behavior of a change in income that is expected to occur in the future. Suppose, for example, that Jennifer is about to finish her college degree in four months, and she lines up a job that starts as soon as she graduates. On landing the job, Jennifer's future income has increased considerably. How would she react to this future increase in income? Clearly, this would imply that she would plan to increase her future consumption, but Jennifer also likes to smooth consumption, so that she should want to have higher current consumption as well. She can consume more currently by borrowing against her future income and repaying the loan when she starts working.

In Figure 8.8 we show the effects of an increase for the consumer in future income, from y_1' to y_2'. This has an effect similar to the increase in current income

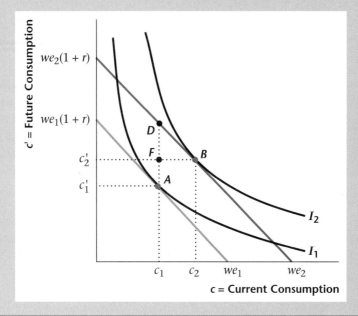

Figure 8.8 An Increase in Future Income

An increase in future income increases lifetime wealth from we_1 to we_2, shifting the lifetime budget constraint to the right and leaving its slope unchanged. The consumer initially chooses point A, and he or she chooses B after the budget constraint shifts. Future consumption increases by less than the increase in future income, saving decreases, and current consumption increases.

on lifetime wealth, with lifetime wealth increasing from we_1 to we_2, and shifting the budget constraint up by the amount $y_2' - y_1'$. Initially, the consumer chooses consumption bundle A, and he or she chooses B after the increase in future income. Both current and future consumption increase; current consumption increases from c_1 to c_2, and future consumption increases from c_1' to c_2'. The increase in future consumption, which is the distance AF in Figure 8.8, is less than the increase in future income, which is the distance AD. This is because, as with the increase in current income, the consumer wants to smooth consumption over time. Rather than spend all the increase in income in the future, the consumer saves less in the current period so that current consumption can increase. The change in saving is given by equation (8-9), where $\Delta t = \Delta y = 0$, and because $\Delta c > 0$, we must have $\Delta s < 0$—that is, savings decreases.

In the case of an expected increase in future income, the consumer acts to smooth consumption over time, just as when he or she receives an increase in current income. The difference is that an increase in future income leads to smoothing backward, with the consumer saving less in the current period so that current consumption can increase, whereas an increase in current income leads to smoothing forward, with the consumer saving more in the current period so that future consumption can increase.

Temporary and Permanent Changes in Income   When a consumer receives a change in his or her current income, it matters a great deal for his or her current consumption-savings choice whether this change in income is temporary or permanent. For example, Allen would respond quite differently to receiving a windfall increase in his income of $1,000, say by winning a lottery, as opposed to receiving a $1,000 yearly salary increase that he expects to continue indefinitely. In the case of the lottery winnings, we might expect that Allen would increase current consumption by only a small amount, saving most of the lottery winnings to increase consumption in the future. If Allen received a permanent increase in his income, as in the second case, we would expect his increase in current consumption to be much larger.

The difference between the effects of temporary and permanent changes in income on consumption was articulated by Milton Friedman in his **permanent income hypothesis**.[2] Friedman argued that a primary determinant of a consumer's current consumption is his or her permanent income, which is closely related to the concept of lifetime wealth in our model. Changes in income that are temporary yield small changes in permanent income (lifetime wealth), which have small effects on current consumption, whereas changes in income that are permanent have large effects on permanent income (lifetime wealth) and current consumption.

In our model, we can show the effects of temporary versus permanent changes in income by examining an increase in income that occurs only in the current period versus an increase in income occurring in the current period and the future period. In Figure 8.9 the budget constraint of the consumer is initially AB, and he or she chooses the consumption bundle represented by point H, on indifference curve I_1. Then, the consumer experiences a temporary increase in income, with current income increasing from y_1 to y_2, so that the budget constraint shifts out to DE. The real interest rate does not change, so that the slope of the budget constraint remains constant. The distance HL is equal to the change in current income, $y_2 - y_1$. Now, the consumer chooses point J on indifference curve I_2, and we know from our previous discussion that the increase in current consumption, $c_2 - c_1$, is less than the increase in current income, $y_2 - y_1$, as saving increases due to consumption-smoothing behavior.

Now, suppose that the increase in income is permanent. We interpret this as an equal increase of $y_2 - y_1$ in both current and future income. That is, initially future income is y_1' and it increases to y_2' with $y_2' - y_1' = y_2 - y_1$. Now, the budget constraint is given by FG in Figure 8.9, where the upward shift in the budget constraint from DE is the distance LM, which is $y_2' - y_1' = y_2 - y_1$. The consumer now chooses point K on indifference curve I_3. At point K, current consumption is c_3. Given that current and future consumption are normal goods, current consumption increases from point H to point J and from point J to point K. Therefore, if income increases permanently, this has a larger effect on current consumption than if income increases only temporarily. If income increases only temporarily, there is an increase in saving, so that consumption does not increase as much as does income. However, if there is a permanent increase in income, then there need not be an increase in saving, and current consumption could increase as much as or more than does income.

----

[2]See M. Friedman, 1957, *A Theory of the Consumption Function,* Princeton University Press, Princeton, NJ.

Figure 8.9 Temporary Versus Permanent Increases in Income

A temporary increase in income is an increase in current income, with the budget constraint shifting from *AB* to *DE* and the optimal consumption bundle changing from *H* to *J*. When there is a permanent increase in income, current and future income both increase, and the budget constraint shifts from *AB* to *FG*, with the optimal consumption bundle changing from *H* to *K*.

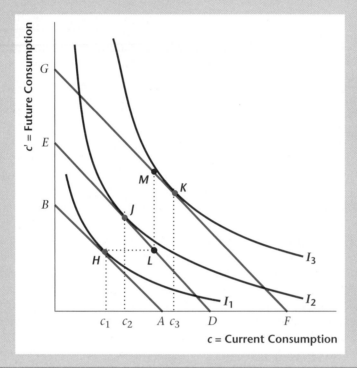

Why is it important that consumers respond differently to temporary and permanent changes in their income? Suppose that the government is considering cutting taxes, and this tax cut could be temporary or permanent. For now, ignore how the government will go about financing this tax cut (we consider this later in the chapter). If consumers receive a tax cut that increases lifetime wealth, then this increases aggregate consumption. However, if consumers expect the tax cut to be temporary, the increase in consumption is much smaller than if they expect the tax cut to be permanent.

An Increase in the Real Interest Rate   To this point, we have examined how changes in a consumer's current income and future income affect his or her choices of consumption in the current and future periods. These are changes that shift the consumer's budget constraint but do not change its slope. In this subsection, we study how the consumer responds to a change in the real interest rate, which changes the slope of the budget constraint. Changes in the market real interest rate are ultimately an important part of the mechanism by which shocks to the economy, fiscal policy, and

Consumption Smoothing and the Stock Market

Thus far, our theory tells us that, in response to increases in their lifetime wealth, consumers increase consumption, but in such a way that their consumption path is smoothed over time. One way in which consumers' wealth changes is through variation in the prices of stocks traded on organized stock exchanges, such as the New York Stock Exchange or NASDAQ.

How should we expect aggregate consumption to respond to a change in stock prices? On the one hand, publicly traded stock is not a large fraction of national wealth. That is, a large fraction of national wealth includes the housing stock and the capital of privately held companies, which are not traded on the stock market. Therefore, even if there is a large change in stock prices, this need not represent a large change in national wealth. On the other hand, financial theory tells us that, when the price of a stock changes, we should expect this price change to be permanent.

Financial theory tells us (with some qualifications) that stock prices are **martingales**. A martingale has the property that the best prediction of its value tomorrow is its value today. In the case of a stock price, the best prediction of tomorrow's stock price is today's stock price. The reason that stock prices follow martingales is that, if they did not, then there would be opportunities for investors to make profits. That is, suppose that a stock price does not follow a martingale, and suppose first that the best forecast is that tomorrow's stock price will be higher than today's stock price. Then, investors would want to buy the stock today so as to make a profit by selling it tomorrow. Ultimately, this would force up the market price of the stock today, to the point where the price today is what it is expected to be tomorrow. Similarly, if the price of the stock today were greater than what the stock's price was

expected to be tomorrow, investors would want to sell the stock today so they could buy it at a cheaper price tomorrow. In this case, investors' actions would force the current stock price down to the point where it was equal to its expected price tomorrow. Because the current price of a stock is the best forecast of its future price, any change in prices is a surprise, and this change in prices is expected to be permanent.

A change in the overall value of the stock market does not represent a change in a large fraction of national wealth, and this would tend to dampen the effect of price movements in the stock market on aggregate consumption. However, the fact that any change in stock prices is expected to be permanent tends to amplify the effects of changes in stock prices, as we know that permanent changes in wealth have larger effects on consumption than do temporary changes in wealth. What do the data tell us? In Figure 8.10 we show a time series plot of the percentage deviations from trend in the Standard and Poor's composite stock price index for the United States, and percentage deviations from trend in real consumption of nondurables and services. The data plotted are quarterly data for the period 1950–2009. Here, note in particular that the stock price index is highly volatile relative to consumption. Deviations from trend in the stock price index of 15 to 20% occur, while the deviations from trend in consumption are at most 1.5%. A close examination of Figure 8.10 indicates that deviations from trend in the stock price index are positively correlated with deviations from trend in consumption. Figure 8.11 shows this more clearly, where we graph the same data as in Figure 8.10, except in a scatter plot. A positively sloped line in Figure 8.11 would provide the best fit to the data in the scatter plot, indicating that the stock price and consumption are positively correlated.

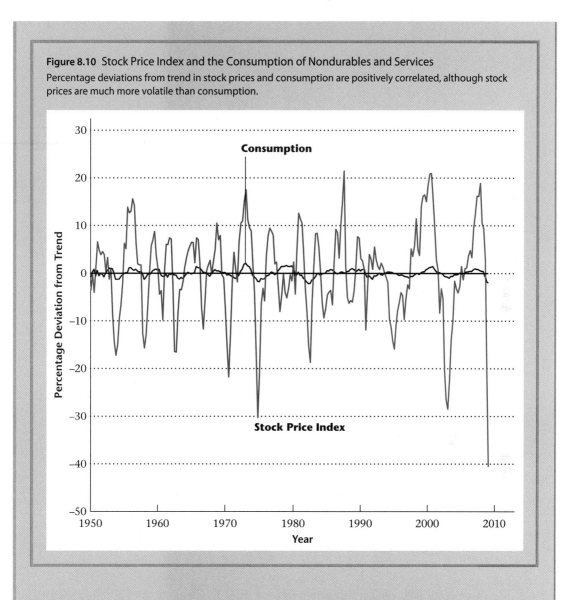

Figure 8.10 Stock Price Index and the Consumption of Nondurables and Services
Percentage deviations from trend in stock prices and consumption are positively correlated, although stock prices are much more volatile than consumption.

The data indicate that the stock market is potentially an important channel for the effects of changes in wealth on aggregate consumption behavior. The fact that consumption and stock prices move together is consistent with the notion that shocks to the financial system that are reflected in the prices of publicly traded stocks can cause significant movements in aggregate consumption. Although the value of publicly traded stock is not a large part of national wealth, the fact that stock price changes are expected to be permanent potentially contributes to the influence of the stock market on consumption behavior.

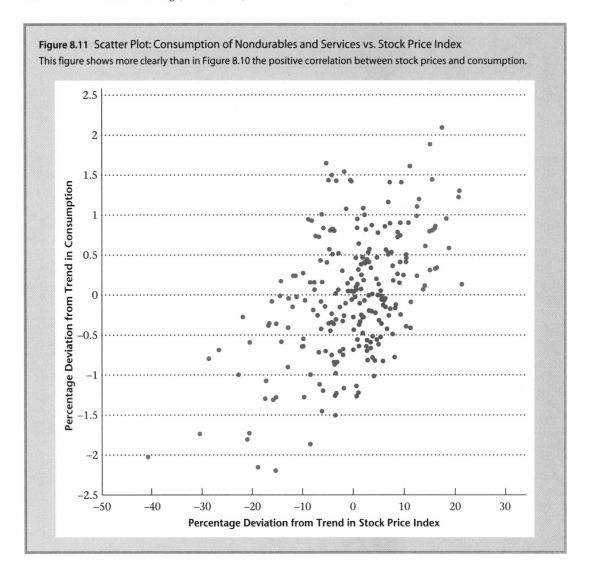

Figure 8.11 Scatter Plot: Consumption of Nondurables and Services vs. Stock Price Index
This figure shows more clearly than in Figure 8.10 the positive correlation between stock prices and consumption.

monetary policy affect real activity, as we show in Chapters 10–13. A key channel for interest rate effects on real activity is through aggregate consumption.

Because $\frac{1}{1 + r}$ is the relative price of future consumption goods in terms of current consumption goods, a change in the real interest rate effectively changes this intertemporal relative price. In Chapter 4, in the consumer's work–leisure choice problem, a change in the real wage was effectively a change in the relative price of leisure and consumption, and a change in the real wage had income and substitution effects. Here, in our two-period framework, a change in the real interest rate also has income and substitution effects in its influence on consumption in the present and the future.

Suppose that the consumer faces an increase in the real interest rate, with taxes and income held constant in both periods. This makes the budget constraint steeper,

Figure 8.12 An Increase in the Real Interest Rate

An increase in the real interest rate causes the lifetime budget constraint of the consumer to become steeper and to pivot around the endowment point E.

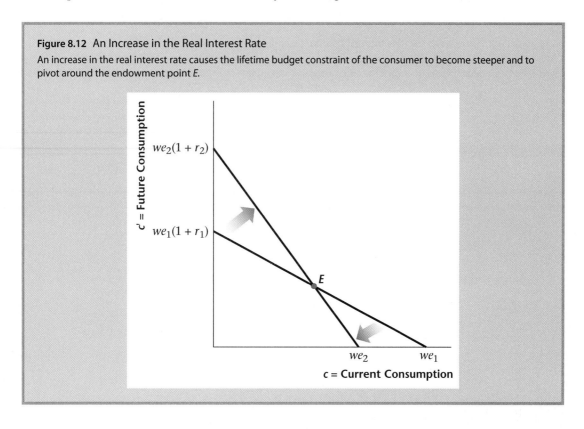

because the slope of the budget constraint is $-(1 + r)$. Further, under the assumption that the consumer never has to pay a tax larger than his or her income, so that $y' - t' > 0$, an increase in r decreases lifetime wealth we, as shown in equation (8-5). Also from equation (8-5), we have

$$we(1 + r) = (y - t)(1 + r) + y' - t',$$

and because $y > t$, there is an increase in $we(1 + r)$ when r increases. Therefore, we know that an increase in r causes the budget constraint to pivot, as in Figure 8.12, where r increases from r_1 to r_2, resulting in a decrease in we from we_1 to we_2. We also know that the budget constraint must pivot around the endowment point E, because it must always be possible for the consumer to consume his or her disposable income in each period, no matter what the real interest rate is.

A change in r results in a change in the relative price of consumption in the current and future periods; that is, an increase in r causes future consumption to become cheaper relative to current consumption. A higher interest rate implies that the return on savings is higher, so that more future consumption goods can be obtained for a given sacrifice of current consumption goods. As well, for a given loan in the first period, the consumer has to forgo more future consumption goods when the loan is repaid. We can use what we learned about income and substitution effects in Chapter 4 to understand how an increase in the real interest rate affects the consumer's behavior. However, it

Figure 8.13 An Increase in the Real Interest Rate for a Lender

When the real interest rate increases for a lender, the substitution effect is the movement from *A* to *D*, and the income effect is the movement from *D* to *B*. Current consumption and saving may rise or fall, while future consumption increases.

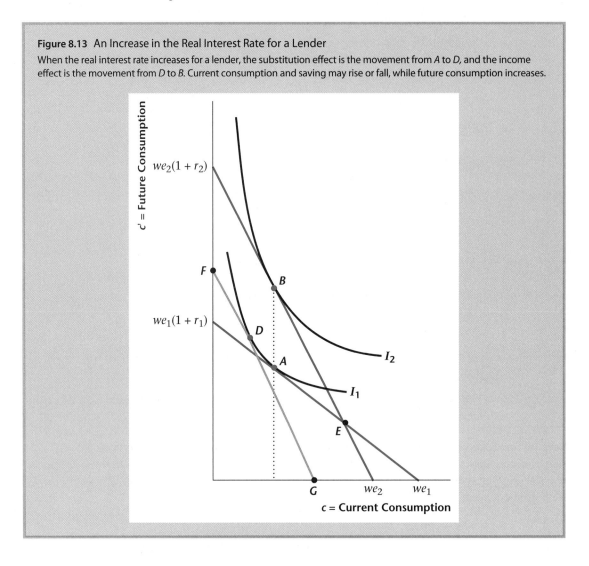

turns out that the income effects of an increase in the real interest rate work in different directions for lenders and borrowers, which is what we want to show next.

First, consider the case of a lender. In Figure 8.13 consider a consumer who is initially a lender and faces an increase in the market real interest rate from r_1 to r_2. Initially, lifetime wealth is we_1, and this changes to we_2. The budget constraint pivots around the endowment point E. Initially, the consumer chose the consumption bundle A, and we suppose that the consumer chooses B after the increase in the real interest rate. To find the substitution effect of the real interest rate increase, we draw an artificial budget constraint FG, which has the same slope as the new budget constraint, and is just tangent to the initial indifference curve I_1. Thus, we are taking wealth away from the consumer until he or she is as well off as before the increase in r. Then, the movement from A to D is a pure substitution effect, and in moving from A to D future consumption increases and current consumption decreases, as future consumption has become cheaper relative to current consumption. The remaining effect, the movement from D to B, is a pure income effect, which causes both current-period and future-period consumption to increase (recall that we assumed that current and future consumption are normal goods). Therefore, future consumption must increase, as both the income and substitution effects work in the same direction. However, current-period consumption may increase or decrease, as the substitution effect causes current consumption to decrease, and the income effect causes it to increase. If the income effect is larger than the substitution effect, then current consumption increases. The effect on savings depends on the change in current consumption, as we are holding constant current disposable income. Thus, saving may increase or decrease. Saving increases if the substitution effect is larger than the income effect, and saving decreases otherwise. An increase in the real interest rate makes saving more attractive, because the relative price of future consumption is lower (the substitution effect), but it makes saving less attractive as there is a positive income effect on period 1 consumption, which tends to reduce saving.

Consider the following example, which shows the intuition behind the income and substitution effects of a change in the real interest rate. Suppose Christine is currently a lender, whose disposable income in the current year is $40,000. She currently saves 30% of her current income, and she faces a real interest rate of 5%. Her income next year will also be $40,000 (in current year dollars), and so initially she consumes $0.7 \times \$40,000 = \$28,000$ this year, and she consumes $\$40,000 + (1 + 0.05) \times \$12,000 = \$52,600$ next year. Now, suppose that the real interest rate rises to 10%. How should Christine respond? If she continues to consume $28,000 in the current year and saves $12,000, then she has future consumption of $53,200, an increase over initial future consumption, reflecting the substitution effect. However, if she consumes the same amount next year, she can now save less in the current year to achieve the same result. That is, she could save $11,454 in the current year, which would imply that she could consume $52,600 next year. Then, she consumes $\$40,000 - \$11,454 = \$28,546$, which is more than before, reflecting the income effect. What Christine does depends on her own preferences and how strong the relative income and substitution effects are for her as an individual.

Now, consider the effects of an increase in r for a borrower. In Figure 8.14, r increases from r_1 to r_2, and lifetime wealth changes from we_1 to we_2. The endowment point is at E, and the consumer initially chooses consumption bundle A; then, he or she chooses B after r increases. Again, we can separate the movement from A to B into substitution and income effects, by drawing an artificial budget constraint FG, which is parallel to the new budget constraint and tangent to the initial indifference curve I_1. Therefore, we are essentially compensating the consumer with extra wealth to make him or her as well off as initially when facing the higher interest rate. Then, the substitution effect is the movement from A to D, and the income effect is the movement from D to B. Here, the substitution effect is for future consumption to rise and current consumption to fall, just as was the case for a lender. However, the income effect in this case is negative for both current consumption and future consumption. As a result, current consumption falls for the borrower, but future consumption may rise or fall, depending on how strong the opposing substitution and income effects are. Savings must rise, as current consumption falls and current disposable income is held constant.

Figure 8.14 An Increase in the Real Interest Rate for a Borrower

When the real interest rate increases for a borrower, the substitution effect is the movement from A to D, and the income effect is the movement from D to B. Current consumption decreases while saving increases, and future consumption may rise or fall.

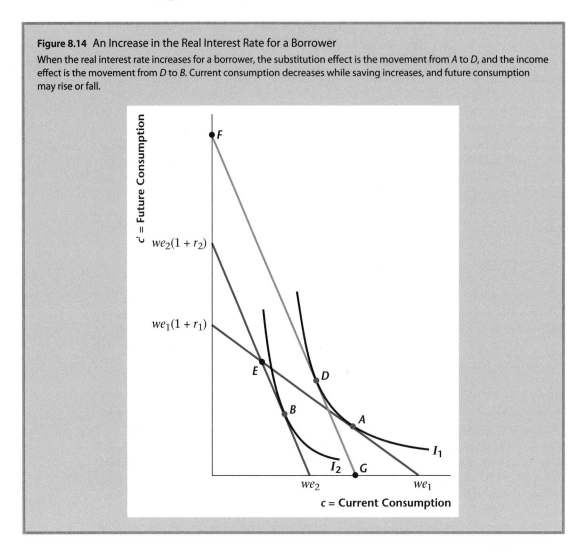

As an example, suppose that Christopher is initially a borrower, whose income in the current year and next year is $40,000 (in current year dollars). Initially, Christopher takes out a loan of $20,000 in the current year, so that he can consume $60,000 in the current year. The real interest rate is 5%, so that the principal and interest on his loan is $21,000, and he consumes $19,000 next year. Now, suppose alternatively that the real interest rate is 10%. If Christopher holds constant his consumption in the future, this must imply that his current consumption goes down, reflecting the negative income effect. That is, if he continues to consume $19,000 next year, given a real interest rate of 10%, he can borrow only $19,091 this year, which implies that his current year consumption is $59,091.

For both lenders and borrowers, there is an **intertemporal substitution effect** of an increase in the real interest rate. That is, a higher real interest rate lowers the relative price of future consumption in terms of current consumption, and this leads to a substitution of future consumption for current consumption and, therefore, to an increase in savings. In much of macroeconomics, we are interested in aggregate effects, but the above analysis tells us that there are potentially confounding income effects in determining the effect of an increase in the real interest rate on aggregate consumption. The population consists of many consumers, some of whom are lenders, and some of whom are borrowers. Although consumption decreases for each borrower when the real interest rate goes up, what happens to the consumption of lenders depends on the strength of opposing income and substitution effects. Although there is a tendency for the negative income effects on the consumption of borrowers to offset the positive income effects on the consumption of lenders, leaving us with only the substitution effects, there is no theoretical guarantee that aggregate consumption will fall when the real interest rate rises.

Tables 8.2 and 8.3 summarize our discussion of the effects of an increase in the real interest rate.

An Example: Perfect Complements A convenient example to work with is the case in which a consumer has preferences with the perfect complements property. Recall from Chapter 4 that if two goods are perfect complements, they are always consumed in fixed proportions. In the case of current consumption and future consumption, the perfect complements property implies that the consumer always chooses c and c' such that

$$c' = ac, \tag{8-10}$$

where a is a positive constant. In Figure 8.15, the consumer's indifference curves, for example I_1 and I_2, are L-shaped with the right angles on the line $c' = ac$. Perfect complementarity is an extreme case of a desire for consumption smoothing, in that the

Table 8.2 Effects of an Increase in the Real Interest Rate for a Lender

Current consumption	?
Future consumption	Increases
Current savings	?

Table 8.3 Effects of an Increase in the Real Interest Rate for a Borrower

Current consumption	Decreases
Future consumption	?
Current savings	Increases

Figure 8.15 Example with Perfect Complements Preferences

The consumer desires current and future consumption in fixed proportions, with $c' = ac$. With indifference curves representing perfect complementarity between current and future consumption, the optimal consumption bundle is at point D on the lifetime budget constraint AB.

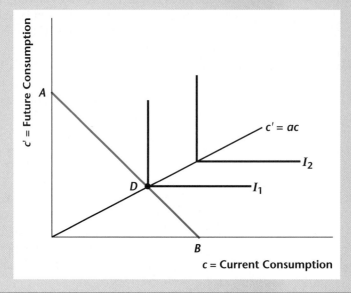

consumer never wants to deviate from having current and future consumption in fixed proportions. The consumer's budget constraint is AB in the figure, which is described by the equation

$$c + \frac{c'}{1 + r} = we, \tag{8-11}$$

where

$$we = y - t + \frac{y' - t'}{1 + r}. \tag{8-12}$$

In Figure 8.15 the optimal consumption bundle is at a point such as D, which is on the consumer's budget constraint and on the line $c' = ac$. Therefore, we can solve algebraically for current and future consumption c and c', respectively, by solving the Equations (8-10) and (8-11) for the two variables c and c', given r and we. Using substitution, we get

$$c = \frac{we(1 + r)}{1 + r + a}, \tag{8-13}$$

$$c' = \frac{awe(1 + r)}{1 + r + a}, \tag{8-14}$$

or substituting for we in (8-13) and (8-14) using (8-12), we obtain

$$c = \frac{(y - t)(1 + r) + y' - t'}{1 + r + a},$$

(8-15)

$$c' = a\left[\frac{(y - t)(1 + r) + y' - t'}{1 + r + a}\right].$$

(8-16)

From equations (8-15) and (8-16), current and future consumption increase with current income y and with future income y'. The effects of a change in the interest rate r are more complicated, but essentially the effect of an increase in r on c and c' depends only on whether the consumer is a lender or a borrower. This is because there are no substitution effects when preferences have the perfect complements property. We explore this further in the problems at the end of this chapter.

Government

Now that we have studied how consumers behave, to complete our description of the model we need only describe what the government does. We can then explore the equilibrium effects of tax policy.

We suppose that the government wishes to purchase G consumption goods in the current period and G' units in the future period, with these quantities of government purchases given exogenously. The aggregate quantity of taxes collected by the government in the current period is T. Recall that there are N consumers who each pay a current tax of t, so that $T = Nt$. Similarly, in the future period total taxes are equal to T', and we have $T' = Nt'$. The government can borrow in the current period by issuing bonds. Recall that government bonds and private bonds are indistinguishable, with these bonds all bearing the same real interest rate r. Letting B denote the quantity of government bonds issued in the current period, the government's current-period budget constraint is

$$G = T + B$$

(8-17)

that is, government spending is financed through taxes and the issue of bonds. Put another way, the current period government deficit, $G - T$, is financed by issuing bonds. In the future period, the government's budget constraint is

$$G' + (1 + r)B = T'.$$

(8-18)

The left-hand side of equation (8-18) is total government outlays in the future, consisting of future government purchases and the principal and interest on the government bonds issued in the current period. These government outlays are financed through future taxes, the quantity on the right-hand side of equation (8-18). The government's budget constraints allow for the possibility that $B < 0$. If $B < 0$ this would imply that the government was a lender to the private sector, rather than a borrower from it. In practice, the government engages in direct lending to the private sector, and it issues debt to private economic agents, so that it is a lender and a borrower.

Recall that, when we analyzed a consumer's budget constraint, we took the budget constraints for the current and future periods and collapsed them into a single lifetime budget constraint. Here, we can accomplish something similar, in taking the government's budget constraints expressed in equations (8-17) and (8-18) and collapsing them into a single **government present-value budget constraint.** We obtain this constraint by first solving equation (8-18) for B to get

$$B = \frac{T' - G'}{1 + r},$$

and then substituting in equation (8-17) for B to get

$$G + \frac{G'}{1 + r} = T + \frac{T'}{1 + r}. \tag{8-19}$$

Equation (8-19) is the government present-value budget constraint, and it states that the present value of government purchases must equal the present value of taxes. This is similar to the consumer's lifetime budget constraint, which states that the present value of consumption is equal to the present value of lifetime disposable income. An interpretation of the government present-value budget constraint is that the government must eventually pay off all of its debt by taxing its citizens.

Competitive Equilibrium

Now that we have described the behavior of the consumers and the government in our model, we can proceed with the final step in putting the model into working order, which is to specify how a competitive equilibrium is achieved.

The market in which the N consumers in this economy and the government interact is the credit market, in which consumers and the government can borrow and lend. In trading in the credit market, consumers and the government are effectively trading future consumption goods for current consumption goods. Recall that the relative price at which future consumption goods trade for current consumption goods is $\frac{1}{1 + r}$, which is determined by the real interest rate r.

In a competitive equilibrium for this two-period economy, three conditions must hold:

1. Each consumer chooses first- and second-period consumption and savings optimally given the real interest rate r.
2. The government present-value budget constraint, equation (8-19), holds.
3. The credit market clears.

The credit market clears when the net quantity that consumers want to lend in the current period is equal to the quantity that the government wishes to borrow. Letting S^p denote the aggregate quantity of private savings—that is, the savings of consumers—the credit market equilibrium condition is

$$S^p = B, \tag{8-20}$$

or the aggregate quantity of private savings is equal to the quantity of debt issued by the government in the current period. Equation (8-20) also states that national saving, which is equal to aggregate private saving minus B, is equal to zero in equilibrium. Recall from Chapter 2 that a national income accounts identity states that $S^p + S^g = I + CA$, where S^g is government savings, I is investment, and CA is the current account surplus. Here, $S^g = -B$, $I = 0$ because there is no capital accumulation in this model, and $CA = 0$ because this is a closed economy model. Also recall that $S = S^p + S^g$, where S is national saving.

The equilibrium condition equation (8-20) implies that

$$Y = C + G, \qquad\qquad (8\text{-}21)$$

where Y is aggregate income in the current period (the sum of incomes across all N consumers) and C is aggregate consumption in the current period (the sum of consumptions across all N consumers). Recall from Chapter 2 that equation (8-21) is the income–expenditure identity for this economy, because there is no investment, and no interaction with the rest of the world (net exports equal zero). To see why equation (8-21) follows from equation (8-20), note that

$$S^p = Y - C - T; \qquad\qquad (8\text{-}22)$$

that is, aggregate private saving is equal to current period income minus aggregate current consumption minus aggregate current taxes. Also, from the government's current-period budget constraint, equation (8-17), we have

$$B = G - T \qquad\qquad (8\text{-}23)$$

Then, substituting in equation (8-20) for S^p from equation (8-22) and for B from equation (8-23), we get

$$Y - C - T = G - T,$$

or, rearranging,

$$Y = C + G.$$

This result proves to be useful in the next section, as the economy can be shown to be in a competitive equilibrium if either equation (8-20) or equation (8-21) holds.

The Ricardian Equivalence Theorem

From Chapter 5, recall that an increase in government spending comes at a cost, in that it crowds out private consumption expenditures. However, in Chapter 5, we could not disentangle the effects of taxation from the effects of government spending, because the government was unable to borrow in the model considered there. That is certainly not true here, where we can independently evaluate the effects of changes in government spending and in taxes.

What we want to show here is a key result in macroeconomics, called the Ricardian equivalence theorem. This theorem states that a change in the timing of taxes by the government is neutral. By neutral, we mean that in equilibrium a change in current taxes, exactly offset in present-value terms by an equal and opposite change in future taxes, has no effect on the real interest rate or on the consumption of individual consumers. This is a very strong result, as it says that there is a sense in which government deficits do not matter, which seems to run counter to standard intuition. As we will see, however, this is an important starting point for thinking about why government deficits *do* matter, and a key message that comes from the logic of the Ricardian equivalence theorem is that *a tax cut is not a free lunch.*

To show why the Ricardian equivalence theorem holds in this model, we need only make some straightforward observations about the lifetime budget constraints of consumers and the government's present-value budget constraint. First, because each of the N consumers shares an equal amount of the total tax burden in the current and future periods, with $T = Nt$ and $T' = Nt'$, substituting in the government's present-value budget constraint, equation (8-19) gives

$$G + \frac{G'}{1 + r} = Nt + \frac{Nt'}{1 + r},$$ (8-24)

and then rearranging we get

$$t + \frac{t'}{1 + r} = \frac{1}{N}\left[G + \frac{G'}{1 + r}\right],$$ (8-25)

which states that the present value of taxes for a single consumer is the consumer's share of the present value of government spending. Next, substitute for the present value of taxes from equation (8-25) in a consumer's lifetime budget constraint, equation (8-4) to get

$$c + \frac{c'}{1 + r} = y + \frac{y'}{1 + r} - \frac{1}{N}\left[G + \frac{G'}{1 + r}\right].$$ (8-26)

Now, suppose that the economy is in equilibrium for a given real interest rate r. Each consumer chooses current consumption and future consumption c and c', respectively, to make himself or herself as well off as possible subject to the lifetime budget constraint, equation (8-26) (the present-value government budget constraint) holds, equation (8-19) holds, and the credit market clears, so current aggregate income is equal to current aggregate consumption plus current government spending, $Y = C + G$.

Next, consider an experiment in which the timing of taxes changes in such a way that the government budget constraint continues to hold at the interest rate r. That is, current taxes change by Δt for each consumer, with future taxes changing by $-\frac{\Delta t}{1 + r}$ so that the government budget constraint continues to hold, from equation (8-24). Then, from equation (8-26) there is no change in the consumer's lifetime wealth, the right-hand side of equation (8-26), given r, because y, y', N, G, and G' remain unaffected. Because the consumer's lifetime wealth is unaffected, then given r the consumer makes the same decisions, choosing the same quantities of current and future consumption. This is true for every consumer, so given r aggregate consumption C is the same. Thus, it is still the case that $Y = C + G$, so the credit market clears. Therefore, with the new timing of taxes and the same real interest rate, each consumer is optimizing, the government's present-value budget constraint holds, and the credit market clears, so r is still the equilibrium real interest rate.

Therefore, we have shown that a change in the timing of taxes has no effect on equilibrium consumption or the real interest rate. Because each consumer faces the same budget constraint before and after the change in the timing of taxes, all consumers are no better or worse off with the change in taxes. We have, thus, demonstrated that the Ricardian equivalence theorem holds in this model.

Although the timing of taxes has no effect on consumption, welfare, or the market real interest rate, there are effects on private saving and government saving. That is, because aggregate private saving is $S^p = Y - T - C$ and government saving is $S^g = T - G$, any change in the timing of taxes that decreases current taxes T increases current private saving and decreases government saving by equal amounts. To give a more concrete example, suppose that there is a cut in current taxes, so that $\Delta t < 0$. Then, the government must issue more debt today to finance the tax cut, and it will have to increase taxes in the future to pay off this higher debt. Consumers anticipate this, and they increase their savings by the amount of the tax cut, because this is how much extra they have to save to pay the higher taxes they will face in the future. In the credit market, there is an increase in savings by consumers, which just matches the increase in borrowing by the government, so there is no effect on borrowing and lending among consumers, and therefore, no effect on the market real interest rate.

Ricardian Equivalence: A Numerical Example
To give a numerical example, assume an economy with 500 consumers who are all identical. Initially, the equilibrium real interest rate is 5%, and each consumer receives income of 10 units in the current period, and income of 12 units in the future period. In the current and future periods, each consumer initially pays taxes of 3 and 4 units, respectively. Lifetime wealth for each consumer is then

$$we = 10 - 3 + \frac{12 - 4}{1.05} = 14.61.$$

Suppose that each consumer initially finds it optimal to consume 6 units in the current period and 9.04 units in the future period. We can verify that this consumption bundle satisfies the consumer's lifetime budget constraint. That is,

$$6 + \frac{9.04}{1.05} = 14.61.$$

Then, each consumer saves $10 - 6 - 3 = 1$ in the current period, so that aggregate private saving is initially 500 units.

The government purchases 2,000 units in the current period and 1,475 units in the future period. Because aggregate taxes are 1,500 in the current period and 2,000 in the future period, the government borrows $B = 500$ in the current period. Thus, national saving is private saving plus government saving, or $500 - 500 = 0$. The government's present-value budget constraint is

$$2{,}000 + \frac{1{,}475}{1.05} = 1{,}500 + \frac{2{,}000}{1.05}.$$

Further, aggregate current income is 5,000, while aggregate current consumption is 3,000. This implies that $Y = C + G$, and so the credit market is in equilibrium.

Now, suppose that the government reduces taxes for each consumer in the current period to 2 units and increases taxes for each consumer in the future period to 5.05 units. Suppose for now that the equilibrium real interest rate is unchanged at 5%. Then, the government's present-value budget constraint still holds, as

$$2{,}000 + \frac{1{,}475}{1.05} = 1{,}000 + \frac{2{,}525}{1.05}.$$

Further, lifetime wealth for each consumer is now

$$we = 10 - 2 + \frac{12 - 5.05}{1.05} = 14.61,$$

which is identical to lifetime wealth before the current tax cut, and so each consumer still wants to consume 6 units in the current period and 9.04 units in the future period. As a result, it must still be the case that $Y = C + G$, that is, the credit market clears. Therefore, 5% is still the equilibrium real interest rate, and each consumer's consumption decisions are unchanged.

Aggregate private saving has now increased by the amount of the tax cut, to 1,000, and government saving has decreased by the amount of the tax cut, to $-1{,}000$, with equilibrium national saving unchanged at 0.

Ricardian Equivalence: A Graph

We can show how the Ricardian equivalence theorem works by considering the effects of a current tax cut on an individual consumer. Here, the consumer also faces an increase in taxes in the future, as the government must pay off the current debt issued to finance the tax cut. Suppose that a consumer initially faces taxes t^* and t'^* in the current period and future period, respectively. In Figure 8.16 he or she has an endowment point E_1, and chooses consumption bundle A. Now, suppose there is a tax cut in the current period, so that $\Delta t < 0$. Therefore, the government must borrow $N\Delta t$ more in period 1 to finance the larger current government deficit, and taxes must rise for each consumer by $-\Delta t(1 + r)$ in the future period to pay off the increased government debt. The effect of this on the consumer is that lifetime wealth we remains unchanged, as the present value of taxes has not changed. The budget constraint is unaffected, and the consumer still chooses point A in Figure 8.16. What changes is that the endowment point moves to E_2; that is, the consumer has more disposable income in the current period and less disposable income in the future period due to the tax cut in the current period. Because the consumer buys the same consumption bundle, what he or she does is to save all of the tax cut in the current period to pay the higher taxes that he or she faces in the future period.

Figure 8.16 Ricardian Equivalence with a Cut in Current Taxes for a Borrower

A current tax cut with a future increase in taxes leaves the consumer's lifetime budget constraint unchanged, and so the consumer's optimal consumption bundle remains at A. The endowment point shifts from E_1 to E_2, so that there is an increase in saving by the amount of the current tax cut.

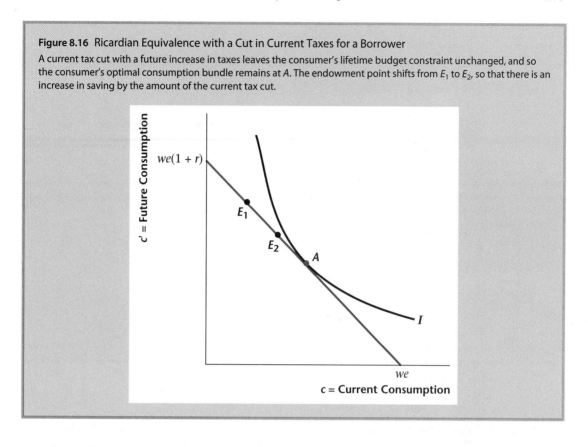

Ricardian Equivalence and Credit Market Equilibrium

Finally, we will consider a graph that shows the workings of the credit market under Ricardian equivalence. In Figure 8.17, the curve $S_1^p(r)$ denotes the private supply of credit, which is the total desired saving of private consumers given the market real interest rate r, drawn given a particular timing of taxes between the current and future periods. We have drawn $S_1^p(r)$ as being upward-sloping, under the assumption that substitution effects outweigh the income effects of changes in interest rates when we add these effects across all consumers. The government demand for credit is B_1, the exogenous supply of bonds issued by the government in the current period. The equilibrium real interest rate that clears the credit market is r_1.

Now, if the government reduces current taxes by the same amount for each individual, this results in an increase in government bonds issued from B_1 to B_2. This is not the end of the story, as savings behavior changes for each consumer. In fact, total savings, or the supply of credit, increases for each consumer by an amount such that the credit supply curve shifts to the right by an amount $B_2 - B_1$ for each r, to $S_2^p(r)$. Therefore, the equilibrium real interest rate remains unchanged at r_1, and private savings increases by the same amount by which government savings falls.

Previously, when we looked at the effects of an increase in a consumer's current disposable income on current consumption, we determined that, because of the consumer's

Figure 8.17 Ricardian Equivalence and Credit Market Equilibrium

With a decrease in current taxes, government debt increases from B_1 to B_2, and the credit supply curve shifts to the right by the same amount. The equilibrium real interest rate is unchanged, and private saving increases by an amount equal to the reduction in government saving.

consumption-smoothing motive, some of the increase in disposable income would be saved. Thus, a temporary increase in disposable income would lead to a less than one-for-one increase in current consumption. In the real world, where individual consumption decisions are made over long horizons, any temporary increase in a consumer's disposable income should lead to a relatively small increase in his or her permanent income, in line with Friedman's permanent income hypothesis. Thus, Friedman's permanent income hypothesis would appear to imply that a temporary change in taxes leads to a very small change in current consumption. The Ricardian equivalence theorem carries this logic one step further by taking into account the implications of a current change in taxes for future taxes. For example, because any current tax cut must be paid for with government borrowing, this government borrowing implies higher future taxes to pay off the government debt. In making their lifetime wealth calculations, consumers recognize that the current tax cut is exactly offset by higher taxes in the future, and they save all of the current tax cut to pay the higher future taxes.

A key message from the Ricardian equivalence theorem is that a tax cut is not a free lunch. While a current tax cut can give all consumers higher current disposable incomes, and this seems like a good thing, consumers must pay for the current tax cut by bearing higher taxes in the future. Under the conditions studied in our model, the costs of a tax cut exactly offset the benefits, and consumers are no better off with the tax cut than without it.

Ricardian Equivalence and the Burden of the Government Debt

At the individual level, debt represents a liability that reduces an individual's lifetime wealth. The Ricardian equivalence theorem implies that the same logic holds for the government debt, which the theorem tells us represents our future tax liabilities as a nation. The government debt is a burden in that it is something we owe to ourselves; the government must pay off its debt by taxing us in the future. In the model in which we explained the Ricardian equivalence theorem above, the burden of the debt is shared equally among consumers. In practice, however, many issues in fiscal policy revolve around how the burden of the government debt is shared, among the current population and between generations. To discuss these issues, we need to address the role played by four key assumptions in our analysis of the Ricardian equivalence theorem.

1. The first key assumption is that when taxes change, in the experiment we considered above, they change by the same amount for all consumers, both in the present and in the future. For example, when a particular consumer received a tax cut in the current period, this was offset by an equal and opposite (in present-value terms) increase in taxes in the future, so that the present-value tax burden for each individual was unchanged. Now, if some consumers received higher tax cuts than others, then lifetime wealth could change for some consumers, and this would necessarily change their consumption choices and could change the equilibrium real interest rate. In the future, when the higher debt is paid off through higher future taxes, consumers might share unequally in this taxation, so that the burden of the debt might not be distributed equally. The government can redistribute wealth in society through tax policy, and the public debate concerning changes in taxes often focuses on how these tax changes affect consumers at different income levels.

2. A second key assumption in the model is that any debt issued by the government is paid off during the lifetimes of the people alive when the debt was issued. In practice, the government can postpone the taxes required to pay off the debt until long in the future, when the consumers who received the current benefits of a higher government debt are either retired or dead. That is, if the government cuts taxes, then the current old receive higher disposable incomes, but it is the current young who will have to pay off the government debt in the future through higher taxes. In this sense, the government debt can be a burden on the young, and it can involve an intergenerational redistribution of wealth. In some instances, intergenerational wealth redistribution can improve matters for everyone, as with some social security programs. We explore this issue in the next chapter.

3. A third assumption made above was that taxes are lump sum. In practice, as mentioned in Chapter 4 and Chapter 5, all taxes cause distortions, in that they change the effective relative prices of goods faced by consumers in the market. These distortions represent welfare losses from taxation. That is, if the government collects $1 million in taxes, the welfare cost to the economy is something greater than $1 million, because of the distortions caused by taxation. The study of optimal taxation in

public finance involves examining how large these welfare costs are for different kinds of taxes. For example, it could be that the welfare cost of income taxation at the margin is higher than the welfare cost of sales taxes at the margin. If the government taxes optimally, it minimizes the welfare cost of taxation, given the quantity of tax revenue it needs to generate. One of the trade-offs made by the government in setting taxes optimally is the trade-off between current taxation and future taxation. The government debt represents a burden, in that the future taxes required to pay off the debt will cause distortions. Some work on optimal taxation by Robert Barro,[3] among others, shows that the government should act to smooth tax rates over time, so as to achieve the optimal trade-off between current and future taxation.

4. A fourth key assumption made above is that there are **perfect credit markets**, in the sense that consumers can borrow and lend as much as they please, subject to their lifetime budget constraints, and they can borrow and lend at the same interest rate. In practice, consumers face constraints on how much they can borrow; for example, credit cards have borrowing limits, and sometimes consumers cannot borrow without collateral (as with mortgages and auto loans).[4] Consumers also typically borrow at higher interest rates than they can lend at. For example, the gap between the interest rate on a typical bank loan and the interest rate on a typical bank deposit can be 6 percentage points per annum or more. Further, the government borrows at lower interest rates than does the typical consumer. While all consumers need not be affected by **credit market imperfections**, to the extent that some consumers are credit-constrained, these credit-constrained consumers could be affected beneficially by a tax cut, even if there is an offsetting tax liability for these consumers in the future. In this sense, the government debt may not be a burden for some segments of the population; it may in fact increase welfare for these groups. We explore this idea further in Chapter 9.

The Ricardian equivalence theorem captures a key reality: Current changes in taxes have consequences for future taxes. However, there are many complications associated with real-world tax policy that essentially involve shifts in the distribution of taxation across the population and in the distribution of the burden of the government debt. These complications are left out of our analysis of the Ricardian equivalence theorem. For some macroeconomic issues, the distributional effects of tax policy are irrelevant, but for other issues they matter a great deal. For example, if you were a macroeconomist working for a political party, how a particular tax policy affected the wealth of different consumers in different ways might be the key to your party's success, and you would want to pay close attention to this. As well, as you will see in Chapter 9, so-called "pay-as-you-go" social security systems work because of the intergenerational redistributional effects of tax policy, and credit market imperfections that cause Ricardian equivalence to fail are key to understanding the current financial crisis.

---

[3]See R. Barro, 1979, "On the Determination of the Public Debt," *Journal of Political Economy* 87, 940–971.

[4]Collateral is the security that a borrower puts up when the loan is made. If the borrower defaults on the loan, then the collateral is seized by the lender. With a mortgage loan, the collateral is the house purchased with the mortgage loan, and with an auto loan, the collateral is the car that was purchased.

THEORY confronts the DATA

George H. W. Bush and the Withholding Reduction

In his State of the Union Address on January 28, 1992, President George H. W. Bush made the following statement:

And I have, this evening, directed the Secretary of the Treasury to change the Federal tax withholding tables. With this change, millions of Americans from whom the Government withholds more than necessary can now choose to have the Government withhold less from their paychecks. Something tells me a number of taxpayers may take us up on this one. This initiative could return about $25 billion back into our economy over the next 12 months, money people can use to help pay for clothing, college, or to get a new car.[5]

The withholding change that President Bush referred to in his State of the Union Address was implemented immediately, as he stated, and continued for 10 months until the end of 1992. Each married person would have a reduction in tax withholding of $28.80 per month, while a single person would have a reduction of $14.40. Those in the highest tax bracket did not receive the benefit. The $25 billion effect appears to represent an estimate of the total withholding reduction for the U.S. population, based on a best guess as to the number of people affected for the 10 months of this program.

The withholding reduction comes as close as one might hope to a real-world Ricardian equivalence experiment. This is because the withholding reduction would not affect anyone's federal income taxes payable for 1992; the taxes were simply deferred until they were due in April 1993. Overlooking the relatively small amount

of interest that consumers would earn on the withholding reduction until their taxes came due, lifetime wealth would be essentially unchanged for U.S. consumers. However, President Bush clearly did not put much stock in the Ricardian equivalence theorem, as he appeared convinced that the withholding reduction would increase private consumption expenditures. The Ricardian equivalence theorem predicts that U.S. taxpayers would essentially save the entire withholding reduction to pay their taxes in spring 1993.

What is the evidence on the effects of the 1992 withholding reduction? In Figures 8.18 to 8.20, we show quarterly real consumption (billions of 1996 dollars, seasonally adjusted at annual rates) of durables, nondurables, and services, respectively, for the period 1991 to 1993. Suppose that we accept that disposable income increased by $25 billion from first quarter 1992 to first quarter 1993, with a decrease of $25 billion in second quarter 1993 (when taxes are paid) as a result of the tax withholding experiment (this is the estimate by President Bush above). If all of the increase in income were spent on consumption goods in the period from 1992 first quarter to 1993 first quarter, with a corresponding reduction in consumption spending in 1993 second quarter, this would make a significant difference for consumption spending that we would see in Figures 8.18 to 8.20 as a sharp increase in some component(s) of consumer expenditure in the first quarter of 1992, with a sharp decrease or decreases in second quarter 1993. However, there appears to be no evidence of this in Figures 8.18 to 8.20. Instead, what we see is a more-or-less smooth recovery in the components of consumer spending from the 1991–92 recession. Thus, there was no apparent effect on aggregate consumption of the withholding reduction, in contrast to what President Bush expected. This evidence is consistent with the Ricardian equivalence theorem.

---

[5]For the full text of President Bush's 1992 State of the Union Address, see http://www.thisnation.com/library/sotu/1992gb.html

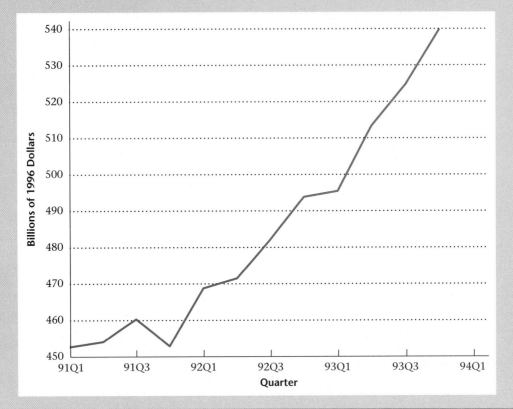

Figure 8.18 Real Consumption of Durables, 1991–1993

There appears to be no significant upward blip in durables consumption associated with the Bush withholding reduction.

Source: Bureau of Economic Analysis, Department of Commerce.

MACROECONOMICS IN ACTION

The Economic Growth and Tax Relief Reconciliation Act and National Saving

The Economic Growth and Tax Relief Reconciliation Act (EGTRRA) was passed into law in the United States by George W. Bush in 2001. As discussed in Chapter 5, the Act reduced marginal federal income tax rates at all levels of income, with larger tax rate reductions for those earning high incomes. The Ricardian equivalence theorem tells us that, if

taxes are lump sum, then the timing of taxes cannot affect national saving. For example, with a current tax cut, government saving decreases, and private saving increases by an equal amount, with total national saving unchanged. However, the tax change brought about in the EGTRRA does not satisfy the conditions required for Ricardian equivalence, for

Figure 8.19 Real Consumption of Nondurables, 1991–1993

There appears to be no significant upward blip in nondurables consumption associated with the Bush withholding reduction.

Source: Bureau of Economic Analysis, Department of Commerce.

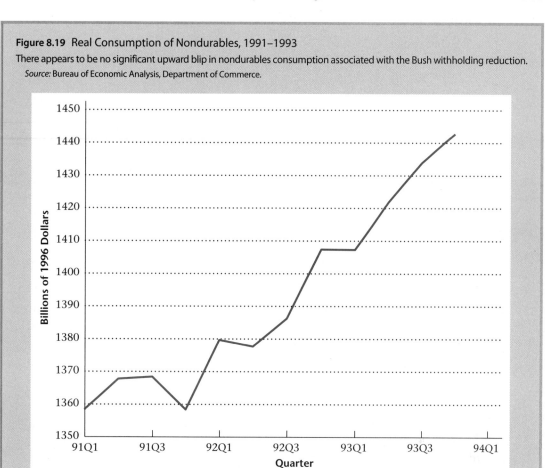

three reasons: (i) a significant fraction of consumers may be credit-constrained; (ii) federal income taxes are not lump-sum—EGTRRA involved changes in tax *rates*; and (iii) there was no guarantee when EGTRRA passed that government spending in the future would remain unchanged.

There are good reasons to think that (i) above would not matter much for the effects of the EGTRRA, since the bulk of the tax cut went to those with high incomes, who are unlikely to be credit-constrained. However, (ii) and (iii) could matter significantly. First, with regard to (ii), in Chapter 5 we studied the effects of changes in income tax rates, and

determined that tax rate decreases will cause a decrease in tax revenue (provided the economy is on the "good side" of the Laffer curve), and an increase in the quantity of labor supplied and real GDP (provided the substitution effect on labor supplied exceeds the income effect). This incentive effect of a decrease in taxes will tend to increase national saving, as private saving will increase with real income, and the government will collect more tax revenue with higher economic activity, thus increasing government saving. Note here that the government will be collecting less tax revenue than would otherwise be the case, because tax rates have gone down, but more

(Continued)

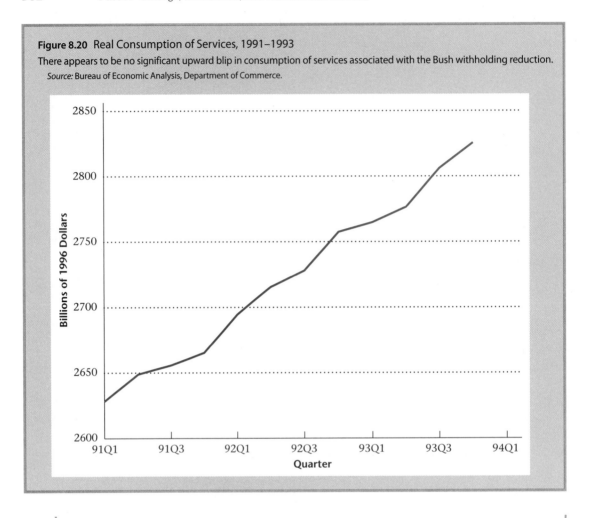

Figure 8.20 Real Consumption of Services, 1991–1993
There appears to be no significant upward blip in consumption of services associated with the Bush withholding reduction.
Source: Bureau of Economic Analysis, Department of Commerce.

than would have been collected if real GDP had not increased because of the tax cut.

Finally, with regard to (iii) above, it can be the case that a large government deficit creates pressure on the government to reduce government spending, perhaps because it is more palatable to the electorate to experience a decrease in government spending than an increase in taxes. Indeed, this tendency is incorporated in a tactic for reducing the size of government, sometimes called "starve the beast." That is, it is easy for the government to reduce taxes, less easy to increase government spending, even less easy to decrease government spending, and very hard to increase

taxes. However, it is much easier to reduce government spending if the government deficit is high than if it is low. Thus, if the goal of the government is to reduce the size of the government, it is easiest to accomplish this by first reducing taxes, thus inducing an increase in the government deficit, and then reduce government spending to balance the budget.

Thus, it would be reasonable to conclude that the EGTRRA would imply a reduction of future government spending rather than a future tax increase (a change in the timing of taxes). Then, the current tax cut would indeed be an increase in wealth for current consumers, and this would increase consumption and reduce national saving. In the future, when government spending falls, our analysis in Chapter 5 tells us that real GDP will fall, which implies lower national saving, as private saving and government saving will fall with real GDP.

In conclusion, theory tells us that the EGTRRA will do the following. First, through effect (ii), there will be positive incentive effects and an increase in national savings in the present and second, through effect (iii) there will be a decrease in current national savings and a decrease in future national savings. However, for practical policy purposes, we are interested in the quantitative effects of the EGTRRA. The effects we understand from theory may be small or large, and theory does not tell us which of the two opposing effects on current national savings is larger. Such a quantitative policy experiment was carried out using a computational macroeconomic model by Alan Auerbach, with the results reported in "The Bush Tax Cut and National Saving."[6]

[6]Auerbach, A. 2002. "The Bush Tax Cut and National Saving," NBER working paper 9012, available at http://www.nber.org/papers/w9012

Auerbach used a model that he designed with Laurence Kotlikoff to simulate the effects of EGTRRA on the computer. Auerbach's conclusion is that EGTRRA would have the effect of reducing national saving in both the present and the future. That is, the incentive effects of the changes in tax rates were not large enough to have a net positive effect on national saving in the short run. Another interesting feature of Auerbach's analysis is that he could measure the effects of "dynamic scoring," which takes account of the effect of changes in economic behavior on government tax revenues. That is, one way to estimate the effects of a change in income tax rates is to assume that income and its distribution across the population remain unchanged. Dynamic scoring takes account of effects like those discussed above, for example the fact that real GDP will tend to increase with a decrease in tax rates, which will offset the tax revenue losses due to the lower tax rates. Auerbach finds that, indeed, it is important to do dynamic scoring, since changes in economic behavior are very important for government tax revenues.

Perspectives on the Financial Crisis

Government Deficits, Taxes, and Government Debt

One of the lessons of this chapter is that a government deficit represents deferred taxation—the government must finance a deficit by issuing debt, and the government must ultimately pay off this debt by increasing taxes in the future. In Figure 8.21 we show the total government surplus in the United States, for all levels of government, for the period 1966–2009, as a percentage of GDP. The government surplus increased from the early 1990s until 2000, then declined sharply as the result of the Bush administration tax cuts

(see the previous Macroeconomics in Action box), the 2001 recession, and a drop in stock market prices, which all acted to reduce tax revenues. There was a modest increase in the surplus from 2004 to 2006, before the government surplus declined precipitously, with the government deficit reaching more than 6% of GDP in the first quarter of 2009. The *Economist* magazine forecasts[7] that the annual U.S. government surplus

[7]See *The Economist*, June 27–July 3, 2009 issue.

(Continued)

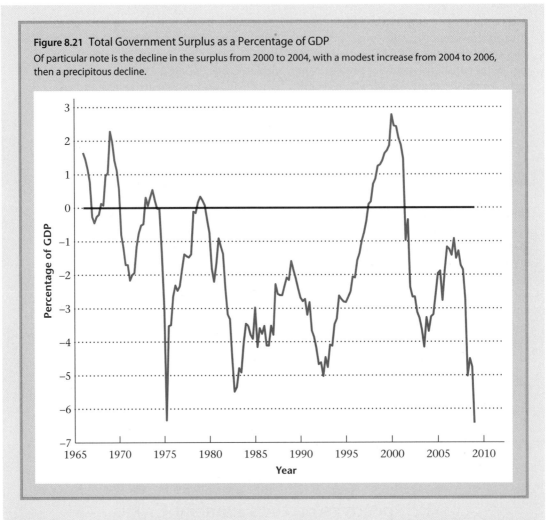

Figure 8.21 Total Government Surplus as a Percentage of GDP

Of particular note is the decline in the surplus from 2000 to 2004, with a modest increase from 2004 to 2006, then a precipitous decline.

will be –13.2% of GDP for 2009, a quantity exceeded (among the 43 countries covered) only by Great Britain, at –13.9% of GDP. Note that, from Figure 8.21, if this forecast is realized, the government deficit would be more than twice as large, as a percentage of GDP, as at any time since 1966.

The government surplus is expected to decline further in the United States from what we see in Figure 8.21 for two reasons. First, the continuing recession in 2009 will act to reduce tax revenues at all levels of government. For example, during a recession, incomes fall, corporate profits decrease, and consumption expenditures fall, which act to reduce income tax revenue, corporate tax revenue,

and sales tax revenue, respectively. Second, as discussed in Chapter 5, the American Recovery and Reinvestment Act (ARRA) was signed into law in early 2009, authorizing a large package of increases in government spending and decreases in taxes.

Focussing on the tax implications of the ARRA, this fiscal policy package includes cuts of $288 billion in personal and corporate taxes, a quantity which amounts to 2% of 2008 GDP, so we can think of this tax cut as contributing 2% to the size of the deficit, as a percentage of GDP. In Figure 8.22, note that taxes are already at a historically low level. Taxes reached a high of about 32% of GDP in 2000, and were at approximately

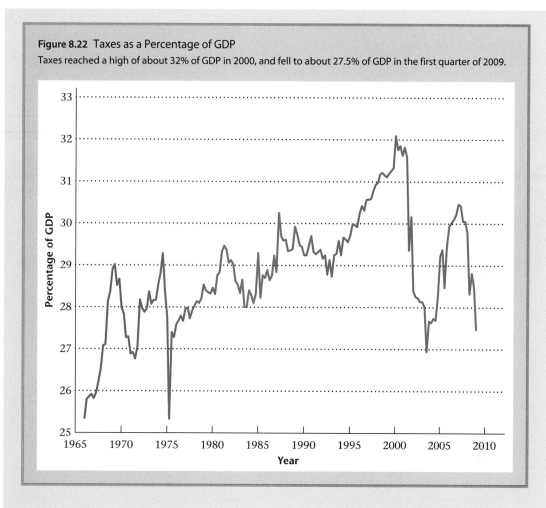

Figure 8.22 Taxes as a Percentage of GDP

Taxes reached a high of about 32% of GDP in 2000, and fell to about 27.5% of GDP in the first quarter of 2009.

27.5% of GDP in 2009, a level as low as in the late 1960s. We can see the results of the recent government deficits on the level of U.S. federal government debt, in Figure 8.23. The quantity of federal government debt peaked at about 70% in the mid-1990s, then decreased during the period of government surpluses in the late 1990s, after which the debt increased gradually, and then at a rapid rate, reaching close to 80% of GDP in early 2009.

The level of GDP essentially represents the tax base which the government can tax to pay off the debt. This then makes the ratio of government debt to GDP a useful measure of the burden of the government debt, or a measure of the future tax

liabilities to be faced by the average American. If the U.S. government ran a deficit of from 5% to 10% of GDP for a long period of time, what would be the consequences for the government debt? How would this matter in the future for the level of taxation faced by the average American?

To address these questions, we will focus on long-term considerations. With that in mind, suppose that GDP grows at a constant rate, g, so that

$$Y_{t+1} = (1 + g)Y_t,$$

where Y_t denotes real GDP in period t. Then, if we start in period 0,

$$Y_t = Y_0(1 + g)^t. \qquad (8\text{-}27)$$

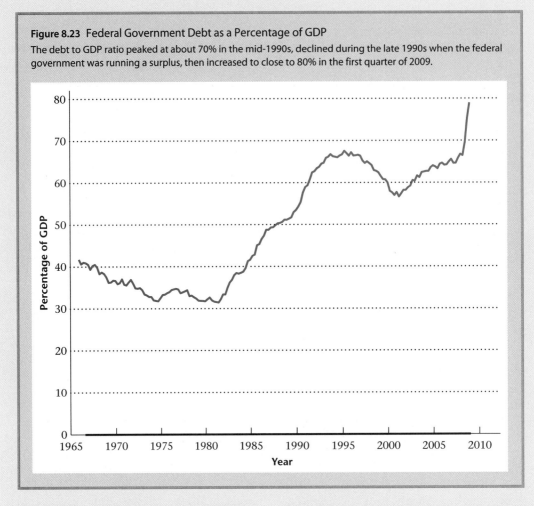

Figure 8.23 Federal Government Debt as a Percentage of GDP

The debt to GDP ratio peaked at about 70% in the mid-1990s, declined during the late 1990s when the federal government was running a surplus, then increased to close to 80% in the first quarter of 2009.

Also suppose that the government needs to finance a primary deficit of dY_t in period t. The primary deficit is the value of the government deficit we obtain after deducting the interest payments on the government debt (see Chapter 2). Here, d is the ratio of the primary deficit to GDP, which we assume is constant forever.

Now, suppose that the market real interest rate r is constant forever. Assume that the government issues one-period debt each period, with one unit of debt in period t paying off $1 + r$ units of consumption goods in period $t + 1$. Then, if B_t is total government debt in period t, we have

$$B_{t+1} = (1 + r)B_t + dY_0(1 + g)^{t+1}, \quad (8\text{-}28)$$

since the debt issued in period $t + 1$ (B_{t+1}) must be just sufficient to pay the interest and principal on the debt issued in period t, and to finance the primary deficit. We have also used equation (8-27) in equation (8-28). Assume that the government starts out in period 0 with no debt outstanding, so using equation (8-28) we have

$$
\begin{aligned}
B_0 &= dY_0, \\
B_1 &= dY_0(1 + r) + dY_0(1 + g) \\
&= dY_0(1 + r + 1 + g), \\
B_2 &= dY_0[(1 + r)^2 \\
&\quad + (1 + r)(1 + g) \\
&\quad + (1 + g)^2],
\end{aligned}
$$

etc. In general, then, we will obtain

$$B_t = dY_0[(1 + r)^t + (1 + r)^{t-1}$$
$$(1 + g) + \ldots + (1 + g)^t] \quad (8\text{-}29)$$

Then, from equations (8-27) and (8-29), the ratio of debt to GDP in period t is

$$\frac{dY_0[(1 + r)^t + (1 + r)^{t-1}(1 + g) + \ldots + (1 + g)^t]}{Y_0(1 + g)^t}$$

$$= d\left[\left(\frac{1 + r}{1 + g}\right)^t + \left(\frac{1 + r}{1 + g}\right)^{t-1} + \ldots + 1\right]. \quad (8\text{-}30)$$

Therefore, if $r \geq g$ so that the real interest rate is at least as large as the rate at which GDP is growing, then the ratio of government debt to GDP will keep on growing over time, and become infinitely large as t gets large. This is because the government keeps issuing more debt to finance the interest payments on its existing debt, but the economy is not growing as fast as the rate at which the debt is growing. Clearly then, if $r \geq g$, then running a deficit forever would be impossible—ultimately, the debt would become so large that there would not be enough lending capacity in the world to absorb it. However, if $r < g$, if t gets very large, then using the formula for the sum of an infinite geometric series in equation (8-30), the ratio of debt to GDP will be approximately

$$\text{long-run debt/GDP ratio} = d\left(\frac{1 + g}{g - r}\right). \quad (8\text{-}31)$$

What this says is that, so long as the real interest rate is smaller than the growth rate of real GDP, the government can permanently run a deficit, provided that people (in the United States and the rest of the world) are willing to hold the debt of the United States government at the interest rate r.

Now, average growth in U.S. GDP over the last 100 years has been about 3% per year, and the short-term real interest rate has been about 1%, so set $g = .03$ and $r = .01$. We then have

$$\text{long-run debt/GDP ratio} = d(51.5)$$

This implies that, if the primary deficit were 5% of GDP, i.e. $d = .05$, then the long-run debt/GDP

ratio would be $.05 \times 51.5 = 2.575$, which is more than three times the current ratio of government debt to GDP (see Figure 8.23). Therefore, if the government runs a permanent primary deficit of 5% of GDP, the government debt will be 257.5% of GDP in the long run. This would imply that the interest payments on the debt in the long run would be $r \times 2.575 = .01 \times 2.575 = .026$, as a fraction of GDP. Thus the actual deficit would be the primary deficit plus the interest payments on the debt or $.05 + .026 = .076$, or 7.6% of GDP. If the primary deficit were permanently larger, say 10% of GDP, then the long-run debt/GDP ratio would be 5.15, or more than 6 times what it is currently, implying a long-run actual deficit of 15.2% of GDP in the long run, including the interest payments on the debt.

The above calculations are intended to give an idea of what would happen if the United States continued to run primary deficits of from 5% to 10% of GDP for the indefinite future. We showed that this would imply a long run increase in the ratio of government debt to GDP of from 3 to 6 times its value in early 2009. It is unclear whether lenders in the world would be willing to hold this much U.S. government debt at a real interest rate of about 1% per annum; such a scenario seems unlikely. Alternatively, suppose that the government debt to GDP ratio increased to, say, 120% over the period 2009–2011. Then, suppose that there were some combination of spending cuts and tax increases so that the debt could be reduced. How long would it take to reduce the debt to zero? Again, assume that $g = .03$ and $r = .01$, and suppose that the primary surplus is 3% ($d = -.03$) of GDP beyond the year 2011 for as long as it would take to reduce the debt to zero. Then, using (8-30), it would take about 75 years to pay off the debt at this rate. This shows that the potential size of the U.S. debt is quite daunting. Given the recent history of government surpluses in Figure 8.21, the federal government would have to acquire a level of discipline hitherto not in evidence, in order to significantly reduce the size of the government debt.

Chapter Summary

- A two-period macroeconomic model was constructed to understand the intertemporal consumption–savings decisions of consumers and the effects of fiscal policy choices concerning the timing of taxes and the quantity of government debt.

- In the model, there are many consumers, and each makes decisions over a two-period horizon where a consumer's incomes in the two periods are given, and the consumer pays lump-sum taxes in each period to the government.

- The lifetime budget constraint of the consumer states that the present value of consumption over the consumer's two-period time horizon is equal to the present value of disposable income.

- A consumer's lifetime wealth is his or her present value of disposable income.

- A consumer's preferences have the property that more is preferred to less with regard to current and future consumption, there is a preference for diversity in current and future consumption, and current and future consumption are normal goods. A preference for diversity implies that consumers wish to smooth consumption relative to income over the present and the future.

- Consumption smoothing yields the result that, if income increases in the current period for a consumer, then current consumption increases, future consumption increases, and current saving increases. If future income increases, then consumption increases in both periods and current saving decreases. A permanent increase in income (when current and future income increase) has a larger impact on current consumption than does a temporary increase in income (only current income increases).

- If there is an increase in the real interest rate that a consumer faces, then there are income and substitution effects on consumption. Because an increase in the real interest rate causes a reduction in the price of future consumption in terms of current consumption, the substitution effect is for current consumption to fall, future consumption to rise, and current saving to rise when the real interest rate rises. For a lender (borrower), the income effect of an increase in the real interest rate is positive (negative) for both current and future consumption.

- The Ricardian equivalence theorem states that changes in current taxes by the government that leave the present value of taxes constant have no effect on consumers' consumption choices or on the equilibrium real interest rate. This is because consumers change savings by an amount equal and opposite to the change in current taxes to compensate for the change in future taxes.

- Ricardian equivalence depends critically on the notion that the burden of the government debt is shared equally among the people alive when the debt is issued. The burden of the debt is not shared equally when: (1) there are current distributional effects of changes in taxes; (2) there are intergenerational distribution effects; (3) taxes cause distortions; or (4) there are credit market imperfections.

Key Terms

Consumption-savings decision The decision by a consumer about how to split current income between current consumption and savings. (p. 262)

Consumption smoothing The tendency of consumers to seek a consumption path over time that is smoother than income. (p. 263)

Credit market imperfections Constraints on borrowing, or differences between borrowing and lending rates of interest. (p. 298)

Endowment point The point on a consumer's budget constraint where consumption is equal to disposable income in each period. (p. 268)

Excess variability The observed fact that measured consumption is more variable than theory appears to predict. (p. 274)

Government present-value budget constraint Condition that the present value of government purchases is equal to the present value of tax revenues. (p. 290)

Intertemporal decisions Decisions involving economic trade-offs across periods of time. (p. 262)

Intertemporal substitution effect Substitution by a consumer of a good in one time period for a good in another time period, in response to a change in the relative price of the two goods. The intertemporal substitution effect of an increase in the real interest rate is for current consumption to fall and future consumption to rise. (p. 286)

Lifetime budget constraint Condition that the present value of a consumer's lifetime disposable income equals the present value of his or her lifetime consumption. (p. 266)

Lifetime wealth The present value of lifetime disposable income for a consumer. (p. 267)

Martingale An economic variable with the property that the best forecast of its value tomorrow is its value today. Finance theory implies that stock prices are martingales. (p. 280)

Perfect credit market An idealized credit market in which consumers can borrow and lend all they want at the market interest rate, and the interest rate at which consumers lend is equal to the interest rate at which they borrow. (p. 298)

Permanent income hypothesis A theory developed by Milton Friedman that implies a consumer's current consumption depends on his or her permanent income. Permanent income is closely related to lifetime wealth in our model. (p. 278)

Present value The value, in terms of money today or current goods, of a future stream of money or goods. (p. 266)

Real interest rate The rate of return on savings in units of consumption goods. (p. 262)

Ricardian equivalence theorem Named for David Ricardo, this theorem states that changes in the stream of taxes faced by consumers that leave the present value of taxes unchanged have no effect on consumption, interest rates, or welfare. (p. 262)

Two-period model An economic model where all decision makers (consumers and firms) have two-period planning horizons, with the two periods typically representing the present and the future. (p. 262)

Questions for Review

All questions refer to the macroeconomic model developed in this chapter.

1. Why do consumers save?
2. How do consumers save in the two-period model?
3. What factors are important to a consumer in making his or her consumption–savings decision?
4. What is the price of future consumption in terms of current consumption?
5. Show how to derive the consumer's lifetime budget constraint from the consumer's current-period and future-period budget constraints.
6. What is the slope of a consumer's lifetime budget constraint?
7. What are the horizontal and vertical intercepts of a consumer's lifetime budget constraint?
8. If a consumer chooses the endowment point, how much does he or she consume in each period, and how much does he or she save?
9. What are the three properties of a consumer's preferences?
10. How is the consumer's motive to smooth consumption captured by the shape of an indifference curve?

11. What are the effects of an increase in current income on consumption in each period, and on savings?

12. Give two reasons why consumption is more variable in the data than theory seems to predict.

13. What are the effects of an increase in future income on consumption in each period, and on savings?

14. What produces a larger increase in a consumer's current consumption, a permanent increase in the consumer's income or a temporary increase?

15. What does theory tell us about how the value of stocks held by consumers should be related to consumption behavior? Does the data support this?

16. What are the effects of an increase in the real interest rate on consumption in each period, and on savings? How does this depend on income and substitution effects and whether the consumer is a borrower or lender?

17. How does the government finance its purchases in the two-period model?

18. State the Ricardian equivalence theorem.

19. Give four reasons that the burden of the government debt is not shared equally in practice.

Problems

1. A consumer's income in the current period is $y = 100$, and income in the future period is $y' = 120$. He or she pays lump-sum taxes $t = 20$ in the current period and $t' = 10$ in the future period. The real interest rate is 0.1, or 10%, per period.
   (a) Determine the consumer's lifetime wealth.
   (b) Suppose that current and future consumption are perfect complements for the consumer and that he or she always wants to have equal consumption in the current and future periods. Draw the consumer's indifference curves.
   (c) Determine what the consumer's optimal current-period and future-period consumption are, and what optimal saving is, and show this in a diagram with the consumer's budget constraint and indifference curves. Is the consumer a lender or a borrower?
   (d) Now suppose that instead of $y = 100$, the consumer has $y = 140$. Again, determine optimal consumption in the current and future periods and optimal saving, and show this in a diagram. Is the consumer a lender or a borrower?
   (e) Explain the differences in your results between parts (c) and (d).

2. Suppose that a consumer's future income increases, and the real interest rate increases as well. In a diagram, determine how the consumer's optimal choice

   of current consumption and future consumption changes and how saving changes. Show how your results depend on income and substitution effects and consider the case where the consumer is initially a lender and where he or she is initially a borrower.

3. An employer offers his or her employee the option of shifting x units of income from next year to this year. That is, the option is to reduce income next year by x units and increase income this year by x units.
   (a) Would the employee take this option (use a diagram)?
   (b) Determine, using a diagram, how this shift in income will affect consumption this year and next year and saving this year. Explain your results.

4. Consider the following effects of an increase in taxes for a consumer.
   (a) The consumer's taxes increase by Δt in the current period. How does this affect current consumption, future consumption, and current saving?
   (b) The consumer's taxes increase permanently, increasing by Δt in the current period and future period. Using a diagram, determine how this affects current consumption, future

consumption, and current saving. Explain the differences between your results here and in part (a).

5. Suppose that the government introduces a tax on interest earnings. That is, borrowers face a real interest rate of r before and after the tax is introduced, but lenders receive an interest rate of $(1 - x)r$ on their savings, where x is the tax rate. Therefore, we are looking at the effects of having x increase from zero to some value greater than zero, with r assumed to remain constant.
   (a) Show the effects of the increase in the tax rate on a consumer's lifetime budget constraint.
   (b) How does the increase in the tax rate affect the optimal choice of consumption (in the current and future periods) and saving for the consumer? Show how income and substitution effects matter for your answer, and show how it matters whether the consumer is initially a borrower or a lender.

6. A consumer receives income y in the current period, income y' in the future period, and pays taxes of t and t' in the current and future periods, respectively. The consumer can borrow and lend at the real interest rate r. This consumer faces a constraint on how much he or she can borrow, much like the credit limit typically placed on a credit card account. That is, the consumer cannot borrow more than x, where $x < we - y + t$, with we denoting lifetime wealth. Use diagrams to determine the effects on the consumer's current consumption, future consumption, and savings of a change in x, and explain your results.

7. A consumer receives income y in the current period, income y' in the future period, and pays taxes of t and t' in the current and future periods, respectively. The consumer can lend at the real interest rate r. The consumer is given two options. First, he or she can borrow at the interest rate r but can only borrow an amount x or less, where $x < we - y + t$. Second, he or she can borrow an unlimited amount at the interest rate r_2, where $r_2 > r$. Use a diagram to determine which option the consumer chooses, and explain your results.

8. Assume a consumer who has current-period income $y = 200$, future-period income $y' = 150$, current and future taxes $t = 40$ and $t' = 50$, respectively, and faces a market real interest rate of $r = .05$, or

5% per period. The consumer would like to consume equal amounts in both periods; that is, he or she would like to set $c = c'$, if possible. However, this consumer is faced with a credit market imperfection, in that he or she cannot borrow at all, that is, $s \geq 0$.
   (a) Show the consumer's lifetime budget constraint and indifference curves in a diagram.
   (b) Calculate his or her optimal current-period and future-period consumption and optimal saving, and show this in your diagram.
   (c) Suppose that everything remains unchanged, except that now $t = 20$ and $t' = 71$. Calculate the effects on current and future consumption and optimal saving, and show this in your diagram.
   (d) Now, suppose alternatively that $y = 100$. Repeat parts (a) to (c), and explain any differences.

9. Assume an economy with 1,000 consumers. Each consumer has income in the current period of 50 units and future income of 60 units and pays a lump-sum tax of 10 in the current period and 20 in the future period. The market real interest rate is 8%. Of the 1,000 consumers, 500 consume 60 units in the future, while 500 consume 20 units in the future.
   (a) Determine each consumer's current consumption and current saving.
   (b) Determine aggregate private saving, aggregate consumption in each period, government spending in the current and future periods, the current-period government deficit, and the quantity of debt issued by the government in the current period.
   (c) Suppose that current taxes increase to 15 for each consumer. Repeat parts (a) and (b) and explain your results.

10. Suppose that a consumer has income y in the current period, income y' in the future period, and faces proportional taxes on consumption in the current and future periods. There are no lump-sum taxes. That is, if consumption is c in the current period and c' in the future period, the consumer pays a tax sc in the current period, and $s'c'$ in the future period where s is the current period tax rate on consumption, and s' is the future period tax rate on consumption. The government wishes to collect total tax revenue in the current and future

periods which has a present value of R. Now, suppose that the government reduces s and increases s' in such a way that it continues to collect the same present value of tax revenue R from the consumer, given the consumer's optimal choices of current-period and future-period consumptions.

(a) Write down the lifetime budget constraint of the consumer.

(b) Show that lifetime wealth is the same for the consumer, before and after the change in tax rates.

(c) What effect, if any, does the change in tax rates have on the consumer's choice of current and future consumption, and on savings? Does Ricardian equivalence hold here? Explain why or why not.

11. Suppose in our two-period model of the economy that the government, instead of borrowing in the current period, runs a government loan program. That is, loans are made to consumers at the market real interest rate r, with the aggregate quantity of loans made in the current period denoted by L. Government loans are financed by lump-sum taxes on consumers in the current period, and we assume that government spending is zero in the current and future periods. In the future period, when the government loans are repaid by consumers, the government rebates this amount as lump-sum transfers (negative taxes) to consumers.

(a) Write down the government's current-period budget constraint and its future-period budget constraint.

(b) Determine the present-value budget constraint of the government.

(c) Write down the lifetime budget constraint of a consumer.

(d) Show that the size of the government loan program (i.e., the quantity L) has no effect on current consumption or future consumption for each individual consumer and that there is no effect on the equilibrium real interest rate. Explain this result.

Working with the Data

1. Calculate and plot the ratio of aggregate consumption to GDP, and plot this data as a time series. Comment on the features of your time series plot. What principle of consumption behavior helps to explain what you see?

2. Calculate the value of real total government receipts by dividing current dollar total receipts by the implicit GDP price deflator. Then, calculate the quarterly percentage change in total government receipts and the quarterly percentage change in real GDP, starting in 1947, until 2009.

   (a) In a scatter plot, show the percentage change in real total government receipts against the quarterly percentage change in real GDP.

   (b) What do you see in the scatter plot in part (a)? Is there a positive or negative correlation between the two time series?

   (c) Is this data consistent with the Ricardian equivalence theorem? Why or why not?

3. Calculate the relative price of housing as the new housing price index divided by the implicit GDP deflator. Then, calculate quarterly percentage increases in the relative price of housing, and plot this against the quarterly percentage increase in real spending on consumer nondurables and services.

   (a) Do you notice a positive or negative correlation in the scatter plot?

   (b) How is your observation in part (a) consistent or not consistent with the theory of consumption behavior in this chapter? Explain.

chapter 9

Credit Market Imperfections: Credit Frictions, Financial Crises, and Social Security

In Chapter 8, we explored the basic elements of consumer behavior in credit markets—how consumers act to smooth consumption over time in response to changes in their incomes and in market interest rates. As well, we studied the aggregate effects of changes in government tax policy. A key theoretical result from Chapter 8 is the Ricardian equivalence theorem, which states that a change in the timing of taxes can have no effects on consumer behavior or interest rates, provided that some special conditions hold. The Ricardian equivalence theorem provides us with a firm foundation for understanding the circumstances under which government tax policy will matter. In particular, as discussed in Chapter 8, the Ricardian equivalence theorem would not hold if the tax burden is not shared equally among consumers, if there is intergenerational redistribution resulting from a change in taxes, if there are tax distortions, or if there are credit market imperfections.

The cases under which Ricardian equivalence does not hold have practical importance in at least two respects. First, credit market imperfections, or "frictions," which cause Ricardian equivalence to fail, are key to understanding some important features of how credit markets work. For example, in practice the interest rates at which consumers and firms can lend are lower than the interest rates at which they can borrow, consumers and firms cannot always borrow up to the quantity they would like at market interest rates, and borrowers are sometimes required to post collateral against a loan. All of these features of actual loan contracts can be understood as arising because of credit market frictions.

In this chapter, we will study two types of credit market frictions: **asymmetric information** and **limited commitment.** Asymmetric information refers to a situation where, in a particular market, some market participant knows more about his or her own characteristics than do other market participants. In the credit market context we examine, asymmetric information exists in that a particular borrower knows more about his or her own creditworthiness than do potential lenders. This credit market friction then leads to differences between the interest rates at which consumers can lend and borrow. The loan interest rate reflects a **default premium**, which acts to compensate lenders for the fact that some borrowers will default on their loans. Even good borrowers who will not default must pay the default premium, as lenders are unable to distinguish between good and bad borrowers. Asymmetric information is an important element that we can use to help understand the 2008–2009 financial crisis, which was characterized by dramatic increases in some **interest rate spreads.** These interest rate spreads are gaps between the interest rates on risky loans and safer loans, or between the rates of interest at which some class of economic agents can lend and borrow. As well, during the financial crisis there was a dramatic decrease in the quantity of lending in some segments of the credit market, which asymmetric information can help explain.

A second credit market friction, limited commitment, refers to situations in which it is impossible for a market participant to commit in advance to some future action. In credit markets, there can be lack of commitment in the sense that a borrower cannot commit to repaying a loan. Given the choice, a rational borrower would choose to default on a loan if there were no penalty to doing so. A typical incentive device used by lenders to prevent this type of strategic default is the posting of collateral. Indeed, most lending in credit markets is collateralized. For example, in consumer credit markets, an individual who takes out a mortgage loan is required to post his or her house as collateral, and when a consumer buys a car with a car loan, the car serves as collateral against the loan. When collateral is posted as part of a credit contract, the borrower gives the lender the right to seize the collateral in the event that the borrower defaults on the loan.

Limited commitment can lead to situations where consumers are constrained in their borrowing by how much wealth they have that can serve as collateral—their **collateralizable wealth.** For a typical consumer, collateralizable wealth is restricted to houses and cars, but could potentially include other assets. If a consumer is collateral-constrained, then a change in the value of collateral will matter for how much they can consume in the present. This effect mattered a great deal recently due to a large decrease in the price of housing, which acted to reduce consumer expenditure. From the late 1990s until the peak in housing prices in the United States in 2006, a significant fraction of consumer expenditure was financed by borrowing, through mortgages and home equity loans, using housing as collateral. With the decrease in housing prices in the United States that began in 2006, the value of collateralizable wealth in the U.S. economy fell, and consumer spending also decreased by a large amount, fueling the 2008–2009 recession. We will explore this idea in depth in this chapter.

A second aspect in which the failure of Ricardian equivalence has practical significance, in addition to credit market frictions, relates to the market failure that creates a role for social security programs. Government social security programs typically mandate some level of saving by the working-age population in order to provide for benefits to retirees. It might seem that such programs can only make us worse off, since rational consumers know best how to save for their own retirement. However, government-provided social security can be rationalized by appealing to a credit market failure—the fact that those currently alive cannot write financial contracts with those as yet unborn. In the absence of such contracts, economic outcomes are not efficient. The first welfare theorem (see Chapter 5) does not hold, and there is a role for government in transferring resources across generations—taxing the working-age population to pay benefits to retirees through social security. We explore how social security works, and the effects of alternative types of social security programs, in this chapter. A key policy issue with respect to social security is the "privatization" of social security—i.e., the replacement of "pay-as-you-go" systems with "fully funded" programs. We will study this issue in detail.

Credit Market Imperfections and Consumption

Our first step in the analysis of credit market imperfections is to show how Ricardian equivalence fails with a standard type of credit market friction—a gap between the interest rates at which a consumer can lend and borrow. Here, we will start with the basic credit market model from Chapter 8, where an individual consumer lives for two periods, the current and future period. The consumer receives income y in the current period, y' in the future period, and consumes c and c' in the current and future periods, respectively. The consumer's savings in the current period is denoted by s.

   We want to show how a consumer who is credit-constrained can be affected by a change in taxes that would not have any effect on the consumer's choices if there were perfect credit markets. Consider a consumer who lends at a real interest rate r_1 and borrows at a real interest rate r_2, where $r_2 > r_1$. This difference in borrowing and lending rates of interest arises in practice, for example, when borrowing and lending is carried out through banks, and it is costly for banks to sort credit risks. If the bank borrows from lenders (depositors in the bank) at the real interest rate r_1, and it makes loans at the real interest rate r_2, the difference $r_2 - r_1 > 0$ could arise in equilibrium to compensate the bank for the costs of making loans. The difference between borrowing and lending rates of interest leads to a more complicated lifetime budget constraint. As in Chapter 8, the current-period budget constraint of the consumer is given by

$$c + s = y - t$$

   Here, because the consumer faces different interest rates if he or she borrows or lends, the future-period budget constraint is

$$c' = y' - t' + s(1 + r_1),$$

if $s \geq 0$ (the consumer is a lender), and

$$c' = y' - t' + s(1 + r_2),$$

if $s \leq 0$ (the consumer is a borrower). Going through the same mechanics as in Chapter 8 to derive the consumer's lifetime budget constraint, we obtain

$$c + \frac{c'}{1 + r_1} = y + \frac{y'}{1 + r_1} - t - \frac{t'}{1 + r_1} = we_1, \tag{9-1}$$

if $c \leq y - t$ (the consumer is a lender), and

$$c + \frac{c'}{1 + r_2} = y + \frac{y'}{1 + r_2} - t - \frac{t'}{1 + r_2} = we_2, \tag{9-2}$$

if $c \geq y - t$ (the consumer is a borrower).

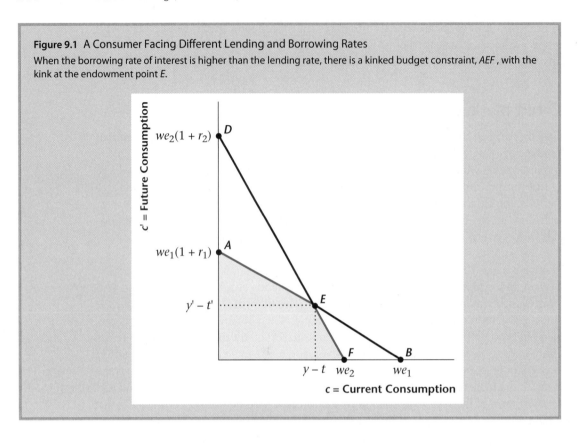

Figure 9.1 A Consumer Facing Different Lending and Borrowing Rates

When the borrowing rate of interest is higher than the lending rate, there is a kinked budget constraint, *AEF* , with the kink at the endowment point *E*.

We graph the consumer's budget constraint in Figure 9.1, where AB is given by equation (9-1) and has slope $-(1 + r_1)$, and DF is given by equation (9-2) and has slope $-(1 + r_2)$. The budget constraint is AEF, where E is the endowment point. Thus, the budget constraint has a kink at the endowment point, because the consumer lends at a lower interest rate than he or she can borrow at.

In a world where there are many different consumers, all having different indifference curves and different incomes, and where each consumer has a kinked budget constraint as in Figure 9.1, there is a significant number of consumers in the population whose optimal consumption bundle is the endowment point. For example, in Figure 9.2 the consumer faces budget constraint AE_1B, and the highest indifference curve on the budget constraint is reached at E_1, the endowment point. For this consumer, at the endowment point, the lending rate is too low to make lending worthwhile, and the borrowing rate is too high to make borrowing worthwhile.

Suppose in Figure 9.2 that the consumer receives a tax cut in the current period—that is, period 1 taxes change by $\Delta t < 0$, with a corresponding change of $-\Delta t(1 + r_1)$ in future taxes. This is the consumer's future tax liability implied by the tax cut, assuming that the interest rate that the government pays on its debt is r_1, the lending rate of interest. Assume that interest rates do not change. The effect of the change in current and future taxes is to shift the endowment point to E_2, and given the way we have drawn the

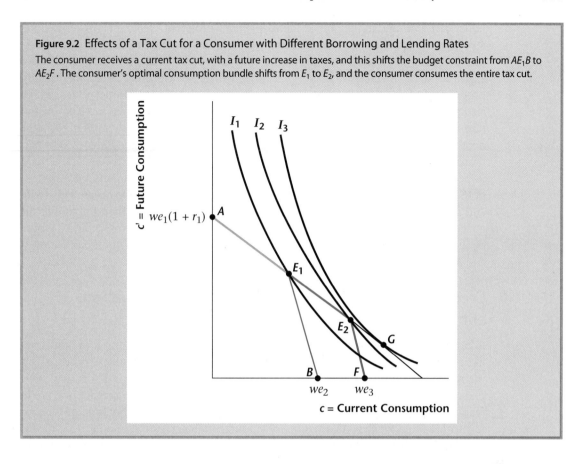

Figure 9.2 Effects of a Tax Cut for a Consumer with Different Borrowing and Lending Rates

The consumer receives a current tax cut, with a future increase in taxes, and this shifts the budget constraint from AE_1B to AE_2F. The consumer's optimal consumption bundle shifts from E_1 to E_2, and the consumer consumes the entire tax cut.

consumer's indifference curves, the consumer now chooses E_2 as his or her optimal consumption bundle on indifference curve I_2. Because he or she chooses the endowment point before and after the tax cut, period 1 consumption increases by the amount of the tax cut, $-\Delta t$. Contrast this with the Ricardian equivalence result in Chapter 8 where the consumer would save the entire tax cut and consumption would be unaffected.

The reason that the consumer's current consumption increases is that the government is effectively making a low interest loan available to him or her through the tax cut scheme. In Figure 9.2, the consumer would like to consume at point G if he or she could borrow at the interest rate r_1. Giving the consumer a tax cut of $-\Delta t$ with a corresponding future tax liability of $-\Delta t(1 + r_1)$ is just like having the government loan the consumer $-\Delta t$ at the interest rate r_1. Because the consumer would take such a loan willingly if it was offered, this tax cut makes the consumer better off.

Therefore, to the extent that credit market imperfections are important in practice, there can be beneficial effects of positive government debt. The government effectively acts like a bank that makes loans at below-market rates. If credit market imperfections matter significantly, then the people that are helped by current tax cuts are those who are affected most by credit market imperfections, and this might suggest to us that tax policy could be used in this way to increase general economic welfare. However, tax policy is quite a blunt instrument for relieving perceived problems due to credit market imperfections. A preferable policy might be to target particular groups of people—for example, small businesses, farmers, or homeowners—with direct government credit programs. In fact, there are many such programs in place in the United States, which are administered through government agencies such as the Small Business Administration. In considering government credit policies, though, careful evaluation needs to be done to determine whether direct lending by the government is a good idea in each particular circumstance. There may be good reasons for a particular private market credit imperfection. For example, real loan interest rates may be high in a particular segment of the credit market because the costs of screening and evaluating loans are very high, and the government would face the same high costs. This would then imply that the government has no special advantage in offering credit to these borrowers, and it would be inefficient for the government to get into the business of lending to them.

Credit Market Imperfections, Asymmetric Information, and the Financial Crisis

A key feature of credit markets that can give rise to a budget constraint for a consumer like the one depicted in Figure 9.1 is asymmetric information. For our purposes, asymmetric information is particularly interesting because of the role it appears to have played in the current financial crisis. In particular, the quality of information in credit markets appears to have declined significantly during 2008, with important implications for market interest rates, the quantity of lending, and aggregate economic activity.

Our first goal is to model asymmetric information in a simple and transparent way, using the tools we have already built up. It will be useful to consider an economy that has banks, in addition to the consumers and the government that were in the Chapter 8 two-period credit model. In our model, as in the real world, a bank is a **financial intermediary** that borrows from one set of individuals and lends to another set. We will study financial intermediaries in more depth in Chapter 16. In the model, a bank borrows from its depositors in the current period, and each depositor is an ultimate lender in the economy, with each depositor receiving a real interest rate on their deposits, held with the bank until the future period, equal to r_1. The bank takes all of its deposits in the current period (which in the model are consumption goods) and makes loans to borrowers. The problem for the bank is that some of the borrowers will default on their loans in the future period. To make things simple, suppose that a fraction a of the borrowers in the economy are good borrowers who have positive income in the future period, while a fraction $1 - a$ of borrowers are bad, in that they receive zero income in the future period, and therefore will default on any loan that is extended to them. However, there is asymmetric information in the credit market. Each borrower knows whether he or she is good or bad, but the bank cannot distinguish bad borrowers from the good borrowers who will pay off their loans with certainty. Assume that the bank can observe a consumer's income at the time it is received, so it knows which are good and bad borrowers once the future period arrives.

Now assume, again for simplicity, that all good borrowers are identical. Then, if the bank charges each borrower a real interest rate r_2 on loans, then each good borrower chooses the same loan quantity, which we will denote L. Bad borrowers do not want to reveal that they are bad to the bank, otherwise they will not receive a loan, so each bad borrower mimics the behavior of good borrowers by also choosing the loan quantity L. Now, one of the reasons that banks exist is that large lending institutions are able to minimize risk by diversifying. In this case, the bank diversifies by lending to a large number of borrowers. This ensures that, as the number of loans gets very large, that the fraction of the bank's borrowers defaulting will be a, the fraction of bad borrowers in the population. For example, if I flip a coin n times, the fraction of flips that turn up heads will get very close to $\frac{1}{2}$ as n gets large, just as the fraction of good borrowers the bank faces gets very close to a as the number of borrowers gets large. For each L units of deposits acquired by the bank, for which the bank will have to pay out $L(1 + r_1)$ to depositors in the future period, the average payoff to the bank will be $aL(1 + r_2)$ in the future period, since fraction a of the bank's loans will be made to good borrowers, who will repay the bank $L(1 + r_2)$, and fraction $1 - a$ of the bank loans will be made to bad borrowers, who will repay zero. Thus, the average profit the bank makes on each loan is

$$\pi = aL(1 + r_2) - L(1 + r_1) = L[a(1 + r_2) - (1 + r_1)]. \qquad (9\text{-}3)$$

In equilibrium, each bank must earn zero profits, since negative profits would imply that banks would want to shut down, and positive profits would imply that banks would want to expand indefinitely. Therefore, $\pi = 0$ in equilibrium, which from equation (9-3) implies that

$$r_2 = \frac{1 + r_1}{a} - 1. \qquad (9\text{-}4)$$

From equation (9-4), note that when $a = 1$ and there are no bad borrowers, that $r_1 = r_2$, and there is no credit market imperfection. This is then just the standard credit model that we studied in Chapter 8. Note also from (9-4) that r_2 increases as a decreases, given r_1, so that the credit market imperfection becomes more severe as the fraction of bad borrowers in the population increases. Each good borrower must pay a default premium on a loan from the bank, which is equal to the difference $r_2 - r_1$. This difference grows as the fraction of good borrowers in the population decreases.

Now, in Figure 9.3, consider what happens to a typical consumer's budget constraint as a decreases, given r_1. Before a decrease in a the budget constraint is AED, where E is the endowment point. When a falls, the budget constraint shifts to AEF. From our previous analysis in Chapter 8, we know that, for a consumer who is a borrower—i.e., who chooses a consumption bundle on ED before the decline in a—consumption in the current period and borrowing must decrease when a falls. That is, with asymmetric information in the credit market and an increase in the incidence of default among borrowers, good borrowers face higher loan interest rates and reduce their borrowing and consumption as a result.

Figure 9.3 Asymmetric Information in the Credit Market and the Effect of a Decrease
in Creditworthy Borrowers

Asymmetric information creates a kinked budget constraint *AED*, with the kink at the endowment point *E*. A decrease in the fraction of creditworthy borrowers in the population shifts the budget constraint to *AEF*.

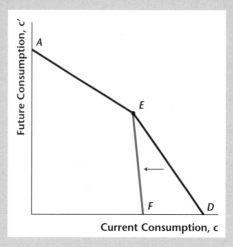

Perspectives on the Financial Crisis
Asymmetric Information and Interest Rate Spreads

Our analysis of asymmetric information in the credit market predicts that, in segments of the credit market where default is possible and lenders have difficulty sorting would-be borrowers, increases in the perceived probability of default will cause increases in interest rates, even for borrowers who are objectively creditworthy. In Figure 9.4, we show the difference in the interest rate on corporate debt rated BAA, and the interest rate on AAA corporate debt. In the United States, there are three dominant private agencies that rate corporate and government debt: Fitch, Moody's, and Standard and Poor's. Debt rated AAA is the highest grade, judged to be essentially default-free, while BAA is judged to have some risk of default. While the objectivity and abilities of the major credit-rating agencies were called

into question in the recent financial crisis, for our purposes we will take the difference in the interest rates (the interest rate spread) on BAA debt and AAA debt shown in Figure 9.4 to represent the difference in interest rates in segments of the credit market that are perceived as somewhat risky, and essentially riskless, respectively.

In Figure 9.4, note that the interest rate spread reached its historical high of close to 6% during the Great Depression in the early 1930s, at about the time of the most severe period in the banking crisis of the Great Depression. After World War II, periods when the interest rate spread is high tend to correspond to recessions, in particular the recessions in 1974–1975, 1981–1982, 1990–1991, 2001, and 2008–2009. However, typically the interest rate spread

Figure 9.4 Interest Rate Spread

The figure depicts the difference between the interest rates on AAA-rated corporate debt (low risk) and BAA-rated corporate debt (moderate risk). The highest spread historically was during the Great Depression, and the spread in generally tends to be high during recessions. The highest spread since the recession occurred during the 2008–2009 recession.

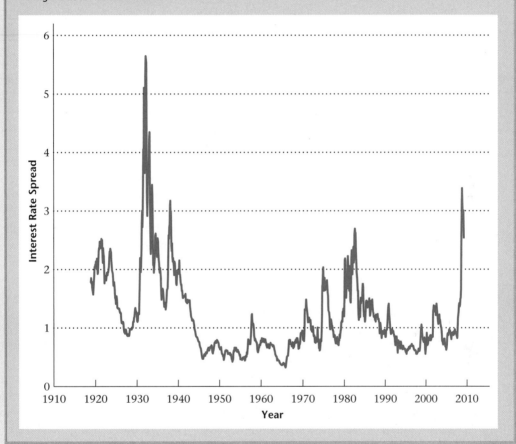

increased toward the end of a recession, when defaults tend to reach their peak. What is unusual about the 2008–2009 recession is not only the size of the interest rate spread, which was larger than at any point since the Great Depression, but the fact that the interest rate spread was high at the beginning of the recession (GDP declined beginning in the fourth quarter of 2008). This high interest rate spread reflected the fact that a principal cause of the recession was the financial crisis, which created a great deal of uncertainty in credit markets. The degree of asymmetric information increased in some segments of the credit market (including the market for BAA corporate debt), due to the fact that lenders were increasingly uncertain about what firms were at risk and what firms were not. Faced with high interest rates, even good borrowers (who had great difficulty identifying themselves as such) reduced their borrowing.

Credit Market Imperfections, Limited Commitment, and the Financial Crisis

Another type of credit market imperfection that is important to how real-world credit markets function, and plays an important role in the current financial crisis, is limited commitment. Any loan contract represents an intertemporal exchange—the borrower receives goods and services in the present in exchange for a promise to give the lender claims to goods and services in the future. However, when the future arrives, the borrower may find it advantageous not to keep his or her promise.

Lenders are not stupid, of course, and will therefore set up loan contracts in a way that gives the borrower the incentive to pay off the loan as promised. One incentive device used widely by lenders is the requirement that a borrower post **collateral.** In general, collateral is an asset owned by the borrower that the lender has a right to seize if the borrower defaults on the loan (does not meet the promised payment). Most people are familiar with the role played by collateral in automobile loans and mortgage loans. For a typical auto loan, the auto itself serves as collateral, while an individual's house is the collateral for his or her mortgage loan. Collateral is also used in short-term lending among large financial institutions. For example, a **repurchase agreement** is a short-term loan where a safe asset, such as government-issued debt, serves as collateral.

For macroeconomic activity, the use of collateral in loan contracts can potentially be very important. For example, mortgages are used by homeowners not only to finance the purchase of homes, but to finance consumption. If the extent to which homeowners can borrow is constrained by the value of houses, and the price of houses falls, then this will cause a decline in the quantity of lending in the economy as a whole, and a drop in current aggregate consumption.

To see how this works, consider an individual consumer exactly like the typical consumer we studied in Chapter 8, who also owns a quantity of an asset, denoted by H, which can be sold in the future period at the price p per unit, so that the value of the asset in the future is pH. To make this example concrete, think of H as the size of the consumer's house, and p as the price of housing per unit. Assume that the house is illiquid, which means that it is difficult to sell quickly. We will represent this by supposing that the consumer cannot sell the house in the current period. The consumer's lifetime wealth is then

$$we = y - t + \frac{y' - t' + pH}{1 + r}, \tag{9-5}$$

which is the same expression as the one for the lifetime wealth of a consumer in Chapter 8, except that we add the quantity $\frac{pH}{1+r}$ to lifetime wealth. This quantity is the future value of the house, discounted to give its value in units of current consumption.

Now, in our model the lenders in the credit market know that there is a limited commitment problem. For simplicity, assume that a borrower will find it advantageous to default on any loan, if he or she can get away with it. However, if the consumer wishes to borrow, he or she can post his or her house as collateral. Lenders will then be willing to lend an amount to the consumer that will imply a loan payment in the future no larger than the value of the collateral, as otherwise the consumer would default on the loan.

That is, given that s is that consumer's saving in the current period, with $-s$ the quantity of borrowing in the current period, then the amount borrowed by the consumer must satisfy the collateral constraint

$$-s(1 + r) \leq pH, \tag{9-6}$$

as $-s(1 + r)$ is the loan payment for the consumer in the future period, and pH is the value of the collateral in the future period. Then, since $s = y - t - c$ for the consumer, we can substitute for s in the collateral constraint (9-6) and rearrange to obtain

$$c \leq y - t + \frac{pH}{1 + r}. \tag{9-7}$$

The collateral constraint, rewritten in the form of (9-7), states that current period consumption can be no greater than current disposable income plus the amount that can be borrowed by the consumer by pledging the future value of the house as collateral.

Now, the consumer's problem is to make himself or herself as well off as possible, given his or her lifetime budget constraint

$$c + \frac{c'}{1 + r} = we, \tag{9-8}$$

and also given the collateral constraint (9-7), where lifetime wealth we is given by equation (9-5). As long as the value of collateral in the future, pH, is small enough, the collateral constraint implies that the budget constraint is kinked, as in Figure 9.5, where the budget constraint is initially ABD. In the figure, the endowment point is E, and if the consumer chose point B, at the kink in the budget constraint, then he or she would have a binding collateral constraint, borrowing up to the full amount that lenders will permit, and consuming future disposable income in the future period, with $c' = y' - t'$.

Next, suppose that the price of houses, p, declines, with everything else held constant. This reduces the quantity of the consumer's collateralizable wealth—i.e., the quantity of wealth that the consumer can borrow against. As a result, in Figure 9.5, the budget constraint shifts from ABD to FGH. Note that the slope of AB is the same as the slope of FG, since the interest rate r has not changed, and that the point G is directly to the left of point B, since future disposable income $y' - t'$ is also unchanged.

If the collateral constraint (9-7) does not bind for the consumer, either before or after the decrease in p, then the consumer is affected in exactly the same way as in our analysis of the effects of a change in future income in Chapter 8. An unconstrained consumer will initially choose a point somewhere between A and B (but not including B) before the decrease in p, and will choose a point between F and G (but not including G) after the decrease in p. The unconstrained consumer can smooth the effects of the decrease in wealth resulting from the fall in p, by reducing consumption in both the current and future periods.

However, suppose that the consumer's collateral constraint binds, both before and after the decrease in p. Then, as in Figure 9.5, the consumer chooses to consume at point B initially, on indifference curve I_1. When p falls, the budget constraint shifts to FGH, and the

Figure 9.5 Limited Commitment with a Collateral Constraint

The consumer can borrow only with collateralizable wealth as security against the loan. As a result, the budget constraint is kinked. Initially, the budget constraint is *ABD* and it shifts to *FGH* with a decrease in the price of collateral. For a constrained borrower, this causes no change in future consumption, but current consumption drops by the same amount as the decrease in the value of collateral if the borrower is collateral-constrained.

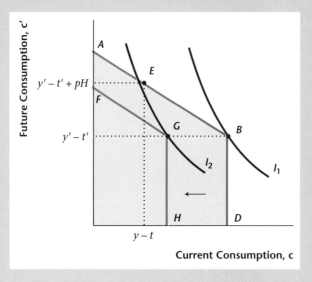

consumer chooses point G on indifference curve I_2. A constrained consumer cannot smooth the effects of the decrease in his or her wealth. For any consumer, a decrease in wealth must be absorbed in a reduction in consumption, either in the present or in the future. However, in this case, since the collateral constraint binds, all of the reduction of consumption occurs in the current period. In the figure, future consumption at points B and G is the same, but current consumption c falls by the reduction in lifetime wealth—i.e., by the change in the present value of collateralizable wealth. To see this another way, if the collateral constraint (9-7) binds, it holds as an equality, so that

$$c = y - t + \frac{pH}{1 + r}$$

and if $y - t$ remains unchanged, then any reduction in the present value of collateralizable wealth, $\frac{pH}{1 + r}$, is reflected in a one-for-one reduction in current consumption, c.

The permanent income hypothesis tells us that, in a world with perfect credit markets, the motive of consumers to smooth consumption over time acts to lessen the impact of changes in wealth on consumer expenditure in the aggregate. Here, our analysis tells us that, if credit market imperfections arising from limited commitment matter in an important way for a significant fraction of the population, then changes in the value of collateralizable wealth (principally housing, for the consumer sector) can matter a great deal for aggregate consumption.

Perspectives on the Financial Crisis
The Housing Market, Collateral, and Consumption

Figure 9.6 shows the relative price of housing in the United States, as measured by the average selling price of houses, divided by the consumer price index, normalized to equal 100 in 1963. A remarkable feature of the figure is the large trend increase in the relative price of housing to the peak in 2006. In particular, the purchasing power of the average house in the United States increased about 220% from 1963 to 2006. Another important feature of Figure 9.6 is the large increase in the relative price of housing occurring from the mid-1990s to 2006, with an acceleration from 2000 to 2006.

In Figure 9.7, we show the percentage deviations from trend in aggregate consumption. In

Figure 9.6 The Relative Price of Housing in the United States

The figure shows the relative price of housing, measured as the average selling price of houses divided by the consumer price index, scaled to equal 100 in 1963. Of particular note is the trend increase in the relative price of housing from 1963 to 2006, the very rapid increase from 2000 to 2006, and the rapid decline after 2006 to 2009.

(Continued)

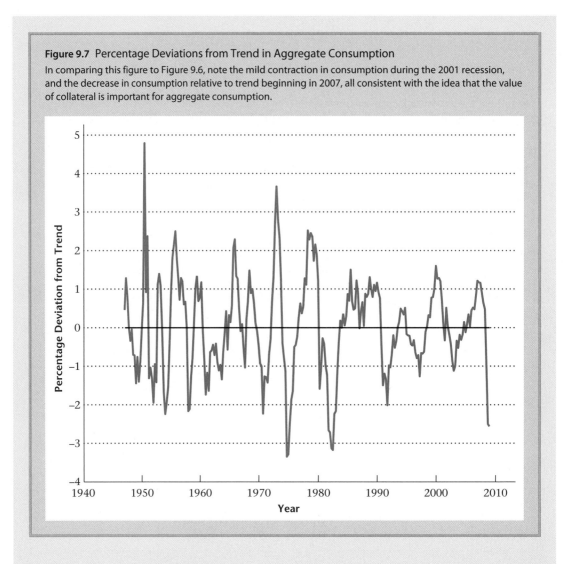

Figure 9.7 Percentage Deviations from Trend in Aggregate Consumption

In comparing this figure to Figure 9.6, note the mild contraction in consumption during the 2001 recession, and the decrease in consumption relative to trend beginning in 2007, all consistent with the idea that the value of collateral is important for aggregate consumption.

the recent history, note in Figure 9.6 that the relative price of housing continues to increase through the 2001 recession, when consumption declines below trend. The 2001 recession was relatively mild, as was the decline in consumption, in part because the value of housing as collateral continued to increase through the recession. Consumers were then able to continue to finance their consumption by borrowing against the value accumulated in their houses. Once the relative price of housing starts to decrease in 2006, this coincides with a subsequent decrease in consumption relative to trend, and the rapid decrease in consumption below trend in 2008–2009. What we see in Figures 9.6 and 9.7 subsequent to the year 2000 is consistent with the idea that the value of collateral in credit markets contributes in an important way to the behavior of aggregate consumption expenditures.

Social Security Programs

Social security programs are government-provided means for saving for retirement. As such they are programs that help individuals smooth their consumption over their lifetimes. But if credit markets work well, then why do we need the government to provide us with consumption smoothing services? As macroeconomists, if we want to provide a rationale for social security, we must be able to find some type of credit market failure that the government can correct. One purpose of this section is to explore this idea, and to examine how social security systems work in practice.

There are essentially two types of programs: **pay-as-you-go** and **fully funded social security**, although in practice social security could be some mix of the two. With pay-as-you-go social security, the program simply involves transfers between the young and the old, while fully funded social security is a government-sponsored savings program where the savings of the young are used to purchase assets, and the old receive the payoffs on the assets that were acquired when they were young. We discuss the two types of social security program in turn.

Pay-As-You-Go Social Security

In the United States, social security operates as a pay-as-you-go system, in that taxes on the young are used to finance social security transfers to the old. While public discussion may make it appear that the system is in fact fully funded, as the difference between social security tax revenue and social security benefits is used to purchase interest-bearing federal government securities, this is merely an accounting convention and is unimportant for the economic consequences of U.S. social security.

To see the implications of pay-as-you-go social security for the distribution of wealth over time and across consumers, we use the basic credit market model of Chapter 8, but modify it to accommodate intergenerational redistribution of income by the government. Assume for simplicity that social security has no effect on the market real interest rate r, which we suppose is constant for all time. Each consumer lives for two periods, youth and old age, and so in any period there is a young generation and an old generation alive. Let N denote the number of old consumers currently alive, and N' the number of young consumers currently alive. Assume that

$$N' = (1 + n)N, \qquad (9\text{-}9)$$

so that the population is growing at the rate n, just as in the Solow growth model used in Chapters 6 and 7, although here people are finite-lived. A given consumer receives income y when young and income y' when old, and we allow (as we did throughout Chapter 8) for the fact that incomes can differ across consumers. For simplicity, assume that government spending is zero in all periods.

Now, suppose that no social security program exists before some date T, and that before date T the taxes on the young and old are zero in each period. Then, pay-as-you-go social security is established at date T and continues forever after. Here, for simplicity we suppose that the social security program guarantees each old-age consumer in periods T and later a benefit of b units of consumption goods. Then, the tax for each old consumer in periods T and after is $t' = -b$. The benefits for old consumers must be financed by taxes on the young, and we assume that each young consumer is taxed an equal amount, t. Then, because total social security benefits equal total taxes on the young, we have

$$Nb = N't, \tag{9-10}$$

and so, using equation (9-9) to substitute for N' in equation (9-10), we can solve for t, obtaining

$$t = \frac{b}{1 + n}. \tag{9-11}$$

How do consumers benefit from social security? Clearly, the consumers who are old when the program is introduced in period T gain, as these consumers receive the social security benefit but do not have to suffer any increase in taxes when they are young. In Figure 9.8, the lifetime budget constraint of a consumer who is old in period T is AB if there is no social security program, where the slope of AB is $-(1 + r)$ and the endowment point with no social security is E_1, determined by disposable income of y when young and y' when old. With the social security program, this consumer receives

Figure 9.8 Pay-As-You-Go Social Security for Consumers Who Are Old in Period T

In the period when social security is introduced, the old receive a social security benefit. The budget constraint of an old consumer shifts from AB to DF, and he or she is clearly better off.

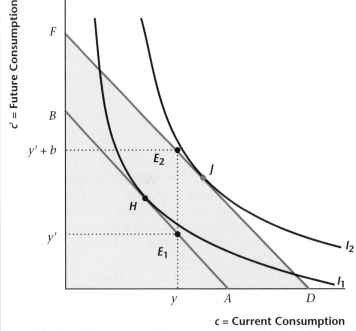

Figure 9.9 Pay-As-You-Go Social Security for Consumers Born in Period T and Later

If $n > r$, the budget constraint shifts out from AB to DF, and the consumer is better off.

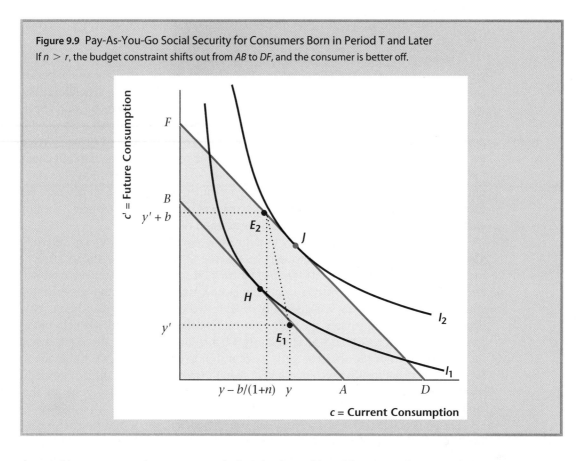

disposable income y when young and $y' + b$ when old and has an endowment point given by E_2 on the budget constraint DF (with slope $-(1 + r)$) in the figure. The optimal consumption bundle shifts from H to J, and the consumer is clearly better off because his or her budget constraint has shifted out and he or she is able to choose a consumption bundle on a higher indifference curve.

What happens to consumers born in periods T and later? For these consumers, in Figure 9.9, the budget constraint would be AB without social security, with an endowment point at E_1 and the budget constraint having slope $-(1 + r)$. With social security, disposable income when young is $y - t = y - \frac{b}{1 + n}$ from equation (9-11) and disposable income when old is $y' + b$, and the endowment point shifts to E_2 in the figure on the budget constraint DF. Because the market real interest rate has not changed, the slope of DF is $-(1 + r)$. The slope of E_1E_2 is $-(1 + n)$, so in the figure we have shown the case where $n > r$. In this case, the budget constraint shifts out for this consumer, with the optimal consumption bundle shifting from H to J, and the consumer is better off. However, the budget constraint would shift in, and the consumer would be worse off if $n < r$.

That is, the consumer's lifetime wealth is given by

$$we = y - \frac{b}{1 + n} + \frac{y' + b}{1 + r} = y + \frac{y'}{1 + r} + \frac{b(n - r)}{(1 + r)(1 + n)}.$$

Whether the consumer is better off or worse off with the social security program is determined by whether *we* increases or decreases, or by whether $n > r$ or $n < r$.

Therefore, social security makes everyone better off here only if the population growth rate is greater than the real interest rate. Otherwise, the old in the initial period are made better off at the expense of the current young in each future generation. The reason why social security can potentially improve welfare is that there is a kind of private market failure here that the government can exploit. That is, there is no way for people to trade with those who are not born yet, and the young and old alive in a given period cannot trade, as the young would like to exchange current consumption goods for future consumption goods, and the old would like to exchange current consumption goods for past consumption goods. The government is able to use its power to tax to bring about intergenerational transfers that may yield a Pareto improvement, whereby welfare increases for all consumers in the present and the future.

For pay-as-you-go social security to improve welfare for the consumers currently alive and those in future generations requires that the "rate of return" of the social security system be sufficiently high. This rate of return increases with the population growth rate *n,* as the population growth rate determines how large a tax burden there is for the young generation in paying social security benefits to the old. The smaller this tax burden is for each young person, the higher the ratio of the social security benefit in old age to the tax paid to support social security when young, and this ratio is effectively the rate of return of the social security system. If n is larger than r, than the rate of return of the social security system is higher than the rate of return in the private credit market, and this is why social security increases welfare for everyone in this circumstance.

The issue of whether social security can bring about a Pareto improvement for consumers in all generations relates directly to contemporary issues facing the U.S. social security system. Currently, the social security taxes paid by the working population are more than sufficient to finance payments of social security benefits to the old. This will change, however, as the baby boom generation retires, roughly between 2010 and 2030. When this large cohort retires, if social security benefits are to remain at their current levels, then this will require either a larger social security tax for the young or more immigration to increase the size of the working population that can pay the tax. Otherwise, benefits will have to be reduced. If we suppose that immigration will not change, then some group will have to lose. That is, if benefits remain at current levels, then the working population that pays the higher social security tax between 2010 and 2030 will receive a low return on social security. If benefits are reduced, then the baby boom generation will receive a low return on social security. The former is a more likely outcome, as the baby boom generation has a great deal of political power due to its size.

Fully Funded Social Security

To analyze fully funded social security, we can use the same apparatus as for the pay-as-you-go case. Again, suppose that government spending is zero forever, and in this case we assume for simplicity that taxes are zero as well.

In the absence of social security a consumer's lifetime budget constraint is given by AB in Figure 9.10, where the slope of AB is $-(1 + r)$. The consumer's endowment is

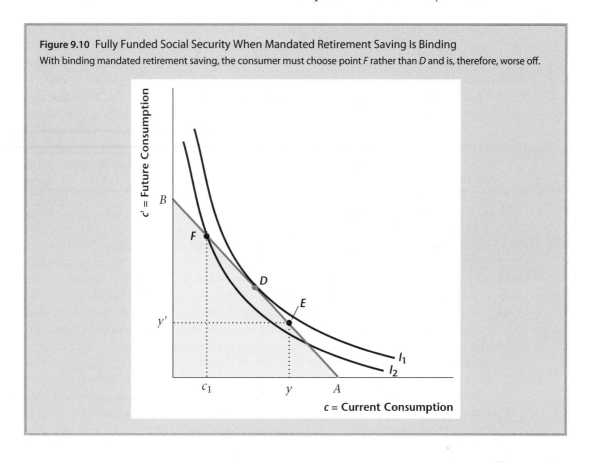

Figure 9.10 Fully Funded Social Security When Mandated Retirement Saving Is Binding
With binding mandated retirement saving, the consumer must choose point *F* rather than *D* and is, therefore, worse off.

given by point E, and we suppose that this consumer optimizes by choosing point D, where saving is positive. Fully funded social security is a program whereby the government invests the proceeds from social security taxes in the private credit market, with social security benefits determined by the payoff the government receives in the private credit market. Alternatively, the government could allow the consumer to choose in which assets to invest his or her social security savings. Here, this makes no difference, as there is a single real rate of return, r, available on the credit market.

In any event, fully funded social security is effectively a forced savings program, and it matters only if the amount of social security saving is a binding constraint on consumers. That is, fully funded social security makes a difference only if the social security system mandates a higher level of saving than the consumer would choose in the absence of the program. Such a case is illustrated in Figure 9.10, where the amount of social security saving required by the government is $y - c_1$, so that the consumer receives the consumption bundle F. Clearly, the consumer is worse off than he or she was at point D in the absence of the program. At best, fully funded social security is ineffective, if the amount of social security saving is not binding, or if consumers can undo forced savings by borrowing against their future social security benefits when young. If fully funded social security is a binding constraint on at least some people in the population, then it can only make things worse for optimizing consumers. Proposals to "privatize" social security in the United States by allowing consumers to invest their social security savings in private assets are essentially proposals to move toward a fully funded rather than pay-as-you-go social security. Such proposals may in fact be welfare-improving for all generations, but this depends critically on how the transition to a fully funded social security system is financed by the federal government (see Macro-economics in Action: Transitions from Pay-As-You-Go to Fully Funded Social Security).

What if the population growth rate is sufficiently low that pay-as-you social security is dominated by saving in the private market? Is there any rationale for establishing a social security system so as to force consumers to save for their retirement? The answer is yes, as social security may be a device that solves a commitment problem for the government. This commitment problem takes the following form. In a perfect world, the government could announce to the public that no one will receive assistance from the government in retirement. In such a world, the public believes this announcement, all individuals save for their retirement, and consumption is optimally smoothed for everyone over their life-times. The problem is that the public understands that the government cannot commit to such a policy. If people are old and destitute, the government will feel obliged to pro-vide for them. Since people then anticipate that they will receive some minimal standard of living on government assistance in retirement in any event, the poor in particular will not save for retirement. It may be preferable, given the government's commitment problem, to establish a government-mandated universal social security program, thus inducing something closer to an optimal amount of saving for retirement.

Now, suppose that we accept the argument that a social security system is a con-venient device to get around the government's inability to commit. Which system is best, pay-as-you-go or fully funded? An argument in favor of the pay-as-you-go system currently in place in the United States is the following. Fully funded programs encounter two problems. First, they potentially allow public pension funds to be run inefficiently because of political interference. This problem occurs if the government manages the public pension fund rather than letting retirees manage their own retirement accounts. The existence of such a large quantity of assets in a public pension fund, seemingly at public disposal, often provides a tempting target for lawmakers and lobbyists. For exam-ple, in Canada, the Canada Pension Plan is a mixed fully funded and pay-as-you-go system and has been the target of groups that advocate socially responsible investing. The theory behind socially responsible investing is that it is possible to change the behavior of firms or to reduce their activities by directing investments away from them. For example, tobacco companies are a typical target of socially responsible investing, for obvious reasons. While socially responsible investing may be well-intentioned, it may at best be ineffective, and at worst have the effect of constraining the management of public pension funds in ways that reduce benefits to retirees. A pay-as-you-go system avoids the issue entirely. With pay-as-you-go, the government is not put in the position of deciding which investments are morally appropriate and which are not, and politi-cal activity can be focussed in ways that are potentially much more productive.

A second problem with fully funded social security programs is that they may be sub-ject to a **moral hazard** problem. Moral hazard is a well-known feature of insurance and refers to the fact that, if an individual is insured against a particular loss, he or she will then take less care to prevent the loss from happening. For example, if a person were fully insured against damages to his or her automobile, then he or she will take less care in driving in parking lots. In the case of a fully funded social security program, suppose that the program allows people to choose how they save for retirement, constraining them only in how much they save. What would happen if an individual chose to invest in a very risky asset, was unlucky, and became destitute in retirement? Given the government's lack of ability to commit, this individual would likely be bailed out by the government. In effect, the government would be called upon to insure retirement accounts, much as it insures the deposits in banks. The moral hazard problem associated with the provision of deposit insurance by the government is well known, and we will study it in Chapter 16. Just as with banks, if retirement accounts were insured, then the managers of retirement accounts would tend to take on too much risk. They would know that, if their highly risky investments pay off, so much the better, but if these assets do not pay off, then they will be bailed out by the government. The moral hazard problem implies that another level of regulation would be needed to make sure that retirement account managers do not take on too much risk. The provision of government insurance for retirement accounts, and the necessary regulation required to solve the moral hazard problem, potentially create enough costs that a pay-as-you-go system is preferable.

MACROECONOMICS IN ACTION
Transitions from Pay-As-You-Go to Fully Funded Social Security

While the United States will not have to address the viability of its pay-as-you-go social security system until the baby boom generation begins to retire, European countries are already being forced to deal with the consequences for social security of an aging population. In some European countries—Germany and Italy, for example—a transition from pay-as-you-go social security to some form of fully funded or partially funded social security is being considered. Research by Assaf Razin and Efraim Sadka analyzes some of the issues associated with such a transition.[1]

[1]A. Razin and E. Sadka. 2002. "The Stability and Growth Pact as an Impediment to Privatizing Social Security," CEPR discussion paper 3621.

In our analysis of pay-as-you-go social security, we showed that the current young, the current old, and all future generations can benefit from such a social security program if the population growth rate exceeds the market real interest rate. However, in circumstances where there exists a very high ratio of current old to young, the current young would benefit from an immediate switch from pay-as-you-go to fully funded social security. The switch implies that the current young do not have to bear a high current tax in exchange for a standard-sized future retirement benefit. However, the transition from pay-as-you-go to fully funded would not be a Pareto improvement if the current old lost their retirement benefits (which they were expecting under the

(Continued)

pay-as-you-go system that was in place when they were young).

An alternative approach to a transition from pay-as-you-go to fully funded social security that could yield a Pareto improvement is to have the government issue debt to finance the payment of social security benefits to the current old. If the government issues debt in the present, this of course implies higher future taxes to pay off this debt. However, these higher future taxes will be paid by those who will benefit from the transition to a fully funded system. If the net benefits of the transition are positive, then the current young and future generations can be made better off as a result, and the current old are no worse off. Any Pareto-improving economic policy is something that the population as a whole will clearly vote for, so political economy arguments tell us that governments with a very old population should choose to abandon pay-as-you-go social security and run temporary deficits to finance benefits for the current old.

A problem with this scenario in Europe is that member countries of the European Monetary Union (EMU) have made commitments to keep their budget deficits within certain bounds. Under the Stability and Growth Pact, which came into effect in 1999 for all EMU countries, the government deficit of an EMU member cannot exceed 3% of GDP without penalties being imposed. Thus, in the case of a transition from pay-as-you-go to fully funded social security, the Stability and Growth Pact could block an economic policy that is Pareto improving. The framers of the Stability and Growth Pact clearly thought that the commitment outlined in the Pact was a good idea, as this would prevent some of the negative effects of large budget deficits. However, the Pact clearly did not account for the role of budget deficits in financing social security. As Razin and Sadka show, there are circumstances when a budget deficit can be a useful device in producing an intergenerational redistribution of wealth that makes an economic policy change (in this case a transition from pay-as-you-go to fully funded social security) produce positive benefits for everyone.

Chapter Summary

- With a credit market imperfection, modeled as a situation where the lending interest rate is less than the borrowing interest rate, Ricardian equivalence does not hold. A current tax cut that just changes the timing of taxes, with no effect on lifetime wealth, will increase current consumption and have no effect on savings.

- One credit market imperfection is asymmetric information, under which lenders cannot perfectly observe the creditworthiness of would-be borrowers. In a credit market with good and bad borrowers, the lending interest rate is less than the borrowing interest rate, reflecting a default premium on the loan interest rate. An increase in the fraction of bad borrowers in the market increases the default premium and reduces the quantity of lending.

- A second credit market imperfection is limited commitment—borrowers have an incentive to default on their debts. Lenders give borrowers the incentive to repay by requiring that borrowers post collateral. However, when borrowers are collateral-constrained, a decrease in the price of collateralizable wealth reduces lending and consumption.

- Social security programs can be rationalized by a credit market failure—the inability of the unborn to trade with those currently alive. There are two types of government-provided social security programs—pay-as-you-go programs and fully funded programs.

- Pay-as-you-go social security, which funds retirement benefits from taxes on the working age population, increases welfare for everyone if the real interest rate is less than the rate of growth in the population.

- Fully funded social security at best has no effect, and at worst constrains retirement savings in ways that make consumers worse off.

- Even if the population growth rate is low, social security can be justified if we think that the government is unable to commit to providing social assistance to destitute senior citizens. In that event, pay-as-you-go systems may in fact be less costly than fully funded systems.

Key Terms

Asymmetric information Refers to a situation where, in a particular market, some market participant knows more about his or her own characteristics than do other market participants. (p. 313)

Collateral An asset owned by the borrower that the lender has a right to seize if the borrower defaults on the loan. (p. 322)

Collateralizable wealth Assets that can serve as collateral. (p. 314)

Default premium The portion of a loan interest rate that compensates the lender for the possibility that the borrower may default on the loan. (p. 313)

Financial intermediary A financial institution that borrows from a large set of ultimate lenders and lends to a large set of ultimate borrowers. Examples are banks, insurance companies, and mutual funds. (p. 318)

Fully funded social security A social security system where the social security payments of the working

population are invested in assets, and the payoffs on these assets finance the social security benefits of those people in old age. (p. 327)

Interest rate spread The gap between interest rates on risky loans and safer loans, or the difference between interest rates at which some class of individuals can lend and borrow. (p. 314)

Limited commitment Refers to situations in which it is impossible for a market participant to commit in advance to some future action. (p. 313)

Moral hazard A situation in which insurance against a potential loss reduces the effort taken by the insured to prevent the loss. (p. 332)

Pay-as-you-go social security A social security system where benefits to the old are financed by taxes on the working population. (p. 327)

Repurchase agreement A short-term loan under which a government security serves as collateral. (p. 322)

Questions for Review

1. What effects do credit market imperfections have on the interest rates faced by lenders and borrowers?

2. What are the effects of a tax cut on consumption and savings in the presence of a credit market imperfections? Does Ricardian equivalence hold?

3. Does the existence of credit market imperfections imply that there is a useful role for government tax policy?

4. What are two sources of credit market imperfections?

5. Explain how a default premium can arise, and what would cause it to increase.

6. If the default premium increases, what is the effect on the consumption and savings of an individual consumer?

7. For a borrower who is collateral-constrained, what happens when the value of collateralizable wealth falls? How does this matter for the financial crisis?

8. Under what conditions will a pay-as-you-go social security system improve welfare for those currently alive and for all future generations?

9. What are the effects of a fully funded social security system?

10. How does the government's ability to commit matter for social security programs?

Problems

1. Suppose that there is a credit market imperfection due to asymmetric information. In the economy, a fraction b of consumers consists of lenders, who each receive an endowment of y units of the consumption good in the current period, and 0 units in the future period. A fraction $(1 - b)a$ consumers are good borrowers who each receive an endowment of 0 units in the current period and y units in the future period. Finally, a fraction $(1 - b)(1 - a)$ of consumers are bad borrowers who receive 0 units of endowment in the current and future periods. Banks cannot distinguish between good and bad borrowers. The government sets $G = G' = 0$, and each consumer is asked to pay a lump-sum tax of t in the current period and t' in the future period. The government also cannot distinguish between good and bad borrowers, but as with banks can observe endowments.

   (a) Write down the government's budget constraint, making sure to take account of who is able to pay their taxes and who does not.

   (b) Suppose that the government decreases t and increases t' in such a way that the government budget constraint holds. Does this have any effect on each consumer's decisions about how much to consume in each period and how much to save? Show, with the aid of diagrams.

   (c) Does Ricardian equivalence hold in this economy? Explain why or why not.

2. Suppose there is a credit market imperfection due to limited commitment. As in the setup with collateralizable wealth we examined in this chapter, each consumer has a component of wealth that has value pH in the future period, cannot be sold in the current period, and can be pledged as collateral against loans. Suppose also that the government requires each consumer to pay a lump-sum tax t in the current period, and a tax t' in the future period. Also suppose that there is

limited commitment with respect to taxation as well. That is, if a consumer refuses to pay his or her taxes, the government can seize the consumer's collateralizable wealth, but cannot confiscate income (the consumer's endowment). Assume that, if a consumer fails to pay off his or her debts to private lenders, and also fails to pay taxes, the government has to be paid first from the consumer's collateralizable wealth.

   (a) Show how the limited commitment problem puts a limit on how much the government can spend in the current and future periods.

   (b) Write down the consumer's collateral constraint, taking into account the limited commitment problem with respect to taxes.

   (c) Now, suppose that the government reduces t and increases t' so that the government budget constraint continues to hold. What will be the effects on an individual consumer's consumption in the present and the future? Does Ricardian equivalence hold in this economy? Explain why or why not.

3. Suppose that there is limited commitment in the credit market, but lenders are uncertain about the value of collateral. Each consumer has a quantity of collateral H, but from the point of view of lender, there is a probability a that the collateral will be worth p in the future period, and probability $1 - a$ that the collateral will be worthless in the future period. Suppose that all consumers are identical.

   (a) Determine the collateral constraint for the consumer, and show the consumer's lifetime budget constraint in a diagram.

   (b) How will a decrease in a affect the consumer's consumption and savings in the current period, and consumption in the future period? Explain your results.

4. Use the social security model developed in this chapter to answer this question. Suppose that the government establishes a social security program

in period T that provides a social security benefit of b (in terms of consumption goods) for each old person forever. In period T the government finances the benefits to the current old by issuing debt. This debt is then paid off in period $T + 1$ through lump-sum taxes on the young. In periods $T + 1$ and later, lump-sum taxes on the young finance social security payments to the old.

(a) Show using diagrams that the young and old alive at time T all benefit from the social security program under any circumstances.

(b) What is the effect of the social security program on consumers born in periods $T + 1$ and later? How does this depend on the real interest rate and the population growth rate?

5. Suppose a pay-as-you-go social security system is established where social security is funded by a proportional tax on the consumption of the young. That is, the tax collected by the government is sc, where s is the tax rate and c is consumption of the young. Retirement benefits are given out as a fixed amount b to each old consumer. Can social security work to improve welfare for everyone under these conditions? Use diagrams to answer this question.

6. Use the social security model developed in this chapter to answer this question. Suppose that a government pay-as-you-go social security system has been in place for a long time, providing a social security payment to each old person of b units of consumption. Now, in period T, suppose that the government notices that $r > n$, and decides to eliminate this system. During period T, the government reduces the tax of each young person to zero, but still pays a social security benefit of b to each old person alive in period T. The government issues enough one-period government bonds, D_T, to finance the social security payments in period T. Then, in period $T + 1$, to pay off the principal and interest on the bonds issued in period T, the government taxes the old currently alive, and issues new one-period bonds D_{T+1}. The taxes on the old in period $T + 1$ are just large enough that the quantity of debt per old person stays constant, that is $D_{T+1} = (1 + n)D_T$. Then, the same thing is done in periods $T + 2, T + 3, \ldots$, so that the government debt per old person stays constant forever.

(a) Are the consumers born in periods $T, T + 1, T + 2, \ldots$ better or worse off than they would have been if the pay-as-you-go social security program had stayed in place? Explain, using diagrams.

(b) Suppose that the government follows the same financing scheme as above, but replaces the pay-as-you-go system with a fully funded system in period T. Are consumers better off or worse off than they would have been with pay-as-you-go? Explain, using diagrams.

Working with the Data

1. Calculate the ratio of durables consumption to GDP, the ratio of nondurables consumption to GDP, and the ratio of consumption of services to GDP, and show each in a scatter plot against the relative price of housing. Do you see any evidence that the price of housing collateral matters for any of the components of consumption expenditure?

2. Calculate the difference between the interest rate on a certificate of deposit (CD) and the three-month treasury bill rate, and plot this in a time series plot. What do you notice? In particular, are there any regularities associated with recessions, and the most recent (2008–2009) recession?

chapter 10

A Real Intertemporal Model with Investment

This chapter brings together the microeconomic behavior we have studied in previous chapters to build a model that can serve as a basis for analyzing how macroeconomic shocks affect the economy and that can be used for evaluating the role of macroeconomic policy. With regard to consumer behavior, we have examined work-leisure choices in Chapter 4 and intertemporal consumption–savings choices in Chapters 8 and 9. From the production side, in Chapter 4 we studied a firm's production technology and its labor demand decision, and then in Chapter 5 we showed how changes in total factor productivity affect consumption, employment, and output in the economy as a whole. In Chapters 8 and 9, we looked at the effects of choices by the government concerning the financing of government expenditure and the timing of taxes. While the Solow growth model studied in Chapters 6 and 7 included savings and investment, in this chapter we examine in detail how investment decisions are made at the level of the firm. This detail is important for our understanding of how interest rates and credit market conditions affect firms' investment decisions.

In this chapter we complete a model of the real side of the economy. That is, the real intertemporal model we construct here shows how real aggregate output, real consumption, real investment, employment, the real wage, and the real interest rate are determined in the macroeconomy. To predict nominal variables, we need to add money to the real intertemporal model, which is done in Chapter 12. The intertemporal aspect of the model refers to the fact that both consumers and firms make intertemporal decisions, reflecting trade-offs between the present and the future.

Recall from Chapter 2 that the defining characteristic of investment—expenditure on plants, equipment, and housing—is that it consists of the goods that are produced currently for future use in the production of goods and services. For the economy as a whole, investment represents a trade-off between present and future consumption. Productive capacity that is used for producing investment goods could otherwise be used for producing current consumption goods, but today's investment increases future productive capacity, which means that more consumption goods can be produced in the future. To understand the determinants of investment, we must study the microeconomic investment behavior of a firm, which makes an intertemporal decision regarding investment in the current period. When a firm invests, it forgoes current profits so as to have a higher capital stock in the future, which allows it to earn higher future profits. As we show, a firm invests more the lower its current capital stock, the higher its expected future total factor productivity, and the lower the real interest rate.

The real interest rate is a key determinant of investment as it represents investment's opportunity cost. A higher real interest rate implies that the opportunity cost of investment is larger, at the margin, and so investment falls. Movements in the real interest rate are an important channel through which shocks to the economy affect investment, as we show in this chapter. Further, monetary policy may affect investment through its influence on the real interest rate, as we show in Chapters 11 to 13.

In addition to the effect of the market interest rates, the investment decisions of firms depend on credit market risk, as perceived by lenders. That is, firms may find it more difficult to borrow to finance investment projects if lenders, including banks and other financial institutions, perceive lending in general to be more risky. Perceptions of an increase in the degree of riskiness in lending have been an important factor in the ongoing worldwide financial crisis. In this chapter, we will show how credit market risk can play a role in investment behavior, by incorporating asymmetric information, a credit market imperfection. The role of asymmetric information in a firm's investment decision will turn out to be very similar to the way in which asymmetric information affects a consumer's consumption–savings decision, as studied in Chapter 9.

A good part of this chapter involves model building, and there are several important steps we must take before we can use this model to address some important economic issues. This requires some patience and work, but the payoff arrives in the last part of this chapter and continues through the remainder of this book, where this model is the basis for our study of monetary factors in Chapter 11, business cycles in Chapters 12 and 13, and for other issues in later chapters.

This chapter focuses on the macroeconomic effects on aggregate output, investment, consumption, the real interest rate, and labor market variables of aggregate shocks to government spending, total factor productivity, the nation's capital stock, and credit market risk. Although we studied elements of some of these effects in Chapters 5 and 9, there are new insights in this chapter involving the effects on the interest rate and investment of these shocks, and the effect of the anticipation of future shocks on current macroeconomic activity. For example, including intertemporal factors shows how credit markets play a role in the effects of government spending on the economy. As well, we will be able to use the real intertemporal model to analyze aspects of the impact of the current financial crisis on aggregate economic activity.

As in Chapters 4 and 5, we work with a model that has a representative consumer, a representative firm, and a government, and, for simplicity, ultimately we specify this model at the level of supply and demand curves. We are able to capture the essential behavior in this model economy by examining the participation of the representative consumer, the representative firm, and the government in two markets: the market for labor in the current period and the market for goods in the current period. The representative consumer supplies labor in the current labor market and purchases consumption goods in the current goods market, while the representative firm demands labor in the current labor market, supplies goods in the current goods market, and demands investment goods in the current goods market. The government demands goods in the current goods market in terms of government purchases.

The Representative Consumer

The behavior of the representative consumer in this model brings together our knowledge of the consumer's work–leisure choice from Chapter 4 with what we know about intertemporal consumption behavior from Chapter 6. In the model we are constructing here, the representative consumer makes a work–leisure decision in each of the current and future periods, and he or she makes a consumption–savings decision in the current period.

The representative consumer works and consumes in the current period and the future period. He or she has h units of time in each period and divides this time between work and leisure in each period. Let w denote the real wage in the current period, w' the real wage in the future period, and r the real interest rate. The consumer pays lump-sum taxes to the government of T in the current period and T' in the future period. His or her goal is to choose current consumption C, future consumption C', leisure time in the current and future periods, l and l', respectively, and savings in the current period, S^p, to make himself or herself as well off as possible, given his or her budget constraints in the current and future periods. The representative consumer is a price-taker who takes w, w', and r as given. Taxes are also given from the consumer's point of view.

In the current period, the representative consumer earns real wage income $w(h - l)$, receives dividend income π from the representative firm, and pays taxes T, so that his or her current-period disposable income is $w(h - l) + \pi - T$, just as in Chapter 4. As in Chapter 8, disposable income in the current period is then split between consumption and savings, and savings takes the form of bonds that earn the one-period real interest rate r. Just as in Chapter 8, savings can be negative, in which case the consumer borrows by issuing bonds. The consumer's current budget constraint is then

$$C + S^p = w(h - l) + \pi - T. \tag{10-1}$$

In the future period, the representative consumer receives real wage income $w'(h - l')$, receives real dividend income π' from the representative firm, pays taxes T' to the government, and receives the principal and interest on savings from the current period, $(1 + r)S^p$. Because the future period is the last period and because the consumer is assumed to make no bequests, all wealth available to the consumer in the future is consumed, so that the consumer's future budget constraint is

$$C' = w'(h - l') + \pi' - T' + (1 + r)S^p. \tag{10-2}$$

Just as in Chapter 8, we can substitute for savings S^p in equation (10-1) using equation (10-2) to obtain a lifetime budget constraint for the representative consumer:

$$C + \frac{C'}{1 + r} = w(h - l) + \pi - T + \frac{w'(h - l') + \pi' - T'}{1 + r}. \tag{10-3}$$

This constraint states that the present value of consumption (on the left-hand side of the equation) equals the present value of lifetime disposable income (on the right-hand side of the equation). A difference from the consumer's lifetime budget constraint in Chapter 8 is that the consumer in this model has some choice, through his or her current and future choices of leisure, l and l', over his or her lifetime wealth.

The representative consumer's problem is to choose C, C', l, and l' to make himself or herself as well off as possible while respecting his or her lifetime budget constraint, as given by equation (10-3). We cannot depict this choice for the consumer conveniently in a graph, as the problem is four-dimensional (choosing current and future consumption and current and future leisure), while a graph is two-dimensional. It is straightforward, however, to describe the consumer's optimizing decision in terms of three marginal conditions we have looked at in Chapters 4 and 8. These are as follows:

1. The consumer makes a work–leisure decision in the current period, so that when he or she optimizes, we have

$$MRS_{l,C} = w, \tag{10-4}$$

   that is, the consumer optimizes by choosing current leisure and consumption so that the marginal rate of substitution of leisure for consumption is equal to the real wage in the current period. This is the same marginal condition as in the work–leisure problem for a consumer that we considered in Chapter 4. Recall that, in general, a consumer optimizes by setting the marginal rate of substitution of one good for another equal to the relative price of the two goods. In equation (10-4), the current real wage w is the relative price of leisure in terms of consumption goods.

2. Similarly, in the future the consumer makes another work–leisure decision, and he or she optimizes by setting

$$MRS_{l',C'} = w', \tag{10-5}$$

   that is, at the optimum, the marginal rate of substitution of future leisure for future consumption must be equal to the future real wage.

3. With respect to his or her consumption–savings decision in the current period, as in Chapter 8, the consumer optimizes by setting

$$MRS_{C,C'} = 1 + r, \tag{10-6}$$

   that is, the marginal rate of substitution of current consumption for future consumption equals the relative price of current consumption in terms of future consumption.

Current Labor Supply

Our ultimate focus is on interaction between the representative consumer and the representative firm in the markets for current labor and current consumption goods, and so we are interested in the determinants of the representative consumer's supply of labor and his or her demand for current consumption goods.

First, we consider the representative consumer's current supply of labor, which is determined by three factors—the current real wage, the real interest rate, and lifetime wealth. These three factors affect current labor supply as listed below.

1. *The current quantity of labor supplied increases when the current real wage increases.* The consumer's marginal condition (10-4) captures the idea that substitution between current leisure and current consumption is governed by the current real wage rate w. Recall from Chapter 4 that a change in the real wage has opposing income and substitution effects on the quantity of leisure, so that an increase in the real wage could lead to an increase or a decrease in the quantity of leisure, depending on the size of the income effect. Here, we assume that the substitution effect of a change in the real wage is always larger than the income effect, implying that leisure decreases and hours worked increases in response to an increase in the real wage. This might seem inconsistent with the fact, pointed out in Chapter 4, that over the long run, income and substitution effects on labor supply appear to cancel. However, the model we are building here is intended mainly for analyzing short-run phenomena. As we argued in Chapter 4, the canceling of income and substitution effects in the long run can be consistent with the substitution effect dominating in the short run, as we assume here.

2. *The quantity of current labor supplied increases when the real interest rate increases.* The consumer can substitute intertemporally not only by substituting current consumption for future consumption, as we studied in Chapter 8, but by substituting current leisure for future leisure. In substituting leisure between the two periods, the representative consumer responds to the current price of leisure relative to the future price of leisure, which is $\frac{w(1 + r)}{w'}$. Here, w is the price of current leisure (labor) in terms of current consumption, w' is the price of future leisure in terms of future consumption, and $1 + r$ is the price of current consumption in terms of future consumption. Therefore, an increase in the real interest rate r, given w and w', results in an increase in the price of current leisure relative to future leisure. Assuming again that the substitution effect is larger than the income effect, the consumer wants to consume less current leisure and more future leisure. An example of how this **intertemporal substitution of leisure** effect works is as follows. Suppose that Paul is self-employed and that the market interest rate rises. Then, Paul faces a higher return on his savings, so that if he works more in the current period and saves the proceeds, in the future he can both consume more and work less. It may be helpful to consider that leisure, like consumption, is a good. When the real interest rate increases, and substitution effects dominate income effects for lenders, current consumption falls (from Chapter 6), just as current leisure decreases when the real interest rate increases and substitution effects dominate.

3. *Current labor supply decreases when lifetime wealth increases.* From Chapter 4, we know that an increase in current nonwage disposable income results in an increase in the quantity of leisure and a decrease in labor supply for the consumer, as leisure is a normal good. Further, in Chapter 8, we showed how income effects generalize to the intertemporal case where the consumer chooses current and

future consumption. That is, an increase in lifetime wealth increases the quantities of current and future consumption chosen by the consumer. Here, when there is an increase in lifetime wealth, there is an increase in current leisure and, thus, a decrease in current labor supply, because current leisure is assumed to be normal. The key wealth effect for our analysis in this chapter is the effect of a change in the present value of taxes for the consumer. Any increase in the present value of taxes implies a decrease in lifetime wealth and an increase in current labor supply.

Given these three factors, we can construct an upward-sloping current labor supply curve as in Figure 10.1. Here, the current real wage w is measured along the vertical axis, and current labor supply N is on the horizontal axis. The current labor supply curve is labeled $N^s(r)$ to indicate that labor supply depends on the current real interest rate. If the real interest rate rises, say from r_1 to r_2, then the labor supply curve shifts to the right, as in Figure 10.2, because labor supply increases for any current real wage w. In Figure 10.3, an increase in lifetime wealth shifts the labor supply curve to the left from $N_1^s(r)$ to $N_2^s(r)$. Such an increase in lifetime wealth could be caused by a decrease in the present value of taxes for the consumer. In Figure 10.3 the real interest rate is held constant as we shift the current labor supply curve to the left.

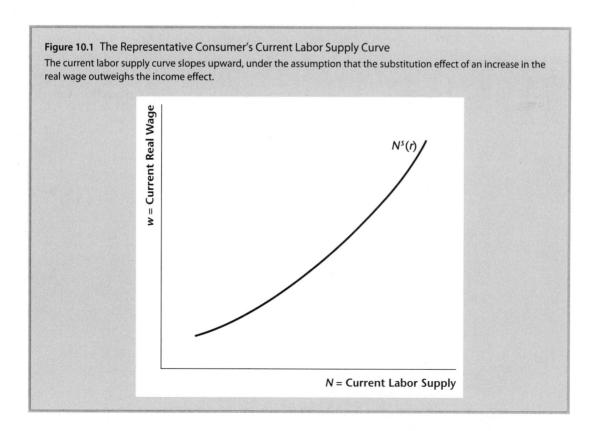

Figure 10.1 The Representative Consumer's Current Labor Supply Curve

The current labor supply curve slopes upward, under the assumption that the substitution effect of an increase in the real wage outweighs the income effect.

Figure 10.2 An Increase in the Real Interest Rate Shifts the Current Labor Supply Curve to the Right

This is because the representative consumer consumes less leisure in the current period and more leisure in the future when r increases.

Figure 10.3 Effects of an Increase in Lifetime Wealth

More leisure is consumed in the present, due to an income effect, and the current labor supply curve shifts to the left.

The Current Demand for Consumption Goods

Now that we have dealt with the determinants of the representative consumer's current labor supply, we can turn to his or her demand for current consumption goods. The determinants of the demand for current consumption goods were studied in Chapter 8, where we showed that the primary factors affecting current consumption are lifetime wealth and the real interest rate. Further, lifetime wealth is affected by current income, and by the present value of taxes.

Given our analysis of the consumption–savings behavior of consumers in Chapter 8, it proves useful here to construct a demand curve that represents the quantity demanded of current consumption goods by the representative consumer, as a function of current aggregate income, Y, as shown in Figure 10.4. Recall from Chapter 8 that, if the real interest rate is held constant and current income increases for the consumer, that current consumption will increase. In Figure 10.4, we graph the quantity of current consumption chosen by the representative consumer, for each level of real income Y, holding constant the real interest rate r. In the figure, the demand for consumption goods is on the vertical axis, and aggregate income is on the horizontal axis. We let $C^d(r)$ denote the demand curve for current consumption goods, indicating the dependence of the demand for consumption on the real interest rate. Recall from Chapter 8 that, if current income increases for the consumer, then consumption and savings both increase, so that the quantity of consumption increases by less than one unit for each unit increase in income. In Figure 10.4, the slope of the curve $C^d(r)$ in the figure is the *MPC* or **marginal propensity to consume**, which is the amount that current consumption increases when there is a unit increase in aggregate real income Y.

When there is an increase in the real interest rate, assuming again that the substitution effect of this increase dominates the income effect, there will be a decrease in the demand for current consumption goods because of the intertemporal substitution of consumption. (recall our analysis from Chapter 8). In Figure 10.5, if the real interest rate increases from r_1 to r_2, the demand curve for current consumption shifts down from $C^d(r_1)$ to $C^d(r_2)$. Also, holding constant r and Y, if there is an increase in lifetime wealth, then, as in Figure 10.6, the demand curve for current consumption shifts up from $C_1d(r)$ to $C_2d(r)$. Such an increase in lifetime wealth could be caused by a decrease in the present value of taxes for the consumer, or by an increase in future income.

The demand for current consumption goods is only part of the total demand in the economy for current goods. What remains for us to consider are the demands for current goods coming from firms (the demand for investment goods) and from the government (government purchases). Total demand for current goods will be summarized later in this chapter by the output demand curve, which incorporates the behavior of the representative consumer, the representative firm, and the government.

The Representative Firm

Now that we have covered the important features of the consumer's current labor supply and current consumption demand decisions, we can turn to the key decisions of the representative firm for the current labor market and the current goods market.

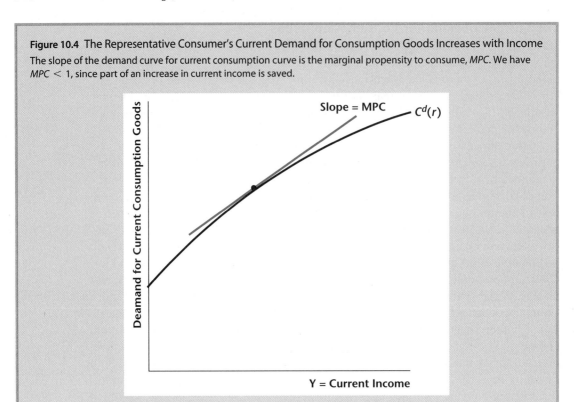

Figure 10.4 The Representative Consumer's Current Demand for Consumption Goods Increases with Income

The slope of the demand curve for current consumption curve is the marginal propensity to consume, *MPC*. We have *MPC* < 1, since part of an increase in current income is saved.

The representative firm, as in Chapter 4, produces goods using inputs of labor and capital. The key differences here are that output is produced in both the current and future periods, and that the firm can invest in the current period by accumulating capital so as to expand the capacity to produce future output. In the current period, the representative firm produces output according to the production function

$$Y = zF(K, N), \tag{10-7}$$

where Y is current output, z is total factor productivity, F is the production function, K is current capital, and N is current labor input. Here, K is the capital with which the firm starts the current period, and this quantity is given. The production function F is identical in all respects to the production function we studied in Chapter 4.

Similarly, in the future period, output is produced according to

$$Y' = z'F(K', N'), \tag{10-8}$$

where Y' is future output, z' is future total factor productivity, K' is the future capital stock, and N' is the future labor input.

Recall from Chapter 2 that investment, as measured in the NIPA, is expenditure on plant, equipment, housing, and inventory accumulation. Here, we model investment

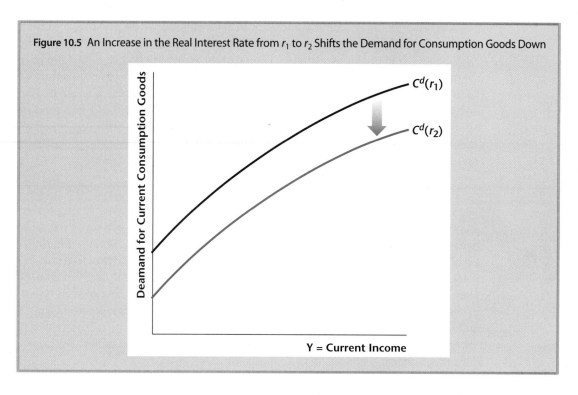

Figure 10.5 An Increase in the Real Interest Rate from r_1 to r_2 Shifts the Demand for Consumption Goods Down

$C^d(r_1)$

$C^d(r_2)$

Deamand for Current Consumption Goods

Y = **Current Income**

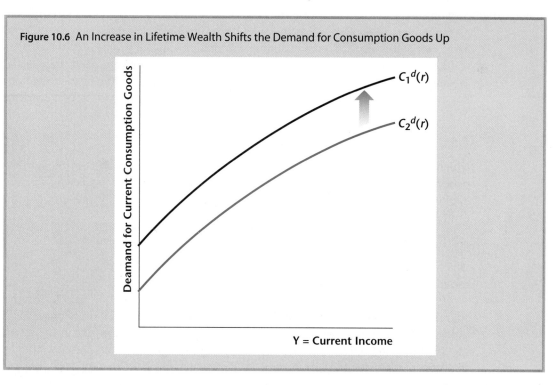

Figure 10.6 An Increase in Lifetime Wealth Shifts the Demand for Consumption Goods Up

$C_1{}^d(r)$

$C_2{}^d(r)$

Deamand for Current Consumption Goods

Y = **Current Income**

goods as being produced from output. That is, for simplicity we assume that it requires one unit of consumption goods in the current period to produce one unit of capital. The representative firm invests by acquiring capital in the current period, and the essence of investment is that something must be forgone in the current period to gain something in the future. What is forgone by the firm when it invests is current profits; that is, the firm uses some of the current output it produces to invest in capital, which becomes productive in the future. As in the Solow growth model introduced in Chapter 6, capital depreciates at the rate d when used. Letting I denote the quantity of current investment, the future capital stock is given by

$$K' = (1 - d)K + I. \tag{10-9}$$

That is, the future capital stock is the current capital stock net of depreciation plus the quantity of current investment that has been added in the current period. Further, the quantity of capital left at the end of the future period is $(1 - d)K'$. Because the future period is the last period, it would not be useful for the representative firm to retain this quantity of capital, and so the firm liquidates it. We suppose that the firm can take the quantity $(1 - d)K'$, the capital left at the end of the future period, and convert it one-for-one back into consumption goods, which it can then sell. This is a simple way to model a firm's ability to sell off capital for what it can fetch on the secondhand market. For example, a restaurant that goes out of business can sell its used tables, chairs, and kitchen equipment secondhand in a liquidation sale.

Profits and Current Labor Demand

Now that we know how the firm produces output in the present and the future and how investment can take place, we are ready to determine present and future profits for the firm. The goal of the firm is to maximize the present value of profits over the current and future periods, and this allows us to determine the firm's demand for current labor, as well as the firm's quantity of investment, which we discuss in the next subsection. For the representative firm, current profits in units of the current consumption good are

$$\pi = Y - wN - I, \tag{10-10}$$

which is current output (or revenue) Y minus wages paid to workers in the current period minus current investment. The firm can produce one unit of capital using one unit of output, so that each unit of investment decreases current profits by one unit. Future profits for the firm are

$$\pi' = Y' - w'N' + (1 - d)K', \tag{10-11}$$

which is future output minus wages paid to workers in the future plus the value of the capital stock net of depreciation at the end of the future period.

Profits earned by the firm in the current and future periods are paid out to the shareholders of the firm as dividend income in each period. There is one shareholder in this economy, the representative consumer, and the firm acts in the interests of this shareholder. That implies that the firm maximizes the present value of the consumer's dividend income, which serves to maximize the lifetime wealth of the consumer. Letting V denote the present value of profits for the firm, the firm then maximizes

$$V = \pi + \frac{\pi'}{1 + r} \tag{10-12}$$

by choosing current labor demand N, future labor demand N', and current investment I.

The firm's choice of current labor demand N affects only current profits π in equation (10-10). As in Chapter 4, the firm hires current labor until the current marginal product of labor equals the current real wage, that is, $MP_N = w$. Also as in Chapter 4, the demand curve for labor in the current period is identical to the marginal product of labor schedule, as the MP_N schedule tells us how much labor the firm needs to hire so that $MP_N = w$. In Figure 10.7 we show the representative firm's demand curve for labor, N^d, with the current real wage w on the vertical axis and the current quantity of labor N on the horizontal axis. Recall from Chapter 4 that the labor demand curve is downward-sloping because the marginal product of labor declines with the quantity of labor employed.

As in Chapter 4, the labor demand curve shifts with changes in total factor productivity z or with changes in the initial capital stock K. A higher current level of total factor

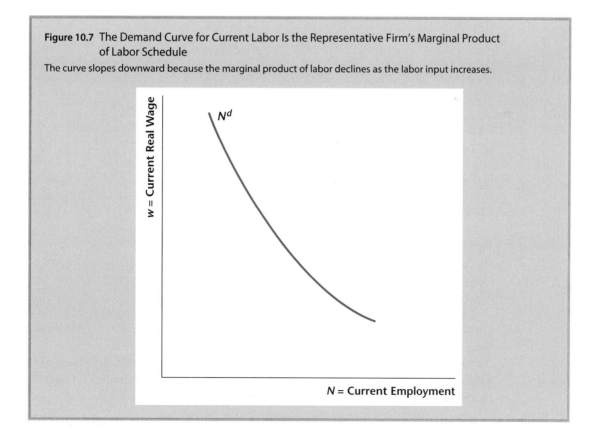

Figure 10.7 The Demand Curve for Current Labor Is the Representative Firm's Marginal Product of Labor Schedule

The curve slopes downward because the marginal product of labor declines as the labor input increases.

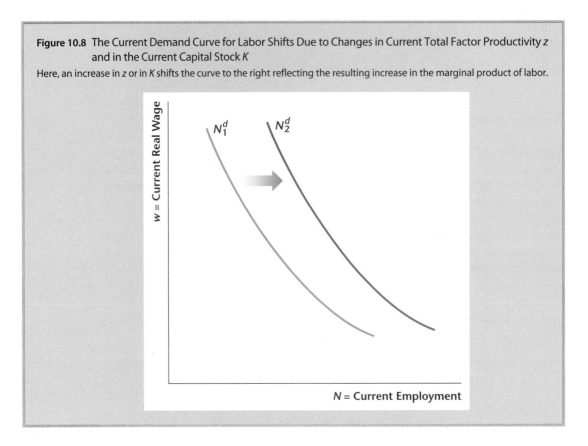

Figure 10.8 The Current Demand Curve for Labor Shifts Due to Changes in Current Total Factor Productivity z and in the Current Capital Stock K

Here, an increase in z or in K shifts the curve to the right reflecting the resulting increase in the marginal product of labor.

productivity z or a higher level of K shifts the labor demand curve to the right, for example, from N_1^d to N_2^d in Figure 10.8.

The firm chooses labor demand in the future period in a similar way to its choice of current-period labor demand. We ignore, however, this future choice in our analysis, as this simplifies our model in a way that makes the model's predictions clearer while doing no harm.

The Representative Firm's Investment Decision

Having dealt with the representative firm's labor demand decision, and given its goal of maximizing the present value of its profits, we can proceed to a central aspect of this chapter, which is analyzing the investment choice of the firm.

A key principle in economic decision-making is that the optimal level of an economic activity is chosen so that the marginal benefit of the activity is equal to its marginal cost. In this respect, there is nothing different about the choice of investment by the representative firm, which will involve equating the marginal cost of investment with the marginal benefit of investment. We let $MC(I)$ denote the **marginal cost of investment** for the firm, where

$$MC(I) = 1. \tag{10-13}$$

That is, the marginal cost of investment for the firm is what it gives up, in terms of the present value of profits, V, by investing in one unit of capital in the current period. This marginal cost is 1, as from equations (10-12) and (10-10), an additional unit of current investment I reduces current profits π by one unit, which reduces the present value of profits V by one unit.

The **marginal benefit from investment,** denoted by $MB(I)$, is what one extra unit of investment in the current period adds to the present value of profits, V. In equation (10-11), all the benefits from investment come in terms of future profits π', and there are two components to the marginal benefit. First, an additional unit of current investment adds one unit to the future capital stock K'. This implies that the firm will produce more output in the future, and the additional output produced is equal to the firm's future marginal product of capital, MP'_K. Second, each unit of current investment implies that there will be an additional $1 - d$ units of capital remaining at the end of the future period (after depreciation in the future period), which can be liquidated. Thus, one unit of additional investment in the current period implies an additional $MP'_K + 1 - d$ units of future profits π'. In calculating the marginal benefit of investment, we have to discount these future profits, so we then have

$$MB(I) = \frac{MP'_K + 1 - d}{1 + r}. \tag{10-14}$$

The firm invests until the marginal benefit from investment is equal to the marginal cost—that is, $MB(I) = MC(I)$—or from equations (10-13) and (10-14),

$$\frac{MP'_K + 1 - d}{1 + r} = 1. \tag{10-15}$$

We can rewrite (10-15) as

$$MP'_K - d = r. \tag{10-16}$$

Equation (10-16) states that the firm invests until the **net marginal product of capital,** $MP'_K - d$, is equal to the real interest rate. The net marginal product of capital, $MP'_K - d$, is the marginal product of capital after taking account of the depreciation of the capital stock. The intuition behind the **optimal investment rule,** equation (10-16), is that the opportunity cost of investing in more capital is the real rate of interest, which is the rate of return on the alternative asset in this economy. That is, in the model there are two assets: bonds traded on the credit market and capital held by the representative firm. If the firm invests in capital, it is foregoing lending in the credit market, where it can earn a real rate of return of r.

Effectively, the representative consumer holds the capital of the firm indirectly, because the consumer owns the firm and receives its profits as dividend income. From the consumer's point of view, the rate of return that he or she receives between the current and future periods when the firm engages in investment is the net marginal product of capital. As the firm acts in the interests of the consumer, it would not be optimal for the firm to invest beyond the point where the net marginal product of capital is equal to the real interest rate, as in equation (10-16), because this would imply that the consumer was receiving a lower rate of return on his or her savings than could be obtained by lending in the credit market at the real interest rate r. Thus, the real interest rate represents the opportunity cost of investing for the representative firm.

Another aspect of the firm's investment decision can help clarify the role of the market real interest rate in the firm's optimal choice. Suppose that, given the optimal choice of investment for the firm, that $\pi = Y - wN - I < 0$. How is this possible? Such a situation is much like what occurs when a consumer chooses to consume more than his or her income during the current period. That is, the firm borrows the amount $I + wN - Y$ so as to help finance current investment, and must repay the quantity $(1 + r)(I + wN - Y)$ in the future period. It will only be optimal for the firm to borrow up to the point where the net rate of return on investment is equal to the market real interest rate, as borrowing any more would be unprofitable. This is just another sense in which the market real interest rate is the opportunity cost of investment for the firm.

The optimal investment rule, equation (10-16), determines a negative relationship between the quantity of capital K' that the firm desires in the future period, and the real interest rate. That is, if the market real interest rate, r, increases, then the firm will choose smaller K', so as to increase MP'_K. However, our interest is in showing how the firm determines investment I given the real interest rate r. But from equation (10-9), we have $K' = (1 - d)K + I$, so effectively there is a negative relationship between I and MP'_K (given K), because one unit of investment yields a one-unit increase in the future capital stock K'. In Figure 10.9 we graph the firm's **optimal investment schedule,** with the interest rate on the vertical axis and the demand for investment goods, I^d, on the horizontal axis. Given equation (10-16), the optimal investment schedule is the firm's net marginal product of capital, as a function of investment, given the initial quantity of capital K. In the figure, if the real interest rate is r_1 then the firm wishes to invest I_1, and if the real interest rate falls to r_2 then investment increases to I_2. Note the similarity here to the firm's current labor demand decision, as represented, for example, in Figure 10.1. When making its current labor demand decision, the relevant price to consider is the current real wage, and the firm hires labor until the marginal product of labor is equal to the real wage. In making its investment decision, the relevant price is the real interest rate, and the firm acquires capital (invests) until the net marginal product of capital is equal to the real interest rate.

Optimal investment I^d is determined in part by the market real interest rate r, as reflected in the negative slope of the optimal investment schedule in Figure 10.9. Also, the optimal investment schedule shifts due to any factor that changes the future marginal product of capital. Primarily, we are interested in the following two types of shifts in the optimal investment schedule:

1. The optimal investment schedule shifts to the right if future total factor productivity z' increases. From Chapter 4, recall that an increase in total factor productivity increases the marginal product of capital, for each level of the capital stock. Therefore, if total factor productivity is expected to be higher in the future, so that z' increases, this increases the future marginal product of capital, and the firm is more willing to invest during the current period. Higher investment in the current period

Figure 10.9 Optimal Investment Schedule for the Representative Firm

The optimal investment rule states that the firm invests until $MP'_K - d = r$. The future net marginal product schedule $MP'_K - d$ is the representative firm's optimal investment schedule, because this describes how much investment is required for the net marginal product of future capital to equal the real interest rate.

I^d = Demand for Investment Goods

leads to higher future productive capacity, so that the firm can take advantage of high future total factor productivity.

2. The optimal investment schedule shifts to the left if the current capital stock K is higher. A higher capital stock at the beginning of the current period implies, from equation (10-9), that for a given level of current investment I, the future capital stock K' will be larger. That is, if K is larger, then there is more of this initial capital left after depreciation in the current period to use in future production. Therefore, higher K implies that the future marginal product of capital, MP'_K, will decrease for each level of investment, and the optimal investment schedule will then shift to the left.

In Figure 10.10 we show a shift to the right in the optimal investment schedule, which could be caused either by an increase in future total factor productivity z', or by a lower current quantity of capital K. Note that the optimal investment schedule also

Figure 10.10 The Optimal Investment Schedule Shifts to the Right if Current Capital Decreases or Future Total Factor Productivity Is Expected to Increase

This is because either of these changes causes the future marginal product of capital to increase. The figure shows the effect of a decrease in current capital from K_1 to K_2

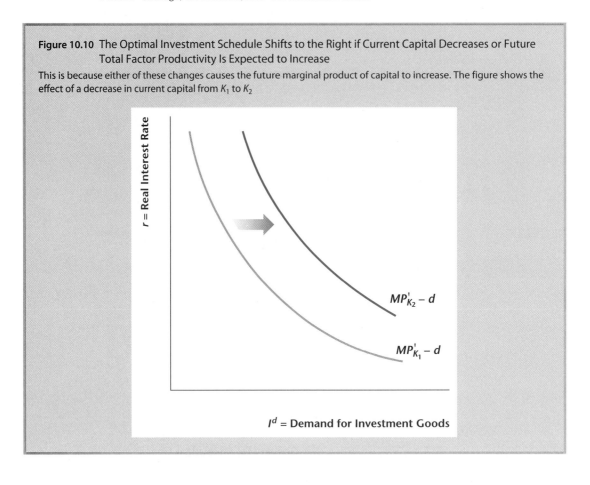

shifts if the depreciation rate d changes, but we ask the reader to determine the resulting shift in the curve as a problem at the end of this chapter.

This theory of investment can potentially explain why aggregate investment expenditures tend to be more variable over the business cycle than aggregate output or aggregate consumption, features of macroeconomic data that we highlighted in Chapter 3. A key implication of consumer behavior is smoothing; consumers wish to smooth consumption over time relative to their income, and this explains why consumption tends to be less variable than income. However, investment behavior is not about smoothing but about the response of the firm's investment behavior to perceived marginal rates of return to investment. Provided that the real interest rate and anticipated future total factor productivity vary sufficiently over the business cycle, our theory of the business cycle can explain the variability in observed investment expenditures. That is, investment is variable if the real interest rate is variable, causing movements along the optimal investment schedule in Figure 10.10, or if there is variability in anticipated future total factor productivity, causing the optimal investment schedule to shift over time.

Optimal Investment: A Numerical Example

To make the firm's optimal investment decision more concrete, consider the following numerical example. Christine, a small-scale farmer, has an apple orchard, which has 10 trees in the current period—that is, $K = 10$. For simplicity, suppose that the quantity of labor required to operate the orchard does not depend on the number of trees Christine has, at least for the number of trees that Christine can plant on her land. In the current period, the 10 trees produce 100 bushels of apples, that is, $Y = 100$. Christine can invest in more trees by taking some of the apples, extracting the seeds (which we assume makes the apples useless), and planting them. Very few of the seeds grow, and it takes 1 bushel of apples to yield 1 tree that will be productive in the future period. The first extra tree that Christine grows is on her best land, and, therefore, it will have a high marginal product, bearing a relatively large amount of fruit. The second tree is planted on slightly worse land, and so will have a smaller marginal product, and so on. Each period, some trees die. In fact, at the end of each period, Christine loses 20% of her trees, and so the depreciation rate is $d = 0.2$. At the end of the future period, Christine can liquidate her trees. Because each bushel of apples can produce a tree, it is possible to exchange 1 tree for 1 bushel of apples on the open market, so that the liquidation value of a tree remaining in the future period, after depreciation, is 1 bushel of apples. The real interest rate is 5%, or $r = 0.05$ in units of apples. Table 10.1 shows the quantity of future output that will be produced when the number of trees Christine has in the future is 8, 9, 10, ..., 15, as well as the associated level of investment, present discounted value of profits (in units of apples), and the net marginal product of capital (trees) in the future.

From Table 10.1, the present value of profits is maximized when the number of trees in the future is 12 and the quantity of investment is 4 bushels of apples. For each unit of investment from 1 to 4, the net marginal product of capital in the future is greater than the real interest rate, which is 0.05, and the net marginal product of capital is less than 0.05 for each unit of investment above 4. Therefore, it is optimal to invest as long as the net marginal product of future capital is greater than the real interest rate.

Table 10.1 Data for Christine's Orchard

$K' =$ trees in the future	I	Y'	V	$MP'_K - d$
8	0	95	196.6	—
9	1	98	199.2	2.8
10	2	100	200.9	1.8
11	3	101	201.6	0.8
12	4	101.5	201.8	0.3
13	5	101.65	201.7	−0.35
14	6	101.75	201.6	−0.10
15	7	101.77	201.4	−0.18

Investment with Asymmetric Information and the Financial Crisis

In Chapter 9, we discussed and analyzed the importance of credit market imperfections in consumer credit markets, and some of the implications for the current world financial crisis. One feature of credit markets that can give rise to credit market imperfections is asymmetric information—a situation where would-be borrowers in the credit market know more about their creditworthiness than do would-be lenders. The purpose of this section is to show how asymmetric information matters for the investment choices of firms, just as it matters for a consumer's saving behavior, and to explore the importance of this for the financial crisis.

As in Chapter 9, it will help to model borrowing and lending in the credit market as occurring only through banks. Anyone who wishes to lend holds a deposit with a bank that bears the market real interest rate r. Assume that these deposits are completely safe—a bank that takes deposits in the current period is always able to pay the rate of return r to each depositor in the future period. Also suppose that, instead of a single representative firm, there are many firms in the economy. Some of these firms will choose to lend in the current period, and these firms will have positive profits in the current period, with $\pi = Y - wN - I > 0$. There will also be some firms that choose to borrow. Among these borrowing firms, there are good firms, which have negative current profits, or $\pi = Y - wN - I < 0$. There are also bad firms that borrow in the credit market, but have no intention of producing anything in the future. The managers of a bad firm are assumed to simply take the amount borrowed in the credit market and consume it as executive compensation rather than investing in new capital.

Unfortunately, a bank is not able to distinguish between a good firm and a bad one, and therefore treats all firms wishing to borrow in the same way. This is the asymmetric information problem—each borrowing firm knows whether it is good or bad, but the bank cannot tell the difference. So that the bank can make good on its promise to pay each depositor a rate of return of r on his or her deposits, the bank must charge each borrower a real interest rate on loans that is greater than r. That is, if we let r^l denote the loan interest rate, we will have $r < r^l$, and the difference $r^l - r$ is a default premium, similar to the default premium we analyzed in Chapter 9. By lending to a large number of borrowers, the bank is able to accurately predict the chances of lending to a bad borrower. Then, the default premium charged to good borrowers will compensate the bank for loans made to bad borrowers that will yield nothing for the bank.

For a firm that is a lender, investment is financed out of retained earnings. Such a firm has revenue remaining after paying its wage bill in the current period (the quantity $Y - wN$), uses some of this revenue to finance investment, and lends the remainder $(Y - wN - I)$ to the bank at the real interest rate r. For such a lending firm, the analysis of the firm's investment decision is identical to what we did in the previous subsection, and the firm's optimal investment rule is given by equation (10-16), with the optimal investment schedule depicted in Figure 10.9.

A good firm that borrows will borrow at the real interest rate

$$r^l = r + x,$$

where x is the default premium, and so the opportunity cost of investment for a good borrowing firm is $r + x$, and the optimal investment schedule for this firm is

$$MP'_K - d = r + x$$

or

$$MP'_K - d - x = r \qquad\qquad (10\text{-}17)$$

In equation (10-17), note that the default premium acts to reduce the net marginal product of capital, given the safe credit market interest rate r. In Figure 10.11, we show the effect on the optimal investment schedule of a good borrowing firm when there is an increase in the default premium. Such an increase in the default premium could occur if banks perceive that bad borrowing firms have become more prevalent. In the figure, the default premium increases from x_1 to x_2. As a result, the optimal investment schedule for the firm shifts down (or to the left), and the firm will choose to invest less at each level of the safe market real interest rate r.

Figure 10.11 The Effect of an Increased Default Premium on a Firm's Optimal Investment Schedule
An increase in the default premium, from x_1 to x_2, shifts the optimal investment schedule down, so that the firm will invest less given any safe real interest rate r.

Perspectives on the Financial Crisis
Investment and the Interest Rate Spread

Theory tells us that we should observe a negative relationship between the default premium and investment expenditures. If the asymmetric information problem worsens in credit markets where firms borrow to finance investment projects, the default premium should increase and we should see a decline in investment expenditures. In Chapter 9, we examined a particular measure of the default premium, the difference between the interest rates on AAA-rated and BAA-rated corporate bonds—i.e., the difference between interest rates on essentially default-free corporate debt, and risky corporate debt.

In Figure 10.12, we show a time series plot of the percentage deviations from trend in aggregate investment expenditures and the deviations from trend in the AAA/BAA interest rate spread. The deviations from trend in the spread are multiplied by 10 to make the comovements more discernible. Note that the two time series are clearly negatively correlated, which is even more apparent in the scatter plot of the same two variables in Figure 10.13. Clearly, a negatively sloped

straight line would provide the best fit to the scatter plot. In Figure 10.12, note in particular the behavior of the spread and investment expenditures around the recessions in 1974–1975, 1981–1982, 1990–1991, 2001, and 2008–2009.

Particularly during the financial crisis leading up to the 2008–2009 recession, an important feature was an increase in financial market uncertainty. Financial institutions, including banks, become increasingly unsure about which firms were likely to default on loans. This uncertainty was reflected in a sharp increase in the interest rate spread in Figure 10.12. As a result, even healthy firms suffered. In our model, a firm may know that it will be able to repay a loan in the future, but in spite of this it will face a higher default premium in the face of increased credit market uncertainty. For a given safe market interest rate (the interest rate r faced by bank depositors), a given firm will choose to invest and borrow less. In the aggregate, investment expenditures will fall, as reflected in the data in Figures 10.12 and 10.13.

Government

We have now shown how the representative consumer and the representative firm behave in the markets for current goods and current labor. We need only to consider government behavior before we show how all these economic agents interact in a competitive equilibrium. Government behavior is identical to what it was in Chapter 8. The government sets government purchases of consumption goods exogenously in each period. The quantity of government purchases in the current period is G, and in the future government purchases are G'. The government finances government purchases in the current period through taxation and by issuing government bonds. Then in the future, the government pays off the interest and principal on its bonds and finances future government spending through future lump-sum taxation. As in Chapter 8, the government must satisfy its present-value budget constraint,

$$G + \frac{G'}{1 + r} = T + \frac{T'}{1 + r}. \tag{10-18}$$

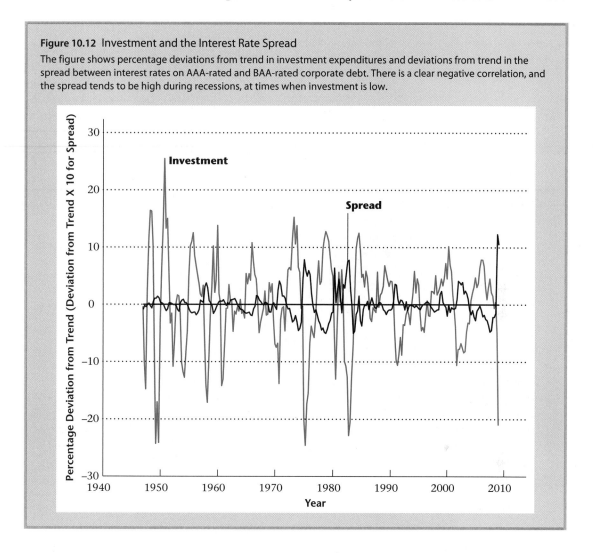

Figure 10.12 Investment and the Interest Rate Spread

The figure shows percentage deviations from trend in investment expenditures and deviations from trend in the spread between interest rates on AAA-rated and BAA-rated corporate debt. There is a clear negative correlation, and the spread tends to be high during recessions, at times when investment is low.

Competitive Equilibrium

Our analysis thus far has focused on the behavior of the representative consumer, the representative firm, and the government in two markets, the current-period labor market and the current-period market for goods. In this real intertemporal model, the representative consumer supplies labor in the current-period labor market, and demands consumption goods in the current-period goods market. The representative firm demands labor in the current period, supplies goods in the current period, and demands investment goods in the current period. Finally, the government demands goods in the current period, in terms of government purchases.

Perceptive readers might wonder why we have neglected the future markets for labor and goods and the market for credit. First, markets in the future are neglected to

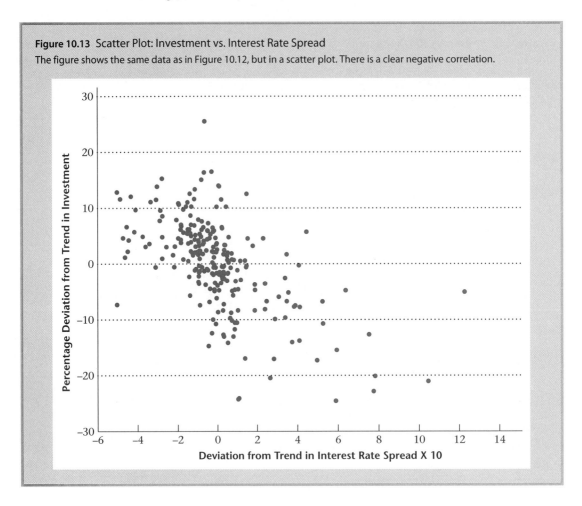

Figure 10.13 Scatter Plot: Investment vs. Interest Rate Spread
The figure shows the same data as in Figure 10.12, but in a scatter plot. There is a clear negative correlation.

make our model simple to work with, and this simplification is essentially harmless at this level of analysis. Second, later in this chapter, we show that we have not actually neglected the credit market, as equilibrium in the current-period goods market implies that the credit market clears, just as we showed in the two-period model in Chapter 8.

This section shows how a competitive equilibrium for our model, where supply equals demand in the current-period labor and goods markets, can be expressed in terms of diagrams. We put together the labor supply and labor demand curves to capture how the labor market functions; then, we derive an output supply curve that describes how the supply of goods is related to the real interest rate. Finally, we derive an output demand curve, which describes how the sum of the demand for goods from the representative consumer (consumption goods), the representative firm (investment goods), and the government (government purchases) is related to the real interest rate. Putting the output demand and supply curves together in a diagram with the labor market gives us a working model, which is used to address some key issues in macroeconomics in the following sections and in later chapters.

The Current Labor Market and the Output Supply Curve

First, we consider how the market for labor in the current period works. In Figure 10.14(a), we show the labor demand curve for the representative firm and the labor supply curve for the representative consumer, as derived in the previous sections, with the current real wage w on the vertical axis and the current quantity of labor, N, on the horizontal axis. Recall from earlier sections in this chapter that the labor supply curve slopes upward, as we are assuming that the substitution effect of an increase in the real wage dominates the income effect, and recall that the position of the labor supply curve depends on the real interest rate r. Also, we determined that an increase (decrease) in the real interest rate causes an increase (decrease) in labor supply for each real wage w, and the labor supply curve shifts to the right (left). Given the real interest rate r, the equilibrium real wage in Figure 10.14(a), is w^*, the equilibrium quantity of employment is N^*, and from the production function in Figure 10.14(b), we determine the quantity of aggregate output supplied (given the real interest rate), which is Y^*. Recall from Chapter 4 that the position of the production function is determined by current total factor productivity z and by the current capital stock K. An increase in z or K would shift the production function up.

Our next step is to use the diagrams in Figure 10.14 to derive an output supply curve, which describes how much output is supplied by firms for each possible level for the real interest rate. In Figure 10.15(a), the labor supply curves for two different interest rates, r_1 and r_2, are shown, where $r_1 < r_2$. Thus, with the increase in the real interest rate, the current labor supply curve shifts to the right, the current equilibrium real wage falls from w_1 to w_2, and current employment increases from N_1 to N_2. Further, current output increases from Y_1 to Y_2, in Figure 10.15(b), from the production function. We can then construct a curve, called the **output supply curve**, which is an upward-sloping curve consisting of all combinations of current output and real interest rates, (Y,r), for which the current labor market is in equilibrium. This curve is denoted Y^s in Figure 10.15(c). Two points on the Y^s curve are (Y_1, r_1) and (Y_2, r_2), because at real interest rate r_1 the labor market is in equilibrium when the representative firm produces current output Y_1 and at real interest rate r_2 the labor market is in equilibrium when the representative firm produces current output Y_2. Thus, the output supply curve slopes upward because of the intertemporal substitution effect on labor supply. If the real interest rate is higher, the representative consumer will choose to supply more labor, resulting in an increase in employment and output.

Shifts in the Output Supply Curve   When we work with our real intertemporal model, we need to know how changes in particular exogenous variables shift supply and demand curves. In this subsection, we show how three factors—lifetime wealth, current total factor productivity, and the current capital stock—can shift the output supply curve. The latter two factors have much the same effect, so we deal with these together.

The output supply curve shifts either because of a shift in the current labor supply curve (not arising because of a change in the real interest rate; the output supply curve already takes this into account), because of a shift in the current labor demand curve, or because of a shift in the production function. From our analysis of consumer behavior, we know that a change in lifetime wealth shifts the labor supply curve, whereas a change in either current total factor productivity or the current capital stock

Figure 10.14 Determination of Equilibrium in the Labor Market Given the Real Interest Rate r

In (a), the intersection of the current labor supply and demand curves determines the current real wage and current employment, and the production function in (b) then determines aggregate output.

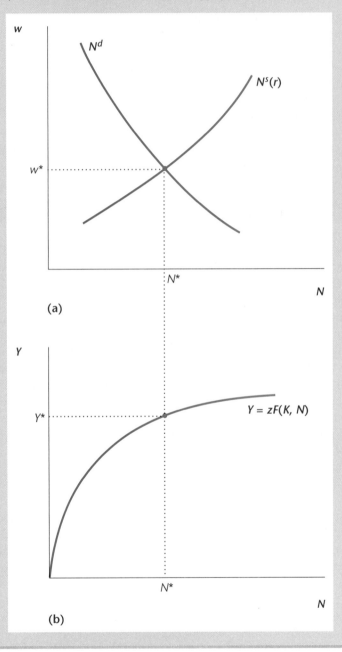

Figure 10.15 Construction of the Output Supply Curve

The output supply curve Y^s is an upward-sloping curve in panel (c) of the figure, consisting of real current output and real interest rate pairs for which the labor market is in equilibrium.

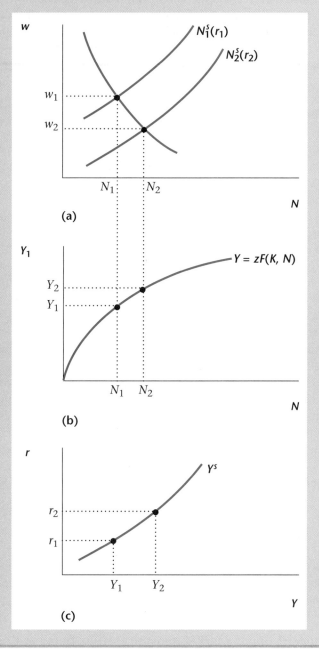

shifts the labor demand curve and the production function. We deal with each of these shifts in turn.

Recall from our discussion of the representative consumer's behavior, earlier in this chapter, that a decrease in lifetime wealth reduces the consumer's demand for current leisure, due to an income effect, and so the consumer supplies more labor for any current real wage. Therefore, the labor supply curve shifts to the right. What would cause a reduction in lifetime wealth for the representative consumer? The key factor, from our point of view, is an increase in government spending, either in the present or the future. From the present-value government budget constraint, equation (10-18), any increase in government spending, either in the present or the future (that is an increase in G or G') must be reflected in an increase in the present value of taxes for the consumer, $T + \frac{T'}{1+r}$. Therefore an increase in G, in G', or in both, results in an increase in the lifetime tax burden for the representative consumer. In Figure 10.16(a), this causes a shift to the right in the labor supply curve from $N_1^s(r_1)$ to $N_2^s(r_1)$, as there is a negative income effect on current leisure.

The shift to the right in the labor supply curve in Figure 10.16(a) implies that, for a given real interest rate, the equilibrium quantity of employment in the labor market is higher; that is, employment rises from N_1 to N_2 in Figure 10.16(a), given a particular real interest rate r_1. From the production function in Figure 10.16(b), output rises from Y_1 to Y_2 given the real interest rate r_1. This then implies that the output supply curve shifts to the right, from Y_1^s to Y_2^s, in 10.16(c). That is, output is higher for each possible value for the real interest rate. The conclusion is that *an increase in G or G' shifts the labor supply curve to the right and shifts the output supply curve to the right, because of the income effect on labor supply.*

From Chapter 4, recall that an increase in total factor productivity or in the capital stock shifts the production function up, because more output can be produced for any level of the labor input, and the labor demand curve shifts to the right, because the marginal product of labor increases. In our model, an increase in current total factor productivity z, or in the current capital stock K, causes the production function to shift up. In Figure 10.17(b) we show the results of an increase in z from z_1 to z_2, but the effect of an increase in K would be identical. The labor demand curve shifts to the right in Figure 10.17(a), from N_1^d to N_2^d. As a result, given the real interest rate r_1, the equilibrium quantity of employment rises from N_1 to N_2. Therefore, from the production function in Figure 10.17(b), as employment is higher and z is higher, output increases from Y_1 to Y_2. The same effects (an increase in employment and output) would happen for any level of the real interest rate, which implies that the output supply curve in Figure 10.17(c) must shift to the right. The results would be identical if there had been an increase in the current capital stock. The conclusion is that *an increase in z or K causes the production function to shift up, the labor demand curve to shift to the right, and the output supply curve to shift to the right.*

The Current Goods Market and the Output Demand Curve

Now that we understand how the current labor market works and how the output supply curve is constructed, we can turn to the functioning of the current-period goods market and the construction of the output demand curve. This then completes our model.

Figure 10.16 An Increase in Current or Future Government Spending Shifts the Y^s Curve

This is because the increase in government spending increases the present value of taxes for the representative consumer, and current leisure falls, shifting the labor supply curve to the right in (a) and shifting the output supply curve to the right in (c).

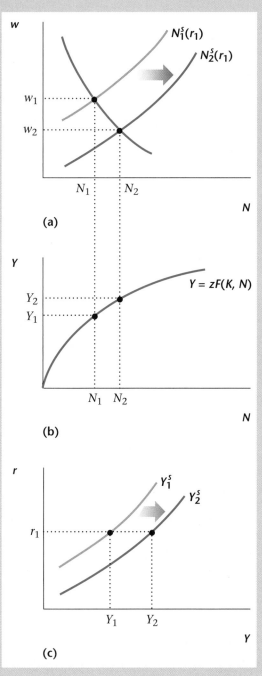

(a)

(b)

(c)

Figure 10.17 An Increase in Current Total Factor Productivity Shifts the Y^s Curve

This is because an increase in z increases the marginal product of current labor, shifting the labor demand curve to the right in (a), and also shifting the production function up in (b). As a result, the output supply curve shifts to the right in (c).

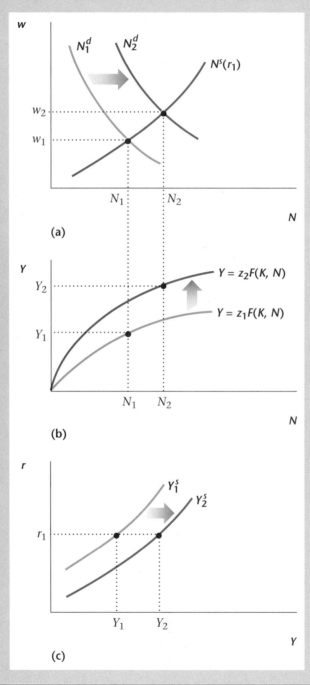

The total current demand for goods Y^d is the sum of the demand for current consumption goods by the representative consumer, $C^d(Y^d, r)$, the demand for investment goods by the representative firm, $I^d(r)$, and government purchases of current goods, G:

$$Y^d = C^d(r) + I^d(r) + G. \tag{10-19}$$

Here, we use the notation $C^d(r)$ and $I^d(r)$ to reflect how the demand for current consumption goods and the demand for investment goods depend negatively on the real interest rate, r. Recall from our treatment of consumer behavior earlier in this chapter that the demand for current consumption goods also depends on the lifetime wealth of the representative consumer, one component of which is current income. In Figure 10.18 we show the total demand for goods, the right-hand side of (10-19), as a function of current aggregate income, Y. Since the demands for investment goods and government purchases do not depend on aggregate income, the slope of the curve $C^d(r) + I^d(r) + G$ in the figure is the marginal propensity to consume, MPC. What will be the equilibrium demand for current goods in the market, given the real interest rate, r? This will be determined by the point at which the curve $C^d(r) + I^d(r) + G$ intersects the 45° line,

Figure 10.18 The Demand for Current Goods

This is an upward-sloping curve, as the demand for consumption goods increases with current income. The slope of the demand curve for current goods is the marginal propensity to consume (*MPC*).

that is where the demand for goods induced by the quantity of income Y (through the dependence of the demand for consumption goods on income) is just equal to Y. Therefore, in Figure 10.18 the demand for current goods is Y_1, which is the quantity of aggregate income that generates a total demand for goods just equal to that quantity of aggregate income.

The next step is to construct the **output demand curve**, which is a negative relationship between current aggregate output and the real interest rate. In Figure 10.19(a), if the real interest rate is r_1, the current demand for goods is $C^d(r_1) + I^d(r_1) + G$. If the real interest rate were r_2 with $r_2 > r_1$, the current demand for goods will fall for each level of aggregate current income Y, as the demand for current consumption goods and for current investment goods will be lower. Thus, the demand for goods will shift down to $C^d(r_2) + I^d(r_2) + G$. As a result, the equilibrium quantity of goods demanded will fall from Y_1 to Y_2. Now, in Figure 10.19(b), we can construct a downward-sloping curve in a diagram with the real interest rate, r, on the vertical axis, and current aggregate income, Y, on the horizontal axis. This curve, Y^d, is the output demand curve, and a point on the curve, (Y,r), represents the level of demand for goods (output), Y, given the real interest rate r. Note that two points on the output demand curve are (Y_1, r_1) and (Y_2, r_2), corresponding to Figure 10.19(a).

Shifts in the Output Demand Curve   Before we put all the elements of our real intertemporal model together—the output demand curve, the output supply curve, the production function, and the current labor supply and demand curves—we need to understand the important factors that shift the output demand curve. The output demand curve shifts as the result of a shift in the demand for current consumption goods, $C^d(r)$, a shift in the demand for investment goods, $I^d(r)$, or because of a change in the current quantity of government purchases G. In Figure 10.20 we show the effects of an increase in the demand for goods coming from an increase in government spending, from G_1 to G_2. In Figure 10.20(a), the demand for current goods shifts up when current government purchases increase from G_1 to G_2. Then, given the real interest rate r_1, the quantity of current goods demanded will increase from Y_1 to Y_2. As a result, in Figure 10.20(b), the output demand curve shifts to the right from Y_1^d to Y_2^d; that is, the quantity of current goods demanded is higher for any real interest rate, including r_1. Other important factors that will shift the Y^d curve to the right, in a manner identical to the results for an increase in G in Figure 10.20 are the following:

- *A decrease in the present value of taxes shifts the Y^d curve to the right.*   A decrease in the present value of taxes is caused by a reduction in current taxes, future taxes, or both. When this happens, the lifetime wealth of the representative consumer rises, and therefore the demand for consumption goods, $C^d(r)$, increases, which causes a shift to the right in the output demand curve.
- *An increase in future income Y' shifts the Y^d curve to the right.*   If the representative consumer anticipates that his or her future income will be higher, then lifetime wealth increases, resulting in an increase in the demand for current consumption goods, $C^d(r)$.

Figure 10.19 Construction of the Output Demand Curve

The output demand curve Y^d in (b) is a downward-sloping one describing the combinations of real output and the real interest rate for which the current goods market is in equilibrium.

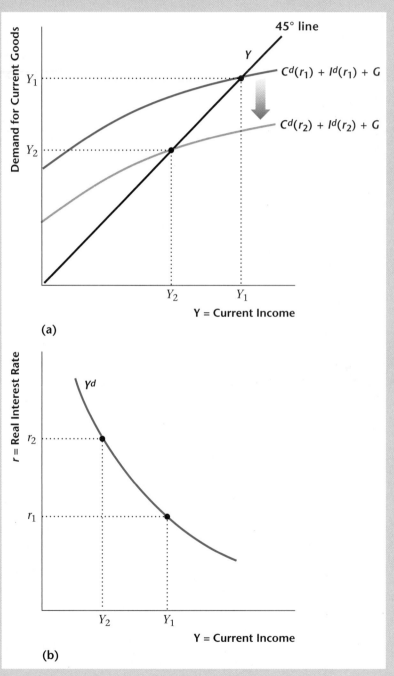

(a)

(b)

Figure 10.20 The Output Demand Curve Shifts to the Right if Current Government Spending Increases

The curve shifts in similar manner if taxes decrease (in the present or the future), if future income is anticipated to increase, if future total factor productivity is expected to increase, or if the current capital stock declines.

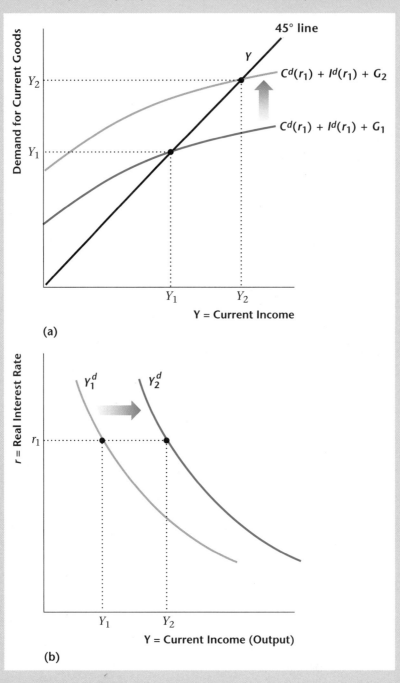

- *An increase in future total factor productivity z' causes the Y^d curve to shift to the right.* If the representative firm expects total factor productivity to be higher in the future, this increases the firm's demand for goods, so that $I^d(r)$ increases.

- *A decrease in the current capital stock K causes the Y^d curve to shift to the right.* When there is a lower current capital stock, perhaps because of destruction, then the demand for investment goods, $I^d(r)$, increases for each r.

The Complete Real Intertemporal Model

We now have all the building blocks for our real intertemporal model, so we can put these building blocks together and use the model to address some interesting economic issues. Our model is presented in Figure 10.21, where a competitive equilibrium consists of a state of affairs where supply equals demand in the current labor market in panel (a) and in the current goods market in panel (b). In Figure 10.21(a), N^d is the current labor demand curve, while $N^s(r)$ is the current labor supply curve, which shifts with the real interest rate r. The equilibrium real wage is given by w^*, and the equilibrium quantity of employment is N^*, where w^* and N^* are determined by the intersection of the demand and supply curves for current labor. Equilibrium output and the equilibrium real interest rate are Y^* and r^*, respectively, in Figure 10.21(b), and they are determined by the intersection of the output demand curve Y^d with the output supply curve Y^s.

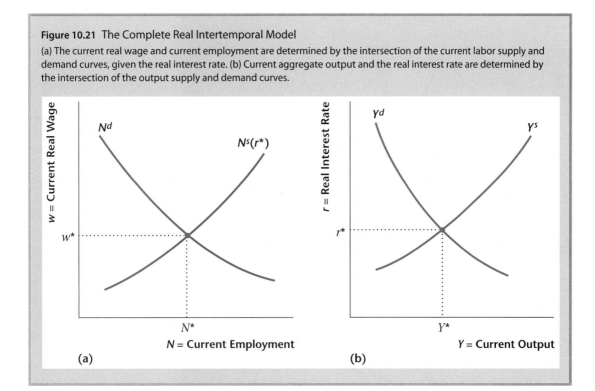

Figure 10.21 The Complete Real Intertemporal Model

(a) The current real wage and current employment are determined by the intersection of the current labor supply and demand curves, given the real interest rate. (b) Current aggregate output and the real interest rate are determined by the intersection of the output supply and demand curves.

To use the model to help us understand how the macroeconomy works, we perform some experiments. These experiments each involve changing the value of some exogenous variable or variables, and then asking how the solution of the model is different as a result. We then show how we interpret the results of these experiments in terms of real-world macroeconomic events. Our experiments answer the following questions:

1. How does an increase in current government purchases, anticipated to be temporary, affect current macroeconomic variables?

2. What are the effects on current macroeconomic variables of a decrease in the current capital stock, brought about by a natural disaster or a war?

3. How does a temporary increase in total factor productivity affect macroeconomic variables, and how does this fit the key business cycle facts?

4. If total factor productivity is expected to increase in the future, how does this affect current macroeconomic variables?

5. How does increased uncertainty in credit markets affect macroeconomic activity?

The Equilibrium Effects of a Temporary Increase in G: Stimulus, the Multiplier, and Crowding Out

This may seem like ground we have covered already, as we analyzed the effects of a change in government purchases in the one-period model in Chapter 5. There, we learned that there is an income effect of government spending which acts to increase labor supply and output, and that government spending acts to crowd out private consumption. What we will learn using the real intertemporal model is, first, how the intertemporal choices of consumers affect the economy's response to a change in government spending. An increase in G will act to increase the real interest rate, and this will introduce additional crowding-out effects on private spending working through both investment and consumption. Further, there will be an intertemporal substitution effect on labor supply as a result of the interest rate increase. Second, we will be able to study in detail the workings of the "Keynesian multiplier," familiar from most introductory macroeconomics courses, and show how the typical approach to the multiplier mechanism can be misleading.

We will model a temporary increase in government spending as an increase in G, the quantity of government purchases in the current period, leaving future government purchases, G', unchanged. When would the government choose to increase its expenditures on goods and services temporarily? An important example is a war. Typically, wars are known to be temporary (although their length can be uncertain), and the government commits spending to the war effort that will not remain in place when the war is over. Another example of an explicitly temporary change in government spending is the spending allocation contained in the American Recovery and Reinvestment Act (ARRA) of 2009, previously discussed in Chapters 5 and 8.

For this particular experiment with the real intertemporal model, it will be useful to start by working with a diagram like Figure 10.18, although this stage of the analysis will not be necessary for the other experiments we will study next. For those experiments, a diagram like Figure 10.21 is all that is necessary.

Now, suppose that government purchases increase from G_1 to G_2 during the current period. In Figure 10.22, to make our arguments simple, suppose that the marginal propensity to consume, MPC, is a constant that does not depend on income or the real interest rate, so that the curve describing the demand for goods is a straight line with slope MPC. In the figure, the initial demand for goods is given by the line $C_1^d(r) + I(r) + G_1$. Now, when current government spending increases, there will be a direct effect on the total demand for goods, equal to the increase in government spending, $G_2 - G_1$. In addition, we have to take account of the effect that government spending has on consumption, as taxes must increase, either in the present or the future to finance government spending. This will then reduce the lifetime wealth of the consumer. From the government's present value budget constraint, equation (10-18), an increase in G on the left-hand side of the equation must be matched by an equal increase in the present value of taxes on the right-hand side of the equation, so that lifetime wealth for the consumer must fall by $G_2 - G_1$. Note here that it is irrelevant whether the increase in government spending is financed by an increase in current taxes or by the issue of government bonds (which results in an increase in future taxes), as we know from the Ricardian equivalence theorem discussed in Chapter 8.

How will the decrease in lifetime wealth affect the demand for consumption goods? This is determined by the marginal propensity to consume. That is, the change in the demand for consumption goods is $-MPC(G_2 - G_1)$, minus the marginal propensity to

Figure 10.22 The Effect of an Increase in G on the Total Demand for Goods

The demand for goods as a function of current income Y shifts up by the amount $(1 - MPC)(G_2 - G_1)$. The increase in total demand for goods is $Y_2^d - Y_1^d$, and the expenditure multiplier is the ratio of the the distance AB to the distance DF, which is 1.

consume multiplied by the decrease in lifetime wealth. Thus, the total change in the demand for goods is the direct effect on government spending plus the indirect effect on consumption, or $(1 - MPC)(G_2 - G_1)$.

Now, given the direct effect on government spending and the indirect effect on the demand for consumption goods, in Figure 10.22, the demand for goods shifts up to $C_2^d(r) + I(r) + G_2$, which is a shift up by $(1 - MPC)(G_2 - G_1)$, that is the difference $C_2^d(r) - C_1^d(r) = -MPC(G_2 - G_1)$ is the indirect effect on consumption of the decrease in lifetime wealth. The net effect on the total demand for goods is then determined by the intersection of the demand relationship with the 45-degree line in Figure 10.22, so that the total demand for output increases from Y_1^d to Y_2^d. From the figure, it is possible to determine exactly the difference $Y_2^d - Y_1^d$. The distance AB is equal to $Y_2^d - Y_1^d$, and since A and F are both on the 45-degree line, the distance AB is equal to the distance BF. Further, since the distance DF is equal to $(1 - MPC)(G_2 - G_1)$, and the slope of AD is equal to MPC, we have

$$MPC = \frac{\text{length}(BD)}{\text{length}(AB)} = \frac{Y_2^d - Y_1^d - (1 - MPC)(G_2 - G_1)}{Y_2^d - Y_1^d} \tag{10-20}$$

Then, solving equation (10-20) for $Y_2^d - Y_1^d$, we obtain

$$Y_2^d - Y_1^d = G_2 - G_1,$$

so that the total increase in the demand for goods generated by the increase in government spending is equal to the increase in government spending. That is, what we will call the **partial expenditure multiplier**, which is the ratio of the total increase in demand for goods to the increase in government spending is

$$\frac{Y_2^d - Y_1^d}{G_2 - G_1} = 1.$$

Figure 10.22 looks much like the "Keynesian cross" analysis that many students are exposed to in introductory macroeconomics courses. Keynesians typically argue that the partial expenditure multiplier for government spending is greater than 1, because they ignore the negative effect of the increase in taxes (present or future) on the demand for consumption goods. Basic Keynesian analysis also ignores production and intertemporal substitution, which will be key elements in the analysis that follows. What we have done so far is only an analysis of the effects of the increase in G on the demand side of the goods market. What remains is to work out the supply-side effects.

Before the increase in current government purchases, G, in Figure 10.23, the economy is in equilibrium with a current real wage, w_1, current employment, N_1, current output, Y_1, and real interest rate, r_1. When G increases, this will have two effects, one on output supply and one on output demand. We have determined the effect on output demand, which is a shift to the right in the output demand curve, from Y_1^d to Y_2^d, where the horizontal shift is equal to the increase in G. Since lifetime wealth decreases due to the increase in the present value of taxes, leisure will decrease (leisure is a normal good) for the representative consumer, given the current real wage, and so the labor

Figure 10.23 A Temporary Increase in Government Purchases

The increase in G shifts the labor supply curve to the right, the output supply curve to the right, and the output demand curve to the right. The real interest rate rises, and aggregate output increases in equilibrium. There is an additional shift to the right in the labor supply curve because of the increase in r, so employment rises and the real wage falls in equilibrium.

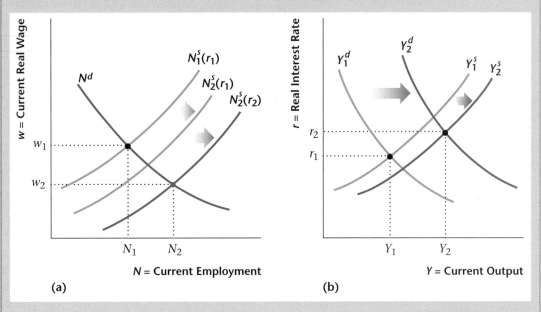

(a)

(b)

supply curve in Figure 10.23(a) shifts to the right from $N_1^s(r_1)$ to $N_2^s(r_1)$, and the output supply curve in Figure 10.23(b) shifts to the right from Y_1^s to Y_2^s.

To determine all the equilibrium effects by using the model, we start first with Figure 10.23(b). It is clear that current aggregate output must increase, as both the output demand and output supply curves shift to the right, and so Y increases from Y_1 to Y_2. It may appear that the real interest rate may rise or fall; however, there is strong theoretical support for an increase in the real interest rate. This is because the temporary increase in government spending should lead to only a small decrease in lifetime wealth for the consumer, which will produce a small effect on labor supply. Therefore, there should be only a small shift to the right in the Y^s curve, and the real interest rate will rise, as in Figure 10.23(b).

What is the **total government expenditure multiplier** here, by which we mean the ratio of the equilibrium increase in real output to the increase in government spending? Since the output demand curve in Figure 10.23(b) shifted to the right by the increase in government spending, the equilibrium increase in current output—the difference $y_2 - y_1$—must be less than the increase in government spending. The total multiplier is less than 1, and it will become smaller as the size of the wealth effect on labor supply falls (this makes the rightward shift in the output supply curve smaller), and as the intertemporal substitution effect of the real interest rate on labor supply falls (this makes the output supply curve steeper).

As mentioned previously, Keynesians typically argue that the total government expenditure multiplier is larger than 1, which makes it appear that society can get something for nothing. In basic Keynesian analysis, each dollar spent by the government increases GDP by more than one dollar. If we followed this idea to its logical conclusion, we would let the government grow infinitely large, which would make everyone infinitely wealthy. Our analysis makes clear that the multiplier must be smaller than 1, that government spending comes at a cost, and that the capacity of the government to increase GDP is limited.

Keynesian ideas are explored in detail in Chapters 12 and 13. These ideas are based on the notion that price and wage inflexibility causes the economy to behave differently in the short run than it does in the long run. A Keynesian might view the analysis done in this chapter as being applicable only to the long run where prices and wages are flexible. However, many modern macroeconomists argue that price and wage inflexibility is unimportant for the behavior of the macroeconomy, and that analysis based on optimal choice by consumers and firms in equilibrium is the appropriate approach to analyzing both short-run and long-run macroeconomic problems.

What happens to current consumption in Figure 10.23? If the real interest rate did not change in equilibrium (for example, if the output supply curve were horizontal), we know from the figure that real income would increase by an amount equal to the increase in government spending. If this occurred, then the change in the consumer's lifetime wealth would be zero, since the increase in the present value of taxes is equal to the increase in current income. As a result, current consumption would be unchanged. However, in Figure 10.23(b) the real interest rate rises in equilibrium, so the representative consumer will substitute future consumption for current consumption, and therefore current consumption declines. As well, investment expenditures must decrease because of the increase in the real interest rate. Thus, both components of private expenditure (current consumption and investment) are crowded out by current government expenditure. Recall from Chapter 5 that when we analyzed the effects of an increase in government spending in the one-period model, without taking intertemporal substitution and investment into account, government spending crowded out only consumption expenditure. Since government spending is shown here to crowd out private investment expenditure, a further cost of government is that it reduces the economy's future productive capacity, as the future capital stock will be lower (than it otherwise would have been).

On the demand side of the goods market, it is the crowding out of private consumption and investment expenditure that causes the total government expenditure multiplier to be less than 1 here. On the supply side, output increases because of two effects on labor supply. First, just as in our Chapter 5 analysis, there is a negative wealth effect on leisure from the increase in lifetime tax liabilities. Second, the increase in the real interest rate makes future leisure cheaper relative to current leisure, and there is a further increase in labor supply. Basic Keynesian analysis, as represented in typical Keynesian cross diagrams, neglects both the crowding-out effects and the effects on the supply side of the goods market.

The next step is to work through the effects of the increase in the real interest rate for the labor market. In Figure 10.23(a), given the initial interest rate r_1, the labor supply curve shifts from $N_1^s(r_1)$ to $N_2^s(r_1)$, because of the negative wealth effect arising from the increase in the present value of taxes. With an increase in the equilibrium real interest rate to r_2, the labor supply curve shifts further to the right, to $N_2^s(r_2)$. Therefore, the equilibrium real wage falls from w_1 to w_2.

What this analysis tells us is that increased temporary government spending, although it leads to higher aggregate output, comes at a cost. With higher current government spending, the representative consumer consumes less and takes less leisure, and he or she also faces a lower real wage rate. Further, current investment spending is lower, which implies that the capital stock will be lower in the future, and the future capacity of the economy for producing goods will be lower.

Perspectives on the Financial Crisis
The Total Government Spending Multiplier: Barro vs. Romer

The value of the total government spending multiplier was a key issue in the U.S. federal government's analysis of the effects of the American Recovery and Reinvestment Act (ARRA) of 2009, and the public debate about these effects. On one side of this debate were economists such as Robert Barro, who wrote on this issue in a Wall Street Journal article on January 22, 2009,[1] arguing essentially along the same lines as what we have laid out in our model in this section. In particular, he stated that "government spending is no free lunch," and that theory tells us that the total government spending multiplier can be at most 1 and will be reduced to the extent that government spending crowds out private expenditures on consumption, investment, and net exports (net exports were of course omitted from our analysis here). Barro also cites his own empirical work on government spending in wartime, suggesting an estimate for the multiplier of 0.8.

Barro's arguments are countered in a speech made by Christina Romer, the Chair of the Council of Economic Advisers, on February 27, 2009.[2] Romer does not lay out much of a theoretical

argument, but relies mainly on empirical work. At the center of her argument is the statement that:

> In estimating the effects of the recovery package, Jared Bernstein [Chief Economist and Economic Policy Adviser to Vice President Joseph Biden] and I used tax and spending multipliers from very conventional macroeconomic models. ... In these models, [the] spending ... multiplier [is] ... about 1.6.

What Romer means by "very conventional models" are large-scale Keynesian models fit to data. Such models are by no means conventional in the sense of being widely accepted. Indeed, a large group of professional economists thinks of these models as essentially useless, principally because they do not satisfy the Lucas critique, discussed briefly in Chapter 1. The principle behind the Lucas critique is that, to be useful for evaluating policy, macroeconomic models need to incorporate the basic building blocks of preferences, endowments, and technology, which are invariant to changes in economic policy. "Conventional" Keynesian macroeconomic models do not satisfy the Lucas critique and therefore give incorrect answers to such questions as "How large is the multiplier?"

[1]See http://online.wsj.com/article/SB123258618204604599.html
[2]See http://news.uchicago.edu/files/newsrelease_20090227.pdf

(Continued)

Romer not only feels confident about making policy recommendations based on a total government spending multiplier of 1.6. She goes even further, in stating, "... I feel quite confident that conventional multipliers are far more likely to be too small than too large."

In our real intertemporal model, one would have to work quite hard to obtain a multiplier of 1.6. We could obtain a multiplier of 1 if the output supply curve were horizontal, which would require an infinitely large elasticity of labor supply with respect to the interest rate—consumers would have to be highly willing to substitute leisure intertemporally in response to interest rate changes. To get a multiplier larger than 1 would require that government spending be financed by borrowing and that Ricardian equivalence not hold. The former is certainly true for the ARRA, which is in fact combined with cuts in taxes.

Thus, all the spending increases in the ARRA represent deferred taxation. For Ricardian equivalence not to hold, however, requires that a large fraction of consumers be credit-constrained and therefore willing to spend each extra dollar of current disposable income on consumption. In fact, Romer argues that the financial crisis likely has made credit constraints matter more for consumers, which is certainly true. However, according to her reasoning, this is an argument for a multiplier larger than 1.6, since she views the 1.6 estimate as coming from "normal" times.

In conclusion, Romer's case looks dubious in light of our analysis here and the arguments in Barro's *Wall Street Journal* article. However, to be fair to Romer, we will need to go into more depth on how Keynesian economics works, as this is at the heart of her argument. This will have to wait until Chapter 13.

The Equilibrium Effects of a Decrease in the Current Capital Stock *K*

Over time, through investment, a nation adds to its capital stock, and this generally occurs slowly, as investment expenditure is typically quite small relative to the total capital stock. Thus, increases in capital do not contribute much to short-run fluctuations in aggregate output and employment. However, sometimes major reductions in the aggregate capital stock occur over a short period of time. For example, a war can leave a country with a much lower capital stock, as happened due to bombing in Germany, Great Britain, and Japan during World War II; in Vietnam during the Vietnam War; and in Iraq during the recent conflict. The capital stock can also be reduced because of natural disasters such as floods and hurricanes.

In this subsection, we examine the effects of an experiment in our model in which the current capital stock K is reduced. That is, suppose that the representative firm begins the current period with a lower capital stock K. This affects both the supply and the demand for output. First, a decrease in K from K_1 to K_2 decreases the current marginal product of labor, which shifts the current demand for labor curve to the left from N_1^d to N_2^d in Figure 10.24(a). The output supply curve then shifts to the left, from Y_1^s to Y_2^s in Figure 10.24(b). Second, a decrease in K increases investment by the firm, because the future marginal product of capital will be higher. This shifts the output demand curve to the right in Figure 10.24(b), from Y_1^d to Y_2^d. The result is that, in equilibrium, in Figure 10.24(b), the real interest rate must rise from r_1 to r_2, but the effect on current aggregate output is ambiguous, depending on whether the output supply effect is

Figure 10.24 The Equilibrium Effects of a Decrease in the Current Capital Stock

If the current capital stock falls—for example, because of a natural disaster—then the output demand curve shifts to the right and the output supply curve shifts to the left. The real interest rate rises, but current output may rise or fall.

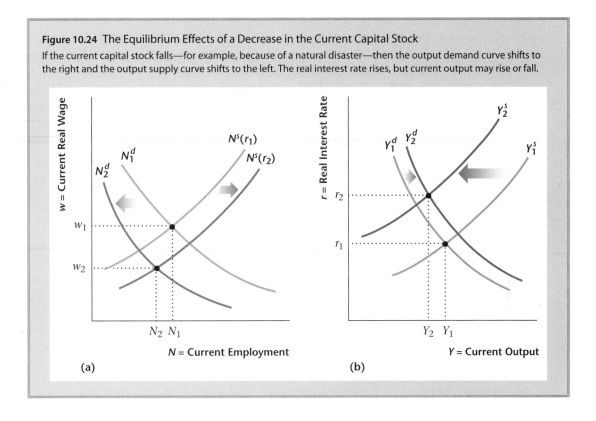

(a)

(b)

larger or smaller than the output demand effect. In the figure, we have drawn the case where the output supply effect dominates, so that current real output falls. Empirically, there may be circumstances, such as with natural disasters, where aggregate output may not fall.

In Figure 10.24 current consumption must fall, because the real interest rate has increased. The effects on investment appear to be ambiguous, because the decrease in K causes investment to increase, while the increase in the equilibrium real interest rate causes investment to fall. However, investment must rise, because less capital would otherwise cause ever-decreasing investment, which would be inconsistent with the fact that the marginal product of capital rises as the quantity of capital falls. That is, as the quantity of capital falls, the marginal product of capital rises, making the return on investment very high, so that ultimately investment must increase if the capital stock decreases.

Because of the increase in the real interest rate, there is intertemporal substitution of leisure, with the representative consumer working harder in the current period for each current real wage w. Therefore, the labor supply curve shifts to the right in Figure 10.24(a) from $N^s(r_1)$ to $N^s(r_2)$. This reinforces the effect of the decrease in labor demand on the real wage, and so the real wage must fall, from w_1 to w_2. The equilibrium effect on the quantity of labor is ambiguous, because the effect on labor demand and on labor supply work in opposite directions on the quantity of employment. In Figure 10.24(a), we show employment falling from N_1 to N_2.

Now, suppose that we interpret these results in terms of the macroeconomic effects of a natural disaster or a war that destroys part of the nation's capital stock. The model shows that there are two effects on the quantity of output. The lower quantity of capital implies that less output can be produced for a given quantity of labor input, which tends to reduce output. However, the lower quantity of capital acts to increase investment to replace the destroyed capital, which tends to increase output. Theoretically, it is not clear whether output increases or decreases, and there appear to be empirical cases in which the output supply and output demand effects roughly cancel, for example during and after large natural disasters such as the Mississippi floods in 1993, and Hurricane Katrina in 2005.

The Equilibrium Effects of an Increase in Current Total Factor Productivity z

Temporary changes in total factor productivity are an important cause of business cycles. Recall from Chapter 4 that an increase in total factor productivity could be caused by good weather, a favorable change in government regulations, a new invention, a decrease in the relative price of energy, or any other factor that results in more aggregate output being produced with the same factor inputs.

The experiment we examine here in our real intertemporal model is to increase current total factor productivity z, and then determine the effects of this change on current aggregate output, the real interest rate, current employment, the current real wage, current consumption, and investment. If current total factor productivity increases, the marginal product of labor goes up for each quantity of labor input, and so in Figure 10.25(a) the demand for labor curve shifts to the right, from N_1^d to N_2^d. Therefore, in Figure 10.25(b), the output supply curve shifts to the right, from N_1^s to N_2^s, and in equilibrium the quantity of output rises and the real interest rate must fall, from r_1 to r_2. The decrease in the real interest rate leads to increases in both consumption and investment.

In the labor market, the decrease in the real interest rate causes intertemporal substitution of leisure between the current and future periods, with current leisure increasing, and so the labor supply curve shifts to the left in Figure 10.25(a), from $N^s(r_1)$ to $N^s(r_2)$. In equilibrium, the real wage must increase from w_1 to w_2, but the net effect on the equilibrium quantity of employment is ambiguous. Empirically, however, the effect of the real interest rate on labor supply is small and, as in Figure 10.25(a), employment rises from N_1 to N_2.

When total factor productivity increases, this increases the current demand for labor, which raises the market real wage. With the real wage increase, workers are willing to supply more labor, employment increases, and output increases. In the goods market, the increased supply of goods decreases the market real interest rate, which results in an increased demand for investment goods and consumption goods, so that the demand for goods rises to meet the increased supply of goods on the market. As well, the increase in current income increases consumption.

From Chapter 3, recall that some key business cycle facts are that consumption, investment, employment, the real wage, and average labor productivity are procyclical. Our real intertemporal model predicts these comovements in the data if the economy receives temporary shocks to total factor productivity. That is, because Figure 10.25 predicts that

Figure 10.25 The Equilibrium Effects of an Increase in Current Total Factor Productivity

When total factor productivity increases temporarily, the output supply curve shifts to the right in(b), with the real interest rate falling and aggregate output rising. Investment and consumption rise, and employment and the real wage increase in (a).

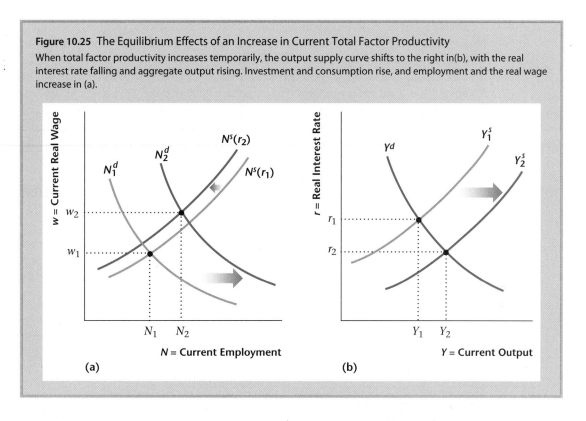

(a)

(b)

a temporary increase in total factor productivity increases aggregate output, consumption, investment, employment, and the real wage, the model predicts that consumption, investment, employment, and the real wage are procyclical, just as in the data. As well, the average product of labor must be higher when z increases, because an increase in z makes the marginal product of labor higher for each quantity of labor, and the marginal product of labor is higher in equilibrium for the last worker hired. Thus, temporary shocks to total factor productivity are a candidate as a cause of business cycles. Indeed, the proponents of real business cycle theory, which we study in detail in Chapter 12, argue that total factor productivity shocks are the most important cause of business cycles.

The Equilibrium Effects of an Increase in Future Total Factor Productivity, z': News About the Future and Aggregate Economic Activity

The anticipation of future events can have important macroeconomic consequences in the present, as when an increase in total factor productivity is expected to happen in the future. For example, firms might learn of a new invention, such as the design for a new production process, which is not available currently but will come on line in the future. We will see that this shock increases current investment, current output, and current employment, and reduces the real wage.

News about future events and the influence of this news has played an important role in macroeconomic theory. For example, Keynes had in interest in the "animal spirits" of financial market investors and the influence of swings in investor sentiment on economic activity. Indeed, the stock market represents a forum in which people take bets on the future health of firms in the economy. Therefore, news that is informative about future productivity will tend to be reflected first in stock prices. In financial market theory, stock prices are typically the reflection of the average stock market participant's views on firms' future dividends, which are in good part determined by the future total factor productivity of firms. Recent empirical research in macroeconomics supports the view that news about future events is a key determinant of aggregate economic activity in the present.[3]

To capture the effect of news about future productivity, suppose in our model that everyone learns in the current period that z' will increase in the future. This implies that the future marginal product of capital increases for the representative firm, and so the firm wishes to invest more in the current period, which increases the demand for current goods, shifting the output demand curve to the right in Figure 10.26(b). In equilibrium, this implies that aggregate output increases from Y_1 to Y_2, and the real interest rate

[3]Beaudry, P. and Portier, F. 2006. "Stock Prices, News, and Economic Fluctuations," *Amercian Economic Review* 96, 1293–1307; and Uribe, M. and Schmitt-Grohe, S. 2008. "What's News in Business Cycles," NBER working paper 14215.

Figure 10.26 The Equilibrium Effects of an Increase in Future Total Factor Productivity
An anticipated increase in future total factor productivity shifts the output demand curve to the right, with current output and the real interest rate increasing in equilibrium. The real wage falls, and employment rises.

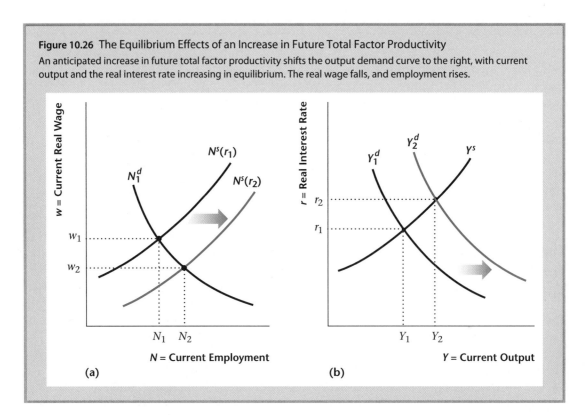

increases from r_1 to r_2. The increase in the real interest rate then causes current consumption to fall, but there is an opposing effect as consumption also tends to rise because of the increase in current income and the anticipated increase in future income (because z' is expected to increase). As a result, consumption could rise or fall. In equilibrium, there are two effects on investment; the increase in z' causes investment to rise, and the increase in r causes it to fall. Consumption may rise or fall, but investment must rise, as the initial shock to the economy works through a positive effect on investment.

What are the effects in the labor market? The increase in the real interest rate leads to a rightward shift of the labor supply curve, from $N^s(r_1)$ to $N^s(r_2)$ in Figure 10.26(a). Therefore, in equilibrium, the quantity of employment increases from N_1 to N_2, and the real wage falls from w_1 to w_2.

In anticipation of a future increase in total factor productivity, firms increase investment expenditure, as the marginal payoff to having a higher future capital stock has increased. The increase in the demand for investment goods raises the market real interest rate, which increases labor supply and employment and generates an increase in aggregate output. The increase in labor supply causes the real wage to fall.

An Increase in Credit Market Uncertainty: Asymmetric Information and the Financial Crisis

In Chapter 9 we analyzed the effects of asymmetric information in consumer credit markets, and early in this chapter we similarly studied how asymmetric information affects a firm's investment decision. In general, some firms or consumers in the economy might default on their debts, and financial institutions that lend to these firms may have difficulty distinguishing creditworthy borrowers from those who are not. This situation then makes lending more costly, even for good borrowers. All borrowers will face loan interest rates that are higher than the safe rates of interest at which financial institutions borrow, as financial institutions need to be compensated for the perceived default risk associated with lending. Thus, asymmetric information in credit markets creates a gap between the interest rates faced by borrowers and lenders, and this gap increases with the degree of uncertainty in credit markets.

The asymmetric information problem has been an important factor in the recent financial crisis. A key feature of the crisis is that financial market participants received critical news about a decrease in the value of assets held by financial institutions, firms, and consumers. However, the degree of credit market uncertainty increased, as there was not good information on which financial institutions, firms, and consumers were holding these bad assets, how bad the bad assets were, and how this would affect the creditworthiness of individual financial institutions, firms, and consumers. We want to use our model to understand the macroeconomic effects of an increase in credit market uncertainty, and this analysis will help us organize our thinking about recent events.

In the real intertemporal model, think of the model as representing a world where there are many different consumers and many different firms, some of whom borrow and some of whom lend, but with aggregate behavior accurately described by the behavior

News, the Stock Market, and Investment Expenditures

The real intertemporal model tells us that news about future total factor productivity could potentially be an important factor affecting investment spending. If there are significant fluctuations in financial market views about the future—i.e., waves of optimism and pessimism—then these fluctuations, through their effects on investment spending, could be very important for business cycles. We have shown that good news about future total factor productivity acts to increase investment, aggregate output, and employment, and bad news works in the opposite direction.

If news about future productivity is important for investment, then we should see this in economic data. In particular, financial theory tells us that stock prices act to aggregate information. That is, an individual stock price moves in a way that immediately incorporates all news about the future prospects of the individual firm that issued the stock. The stock simply represents a claim to the future dividends that the firm will pay, which will be determined by the performance of the firm in the future. A stock price index that averages all stock market prices then captures all of the news about the future prospects of all firms in the economy, and should include information about what is collectively known about what will happen to aggregate productivity in the future.

Therefore, if news about the future is an important determinant of aggregate investment, stock prices and investment expenditures should be highly positively correlated. In Figure 10.27, we show percentage deviations from trend in aggregate real investment spending and in the Standard and Poor's 500 stock price index, for the period 1950–2009. What we observe in the figure is a remarkably high degree of correlation between the two time series, that is investment spending tracks the stock price index remarkably closely. Further, stock prices tend to lead investment in the figure, which is consistent with our theory. News about the future can affect stock prices and investment plans simultaneously, but it takes time to build capital equipment, plants, and housing. Therefore, stock prices should lead investment, just as we observe.

Figure 10.27 is consistent with the view that news about the future is a key determinant of investment spending. Therefore, since investment is a highly volatile component of GDP (for example much more volatile than consumption or government spending), fluctuations in sentiment about the future are likely a key source of business cycles.

of a single representative consumer and a single representative firm. Now, suppose there is an increase in credit market uncertainty. For simplicity, we will focus on credit market uncertainty that affects only firms, in that the gap between borrowing and lending rates remains the same for consumers, but increases for firms.

In our model, the real interest rate r will denote the safe real rate of interest at which consumers and firms lend. However, the decisions of borrowers are determined by a loan rate that is higher than r. In Figure 10.28, the economy is initially in equilibrium with the real interest rate r_1, level of real income Y_1, real wage w_1, and level of employment N_1. Then, credit market uncertainty increases for firms, which causes an increase in the gap between the rates of interest at which firms lend and borrow. The effect of this shock to the economy, which we will assume is temporary and does not

Figure 10.27 Percentage Deviations from Trend in Investment and a Stock Price Index, 1950–2009

Investment and the stock price index are highly positively correlated, with stock prices leading GDP. This is consistent with the view that fluctuations in news about the future are an important source of business cycles.

continue to the future period, is to shift the output demand curve to the left from Y_1^d to Y_2^d. That is, any firm that borrows now faces a higher real interest rate for any level of the safe lending rate r. Therefore, given r, a borrowing firm will face a higher real interest rate and will choose to invest less, but a lending firm will still face the same interest rate r. The demand for goods falls then, for each r, given the decrease in demand for investment goods.

The increase in credit market risk then has the same aggregate effects as bad news about future total factor productivity (see the previous section). In Figure 10.28(b), the real interest rate (the safe interest rate faced by lenders) must decrease, and aggregate output must fall. Investment will decrease, but consumption may increase or decrease, following our analysis in the previous section (except in reverse). In the labor market in Figure 10.28(a), the decrease in the real interest rate shifts the labor supply curve to the left from $N^s(r_1)$ to $N^s(r_2)$. The real wage rises in equilibrium and employment falls.

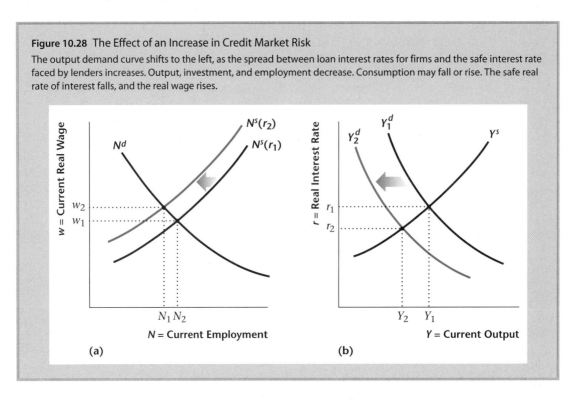

Figure 10.28 The Effect of an Increase in Credit Market Risk

The output demand curve shifts to the left, as the spread between loan interest rates for firms and the safe interest rate faced by lenders increases. Output, investment, and employment decrease. Consumption may fall or rise. The safe real rate of interest falls, and the real wage rises.

(a)

(b)

In our model, increased credit market uncertainty leads to a contraction in investment, output, and employment, as we have observed during the 2008–2009 recession. Real wages have most likely fallen rather than increased, but as we have argued previously, there are elements of the current recession that can be interpreted as a decrease in productivity, which would shift the labor demand curve to the left and reduce real wages. This would also shift the output supply curve to the left and reduce consumption.

Does our model tell us that there is some appropriate policy response to this shock to credit market uncertainty? Certainly we could say that the revelation of hidden information would cure the problem—if consumers, firms, and financial institutions were all fully aware of who was holding bad assets and how bad these assets are, then much of the problem would be solved. Borrowers in credit markets would then face interest rates that are appropriate, given their true creditworthiness. However, the revelation of hidden information is something that would have been achieved had there been better financial disclosure and adequate regulatory supervision of credit markets, so that shocks to credit market uncertainty would not occur, or would be dampened. Once the shock has hit the economy, it is not obvious that any type of government intervention will help. The government could attempt to use fiscal policy to extend credit to consumers and firms, sidestepping private financial institutions, but why should the government know any more than private lenders about evaluating creditworthiness? There may be a role for monetary policy in this context, but that is a topic for later in this book, when we study monetary economics, monetary policy, and banking.

Perspectives on the Financial Crisis
Interest Rate Spreads and Aggregate Economic Activity

The predictions of the real intertemporal model in this section help explain features of the recent financial market crisis and its implications for the 2008–2009 recession in the United States and the rest of the world. However, we would like more evidence from the historical record that credit market risk has played an important role in generating aggregate economic fluctuations. What the model suggests we should observe is that the difference between the interest rates at which consumers and firms lend and borrow (the interest rate spread) should be negatively correlated with aggregate economic activity.

From earlier in this chapter, we know that the interest rate spread between AAA-rated corporate debt and BAA-rated corporate debt is negatively correlated (in terms of deviations from trend) with aggregate investment. The results from

our model predict that we should observe a similar correlation between the interest rate spread and aggregate output. Indeed, in Figure 10.29, that is exactly what we see in the data. In the figure we show the percentage deviations from trend in real GDP, and the deviations from trend in the spread between AAA-rated bonds and BAA rated bonds. The spread is multiplied by 10 so as to put it on a similar scale with the percentage deviations from trend in real GDP.

In Figure 10.29, note in particular the large positive deviations from trend in the interest rate spread during the recessions of 1974–1975, 1981–1982, 1990–1991, 2001, and 2008–2009. The figure indicates that riskiness in credit markets, as measured by interest rate spreads, is a key element in business cycle phenomena in the United States.

Now that we have gained an understanding of the workings of our real intertemporal model, we can go on to use this model further, adding money and nominal variables in Chapter 11, and then using the model as a basis for studying business cycles in Chapters 12 and 13.

Chapter Summary

- We developed a real intertemporal macroeconomic model that is useful for evaluating the macroeconomic effects of shocks to the economy, and that we can build on in later chapters. This model allows us to study the determinants of investment, consumption, aggregate output, the real interest rate, and employment, in an intertemporal setting.

- The model has two periods, the present and the future, and the representative consumer makes a work—leisure decision in each period and a consumption—savings decision in the current period. As the real interest rate increases, the consumer's demand for current consumption goods decreases, and his or her current labor supply increases. These effects are due to the intertemporal substitution of consumption and leisure between the present and the future in response to changes in the real interest rate.

- The representative firm produces output using labor and capital in each period. The firm's current demand for labor is determined by the usual marginal productivity condition (the

Figure 10.29 Real GDP and the Interest Rate Spread

The figure shows the percentage deviations from trend in real GDP, and the deviations from trend (multiplied by 10 for scaling) in the difference between the interest rate on BAA-rated corporate debt and AAA-rated corporate debt. The two time series are negatively correlated, and the interest rate spread exhibits large positive deviations from trend during recessions.

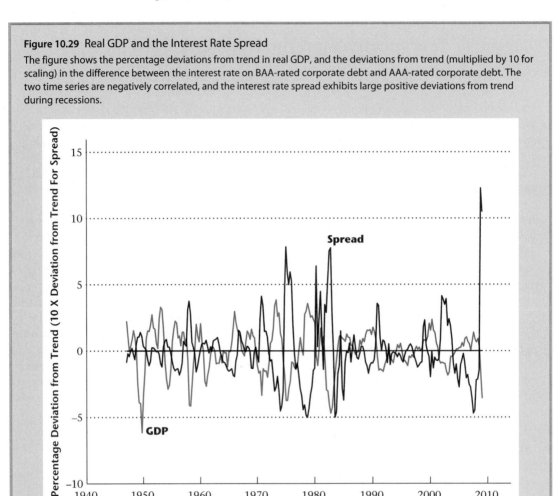

marginal product of labor equals the real wage in the current period when the firm optimizes), and the firm invests in new capital in the current period until the net marginal product of capital in the future is equal to the real interest rate. An increase in the real interest rate leads to a decrease in the firm's optimal quantity of investment, and investment increases if the firm's initial quantity of capital decreases, if there is an anticipated increase in future total factor productivity, or if there is a decrease in credit market uncertainty.

- In equilibrium, the current goods market and the current labor market clear, and this implies that the credit market clears as well. For simplicity, we ignore markets in the future period.

- In the graphical representation of the model, there are two key elements: (1) output demand and supply, determining current aggregate output and the real interest rate; (2) current labor supply and current labor demand, determining current employment and the current real wage given the real interest rate.

- We conducted five experiments using the model:

1. If current government purchases increase (a temporary increase in government spending), this increases the present value of taxes for the consumer, reducing lifetime wealth. Labor supply increases, and on net the demand for current goods rises by the amount of the increase in government spending. In equilibrium, current output rises, current employment rises, the current real wage falls, and the real interest rate increases given that a temporary increase in government purchases implies that the output supply effect is small. Consumption and investment are crowded out. The total government expenditure multiplier must be less than one, due to the crowding out of private expenditure by government spending.

2. If the current capital stock decreases—for example, because of a natural disaster—then the optimal quantity of investment increases for the firm, given the real interest rate, so that output demand increases. Current output supply decreases, because the representative firm can produce less current output with a given input of labor. The real interest rate increases in equilibrium, but current aggregate output may rise or fall. If the output demand effect is small, then output falls.

3. If current total factor productivity increases (a temporary increase in total factor productivity), then output supply increases, the real interest rate falls, and consumption and investment increase in the current period. Current employment may rise or fall, but it rises provided the interest rate effect on labor supply is small. The current real wage rises. These predictions of the model replicate some of the key business cycle facts from Chapter 3.

4. An anticipated increase in future total factor productivity implies that the representative firm demands more investment goods, because the future marginal product of capital is expected to be higher. The demand for goods increases, causing the real interest rate and current aggregate output to rise. In the labor market, the real wage falls and employment rises, as the representative consumer substitutes leisure intertemporally in response to the real interest rate increase.

5. An increase in credit market uncertainty, affecting only the credit markets in which firms borrow, acts in similar fashion to bad news about future total factor productivity. The output demand curve shifts to the left, and the real interest rate and aggregate output fall in equilibrium. Employment decreases, the real wage increases, investment falls, and consumption may rise or fall. A negative correlation between credit market uncertainty (as measured by the interest rate spread) and real GDP is evident in the data.

Key Terms

Intertemporal substitution of leisure The substitution of leisure between the current and future periods in response to the market real interest rate. (p. 342)

Marginal benefit from investment The future marginal product of capital plus $1 - d$, where d is the depreciation rate. (p. 351)

Marginal cost of investment The profit forgone by the firm in the current period from investing in an additional unit of capital. (p. 350)

Marginal propensity to consume The amount by which the demand for consumption goods increases when there is a one-unit increase in lifetime wealth. (p. 345)

Net marginal product of capital The marginal product of capital minus the depreciation rate. (p. 351)

Optimal investment rule Rule stating that the firm invests until the future net marginal product of capital is equal to the real interest rate. (p. 351)

Optimal investment schedule   A negative relationship between the firm's optimal quantity of investment and the market real interest rate. (p. 352)

Output demand curve   A negative relationship between the quantity of output demanded (in the form of consumption expenditures, investment expenditures, and government expenditures) and the real interest rate. (p. 368)

Output supply curve   A positive relationship between the quantity of output supplied by firms and the real interest rate. (p. 361)

Partial expenditure multiplier   The ratio of the increase in the demand for current goods to the increase in government expenditures in the current period. (p. 374)

Total government expenditure multiplier   The ratio of the equilibrium increase in current output to the increase in government expenditure. (p. 375)

Questions For Review

All questions refer to the macroeconomic model developed in this chapter.

1. Explain how intertemporal substitution is important for current labor supply and for the current demand for consumption goods.

2. What are three factors that determine current labor supply?

3. What determines the current demand for labor?

4. What is the goal of the representative firm in the real intertemporal model?

5. What rule does the representative firm follow in determining its optimal level of investment?

6. How is optimal investment for the firm affected by an increase in the current capital stock?

7. How is optimal investment affected by an increase in future total factor productivity?

8. Explain how credit market uncertainty affects the investment decision of the firm.

9. What is the government's budget constraint in the real intertemporal model? Can the government run a deficit or run a surplus in the current period?

10. What are the factors that shift the output supply curve?

11. What are the factors that shift the output demand curve?

12. How are aggregate output and the real interest rate determined in competitive equilibrium?

13. What are the effects of a temporary increase in government purchases on the real interest rate, aggregate output, employment, the real wage, consumption, and investment?

14. What are the effects of a decrease in the current capital stock on the real interest rate, aggregate output, employment, the real wage, consumption, and investment?

15. What are the effects of an increase in total factor productivity on the real interest rate, aggregate output, employment, the real wage, consumption, and investment? Explain how these results relate to key business cycle facts and the causes of business cycles.

16. Determine the equilibrium effects of an anticipated increase in future total factor productivity in the real intertemporal model. Explain why these effects are different from the effects of an increase in current total factor productivity.

17. How does credit market uncertainty affect aggregate economic activity? Explain the importance of this for the financial crisis and the 2008–2009 recession.

Problems

1. What is the effect of an increase in d, the depreciation rate, on the representative firm's investment decision, and on its optimal investment schedule? Explain your results carefully.

2. Tom lives on an island and has 20 coconut trees in the current period, which currently produce 180 coconuts. Tom detests coconuts, but he can trade them with people on other neighboring islands for things that he wants. Further, Tom can borrow and lend coconuts with neighboring islands. In the coconut credit market, a loan of 1 coconut in the current period is repaid with 2 coconuts in the future period. Each period, Tom's trees produce, and then 10% of them die. If Tom plants a coconut in the ground in the current period, it will grow into a productive coconut tree in the future period. At the end of the future period, Tom can sell any remaining coconut trees for 1 coconut each. When Tom plants coconuts in the current period, he plants them in successively less fertile ground, and the less fertile the ground, the less productive is the coconut tree. For convenience, we assume here that fractions of coconuts can be produced by trees. Output in the future period, for given numbers of trees in production in the future period, is given in the following table:
   (a) Plot the level of output against the quantity of capital for the future period.

Trees in Production in the Future	Future Output of Coconuts
15	155
16	162
17	168
18	173
19	177
20	180
21	182
22	183.8
23	184.8
24	185.2
25	185.4

   (b) Plot the marginal product of capital against the quantity of capital for the future period.
   (c) Calculate Tom's present value of profits given each quantity of future trees.
   (d) Calculate the net marginal product of capital for each quantity of future trees.
   (e) Determine Tom's optimal quantity of investment, and explain your results.

3. The government wishes to bring about an increase in investment expenditures, and is considering two tax policies that policymakers think could bring this about. Under the first tax policy, firms would receive a subsidy in the current period of t per unit of current output produced. Policymakers reason that firms will use this subsidy for investment. The second policy under consideration is an investment tax credit, by which firms would receive a subsidy of s per unit of investment in the current period. Determine which tax policy would be more effective in accomplishing the government's goal of increasing current investment expenditures, and carefully explain your results.

4. Suppose that we modify the model of the firm's investment behavior by supposing that any capital the firm has remaining at the end of the period can be sold at the price p'_K (in our model we assumed the capital could be sold at a price of one, in terms of consumption goods).
   (a) Determine how this change affects the optimal investment rule for the firm.
   (b) Suppose that we interpret p'_K as the firm's stock price. If p'_K increases, what effect does this have on the firm's optimal investment schedule? What does this imply about the relationship between investment expenditures and stock prices?

5. Determine how the following affects the slope of the output demand curve, and explain your results:
   (a) The marginal propensity to consume increases.
   (b) The intertemporal substitution effect of the real interest rate on current consumption increases.
   (c) The demand for investment goods becomes less responsive to the real interest rate.

6. The government decreases current taxes, while holding government spending in the present and the future constant.
   (a) Using diagrams, determine the equilibrium effects on consumption, investment, the real

interest rate, aggregate output, employment, and the real wage. What is the multiplier, and how does it differ from the government expenditure multiplier?

(b) Now, suppose that there are credit market imperfections in the market for consumer credit, for example due to asymmetric information in the credit market. Repeat part (a), and explain any differences in your answers in parts (a) and (b).

7. Determine how the following affects the slope of the output supply curve, and explain your results:

(a) The marginal product of labor decreases at a faster rate as the quantity of labor used in production increases.

(b) The intertemporal substitution effect of the real interest rate on current leisure decreases.

8. Suppose that there is a shift in the representative consumer's preferences. Namely, the consumer prefers, given the market real interest rate, to consume less current leisure and more current consumption goods.

(a) Determine the effects of this on current aggregate output, current employment, the current real wage, current consumption, and current investment.

(b) Explain your results. What might cause such a change in the preferences of consumers?

9. Suppose that there is a permanent increase in total factor productivity. Determine the implications of this for current macroeconomic variables, and show how the impact differs from the case where total factor productivity is expected to increase only temporarily. Explain your results.

10. Suppose that z' increases and that K increases at the same time. Show that it is possible for the real interest rate to remain constant as a result. What

does this say about the model's ability to explain the differences between poor and rich countries and to explain what happens as a country's economy grows?

11. There is a temporary increase in the relative price of energy. Determine how the response of current aggregate output to this shock depends on the marginal propensity to consume, and explain carefully why you get this result.

12. The nation experiences a major hurricane that destroys significant capital stock. Policymakers in the federal government reason that the destruction caused by the hurricane will reduce national income and that this should be counteracted through an increase in government expenditures.

(a) Is the action suggested by these policymakers necessary, given what their goals appear to be?

(b) What would be the net effects on the economy if government expenditures were temporarily increased after the hurricane?

(c) Are there any circumstances when this course of action would make sense? Explain.

13. A war breaks out that is widely expected to last only one year. Show how the effect of this shock on aggregate output depends on the size of the intertemporal substitution effect of the real interest rate on current leisure, and carefully explain your results.

14. There is an increase in aggregate credit market risk, and the government responds to this aggregate shock by increasing government spending so that aggregate income remains unchanged. Using diagrams, determine the aggregate economic effects of the combination of the shock to the economy and the government's response to it. Is the government policy response to the aggregate shock a good idea or not? Explain why or why not.

Working with the Data

1. Calculate the ratio of real investment expenditures to GDP, quarterly, for the period 1947–2009, and calculate the real interest rate as the three-month treasury bill rate minus the inflation rate (be careful that you calculate the inflation rate as an annualized rate), then plot the first variable against the second in a scatter plot. The theory of investment in this chapter predicts an optimal investment schedule that is a negative relationship between investment and the real interest rate. Is this what you observe in the data? Explain.

2. Calculate the ratio of total real government purchases to real GDP, quarterly, from 1947 to 2009. Also, calculate the real interest rate on a quarterly basis, as the 91-day Treasury bill rate in the last month of the quarter minus the inflation rate (measured as the percentage increase in the consumer price index from the last month of the previous quarter to the last month of the current quarter, multiplied by four to make this an annual rate).

   (a) Construct a scatter plot of the ratio of government purchases to GDP against the real interest rate.

   (b) Our real intertemporal model predicts that a temporary increase in government purchases causes an increase in the real interest rate. Is this implication of the model consistent with what you see in the scatter plot from part (a)? Explain why or why not.

3. Large increases in the relative price of energy occurred in 1974–75, 1979–80, in 1991 during the Persian Gulf War, in 2000, and after 2003. Is the behavior of detrended quarterly investment expenditures consistent with the interpretation that increases in the relative price of energy are negative shocks to total factor productivity? Explain.

PART V

Money and Business Cycles

In this part, our first task is to integrate monetary factors into the real intertemporal model that was developed in Chapter 10. The resulting model, a monetary intertemporal model, is used in Chapter 11 to study the role of currency and the banking system in transactions, the effects of changes in the quantity of money, the interaction between real and nominal phenomena, and monetary policy. In Chapters 12 and 13, we then use the monetary intertemporal model to study the causes of business cycles and the role of fiscal and monetary policy over the business cycle. In Chapter 12, we examine three equilibrium models of the business cycle, the first two of which imply that the government can at best make matters worse by smoothing business cycles, whereas the third is a modern Keynesian model in which government intervention to smooth business cycles can improve welfare. Chapter 13 is devoted to the examination of a New Keynesian sticky price model, which justifies a role for government intervention to smooth business cycles. The alternative business cycle models we study highlight the many possible causes of business cycles, and in Chapters 12 and 13 we pay careful attention to the match between the predictions of business cycle models and the business cycle facts studied in Chapter 3.

chapter **11**

Money, Banking, Prices, and Monetary Policy

Money is important to the economy, for two reasons. First, the economy functions better with money than without it, because carrying out transactions by trading one kind of good for another is difficult, and because using credit in some transactions is costly or impossible. Second, changes in the quantity of money in existence matter for nominal quantities—for example, the price level—and can also affect real economic activity. The quantity of money in circulation is governed in most countries by a central bank, and the primary monetary policy decisions of the central bank concern the control of the money supply.

In this chapter, we construct a monetary intertemporal model, which builds on the real intertemporal model in Chapter 10. In the monetary intertemporal model, consumers and firms choose among means of payment to carry out transactions. That is, they use government-supplied currency for some transactions, and they also use the transactions services supplied by banks. In practice these transactions services include the use of debit cards, credit cards, and checks, but for simplicity we represent these alternative payments services with one type of payments instrument, a credit card. A key part of the model is that consumers and firms make choices about their usage of credit cards versus cash, and this is important for determining the demand for money. Building up a knowledge of the role of banks in the monetary system and in credit markets will be critical for our understanding of the current financial crisis. The monetary intertemporal model resulting from our work in this chapter will also serve as the basis for our study of business cycles in Chapters 12 and 13.

The first result we show using the monetary intertemporal model is the **neutrality of money**, under which a one-time change in the money supply has no real consequences for the economy. Consumption, investment, output, employment, the real interest rate, and economic welfare remain unaffected. The neutrality of money is a good starting point for examining the role of money in the economy, but most macroeconomists agree that money is neutral only in the long run and that for various reasons changes in the money supply have real effects on the economy in the short run. We study these short-run non-neutralities of money in Chapters 12 and 13.

Our model determines a **money demand function**, which is a relationship between the quantity of money that is held in equilibrium and other macroeconomic variables.

In the monetary intertemporal model, the demand for money, in conjunction with the supply of money, determined by the central bank, will determine the price level—the price of goods in terms of money. Changes in the price level will then be the result of changes in any of the factors affecting the demand and supply of money. This analysis will yield a basic understanding of the determinants of money prices in the economy, and of the role of monetary policy in determining money prices. We use the model to explore how alternative monetary policy rules perform if the goal of monetary policy is to produce price stability.

What is Money?

A traditional view of money is that it has three important functions. Namely, money is a **medium of exchange**, it is a **store of value**, and it is a **unit of account**. Money is a medium of exchange in that it is accepted in exchange for goods for the sole reason that it can in turn be traded for other goods, not because it is wanted for consumption purposes. Money is a store of value, like other assets such as stocks, bonds, housing, and so on, as it allows consumers to trade current goods for future goods. Finally, money is a unit of account because essentially all contracts are denominated in terms of money. For example, in the United States a typical labor contract is a promise to pay a specified number of U.S. dollars in exchange for a specified quantity of labor, and a typical loan contract is a promise to pay a specified number of U.S. dollars in the future in exchange for a specified quantity of U.S. dollars in the present. As well, U.S. firms keep their books in terms of U.S. dollars.

The distinguishing economic feature of money is its medium-of-exchange role. As mentioned above, there are other assets such as stocks, bonds, and housing that serve the store-of-value role that is served by money. However, there are difficulties in using these other assets in exchange. First, there is often imperfect information concerning the quality of assets. For example, it may be difficult to get the clerk in a convenience store to accept a stock certificate in exchange for a newspaper, as the clerk probably does not know the market value of the stock certificate, and it would be costly for him or her to sell the stock certificate. Second, some assets come in large denominations and are, therefore, difficult to use for small purchases. Even if the clerk in the convenience store knows the market value of a U.S. Treasury bill (a short-term debt instrument issued by the U.S. government), Treasury bills do not come in denominations less than $10,000, and so the clerk likely cannot make change for the purchase of a newspaper. Third, some assets take time to sell at their market value. For example, if I attempted to sell my house to the convenience store clerk, he or she would likely offer me much less for the house than I would receive if I searched the market for a buyer whose preferences best matched my house.

Measuring the Money Supply

As we discuss in more detail in Chapter 16, money has taken many forms historically. Money has circulated as commodity money (primarily silver and gold), circulating private bank notes (as was the case prior to the Civil War in the United States), commodity-backed paper currency (for example, under the gold standard), fiat money (for example, Federal Reserve notes in the United States), and transactions deposits at private banks. In the United States today, money consists mainly of objects that take the latter two forms, fiat money and transactions deposits at banks.

In modern developed economies, there are potentially many ways to measure the supply of money, depending on where we want to draw the line defining which assets satisfy the medium-of-exchange property and which do not. What is defined as money is somewhat arbitrary, and it is possible that we may want to use different definitions of money for different purposes. Table 11.1 shows measures of the standard **monetary aggregates** for June 2009, taken from the *Federal Reserve Bulletin*. A given monetary aggregate is simply the sum of a number of different assets for the U.S. economy.

The most narrowly defined monetary aggregate is M0, which is sometimes referred to as the **monetary base** or **outside money**. The monetary base consists entirely of liabilities of the **Federal Reserve System** (the **Fed**), which is the central bank of the United States. The chief role of a central bank is to issue outside money. The liabilities making up M0 are U.S. currency outside the Fed and the deposits of depository institutions with the Fed. The quantity of M0 is called outside money, as it is the quantity of money outside of the banking system. The quantity of M1 is obtained by adding currency (outside the U.S. Treasury, the Fed, and the vaults of depository institutions), travelers' checks, demand deposits, and other transactions accounts at depository institutions. Thus, M1 is intended as a measure of the assets that are most widely used by the private sector in making transactions. An interesting feature of the numbers reported in Table 11.1 is that the monetary base in June 2009 was actually larger than M1, which is historically unusual. This state of affairs occurred because depository institutions were holding large quantities of outside money, and a significant fraction of this outside money was borrowed from the Fed. The quantity of M2 is M1 plus savings deposits, small-denomination savings deposits, and retail money market mutual funds. These additional assets are not directly used in transactions, but they are easily exchanged for currency and transactions deposits, which can then be used in transactions.

The monetary aggregates are important, because they can be useful indirect measures of aggregate economic activity that are available on a more timely basis than GDP. Further, there are key regularities in the relationship between monetary aggregates and other aggregate variables, which make monetary aggregates useful in economic forecasting and in policy analysis. Finally, the paths followed by monetary aggregates over time can be useful in evaluating the performance of the Fed.

Table 11.1	Monetary Aggregates, June 2009 (in $billions)
M0	1684.0
M1	1655.1
M2	8363.6

Source: Federal Reserve Bulletin

A Monetary Intertemporal Model

Why do we use money in exchange? A useful analogy is that money is to economic exchange as oil is to an engine; money overcomes "frictions." Two important economic frictions that make money useful are the following. First, in modern economies, barter exchange—the exchange of goods for goods—is difficult. As Adam Smith recognized in his *Wealth of Nations,* specialization is key to the efficiency gains that come from economic development. Once economic agents become specialized in what they produce and what they consume, it becomes very time-consuming to trade what one has for what one wants through barter exchange. For example, if Sara specializes in giving economics lectures and wants to buy car repairs, to make a barter exchange she must not only find someone willing to repair her car—a **single coincidence of wants**—but the car repair person must also want to receive a lecture in economics—a **double coincidence of wants.** Clearly, Sara may have to spend a great deal of time and energy searching for a trading partner! The double coincidence problem was first studied by William Stanley Jevons in the nineteenth century.[1] Money solves the double-coincidence problem because, if everyone accepts money in exchange, then would-be buyers need only satisfy a single-coincidence problem to buy a good, which is much easier. Sara can sell economics lectures for money and then exchange this money for car repairs.

A second reason that money is useful in exchange is that there are circumstances where credit transactions may be difficult or impossible to make. For example, it would be unlikely that a street vendor in New York City would accept my personal IOU in exchange for a hot dog. Because the street vendor does not know me or my credit history, he or she cannot evaluate whether my IOU is good, and it would be costly for him or her to take legal action should I not be willing to pay off my IOU. While modern credit card systems solve some of the information problems connected with the use of personal credit in transactions, these systems are costly to operate, and there are sellers of goods who do not accept credit under any circumstances. Because money is easily recognizable, there are essentially no information problems associated with the use of money in exchange, other than the problems that arise from counterfeiting.

There is much heated debate concerning how monetary exchange should be represented in macroeconomic models. According to one view,[2] if we are to understand the role of money in the economy and how monetary policy works, we need to model money at a deep level. That is, we need to model the fundamental reasons money is held—the frictions that make money useful—to make progress. In Chapter 16, we study a model that takes explicit account of the double-coincidence-of-wants problem in barter exchange discussed above and show how this problem gives rise to a role for money. An alternative view is that, in many circumstances, it is sufficient in modeling money in a macroeconomic context to simply assume that money is used in all or some transactions and then proceed from there. This approach is relatively

---

[1] See S. Jevons, 1910. *Money and the Mechanism of Exchange,* 23rd edition, Kegan Paul, London.
[2] See J. Kareken and N. Wallace, 1980. "Introduction," in J. Kareken and N. Wallace, eds., *Models of Monetary Economies,* Federal Reserve Bank of Minneapolis, Minneapolis, MN, pp. 1–12; and N. Wallace, 1998. "A Dictum for Monetary Theory," *Federal Reserve Bank of Minneapolis Quarterly Review,* Winter, 20–26.

simple, but the deep approach to modeling money has much merit, particularly in advanced monetary economics.

In the model we construct here, we assume at the outset that some goods must be purchased with cash on hand or by using the costly transactions services provided by banks through debit cards, credit cards, or checks. This type of model is a version of a **cash-in-advance model**, which has been used extensively in macroeconomics. The idea behind the cash-in-advance model originated with Robert Clower,[3] and Robert Lucas made important contributions to its development and applications.[4]

We use the details of the monetary intertemporal model in this chapter to examine the neutrality of money, the effects of shocks to the economy on nominal variables, and monetary policy issues.

Real and Nominal Interest Rates and the Fisher Relation

In the monetary intertemporal model that we construct, there are many periods but, just as in the economic growth models studied in Chapters 6 and 7, our analysis is mainly in terms of an arbitrary *current period* and the following period, which we refer to as the *future period*. There are two primary assets, money and nominal bonds, and later we will introduce banks, which have some other assets and liabilities. For simplicity, the entire stock of outside money is assumed to consist of currency. We use money as the numeraire here (recall that the numeraire is the object in which all prices are denominated in an economic model) with P denoting the current price level, or the current price of goods in terms of money. Similarly, P' denotes the price level in the future period. A **nominal bond** is an asset that sells for one unit of money (e.g., one dollar in the United States) in the current period and pays off $1 + R$ units of money in the future period. Therefore, R is the rate of return on a bond in units of money, or the **nominal interest rate.** Nominal bonds can be issued by the government, by consumers, or by firms, and all bonds bear the same nominal interest rate, as we are assuming that no one defaults on their debts.

As in Chapters 8–10, the real rate of interest, r, is the rate of interest in terms of goods. The real interest rate is the real rate of return that someone receives when holding a nominal bond from the current period to the future period. The real interest rate can be determined from the nominal interest rate, and the **inflation rate** i, which is defined by

$$i = \frac{P' - P}{P}. \tag{11-1}$$

That is, the inflation rate is the rate of increase in the price level from the current period to the future period. Then, the real interest rate is determined by the **Fisher relation**, named after Irving Fisher, which is

$$1 + r = \frac{1 + R}{1 + i}. \tag{11-2}$$

---

[3]See R. Clower, 1967. "A Reconsideration of the Microfoundations of Monetary Theory," *Western Economic Journal* 6, 1–8.

[4]See R. Lucas, 1980. "Equilibrium in a Pure Currency Economy," in J. Kareken and N. Wallace, eds., *Models of Monetary Economies,* pp. 131–146, Federal Reserve Bank of Minneapolis, Minneapolis, MN; and R. Lucas and N. Stokey, 1987. "Money and Interest in a Cash-in-Advance Economy," *Econometrica* 55, 491–514.

To derive the Fisher relation, recall that $1 + R$ is the return in terms of money in the future period from giving up one unit of money in the current period to buy a nominal bond. In real terms, someone acquiring a nominal bond gives up $\frac{1}{P}$ goods in the current period and receives a payoff of $\frac{1+R}{P'}$ goods in the future period. Therefore, from equation (11-1), the gross rate of return on the nominal bond, in real terms, is

$$1 + r = \frac{\frac{1+R}{P'}}{\frac{1}{P}} = \frac{1+R}{\frac{P'}{P}} = \frac{1+R}{1+i},$$

which gives us the Fisher relation (11-2).

Given a positive nominal interest rate on nominal bonds—that is, $R > 0$—the rate of return on nominal bonds exceeds the rate of return on money. The nominal interest rate on money is zero, and the real interest rate on money can be determined just as we determined the real interest rate associated with the nominal bond above. That is, if r^m is the real rate of interest on money, then as in equation (11-2), we have

$$1 + r^m = \frac{1+0}{1+i} = \frac{1}{1+i},$$

and so if $R > 0$ then $r^m < r$, or the real interest rate on money is less than the real interest rate on the nominal bond. In our monetary intertemporal model, we need to explain why people are willing to hold money if they can receive a higher rate of return on the alternative asset, nominal bonds, when the nominal interest rate is positive.

Now, the Fisher relation can be rewritten by multiplying each side of equation (11-2) by $1 + i$ and rearranging to get

$$r = R - i - ir.$$

Then, if the real interest rate and the inflation rate are small, ir is negligible; for example, if the inflation rate is 10% and the real interest rate is 8%, then $i = 0.1$, $r = 0.08$, and $ir = 0.008$. We can say that, for small inflation rates and interest rates,

$$r \approx R - i \tag{11-3}$$

that is, the real interest rate is approximately equal to the nominal interest rate minus the inflation rate. For example, if the nominal interest rate is 5%, or 0.05, and the inflation rate is 3%, or 0.03, then the real interest rate is approximately 2%, or 0.02.

Empirically, there is a problem in measuring the real interest rate. Nominal interest rates on many different assets can be observed, but economic agents do not know the inflation rate that will be realized over the time they hold a particular asset. The correct inflation rate to use might be the one that an economic agent expects, but expectations cannot be observed. However, one approach to measuring the real rate of interest is to calculate it based on equation (11-3), using the realized inflation rate for i. In Figure 11.1 we show data on the nominal interest rate, measured as the interest rate on 91-day U.S. Treasury bills over the period 1948–2009 and the corresponding real rate, calculated as the nominal interest rate minus the inflation rate. The measured real interest rate has varied considerably over time, and it has sometimes been quite low, dipping

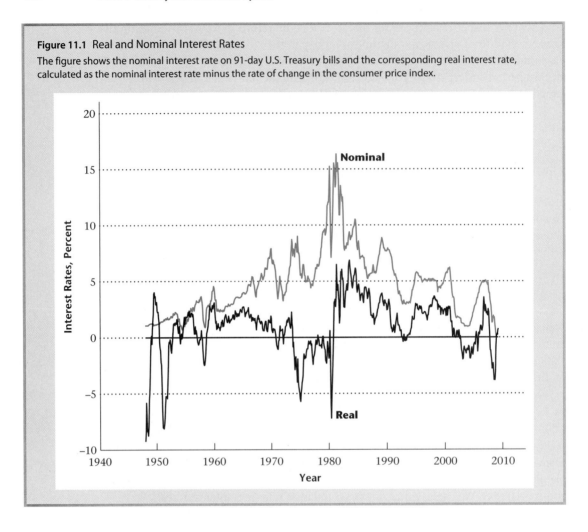

Figure 11.1 Real and Nominal Interest Rates

The figure shows the nominal interest rate on 91-day U.S. Treasury bills and the corresponding real interest rate, calculated as the nominal interest rate minus the rate of change in the consumer price index.

below 0% several times over this sample period, particularly during the early and late 1940s, early 1950s, and 1970s.

Banks

In constructing the monetary intertemporal model, we need to modify the real intertemporal model of Chapter 10 to account for how transactions are carried out using currency and transactions services supplied by banks. For the analysis that we do in this chapter and in Chapters 12 and 13, we do not have to alter how we model demand and supply in the labor market and goods market. However, we need to introduce a new market, the market for money. In the model, the money stock corresponds to the most narrow definition of money—outside money or the monetary base. Here the demand for money is determined by the behavior of the representative consumer and the representative firm, and the supply of money is determined by the central bank.

As we will see, the demand for money is a quite different concept from the demand for a good or service. In contrast to goods and services, we want money not because it contributes directly to our happiness, but because it allows us to acquire the goods and services that ultimately make us happy. To understand the determinants of the demand for money, we need to be specific about how consumers and firms make choices between using currency and the services of banks in making transactions.

In practice, banks have two roles. First, they serve to facilitate transactions among consumers, firms, and the government. Second, banks serve as financial intermediaries that manage the savings of their depositors in a more efficient way than could be accomplished by each depositor on his or her own. In our model, banks serve both of these roles, although we will explore the second role of banks in much more detail in Chapter 16.

A bank in the monetary intertemporal model offers two kinds of deposits, transactions deposits and savings deposits. A transactions deposit can be held by a consumer, a firm, or the government and can be transferred at any time to some other individual, just as we transfer the claims to deposits in practice by using a debit card or a check. As well, the individual holding the transactions deposit can withdraw it as cash. A savings deposit is held by a consumer or a firm. For the consumer or firm, the savings deposit is an asset that is acquired at the beginning of a period and is held until the beginning of next period. A one-dollar savings deposit acquired in the current period pays off $1 + R$ dollars at the beginning of the future period, and it cannot be used in transactions or withdrawn before it matures.

A bank can hold three types of assets: money, credit card balances, and nominal government bonds. Money is held so that the bank can satisfy the demand for withdrawals of cash from its depositors. Note that money in the model is currency, which does not bear interest. In practice, the central bank can pay interest on the portion of outside money that is held by banks as deposits with the central bank. In some countries, central banks have for some time paid interest on deposits with the central bank, and in the United States this has been the practice since late 2008. Including central bank deposits is something we could do to extend the model, but for our purposes here, that is not necessary. In the model, credit card balances are loans made by a bank during the period, and each dollar extended as a loan during the current period must be paid back at the end of the period. That is, the credit card balances of consumers and firms must be paid off at the end of the period. As well, the bank charges a fee on credit card balances, which is a price of q units of consumption goods for each unit of credit card balances, in real terms, during the period, payable at the end of the period. Nominal government bonds earn a nominal interest rate of R from the current period to the future period.

The balance sheet for a typical bank is shown in Table 11.2. Assets of the bank (what other individuals owe to the bank) are on the left side of the balance sheet, and liabilities (what the bank owes to other individuals) are on the right side. The balance sheet balances, in that the value of total assets equals the value of total liabilities. Further, the bank is in some sense two separate businesses, in that each dollar of savings deposits on the liabilities side is matched by one dollar of government bonds on the asset side. The nominal interest rate on savings deposits, R, is the same as the nominal interest rate on nominal government

Table 11.2 A Typical Bank's Balance Sheet

Assets	Liabilities
Money	Transactions Deposits
Credit Card Balances	
Nominal Government Bonds	Savings Deposits

bonds since, with free entry into banking, the bank must make zero profits on the business of issuing savings deposits and acquiring government bonds.

The second part of a bank's business involves the transactions deposits of consumers, firms, and the government, with each dollar of these deposits matched on the asset side of the balance sheet either by one dollar in money or one dollar in credit card balances. A bank acquires a transactions deposit in one of two ways. First, an individual could deposit some money with the bank, in which case the deposited money shows up on the balance sheet as an asset (money) and a liability (transactions deposit). Second, an individual could receive a loan from the bank by using his or her bank credit card. Then, suppose, for example, that the credit card was used by a consumer to buy $100 in goods from a firm. Then, the credit card transaction gives the firm a $100 transactions balance at the bank, and the consumer a $100 credit card balance as a liability to the bank (and an asset for the bank). Real-world credit card transactions are somewhat more complicated, but we capture the essence of what is involved here. The credit card transaction is reflected in an increase in credit card balances on the asset side of the bank balance sheet and by an equal increase in transactions deposits on the liability side of the bank balance sheet.

Transactions deposits pay no interest, but unlike government bonds or savings deposits, these transactions deposits can either be withdrawn as cash at the ATM machine or the depositor can make use of the bank's ability to transfer the claim to the deposit to someone else (for example, when we use a check or debit card).

A critical feature of the model is that extending credit balances is costly for the bank, because it is costly to set up and use an electronic credit card system. The costs of lending generate a market supply curve for credit card balances. In Figure 11.2, the quantity of credit card balances supplied, in units of consumption goods, is denoted by X^s on the horizontal axis, and q, the price of credit card balances, is on the vertical axis. An increase in q increases the profitability of extending credit balances, and banks will therefore increase the quantity supplied.

Transactions

It is useful to think of a period in the monetary intertemporal model as being a day, as this will most closely match reality in terms of the flow of transactions and payments among consumers, firms, banks, and the government. The fit with reality is not perfect, as consumers and firms in the model will pay off their credit card balances each day, whereas in reality it is customary for credit card balances to be settled once per month, with outstanding balances at the end of the month subject to interest charges. The setup in the model keeps the story simple, without losing anything that is essential for what we want to accomplish.

Figure 11.2 The Supply Curve for Credit Card Balances

The supply curve is upward-sloping as the profitability of extending credit balances increases as q increases, so banks increase quantity supplied.

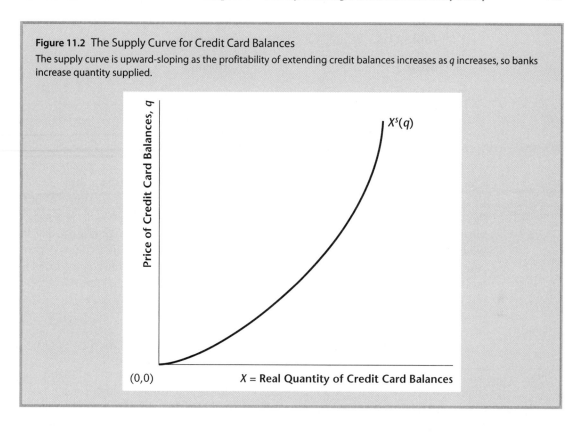

The model captures a world where there are many consumers and firms, but for simplicity we will mesh the constraints that consumers and firms face into constraints that apply to all of them as a group. In the morning of the day, consumers and firms have nominal quantities of transactions deposits and savings deposits held over from the previous day. The government does not hold any transactions deposits at the beginning of the day. For all banks in the economy, the collective balance sheet at the beginning of the day is as in Table 11.3.

To make transactions during the day, consumers and firms have available their transactions deposits M^- and the payoff on their savings deposits acquired the previous day, $B^-(1 + R^-)$, where R^- is the nominal interest rate from the previous period. Consumers and firms can also use their credit cards to finance their transactions during the day, and we let X^d denote the real value, and PX^d the nominal value, of the borrowing that consumers and firms plan to do during the period on their credit cards. During the period, consumers and firms will purchase consumption and investment goods C and I, respectively, they will pay taxes T to the government, all in units of goods, and they will acquire nominal savings deposits B^d. Therefore, consumers and firms will collectively face the **transactions constraint**

$$P(C + I + T) + B^d = M^- + B^-(1 + R^-) + PX^d \qquad (11\text{-}4)$$

Table 11.3 Banks' Balance Sheet in the Morning	
Assets	**Liabilities**
Money $= M^-$	Transactions Deposits $= M^-$
Credit Card Balances $= 0$	
Nominal Government Bonds $= B^-$	Savings Deposits $= B^-$

Equation (11-4) is related to the **cash-in-advance constraint** that appears in typical cash-in-advance models, which usually states simply that cash on hand for a consumer or firm be sufficient to finance planned expenditures. The transactions constraint (11-4) is somewhat more sophisticated in that it states that total nominal expenditures during the day on goods and assets cannot exceed cash available in the transactions deposit accounts of consumers and firms at the beginning of the day, in dollars, plus the amount that consumers and firms plan to borrow on their credit cards during the day, in nominal terms.

In addition to the transactions constraint, consumers and firms must collectively meet their budget constraint, which is

$$P(C + I + T) + B^d + M^d + PqX^d = M^- + B^-(1 + R^-) + PY \qquad (11-5)$$

Total purchases of goods, services, and assets, and tax payments are on the left-hand side of equation (11-5). That is, during the day consumers and firms purchase consumption goods and investment goods and pay their taxes, spending a total nominal quantity $P(C + I + T)$. They also acquire assets that are savings deposits at banks B^d and money balances M^d, both in nominal terms. Finally, they purchase credit card services from banks, with total nominal expenditure for this purpose equal to PqX^d. On the right hand side of equation (11-5) is total assets available at the beginning of the period, plus total income received during the period by consumers and firms. The quantity $M^- + B^-(1 + R^-)$ is the amount of cash available in the transactions deposit accounts of consumers and firms at the beginning of the period, while PY is total nominal income earned by consumers and firms during the day. An important feature captured in the transactions constraint (11-4) and the budget constraint (11-5) is that current nominal income PY is not available to spend during the day, unless consumers and firms use their credit cards to borrow against this income. Note that the credit balances of consumers and firms PX^d do not appear in the budget constraint (11-5) as these balances are paid off at the end of the day.

Equilibrium in the Market for Credit Card Balances and the Demand for Money

In Figure 11.2 we showed the supply side of the market for credit balances, determined by the behavior of banks. What remains is to show how the optimizing behavior of consumers and firms determines a demand curve for credit card balances, so that we can determine equilibrium in the market for credit card balances. From there, it will be straightforward to show how equilibrium in the market for credit card balances determines the demand for money.

During the day, consumers and firms need to choose consumption C, investment I, the quantity of savings deposits to hold into the next day B^d, the quantity of money to hold into the next day, M^d, and the quantity of credit card balances X^d. Consumption and investment are chosen by consumers and firms, respectively, just as in the real intertemporal model. Then, in spite of the fact that it appears there are three choices left to determine for consumers and firms $(B^d, M^d, \text{ and } X^d)$, once we determine one of these choices we determine the other two from the constraints (11-4) and (11-5).

Now, if we use equation (11-4) to substitute the quantity on right-hand side of equation (11-5) for the quantity on the left-hand side of equation (11-4), we obtain

$$M^- + B^-(1 + R^-) + PX^d + M^d + PqX^d = M^- + B^-(1 + R^-) + PY$$

Then, simplifying the above equation, we obtain

$$M^d = PY - P(1 + q)X^d \tag{11-6}$$

Equation (11-6) states that the quantity of money carried into the next day by consumers and firms is equal to total nominal income earned during the day, minus nominal income spent by borrowing on credit cards during the day (PX^d), minus the nominal cost of carrying a credit card balance during the day (PqX^d).

As we noted above, we need only determine one of the remaining three decisions for consumers and firms and then we are done, and we will choose to focus here on the choice of credit card balances. To determine the demand for credit card balances X^d, we need to look at the marginal benefit and marginal cost of credit card balances for consumers and firms.

What do consumers and firms gain, at the margin, from an additional unit of credit card balances? In equation (11-4), $M^- + B^-(1 + R^-)$ is determined from the previous period, and we analyzed how C and I are determined in Chapter 10. This leaves the quantities B^d and X^d for consumers and firms to determine in equation (11-4). Then, if X^d increases by one unit on the right-hand side of equation (11-4), B^d increases by P units on the left-hand side of equation (11-4). That is, if consumers and firms borrow more on their credit cards, they can hold their spending constant on goods and taxes and hold more savings deposits. The benefit of holding P more units in savings deposits is a payoff of $(1 + R)P$ units of money at the beginning of the next day, and this is the marginal benefit of credit card balances.

What do consumers and firms lose at the margin from an additional unit of credit card balances? From equation (11-6), if X^d increases by one unit, consumers and firms will carry over $P(1 + q)$ less money balances into the next day, and this is the marginal cost of credit card balances.

Our analysis of the marginal benefit and marginal cost of holding credit card balances makes clear that adjusting credit balances also represents a tradeoff between holdings of cash (which does not bear interest) and savings deposits (which do) going forward into the next day. If consumers and firms borrow more on their credit cards during the day, they can hold more savings deposits and less cash going into the next day.

Now, the marginal benefit minus the marginal cost of credit card balances for the consumers is given by

$$(1 + R)P - P(1 + q) = P(R - q).$$

Therefore, if $R > q$, then the marginal benefit of an extra unit of credit card balances is always positive, and so consumers and firms will borrow as much as possible on their credit cards during the period. From equation (11-6), this will be the quantity X^d that makes money balances $M^d = 0$ at the beginning of the next day, or

$$X^d = \frac{Y}{1 + q},$$

so that credit card borrowing is just large enough that all income received during the period is sufficient to pay off the credit balance and pay credit card fees.

However, if $R < q$, then marginal benefit is smaller than marginal cost, and consumers and firms will choose $X^d = 0$. Finally, if $R = q$, then consumers and firms are indifferent concerning how much they use their credit cards.

The conclusion is that the demand curve X^d for credit card balances is horizontal at $q = R$, as depicted in Figure 11.3, and we have $X^d = \frac{Y}{1 + q}$ for $q < R$. Therefore in equilibrium, as in Figure 11.3, the equilibrium price that banks charge for carrying credit card balances is $q = R$, and the equilibrium quantity of credit card balances is X^* in real terms. We have assumed here that it will always be the case in equilibrium that $M^d > 0$ or $X^d < \frac{Y}{1 + q}$. This equilibrium outcome reflects the fact that, if consumers

Figure 11.3 Equilibrium in the Market for Credit Card Balances
The demand curve for credit balances is horizontal at the price $q = R$, up to the maximum amount that consumers and firms can borrow, $\frac{Y}{1+q}$. In equilibrium, the price of credit card balances is $q = R$ and the quantity is X^*.

Figure 11.4 The Effect of an Increase in the Nominal Interest Rate on the Market for Credit Card Balances
An increase in the nominal interest rate from R_1 to R_2 shifts the demand curve for credit balances up from X_1^d to X_2^d. The equilibrium price of credit card balances increases from R_1 to R_2 and the equilibrium quantity increases from X_1^* to X_2^*.

and firms borrow more on their credit cards, they are making a decision to hold less cash and more savings deposits going into the next day. At the margin they will pay a fee q for the privilege of borrowing more on their credit cards, but they benefit from the extra interest earnings R on their savings deposits relative to holding non-interest-bearing cash.

If the nominal interest rate R were to rise, say from R_1 to R_2 as in Figure 11.4, then this will shift up the demand for credit card balances from X_1^d to X_2^d, increasing the equilibrium quantity of credit card balances from X_1^* to X_2^*. Therefore, it is convenient to write the equilibrium quantity of credit card balances, in real terms as $X^*(R)$, which is an increasing function of the nominal interest rate. Then, since $X^d = X^*(R)$ and $q = R$ in equilibrium, we can write the demand for money balances by consumers and firms, as of the end of the day, from (11-6), as

$$M^d = P[Y - (1 + R)X^*(R)]\tag{11-7}$$

For simplicity, we can then write equation (11-7) as

$$M^d = PL(Y, R),\tag{11-8}$$

where the function L is increasing in real income Y and decreasing in the nominal interest rate R, since $(1 + R)X^*(R)$ is an increasing function of R. Then $PL(Y, R)$ is a money demand function, although it would be quite misleading to think of the money demand function as being much like the demand function for a good or service. In our model, the money demand function is derived as an equilibrium relationship, given the choices of banks concerning the supply of credit card balances and the choices of consumers and firms concerning how they will use cash or credit cards in making transactions.

The nominal demand for money is proportional to the price level, because the quantity that matters to consumers and firms in their choice of means of payment is the real quantity of money, $\frac{M^d}{P}$. Money demand increases with real income as consumers and firms wish to engage in a larger real volume of transactions as real income rises, and the capacity of the banking system to supply alternative means of payment is limited. Finally, money demand falls as the nominal interest rate rises, because a higher nominal interest rate increases the opportunity cost of holding cash, thus consumers and firms are more inclined to use alternative means of payment such as credit cards.

Now, taking the approximate Fisher relation (11-3) as an equality (that is, assuming the real interest rate and the inflation rate are small) implies that we can substitute $r + i$ for R in equation (11-8), to get

$$M^d = PL(Y, r + i). \tag{11-9}$$

For most of the analysis that we do in this chapter and in Chapters 12 and 13, we look at economic experiments that do not deal with the effects of changes in long-run inflation. That is, most of the experiments we consider in these chapters leave i unaffected. When i is constant in equation (11-9), it is harmless to set it to zero for convenience, which implies that equation (11-9) becomes

$$M^d = PL(Y, r). \tag{11-10}$$

With Y and r given, the function on the right-hand side of equation (11-10) is linear in P with slope $L(Y, r)$, and we depict this function in Figure 11.5. If real income increases, for example from Y_1 to Y_2, then in Figure 11.6 the money demand curve shifts to the right from $PL(Y_1, r)$ to $PL(Y_2, r)$. We would obtain the same type of rightward shift in the money demand curve if the real interest rate r were to decrease.

Government

We have to expand on our treatment of government from Chapter 10 to take into account the ability of the government to issue money. For our purposes, it is convenient to assume that there is a single institution in our model called the government, which is responsible for both fiscal and monetary policy. Therefore, the government entity in this model is essentially what we would get if we merged the U.S. Treasury with the Federal Reserve System and placed them both under the control of the Congress. In the United States, the Federal Reserve System, which is the monetary

Figure 11.5 The Nominal Money Demand Curve in the Monetary Intertemporal Model

Nominal money demand is a straight line and it shifts with changes in real income Y and the real interest rate r.

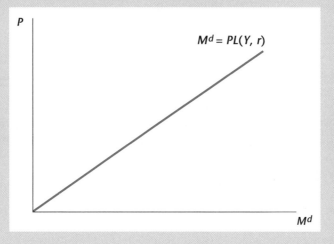

$$M^d = PL(Y, r)$$

Figure 11.6 The Effect of an Increase in Current Real Income on the Nominal Money Demand Curve

The current nominal money demand curve shifts to the right with an increase in current real income Y. The curve shifts in the same way if there is a decrease in the real interest rate r.

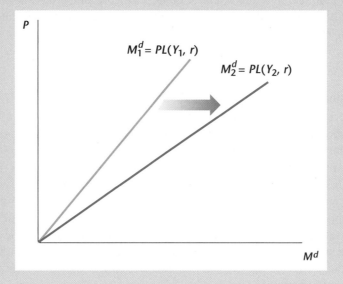

$$M_1^d = PL(Y_1, r)$$

$$M_2^d = PL(Y_2, r)$$

authority, is essentially independent of the Treasury, which is the federal fiscal authority controlled by the U.S. government. The arrangement between the central bank and the federal government varies considerably across countries. In some countries, such as the United States, the central bank has considerable independence, while in other countries it does not.

In the current period, the government purchases G goods and pays the nominal interest and principal on the government debt outstanding from the last period, $(1 + R^-)B^-$, where B^- is the quantity of one-period nominal bonds issued by the government in the previous period, which come due in the current period, with each of these bonds bearing a nominal interest rate of R^-. Current government purchases and the interest and principal on government debt, which sum to total current government outlays, are financed through taxation, the issue of new bonds, and by printing money. The government budget constraint in the current period is, therefore, given by

$$PG + (1 + R^-)B^- = PT + B + M - M^-. \qquad (11\text{-}11)$$

The government budget constraint, equation (11-11) is expressed in nominal terms, with the left-hand side denoting total government outlays during the period, and the right-hand side denoting total government receipts. On the right-hand side, PT denotes nominal taxes, B denotes government bonds issued in the current period, which come due in the future period, and the final term, $M - M^-$, is the change in the nominal money supply, where M is the total quantity of money outstanding in the current period, and M^- is the previous period's money supply.

Adding money creation, $M - M^-$, to the government budget constraint is an important step here over the kinds of models we considered in Chapters 5, 8, 9, and 10, where we did not take account of the monetary transactions that take place in the economy. We are now able to consider the effects of monetary policy and how monetary and fiscal policy interact.

Competitive Equilibrium—The Complete Monetary Intertemporal Model

In the monetary intertemporal model there are three markets to consider—the market for current goods, the market for current labor, and the money market. As in the real intertemporal model studied in Chapter 10, equilibrium in the credit market is implied by equilibrium in these three other markets. The markets for current goods and current labor operate exactly as in the real intertemporal model, so the only important difference here from the model of Chapter 10 is the addition of the money market. In adding money to the model, we needed to analyze the behavior of banks, consumers, and firms, in the market for credit card balances. However, in the work we did above, we showed how all of that behavior could be summarized in a money demand function.

In the new market we need to include in the model, the market for money, we will assume that the money supply M^s is determined exogenously by the government as

Figure 11.7 The Current Money Market in the Monetary Intertemporal Model

The figure shows the current nominal demand for money curve M^d and the money supply curve M^s. The intersection of these two curves determines the equilibrium price level, which is P^* in the figure.

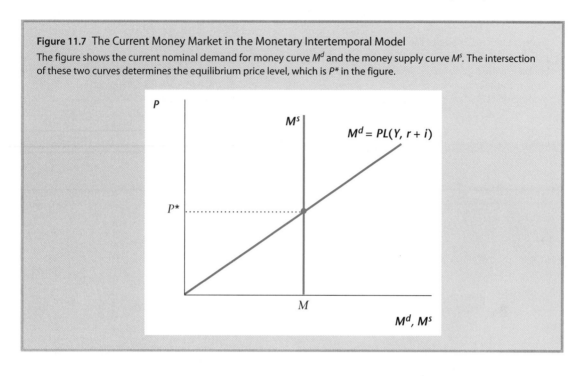

$M^s = M$. Then, for the money market to be in equilibrium, the nominal quantity of money supplied equals the quantity of money demanded, or

$$M = PL(Y, r). \qquad (11\text{-}12)$$

In Figure 11.7 we illustrate the workings of the money market, with the nominal money demand curve M^d being upward sloping and linear in P, as we saw previously. Here, we have added the money supply curve, which is a vertical line at the quantity M, because the money supply is exogenous. The intersection of the nominal money demand and nominal money supply curves determines the price level P. In the figure, the equilibrium price level is P^*.

Next, integrating the money market into the real intertemporal model of Chapter 10, we show in Figure 11.8 how the endogenous variables in the monetary intertemporal model are determined. In Figure 11.8(b), we depict equilibrium in the current goods market, where the output demand curve Y^d and the output supply curve Y^s jointly determine the equilibrium real interest rate r^* and the equilibrium quantity of aggregate output, Y^*. Then, in Figure 11.8(a), given the equilibrium real interest rate r^*, which determines the position of the labor supply curve $N^s(r^*)$, the labor demand curve N^d and the labor supply curve $N^s(r^*)$ jointly determine the equilibrium real wage w^* and the equilibrium quantity of employment, N^*. Then, in Figure 11.8(c), the equilibrium quantity of output, Y^*, and the equilibrium real interest rate r^* determine the position of the money demand curve M^d. Then, the money demand curve and the money supply curve in Figure 11.8(c) determine the equilibrium price level P^*.

Figure 11.8 The Complete Monetary Intertemporal Model

In the model, the equilibrium real interest rate r and equilibrium current aggregate output Y are determined in panel (b). Then, the real interest rate determines the position of the labor supply curve in panel (a), where the equilibrium real wage w and equilibrium employment N are determined. Finally, the equilibrium price level P is determined in the money market in panel (c), given the equilibrium real interest rate r and equilibrium output Y.

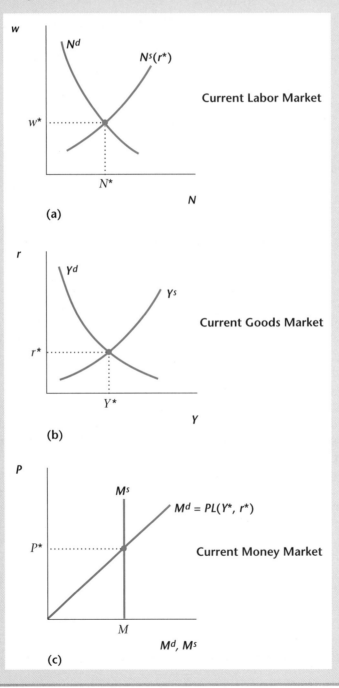

A Level Increase in the Money Supply and Monetary Neutrality

A government, through its central bank, has the power to increase the money supply by several different means. Historically, the power of a government to print money has been important, as the issue of new money can finance transfers to the private sector, can involve changing the quantity of interest-bearing assets held by the private sector, and can finance government expenditures. In this section, we would like to determine the effects on current macroeconomic variables of a one-time increase in the money supply. As we will see, a change in the level of the money supply of this sort is **neutral,** in that no real variables change, but all nominal quantities change in proportion to the change in the money supply. The neutrality of money is an important concept in monetary economics, and we want to understand the theory behind it and what it means in practice.

In the experiment we perform in the model, we suppose that the money supply is fixed at the quantity $M = M_1$ until the current period, as in Figure 11.9. Until the current period, everyone anticipates that the money supply remains fixed at the quantity M_1 forever. During the current period, however, the money supply increases from M_1 to M_2 and then remains at that level forever. What could cause such an increase in the money supply? From the government budget constraint, equation (11-11), the change in the money supply in the current period, $M - M^- = M_2 - M_1$, is positive, and so this positive change in the money supply in the current period needs to be offset by some

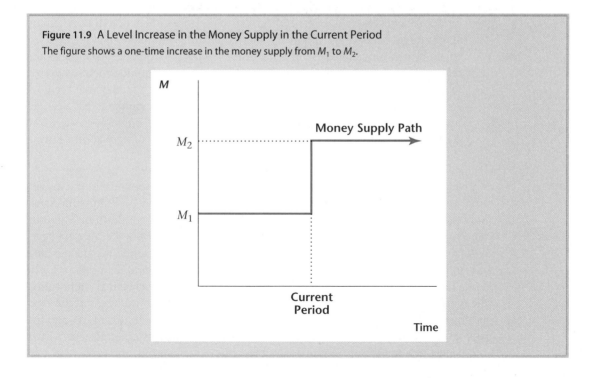

Figure 11.9 A Level Increase in the Money Supply in the Current Period
The figure shows a one-time increase in the money supply from M_1 to M_2.

other term in equation (11-11). Because the nominal interest rate from the previous period, R^-, and the quantity of bonds issued by the government in the previous period, B^-, were determined last period based on the expectation that the quantity of money in circulation would be M_1 forever, only the other terms in equation (11-11) could be affected. There are three possibilities:

1. The government could reduce current taxes T. The money supply increase, therefore, is reflected in a decrease in taxes on the household, which is the same as an increase in transfers. Milton Friedman referred to this method of increasing the money stock as a " **helicopter drop,**" because it is much like having a government helicopter fly over the countryside spewing money.

2. The government could reduce the quantity of bonds, B, that it issues during the current period. This is an **open market operation,** which in practice is carried out when the fiscal authority issues interest-bearing government debt, and then the monetary authority—the central bank—purchases some of this debt by issuing new money. An **open market purchase** is an exchange of money for interest-bearing debt by the monetary authority, and an **open market sale** is the sale of interest-bearing debt initially held by the monetary authority in exchange for money. In the case we examine here, where the money supply increases, there is an open market purchase. The day-to-day control of the money supply is accomplished in the United States mainly through open market operations by the Fed.

3. The government could temporarily increase the quantity of government spending, G, in the current period. Thus, the government would be printing money in order to finance government spending. When the government does this, it collects **seigniorage.** Seigniorage originally referred to the profit made by a seigneur, or ruler, from issuing coinage, but it has come to take on a broader meaning as the revenue earned by the government from issuing money. Seigniorage is also referred to as the revenue from the **inflation tax,** because the extra money that the government prints in general increases prices. Historically, seigniorage has been an important revenue-generating device. In the United States, seigniorage was a key source of revenue for the federal government during the Civil War and during World War I.

For our purposes here, it is most convenient for now to suppose that the money supply increase occurs through the first aforementioned method—a lump-sum transfer of money to the representative consumer. What happens in equilibrium when the money supply increases in the current period from M_1 to M_2? Here, because the level of the money supply does not matter for labor supply, labor demand, and the demand and supply of goods, the equilibrium determination of N, Y, r, and w in Figure 11.10 is unaffected by the current money supply M. That is, there a **classical dichotomy:** The model solves for all the real variables (output, employment, the real interest rate, and the real wage) in the labor market and the goods market in Figure 11.10, and the price level is then determined, given real output, in the money market. Real activity is completely separated from nominal variables (the money supply, the price level). In

Figure 11.10 The Effects of a Level Increase in M—The Neutrality of Money

A level increase in the money supply in the monetary intertemporal model from M_1 to M_2 has no effects on any real variables, but the price level increases in proportion to the increase in the money supply. Money is neutral.

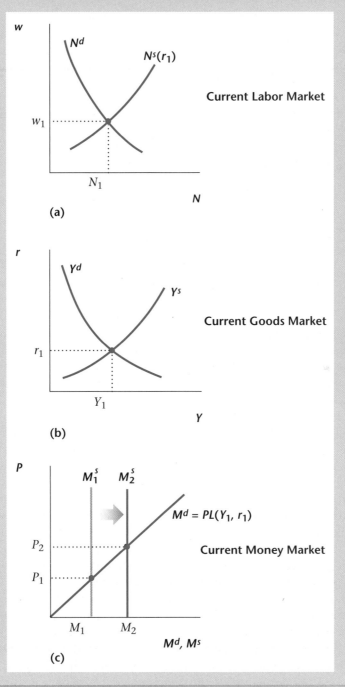

Figure 11.10(b), the real interest rate and current real output are given by r_1 and Y_1, respectively, and in Figure 11.10(a), the equilibrium real wage and level of employment are w_1 and N_1, respectively.

In the model, we want to investigate the effects of having a money supply of M_2 from the current period on, rather than a money supply of M_1. In Figure 11.10 there is no effect on real activity, because the labor market and goods market are unaffected by the level of the money supply. However, there is an effect on the price level. In Figure 11.10(c), the money supply curve shifts to the right because of the increase in the money supply from M_1 to M_2. The money demand curve is unaffected, because Y does not change and r does not change. As a result, the price level increases in equilibrium from P_1 to P_2. Further, we can say something about how much the price level increases. Because $M = PL(Y, r)$ in equilibrium (money supply equals money demand) and because Y, and r are unaffected by the increase in M, P must increase in proportion to M, so that $\frac{M}{P} = L(Y, r)$ remains unchanged. That is, if M increases by 10%, then P increases by 10%, so that the real money supply $\frac{M}{P}$ is unaffected. Note that the level increase in the money supply causes a level increase in the price level. There is only a one-time increase in the inflation rate (the rate of change in the price level), from the previous period to the current period, and no long-run increase in the inflation rate.

In this model, then, money is neutral. Money neutrality is said to hold if a change in the level of the money supply results only in a proportionate increase in prices, with no effects on any real variables. Thus, a change in the level of the money supply does not matter here. This does not mean, however, that money does not matter. In this model, if there were no money, then no goods could be consumed, because money is necessary to acquire these goods. In the real world, even if money were neutral, we know that if we eliminated money, then people would have to use more cumbersome means, such as barter, for making transactions. This would be much less efficient, and, in general, people would be worse off.

Is monetary neutrality a feature of the real world? In one sense, it almost obviously is. Suppose that the government could magically add a zero to all Federal Reserve notes. That is, suppose that overnight all $1 bills become $10 bills, all $5 bills become $50 bills, and so on. Suppose further that this change was announced several months in advance. It seems clear that, on the morning when everyone wakes up with their currency holdings increased by ten times, all sellers of goods would have anticipated this change and would have increased their prices by ten times as well, and that there would be no real change in aggregate economic activity. Although this thought experiment helps us understand the logic behind monetary neutrality, real-world increases in the money supply do not occur in this way, and there is in fact much debate about the extent of money neutrality in the short run.

Later, in Chapters 12 and 13, we explore the role of money in causing short-run fluctuations in real macroeconomic activity. Whether money is neutral in the short run can depend on how changes in the money supply are brought about, for example, through transfer payments, open market operations, or money-financed increases in government purchases. Also, it can matter whether a change in the money supply is widely anticipated. Key macroeconomic debates hinge on whether money is an important contributor to short-run fluctuations in aggregate economic activity and just what mechanism causes money to be nonneutral in the short run. However, macro-economists generally agree that money is neutral in the long run.

Short–Run Analysis in the Monetary Intertemporal Model: A Temporary Decrease in Total Factor Productivity

The monetary intertemporal model developed here is a foundation for the analysis of business cycles in Chapters 12 and 13. We must understand, therefore, how the model is used to analyze short-run issues. As an example, we examine here the effects in the current period of a temporary decrease in total factor productivity. From Chapter 10, we already know the real effects of such a shock to the economy, which are a decrease in aggregate output, consumption, investment, the real wage, and employment and an increase in the real interest rate. We show here that a temporary decrease in total factor productivity also causes an increase in the price level.

As mentioned earlier, it is convenient to consider the case in which the current inflation rate is zero, or $i = 0$, so that nominal and real interest rates are equal. Our analysis would not change if the inflation rate i were positive or negative; setting $i = 0$ is simply a convenience.

In Chapters 5 and 10, we examined the effects on the real side of the economy of a change in total factor productivity. Recall that a decrease in total factor productivity z could arise because of an increase in the relative price of energy or because of new government regulations, among other causes. In Figure 11.11 we show the equilibrium effects in the monetary intertemporal model of a temporary decrease in current total factor productivity z. In Figure 11.11(a) and (b), the effects are exactly the same as in the real intertemporal model in Chapter 9. That is, a decrease in z decreases the current marginal product of labor, which shifts the labor demand curve to the left from N_1^d to N_2^d in Figure 11.11(a), and the output supply curve shifts to the left from Y_1^s to Y_2^s in Figure 11.11(b). In equilibrium, the real interest rate rises from r_1 to r_2, and current aggregate output falls from Y_1 to Y_2. Because of the increase in the real interest rate, current consumption and current investment decrease. Also, the higher real interest rate results in intertemporal substitution of leisure, and the labor supply curve in Figure 11.11(a) shifts to the right, from $N^s(r_1)$ to $N^s(r_2)$. In equilibrium, the shift in the labor supply curve is sufficiently small that employment falls from N_1 to N_2 and the real wage falls from w_1 to w_2.

The effects that are new in the monetary intertemporal model occur in the money market in Figure 11.11(c). The equilibrium decrease in current real income Y reduces money demand, and the increase in the real interest rate r also reduces money demand. Therefore, the money demand curve shifts to the left, from $PL(Y_1, r_1)$ to $PL(Y_2, r_2)$. The money supply is fixed at M, thus in equilibrium the price level must rise from P_1 to P_2. The price level rises because, given the reduced real demand for money and the constant nominal money supply, it must rise to reduce the real supply of money so that it is equal to real money demand. Effectively, the same quantity of money is chasing a smaller quantity of goods, and so the price of goods, P, must rise.

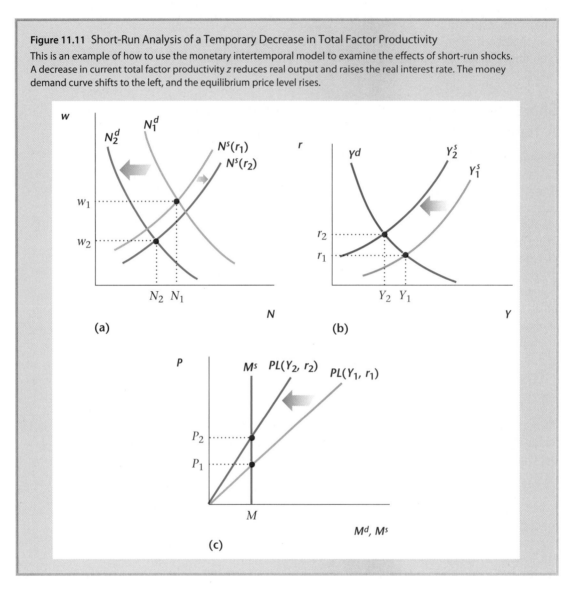

Figure 11.11 Short-Run Analysis of a Temporary Decrease in Total Factor Productivity
This is an example of how to use the monetary intertemporal model to examine the effects of short-run shocks. A decrease in current total factor productivity z reduces real output and raises the real interest rate. The money demand curve shifts to the left, and the equilibrium price level rises.

Recall from Chapter 10 that the real intertemporal model responded to a change in total factor productivity in a manner consistent with the key business cycle facts that we studied in Chapter 3. That is, in the data, consumption, investment, employment, and the real wage are procyclical, just as the model predicts. The monetary intertemporal model not only matches these real business cycle facts, but it also is consistent with observed price level behavior. That is, the price level is observed to be counter-cyclical in post–World War II data, from Chapter 3, and the monetary intertemporal model predicts this countercyclical price level behavior. When total factor productivity decreases, real output falls and the price level increases. Therefore, aggregate output and the price level move in opposite directions in response to total factor productivity shocks.

THEORY confronts the DATA

Changes in the Relative Price of Energy and the Price Level

The monetary intertemporal model predicts that increases in the price level are associated with decreases in total factor productivity, and in Chapter 3 we discussed how an increase in the relative price of energy can be interpreted as a decrease in total factor productivity. In Figure 11.12 we plot percentage deviations from trend in the price level and the relative price of energy. So as to better observe comovements, the percentage deviation from trend in the relative price of energy is divided by 10. What we observe in the figure is a clear positive correlation between the two time series, which is consistent with the idea that shocks to the

Figure 11.12 Percentage Deviations from Trend in the Price Level and in the Relative Price of Energy

In the figure, the two time series are positively correlated, particularly after 1970, which is consistent with the view that shocks to the relative price of energy are essentially negative aggregate productivity shocks.

(Continued)

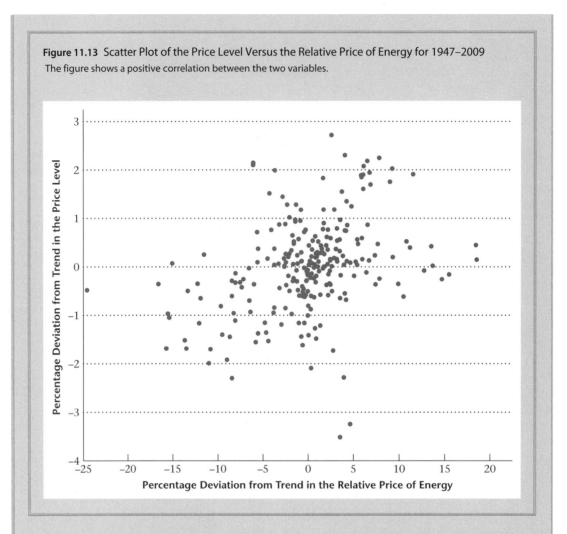

Figure 11.13 Scatter Plot of the Price Level Versus the Relative Price of Energy for 1947–2009
The figure shows a positive correlation between the two variables.

relative price of energy are essentially negative aggregate productivity shocks. The positive correlation in Figure 11.12 is particularly striking after 1970, when the extreme volatility in the relative price of energy occurs. We show the same variables in a scatter plot in Figure 11.13, where we can more readily observe the positive correlation between the percentage deviations from trend in the relative price of energy and the price level. The correlation coefficient for the two variables is 0.36.

Shifts in Money Demand

In the monetary intertemporal model, the demand for money is determined by the choices of consumers and firms concerning the means of payment to be used in transactions, and the choices of banks concerning the supply of credit card balances. Any factor that affects either the demand or supply of credit card balances will bring about a shift in the demand for money.

   Here, we will focus on the effects of a shift in the supply of credit card balances. In Figure 11.14, suppose that the supply curve for credit balances shifts to the left from $X_1^s(q)$ to $X_2^s(q)$. Such a shift could be caused, for example, by a widespread power failure that shuts down communications between some retailers and credit card issuers. As a result, while the price of credit card balances remains constant at $q = R$, the market quantity of credit balances falls from X_1^* to X_2^*. Therefore, the equilibrium quantity of credit card balances decreases for each R. Recall that the nominal demand for money is given by

$$M^d = PL(Y, R) = P[Y - (1 + R)X^*(R)],$$

so the demand for money is now higher for each P, Y, and R, since $X^*(R)$ is smaller for each R.

Figure 11.14 A Decrease in the Supply of Credit Card Balances
The equilibrium price does not change, but equilibrium quantity falls.

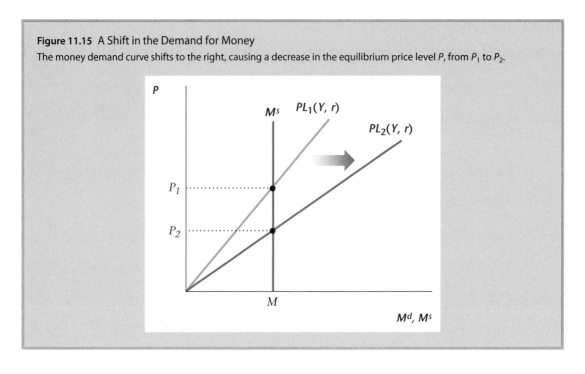

Figure 11.15 A Shift in the Demand for Money
The money demand curve shifts to the right, causing a decrease in the equilibrium price level P, from P_1 to P_2.

We will again set $i = 0$, so that the nominal interest rate equals the real interest rate, or $R = r$. Then, in Figure 11.15 the demand for money increases and the money demand curve shifts to the right, from $PL_1(Y, r)$ to $PL_2(Y, r)$. Now, Y and r are determined in the goods market and labor market, and they are unaffected by what happens to the supply and demand for money. Thus, the price level falls from P_1 to P_2. That is, because the real demand for money has risen, the real money supply (M/P) must rise to meet the increased demand, and this can only happen if P falls.

What would cause shifts in the supply and demand curves for credit card balances, other than our power-failure example, leading to shifts in the money demand function?

1. *New information technologies that lower the cost for consumers of accessing bank accounts.* In 1970, banks did not provide ATM machines or debit cards. A typical transactions account could typically be accessed only by going to the bank or by making a transaction with a check. ATM machines dramatically reduced the cost of communicating with banks. As well, a typical debit card transaction, handled electronically, can be done at much lower cost than a transaction involving a check, which requires depositing the check in the bank and routing it through the check-clearing system. Thus, replacing the use of checks with debit cards has reduced the cost of banking. Online banking is another technological development that has lowered the cost of banking transactions and reduced the demand for money. In the context of our model, we can think of these advances as reducing the average length of time between trips to replenish cash balances, which tends to reduce the average quantity of cash that each individual holds. For example,

the wider availability of ATMs and debit cards may mean that an individual will switch to visiting the ATM once every two days, withdrawing $40 each time, and holding an average cash balance of $20, from visiting the ATM once per week, withdrawing $140 each time, and holding an average cash balance of $70.

2. *New financial instruments that lower the cost of banking.* An example of such an instrument is a *sweep account*. These are accounts offered by banks that are held by businesses and that automatically minimize the money balances held in transactions accounts by making transfers in and out of interest-earning accounts. For a bank, a transactions account is more costly to offer, in part because it is subject to reserve requirements (discussed in Chapter 16), so reducing total balances in transactions accounts will lower costs for banks. Sweep accounts therefore lower the cost of banking and reduce the demand for money.

3. *A change in government regulations.* An example is the Depository Deregulation and Monetary Control Act of 1980, which permitted depository institutions (banks, savings and loan institutions, and credit unions) to pay interest on transactions accounts. This acted to lower the cost of banking and to reduce the demand for money.

4. *A change in the perceived riskiness of banks.* If consumers and firms perceive that holding a banking deposit is a more risky proposition—for example, if they think that banks could fail and they might lose their deposits—then consumers and firms may forego dealing with the banking system and simply conduct transactions using currency. During the Great Depression in the United States, and around the world during the recent financial crisis, the perceived instability of banks made households more uncertain about the value of their bank deposits, and there was an increase in the demand for currency. This therefore increased the demand for money. Bank riskiness is currently not an issue for small depositors in banks, because of government-provided deposit insurance, but it potentially matters for large depositors. We will discuss this further in Chapter 16.

5. *Changes in hour-to-hour, day-to-day, or week-to-week circumstances in the banking system.* There are times of the day, times of the week, or times of the month when the volume of financial transactions is particularly high or particularly low. For example, the volume of transactions among banks and other financial institutions tends to increase as financial traders get close to the end of the financial trading day. As the volume of transactions rises, the marginal cost of making financial transactions rises, due to congestion. In our model, this works as a shift to the left in the supply curve for credit card balances. Many such effects are predictable, but there are sometimes unpredictable shocks to the financial system, such as the failure of a large financial institution or a breakdown in the financial network because of a power failure or terrorist attack. Such failures and breakdowns tend to increase the demand for money.

Monetary Policy: Targets and Policy Rules

The analysis so far in this chapter shows that, if the central bank has control over the money supply, M, then changing M has no real consequences, only changing the price level in proportion to the change in the money supply. Why then should we care about monetary policy, if the model tells us that it does not matter for anything that consumers ultimately care about? As it turns out, inflation (persistent change in the price level) does matter for the economic welfare of consumers in the monetary intertemporal model, and we will explore this further in Chapter 16. Also, changes in the money supply may not be neutral in the short run, for reasons we have not yet modeled, and in Chapters 12 and 13 we explore this idea in detail.

For now, we will focus on the role of monetary policy in controlling inflation. Suppose that the monetary authority has a target inflation rate, which we denote by π^*. Recent behavior by the Federal Reserve System might seem to indicate that the Fed's optimal inflation rate is in the neighborhood of 2% to 3% per year. For our analysis, it does not particularly matter exactly what π^* is, as long as it is constant, so suppose that $\pi^* = 0$, which implies that the goal of the monetary authority is price stability, or a constant price level forever.

Now, what might get in the way of the monetary authority achieving its goal of price stability? First, as we studied in the previous section, there can be shocks to the money demand function which will change the price level. In Figure 11.16, if the money demand function shifts to the right from $PL_1(Y, r)$ to $PL_2(Y, r)$, then the price level will fall in equilibrium from P_1 to P_2, given the quantity of money supplied M_1. Second, there could be shocks to output demand. For example, suppose that an increase in future total factor productivity is expected. In Figure 11.17(a), this shifts the output demand curve to the right from Y_1^d to Y_2^d, which increases real output from Y_1 to Y_2, and increases the

Figure 11.16 A Shift in the Demand for Money

The money demand curve shifts to the right from $PL_1(Y, r)$ to $PL_2(Y, r)$. The price level will fall from P_1 to P_2 unless the monetary authority increases the money supply from M_1 to M_2.

Figure 11.17 A Shift in the Output Demand Curve

The output demand curve shifts to the right in panel (a), so Y increases and r increases. Assuming that the income effect on money demand is larger than the interest rate effect, the money demand curve shifts to the right in panel (b). The price level will fall from P_1 to P_2 unless the monetary authority increases the money supply from M_1 to M_2.

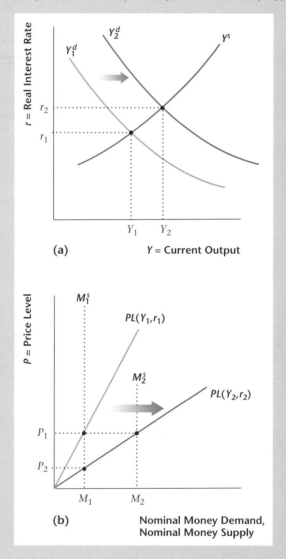

real interest rate from r_1 to r_2. In Figure 11.17(b), this could potentially shift the money demand curve to the left or the right, as an increase in Y will increase money demand, and an increase in r will reduce money demand. We assume that the effect of the increase in income on money demand dominates, so that the money demand curve in the figure shifts to the right from $PL(Y_1, r_1)$ to $PL(Y_2, r_2)$. As a result, the price level will fall

Figure 11.18 A Shift in the Output Supply Curve

The output demand curve shifts to the right in panel (a), so Y increases and r decreases. The money demand curve shifts to the right in panel (b). The price level will fall from P_1 to P_2 unless the monetary authority increases the money supply from M_1 to M_2.

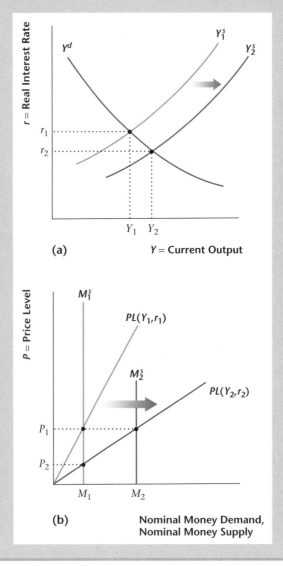

from P_1 to P_2. Third, there could be shocks to output supply. For example, if there is a temporary increase in total factor productivity, then in Figure 11.18(a) the output supply curve shifts to the right from Y_1^s to Y_2^s, which results in an increase in output from Y_1 to Y_2, and a decrease in the real interest rate from r_1 to r_2. In Figure 11.18(b), the money demand curve shifts to the right from $PL(Y_1, r_1)$ to $PL(Y_2, r_2)$ and the price level falls in equilibrium from P_1 to P_2.

Now, as long as the monetary authority has full information about all events in the economy, it is clear what it should do in response to a shift in money demand, a shift in output demand, or a shift in output supply. Since the monetary authority's goal is price stability, it should increase the money supply in response to any shock that increases money demand. That is, changes in money demand stemming from shifts in the money demand function, changes in income, or changes in the real interest rate should all be accommodated by moving the money supply in the same direction as the change in money demand. In Figures 11.16, 11.17(b), and 11.18(b), the money supply should increase from M_1 to M_2 when the money demand curve shifts to the right.

This may seem to make monetary policy look easy. In practice, monetary policy is not easy, in part because the Fed never has full information about the current state of the economy, and this makes monetary policy decision making costly and time-consuming. To simplify policy decisions, discussion of monetary policy typically focusses on a small set of simple **monetary policy rules**. A monetary policy rule, once set, determines how the monetary authority should control the money supply in response to variables in the economy that it can observe. In the next two sections, we discuss two different policy rules, which are money supply targeting and nominal interest rate targeting. We are interested in how these rules perform in response to particular shocks to the economy.

Money Supply Targeting

Money supply targeting is an approach to monetary policy recommended by Milton Friedman in 1968.[5] Friedman's recommendation is part of the **monetarist** approach to monetary policy making. Friedman argued that the economy would perform best if the central bank set a target for the growth rate in some monetary aggregate, say a 4% per year target for the annual growth rate in M1, and then stuck to this target growth rate forever. Money supply targeting was a popular approach to monetary policy by the world's central banks in the 1970s and 1980s and was typically implemented in the form of target growth ranges for one or more monetary aggregates.

In terms of performance in response to shocks to the economy, money supply targeting performs poorly, which is why money supply targeting has been virtually abandoned by most central banks. If the monetary authority's goal is price stability, and there is a shift in money demand, output demand, or output supply, and if the money supply is held constant at M_1 in Figures 11.16, 11.17(b), and 11.18(b), then the price level will fall in each case, and the monetary authority does not achieve its goal. The only feature of money supply targeting that recommends itself is that, if the money supply has been growing at a high rate, thus causing a high rate of inflation, then targeting money supply growth at a low rate commits the monetary authority to reducing long-run inflation. We will explore the role of commitment in monetary policy in Chapter 18.

Nominal Interest Rate Targeting

Given the Fisher relation, the nominal interest rate is $R = r + \pi$, where r is the real interest rate and π is the inflation rate. Suppose that the monetary authority commits

---

[5]See M. Friedman, 1968. "The Role of Monetary Policy," *American Economic Review* 58, 1–17.

to a nominal interest rate target R^*, where $R^* = r_1$, with r_1 being the current real interest rate. Therefore, as long as the real interest rate stays constant, this rule is consistent with price stability, or $\pi = 0$.

Given the nominal interest rate target R^*, suppose that there is a temporary shift in the money demand function, as in Figure 11.16. If the money supply did not change, then the price level would fall from P_1 to P_2, so since the current price level is temporarily low, the inflation rate is expected to be high, which will tend to increase the nominal interest rate. To hold the nominal interest rate constant at R^* requires that the monetary authority increase the money supply from M_1 to M_2. As a result, the price level is stabilized while the monetary authority maintains its nominal interest rate target. Therefore, nominal interest rate targeting achieves the desired outcome in the face of shocks to money demand.

Now, suppose instead that there is a shift to the right in the output demand curve, as in Figure 11.17(a). The real interest rate then increases from r_1 to r_2. Now, if the central bank wants to maintain price stability, we know that this requires an increase in the money supply from M_1 to M_2. But if the price level then does not change, the nominal interest rate must then rise by the amount $r_2 - r_1$, so maintaining a constant nominal interest rate target R^* in the face of an aggregate shock that shifts the output demand curve is not feasible. Similarly, if there is a shift to the right in the output supply curve, as in Figure 11.18(a), the real interest rate falls. Maintaining price stability again requires increasing the money supply, in Figure 11.18(b), but this is inconsistent with holding constant the nominal interest rate target, as the target should fall to achieve the central bank's goals. Therefore, the nominal interest rate rule does not give good performance under shocks that shift the output demand curve or the output supply curve.

The current policy approach of the Federal Reserve System could be characterized as one of nominal interest rate targeting, at least between the dates at which the decision-making arm of the Federal Reserve System, the **Federal Open Market Committee (FOMC)** meets. The FOMC meets about every six weeks, and at its meeting a decision is made on a new target for the nominal **federal funds rate,** which is the interest rate on interbank overnight lending, a key interest rate in the financial market. The Fed's nominal-interest-rate-targeting procedure makes sense, first, because the shocks that matter most over a very short horizon, such as a few weeks, are money demand shocks, which a nominal interest rate target is well suited to accommodate in an appropriate way, with the result being price level stabilization. Shocks which shift the output demand or output supply curves are typically much slower to develop, although it is difficult to detect exactly what shocks are affecting the economy, as information is imperfect, and economic variables sometimes move in confusing ways. It makes sense for the Fed to set a nominal interest rate target at intervals of about six weeks and to re-evaluate the state of economy at each FOMC meeting to determine whether the real interest rate (which is a variable that cannot be directly observed) has changed. In terms of our model, a shift to the right in the output demand curve, which increases the real interest rate, would necessitate an increase in the nominal federal funds rate target, and a shift to the right in the output supply curve would imply the need for a reduction in the nominal federal funds rate target.

MACROECONOMICS IN ACTION
Should Monetary Policy Respond to Asset Prices?

As we will show in Chapter 15, the monetary intertemporal model implies that an increase in the inflation rate will reduce economic welfare. Therefore, the model provides a reason for the central bank to care about the inflation rate, and justifies an inflation target as a long-run objective for monetary policy. If the central bank has an inflation target, we showed in this chapter how the central bank can hit this target by using a nominal interest rate targeting approach as a policy rule, provided that it has full information on the shocks hitting the economy. The central bank should increase its nominal interest rate target in response to a positive shift in output demand and reduce it in response to a positive shift in output supply. We also showed how a nominal interest rate target, revised every few weeks, works well in getting close to the inflation target, when the central bank has poor information about the state of the economy.

It is sometimes argued that central bankers should care about financial market conditions (among other things), in addition to the inflation rate. For example, Alan Greenspan's comments about "irrational exuberance" in the stock market in 1996 appeared to reflect his concern with the rate of change in the prices of stocks at that time.[6] It could be that good or bad performance of the financial system could affect the banking system, thus changing the costs of banking and shifting the money demand function. Another mechanism by which the financial system could matter for monetary policy is through a "financial accelerator" effect, studied by Ben Bernanke, Mark Gertler, and Simon Gilchrist.[7]

The financial accelerator effect tends to amplify the effects of shocks to the economy, through financial market frictions, which could make a difference for how monetary policy should be conducted.

In an article on monetary policy, delivered at the 1999 Federal Reserve Bank of Kansas City annual policy conference in Jackson Hole, Wyoming, Ben Bernanke and Mark Gertler evaluate whether stock market behavior should be taken into consideration in formulating monetary policy.[8] This article is interesting in part because Ben Bernanke is now the Chairman of the Federal Reserve Board, and the article was written while he was a Professor at Princeton University. The article therefore gives some insight into how the current Fed Chairman thinks.

Bernanke and Gertler study the behavior of a computational economic model, complete with a financial accelerator effect, when the model is subjected to financial shocks that could be characterized as irrational exuberance. Fundamentally, Bernanke and Gertler are interested in whether the central bank's policy rule should respond to such irrational exuberance episodes. Bernanke and Gertler's conclusion is that a flexible approach to inflation targeting is what works best. That is, Bernanke and Gertler favor a kind of modified Taylor rule, which acts to indirectly mitigate any financial market inefficiencies. That is, according to Bernanke and Gertler, central banks need not be directly concerned with the behavior of financial markets and of asset prices in particular, as a flexible inflation-targeting approach looks after inflation and financial market instability at the same time.

---

[6]See http://www.federalreserve.gov/BOARDDOCS/SPEECHES/19961205.htm

[7]See Bernanke, B., Gertler, M., and Gilchrist, S. 1996. "The Financial Accelerator and the Flight to Quality," *Review of Economics and Statistics* 78, 1–15.

[8]See Bernanke, B., and Gertler, M. 1999. "Monetary Policy and Asset Price Volatility," Federal Reserve Bank of Kansas City *Quarterly Review*, December.

Perspectives on the Financial Crisis
Increases in the Monetary Base and the Fed's Balance Sheet

From Chapter 1, we know that there is not a tight relationship between prices and the quantity of money, however measured. Whether we look at the relationship between a measure of the price level and a measure of money, or the relationship between the rate of change in the price level (the inflation rate) and the rate of growth in the money supply, movements in the money supply do not appear to have much to do with movements in the price level over the short run. However, this could simply be due to the fact that there are short-run fluctuations in income and interest rates that affect the quantity of money demanded in the short run, along with other factors that shift the money demand function in the short run. This tends to cause the price level to fluctuate independently of what is happening to the money supply. It would be interesting to see what would happen if there were a very large injection of outside money into the economy by the central bank so that we could study the effects, as such an injection would swamp whatever other shocks were occurring at the time.

It turns out that the Fed has recently run this experiment for us. In Figure 11.19 we show the monetary base, or M0, for the United States, and the price level, as measured by the consumer price index, for the period 1980–2009. In the figure, the monetary base and the price level are both indexed to equal 100 in 1980. What we observe in the figure is that, between 1980 and late 2008, the price level and the monetary base both grow smoothly, but the monetary base grows at a higher rate. This difference in growth rates can potentially be explained by growth in real income over this period, which causes growth in the demand for money, thus implying a gap between the rate of growth in money and the rate of growth in prices. However, beginning in late 2008, there was a dramatic increase in the monetary base in

the figure, with the base more than doubling in the course of a few months. Such an increase in the quantity of outside money is unprecedented since the founding of the Fed in 1914. A puzzling feature of Figure 11.19 is that this huge increase in the stock of outside money apparently had no effect on prices. In fact, there was a downward blip in the consumer price index at about the same time that the money stock was increasing dramatically. If money were neutral in the short run, we should have observed roughly a doubling in the consumer price index from late 2008 to early 2009.

What is going on here? To get some perspective on this, it will be informative to examine what is on both the asset and liability sides of the Federal Reserve's balance sheet, displayed in Table 11.4 for July 15, 2009.[9]

The Fed is in some ways just like any other bank in that it has assets and liabilities, and the liabilities are used in transactions. However, the Fed has the special power to issue outside money, which makes it different from private banks. Also, traditionally, the Fed has restricted the types of assets on its balance sheet mainly to interest-bearing securities issued by the U.S. Treasury and discount window loans, issued to depository financial institutions as part of the Fed's role as lender of last resort (to be discussed in detail in Chapter 16). The Fed's assets have traditionally been essentially default-free, making them different from the assets on the balance sheet of a private bank. Private banks spend time and effort screening the assets they hold, and these assets—for example, business loans and consumer loans—are typically subject to default.

---

[9]For more information, see http://www.federalreserve.gov/monetarypolicy/bst_fedsbalancesheet.htm

The balance sheet in Table 11.4 certainly does not look like a traditional central bank balance sheet, at the Fed or most other central banks in the world. The large increase in the monetary base, represented on the liabilities side of the balance sheet by increases in currency in circulation and in reserves (deposits of banks with the Fed and currency held by banks), was used by the Fed to finance the purchase of non-traditional central bank assets, including agency securities, mortgage-backed securities, loans that were not typical discount window loans, and commercial paper.

What are these unusual items on the asset side of the Fed's balance sheet? The agency securities on the Fed's balance sheet are primarily the debt obligations of FNMA and FHLMC ("Fannie Mae" and "Freddie Mac"), which are government agencies set up to promote mortgage lending in the United States. Mortgage-backed securities are tradable packages of mortgage loans, typically put together by agencies such as FNMA, FHLMC, private banks, or investment banks. The Fed acquired these agency securities and mortgage-backed securities in an attempt to reallocate credit in the U.S. economy toward mortgage lending. Some of the loans held as assets by the Fed are typical discount window loans to banks, but this quantity also includes loans to an insurance company, AIG, and to other nontraditional recipients of Fed lending. Commercial paper is short-term debt obligations of private firms, and it is an item that the Fed would not normally buy. All of the unusual items on the Fed's balance sheet make it look more like a private bank in that it is engaging in some kinds of lending activities that are more risky than is typical for a central bank.

What reasons could there be for the disconnect between the growth in the monetary base from late 2008 to early 2009 and the behavior of the price level for the same period? Potential explanations are the following:

1. *There is a liquidity trap.* A **liquidity trap** occurs when the nominal interest rate is zero, or essentially zero. Once the nominal interest rate is zero, there is no opportunity cost to holding money. Therefore, if the Fed injects more outside money into the economy, through whatever means, the private sector is willing to hold this extra outside money and not spend it. In fact, from late 2008 to early 2009, the nominal interest rate on short-term U.S. treasury bills was about 0.25 %, and the Fed was paying interest on reserves held by banks at a rate of 0.25%. Thus, for a typical bank, holding reserves was equivalent to holding treasury bills. Further, most of the extra outside money injected by the Fed was held as reserves (not as currency), which is consistent with the liquidity trap story. In terms of our model, if there is a liquidity trap, then when the nominal interest rate is zero, the money demand function in Figure 11.7 would be horizontal at the current price level, so that changes in the money supply would have no effect on the price level.

2. *The effects of a change in the money supply are determined by how it is backed.* By "backing" we mean the assets on the Fed's balance sheet that the Fed buys with the outside money that is issued. In the experiment we conducted in our model to show the neutrality of money in Figure 11.10, the increase in the money supply was not backed, in the sense that the money supply increased permanently, and there was no intention by the central bank to reverse this increase in the future. In contrast, the Fed could buy $1 billion in mortgage-backed securities in December 2008 by issuing outside money, and then sell those mortgage-backed securities in December 2009 (at the existing market price) and retire the money it received in exchange for the mortgage-backed securities. In this sense, the entire increase in the money supply that was engineered by the Fed from late 2008 to early 2009 could later be reversed through the sale of the assets on the Fed's balance sheet. Consistent with the liquidity trap story above,

banks that in early 2009 were hoarding reserves may be pleased in the future to sell those reserves back to the Fed in exchange for commercial paper, mortgage-backed securities, and agency securities, for example. In this way, the increase in outside money could be held by banks (and therefore not be spent) in the present and then returned to the Fed in the future.

One could then argue that the Fed's strategy of more than doubling the monetary base could have no inflationary consequences, as long as the public believes that the Fed will ultimately reverse the outside money injection by selling off the assets it acquired, thus retiring the excess outside money. The risk is that the public comes to distrust the Fed's stated intentions of executing an "exit strategy" from its dramatic monetary intervention. If the private sector does not believe that the 2008–09 money injection by the Fed is temporary, but is instead permanent, then a large increase in the price level will have to result.

Figure 11.19 The Monetary Base and the Price Level, 1980–2009

The monetary base (M0) and the price level (the CPI) are scaled to equal 100 in 1980. Both series show a smooth increase from 1980 to late 2008, with the monetary base growing faster than the price level. From later 2008 to early 2009, the monetary base more than doubles, but there is no corresponding increase in the price level.

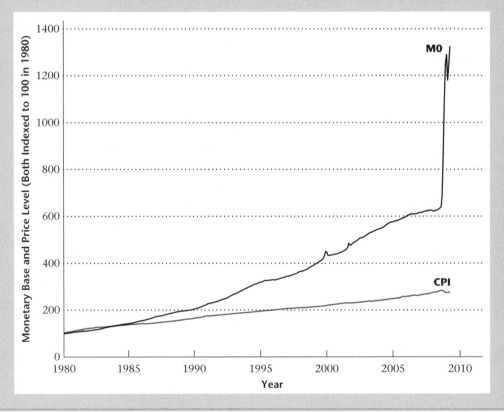

Table 11.4   The Federal Reserve Balance Sheet, July 15, 2009 (in $billions)

Assets: $2,011.7	Liabilities: $2,011
Treasury Securities: $677.2	Currency in Circulation: $910.6
Agency Securities: $99.5	Reserves: $781.7
Mortgage-backed Securities: $489.1	Deposits other than Reserves: $249.9
Loans: $385.6	Other: $68.8
Commercial paper: $112.3	
Other: $248.0	

Chapter Summary

- Money has three functions in the economy—it is a medium of exchange, a store of value, and a unit of account.

- The key measures of money are the monetary aggregates, which are the sums of quantities of assets having the functions of money. The monetary base, or M0, is the narrowest monetary aggregate, and it consists only of liabilities of the Federal Reserve System, in particular currency and the reserves of depository institutions. Other broader monetary aggregates, which include bank deposits and other assets, are M1 (broader than M0), M2 (broader than M1), and M3 (broader than M2).

- The monetary intertemporal model builds on the real intertemporal model of Chapter 10 by including supply and demand in the market for money. An important element of the monetary intertemporal model is the transactions constraint, which states that purchases by consumers and firms must be financed with cash on hand and by using credit cards.

- The demand for money is determined by first determining the equilibrium price and quantity of credit card balances. Credit balances are supplied by banks.

- In the monetary intertemporal model, money is neutral, in the sense that an increase in the level of the money supply leaves real variables—employment, output, consumption, the real interest rate, the real money supply, and the real wage—unaffected, and causes only a proportionate increase in all money prices.

- In the monetary intertemporal model, a short-run decrease in total factor productivity leads to an increase in the price level, which is consistent with evidence from U.S. historical episodes when the relative price of energy increased.

- Shifts in money demand can occur because of new information technologies, new financial instruments, changes in government regulations, changes in the perceived riskiness of banks, or changes in hour-to-hour, day-to-day, or week-to-week circumstances in the banking system.

- When the central bank cannot observe all the shocks hitting the economy, money supply policy rules tend to work poorly, and nominal interest rate policy rules tend to work well.

Key Terms

Cash-in-advance constraint A condition stating that a consumer's cash on hand must be at least as large as the nominal quantity of purchases of cash goods he or she wants to make. (p. 406)

Cash-in-advance model A macroeconomic model in which it is assumed that some goods must be purchased with cash on hand at the beginning of the period. (p. 400)

Classical dichotomy Situation in an economic model where real variables are determined by real factors, and the money supply determines only the price level. (p. 416)

Double coincidence of wants Situation in which two people meet and the first person has what the second person wants and the second has what the first wants. (p. 399)

Federal funds rate A key financial market interest rate, which is the interest rate on overnight lending among banks and other financial institutions. The FOMC typically sets a target for the federal funds rate. (p. 430)

Federal Open Market Committee (FOMC) The monetary policy decision-making arm of the Federal Reserve System. (p. 430)

Federal Reserve System (the Fed) The central bank of the United States. (p. 398)

Fisher relation Condition stating that $1 + r = \frac{1 + R}{1 + i}$, where r is the real interest rate from the current period to the future period, R is the nominal interest rate from the current period to the future period, and i is the rate of inflation between the current period and the future period. (p. 400)

Helicopter drop Milton Friedman's thought experiment, which corresponds to an increase in the money supply brought about by transfers. (p. 416)

Inflation rate The rate of change in the price level. (p. 400)

Inflation tax Inflation arising when the government prints money to extract seigniorage; this effectively taxes the private sector. (p. 416)

Liquidity trap A situation where the nominal interest rate is zero, and injections of outside money into the economy are willingly held as assets by the private sector and not spent on goods and services. (p. 433)

Medium of exchange A property of money; a medium of exchange is accepted in transactions for the sole reason that it can in turn be exchanged for other goods and services. (p. 397)

Monetarist An adherent of ideas shared by Milton Friedman, who argued for money supply targeting as a monetary policy rule. (p. 429)

Monetary aggregates These are measures of the money supply; each is the sum of a number of different types of assets in the economy. (p. 398)

Monetary base The quantity of M0, consisting of U.S. currency outside the Federal Reserve System and the deposits of depository institutions with the Fed. (p. 398)

Monetary policy rules Relationships between the actions of the central bank and the economic variables that the central bank can observe. (p. 429)

Money demand function The relationship between the quantity of money that economic agents wish to hold and other macroeconomic variables. (p. 396)

Neutral Describes a government policy that has no real effects. (p. 415)

Neutrality of money Money is neutral if a change in its level has no real effects and causes only a proportionate increase in the price level. (p. 396)

Nominal bond A bond for which the payoff is defined in terms of money. (p. 400)

Nominal interest rate If R is the nominal interest rate on an asset, then if 1 unit of money is exchanged for a given quantity of the asset in the current period, then this quantity of the asset pays off $1 + R$ units of money next period. (p. 400)

Open market operation A purchase or sale of interest-bearing government debt by the central bank. (p. 416)

Open market purchase An open market operation in which interest-bearing government debt is purchased by the central bank, increasing the money supply. (p. 416)

Open market sale An open market operation in which interest-bearing government debt is sold by the central bank, decreasing the money supply. (p. 416)

Outside money This is identical to the monetary base. (p. 398)

Seigniorage Revenue generated by the government through printing money. (p. 416)

Single coincidence of wants Situation in which two people meet and one person has what the other wants. (p. 399)

Store of value A property of money that is shared with other assets that permit current goods and services to be traded for future goods and services. (p. 397)

Transactions constraint A constraint for consumers and firms, stating that purchases of goods and assets must be financed with money or an increase in credit card balances. (p. 405)

Unit of account The object in an economy in which prices and contracts are denominated. (p. 397)

Questions for Review

1. What are the three functions of money?
2. List three monetary aggregates and the assets that these monetary aggregates include.
3. Why is money used in exchange when people could carry out transactions by trading goods or using credit?
4. How are the real interest rate, the nominal interest rate, and the inflation rate related to one another?
5. What is the real rate of interest on money?
6. What determines the demand for money in the monetary intertemporal model?
7. What are the effects of an increase in the money supply in the monetary intertemporal model?
8. What are three ways in which the government could bring about a change in the money supply?
9. What are the effects of a short-run decrease in total factor productivity in the monetary intertemporal model?
10. How does a shift in the demand for credit card balances affect the demand for money, and why?
11. List the factors that lead to an increase in money demand.
12. What is the goal of monetary policy in the monetary intertemporal model?
13. What is a monetary policy rule? List two of them.
14. How do the two monetary policy rules you listed in question 13 perform in response to shifts in money demand, shifts in output demand, and shifts in output supply?

Problems

1. In the monetary intertemporal model, show that it is possible to have an equilibrium where money is not held and only credit cards are used in transactions. Is there such a thing as a price level in this equilibrium? Does monetary policy work? If so, how? Explain your results, and what they mean for actual economies.

2. The government decides that the use of credit cards is bad and introduces a tax on credit card balances. That is, if a consumer or firm holds a credit card balance of X (in real terms), he or she is taxed tX, where t is the tax rate. Determine the effects on the equilibrium price and quantity of credit card balances, the demand for money, and the price level, and explain your results.

3. Suppose that the nominal interest rate is zero, that is $R = 0$.
   (a) What is the equilibrium quantity of credit card balances?
   (b) In what sense does the economy run more efficiently with $R = 0$ than with $R > 0$?
   (c) Explain your results in parts (a) and (b). Discuss the realism of these predictions.

4. In the monetary intertemporal model, suppose that the money supply is fixed for all time. Determine the effects of a temporary increase in the quantity of government purchases on current equilibrium output, employment, the real wage, the real interest rate, the nominal interest rate, and the price level. Explain your results.

5. In the monetary intertemporal model, suppose that the money supply is fixed for all time and determine the effects of a decrease in the capital stock, brought about by a war or natural disaster, on current equilibrium output, employment, the real wage, the real interest rate, the nominal interest rate, and the price level. Explain your results.

6. A new technological innovation is announced that will come on line in the future period. What are the current effects on aggregate output, consumption, investment, employment, the real wage, the real interest rate, the nominal interest rate, and the price level? Explain your results.

7. Suppose that there is an increase in the number of ATM machines in service. What are the effects of this innovation on the demand for money and on the price level?

8. Suppose that the monetary authority's goal is stabilize the price level, and suppose also that the monetary authority uses a nominal interest rate policy rule. Suppose that in the short run the monetary authority can only observe the market nominal interest rate and the money supply and cannot observe any other economic variables, except for surprise pieces of news.
   (a) The monetary authority observes an increase in the nominal interest rate and also gets a surprise piece of news that housing construction has increased. What should it do?
   (b) The monetary authority observes an increase in the nominal interest rate and receives a surprise piece of news that there has been a power failure in New York City. What should it do?
   (c) The monetary authority observes a decrease in the nominal interest rate, and receives a surprise piece of news that the automobile industry has become dramatically more productive. What should it do?

9. Suppose that we allow for the fact that cash can be stolen, but assume that a stolen credit card cannot be used, as it is instantly cancelled, so no one steals credit cards. Determine the effects this has on the quantity and price of credit card balances, the demand for money, and the price level. Explain your results.

Working with the Data

1. The income velocity of money, V, is defined by

$$V = \frac{PY}{M},$$

where PY is nominal GDP and M is the money supply. Calculate the income velocities of M0, M1, and M2 over the period 1959–2009, and plot these time series, that is use M0, M1, and M2, respectively, as the measure of M in the above equation. What do you notice in these time series, and how might our theory of money demand in this chapter make sense of what you see?

2. Construct a scatter plot of M1 against real GDP for the period 1959–2009.
   (a) Is there a positive or negative correlation in the scatter plot?
   (b) Is the correlation you observed in part (a) evidence that money is not neutral? Why or why not?

3. Plot the income velocity of M1 against the three-month Treasury bill rate for 1959–2009. What do you observe? Is this consistent with the theory of money demand in this chapter?

chapter 12

Market-Clearing Models of the Business Cycle

The publication of John Maynard Keynes's *A General Theory of Employment, Interest, and Money*[1] was a key departure from previous views of the causes of business cycles and the role of government policy. By the 1960s, Keynesian thought had come to dominate macroeconomics. At that time, most macroeconomists accepted Keynesian business cycle models as capturing the behavior of the economy in the short run. There appeared to be broad agreement that money was not neutral in the short run, and most macroeconomists viewed this nonneutrality as arising from the short-run inflexibility of wages and prices. Price and wage inflexibility, and the resulting possibility that all markets may not clear at each point in time, were the key to the mechanism by which shocks to the economy could cause aggregate output to fluctuate in Keynesian models. In the Keynesian view, the fact that prices and wages are slow to move to clear markets implies that there is a role for monetary and fiscal policy in stabilizing the economy in response to aggregate shocks.

By the 1960s, the main disagreements in macroeconomics were between monetarists and Keynesians. Monetarists tended to believe that monetary policy was a more effective stabilization tool than fiscal policy, but they were skeptical about the ability of government policy to fine-tune the economy; some monetarists argued that the short run over which policy could be effective was very short indeed. Keynesians believed that monetary policy was unimportant relative to fiscal policy and that government policy should take an active role in guiding the economy along a smooth growth path. It may have seemed at the time that all the theoretical issues in macroeconomics had been resolved, in that most everyone agreed that the Keynesian model was a satisfactory model of the macroeconomy and all that remained was for empirical work to sort out the disagreements between monetarists and Keynesians.

This view changed dramatically, however, with the advent of the rational expectations revolution in the early 1970s. Some important early contributors to the rational expectations revolution were Robert Lucas, Thomas Sargent, Neil Wallace, and

---

[1]See J. M. Keynes, 1936. *The General Theory of Employment, Interest, and Money*, Macmillan, London.

Robert Barro. Two key principles coming out of the rational expectations revolution were the following: (1) Macroeconomic models should be based on microeconomic principles—that is, they should be grounded in descriptions of the preferences, endowments, and technology and the optimizing behavior of consumers and firms; and (2) equilibrium models (as opposed to models with price and wage inflexibility where all markets need not clear) are the most productive vehicles for studying macroeconomic phenomena. There was some resistance to following these two principles, but there was wide acceptance, at least of the first principle, by the 1980s. It became clear as well, with respect to the second principle, that equilibrium modeling does not automatically rule out an active role for government policy. Indeed, as we see in this chapter, some Keynesian ideas can be exposited using equilibrium models.

In this chapter, we study three models of the business cycle, which were each developed as explicit equilibrium models with optimizing consumers and firms. These models are the real business cycle model, the segmented markets model, and the Keynesian coordination failure model. Each model differs from the others in terms of what is important in causing business cycles and the role implied for government policy. However, we will show that we can describe each of these models by building on the monetary intertemporal model of Chapter 11 in straightforward ways. We study each model in turn, examine how well each matches the business cycle facts discussed in Chapter 3, and discuss each model's shortcomings.

We study equilibrium models of the business cycle first in this chapter, as this follows naturally from the theory we have developed in Chapters 4, 5, 8, 9, 10, and 11. We study a modern Keynesian (or "New Keynesian") model with inflexible (or "sticky") prices in Chapter 13.

Why is it necessary to study several different business cycle models? As we discussed in Chapter 3, business cycles are remarkably similar in terms of the comovements among macroeconomic time series. However, business cycles can have many causes, and fiscal and monetary policymakers are constantly struggling to understand what macroeconomic shocks are driving the economy and what this implies for future aggregate activity. Each business cycle model we study allows us to understand one or a few features of the economy and some aspects of the economy's response to macroeconomic shocks. Putting all of these features into one model would produce an unwieldy mess that would not help us understand the fundamentals of business cycle behavior and government policy.

Different business cycle models, however, sometimes give contradictory advice concerning the role of government policy. Does this mean that business cycle theory has nothing to say? The contradictory advice that different business cycle models give concerning the role of government policy reflects the reality of macroeconomic policymaking. Policymakers in federal and state governments and in central banks often disagree about the direction in which policy should move. To make persuasive arguments, however, policymakers have to ground their arguments in well-articulated macroeconomic models. This chapter shows, in part, how we can evaluate and compare macroeconomic models and come to conclusions about their relative usefulness.

The Real Business Cycle Model

Real business cycle theory was introduced by Finn Kydland and Edward Prescott[2] in the early 1980s. Kydland and Prescott asked whether a standard model of economic growth subjected to random productivity shocks (that is, "real" shocks, as opposed to monetary shocks) could replicate, qualitatively and quantitatively, observed business cycles. Kydland and Prescott were perhaps motivated to pursue this question by the observation we made in Chapter 6, and replicate in Figure 12.1, that the detrended Solow residual (a measure of total factor productivity z) closely tracks detrended real GDP. Thus, productivity shocks appear to be a potential explanation for business cycles.

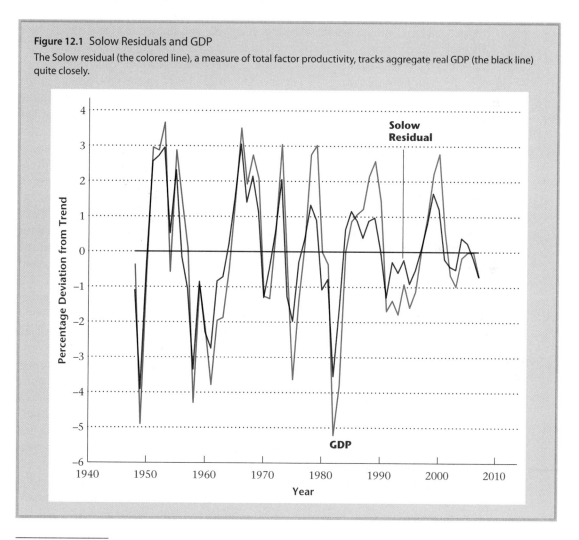

Figure 12.1 Solow Residuals and GDP

The Solow residual (the colored line), a measure of total factor productivity, tracks aggregate real GDP (the black line) quite closely.

[2]See F. Kydland and E. Prescott, 1982. "Time to Build and Aggregate Fluctuations," *Econometrica* 50, 1345–1370.

Recall that many factors can lead to changes in total factor productivity. Essentially, any change implying that an economy can produce more aggregate output with the same factor inputs is an increase in total factor productivity, that is, an increase in z. Factors that increase z include good weather, technological innovations, the easing of government regulations, and decreases in the relative price of energy.

The version of the real business cycle model we study here is the monetary intertemporal model from Chapter 10. Although Kydland and Prescott studied a model where there was no role for money, Thomas Cooley and Gary Hansen showed, in a cash-in-advance real business cycle model, that adding money made little difference to the results.[3]

The Solow residual, as observed in Figure 12.1, is a persistent variable. When it is above (below) trend, it tends to stay there. This tells us that total factor productivity shocks are persistent, so that when there is a current increase in z, we would expect future total factor productivity z' to be higher as well. This implies that, in analyzing how the real business cycle model reacts to a total factor productivity shock, we need to combine the results of two different shocks from Chapter 10, a shock to z and a shock to z'.

Now, suppose that there is a persistent increase in total factor productivity in the monetary intertemporal model, so that there are increases in z and z', current and future total factor productivity respectively. In Figure 12.2 we show the equilibrium effects. The increase in current total factor productivity z increases the marginal product of labor for each quantity of labor input, so that the labor demand curve shifts rightward from N_1^d to N_2^d in Figure 12.2(a), and this shifts the output supply curve rightward from Y_1^s to Y_2^s in Figure 12.2(b). There are additional effects because of the anticipated increase in future total factor productivity z'. First, the demand for investment goods increases as the representative firm anticipates an increase in the future marginal productivity of capital. Second, the representative consumer anticipates that higher future total factor productivity implies higher future income, so that lifetime wealth increases and the demand for consumption goods goes up. Both of these factors cause the output demand curve Y^d to shift rightward from Y_1^d to Y_2^d.

In equilibrium, in Figure 12.2(b), aggregate output must rise, but it may seem that the real interest rate may rise or fall, depending on whether the shift in output demand dominates the shift in output supply, or vice versa. However, the real interest rate will fall for the following reasons. The consumer now expects that current and future income will be higher because of the positive and persistent productivity shock. However, because the shock is in part temporary (i.e., the increase in z' is not as large as the increase in z), consumers are expecting their real income to fall. The consumer wishes to smooth consumption over time, and so he or she tries to save more so as to consume less in the current period and more in the future, but this has the effect of driving down the market real interest rate, from r_1 to r_2 in Figure 12.2(b). Current consumption expenditures then increase because of the decrease in the real interest rate, the increase in current real income, and the increase in future real income stemming from the increase in future total factor productivity. Current investment rises because of the decrease in the real interest

---

[3]See T. Cooley and G. Hansen, 1989. "The Inflation Tax in a Real Business Cycle Model," *American Economic Review* 79, 733–748.

Figure 12.2 Effects of a Persistent Increase in Total Factor Productivity in the Real Business Cycle Model

With a persistent increase in total factor productivity, the output supply curve shifts to the right because of the increase in current total factor productivity, and the output demand curve shifts to the right because of the anticipated increase in future total factor productivity. The model replicates the key business cycle facts.

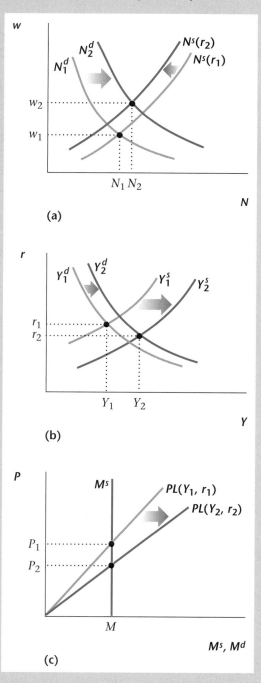

(a)

(b)

(c)

rate and the increase in future total factor productivity. In the money market, in Figure 12.2(c), because equilibrium real output rises and the real interest rate falls, money demand increases, and the nominal money demand curve shifts rightward from $PL(Y_1, r_1)$ to $PL(Y_2, r_2)$. Therefore, in equilibrium, the price level falls from P_1 to P_2. In the labor market, in Figure 12.2(a), the labor supply curve shifts leftward from $N^s(r_1)$ to $N^s(r_2)$ because of the fall in the real interest rate. However, as in Chapter 7, the labor supply curve shifts less than the labor demand curve, since the intertemporal substitution effect on labor supply from the change in the real interest rate is relatively small. Hence, current equilibrium employment rises from N_1 to N_2, and the current real wage rises from w_1 to w_2. In Figure 12.3, we show the response of average labor productivity. Initially, employment is N_1 and output is Y_1, and average labor productivity is the slope of AB. After the increase in current and future total factor productivity, employment increases to N_2 and output to Y_2, with average labor productivity being the slope of AD in the figure. Thus, average labor productivity increases. We could have drawn the figure so that employment increased sufficiently that the slope of AD was smaller than the slope of AB. However, Figure 12.3 is consistent with the results from Kydland and Prescott's model, where N would increase in this circumstance but not enough that Y/N would decrease.

Figure 12.3 Average Labor Productivity with Total Factor Productivity Shocks

When output and employment are high, average labor productivity is also high, as in the data.

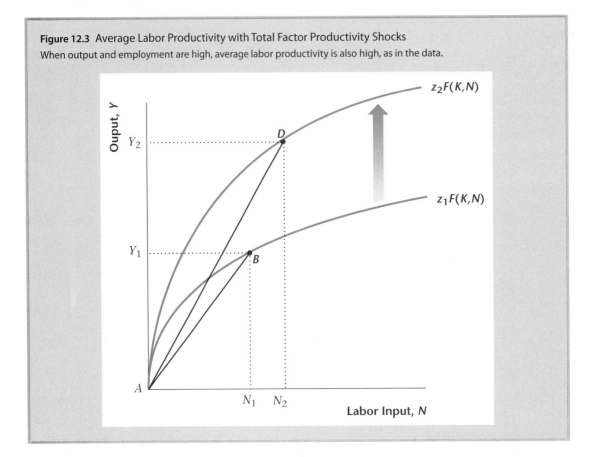

Table 12.1   Data Versus Predictions of the Real Business Cycle Model with Productivity Shocks

Variable	Data	Model
Consumption	Procyclical	Procyclical
Investment	Procyclical	Procyclical
Price Level	Countercyclical	Countercyclical
Money Supply	Procyclical	-
Employment	Procyclical	Procyclical
Real Wage	Procyclical	Procyclical
Average Labor Productivity	Procyclical	Procyclical

Therefore, as shown in Table 12.1, the real business cycle model qualitatively explains essentially all of the key business cycle regularities. Consumption, investment, employment, the real wage, and average labor productivity are procyclical, and the price level is countercyclical. Perhaps more important, the real business cycle model can also quantitatively replicate some important observations about business cycles, as can be shown if a more sophisticated version of this model is put on a computer and simulated. The model can explain the fact that consumption is less variable than output and that investment is more variable than output. Further, it can approximately replicate the observed relative variabilities in consumption, investment, output, and employment, which were discussed in Chapter 3.[4] As we see in Table 12.1, one feature of the data that the model in this form cannot replicate is the procyclicality of the money supply. We discuss this further in the next subsection.

Real Business Cycles and the Behavior of the Money Supply

In the real business cycle model, money is neutral; level changes in M have no effect on real variables and cause a proportionate increase in the price level. It might seem, then, that the real business cycle model cannot explain two key business cycle regularities from Chapter 3, which are the following:

1. The nominal money supply is procyclical.
2. The nominal money supply tends to lead real GDP.

As we show, however, the real business cycle model can be made consistent with these two facts through some straightforward extensions.

First, in the real business cycle model, the procyclicality of the nominal money supply can be explained by way of **endogenous money**. That is, in practice, the money supply is not determined exogenously by the monetary authority but responds to

---

[4]See E. Prescott, 1986. "Theory Ahead of Business Cycle Measurement," *Federal Reserve Bank of Minneapolis Quarterly Review*, Fall, 9–22.

conditions in the economy. Endogenous money can explain the procyclicality of money in two ways, supposing that business cycles are caused by fluctuations in z. First, if our money supply measure is M1, M2, or some broader monetary aggregate, then part of the money supply consists of bank deposits. When aggregate output increases, all sectors in the economy, including the banking sector, tend to experience an increase in activity at the same time. An increase in banking sector activity is reflected in an increase in the quantity of bank deposits and, therefore, in an increase in M1, M2, and the broader monetary aggregates, and we observe the money supply increasing when total factor productivity increases.

Second, the money supply could increase in response to an increase in z because of the response of monetary policy. Suppose that the central bank wishes to stabilize the price level. When there is a persistent increase in total factor productivity, this causes an equilibrium increase in Y, and the real interest rate falls, as we showed above. In Figure 12.4 output increases from Y_1 to Y_2 and the real interest rate falls from r_1 to r_2, so that the nominal money demand curve shifts rightward from $PL(Y_1, r_1)$ to $PL(Y_2, r_2)$. If the central bank did nothing, the price level would fall from P_1 to P_2. However, because the central bank wishes to stabilize the price level, it increases the money supply from M_1 to M_2, shifting the money supply curve from M_1^s to M_2^s. As a result, the money supply is procyclical, because it increases when output increases in response to the persistent total factor productivity increase.

Figure 12.4 Procyclical Money Supply in the Real Business Cycle Model with Endogenous Money

A persistent increase in total factor productivity increases aggregate real income and reduces the real interest rate, causing money demand to increase. If the central bank attempts to stabilize the price level, this increases the money supply in response to the total factor productivity shock.

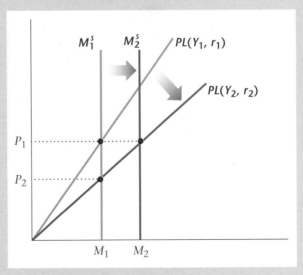

Fact (2) above, that the nominal money supply tends to lead real GDP, appears to be a particular problem, because this might be viewed as strong evidence that money supply fluctuations cause the fluctuations in real GDP. Indeed, this was the interpretation given to fact (2) by Milton Friedman and Anna Schwartz.[5] However, the weak link in Friedman and Schwartz's interpretation of the data is that **statistical causality** need not tell us anything about true causality. A variable a statistically causes a variable b if current a helps predict future b. For example, every year we observe birds flying south before the onset of winter, and so the flight patterns of birds statistically predict the winter. However, birds flying south do not cause winter; it is winter that is causing the birds to fly south.

There is an explanation for the tendency of money to lead output that is analogous to the example of birds flying south for the winter. There are two reasons that productivity shocks could cause money to lead output, again through the process of endogenous money. First, the banking sector tends to lead other sectors of the economy, as banks provide loans for real activity that will occur at a later date. When bank loans increase, so do bank deposits, as a bank borrows by way of bank deposits to finance its lending. Thus, bank deposits tend to be procyclical and to lead real GDP, and, therefore, M1, M2, and broader monetary aggregates tend to lead real GDP. Second, if the monetary authority is trying to stabilize prices, and it uses all available information efficiently, it can predict an increase in output due to an increase in z before the output increase is observed. Because an increase in the money supply may take time to affect prices, the monetary authority may want to act on this information before the increase in output and the decrease in the price level actually occur. Thus, money can lead real GDP because of preemptive monetary policy actions.

Implications of Real Business Cycle Theory for Government Policy

Now that we know how the real business cycle model works and have discussed how it fits the data, we can explore what the model implies for government policy. In the basic real business cycle model, there is no role for government stabilization policy. First, level changes in the money supply are neutral, thus attempts to smooth out business cycles through monetary policy actions have no effect. Second, because all markets clear, and there are no inefficiencies (for example, distorting taxes or externalities) in the basic model that government policy should correct, there is also no reason that the government should vary its spending in response to fluctuations in total factor productivity. Government spending can have an effect on output, but the level of such spending should be set according to the appropriate long-run role of the government in providing public goods (goods and services, such as national defense, that cannot or should not be provided by the private sector), not to smooth short-run fluctuations in aggregate GDP. In the basic real business cycle model, business cycles are essentially optimal responses of the economy to fluctuations in total factor productivity, and nothing should be done about them. Given the first fundamental theorem of welfare

[5]See M. Friedman and A. Schwartz, 1963. *A Monetary History of the United States, 1867–1960,* National Bureau of Economic Research, Cambridge, MA.

economics, from Chapter 5, if the allocation of resources in the economy is Pareto optimal, there is no need for the government to intervene, unless we think the government should redistribute income and wealth.

Although there is no role for government in the basic real business cycle model, other more elaborate versions of this model explain a role for government arising from the need to correct market failures and distortions.[6] For example, in practice all taxes are distorting. Income taxes distort labor supply decisions because firms and workers face different effective wage rates, and sales taxes distort consumer purchasing patterns because firms and consumers do not face the same effective prices for all goods. Over time, it is efficient for the government to smooth out these distortions, or welfare losses, that arise from taxation. This can tell us that tax rates should be smooth over time, which then implies that the government should let total tax revenues rise in booms and fall in recessions, as tax revenue increases with income if the income tax rate is constant. This is a kind of countercyclical government policy, which may look like it is intended to stabilize output but is actually aimed at smoothing tax distortions.

Critique of Real Business Cycle Theory

The real business cycle model clearly does a good job of fitting the key business cycle facts. Real business cycle theory is also internally consistent, and it helps focus our attention on how government policy should act to correct market failures and distortions, rather than on attempting to correct for the fact that prices and wages may not clear markets over short periods of time, as in Keynesian models of the type we study in Chapter 13.

Real business cycle theory certainly has shortcomings, however, in its ability to explain business cycles. One problem is that the assessment of whether real business cycle theory fits the data is based on using the Solow residual to measure total factor productivity. There is good reason to believe that there is a large cyclical error in how the Solow residual measures total factor productivity z, and that the close tracking of detrended GDP by the Solow residual in Figure 12.1 might at least partly be accounted for by measurement error. During a boom, the aggregate capital stock is close to being fully utilized. Most machinery is running full time, and many manufacturing plants are in operation 24 hours per day. Further, the workers who are operating the plant and equipment are very busy. These workers are under pressure to produce output, because demand is high. There are few opportunities to take breaks, and overtime work is common. Thus, workers are being fully utilized as well. Alternatively, in a temporary recession, the aggregate capital stock is not fully utilized, in that some machinery is sitting idle and plants are not running 24 hours per day. Further, during a temporary recession, a firm may not wish to lay workers off (even though there is not much for them to do), because this may mean that these workers would get other jobs and the firm would lose workers having valuable skills that are specific to the firm. Thus, workers employed at the firm during a recession might not be working very hard—they might take long breaks and produce little. In other words, the workforce tends to be

---

[6]See T. Cooley, 1995. *Frontiers of Business Cycle Research,* Princeton University Press, Princeton, NJ.

underutilized during a recession, just as the aggregate capital stock is. This phenomenon of underutilization of labor during a recession is sometimes called **labor hoarding**.

The underutilization of capital and labor during a recession is a problem for the measurement of total factor productivity, because during recessions the capital stock and the labor input would be measured as being higher than they actually are. Thus, in terms of measurement, we could see a drop in output during a recession and infer that total factor productivity dropped because the Solow residual decreased. But output may have dropped simply because the quantity of inputs in production dropped, with no change in total factor productivity.

To see how this works, consider the following example. Suppose that the production function is Cobb-Douglas with a capital share in output of 36%, as we assumed in calculating Solow residuals in Chapter 6. That is, the production function takes the form

$$Y = zK^{0.36}N^{0.64}, \tag{12-1}$$

where Y is aggregate output, z is total factor productivity, K is the capital stock, and N is employment. Now, suppose initially that $z = 1$, $K = 100$, and $N = 50$, so that, from equation (12-1), we have $Y = 64.2$, and capital and labor are full utilized. Then, suppose that a recession occurs that is not the result of a drop in total factor productivity, so that $z = 1$ as before. Firms still have capital on hand equal to 100 units, and employment is still 50 units, and so measured capital is $K = 100$ and measured employment is $N = 50$. However, suppose only 95% of the capital in existence is actually being used in production (the rest is shut down), so that actual capital is $K = 95$. Further, suppose the employed workforce is being used only 90% as intensively as before, with workers actually only putting in 90% of the time working than they were formerly. Thus, actual employment is $N = 45$. Plugging $z = 1$, $K = 95$, and $N = 45$ into equation (12-1), we get $Y = 58.9$. Now, if we mistakenly used the measured capital stock, measured employment, and measured output to calculate the Solow residual, we would obtain

$$\hat{z} = \frac{58.9}{(100)^{0.36}(50)^{0.64}} = 0.918,$$

where $\hat{z}$ is the Solow residual or measured total factor productivity. Therefore, we would measure total factor productivity as having decreased by 8.2%, when it really had not changed at all. This shows how decreases in the utilization of factors of production during recessions can lead to biases in the measurement of total factor productivity and to biases in the evaluation of the importance of total factor productivity shocks for business cycles.

The Segmented Markets Model

In Chapter 10, we introduced the monetary intertemporal model, in which money plays a role in the economy in facilitating transactions. In that model, money is neutral since, if the central bank increases the stock of money in circulation, this will serve only to increase all prices and wages in proportion to the money supply increase. There are no effects on any real variables. However, there is ample empirical evidence, including the work of Friedman and Schwartz mentioned in the previous section, that supports the view that money is neutral in the long run but is not neutral in the short run.

In the 1960s, most macroeconomists regarded any short-run nonneutralities of money as being the result of out-of-equilibrium behavior of the economy arising from sticky wages or prices. With the rational expectations revolution in the 1970s, however, macroeconomists began to construct models in which money was not neutral and that could explain features of aggregate data such as the co-movements among nominal and real variables. In these models, all prices and wages were fully flexible, with all markets clearing all the time. For example, in Robert Lucas's "money surprise" model,[7] money is not neutral because of imperfect information; workers supply more labor and output increases when the money supply increases because workers mistake a nominal wage increase for a real wage increase. We will use the money surprise model when we discuss policy commitment issues in Chapter 18.

While the money surprise model was important in its time, it is currently not taken that seriously by macroeconomists as a model explaining the short-run nonneutrality of money. A more modern market-clearing model in which money is not neutral in the short run is the segmented markets model. Early work on segmented markets models of money was done by Sanford Grossman and Laurence Weiss,[8] and by Julio Rotemberg,[9] with later important breakthroughs by Robert Lucas and Timothy Fuerst.[10]

A key feature of the segmented markets model is that some economic agents participate more actively in financial markets than do others. In practice, financial institutions such as banks life insurance companies, and investment banks are well-connected to financial markets, as are many non-financial firms and some individual consumers. These institutions and individuals trade on a regular basis in markets for stocks, bonds, and money market instruments, and when the central bank intervenes in financial markets, these economic agents will receive the brunt of the first-round effects of monetary policy. Some businesses, and particularly some consumers, are not as well-connected to financial markets, in that they hold most of their wealth in savings accounts, transactions accounts, and housing. In the 2004 Survey of Consumer Finances for the United States, the Federal Reserve Board found that 8.6% of U.S. families surveyed had no checking account and 6.6% had no financial assets. Low income families hold very little in the way of stocks, bonds, or investment accounts.[11]

When the central bank increases the money supply through an open market purchase of interest-bearing government securities, it is economic agents who are well-connected to financial markets who will be on the receiving end of the money supply increase, and the initial effects will be felt most in financial markets. One of these initial effects will be a **liquidity effect**—a short-run decrease in the real interest rate as the

[7]See R. Lucas, 1972. "Expectations and the Neutrality of Money," *Journal of Economic Theory* 4, 103–124.

[8]Grossman, S. and Weiss, L. 1983. "A Transactions-Based Model of the Monetary Transmission Mechanism," *American Economic Review* 73, 871–880.

[9]Rotemberg, J. 1984. "A Monetary Equilibrium Model with Transactions Costs," *Journal of Political Economy* 92, 40–58.

[10]See Lucas, R. 1990. "Liquidity and Interest Rates," *Journal of Economic Theory* 50, 237–264 and Fuerst, T. 1992. "Liquidity, Loanable Funds, and Real Activity," *Journal of Monetary Economics* 29, 3–24.

[11]See http://www.federalreserve.gov/PUBS/oss/oss2/2004/scf2004home.html#scfdata2004

result of a money supply increase. As well, employment and output will increase temporarily. In the long run, the effects of a money supply increase are felt by all economic agents, with prices and wages increasing in proportion to the money supply increase. That is, money is neutral in the long run. The segmentation effect refers to the short run segmentation between goods markets and financial markets resulting from the limited participation of some economic agents in financial markets.

To show how the segmented markets theory works, we need to modify our monetary intertemporal model from Chapter 11. To simplify our approach, suppose that the consumers in our model access financial markets infrequently so that, within the current time period represented in the model, they do not trade on financial markets and are not affected by central bank actions. This requires modifying our treatment of the market for money, in which the price level is determined. The demand for money in the money market of the segmented markets model reflects only the money that consumers hold for transactions purposes. Since in the model consumers do not trade interest-bearing assets (including savings accounts), the market interest rate is irrelevant for their decisions concerning how much money to hold. Therefore, we can now write the money demand function as

$$M^d = PL(Y),$$

so that money demand in the segmented markets model depends only on the price level P and real income Y.

In contrast to consumers, firms are active participants in financial markets in the segmented markets model. These firms exchange nominal bonds for money in financial markets and also pay their workers using money. An important feature of the segmented markets model is that firms come into the period with a quantity of cash balances that they have planned to hold given what they expect to happen during the period. During the period, firms trade cash and nominal bonds on financial markets and pay their workers from available cash balances. Thus, firms are liquidity constrained in buying labor. One of the events that may occur within the period is that the central bank could increase the money supply. In equilibrium, since firms are the only financial market participants, firms will have to end up holding this money after trading on financial markets. To induce them to hold this extra cash, the nominal interest rate will have to fall, which reduces the opportunity cost of holding money. Firms, which now have more cash than what they had planned for, will use the extra cash to purchase more labor. As a result, the demand for labor will rise. This will cause the real wage to increase.

To see how this works in our model, suppose that the central bank increases the money supply. Liquidity-constrained firms, as financial market participants, receive this money supply increase, so their demand for labor increases, and in Figure 12.5(a) the labor demand curve shifts to the right, from N_1^d to N_2^d. This then implies a shift to the right in the output supply curve in Figure 12.5(b) from Y_1^s to Y_2^s. In Figure 12.5 (c), the money supply is determined by what is available for consumers to spend in the goods market. During the period, consumers do not participate in financial markets, so they are not immediate recipients of the money supply increase. Thus, in Figure 12.5(c), the money supply curve does not shift.

Figure 12.5 Effects of an Unanticipated Increase in the Money Supply in the Segmented Markets Model

An unanticipated increase in money supply shifts the labor demand curve to the right because the firm has more cash on hand to hire workers. The output supply curve shifts right, output rises, the real interest rate falls, and the price level falls because money demand increases. The real wage rises and employment rises. The goods market is not initially directly affected by the money supply increase.

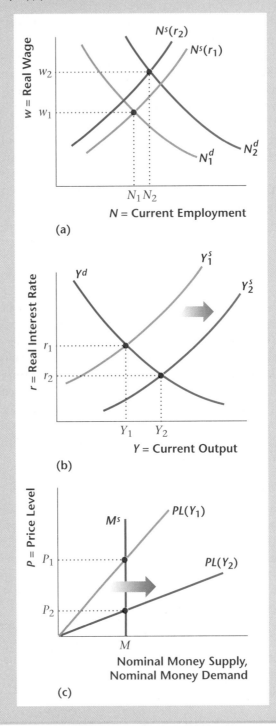

As a result, in Figure 12.5(b) the equilibrium real interest rate falls from r_1 to r_2, and real output rises from Y_1 to Y_2. The demand for money rises, as real income has risen, so the money demand curve shifts to the right in Figure 12.5(c), from $PL(Y_1)$ to $PL(Y_2)$. As a result, the equilibrium price level must fall from P_1 to P_2. With the decrease in the real interest rate, the labor supply curve shifts to the left from $N^s(r_1)$ to $N^s(r_2)$ in Figure 12.5(a), but not enough that employment falls, because we know that employment must have increased to give an increase in output (total factor productivity and the capital stock have not changed). In Figure 12.5(a), the real wage rises from w_1 to w_2 and employment increases from N_1 to N_2.

Money is not neutral in the short run in the segmented markets model, since an unanticipated increase in the money supply causes changes in real variables. The real interest rate falls, real output rises, the real wage rises, and employment increases. The fall in the real interest rate in response to the money supply increase is the liquidity effect that we referred to above. Money is not neutral in the short run in the segmented markets model because liquidity-constrained firms, who are active in financial markets, receive the new money that is injected into the economy by the central bank and use this money to buy labor. The money supply increase would be neutral if consumers were active in financial markets, as we assumed in the basic monetary intertemporal model in Chapter 11. In the segmented markets model, money will ultimately be neutral in the long run. That is, the money supply increase that was initially received only by firms will find its way back to consumers due to the fact that the increase in the money supply is used in part to purchase labor services. The long run effects are described by Figure 11.10 in Chapter 11, where money is neutral.

How do the predictions of the model with monetary shocks match the business cycle facts from Chapter 3? The results are summarized in Table 12.2. First, since real income increases and the real interest rate falls, consumption increases, so consumption is procyclical in response to shocks to the money supply. Second, investment increases because of the decrease in the real interest rate, so investment is also procyclical. The price level is countercyclical, because the price level falls due to the increase in money demand resulting from higher real income. It may seem odd that the price level falls, but this is

---

Table 12.2 Data Versus Predictions of the Segmented Markets Model with Monetary Shocks

Variable	Data	Model
Consumption	Procyclical	Procyclical
Investment	Procyclical	Procyclical
Price Level	Countercyclical	Countercyclical
Money Supply	Procyclical	Procyclical
Employment	Procyclical	Procyclical
Real Wage	Procyclical	Procyclical
Average Labor Productivity	Procyclical	Countercyclical

because the new money injected into the economy does not find its way immediately into the market for goods. As well, an important prediction of the model is that the money supply is procyclical. In the labor market, the real wage and employment are both procyclical.

In terms of all of the above predictions, the model matches the qualitative business cycle facts. However, the model fails to predict procyclical average labor productivity. This is because the production function does not shift in response to the money supply increase, but employment increases. As the marginal product of labor decreases with the quantity of labor employed, the new workers added must reduce the average product of labor. Therefore, average labor productivity must decrease in response to the money supply increase, so average labor productivity is countercyclical. The segmented markets model thus does not do as well as the real business cycle model in fitting the business cycle facts.

Government Policy in the Segmented Markets Model

It may seem that by engineering an increase in the money supply that the monetary authority can get something for nothing. Real GDP and consumption increases, and this may seem like a good thing. However, the reason that real output increased in Figure 12.5 was that firms did not correctly predict what the monetary authority would do. In some sense, firms were fooled into hiring more workers and producing more output than they otherwise would have. If the central bank changes the money supply in an unexpected way, the outcome will be economic inefficiency.

In the segmented markets model, the central bank can introduce unpredictable variability in the money supply, and real variables will fluctuate as a result. However, this unsystematic monetary variability will only add uncertainty to the environment in which economic agents have to make decisions, and this can only be a bad thing. An important lesson from this model is that monetary policy should be predictable, and many central banks have taken this message seriously. For example, the Federal Reserve is now more open than it once was in revealing its decisions and the deliberations that went on behind the scenes.

Engineering money surprises is clearly bad policy for the central bank in this model, but one might then ask whether the segmented markets model provides a justification for some other type of active monetary policy. Is there any sense in which the monetary authority should change the money supply in response to economic events, or should it just do nothing? What the model tells us is that the monetary authority can improve matters, but only if it can react to economic events more quickly than private economic agents do. For example, suppose that there is a temporary increase in total factor productivity during the period, but this happens after the firm has locked in its decision concerning how much money to hold as of the beginning of the period. The firm now finds itself with too little money on hand to purchase the quantity of labor it would like to hire. In Figure 12.6, the output supply curve shifts to the right from Y_1^s to Y_2^s because of a shift to the right in the labor demand curve. However, if the firm were not constrained by the amount of cash it has on hand, it would be socially efficient for the output supply curve to shift further to the right, to Y_3^s. Therefore, because the firm is liquidity constrained, the real interest rate does not fall by enough, and output does

Figure 12.6 A Welfare-Improving Role for Active Monetary Policy

A temporary increase in total factor productivity occurs after the firm has locked in its cash management decisions. The firm finds itself cash-constrained in hiring workers. The output supply curve shifts right, but by a socially inefficient amount, from Y_1^s to Y_2^s. An increase in the money supply in response to the productivity shock can shift the output supply curve to its socially efficient position at Y_3^s.

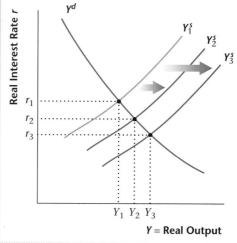

Y = Real Output

not increase by enough. The monetary authority can solve this problem if it can observe the increase in total factor productivity and react to it with an increase in the money supply that is just enough to shift the output supply curve to Y_3^s.

For active monetary policy to work here requires that the central bank not only be able to act more quickly than private sector economic agents do, but that it also have good and accurate information. In the productivity shock example above, the monetary authority needs to observe the total factor productivity shock and to respond to it appropriately.

A Critique of the Segmented Markets Model

The segmented markets model tells a coherent story about the nonneutrality of money based on the actions of optimizing consumers and firms. Money is not neutral because there are frictions in the model—goods markets and financial markets are not completely integrated, and firms are liquidity constrained in making their employment decisions. The model did not do badly in terms of explaining some key business cycle facts, so it is plausible that monetary shocks could have contributed to business cycles over the period 1947–2009, although the model fails to predict procyclical average labor productivity.

However, as a model of how money supply fluctuations might contribute to business cycles, the model may leave something to be desired. The model does not tell us why a central bank would want to make real variables fluctuate by causing the money supply to fluctuate over time in a way unrelated to economic activity. The central bank would have to naively believe that it is a good idea to fool firms into hiring more workers than they would have planned to. The model could, however, explain the observed procyclicality of the money supply through endogenous money. That is, the central bank could be efficiently responding to total factor productivity shocks by increasing the money supply in response to positive productivity shocks and decreasing it in response to negative productivity shocks, which acts to adjust the firm's available money balances appropriately, and to bring about an efficient allocation of resources.

A key defect in the model may be the reliance on liquidity-constrained firms to explain why employment would expand in response to a money supply increase. While it may seem plausible that a significant fraction of consumers in the economy are financially constrained in some way, it seems less plausible for firms. Therefore, the mechanism by which a money supply increase causes an increase in employment and output is questionable.

Monetary Shocks, Real Shocks, and U.S. Experience During Some Pre-Financial Crisis Recessions

THEORY confronts the DATA

If the Solow residual were a highly accurate measure of total factor productivity, we would take Figure 12.1 as strong evidence that the primary cause of business cycles in the United States after World War II was fluctuations in total factor productivity. We would then have little reason to go beyond the real business cycle model to explain why we have booms and recessions. However, as we explained above, there is good reason to believe that there is significant bias in the Solow residual as a measure of total factor productivity. Therefore, in determining the causes of particular recessions, for example, it is useful to look at other sources of evidence than just the behavior of the Solow residual. This is also important because movements in the Solow residual, even if they accurately reflect movements in total factor productivity, may be due to many different factors.

As an example of how we can use available evidence to sort out the causes of particular business cycle events, suppose that we focus on recessions that have occurred since 1970, but before

the 2008–2009 financial crisis and recession (we will address that later in this chapter). These are the recessions of 1974–1975, 1981–1982, 1990–1991, and 2001. Further, in terms of evidence on what the underlying shocks were that caused these recessions, we focus on movements in the monetary base (M0) and interest rates as indicators of monetary shocks and on movements in the relative price of energy as a source of total factor productivity shocks. This evidence is displayed in Figures 12.7, 12.8, and 12.9, where for Figure 12.7 we include data only up to the end of 2007, so as to leave out the extremely large monetary policy intervention that occurred in the recent financial crisis.

First, consider the 1974–1975 recession. Conventional wisdom is that this recession was caused by a negative shock to total factor productivity arising from a sharp increase in the relative price of energy. This is certainly consistent with Figures 12.7–12.9. In Figure 12.9, there was a large increase in the relative price of energy in 1973, which resulted from a cutback in crude oil

Figure 12.7 Percentage Deviations from Trend in the Monetary Base and Real GDP

In the 1974–1975 recession, there is a small decrease in the money supply below trend, and the money supply decreases significantly below trend during the 1981–1982 recession. After that, the monetary base displays erratic behavior, probably caused by volatility in money demand.

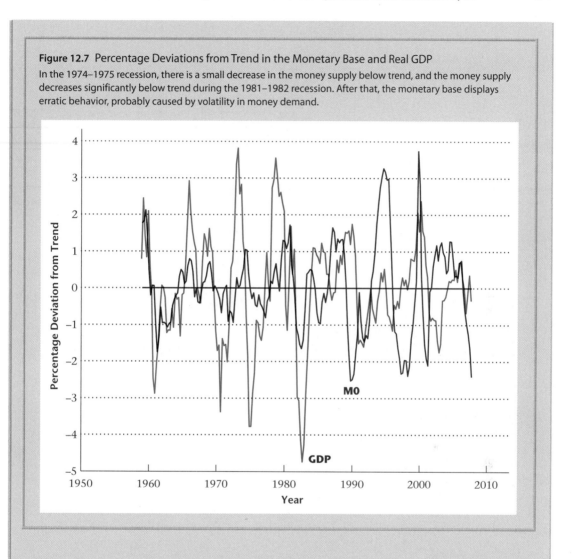

output by OPEC countries. While Figure 12.7 shows a reduction in the money supply below trend in 1974–1975 that leads the decrease in real GDP below trend, the movement in the stock of outside money is small relative to the size of the downturn in real GDP, so this is unlikely to have been important. As well, there is a decline in the real interest rate in 1974–1975 in Figure 12.8, indicating perhaps that monetary policy was actually accommodating in this instance. As discussed in Chapter 11, we need to be careful about interpreting movements in the monetary base as representing policy decisions, because these movements could simply be there to accommodate changes in money demand.

What about the recession of 1981–1982? This is often referred to as the "Volcker recession," as it is commonly believed that the Federal Reserve Chairman, Paul Volcker, instigated a tightening in monetary policy to reduce inflation, which then caused the recession. There is certainly evidence for this, as Figure 12.7 shows the

(Continued)

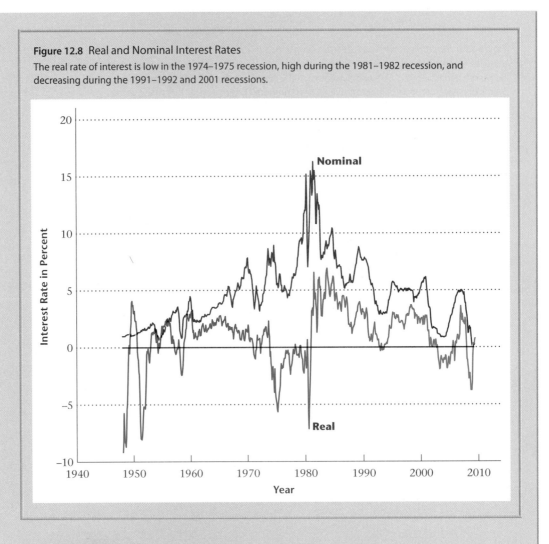

Figure 12.8 Real and Nominal Interest Rates

The real rate of interest is low in the 1974–1975 recession, high during the 1981–1982 recession, and decreasing during the 1991–1992 and 2001 recessions.

money supply dropping below trend during the 1981–1982 recession, and in Figure 12.8 there is a sharp jump in the real interest rate in 1981 to unprecedented high levels. However, we cannot entirely discount real factors as a contributing cause to the 1981–1982 recession, as there was a very large increase in the relative price of energy, shown in Figure 12.9, in 1979–1980.

For the 1990–1991 recession, it is somewhat more difficult to pinpoint causes. There was a spike in the relative price of energy in late 1990/early 1991 caused by the Persian Gulf War, as shown in Figure 12.9, but it seems unlikely that this

temporary price increase would have had much effect on total factor productivity. With regard to monetary policy, the money supply was well below trend before 1990–1991 in Figure 12.7, but M0 is particularly erratic in the period after mid-1980, and therefore somewhat disconnected from real economic activity, probably due to volatility in the demand for money. In Figure 12.8 the real interest rate was falling before the 1990–1991 recession. Thus, the recession does not appear to have been caused by tight monetary policy, although we could say that monetary policy likely prevented the recession from being more severe.

Figure 12.9 Relative Price of Energy

Large increases in the relative price of energy are associated with each of the recessions of 1974–1975, 1981–1982, 1991–1992, and 2001. However, the increase in the relative price of energy preceded the 1981–1982 recession by at least a year, and the increase in the relative price of energy prior to the 1991–1992 recession was very short-lived.

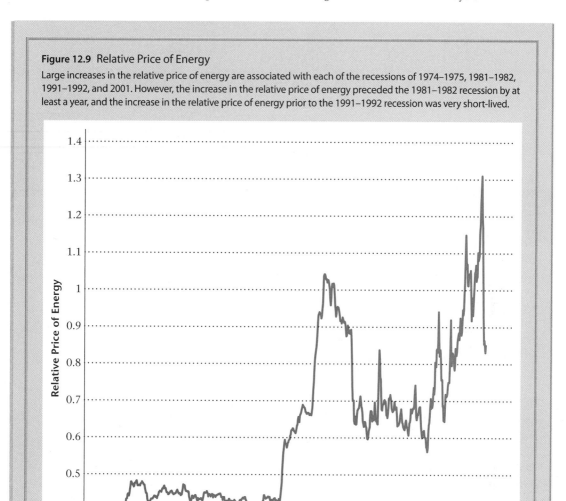

The most likely primary cause of the 2001 recession was a collapse in investment spending, something that is not explicitly part of either of the business cycle theories we have studied so far in this chapter. However, the shock that produced this drop in investment spending fits the characteristics of bad news about future productivity, as studied in Chapter 10. This does not show up in Figures 12.7–12.9, but is instead reflected in stock prices, as we showed in Chapter 10. Another important cause of the 2001 recession would appear to be the increase in the relative price of energy in 2000, observed in Figure 12.9. As with the 1990–1991 recession, monetary policy appears to have made the recession less severe, as the real interest rate was falling, in Figure 12.8. Just as for the 1990–1991 recession, the behavior of M0 around the 2001 recession in Figure 12.7 does not tell us much. All that we can say is that the money supply behaves erratically.

MACROECONOMICS IN ACTION
Business Cycle Models and the Great Depression

The Great Depression was a unique event in U.S. macroeconomic history. The Great Depression began in 1929, and real GDP declined for about four years, decreasing by 31% from 1929 to 1933. It then took another seven years for real GDP to recover to its 1929 level. Relative to the average post–World War II recession, the length and size of the decline in output during the Great Depression were very large, and the recovery took a particularly long time. In the average post–World War II recession, GDP declined by 2.9% after about one year and then recovered in one-and-a-half years. Was the Great Depression essentially a larger-scale version of a recession that otherwise looks much like a typical post–World War II recession, or do standard macroeconomic theories of the business cycle fail to explain the behavior of the U.S. economy during the Great Depression? In an article in the *Federal Reserve Bank of Minneapolis Quarterly Review*, Harold Cole and Lee Ohanian set out to answer this question.[12]

Cole and Ohanian look at versions of the three business cycle theories that we have examined or will examine—a Keynesian sticky wage model, a money surprise model, and a real business cycle model (among other explanations)—to see how well these models fit the data for the Great Depression. The Keynesian sticky wage model does not fare very well. During the Great Depression, there was a large decline in the money supply. In a

typical Keynesian sticky wage model, this would reduce the price level, and then, given a sticky nominal wage, the real wage would rise, and this would cause firms to hire less labor, with output decreasing. In the manufacturing sector, real wages increased while output was declining from 1929 to 1933, but outside of manufacturing, the real wage fell precipitously over this period, and nonmanufacturing real wages were still much below trend in 1939. These data do not appear to be consistent with broad-based stickiness in nominal wages being a major influence during the Great Depression.

Cole and Ohanian find that shocks to total factor productivity can explain the decline in aggregate output from 1929 to 1933, but cannot explain the slow recovery. Similar results are obtained for the money surprise model. Estimated total factor productivity shocks and money surprises during the Great Depression predict that the recovery should have happened much earlier than it did.

Thus, the problem with standard theories of the business cycle, when confronted with the Great Depression, is primarily in explaining the long and weak recovery. What is Cole and Ohanian's alternative explanation for the length of the recovery during the Great Depression? They conjecture that regulation was the culprit. The National Industrial Recovery Act of 1933 suspended U.S. antitrust laws and permitted more collusion among firms, particularly in the manufacturing sector. More collusion among firms in an industry tends to reduce output, raise prices, and lower investment—all features consistent with the Great Depression.

---

[12]See H. Cole and L. Ohanian, 1999. "The Great Depression in the United States from a Neoclassical Perspective," *Federal Reserve Bank of Minneapolis Quarterly Review*, Winter, 2–24.

A Keynesian Coordination Failure Model

The two equilibrium theories of the business cycle that we have discussed thus far in this chapter—the real business cycle theory and the segmented markets theory—imply that the government has either no role or a limited role in stabilizing the economy. However, this does not mean that all equilibrium theories of the business cycle imply skepticism about the role of the government in smoothing business cycles. Many modern Keynesians adopt an approach to macroeconomics very similar to that of classical economists, in assuming that prices and wages are fully flexible and that all markets clear. Some of these modern Keynesians explore an idea that one can find in Keynes's *General Theory,* the notion of **coordination failure.** In macroeconomics, coordination failures were first studied rigorously by Peter Diamond in the early 1980s,[13] and later contributions were by Russell Cooper and Andrew John,[14] Jess Benhabib and Roger Farmer,[15] and Roger Farmer and Jang-Ting Guo.[16] The basic idea in coordination failure models is that it is difficult for private sector workers and producers to coordinate their actions, and there exist **strategic complementarities,** which imply that one person's willingness to engage in some activity increases with the number of other people engaged in that activity.

An example of an activity with a strategic complementarity is a party. If Paul knows that someone wishes to hold a party and that only a few other people will be going, he will probably not want to go. However, if many people are going, this will be much more fun, and Paul will likely go. Paul's potential enjoyment of the party increases with the number of other people who are likely to go. We might imagine that there are two possible outcomes (equilibria) here. One outcome is that no one goes, and another is that everyone goes. These are equilibria because, if no one goes to the party, then no individual would want to go, and if everyone goes to the party, then no individual would want to stay at home. If Paul could coordinate with other people, then everyone would certainly agree that having everyone go to the party would be a good idea, and they could all agree to go. However, without coordination, it is possible that no one goes.

If we use the party as an analogy to aggregate economic activity, the willingness of one producer to produce may depend on what other producers are doing. For example, if Jennifer is a computer software producer, the quantity of software she can sell depends on the quantity and quality of computer hardware that is sold. If more hardware is sold, it is easier for Jennifer to sell software, and if Jennifer sells more software, it is easier to sell hardware. Computer hardware and computer software are complementary. Many such complementarities exist in the economy, and different producers find it difficult to coordinate their actions. Thus, it is possible that there may be **multiple equilibria** for the aggregate economy, whereby output and employment might be high, or output and

---

[13]See P. Diamond, 1982. "Aggregate Demand in Search Equilibrium," *Journal of Political Economy* 90, 881–894.

[14]R. Cooper and A. John, 1988. "Coordinating Coordination Failures in Keynesian Models," *Quarterly Journal of Economics* 103, 441–463.

[15]See J. Benhabib and R. Farmer, 1994. " Indeterminacy and Increasing Returns," *Journal of Economic Theory* 63, 19–41.

[16]See R. Farmer and J. Guo, 1994. "Real Business Cycles and the Animal Spirits Hypothesis," *Journal of Economic Theory* 63, 42–72.

employment might be low. Business cycles might simply be fluctuations between these high and low equilibria, driven by waves of optimism and pessimism.

To formalize this idea in an economic model, we start with the notion that there are aggregate increasing returns to scale, which implies that output more than doubles if all inputs double, as discussed in Chapter 4. Until now, we have assumed constant returns to scale, which implies that the marginal product of labor is diminishing when the quantity of capital is fixed. Increasing returns to scale at the aggregate level can be due to the strategic complementarities that we discussed above. We can then have increasing returns to scale at the aggregate level in a situation where, for each individual firm, there are constant returns to scale in production. With sufficient aggregate increasing returns to scale, the aggregate production function, fixing the quantity of capital, can be convex, as in Figure 12.10. Then, because the slope of the production function in the figure increases with the labor input, the marginal product of labor for the aggregate economy is increasing rather than decreasing. Because the aggregate demand for labor is just the aggregate marginal product of labor schedule, this implies that the aggregate labor demand curve N^d can be upward sloping as in Figure 12.11.

Now, for the coordination failure theory to work, the aggregate labor demand curve must have a greater slope than the labor supply curve, as in Figure 12.12. To repeat the

Figure 12.10 A Production Function with Increasing Returns to Scale

Strategic complementarities among firms imply that there can be increasing returns to scale at the aggregate level, which can give a convex production function as depicted, where the marginal product of labor increases as the quantity of labor input increases.

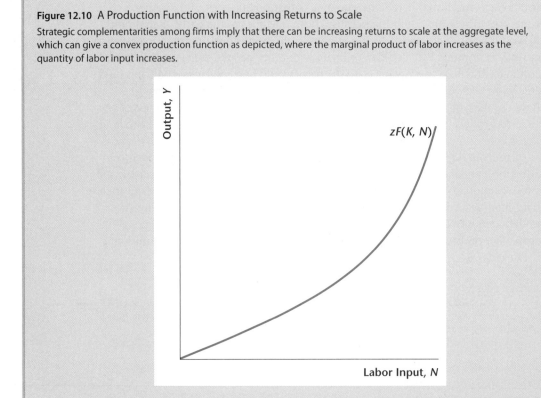

Figure 12.11 Aggregate Labor Demand with Sufficient Increasing Returns to Scale

With sufficient increasing returns to scale, the aggregate labor demand curve slopes upward, as the aggregate marginal product of labor increases with aggregate employment.

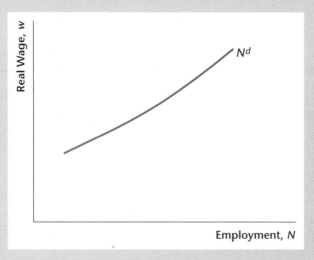

Figure 12.12 The Labor Market in the Coordination Failure Model

With sufficient increasing returns, the labor demand curve is steeper than the labor supply curve, which is required for the coordination failure model to work.

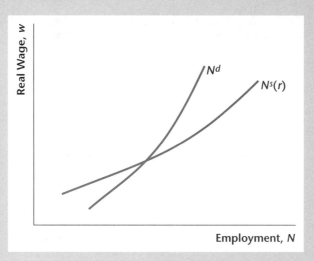

exercise from Chapter 9 where we derived the output supply curve Y^s, suppose that the real interest rate is r_1, with the labor supply curve $N^s(r_1)$ in Figure 12.13(c). Then the equilibrium quantity of employment would be N_1 and output would be Y_1, from the production function in Figure 12.13(b). Therefore, an output-real interest rate pair implying equilibrium in the labor market is (Y_1, r_1) in Figure 12.13(a). Now, if the real

Figure 12.13 The Output Supply Curve in the Coordination Failure Model

The figure shows the construction of the output supply curve Y^s in the coordination failure model. An increase in the real interest rate shifts the labor supply curve to the right, reducing employment and output.

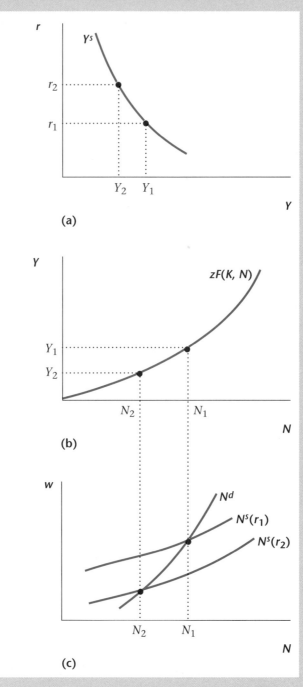

interest rate is higher, say r_2, then the labor supply curve shifts rightward to $N^s(r_2)$ in Figure 12.13(c), because workers wish to substitute future leisure for current leisure. As a result, the equilibrium quantity of employment falls to N_2 and output falls to Y_2. Thus, another point on the output supply curve in Figure 12.13(a) is (Y_2, r_2), and the Y^s curve is downward sloping.

The Coordination Failure Model: An Example

We now consider a simple example that shows some of the key insights that come from coordination failure models. Suppose that the downward-sloping Y^s curve and the downward-sloping Y^d curve intersect in just two places (although this need not be the case; there could be more than two intersections, or there could be only one), as in Figure 12.14(b). Here, the economy could be in one of two equilibria. In the first, the "bad equilibrium," output is Y_1, the real interest rate is r_1, the price level is P_1, the real wage is w_1, and employment is N_1. In the second, the "good equilibrium," output is Y_2, the real interest rate is r_2, the price level is P_2, the real wage is w_2, and employment is N_2. In a more explicit version of this model, which would have a description of consumers' preferences, consumers would be better off in the good equilibrium with high output and employment than in the bad equilibrium with low output and employment.

Will the economy be in the good equilibrium or the bad equilibrium? There is certainly nothing to prevent the bad equilibrium from arising. Even though everyone prefers the good equilibrium, the bad equilibrium could arise if everyone is pessimistic and expects bad things to happen. Similarly, the good equilibrium arises if everyone is optimistic. In this model, business cycles could result if consumers and firms are alternately optimistic and pessimistic, so that the economy alternates between the good equilibrium and the bad equilibrium. This seems much like what Keynes referred to as "animal spirits," the waves of optimism and pessimism that he viewed as being an important determinant of investment.

In the coordination failure model, it is possible that extraneous events that are completely unrelated to economic fundamentals (technology, preferences, and endowments) can "cause" business cycles. Macroeconomists sometimes call such extraneous events **sunspots,** in analogy to the irregular occurrence of dark spots observed on the sun, because a dark spot on the sun does not affect production possibilities, preferences, or available resources (i.e., anything fundamental) on Earth. However, sunspots are in principle observable to everyone. Therefore, if workers and firms all treat the observation of a sunspot as a sign of optimism, then the economy goes to the good equilibrium when a sunspot is observed, and it goes to the bad equilibrium when no sunspot is observed. It then appears that sunspots are causing business cycles. The behavior of the stock market is perhaps most indicative of the presence of "sunspot behavior," in that there is much more variability in stock prices than can be explained by fluctuations in fundamentals (the earnings potential of firms). Alan Greenspan, the former chairman of the Federal Reserve Board, once referred to the stock market as being under the influence of "irrational exuberance." Sunspot behavior in the economy need not literally be driven by sunspots, but by events with no connection to anything fundamentally important to preferences, endowments, and technology.

Figure 12.14 Multiple Equilibria in the Coordination Failure Model

Because the output supply curve is downward-sloping in the coordination failure model, there can be two equilibria, as in this example. In one equilibrium, aggregate output is low and the real interest rate is high; in the other, aggregate output is high and the real interest rate is low.

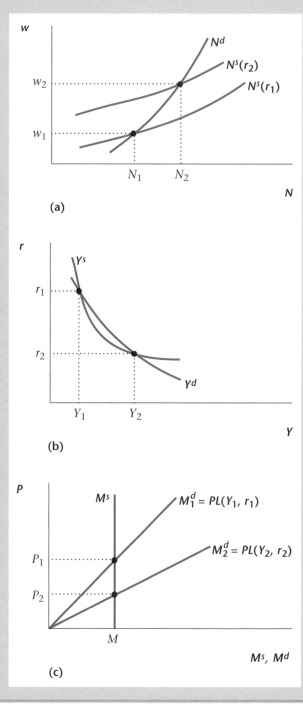

(a)

(b)

(c)

Predictions of the Coordination Failure Model

From Figure 12.14, the good equilibrium has a low real interest rate, a high level of output, a low price level, a high level of employment, and a high real wage. The bad equilibrium has a high real interest rate, a low level of output, a high price level, a low level of employment, and a low real wage. Thus, given the low (high) real interest rate, the good (bad) equilibrium has a high (low) level of consumption and investment. Therefore, if business cycles are fluctuations between the good and bad equilibrium, then, as in Table 12.3, consumption, investment, and employment are procyclical, the price level is countercyclical, and the real wage is procyclical, just as observed in the data. As well, in Figure 12.15 average labor productivity (the slope of a ray from the origin to the relevant point on the production function) must be procyclical, as it is higher in the good equilibrium than in the bad equilibrium. Further, Roger Farmer and Jang-Ting Guo have shown that a version of the coordination failure model does essentially as well as the real business cycle model in quantitatively replicating U.S. business cycle behavior.[17]

Although money is neutral in the coordination failure model, as it is in the real business cycle model, the coordination failure model can explain why the nominal money supply is procyclical. Suppose that the money supply fluctuates between M_1 and M_2, where $M_2 > M_1$. Also, suppose that money acts as a sunspot variable. That is, when consumers and firms observe a high money supply, they are optimistic, and when they observe a low money supply, they are pessimistic. Therefore, when the money supply is high, the economy is in the good equilibrium, and when the money supply is low, the economy is in the bad equilibrium, and people's expectations are self-fulfilling. In Figure 12.16, we can still have the price level moving countercyclically, provided money supply does not fluctuate too much. In the good equilibrium, nominal money demand is $PL(Y_2, r_2)$, and in the bad equilibrium, nominal money demand is $PL(Y_1, r_1)$. Money supply increases in the good equilibrium from M_1 to M_2, and the price level falls from P_1 to P_2. Here, though money is actually neutral, it can appear to be causing business cycles.

Table 12.3   Data Versus Predictions of the Coordination Failure Model

Variable	Data	Model
Consumption	Procyclical	Procyclical
Investment	Procyclical	Procyclical
Price Level	Countercyclical	Countercyclical
Money Supply	Procyclical	Procyclical
Employment	Procyclical	Procyclical
Real Wage	Procyclical	Procyclical
Average Labor Productivity	Procyclical	Procyclical

---

[17]See R. Farmer and J. Guo, 1994. "Real Business Cycles and the Animal Spirits Hypothesis," *Journal of Economic Theory* 63, 42–72.

Figure 12.15 Average Labor Productivity in the Keynesian Coordination Failure Model

In the good (bad) equilibrium, output is high (low), employment is high (low), and average labor productivity is high (low).

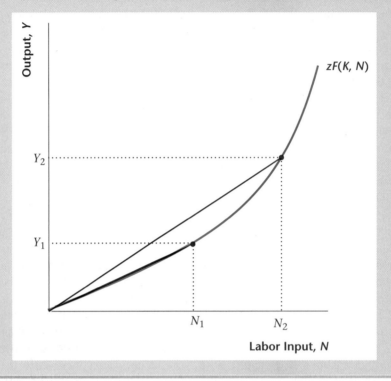

Figure 12.16 Procyclical Money Supply in the Coordination Failure Model

If the money supply is a sunspot variable in the coordination failure model, then money may appear to be nonneutral because people believe it to be. When the money supply is high (low), everyone is optimistic (pessimistic), and output is high (low).

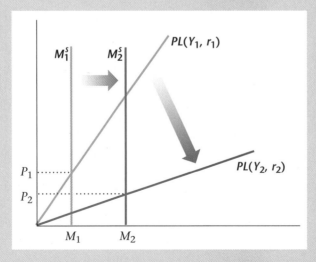

Policy Implications of the Coordination Failure Model

In terms of how they match the data, the coordination failure and real business cycle models are essentially indistinguishable. However, the two models have very different policy implications. In the real business cycle model, decreases in output and employment are just optimal responses to a decline in total factor productivity, while in the coordination failure model, the good equilibrium is in principle an opportunity available in the aggregate economy when the bad equilibrium is realized. Thus, if we believe this model, then government policies that promote optimism would be beneficial. For example, encouraging statements by public officials, such as the treasury secretary or the chairman of the Federal Reserve Board, could in principle bump the economy from the bad equilibrium to the good equilibrium.

Policy could also be designed to smooth business cycles or to eliminate them altogether in the coordination failure model. As an example, consider Figure 12.17, where there are initially two equilibria, a bad equilibrium where the real interest rate is r_1 and the level of output is Y_1, and a good equilibrium where the real interest rate is r_2 and the level of output is Y_2. Then, suppose that the government reduces current government spending G. Recall from Chapter 10 that a decrease in current government spending reduces the present value of taxes, causing a decrease in current labor supply. Here, this shifts the output supply curve to the right (not to the left as in Chapter 10) from Y_1^s to Y_2^s in the figure. Further, recall from Chapter 10 that we know that a decrease in G shifts the output demand curve leftward from Y_1^d to Y_2^d. If the government reduces G by just the right amount, then there is only one equilibrium, where $Y = Y^*$ and $r = r^*$, as in the figure. Effectively, the bad equilibrium gets better and the good equilibrium gets worse, because of the decrease in G, and there are no business cycles. It is not clear whether eliminating business cycles in this manner is advantageous. For example, if in the absence of the decrease in G the economy was in the good equilibrium most of the time, then average welfare could go down when business cycles are eliminated. It could be, however, that there are benefits from reduced uncertainty when business cycles are eliminated, so that even though average output might go down, the benefits from reduced uncertainty from smoothing business cycles could be beneficial.

Critique of the Coordination Failure Model

The key insight of the coordination failure model is that business cycles can result simply from self-fulfilling waves of optimism and pessimism. As mentioned previously, the existence of these self-fulfilling expectations appears to be most evident in the case of the stock market, where it seems difficult to explain the wild gyrations that occur daily as being the result of changes in fundamental economic factors.

There are some potential weaknesses, however, in coordination failure theories of the business cycle. First, a critical element of the coordination failure theory is that there exist sufficient increasing returns to scale in aggregate production that the aggregate labor demand curve slopes upward and is steeper than the aggregate labor supply curve. If aggregate production is subject to constant returns to scale or decreasing returns to scale, then this theory is a nonstarter. In practice, the

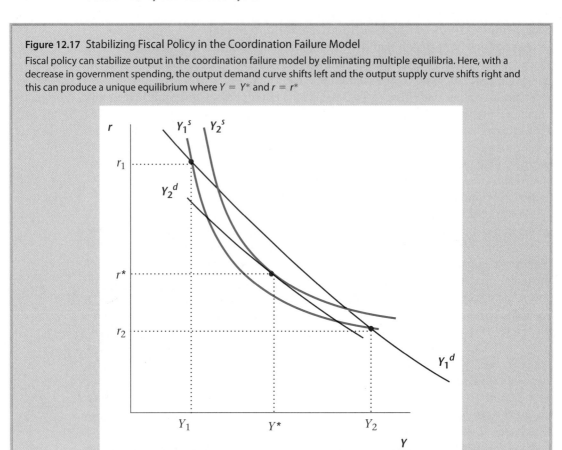

Figure 12.17 Stabilizing Fiscal Policy in the Coordination Failure Model

Fiscal policy can stabilize output in the coordination failure model by eliminating multiple equilibria. Here, with a decrease in government spending, the output demand curve shifts left and the output supply curve shifts right and this can produce a unique equilibrium where $Y = Y^*$ and $r = r^*$

measurement of returns to scale in aggregate production is very imprecise. Some researchers claim to find evidence of increasing returns in the data, but others do not. A good reference for this issue is the work of Harold Cole and Lee Ohanian.[18] At best, the evidence supporting the existence of increasing returns to scale at the aggregate level is weak.

Second, a problem with this model is that the underlying shocks that cause business cycles are expectations, and expectations are essentially unobservable. This makes it difficult to use the theory to understand historical recessions and booms.

This completes our study of equilibrium models of the business cycle. In Chapter 13 we analyze a New Keynesian model with sticky prices, in which some markets fail to clear in the short run.

----

[18]See H. Cole and L. Ohanian, 1999. "Aggregate Returns to Scale: Why Measurement Is Imprecise," *Federal Reserve Bank of Minneapolis Quarterly Review,* Summer, 19–28.

Perspectives on the Financial Crisis

How Do the Equilibrium Business Cycle Theories in Chapter 12 Help Us Understand the 2008–2009 Recession?

From the second quarter of 2008, when the turning point in real GDP occurred, to the first quarter of 2009, real GDP decreased from 11,727.4 billion (2000) dollars to 11,353.7 billion (2000) dollars, a decrease of 3.19%. Over the same period, aggregate employment fell from 145,990 thousand to 141,578 thousand, a decrease of 3.02%. Part of what is unusual about these observations is the large decrease in employment relative to GDP. Recall from Chapter 3 that the percentage deviation from trend in employment is about two-thirds as volatile as for real GDP. Thus, for a decrease of 3.19% in real GDP, we would expect a decrease in employment on the order of a little more than 2%, rather than 3%. According to conventional wisdom, this is not all that is unusual about the 2008–2009 recession. The role of financial factors in the most recent recession is thought to be out of the ordinary, and comparisons to the Great Depression have been common.[19] This is in spite of the fact that the percentage decline in aggregate output in the Depression was an order of magnitude larger.

Suppose that we adopted a real business cycle theorist's view of the world. What would this tell us about the 2008–2009 recession? A first step would be to measure the extent of the change in total factor productivity from the second quarter of 2008 to the first quarter of 2009. To measure total factor productivity, assume the same production function that we used in Chapters 4 and 6 to come up with a

Solow residual as a measure of productivity. The function we used was the Cobb-Douglas production function

$$Y = zK^{.36}N^{.64}, \tag{12-2}$$

where Y is aggregate output, measured by real GDP, z is total factor productivity, K is the capital stock, and N is employment. Then, if we let the subscript 1 denote observations for the second quarter of 2008, and the subscript 2 denote observations for the first quarter of 2009, equation (12-2) implies that we can express the ratio of total factor productivity in the second quarter of 2009 to total factor productivity in 2010 as

$$\frac{z_2}{z_1} = \frac{\dfrac{Y_2}{K_2^{.36}N_2^{.64}}}{\dfrac{Y_1}{K_1^{.36}N_1^{.64}}} = \frac{Y_2}{Y_1}\left(\frac{K_1}{K_2}\right)^{.36}\left(\frac{N_1}{N_2}\right)^{.64} \tag{12-3}$$

A problem in measuring $\frac{z_2}{z_1}$ is that we do not yet have measures of the capital stock for 2008 and 2009. However, investment expenditures were low enough in 2008–2009 so as to be close to just replacing the capital that was depreciating, so a safe assumption is that $K_2 = K_1$ in equation (12-3). Then, if we use the real GDP and employment measures mentioned above in equation (12-3), we obtain

$$\frac{z_2}{z_1} = \frac{11,353.7}{11,727.4}\left(\frac{145,990}{141,578}\right)^{.64} = .9873$$

Therefore, the decline in total factor productivity, from second quarter 2008 to first quarter 2009, as measured by the Solow residual, was $100 \times (1 - .9873)\% = 1.27\%$. Thus, while measured productivity declined in the 2008–2009 recession, note from Figure 12.1 that

[19]See, for example, Christina Romer, 2009. "The Lessons of 1937," *The Economist*, June 18, available at http://www.economist.com/businessfinance/displaystory.cfm?story_id=13856176

(Continued)

the decline in productivity relative to the decline in real GDP was smaller than in typical post-World War II recessions. This is just another way of saying that the decline in employment relative to the decline in real GDP was larger in the 2008–2009 recession than was usual.

Thus, we can at least say that the evidence appears to indicate that total factor productivity contributed less to the 2008–2009 recession than was typical of recent recessions in the United States. However, measured total factor productivity seems to have declined nevertheless. We then have to address the problem of measurement error in using the Solow residual to represent productivity. As usual, the Solow residual could have decreased due to an upward bias in the measurement of the decline in the labor input. However, we do have some direct evidence of a factor contributing to the productivity decline, which is the increase in the relative price of energy that occurred into 2008, as we see in Figure 12.9.

Monetary factors have, if anything, been a mitigating factor in the 2008–2009 downturn. In late 2008, short-term nominal interest rates fell close to zero (see Figure 12.8), and there was a large increase in the monetary base, as we observed in Chapter 11. Thus, monetary policy has been highly accommodative and could not be said to have been an immediate factor in causing the recession. However, one could make a case that the regulatory activities of the Fed (or lack of such activities) was a contributing factor to the financial crisis and the ensuing recession. In terms of our segmented markets model, we could think of the financial crisis as leading to circumstances where firms were more liquidity constrained than they might otherwise

have been. Thus, we could view part of the Fed's monetary accommodation as being an appropriate reaction to more stringent liquidity constraints for firms, with this monetary accommodation acting to increase economic efficiency.

It is not clear that the Keynesian coordination failure model applies directly to the 2008–2009 recession. However, there are features of the financial crisis that may be interpreted as involving a kind of coordination failure problem. In credit markets, a coordination failure problem could potentially occur through a "credit chain" effect. In a credit chain, credit relationships work efficiently if everyone in the chain believes that the person or institution to which they lend will not default. However, if, for example, bank A has been lending to insurance company B and believes that insurance company B is likely to default on its debt, then bank A may choose not to lend to insurance company B. Because insurance company B cannot borrow, it cannot provide insurance to investment bank C, and investment bank C then cannot meet some financial obligations to bank D, etc. As the theory goes, this could then lead to a chain of defaults in financial markets or, in the worst possible case, to systemic failure.

This idea is closely related to what occurs in the Keynesian coordination failure model. With the credit chain effect, the good equilibrium occurs when there is widespread confidence in the ability of borrowers to repay their debts, and a bad equilibrium when there is a widespread, self-fulfilling belief that borrowers are going to default. Whether such systemic risk problems are a feature of actual economies is a subject of debate among professional economists.

Chapter Summary

- In this chapter, we constructed three different equilibrium models of the business cycle, and we evaluated these models in terms of how they fit the data, their policy predictions, and their plausibility.
- The first model studied in this chapter is the real business cycle model, in which business cycles are explained by persistent fluctuations in total factor productivity. The real business cycle model

is consistent with all the business cycle facts from Chapter 3, and endogenous money can explain the regularities in the behavior of the nominal money supply relative to real aggregate output.

- The basic real business cycle model has no role for government policy, since business cycles are simply optimal responses to fluctuations in total factor productivity.

- The real business cycle model is not always successful in explaining historical business cycle events, and there are measurement problems in using the Solow residual as a measure of total factor productivity.

- In the second model, the segmented markets model, firms commit to a cash-management policy in advance of knowing the action of the monetary authority in the bond market. An unanticipated increase in the money supply is not neutral, as cash-constrained firms hire more labor, output increases, the real wage rises, and the real interest rate falls. The decrease in the real interest rate is a liquidity effect. The price level decreases. The model matches all of the key business cycle facts from Chapter 3, except that average labor productivity is countercyclical in response to unanticipated money shocks.

- In the segmented markets model, unanticipated changes in the money supply that are not responses to events in the economy are always inefficient, as this just creates uncertainty. However, there can be a role for monetary policy in responding to unanticipated shocks to the economy, if the monetary authority can react to events more quickly than does the private sector.

- The third model studied here is the Keynesian coordination failure model, which is based on the existence of strategic complementarities giving rise to increasing returns to scale at the aggregate level. This implies that there can be multiple equilibria, and we considered an example in which the model had two equilibria: a good equilibrium with high output, consumption, investment, employment, and real wage, and a low real interest rate and price level; and a bad equilibrium with low output, consumption, investment employment, and real wage, and a high real interest rate and price level. The economy could then fluctuate between these two equilibria, with fluctuations driven by waves of optimism and\break pessimism.

- Money is neutral in the Keynesian coordination failure model, but it could be a sunspot variable that produces optimism and pessimism, thus making it appear that money is not neutral.

- The coordination failure model does as well as the real business cycle model in fitting the data. The role for government policy in the coordination failure model could be to produce optimism, and there may be a role for fiscal policy in smoothing out business cycles.

Key Terms

Coordination failure Situation in which economic agents cannot coordinate their actions, producing a bad equilibrium. (p. 461)

Endogenous money The concept that the money supply is not exogenous but depends on other aggregate economic variables because of the behavior of the banking system and the central bank. (p. 445)

Labor hoarding The process by which firms may not lay off workers during a recession, even though those workers are not as busy on the job as they might be. (p.449)

Liquidity effect A decrease in the real interest rate in response to an increase in the money supply. (p. 450)

Multiple equilibria The presence of more than one equilibrium in an economic model. (p. 461)

Statistical causality When an economic variable a helps predict the future values of an economic variable b, we say that a statistically causes b. (p. 447)

Strategic complementarities Relationships in which actions taken by others encourage a particular firm or consumer to take the same action. (p. 461)

Sunspot An economic variable that has no effect on aggregate production possibilities or on consumers' preferences. (p. 465)

Questions for Review

1. What were the two main principles introduced in the rational expectations revolution?
2. Why is it useful to study different models of the business cycle?
3. What causes output to fluctuate in the real business cycle model?
4. Why is money neutral in the real business cycle model?
5. How can the real business cycle model explain the behavior of the money supply over the business cycle?
6. Should the government act to stabilize output in the real business cycle model?
7. Does the real business cycle model fit the data?
8. What are the important shortcomings of the real business cycle model?
9. Explain why money is nonneutral in the market segmentation model.
10. Should the government act to stabilize output in the market segmentation model? Why or why not?
11. Does the market segmentation model fit the data?
12. Describe an example of a coordination failure problem.
13. What causes business cycles in the coordination failure model?
14. Why is money neutral in the coordination failure model?
15. Does the coordination failure model fit the data?
16. Which is the better macro model, the real business cycle model or the coordination failure model? Explain.

Problems

1. In the real business cycle model, suppose that government spending increases temporarily. Determine the equilibrium effects of this. Could business cycles be explained by fluctuations in G? That is, does the model replicate the key business cycle facts from Chapter 3 when subjected to temporary shocks to government spending? Explain carefully.

2. Suppose that temporary increases in government spending lead to permanent increases in total factor productivity, perhaps because some government spending improves infrastructure and makes private firms more productive. Show that temporary shocks to government spending of this type could lead to business cycles that are consistent with the key business cycle facts and explain your results.

3. In the real business cycle model, suppose that firms become infected with optimism, and they expect that total factor productivity will be much higher in the future.
   (a) Determine the equilibrium effects of this.

   (b) If waves of optimism and pessimism of this sort cause GDP to fluctuate, does the model explain the key business cycle facts?
   (c) Suppose that the monetary authority wants to stabilize the price level in the face of a wave of optimism. Determine what it should do, and explain.

4. Suppose that the central bank wishes to reduce the price level and announces that it will reduce the money supply to accomplish this. Use the market segmentation model to answer the following questions:
   (a) Suppose that the public does not believe that the central bank is serious about reducing the price level. What happens to real aggregate variables and the price level?
   (b) Suppose, alternatively, that the public believes the central bank announcement. What happens to real variables and the price level now?
   (c) Compare your results in parts (a) and (b). In which case does the price level change more for a given reduction in the money supply?

What do you think a central bank can do to make its policy announcements more credible?

5. In the market segmentation model, compare the performance of the economies in two countries, which in all respects but one are identical. In country *a*, the money supply is highly variable, while in country *b*, there is little variability in the money supply. For a given surprise increase in the money supply, determine with the aid of diagrams how the economy in country *a* responds relative to the economy in country *b*. Explain your results.

6. In the market segmentation model, suppose that the goal of the central bank is price stability; that is, the central bank would like to keep the price level at a constant level. Now, suppose that there is a temporary shift in money demand; that is, money demand will increase temporarily for one period. What will happen if the central bank increases the money supply in response? Will the central bank achieve its goal? What is the best response for the central bank to the temporary shift in money demand? Explain with the aid of diagrams.

7. Suppose that money plays the role of a sunspot variable in the coordination failure model, so that the economy is in the bad equilibrium when the money supply is low and in the good equilibrium when the money supply is high. Explain what the monetary authority could do to make consumers

better off. Compare this prescription for monetary policy with the one coming from the money surprise model and discuss.

8. In the coordination failure model, suppose that consumers' preferences shift so that they want to consume less leisure and more consumption goods. Determine the effects on aggregate variables in the good equilibrium and in the bad equilibrium, and explain your results.

9. Suppose that there is a natural disaster that destroys some of the nation's capital stock. The central bank's goal is to stabilize the price level. Given this goal, what should the central bank do in response to the natural disaster? Explain with the aid of diagrams.

10. Suppose that the central bank observes a drop in real GDP, but does not know what caused this drop.
    (a) How would the central bank respond if it believed that GDP dropped because of a decline in total factor productivity and that real business cycle theory is correct?
    (b) How would the central bank respond if it believed that GDP dropped because of a wave of pessimism and that the Keynesian coordination failure model is correct?
    (c) Explain your answers to (a) and (b) with the aid of diagrams.

Working with the Data

1. Construct scatter plots of: (i) detrended monetary base vs. detrended real GDP; (ii) detrended M1 vs. detrended real GDP; (iii) detrended M2 vs. detrended real GDP.
   (a) What differences do you notice among the scatter plots?
   (b) How would you explain the differences you observed in part (a), if any?

2. Construct a times series plot of detrended real government expenditures and detrended real GDP and construct a scatter plot of these two variables.
   (a) What do you observe in the plots you constructed? Is government spending a countercyclical or procyclical variable? Does it appear to be a leading, lagging, or coincident variable?
   (b) Do any of the business cycle models studied in this chapter explain the features of the data in your answer to part (a)? If not, suggest an explanation or explanations for these regularities in the data.

3. Construct a times series plot of the detrended S&P 500-stock price index and detrended real GDP and construct a scatter plot of these two variables.
   (a) What do you observe in the plots you constructed?
   (b) With what business cycle theory or theories are the observations from part (a) consistent? Explain.

chapter 13

New Keynesian Economics: Sticky Prices

Keynesian ideas have been with us since Keynes wrote his *General Theory*[1] in 1936. Keynesians argue that wages and prices are not perfectly flexible or "sticky" in the short run, with the result that supply may not equal demand (in the usual sense) in all markets in the economy at each point in time. The implication, as Keynesians argue, is that government intervention through fiscal and monetary policy can improve economic aggregate economic outcomes by smoothing out business cycles.

Business cycle models based on these Keynesian ideas have been very influential among both academics and policymakers, and continue to be so. The basic formal modelling framework underlying these models was developed by Hicks in the late 1930s[2] in his "IS-LM" model, and popularized in Paul Samuelson's textbook in the 1950s. In the 1960s, large-scale versions of these Keynesian business cycle models were fitted to data, and used in policy analysis.

Since the 1960s, Keynesians have adapted their models and ideas to the newer methods and ideas coming from other schools of thought in macroeconomics. In the 1960s and 1970s, monetarist approaches, represented primarily by the work of Milton Friedman, were in part adopted by Keynesians in what was called the "neoclassical synthesis." In the 1980s, the influence of equilibrium models with optimizing consumers and firms, of the type studied in Chapter 12, were influential in the development of Keynesian "menu cost" models, which explained sticky prices as arising from the costs to firms of changing prices.[3] More recently, Keynesian models with sticky prices have been constructed that have as their core a basic real business cycle framework, but incorporate sticky prices.[4] Those who work in this research program call it "New Keynesian Economics" and argue that it represents the newest synthesis of ideas in macroeconomics.

---

[1] See J. M. Keynes, 1936, *The General Theory of Employment, Interest, and Money*, Macmillan, London.

[2] J. Hicks, 1937, "Mr. Keynes and the Classics: A Suggested Interpretation," *Econometrica* 5, 147–159.

[3] L. Ball and N. G. Mankiw, 1994, "A Sticky-Price Manifesto," *Carnegie-Rochester Conference Series on Public Policy* 41, 127–151.

[4] R. Clarida, J. Gali, and M. Gertler, 1999, "The Science of Monetary Policy: A New Keynesian Perspective," *Journal of Economic Literature* 37, 1661–1707; M. Woodford, 2003, *Money, Interest, and Prices*, Princeton University Press, Princeton, NJ.

The primary feature that makes a Keynesian macroeconomic model different from the models we have examined thus far is that some prices and wages are not completely flexible—that is, some are "sticky." That some prices and wages cannot move so as to clear markets will have important implications for how the economy behaves and for economic policy. The New Keynesian model studied in this chapter is essentially identical to the monetary intertemporal model in Chapter 11, except that the price level is not sufficiently flexible for the goods market to clear in the short run. Given the failure of the goods market to clear, the New Keynesian model will have far different properties from the monetary intertemporal model, but constructing the model will be a straightforward extension of our basic monetary intertemporal framework.

Although Keynesian models certainly have some strong adherents, they have many detractors as well.[5] Part of what we will do in this chapter is to critically evaluate the New Keynesian model, just as we evaluated equilibrium business cycle models in Chapter 12. We will see how well the New Keynesian model fits the key business cycle facts we discussed in Chapter 3, and we will examine how useful it is for guiding the formulation of economic policy.

In contrast to the monetary intertemporal model in Chapter 11, the New Keynesian model will have the property that money is not neutral. When the monetary authority increases the money supply, there will be an increase in aggregate output and employment. In general, monetary policy can then be used to improve economic performance and welfare. Keynesians typically believe strongly that the government should play an active role in the economy, through both monetary and fiscal policy, and Keynesian business cycle models support this belief.

As in most New Keynesian analysis, we take a different approach in this chapter to the conduct of monetary policy than in Chapters 11 and 12. Rather than setting up our model as one where the instrument that the central bank controls is the money supply, here the central bank will use the market interest rate as its policy target. This is consistent with how most central banks behave—in particular, the Fed targets the federal funds rate (discussed in Chapter 11) in the short run and typically considers changing the target for the fed funds rate about every six weeks. As we will show, however, what the central bank controls directly is the money supply, so any target for the market interest rate must be supported with appropriate money supply control. Once we treat the market interest rate as the central bank's policy target, we will eliminate a feature of traditional Keynesian textbook analysis, Hicks's "LM curve," which was included in older Keynesian models to summarize money demand, money supply, and equilibrium in the money market.

In our New Keynesian model, we will show how active monetary and fiscal policy can smooth out business cycles by reacting to extraneous shocks to the economy. Given well-informed fiscal and monetary authorities that can act very quickly, there is little difference between monetary and fiscal policy in terms of their effects on stabilizing aggregate output. However, the active use of fiscal policy in stabilizing the economy will matter for the division of aggregate spending between the public and private sectors.

---

[5]See R. Lucas, 1980, "Methods and Problems in Business Cycle Theory," *Journal of Money, Credit, and Banking* 12, 696–715; S. Williamson, 2008, "New Keynesian Economics: A Monetary Perspective," *Economic Quarterly*, *94*, Federal Reserve Bank of Richmond, 197–218.

The New Keynesian Model

Our New Keynesian model will have very different properties from the basic monetary intertemporal model that we constructed in Chapter 11. However, there is only one fundamental difference in the New Keynesian model, which is that the price level is sticky in the short run and will not adjust quickly to equate the supply and demand for goods.

Why might goods prices be sticky in the short run? Some Keynesians argue that it is costly for firms to change prices, and even if these costs are small, this could lead firms to fix the prices for their products for long periods of time. Consider a restaurant, which must print new menus whenever it changes its prices. Printing menus is costly, and this causes the restaurant to change prices infrequently. Given that prices change infrequently, there may be periods when the restaurant is full and people are being turned away. If menus were not costly to print, the restaurant might increase its prices under these circumstances. Alternatively, there may be periods when the restaurant is not full and prices would be lowered if it were not for the costs of changing prices. The restaurant example is a common one in the economic literature on sticky price models. Indeed, sticky price models are sometimes referred to as **menu cost models.**

In typical New Keynesian models, it is assumed that, among the many firms in the economy, some will change their prices during any given period of time, and some will not. This could be modeled the hard way, by assuming a fixed cost for a firm associated with changing its price. Then, a firm will change its price only when the firm's existing price deviates enough from the optimal price, making it profit-maximizing for the firm to bear the menu cost and shift to the optimal price. An easier approach is to simply assume that a firm receives an opportunity at random to change its price. Every period, the firms that are lucky receive this opportunity and change their prices, while the unlucky firms are stuck charging the price they posted in the previous period.

Whichever way sticky prices are modeled, this tends to lead to forward-looking behavior on the part of firms. Whenever a firm changes its price, it knows that it may be charging this price for some time into the future, until it can change its posted price again. Thus, in making its price-setting decision the firm will attempt to forecast the shocks that are likely to affect future market conditions and the firm's future profitability. While this forward-looking behavior can play an important role in New Keynesian economics, we will need to simplify here by assuming that all firms charge the price P for goods in the current period and that this price is sticky and will not move during the period in response to shifts in the demand for goods.

In Figure 13.1, we display the basic apparatus for the New Keynesian model, which includes the same set of diagrams we used for the basic monetary intertemporal model in Chapter 11, with the addition of the production function. That is, the labor market is in panel (a) of the figure, the goods market in panel (b), the money market in panel (c), and the production function in panel (d).

Now, start with panel (c), the money market. Here, the price level is fixed at P^*, which is the sticky price charged by all firms. Assume that this price was set in the past, and firms cannot change it during the current period. Then, in panel (b), r^* is the interest rate target of the central bank. Here we assume, as in Chapter 12, that the inflation rate is a constant—zero for convenience—so that the Fisher relation tells us that the nominal interest rate R is identical to the real interest rate r. In practice we know that

Figure 13.1 The New Keynesian Model

Given the fixed price level P^* and the target interest rate r^*, output is Y^*, determined by the output demand (*IS*) curve, and the central bank must supply M^* units of money to hit its interest rate target. Firms hire N^* units of labor at the real wage w^*. The natural rate of interest is r_m, and the output gap is $Y_m - Y^*$.

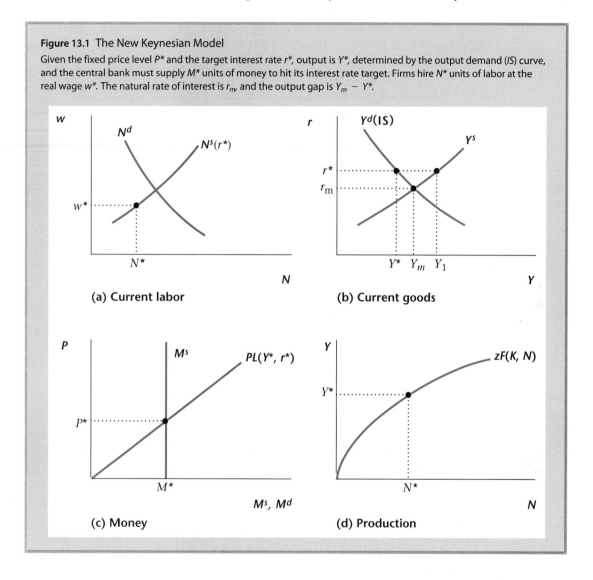

(a) Current labor

(b) Current goods

(c) Money

(d) Production

central banks typically target a nominal interest rate, which is consistent with what the central bank does in the model, where setting r is the same as setting R.

Given the interest rate target r^*, output is determined by the output demand curve in Figure 13.1(b), so aggregate output is Y^*. Note that, in Keynesian models with sticky prices or wages, in line with the tradition of Hicks, what we have called the output demand curve, Y^d is typically called the *IS* curve. Thus, we have labeled the output demand curve "$Y^d(IS)$" in Figure 13.1(b).

Given the level of output Y^*, and the interest rate r^*, in the money market in 13.1(c), the quantity of money demanded is $PL(Y^*, r^*)$, so in order to hit its target market interest rate of r^*, given the price level P^*, the central bank must supply M^* units of money. From the production function in panel (d), firms hire the quantity of labor N^*, which is just sufficient to produce the quantity of output demanded in the goods market, Y^*. In the labor market in panel (a), the labor supply curve is $N^s(r^*)$, determined by the equilibrium real interest rate r^*. The real wage w^* is the wage rate at which the quantity of labor that consumers are willing to supply is N^*.

A critical feature of the model is that some markets clear, while others do not. The money market clears in Figure 13.1(c), since the central bank needs to supply a sufficient quantity of money, that money demand equals money supply at the central bank's target interest rate r^*, given the fixed price level P^* and the level of output Y^*. The goods market need not clear however. In panel (b), firms would like to supply the quantity of output Y_1 at the interest rate r^*, but firms actually produce only the quantity demanded, which is Y^*. If firms could, they would lower prices, but prices are rigid in the short run. Note that the quantity of output Y_m is the market-clearing level of output that would be determined in the monetary intertemporal model. The market-clearing interest rate r_m is sometimes referred to as the **natural rate of interest** in the New Keynesian literature. As well, New Keynesians call the difference between the market-clearing level of output and actual level of output, $Y_m - Y^*$, the **output gap.**

In the New Keynesian model, the labor market need not clear in the short run. In particular, in Figure 13.1(a), at the market real wage w^*, firms would like to hire more labor than N^*, but firms know that if they hired more labor, they would not be able to sell the larger amount of produced output at the price P^*.

The Non-neutrality of Money in the New Keynesian Model

Given our short-run New Keynesian model, we can proceed with an experiment, which will illustrate how money fails to be neutral in this model. Keynesian price stickiness is an alternative theory to the segmented markets model studied in Chapter 12 for explaining why changes in monetary policy can have real effects on aggregate economic activity in the short run.

In Figure 13.2, suppose initially that the economy is in a long-run equilibrium with level of output Y_1, real interest rate r_1, price level P_1, employment N_1, and real wage w_1, given the money supply M_1. Then, the central bank lowers its interest rate target to r_2, implying that output increases to Y_2 in Figure 13.2(b), as firms supply the extra output demanded since the price of output is fixed in the short run at P_1. In Figure 13.2(c), money demand shifts to the right from $PL(Y_1, r_1)$ to $PL(Y_2, r_2)$, as real income has risen and the real interest rate has fallen, both of which act to increase money demand. Therefore, to support the lower nominal interest rate target, the central bank must increase the money supply to M_2. In the labor market in Figure 13.2(a), the labor supply curve shifts to the left from $N^s(r_1)$ to $N^s(r_2)$, as a result of intertemporal substitution in response to the lower interest rate. Therefore, the real wage must rise so as to induce consumers to supply the extra labor required to produce the higher level of output.

Another way to view this is that the central bank increases the money supply, which results in an excess supply of money at the interest rate r_1, and so the interest rate falls so as to equate money supply and demand. The decrease in the real interest rate then increases the demand for consumption goods and investment goods, so firms supply the extra output given that prices are fixed in the short run. Money is not neutral,

Figure 13.2 A Decrease in the Central Bank's Interest Rate Target in the New Keynesian Model

Money is not neutral with sticky prices. A decrease in the interest rate target results in an increase in output, and the central bank must increase in the money supply to achieve its interest rate target. Employment, the real wage, consumption, investment, and the money supply all increase.

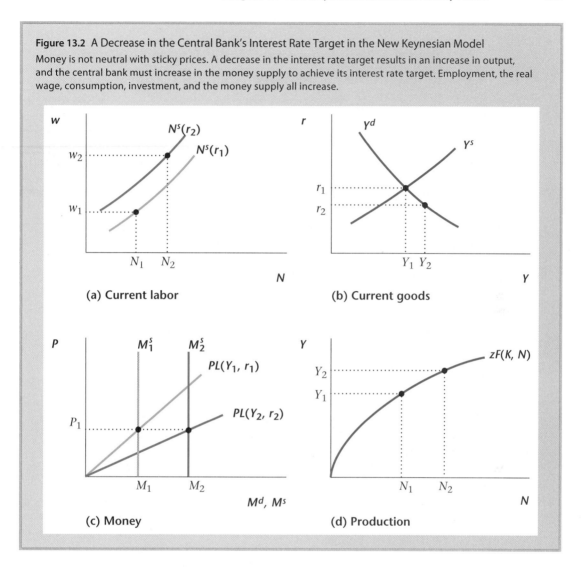

(a) Current labor

(b) Current goods

(c) Money

(d) Production

because the increase in the money supply has real effects; the real interest rate falls, real output increases, the real wage increases, and employment increases. Keynesians think of money as having these real effects through the above-described **Keynesian transmission mechanism for monetary policy.** That is, an increase in the money supply has its first effects in financial markets; the real interest rate falls to equate money demand with the increased money supply, and this acts to increase the demand for goods.

Most Keynesians regard money as being neutral in the long run. Although Keynesians argue that money is not neutral in the short run because of sticky prices (or wages), they also believe that prices will eventually adjust so that supply equals demand in the goods and labor markets, in which case money will be neutral, just as in the monetary intertemporal model we studied in Chapter 11.

Can the New Keynesian Model Under Fluctuations in the Interest Rate Target Explain Business Cycles?

Since changes in the central bank's interest rate target can cause output to change in the New Keynesian model, a key prediction of the model is that, if the interest rate target fluctuates, so will aggregate output. The model then gives a monetary theory of business cycles. That is, the model predicts that policy-induced fluctuations in the central bank's interest rate target could cause business cycles. As economists, we would then like to ask whether this is a good or bad theory of business cycles. To answer this question, we have to ask how the predictions of the model fit the key business cycle regularities that we outlined in Chapter 3.

In Table 13.1 we show how the predictions of the New Keynesian model with interest rate target fluctuations fit features of the data we examined in Chapter 3. Some features of the model clearly fit the data. For example, when the interest rate target falls and the money supply increases, output increases, which is consistent with the fact that money is procyclical in the data. As well, when the interest rate target falls, this causes investment and consumption to rise, so that investment, I, and consumption, C, are procyclical, as is true for the data. Further, a decrease in the interest rate target

causes an increase in employment and the real wage, and so employment and the real wage will be procyclical, as is the case in the data.

However, other results do not fit. First, when the interest rate target falls, the price level does not change (prices are assumed to be sticky), so the price level is acyclical, and not countercyclical, as is the case in the data. If we modified the model so that some firms in the economy could change their prices, with only some firms facing sticky prices, then the decrease in the interest rate target would tend to increase the price level, the price level would be procyclical, and the fit with the data would be even worse. Second, since the interest rate target decrease does not shift the production function, the increase in the level of employment and output must result in a decrease in average labor productivity. Therefore, under fluctuations in the interest rate target, labor productivity is countercyclical and not procyclical, as in the data.

We conclude that, at least for the time period in the United States we examined in Chapter 3, it does not appear that fluctuations in central bank's interest rate target could have been the most important cause of business cycles, if money affects the economy as captured in the New Keynesian model.

Table 13.1   Data Versus Predictions of the New Keynesian Model with Fluctuations in the Central Bank's Interest Rate Target

Variable	Data	Model
Consumption	Procyclical	Procyclical
Investment	Procyclical	Procyclical
Price Level	Countercyclical	Acyclical
Money Supply	Procyclical	Procyclical
Employment	Procyclical	Procyclical
Real Wage	Procyclical	Procyclical
Average Labor Productivity	Procyclical	Countercyclical

It is possible, however, that fluctuations in the Fed's interest rate target, acting through the Keynesian transmission mechanism for monetary policy, made significant contributions (though not the primary ones) to fluctuations in GDP over this period. As well, before World War II in the United States, the price level was procyclical, rather than countercyclical as in the later period we examined, which is consistent with monetary policy shocks being important for business cycles during this earlier period.

We must regard conclusions from Table 13.1 with caution, as in practice the Fed's interest rate target changes with events in the economy. Fed policymakers living in the New Keynesian world

would come to realize that fluctuations in the Fed's interest rate target could cause output and employment to fluctuate. In circumstances where no other shocks were impinging on the economy, the Fed would have no reason to change its interest rate target, and so we would not observe events where a change in the interest rate target was the obvious cause of a change in output. As we will study in more detail later in this chapter, the Fed might have good reasons to change the interest rate target in response to other shocks to the economy, but then it would be hard to disentangle the effects of monetary policy on real activity from the effects of other shocks.

MACROECONOMICS IN ACTION
Monetary Policy and the "Volcker Recession"

Although the evidence from the previous section appears to indicate that monetary policy was relatively unimportant in causing business cycles during the post–World War II period, the 1981–1982 recession is widely attributed to the actions of the Federal Reserve System under Chairman Paul Volcker. Volcker was appointed as chairman of the Federal Reserve Board by President Carter in 1979, at a time when the inflation rate in the United States was at a historically high level. Under a Keynesian interpretation of subsequent events, Volcker decided that inflation had to be reduced through contractionary monetary policy, which had the side effect of producing a severe recession in 1981–1982, dubbed the "Volcker recession." Then, according to the story, once U.S. residents had borne the short-run pain of a recession, they could enjoy the relatively low inflation rates of the later 1980s and 1990s.

An examination of the behavior of real GDP, the money supply, and interest rates certainly appears to support this view. In Figure 13.3 the

money supply dips below trend beginning in 1979–1980, and this is followed by a large drop in real GDP below trend in 1981–1982, as it took some time for the tightening in monetary policy to have its real effects on the economy. In Figure 13.4 there is an increase in the real interest rate in 1980, which is consistent with the monetary tightening seen in the behavior of the money supply. The data in Figures 13.3 and 13.4, therefore, appear consistent with the New Keynesian model and with the view that monetary policy can have large effects on real output.

The evidence from Figures 13.3 and 13.4 is not, however, the end of the story. Typically, there are many different shocks hitting the economy simultaneously, and sophisticated statistical analysis is required to separate out the effects of these shocks from the effects of monetary policy. It turns out that the results from this type of sophisticated statistical analysis are not entirely conclusive. Work by Eric Leeper, Christopher Sims, and Tao Zha summarizes much of the research in this area. They generally
(Continued)

find that contractionary monetary policy has significant negative effects on real output.[6] Harald Uhlig argues, however, that much of this research is tainted, and he suggests that the evidence is consistent with money being neutral.[7]

During the 1981–1982 recession in the United States, most casual observers attributed the severity of the recession to high interest rates, and they assigned responsibility for those high interest rates to the Federal Reserve System and Chairman Volcker. The statistical evidence, however, although tending to favor this view of the cause of the 1981–1982 recession, is not entirely conclusive.

[6]See E. Leeper, C. Sims, and T. Zha, 1996. "What Does Monetary Policy Do?" *Brookings Papers on Economic Activity*, series 2, 1–63.

[7]See H. Uhlig, 2001, "What Are the Effects of Monetary-Policy on Output? Results from an Agnostic Identification Procedure," working paper, Humboldt University.

Figure 13.3 Percentage Deviations from Trend in the Money Supply and Real GDP

The figure shows detrended money supply and detrended real GDP from 1947–2009 in the United States. A drop in the money supply precedes the 1981–1982 recession.

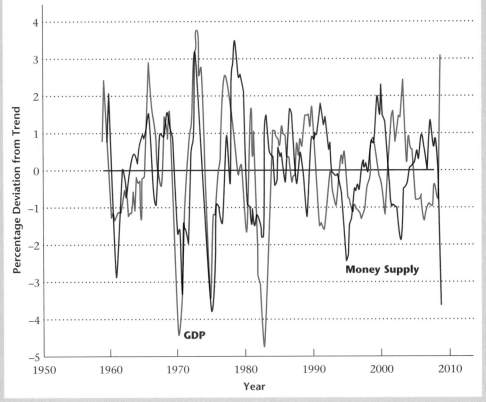

Figure 13.4 Real Interest Rate

The figure shows the short-term real interest rate, measured as the nominal interest rate minus the inflation rate. An increase in the real interest rate precedes the 1981–1982 recession.

THEORY confronts the DATA

Keynesian Aggregate Demand Shocks as Causes of Business Cycles

Although monetary policy shocks in the New Keynesian model may not be able to explain all the key business cycle regularities discussed in Chapter 3, some other shock to the economy might successfully explain observed business cycles in this model. Keynes argued in his *General Theory of Employment, Interest, and Money* that a principal cause of business cycles is fluctuations in aggregate demand. What he appears to have had in mind was shocks to investment, which would be captured here as shifts in the Y^d curve. That is, suppose that firms become more optimistic about future total factor productivity, so that they view the future marginal product of capital as having increased (Keynes referred to such waves

(Continued)

of optimism as being due to the "animal spirits" of investors). This increases the demand for investment goods, and shifts the Y^d curve to the right.

In Figure 13.5, suppose that the economy is initially in long-run equilibrium, with all markets clearing. The level of output is Y_1, the central bank's interest rate target is r_1, the price level is P_1, the money supply is M_1, the real wage is w_1, and the level of employment is N_1. Then, an increase in the demand for investment goods leads to a rightward shift in the Y^d curve from Y_1^d to Y_2^d

in Figure 13.5(b). An important factor in determining the effects on the economy will be the central bank's response to this aggregate shock. Here, we will assume that the interest rate target does not change, remaining at r_1. As a result, in Figure 13.5(b), the level of output increases to Y_2, with firms increasing output to meet the increase in demand for goods.

In Figure 13.5(c), the money demand curve shifts to the right from $PL(Y_1, r_1)$ to $PL(Y_2, r_1)$, due to the increase in real aggregate income.

Figure 13.5 An Increase in the Demand for Investment Goods in the New Keynesian Model
The output demand curve shifts to the right, with the central bank's target interest rate unchanged. Output, investment, consumption, the money supply, employment, and the real wage all increase. In panel (d), average labour productivity must fall.

(a) Current labor

(b) Current goods

(c) Money

(d) Production

Then, in order for the central bank to meet its interest rate target r_1, it must increase the money supply from M_1 to M_2 so as to accommodate the increase in the demand for money. In Figure 13.5(d), firms must increase employment to N_2 from N_1 so as to produce the higher level of output required to meet the increase in demand for goods. In Figure 13.5(a), this requires that the market real wage increase so that consumers are willing to supply a higher quantity of labor.

Now, investment must rise, as the real interest rate is unchanged and firms expect productivity to be higher in the future. Consumption also increases, since real income has risen and the interest rate is unchanged. The price level is sticky in the short run, and therefore unchanged, while in Figure 13.5(d), average labor productivity must fall, since employment and output increase and the production function does not shift.

Table 13.2 summarizes the key business cycle facts from Chapter 3 and the predictions of the New Keynesian model under investment shocks. From Figure 13.5, an increase in output coincides with an increase in investment, an increase in consumption, no change in the price level, an increase in the money supply, an increase in employment, an increase in the real wage, and a decrease in average labor productivity. Therefore, in contrast to the data, the price level is acyclical (or worse, procyclical, if the prices of some goods are not sticky), and average labor productivity is countercyclical. Our conclusion is that the fit to the data is not the best, and so investment shocks in the New Keynesian model do not appear to completely explain business cycle facts.

Table 13.2 Data Versus Predictions of the New Keynesian Model with Investment Shocks

Variable	Data	Model
Consumption	Procyclical	Procyclical
Investment	Procyclical	Procyclical
Price Level	Acyclical	Procyclical
Money Supply	Procyclical	Procyclical
Employment	Procyclical	Procyclical
Real Wage	Procyclical	Procyclical
Average Labor Productivity	Procyclical	Countercyclical

The Role of Government Policy in the New Keynesian Model

In macroeconomics, some important disagreements focus on the issue of whether the government should act to smooth out business cycles. This smoothing, or what is sometimes referred to as **stabilization policy,** involves carrying out government actions that will increase aggregate real output when it is below trend and decrease it when it is above trend. Using government policy to smooth business cycles may appear to be a good idea. For example, we know that a consumer whose income fluctuates will behave optimally by smoothing consumption relative to income, so why shouldn't the government take actions that will smooth aggregate real income over time? As we saw in Chapter 12, this logic need not apply when considering the rationale for government policy intervention with respect to macroeconomic events. For example, in a real business cycle model, stabilization policy must be detrimental, as business cycles are just optimal responses to aggregate productivity shocks.

Keynesians tend to believe that government intervention to smooth out business cycles is appropriate, and the New Keynesian model provides a justification for this belief. We will start by considering a situation where an unanticipated shock has hit the economy, causing the price level to be higher than its equilibrium level in the goods market, as in Figure 13.6. Alternatively, the central bank's interest rate target r_1 is too high, so there exists a positive output gap of $Y_2 - Y_1$ in Figure 13.6 or, in other words, a situation where firms would like to supply more output than is demanded given the price level P_1 and the interest rate target r_1.

Now, after the shock has hit the economy, the allocation of resources is not economically efficient. Recall from Chapter 5 that the first fundamental theorem of welfare economics implies that a competitive equilibrium is Pareto-optimal, but in Figure 13.6 the economy is not in a competitive equilibrium, as initially the quantity of output demanded is not equal to the quantity of output that firms would like to supply. One response of the government to the economic inefficiency caused by the shock to the economy would be to do nothing and let the problem cure itself. Since the price level P_1 is initially above its long-run equilibrium level, with the quantity of goods demanded less than what firms would like to supply, the price level will tend to fall over time. If the central bank does nothing, this means that it does not change the quantity directly under its control, which is the quantity of money. The money supply remains fixed at M_1, as in Figure 13.6(b). Then, as the price level falls over time, money demand must increase, so the central bank's interest rate target must fall until ultimately, in the long run, the interest rate target is r_2, output is Y_2, and the price level is P_2, as in Figure 13.6, and the economy is again in equilibrium and operating efficiently.

Keynesian macroeconomists argue that the long run is too long to wait. In Figure 13.6 suppose alternatively, that instead of doing nothing in response to the shock to the economy, the central bank immediately reduces its interest rate target from r_1 to r_2. To hit this lower interest rate target requires that the central bank increase the money supply from M_1 to M_2 in Figure 13.6. This immediately closes the output gap and restores economic efficiency in the short run. The price level is P_1 and the level of output is Y_2.

Note that after the increase in the money supply, the economy is in exactly the same situation, in real terms, as it would have been in the long run if the central bank did nothing and allowed the price level to fall. The only difference is that the price level is higher in the case where the central bank intervenes. The advantage of intervention is that an efficient outcome is achieved faster than if the central bank let events take their course.

The return to full employment could also be achieved through an increase in government expenditures, G, but with some different results. In Figure 13.7, we show a

Figure 13.6 Stabilization Using Monetary Policy

Initially the level of output is Y_1 given the interest rate target r_1 and the price level P_1. In the long run, the price level will fall to P_2, but the central bank can achieve Y_2 in the short run by reducing the interest rate target to r_2.

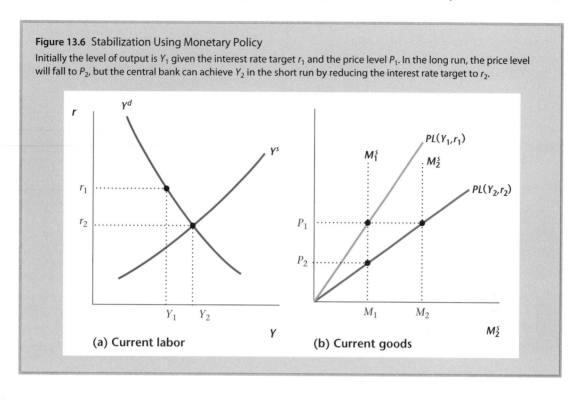

(a) Current labor   **(b) Current goods**

similar initial situation to Figure 13.6, where initial output is Y_1, which is less than the quantity of output that firms want to supply given the price level P_1 and the interest rate target r_1. Now, suppose that the central bank maintains its interest rate target at r_1, in anticipation that the government fiscal authority will increase government spending to correct the inefficiency problem that exists in the short run. If the government increases government purchases, G, by just the right amount, then the output demand curve shifts to the right from Y_1^d to Y_2^d and the output supply curve shifts to the right from to Y_1^s to Y_2^s (recall our analysis from Chapter 10, where we analyzed the effects of temporary increases in G). In Figure 13.7(b), the price level is sticky in the short run at P_1, and the increase in output shifts the money demand curve to the right from $PL(Y_1, r_1)$ to $PL(Y_2, r_1)$, and so to maintain its interest rate target the central bank increases the money supply from M_1 to M_2.

Now, note the differences in final outcomes between Figures 13.6 and 13.7. Recall from Chapter 10 that the entire increase in output from Y_1 to Y_2 in Figure 13.7 is due to the increase in government spending, as the interest rate is unchanged. That is, the fiscal policy response to the shock results in no increase in consumption or investment, with the only component of spending that increases being government spending, with output increasing one-for-one with government spending. After government intervention, output is higher in Figure 13.7 than in Figure 13.6, but with monetary policy intervention, consumption and investment are higher in Figure 13.7 than in Figure 13.6 because of the decrease in the target central bank interest rate. Thus, the key differences

Figure 13.7 Stabilization Using Fiscal Policy

Given the central bank's interest rate target r_1, an increase in government spending shifts the output demand and supply curves to the right and restores efficiency in the short run.

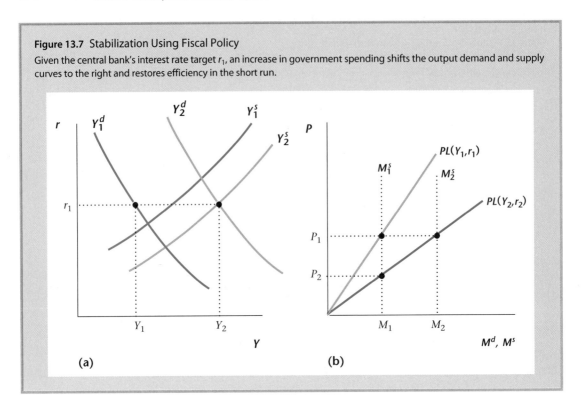

(a)   (b)

that fiscal policy intervention makes, relative to monetary policy intervention to stabilize the economy, is that output needs to change more in response to fiscal policy in order to restore efficiency, and the composition of output is different with fiscal policy, with a greater emphasis on public spending relative to private spending, compared to what happens with monetary policy intervention.

Whether fiscal or monetary policy is used to smooth business cycles, the New Keynesian model provides a rationale for stabilization policy. If shocks kick the economy out of equilibrium, because of a failure of private markets to clear in the short run, fiscal or monetary policymakers can, if they move fast enough, restore the economy to equilibrium before self-adjusting markets achieve this on their own. Thus, the important elements of the Keynesian view of government's role in the macroeconomy are:

1. Private markets fail to operate smoothly on their own, in that not all wages and prices are perfectly flexible, implying that supply is not equal to demand in all markets, and economic efficiency is not always achieved in a world without government intervention.

2. Fiscal policy and/or monetary policy decisions can be made quickly enough, and information on the behavior of the economy is good enough, that the fiscal or monetary authorities can improve efficiency by countering shocks that cause a deviation from a full-employment equilibrium.

Perspectives on the Financial Crisis

The Effects of Monetary Policy When the
Nominal Interest Rate Is Zero

About every six weeks, the Federal Open Market Committee (FOMC) of the Federal Reserve System meets, and the primary decision made at this meeting is the setting of a target for the federal funds rate (or fed funds rate), the short-term interest rate at which banks borrow and lend. In Figure 13.8 we show the actual fed funds rate for the period 1954–2009. Typically, the Fed comes very close to hitting its target, but there is usually a small difference between the actual fed funds rate and the target for this rate. For example, in July 2007 the target fed funds rate was 5.25%, but the actual fed funds rate was 5.26%. July 2007 is significant, as this was the most recent peak in the value for the fed funds rate. In the latter half of 2007, the Fed began reducing its target for the fed funds rate in response to a lower inflation rate and a weakening in aggregate economic activity.

Figure 13.8 The Federal Funds Rate

The fed funds rate was targeted at 0%–0.25% from December 2008 until the end of the sample period in the figure.

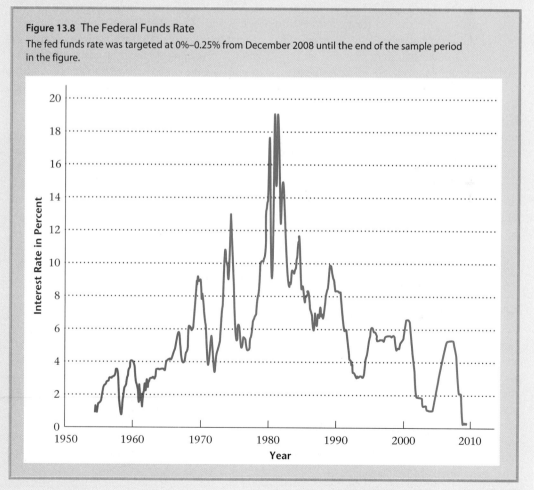

(*Continued*)

Fed funds rate reductions continued in response to the failure of the investment banking firm Bear Stearns in March 2008, with a crisis point reached after the failure of another investment bank, Lehman Brothers, in September 2008, and the subsequent solvency problems of the insurance company American International Group. In December 2008, the FOMC officially stated that the target for the fed funds rate was to be 0 to 0.25%, and the target has remained in that range to this date (August 2009). Note in Figure 13.8 that the fed funds rate has never been this low during the previous 55-year period in the figure. Clearly 0% is as low as the interest rate on fed funds can go. The fed funds rate cannot be negative, as then banks could make infinite profits by borrowing on the fed funds market and simply holding the borrowed outside money. The possibility of making infinite profits is an arbitrage opportunity that cannot exist in practice.

When the short-term nominal interest rate is at or close to zero, this is a very special circumstance. Since the nominal interest rate represents the opportunity cost of holding outside money, money is then costless to hold at a zero nominal interest rate. Typically, when the nominal interest rate is greater than zero, if the central bank conducts an open market purchase of short-term government securities (the most common vehicle the central bank uses for injecting money into the economy) the financial market participants who receive the new money balances will want to spend them. No one wants to hold the extra outside money as an asset, as there are other safe assets that bear a positive rate of interest. However, if the nominal interest rate is zero, then, from the viewpoint of financial market participants, money and interest-bearing government securities are essentially identical. Then, when an open market purchase of government securities is conducted by the central bank, financial market participants may want to hold the additional outside money rather than spending it, as safe government securities do not offer a better return. Such a situation is sometimes referred to as a "liquidity trap," as we discussed in Chapter 11.

In the New Keynesian model, we represent a liquidity trap in Figure 13.9. In panel (a) of the figure, the central bank's interest rate target is zero, and the quantity of aggregate output is Y_1. Even with a zero interest rate target, there is a positive output gap in panel (a) of the figure. In panel (b), since the interest rate is zero, the demand for money is infinitely elastic at the price level P_1, and changes in the money supply will be irrelevant—any level of the money supply is consistent with the zero interest rate target. The interest rate target cannot go lower than zero, so in the model monetary policy is powerless to eliminate the positive output gap in the short run through reductions in the target interest rate.

Thus, simple New Keynesian models are consistent with the possibility of a liquidity trap phenomenon. As well, observed behavior of financial institutions during the financial crisis appears consistent with the existence of a liquidity trap. In particular, much of the outside money that was injected into the U.S. economy by the Fed from late 2008 on has been held as reserve balances by banks. Essentially, banks are hoarding outside money, and this certainly looks like a liquidity trap phenomenon. The Fed's reaction to this, in light of the fact that U.S. GDP and employment remain well below trend in mid-2009, has been to resort to other means of injecting money into the economy other than traditional central bank open market operations in short-term government securities. This alternative central bank intervention is sometimes referred to as "quantitative easing." Alternative interventions have included the purchase of long-term government securities, long-term government agency securities and mortgage-backed securities, as well as lending to financial institutions that have not traditionally received central bank loans. The Fed hopes that, in pursuing such policies, it can reduce the output gap through means other than reducing the short-term market interest rate. That is, Fed policymakers believe that their actions can relieve some of the credit market problems which caused the financial crisis and the 2008–2009 recession.

Figure 13.9 A Liquidity Trap in the New Keynesian Model

With the central bank's interest rate target at zero, real output is Y_1 and there is a positive output gap. Since the nominal interest rate is zero, the demand for money is perfectly elastic (i.e. horizontal) at the fixed price P_1. Increasing the money supply above M will have no effect.

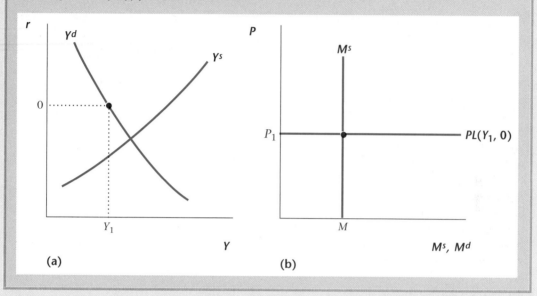

(a)   (b)

The risk associated with the Fed's massive intervention in 2008–2009 is that the liquidity will not remain trapped forever. The stock of outside money more than doubled in the United States from late 2008 to mid-2009, and if this outside money is spent on goods rather hoarded by banks as reserves, it would result in a very large inflation, which would be costly in its effects, and costly for the Fed to ultimately control. We will study some issues in inflation control later, in Chapters 16 and 18.

Perspectives on the Financial Crisis

The Timing of the Effects of Fiscal and Monetary Policy

While the effects of fiscal and monetary policy are instantaneous in the New Keynesian model, in practice it takes time to formulate policy, and it takes time for policy to affect the economy. First, policymakers do not have complete information. The national income accounts, employment data, and price data are time-consuming to compile, and policymakers in the federal government and at the Fed have good information only for what was happening in the economy months previously. Second, when information is available, it may take time for policymakers to agree among themselves concerning a course of action. Finally, once policy is implemented, there is a

(Continued)

time lag before policy has its effects on aggregate economic activity. The awkward lags in macroeconomic policymaking were recognized at least as early as 1948, by Milton Friedman.[8]

While the first stage of policymaking (information collection) is essentially the same for fiscal and monetary policy, it is generally recognized that the second stage (decision making) takes much longer for fiscal policy than for monetary policy in the United States. The congressional process of passing a budget can take months, while the Federal Open Market Committee, the decision-making body of the Fed, meets every six weeks, and it can make decisions between these meetings if necessary. For the third stage in the timing of the effects of fiscal and monetary policy—that is, the lag between a policy decision and when its effects are realized in the economy—it is not clear whether fiscal or monetary policy takes longer. For fiscal policy, the results will depend on whether the fiscal policy changes are to taxes or government spending. Tax changes can in principle have their effects quickly. For example, the government can send out checks in the mail at short notice, with essentially immediate effects on consumption/savings decisions. However, new spending takes longer to allocate, and for public works projects there are long lags in getting the projects off the ground. With regard to monetary policy, one of the points of Milton Friedman and Anna Schwartz's study of the role of money in the U.S. economy, *A Monetary History of the United States, 1867–1960*, is that the lag between a monetary policy action and its effects is "long and variable." That is, it can take a long time for monetary policy to have its effects, perhaps six months to a year, and this length of time is always uncertain.

Factors relating to time-consuming policymaking and implementation came into play in the policy responses of the U.S. federal government and the Fed to the financial crisis and the ensuing

2008–2009 recession. For monetary policy, some viewed the Fed as being overly complacent and oblivious to the problems developing in the mortgage market, beginning with the decline in the price of housing in 2006. However, with the developing recession in 2008 and the clear financial crisis in the fall of 2008, the Fed acted quickly to reduce the target federal funds rate and to implement other measures to intervene in credit markets. Whether the Fed is doing the right things or doing too much continues to be a subject of debate, but the ability of the central bank to act quickly is certainly in evidence in its responses to the financial crisis.

With respect to fiscal policy, two main programs were put in effect. The first was the Emergency Economic Stabilization Act of 2008 (EESA), which authorized $700 billion for the Troubled Asset Relief Program (TARP). The Act was passed by Congress in October 2008 and was a very unusual fiscal policy program. The Act gave the Secretary of the Treasury a great deal of discretion in implementing the legislation, in consultation with the Federal Reserve Chairman. Originally, the intention appeared to be for the federal government to buy up "troubled assets," for which organized markets had essentially shut down. These assets would be purchased from financial institutions, including banks. In this respect, this program looked more like monetary policy than fiscal policy in that the federal government would essentially be issuing its own debt to finance the purchase of assets, and therefore be acting as a financial intermediary. Ultimately, the program evolved into a scheme to "bail out" banks and other financial institutions. Funds were transferred by the federal government to financial institutions in exchange for equity claims, with some restrictions then placed on the terms of hiring and employee compensation of these financial institutions. The goal of the program was to temporarily stabilize financial markets and to encourage lending by banks and other financial institutions. This program was certainly implemented much more quickly

---

[8]M. Friedman, 1948, "A Monetary and Fiscal Framework for Economic Stability," *American Economic Review* 38, 245–264.

than is typically the case for fiscal policy programs, although the program has frequently been criticized as poorly thought-out and as a simple redistribution from taxpayers to the financial sector of the economy. Whether it has had its intended effects is debatable.

The second key fiscal policy program was the American Recovery and Reinvestment Act (ARRA), discussed in earlier chapters, particularly Chapter 5. This act of Congress was passed in February 2009 and included a range of government expenditure, tax, and transfer programs. Of all the monetary and fiscal policy interventions carried out in response to the financial crisis and the 2008–2009 recession, this program was the one most strongly motivated by traditional Keynesian economics, and the one also most clearly subject to Milton Friedman's concerns about policy timing issues. Although the ARRA was quickly put together and passed by Congress (a concern in itself, as little thought was given to the economic efficiency of the components of the program), much of the spending authorized by the program will not take place until late 2009, 2010, and even on into 2011. Even if we accept that fiscal policy works as Keynesian theorists say it

does, it is quite possible that the U.S. economy will have closed the output gap on its own long before all of the new government spending comes on line. One concern of Friedman's was that attempts to stabilize the economy through government policy could actually contribute to instability. This is what could happen due to the ARRA, if the U.S. economy continues to be "stimulated" long after the problem has gone away.

The conclusion is that, even if we believe that stabilizing the economy through the use of fiscal and monetary policy is appropriate, as the New Keynesian model tells us, there is still much that can go wrong. Guiding the economy can be much like trying to steer a car with a faulty steering mechanism; one has to see the bumps and curves in the road well in advance to avoid driving into the ditch or otherwise having a very uncomfortable ride. This is in part why Milton Friedman, among others, encouraged abstinence from stabilization policy altogether. Friedman argued that well-intentioned stabilization policy could do more harm than good, as the lags in policy could lead to stimulative action being taken when tightening the screws on the economy would be more appropriate, and vice versa.

Total Factor Productivity Shocks in the New Keynesian Model

The New Keynesian Model responds quite differently to shocks to total factor productivity from the real business cycle model of Chapter 12. This different behavior is important, as we can then use the data to draw conclusions about the relative performance of the two models.

First, consider the response of the New Keynesian model to a positive shock to total factor productivity. In Figure 13.10(a), initially the level of output is Y_1 with the central bank target interest rate r_1, and we have assumed that the economy is initially in equilibrium with output demand curve Y^d and output supply curve Y_1^s. In Figure 13.10(b), the price level is P_1, with the price level inflexible in the short run, and the money supply is M_1. In Figure 13.10(c), the initial production function is $z_1 F(K, N)$ and, given the level of output Y_1, employment is N_1.

Now, if total factor productivity increases from z_1 to z_2, then the production function shifts up to $z_2 F(K, N)$ in Figure 13.10(c), and the output supply curve shifts to the

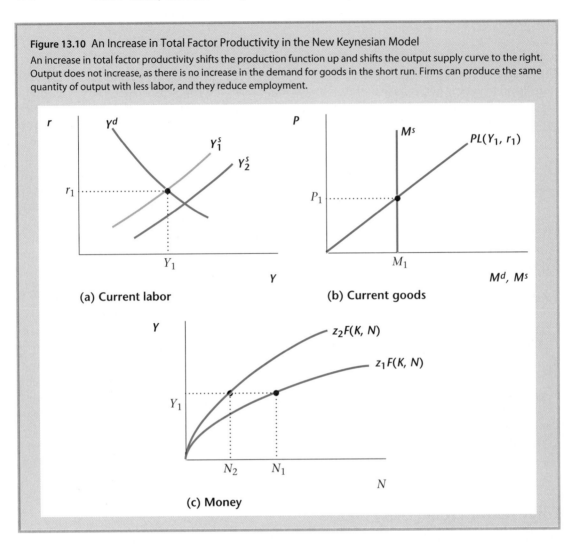

Figure 13.10 An Increase in Total Factor Productivity in the New Keynesian Model

An increase in total factor productivity shifts the production function up and shifts the output supply curve to the right. Output does not increase, as there is no increase in the demand for goods in the short run. Firms can produce the same quantity of output with less labor, and they reduce employment.

(a) Current labor

(b) Current goods

(c) Money

right from Y_1^s to Y_2^s in Figure 13.10(a). Supposing that the central bank's interest rate target remains unchanged, output remains at the level Y_1, as output is demand-determined in the goods market. Therefore, after the productivity shock, a positive output gap opens up, since output is below its equilibrium level. Given that there is no change in the interest rate or in output, the money demand curve does not shift, and so there are no changes in Figure 13.10(b). However, given that the level of output is unchanged, in Figure 13.10(c) employment must fall to N_2. That is, since the price level is sticky, the increase in the quantity of output that firms wish to supply has no effect on the quantity of goods demanded, or the quantity that is actually produced. As productivity has increased, firms can now produce the same quantity of output with less labor, and employment must fall.

We can contrast these results to what we obtained in the real business cycle model in Chapter 12, where an increase in total factor productivity resulted in an increase in output and employment, and a decrease in the real interest rate and the price level. Given our assumptions, productivity shocks in the New Keynesian model do not produce business cycles as we know them. Productivity shocks will not cause output to fluctuate in the short run, and will only produce a negative correlation between employment and total factor productivity. If price stickiness is important, and the central bank does not move its target interest rate in response to productivity shocks (this is important), then productivity shocks cannot be an important cause of business cycles.

What do the data tell us about this issue? Jordi Gali has argued that statistical evidence supports the idea that, when the U.S. economy is hit by a positive productivity shock, employment declines in the short run.[9] This would appear to be consistent with the New Keynesian model and inconsistent with the real business cycle model. However, this is not the end of the story. V.V. Chari, Ellen McGratten, and Patrick Kehoe simulate a real business cycle model on the computer, producing some artificial data, which they then treat in the same way that Gali treated his actual data when he did his statistical tests.[10] They get the same results as did Gali, but Chari, McGratten, and Kehoe know that their data come from a real business cycle world. This makes Gali's results seem suspicious. Obviously, the debate about which business cycle model best fits reality is far from over.

Criticisms of Keynesian Models

Critics of Keynesian models, who we might call **classical macroeconomists**, argue that these models fall short in several respects. First, as we have already pointed out, the New Keynesian model does not fully replicate the key business cycle regularities. The New Keynesian model cannot replicate the countercyclicality of the price level and procyclicality of average labor productivity, as is observed in the data. Second, classical economists argue that the theory underlying sticky wage and sticky price models is poor or nonexistent. Typically, these models do not capture the underlying reasons for wage and price stickiness—the stickiness is simply assumed. To properly understand why wages might be sticky and exactly how this matters for macroeconomic activity, we need to be explicit in our theories about the features of the world that are important to the setting of wages and prices and to show how a model with such features explains reality.

Menu cost models are a response to the criticisms by classical economists of Keynesian models. In these models, firms face explicit costs of changing prices, firms maximize profits in the face of these costs, and the result is that prices are in fact sticky, and the models have implications much like those of our New Keynesian model. However, menu cost models have certainly not been immune from criticism. Classical economists point out that the costs of changing prices are minuscule compared with the short-run costs of changing the quantity of output. Consider the case

---

[9]See J. Gali, 2004, "Technology Shocks and Aggregate Fluctuations: How Well Does the RBC Model Fit Postwar US Data?" *NBER Macreconomics Annual 2004*, 225–228.

[10]V.V. Chari, E. McGratten, and P. Kehoe, 2006, "A Critique of Structural VARs Using Real Business Cycle Theory," working paper, University of Minnesota and Federal Reserve Bank of Minneapolis.

of a restaurant. On the one hand, the cost of changing menu prices is the cost of making a few keystrokes on a computer keyboard, and then running off a few copies of the menu on the printer in the back room. Indeed, a restaurant will be printing new menus frequently anyway, because restaurant patrons tend to spill food on the menus. On the other hand, if the restaurant wants to increase output in response to higher demand, it will have to move in more tables and chairs and hire and train new staff. Why would the restaurant want to change output in response to a temporary increase in demand rather than just increasing prices temporarily?

The questions we have raised above help in framing the debate as to whether Keynesian sticky wage and sticky price models on the one hand or equilibrium business cycle models on the other hand are more useful. As we saw in Chapter 12, equilibrium models in general have quite different implications for the role of fiscal and monetary policy than does the New Keynesian model, with some equilibrium models implying that government intervention is detrimental. However, in the Keynesian coordination failure model (an equilibrium business cycle model) active government stabilization policy could be justified, and there is a limited role for monetary policy in the segmented markets model. The reader may wonder at this point why we should study different business cycle models that appear to have contradictory implications. The reason is that business cycles can have many causes, and each of the business cycle models we have examined contains an element of truth that is useful in understanding why business cycles occur and what, if anything, can or should be done about them.

This chapter completes our study of the macroeconomics of business cycles in closed economies. We go on in Chapters 14 and 15 to study macroeconomics in an open economy context.

Chapter Summary

- A New Keynesian model was constructed in which the price level is sticky in the short run, and the central bank manipulates the money supply so as to maintain a target interest rate. Otherwise, the model is identical to the monetary intertemporal model of Chapter 11. Price stickiness implies that the goods market and labor market need not clear in the short run, although the money market does clear.
- Monetary policy is not neutral in the New Keynesian model. A decrease in the central bank's target interest rate, brought about by an increase in the money supply, will increase output, employment, consumption, investment, and the real wage.
- Under either monetary policy shocks or shocks to the demand for investment goods, the New Keynesian model replicates most of the key business cycle facts from Chapter 3, but the price level is not countercyclical in the model and average labor productivity is countercyclical rather than procyclical, as it is in the data.
- Although some markets do not clear in the short run and the economy does not achieve a Pareto-optimal outcome, in the long run prices will adjust so that economic efficiency holds. Keynesians argue that the long run is too long to wait and that better results can be achieved through monetary and fiscal policy intervention in the short run in response to shocks to the aggregate economy.

MACROECONOMICS IN ACTION
How Sticky Are Nominal Prices?

Casual observation tells us that some prices appear to be quite sticky. For example, the prices of newspapers and magazines tend to remain fixed for long periods of time. As well, there are some prices that clearly change frequently. The prices of fresh vegetables change week-to-week in the supermarket, and the prices of gasoline posted by gas stations can change on a daily basis. However, to evaluate the importance of Keynesian sticky price models, it is important to quantify the degree of price stickiness for a broad array of consumer goods. If there is little actual price stickiness for the average good or service in the economy, then price stickiness will be relatively unimportant in contributing to business cycles and the nonneutrality of money. As well, we would like to know whether the pattern of price changes we observe in the economy is consistent with the type of price stickiness that Keynesian theorists typically build into their models.

Until recently, economists had not gathered comprehensive evidence on the nature of price changes across the economy's goods and services. However, Mark Bils and Peter Klenow gained access to Bureau of Labor Statistics data on the prices of goods and services that was heretofore unavailable to researchers.[11] Their findings are surprising. Bils and Klenow found that, for half of the goods and services in their

data set, prices changed every 4.3 months or less, which is a much higher frequency of price changes than indicated by previous studies. While this does not entirely preclude significant effects from the sticky price mechanism for business cycles and the nonneutrality of money, it raises questions about previous results in Keynesian macroeconomics that would have exaggerated Keynesian sticky price effects.

Another feature of the data that Bils and Klenow find is that the rates of change in prices for particular goods and services are far more variable than is consistent with sticky price models. In a typical sticky price model of the type in common use by Keynesian researchers, a shock to the economy that causes prices to increase will lead to staggered price increases over time, because individual firms do not coordinate their price increases. As a result, the rate of change in the price of an individual good or service should be persistent over time, and not very volatile, but this is not so in the data.

The work of Bils and Klenow points to some key faults in the sticky price models typically used in practice. Their work does not definitively resolve issues about the value of Keynesian business cycle models relative to the alternatives. However, Bils and Klenow have cast doubt on whether the sticky price mechanism is of key importance in understanding business cycles and how monetary policy works.

---

[11]M. Bils and P. Klenow, 2004, "Some Evidence on the Importance of Sticky Prices," *Journal of Political Economy* 112, 947–985.

- Aggregate stabilization through monetary policy has different effects from fiscal policy stabilization. Monetary policy stabilization achieves the same result that would occur in long run when prices adjust, in terms of real economic variables, but fiscal policy stabilization alters the mix of public versus private spending in the goods market.

- Changes in total factor productivity have very different effects in the New Keynesian model than in the real business cycle model of Chapter 12. In the New Keynesian model, a positive productivity shock has no effect on output in the short run, and employment falls.

- Classical economists find the assumptions made in sticky-price and sticky-wage Keynesian models implausible, and empirical evidence on the behavior of individual prices seems inconsistent with elements of Keynesian models.

Key Terms

Classical macroeconomists   The alternative to Keynesian macroeconomists; a classical macroeconomist believes that market-clearing models are useful and tends to believe that the government should not engage in stabilization policy. (p. 497)

Keynesian transmission mechanism for monetary policy   The real effects of monetary policy in the Keynesian model. In the model, money is not neutral, because an increase in the money supply causes the real interest rate to fall, increasing the demand for consumption and investment, and causing the price level to increase. The real wage then falls, the firm hires more labor, and output increases. (p. 481)

Menu cost models   Sticky price models with explicit costs of changing prices. (p. 478)

Natural rate of interest   The real interest rate that would be determined in equilibrium when all prices and wages are flexible. (p. 480)

Output gap   The difference between actual aggregate output and the efficient level of aggregate output. (p. 480)

Stabilization policy   Fiscal or monetary policy justified by Keynesian models, which acts to offset shocks to the economy. (p. 487)

Questions for Review

1. Are Keynesian business cycle models still used? If so, what for?
2. What is the key difference between the New Keynesian model and the models studied in Chapter 12?
3. Which markets clear in the New Keynesian model, and which do not?
4. How is monetary policy determined in the New Keynesian model? What is the central bank's target, and what does the central bank control directly?
5. Why is monetary policy not neutral in the New Keynesian model? What are the effects of a change in the central bank's target interest rate?
6. How does the New Keynesian model fit the key business cycle facts from Chapter 3?
7. What happens in the long run in the New Keynesian model?
8. How do Keynesians justify intervention in the economy through monetary and fiscal policy?
9. How does monetary policy stabilization differ from fiscal policy stabilization?
10. Explain the differences in how the New Keynesian model and the real business cycle model respond to changes in total factor productivity.
11. What are the faults of the New Keynesian model?

Problems

1. Suppose government spending increases temporarily in the New Keynesian model.
   (a) What are the effects on real output, consumption, investment, the price level, employment, and the real wage?
   (b) Are these effects consistent with the key business cycle facts from Chapter 3? What does this say about the ability of government spending shocks to explain business cycles?

2. In the New Keynesian model, suppose that supply is initially equal to demand in the goods market and that there is a negative shock to the demand for investment goods, because firms anticipate lower total factor productivity in the future.
   (a) Determine the effects on real output, the real interest rate, the price level, employment, and the real wage if the government did nothing in response to the shock.
   (b) Determine the effects if monetary policy is used to stabilize the economy, with the goal of the central bank being zero economic efficiency.
   (c) Determine the effects if government spending is used to stabilize the economy, with the goal of the fiscal authority being economic efficiency.
   (d) Explain and comment on the differences in your results among parts (a), (b), and (c).

3. Suppose that the nominal interest rate is zero, there is a liquidity trap, and there exists a positive output gap. What are the effects of an increase in this government expenditures in this circumstance? Can an increase in government spending eliminate the output gap in the short run? Discuss your results.

4. Suppose that the goal of the fiscal authority is to set government spending so as to achieve economic efficiency, while the goal of the monetary authority is to achieve stability of the price level over the long run. Assume that the economy is initially in equilibrium and that there is then a temporary decrease in total factor productivity. Show that there are many ways in which the fiscal and monetary authority can achieve their separate goals. What could determine what fiscal and monetary policy settings are actually used in this context? Discuss.

5. Some macroeconomists have argued that it would be beneficial for the government to run a deficit when the economy is in a recession, and a surplus during a boom. Does this make sense? Carefully explain why or why not, using the New Keynesian model.

6. In the New Keynesian model, how should the central bank change its target interest rate in response to each of the following shocks. Use diagrams, and explain your results.
   (a) There is a shift in money demand.
   (b) Total factor productivity is expected to decrease in the future.
   (c) Total factor productivity decreases in the present.

7. Suppose that the central bank sets its interest rate target to achieve efficiency in response to temporary shocks to total factor productivity. Using diagrams, determine what the economy's responses will then be to the total factor productivity shocks. How will this differ from what happens in a real business cycle model? Explain your results, and discuss the implications for what the data can reveal about what is the better business cycle model, the real business cycle model or the New Keynesian model.

8. In the New Keynesian model, suppose that in the short run the central bank cannot observe aggregate output or the shocks that hit the economy. However, the central bank would like to come as close as possible to economic efficiency. That is, ideally the central bank would like the output gap to be zero. Suppose initially that the economy is in equilibrium with a zero output gap.
   (a) Suppose that there is a shift in money demand. That is, the quantity of money demanded increases for each interest rate and level of real income. How well does the central bank perform in relative to its goal? Explain using diagrams.
   (b) Suppose that firms expect total factor productivity to increase in the future. Repeat part (a).
   (c) Suppose that total factor productivity increases in the current period. Repeat part (a).
   (d) Explain any differences in your results in parts (a)–(c), and explain what this implies about the wisdom of following an interest rate rule for the central bank.

Working with the Data

1. Construct a time series plot of the percentage deviations from trend in the monetary base and in real GDP, and construct a scatter plot of the two variables. Are these plots consistent or inconsistent with the nonneutrality of money that the Keynesian sticky wage model predicts? Explain.

2. Construct a time series plot of the percentage deviations from trend in total real government expenditures and in real GDP, and construct a scatter plot of the two variables. Does it appear from these plots that the government is engaging in stabilizing fiscal policy? Explain.

PART VI

International Macroeconomics

Because of globalization—the continuing integration of world markets in goods, services, and assets—international factors are increasingly important for the performance of the domestic economy and for the conduct of fiscal and monetary policy. In this part, we study models of open economies in which there is trade between the domestic economy and the rest of the world. We use these models in Chapter 14 to study the benefits from international trade, the effects of changes in world prices and interest rates, the determinants of the current account surplus, and the implications of current account deficits. In Chapter 15, we examine the role of money in the world economy, the determination of exchange rates, the effects of fixed and flexible exchange rates, and the implications of shocks occurring abroad for domestic business cycles.

chapter 14

International Trade in Goods and Assets

Our goal in this chapter is to extend the models developed in Chapters 5, 8, and 10 so that they can address issues in international macroeconomics. Until now, we have looked at closed-economy macroeconomic issues using closed-economy models, but for many interesting macroeconomic problems, we must do our analysis in an open-economy context. This chapter is confined to issues relating to real international macroeconomics. In Chapter 15, we address the monetary side of international interaction.

During the twentieth and twenty-first centuries, international trade has become increasingly important for two reasons. First, the costs of transporting goods and assets across international boundaries has fallen dramatically, permitting a freer flow of international trade. Second, government-imposed barriers to trade, such as import quotas, tariffs, and restrictions on international financial activity, have been relaxed. A relaxation of trade restrictions was carried out under the General Agreement on Tariffs and Trade (GATT) between 1947 and 1995, when the GATT framework was replaced by the World Trade Organization. Trade restrictions have also been reduced through regional agreements, for example, the North American Free Trade Agreement (NAFTA), signed in 1992, and the European Union (EU). Given the increasing importance of trade in the world economy, there is much to be gained from understanding its implications for domestic macroeconomic activity.

In this chapter, we study the importance for domestic aggregate economic activity of trade with the rest of the world in goods and assets. We are interested particularly in how the current account surplus and domestic output, employment, consumption, and investment are affected by events in the rest of the world. To study this, we extend some of the models we have worked with in Chapters 5, 8, and 10.

Throughout this chapter, we confine attention to small open-economy models, which are models in which actions by consumers and firms in the domestic economy have no collective effect on world prices. Some countries are clearly small relative to the rest of the world, such as New Zealand, Singapore, and Luxembourg, and for these countries it is clear that the small open-economy assumption is quite realistic. However, for large countries such as the United States, which play a particularly important role in the world economy, the assumption of price-taking on world markets is perhaps less plausible. There are three reasons that we study small open-economy models here and use them to explain events in large open economies (the United States in particular).

The first is that small open-economy models are relatively simple to work with; for example, it is easy to modify closed-economy models in constructing small open-economy models. Second, many of the conclusions we derive from small open-economy models are identical to the ones we would obtain in more complicated large open-economy models. Third, as time passes, the small open-economy assumption becomes more realistic for a country such as the United States. Given development in the rest of the world, GDP in the United States relative to GDP in the rest of the world falls, and it becomes a closer approximation to the truth that the United States is a price-taker in world goods and asset markets.

In this chapter, we study three small open-economy models that build, respectively, on the one-period model in Chapter 5, the two-period model in Chapter 8, and the real intertemporal model in Chapter 10. The first model focuses on the determinants of domestic production and consumption of goods and the volume of trade between the domestic economy and the rest of the world. This model is used to study how the welfare of domestic consumers can be improved through free trade in goods with the rest of the world and to study the effects of changes in world prices on domestic consumption, production, and the volume of trade.

In the second model, there are two periods, so that we can examine the impact of borrowing and lending between the domestic economy and the rest of the world. Here, we are primarily interested in the determinants of the current account surplus and the importance of the current account surplus in domestic policymaking. An important idea is that international borrowing and lending permits the smoothing of aggregate consumption over time for the domestic economy, just as a single consumer can smooth consumption by borrowing and lending.

In the third and final model, we include investment and production, so that we can study the relationships among domestic consumption, output, investment, government spending, and the current account balance. This model is used to examine the relationship between the current account deficit and the government budget deficit, and we can apply this analysis to understanding the so-called twin deficits problem of the 1980s. We also examine the role of investment in determining the current account deficit, and we address to what extent a current account deficit is good or bad for a nation's welfare.

A Two-Good Model of a Small Open Economy

The first international model we consider is closely related to the one-period model we constructed in Chapter 5, and the analysis we developed there is also useful here. We use this international model to understand why countries trade, and the primary determinants of the volume of trade. This is a model of a **small open economy (SOE)**. The economy is small, in the sense that economic activity in this country does not affect the world prices of goods. That is, the firms and consumers in this economy are individual price-takers—they treat market prices as being given—and collective price-takers—their collective actions have no effect on the world prices for goods. The economy is also open, in that we explore the consequences of trade between this economy and the rest of the world. Until now, we have considered macroeconomic models of closed economies where there is no trade with the rest of the world.

In the SOE, there are two goods that are produced and consumed, which we will call good a and good b. From the viewpoint of people in the SOE, the price of good a in terms of good b, denoted by TOT_{ab}, is given. This price is the **terms of trade** or the **real exchange rate,** because TOT_{ab} is the rate at which the residents of the SOE can trade good b for good a on world markets. The model tells us under what conditions the SOE imports good a and exports good b, or exports good a and imports good b.

Allowing the two goods in the model, a and b, to stand in for all of the goods produced and consumed in the economy is an important simplification. Clearly, a given country imports and exports many different kinds of goods, and so assuming that there are only two goods may seem unrealistic. For many countries, however, the assumption of two broad categories of goods fits the facts of their trade patterns well. For example, New Zealand's exports are primarily agricultural products, and its main imports are manufactured goods. Similarly, Kuwait exports crude oil and imports manufactured goods. For the United States, the story is somewhat more complicated, as the United States imports and exports goods that may appear to be the same. For example, the United States exports wine produced in California and imports wine from Australia and France. Also, a good portion of trade between the United States and its largest trading partner, Canada, is trade in automobiles. The Ford Motor Company, for example, assembles cars in Oakville, Ontario, for export to the United States, and it also builds cars in Detroit, Michigan, for export to Canada. For our purposes, however, it is convenient to think of exports and imports as different goods. For wine, this is clearly the case. Wine consumers definitely draw a distinction between California wine and French wine. However, most of the trade between the United States and Canada in automobiles is explained by factors that are quite specific to the nature of production in the auto industry. These factors are unimportant for the issues we wish to address.

The SOE has a production possibilities frontier (*PPF*), which describes the combinations of good a and good b that the SOE can produce, and this *PPF* is depicted in Figure 14.1. The *PPF* is similar to the ones that we constructed in Chapter 5, where we considered the combinations of consumption and leisure that could be produced in a closed economy. We do not formally derive the *PPF* for the SOE in the figure as we did in Chapter 5, but we can give some intuition for why it has the shape that it does. In the SOE, goods a and b are produced using labor and capital. At point A on the *PPF* in the figure, only good a is produced; at point B, only good b is produced. Now, consider what happens if we begin at point B and move along the *PPF* toward point A. As we do so, more of good a is produced and less of good b is produced, with labor and capital being reallocated from production of good b to production of good a. Because the *PPF* represents combinations of goods b and a that can be produced efficiently in the SOE, when labor and capital are reallocated from production of good b to production of good a, these factors of production are those that are most productive at the margin in producing good a relative to good b. Thus, the *PPF* is not very steep at point B, as only a small amount of good b is sacrificed at the margin to obtain another unit of good a. As we move down the *PPF* from point B to point A, however, the *PPF* becomes steeper, as the labor and capital reallocated from production of good b to production of good a

Figure 14.1 Production Possibilities Frontier for the SOE

The figure depicts the production possibilities frontier (*PPF*) for the small open economy. The slope of the *PPF* is minus the marginal rate of transformation, and the *PPF* is concave.

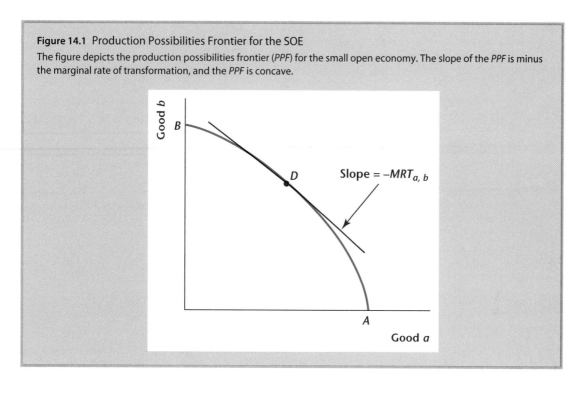

become relatively more productive at the margin in industry b than in industry a, and we need to sacrifice more of good b at the margin to obtain another unit of good a. Recall that the slope of the *PPF* is minus the marginal rate of transformation, which is denoted by $MRT_{a,b}$. The marginal rate of transformation, $MRT_{a,b}$, is the quantity of good b that must be forgone in the economy if another unit of good a is produced. At point D in Figure 14.1, $MRT_{a,b}$ is minus the slope of a tangent to the *PPF*. Thus, as for the *PPF* in Chapter 5, the marginal rate of transformation increases as we move down the *PPF* from point B to point A. That is, the *PPF* is concave.

The residents of the SOE consume only goods a and b, and we assume that we can capture their preferences using the representative consumer device, as in Chapter 4. That is, there is a representative consumer in the SOE whose preferences are represented by indifference curves, as in Figure 14.2. As we assumed in Chapter 4, the representative consumer prefers more to less and has a preference for diversity, so that the indifference curves in Figure 14.2 slope downward and are convex. Further, goods a and b are both normal in that an increase in income, holding prices constant, will imply that domestic consumption of both goods increases.

Competitive Equilibrium in the Small Open Economy Without Trade

Now that we know the basic characteristics of the SOE, given by the production possibilities frontier and the representative consumer's indifference curves, our first goal is

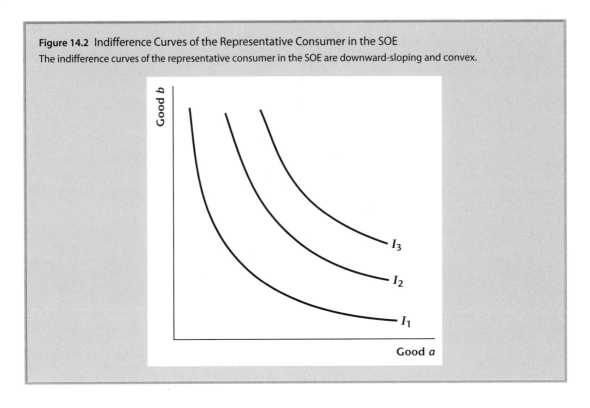

Figure 14.2 Indifference Curves of the Representative Consumer in the SOE
The indifference curves of the representative consumer in the SOE are downward-sloping and convex.

to understand what determines the pattern of trade. That is, we want to know what factors determine whether the SOE imports a and exports b, or vice versa, and how this is important for the welfare of consumers in the SOE.

To show the effects of trade in the SOE, we want to first determine the characteristics of a competitive equilibrium if the SOE could not engage in trade. Just as in Chapter 5, a competitive equilibrium for this economy is Pareto-optimal, and the competitive equilibrium quantities of goods a and b produced and consumed are determined by the point at which an indifference curve is tangent to the PPF. That is, the competitive equilibrium is point A in Figure 14.3. Recall that, at the competitive equilibrium point A, the marginal rate of substitution of good a for good b is equal to the marginal rate of transformation, or

$$MRS_{a,b} = MRT_{a,b},$$

because the marginal rate of substitution is minus the slope of the indifference curve at point A, and the marginal rate of transformation is minus the slope of the PPF at point A. Further, the equilibrium price of good a relative to good b, or p_{ab}, is minus the slope of a line tangent to the indifference curve and the PPF at point A. This is because, first, in equilibrium the representative consumer optimizes by setting

$$MRS_{a,b} = p_{ab}. \tag{14-1}$$

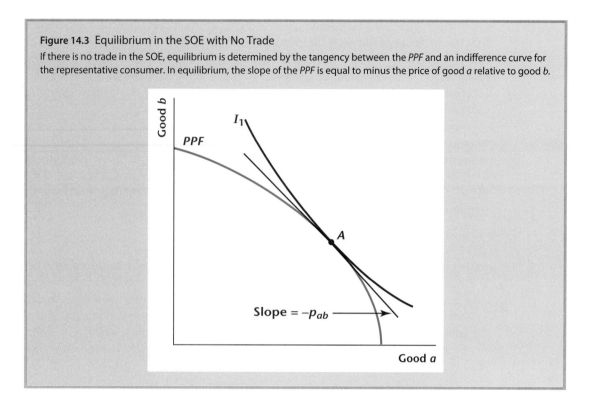

Figure 14.3 Equilibrium in the SOE with No Trade
If there is no trade in the SOE, equilibrium is determined by the tangency between the *PPF* and an indifference curve for the representative consumer. In equilibrium, the slope of the *PPF* is equal to minus the price of good *a* relative to good *b*.

Recall from Chapter 4 that consumer optimization implies that a consumer sets the marginal rate of substitution of one good for another equal to the price of one good relative to the other, which implies that equation (14-1) holds in this model in equilibrium. Second, optimization by firms will imply that

$$MRT_{a,b} = p_{ab}. \qquad (14\text{-}2)$$

This second condition holds for the following reason. The marginal rate of transformation, $MRT_{a,b}$, tells us how many units of good *b* must be given up to produce one additional unit of good *a*, while p_{ab} is the price that can be received in the market for one unit of good *a* in units of good *b*. If $MRT_{a,b} < p_{ab}$, then a firm could profit by taking capital and labor from the production of good *b* and producing good *a*, whereas if $MRT_{a,b} > p_{ab}$, then a firm could profit by taking capital and labor from the production of good *a* and producing good *b*. Therefore, profit maximization implies that equation (14-2) holds in equilibrium.

The Effects of Trade in the Small Open Economy
We now know the characteristics of a competitive equilibrium in the SOE in the case where there is no trade with the rest of the world. Of course, our objective is to show the determinants of the pattern and volume of trade between the SOE and the rest of

the world and to show how trade affects welfare. Thus, at this stage, we will suppose that the SOE can trade with the rest of the world at world prices given by TOT_{ab}; that is, the relative price of good a in terms of good b is now determined on world markets, rather than in domestic markets in the SOE. Recall that the SOE is a price-taker on world markets, so that economic activity in the SOE does not affect the terms of trade TOT_{ab}.

Trade opens up consumption opportunities that are not available to the representative consumer in the SOE in the absence of trade. That is, in equilibrium, the representative consumer need no longer consume the consumption bundle that is produced in the SOE, as was the case in Figure 14.3. When the SOE can trade with the rest of the world, the terms of trade determine what is produced. Namely, optimization by firms implies that

$$MRT_{a,b} = TOT_{ab},$$

so that the quantities of goods a and b that are produced in the SOE are given by point D in Figure 14.4, where the slope of DE is equal to $-TOT_{ab}$. The quantity of good a produced is a_1, and the quantity of good b produced is b_1. To determine what is consumed in a competitive equilibrium with trade, we think of the consumption bundle that is produced in the SOE as being an endowment available to the consumer, which then determines the representative consumer's budget constraint. Essentially, the representative

Figure 14.4 Production and Consumption in the SOE with Trade

When the SOE trades with the rest of the world at market prices given by the terms of trade, consumption occurs at point E and production occurs at point D, with the slope of DE equal to minus the terms of trade.

consumer receives what is produced as income, through wages and the dividends distributed by firms. Then, if the consumer is endowed with a_1 units of good a and b_1 units of good b and can exchange good b for good a on world markets at the rate TOT_{ab}, the terms of trade, then the representative consumer's budget constraint is

$$TOT_{ab}q_a + q_b = TOT_{ab}a_1 + b_1. \tag{14-3}$$

In the consumer's budget constraint, q_a and q_b are the quantities of good a and good b consumed, respectively, and the budget constraint is written in terms of good b. Thus, the quantity on the right-hand side of equation (14-3) is the representative consumer's income in terms of good b, and the quantity on the left-hand side is the consumer's expenditure on goods a and b, again in units of good b. The budget constraint, equation (14-3) then runs through points D and E in Figure 14.4.

Next, the representative consumer optimizes, just as in Chapter 4, by choosing the consumption bundle for which an indifference curve is tangent to his or her budget constraint. In Figure 14.4, the consumer chooses point E, where the quantity of good a consumed is $q_a = a_2$ and the quantity of good b consumed is $q_b = b_2$. In the figure, the SOE then is an importer of good a and an exporter of good b, because $a_2 > a_1$ and $b_2 < b_1$. The value of imports, in units of good b, is $TOT_{ab}(a_2 - a_1)$, and the value of exports is $b_1 - b_2$. Recalling the definition of the current account surplus from Chapter 2, which is net exports plus net factor payments from abroad, the current account surplus in the SOE in units of good b, is the value of exports minus the value of imports (because net factor payments are zero here), which is

$$CA = b_1 - b_2 - TOT_{ab}(a_2 - a_1).$$

But from the consumer's budget constraint, equation (14-3), we then have $CA = 0$; that is, the current account surplus is zero. This is a one-period model where the SOE cannot borrow and lend abroad, which implies that the current account surplus must be zero in equilibrium. In this model, the value of goods exported always equals the value of goods imported in equilibrium.

The pattern of trade between the SOE and the rest of the world is determined in part by two factors. The first is the principle of **comparative advantage.** In Figure 14.4, the SOE imports good a and exports good b, so that the SOE tends to have a comparative advantage in producing good b. Comparative advantage is determined by the slope of the production possibilities frontier. The steeper the production possibilities frontier, the greater is the SOE's comparative advantage in producing good b relative to good a, because more of good b needs to be sacrificed at the margin to produce another unit of good a. A steeper PPF also implies that more of good b is produced, and less of good a is produced, when the SOE can trade with the rest of the world, and so there is a tendency to export more of good b.

The second factor that determines the pattern of trade is consumer preferences. Even if the SOE has a strong comparative advantage in producing a good, if the representative consumer has a strong preference for that good, it could be imported rather than exported. The important characteristic of consumer preferences for determining

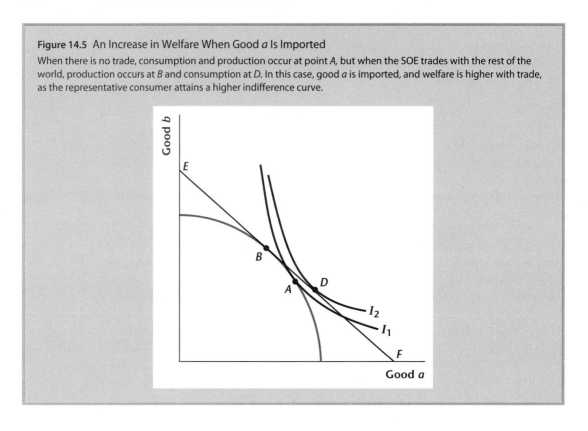

Figure 14.5 An Increase in Welfare When Good *a* Is Imported

When there is no trade, consumption and production occur at point *A*, but when the SOE trades with the rest of the world, production occurs at *B* and consumption at *D*. In this case, good *a* is imported, and welfare is higher with trade, as the representative consumer attains a higher indifference curve.

the pattern of trade is the marginal rate of substitution, $MRS_{a,b}$. As $MRS_{a,b}$ increases, the indifference curves of the representative consumer become steeper, and the SOE has a greater tendency to import good *a* and export good *b*.

An important result is that the representative consumer is always better off with trade than without it. To show this, we consider two cases. In the first case, the domestic price of good a in terms of good b (when there is no trade) is greater than the terms of trade, as in Figure 14.5. Here, when there is no trade, the consumption bundle produced and consumed is given by point A, but when the SOE is opened up to world trade, production occurs at point B, and the representative consumer chooses point D. The terms of trade are given by minus the slope of the line EF. With trade, the consumer is on a higher indifference curve; that is, indifference curve I_2 represents a higher level of welfare than indifference curve I_1. In the second case, as in Figure 14.6, the domestic price of good a in terms of good b (when there is no trade) is smaller than the terms of trade. In this case, consumption and production when the economy is closed are at point A, but when the economy is open, production occurs at point B and consumption at point D. Again, the representative consumer's welfare improves with free trade. This result—trade increases opportunities and makes the nation better off—is a fundamental economic principle.

Figure 14.6 An Increase in Welfare When Good *b* Is Imported

Here, in contrast to Figure 14.5, good *b* is imported when the SOE can trade with the rest of the world. Trade improves welfare, as the consumer attains a higher indifference curve.

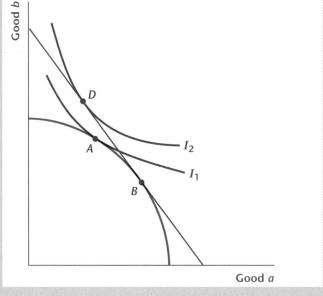

Our model captures the effects of trade on the average consumer, showing that trade always makes this average consumer (the representative consumer) better off. In practice, however, eliminating trade restrictions typically harms some people while benefiting others, although we argue the net effect on welfare is positive. For example, U.S. residents were not all in agreement that NAFTA, signed in 1992 by Canada, Mexico, and the United States, was a good idea. NAFTA tended to harm those industries in the United States for which Mexico and Canada had comparative advantages. In those industries, product prices and real wages tended to fall, and workers were displaced. However, in industries for which the United States has a comparative advantage relative to Mexico and Canada, prices and real wages tended to rise, and employment expanded. The fact that someone almost always stands to lose in circumstances where trade restrictions are relaxed makes it difficult to pass laws that free up international trade.

A Change in the Terms of Trade:
Effects on Production, Consumption, and Welfare

A key macroeconomic shock for an open economy is a change in the price of imports relative to the price of exports, that is, a change in the terms of trade. The terms of trade could move against a country if imports became more expensive relative to exports, as, for example, in New Zealand if the prices of manufactured goods were to increase relative to the prices of agricultural goods. In this case, economic welfare would decrease in New Zealand. The terms of trade could also move in favor of a country if imports became cheaper relative to exports. This would happen in Kuwait if there were an increase in the relative price of crude oil, which would increase economic welfare for the residents of Kuwait. As we show in this section, a change in the terms of trade has similarities to a change in total factor productivity in a closed economy, as considered in Chapter 5. This is because there are in general income and substitution effects associated with a change in the terms of trade.

In an open economy, changes in the terms of trade affect domestic production, domestic consumption, exports, and imports. In the model, we must consider the two cases where the terms of trade move in favor of, and against the SOE. In the first case, the SOE imports good a before an increase in the terms of trade, and in the second, the SOE initially imports good b. This matters for the results because of the effects on economic welfare and because there is a difference in income effects on consumption of both goods. In the first case, there is a negative income effect on consumption and in the second case a positive income effect. Substitution effects work in the same way in each case.

In Figure 14.7 we show the first case, where initially the consumption bundle produced is given by point A, and the initial terms of trade are given by the negative of

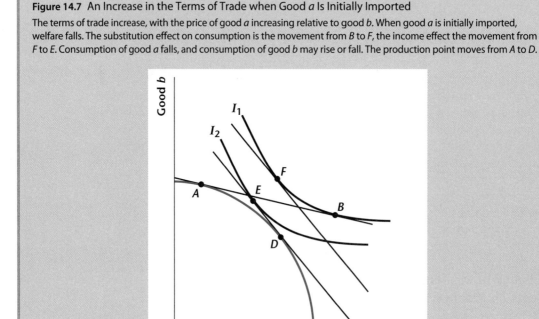

Figure 14.7 An Increase in the Terms of Trade when Good a Is Initially Imported

The terms of trade increase, with the price of good a increasing relative to good b. When good a is initially imported, welfare falls. The substitution effect on consumption is the movement from B to F, the income effect the movement from F to E. Consumption of good a falls, and consumption of good b may rise or fall. The production point moves from A to D.

the slope of a line tangent at point A. The initial consumption bundle is at point B, where this line is tangent to indifference curve I_1. With an increase in the terms of trade, production is at point D, where the terms of trade (minus the slope of a line tangent to the PPF at point D) is higher. Production of good a must increase, while production of good b decreases, as the relative price of good a has risen, encouraging more production of a and less production of b. The new consumption bundle is given by point E, where in this case the representative consumer consumes less of good a and more of good b. In fact, the SOE now imports good b and exports a.

We can separate the effect of the change in the terms of trade on consumption into income and substitution effects. Namely, if we draw a tangent to the initial indifference curve I_1 in Figure 14.7, the slope of which is minus the new terms of trade, then this line is tangent to I_1 at point F, and the substitution effect of the change in the terms of trade is the movement from B to F. That is, the substitution effect is for consumption of good a to decrease and that of good b to increase. There is a negative income effect, which is the movement from F to E. Recall that we assumed that both goods are normal, so that the income effect is for consumption of goods a and b to decrease.

On net, then, the consumption of good a must decrease, and the consumption of good b may increase or decrease, depending on the size of the income effect relative to the substitution effect. Production of good a increases, and production of good b decreases. The quantity of a good imported is given by consumption minus production. Therefore, we can conclude that the quantity of good a imported must decrease, as consumption decreases and production increases. For good b, however, there is an ambiguous effect on the quantity imported, as production decreases, but consumption may increase or decrease. However, if substitution effects dominate income effects, then the quantity of good b imported rises.

In terms of the value of imports and exports, in units of good b, the results are ambiguous. The value of imports is

$$\text{Quantity of imports} \times TOT_{ab},$$

and although we know that the quantity of imports decreases, the terms of trade TOT_{ab} increases, and so the product of quantity and terms of trade could either increase or decrease. Because we have already determined that the quantity of good b exported could increase or decrease, we know that the value of good b exported, in units of good b (which is the same thing), could increase or decrease. Although the effects on the value of exports and imports are ambiguous here, we know that there is no effect on the current account surplus from a change in the terms of trade, because the current account surplus is always zero in this model.

Now consider the second case, in Figure 14.8, where there is an increase in the terms of trade when the SOE initially imports good b and exports good a. Initially, production of goods a and b is given by point A, with consumption at point B. The slope of the line AB is equal to minus the initial terms of trade. When the terms of trade increase, the production point shifts to D, with domestic output of good a rising and output of good b falling, just as in the first case. The representative consumer now chooses point E, with the slope of DE equal to minus the new terms of trade. Here,

Figure 14.8 An Increase in the Terms of Trade when Good *b* Is Initially Imported

An increase in the terms of trade increases welfare when good *b* is initially imported. The substitution effect on consumption is the movement from *B* to *F*, the income effect the movement from *F* to *E*. Consumption of good *a* may rise or fall, and consumption of good *b* rises. Production moves from *A* to *D*.

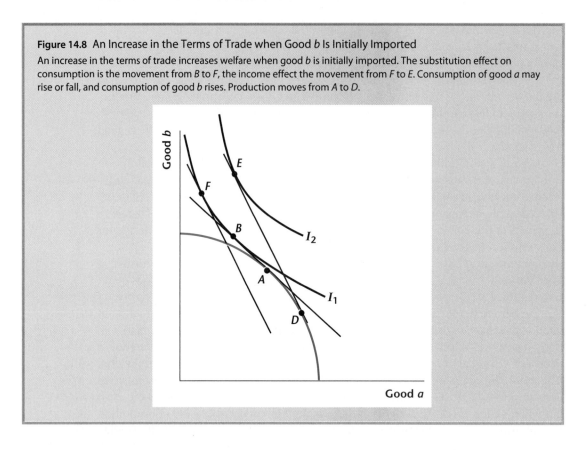

there is a positive income effect on consumption of goods *a* and *b*. Separating the effect of the change in the terms of trade into income and substitution effects, the substitution effect is the movement from *B* to *F*, while the income effect is the movement from *F* to *E*. As before, the substitution effect leads to an increase in consumption of good *b* and a decrease in consumption of good *a*. Here, however, the income effect leads to an increase in consumption of both goods *a* and *b* (again under the assumption that both goods are normal). Therefore, consumption of good *b* must rise, but consumption of good *a* may rise or fall.

In the second case, then, imports of good *b* increase. Exports of good *a* may also rise or fall, because more is produced, but consumption may increase or decrease. What happens to the value of imports and exports is also ambiguous, but again there is no effect on the current account surplus, which is always zero.

What happens to the representative consumer's welfare differs between the first case and the second. When good *a* is initially imported, and the terms of trade change so that the relative price of good *a* increases, the representative consumer is worse off. That is, in Figure 14.7, the representative consumer initially chooses a consumption bundle on indifference curve I_1 and chooses a consumption bundle on a lower indifference curve, I_2, when the terms of trade changes. This is the case in which the terms of trade

MACROECONOMICS IN ACTION

How Important Are Shocks to the Terms of Trade for Business Cycles?

Because the terms of trade cause changes in the makeup of domestic consumption and production and they affect aggregate economic welfare, shocks to the terms of trade could be sources of business cycles. Indeed, one of the shocks to the economy that we have previously analyzed as a shock to total factor productivity—a change in the relative price of energy—can also be modeled as a change in the terms of trade. The large increases in the world price of crude oil that occurred in 1973, in the late 1970s, in 1991, and from 2000 to 2008, were adverse changes in the terms of trade for the United States. In all these cases, the terms of trade turned against the United States, which is a net importer of crude oil. After the shifts in the terms of trade in these episodes, the results in the United States were just as our model predicts. Domestic production of crude oil and other alternative sources of energy increased, while domestic consumption of energy decreased. A reduction in economic welfare was reflected in a short-run decrease in GDP.

Although the United States can be vulnerable to terms of trade shocks, particularly those resulting from changes in the world price of crude oil, it is not as sensitive to changes in the terms of trade as some other countries. Although imports and exports are significant relative to GDP in the United States, foreign trade is much more important for some other countries, particularly Canada, Mexico, and the countries of Western Europe. As well, U.S. imports and exports are diversified across a wide array of goods and services. In some countries, there is a dependence on one commodity as a major export. For example, Kuwait is primarily an exporter of crude oil, so fluctuations in the world price of this one commodity can have dramatic effects for the economy of Kuwait.

For all countries of the world, how important are terms of trade shocks for business cycles? Using a real business cycle model and data from many countries, Enrique Mendoza finds that half of the variability in real GDP is explained by terms of trade shocks.[1] This is a highly significant finding, and it indicates that accounting for shocks from abroad is very important for analyzing business cycles. If attention is confined to a closed-economy analysis of the factors determining business cycles, we lose at least half of the picture.

---

[1]See E. Mendoza, 1993, "The Terms of Trade, the Real Exchange Rate, and Economic Fluctuations," *International Economic Review* 36, 101–138.

turn against the SOE, in the sense that the goods that are being sold abroad (good *b*) become cheaper relative to the goods that are purchased abroad (good *a*). In Figure 14.8, however, the change in the terms of trade is favorable to the SOE, in that the representative consumer is on a higher indifference curve after the terms of trade change. In this case, imported goods (good *b*) become cheaper relative to exports, and this is good for economic welfare in the SOE.

A Two-Period Small Open-Economy Model: The Current Account

The previous one-period model was useful for understanding the benefits from trade and the effects of changes in the terms of trade. However, some important issues in international macroeconomics are related to intertemporal choices. In particular, we would like to study the determinants of the current account surplus. We know from Chapter 2 that a current account surplus must always be reflected in an excess of domestic savings over domestic investment and by an increase in the net claims of domestic residents on foreign residents. Thus, to analyze the current account, we need a model where, at the minimum, consumers make borrowing and lending and consumption–savings decisions. A useful model of borrowing and lending and consumption–savings decisions is the two-period model we developed in Chapter 8. Here, we modify that model by having a single representative consumer, capturing the average behavior of all domestic consumers, and we allow borrowing and lending between domestic and foreign residents.

We suppose that there is a single representative consumer in the SOE, and that this consumer lives for two periods, the current and future periods. For the representative consumer, income is exogenous in both periods, with Y denoting current real income and Y' future real income. The consumer also pays lump-sum taxes to the SOE government of T in the current period and T' in the future period. Because this economy is small and open, the actions of the representative consumer do not affect the world real interest rate, and so we assume that the consumer in the SOE can borrow and lend as much as he or she wishes at the world real interest rate r. Just as in Chapter 8, the representative consumer chooses consumption in the current and future periods, C and C', respectively, to make himself or herself as well off as possible given his or her lifetime budget constraint

$$C + \frac{C'}{1 + r} = Y - T + \frac{Y' - T'}{1 + r}. \tag{14-4}$$

In Figure 14.9 we show the consumer's lifetime budget constraint as the line AB. Point E is the endowment point, and the representative consumer chooses point D on his or her lifetime budget constraint, which is the point where an indifference curve is tangent to the lifetime budget constraint. In the figure, consumption in the current and future periods is C^* and C'^*, respectively. Private saving in the current period is then given by $S^p = Y - T - C = Y - T - C^*$, thus in the figure the consumer saves a positive amount.

Now, to complete the model, we need to describe the behavior of the government in the SOE. Government spending in the current and future periods is G and G', respectively, and these quantities are exogenous. The government then sets current and future taxes on the representative consumer, T and T', respectively, to satisfy the government's present-value budget constraint

$$G + \frac{G'}{1 + r} = T + \frac{T'}{1 + r}. \tag{14-5}$$

Figure 14.9 The Two-Period Small Open-Economy Model
The representative consumer's budget constraint is *AB*, the endowment point is *E*, and the consumer chooses point *D*.

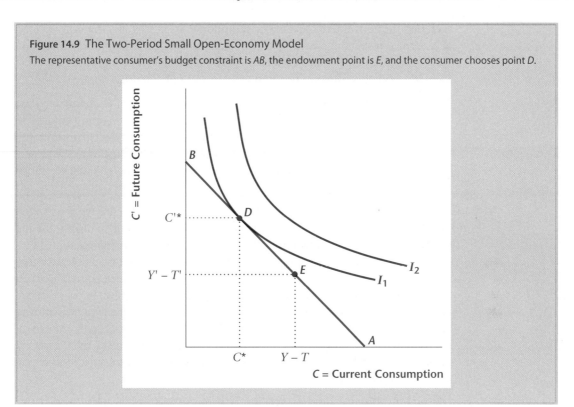

Then, the quantity of government saving is given by $S^g = T - G$, and in this economy where there is no investment, the current account surplus in the current period, from Chapter 2, is

$$CA = S - I = (S^p + S^g) - 0 = Y - C - G.$$

In this model, we are interested in understanding the key factors that affect the current account surplus *CA*, which are the following:

- *Current period income.* Recall from Chapter 8 that an increase in current income increases current consumption and future consumption, and current consumption increases by less than the increase in current income, because the consumer wishes to smooth consumption over his or her lifetime. An increase in *Y*, therefore, leads to an increase in the current account surplus. Because of the consumption-smoothing motive, a country that experiences an increase in current income saves more by lending abroad, and this is reflected in an increase in the current account surplus.
- *Current government spending.* An increase in government spending, given the government's present-value budget constraint, equation (14-5), leads to an increase by an equal amount in the present value of taxes for the consumer. Therefore, the consumer's lifetime wealth falls by the increase in government spending. We know

then that the consumer's current consumption falls, but by less than the increase in government spending, because the consumer smooths consumption between the current and future periods. The current account surplus, therefore, decreases with an increase in government spending.

- *Taxes.*   Given the Ricardian equivalence theorem from Chapter 8, changes in taxes have no effect on aggregate consumption, because consumers simply adjust savings to account for the change in their future tax liabilities. As consumption is unaffected, there is no effect on the current account surplus. Just as in the closed-economy model in Chapter 8, however, if there are significant credit market imperfections, then a change in current taxes in general affects current consumption, and this matters for the trade balance.

- *The real interest rate.*   Recall from Chapter 8 that the effect of a change in the real interest rate on current consumption depends on whether the representative consumer is initially a net borrower or a net lender. If the consumer is a net lender, then current consumption may rise or fall when the real interest rate rises, because there is a positive income effect on consumption, and the substitution effect implies that current consumption falls and future consumption rises. If the consumer is a net borrower, the income and substitution effects work in the same direction, and an increase in the real interest rate causes a decrease in current consumption. In general, then, if income effects are not too large, an increase in the real interest rate causes a decrease in current consumption and an increase in the current account surplus.

THEORY confronts the DATA

Is a Current Account Deficit a Bad Thing?

It may seem that a current account deficit is undesirable, because if a country runs a current account deficit, it is borrowing from the rest of the world and accumulating debt. However, just as is the case for individual consumers, lending and borrowing is the means by which a nation smooths consumption. If a given country runs current account deficits when aggregate income is low and runs current account surpluses when aggregate income is high, this allows the residents of that country to smooth their consumption over time. This state of affairs is preferable to one in which the country always has a current account surplus of zero and consumption is as variable as income.

Thus, there are good reasons for expecting that countries should run current account surpluses in good times and current account deficits in bad times. Government policy aimed at correcting this tendency could be counterproductive. But do countries actually smooth consumption over time as theory predicts? In Figure 14.10 we show the deviations from trend in real GDP and the current account surplus for the United States over the period 1960–2008. For real GDP, the deviations are percentage deviations from trend, and for the current account surplus these are the absolute deviations from trend, scaled to match reasonably closely the average percentage deviation from trend in real GDP. In the figure, there is a tendency for the current account surplus to

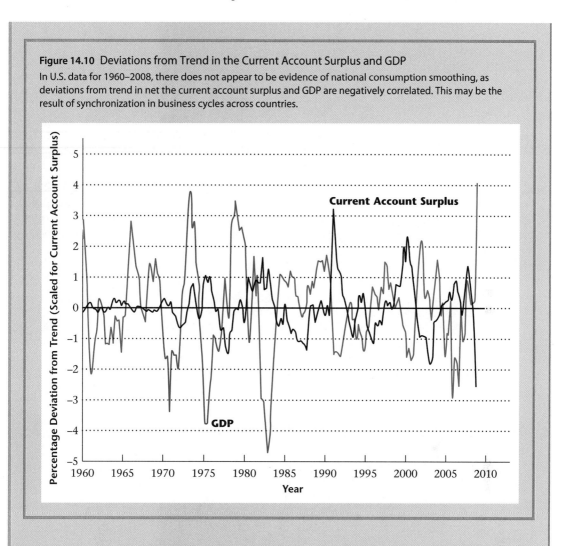

Figure 14.10 Deviations from Trend in the Current Account Surplus and GDP

In U.S. data for 1960–2008, there does not appear to be evidence of national consumption smoothing, as deviations from trend in net the current account surplus and GDP are negatively correlated. This may be the result of synchronization in business cycles across countries.

be above (below) trend when real GDP is below (above) trend, so that deviations from trend in GDP and the current account surplus are negatively correlated. This is the opposite of consumption smoothing, in that the United States tended to export goods and lend more abroad when output was low and to borrow more abroad when output was high.

Why would the data not exhibit obvious evidence of consumption smoothing when economic theory tells us that nations should smooth consumption by lending (borrowing) abroad when income is high (low)? A potential explanation may be that the timing and severity of business cycles in the rest of the world and in the United States are similar. For example, the data in Figure 14.10 are consistent with consumption smoothing if business cycles coincided in the United States and the rest of the world, but the upturns and downturns were more severe in the rest of the world. Then, the United States could in equilibrium be lending to other countries when its own output was low and borrowing from other countries when its own output was high.

The Twin Deficits

Our two-period small open-economy model predicts that an increase in government spending causes a decrease in the current account surplus and that, given Ricardian equivalence, a decrease in current taxes has no effect. With a decrease in current taxes, consumers understand that their future taxes have increased by an equal amount, in present-value terms, and current consumption is

unaffected, leaving the current account surplus unchanged.

During the 1980s, an interesting fiscal policy experiment was carried out by the Reagan administration in that there was a sharp increase in government spending, accounted for mainly by an increase in defense spending, coupled with a sharp reduction in income taxes. In Figure 14.11, the resulting decrease in the government surplus in the 1980s corresponds to a decrease in the

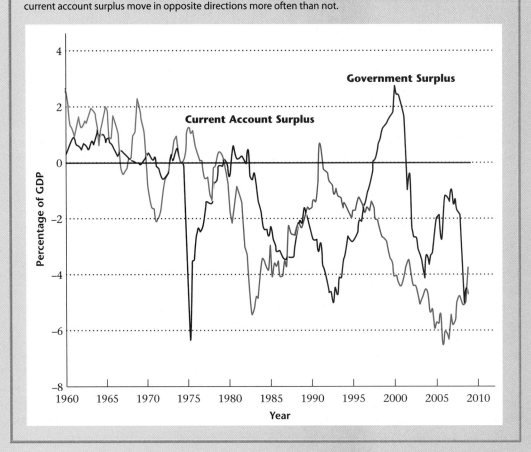

Figure 14.11 The Twin Deficits?
The twin deficits phenomenon is apparent in the 1980s but otherwise the government budget surplus and current account surplus move in opposite directions more often than not.

current account surplus. While many other factors could have influenced the current account surplus during the 1980s, this is a case where there appears to be a clear connection between the government budget surplus and the current account surplus. This is often referred to as the **twin deficits,** as both the government surplus and the current account surplus were negative in the 1980s. The data for the 1980s are consistent with the increase in government spending causing an increase in the government budget deficit and the current account deficit and the decrease in taxes having no effect on the current account deficit because of Ricardian equivalence.

The clear connection between the government budget deficit and the current account deficit in the 1980s certainly does not appear to apply generally in Figure 14.12. Outside the 1980s, the government surplus and current account surplus move in opposite directions more often than not. Recall from Chapter 2 that national income accounts identities imply that

$$CA = S - I;$$

that is, the current account surplus is equal to national saving minus investment expenditures. If private saving and investment are unchanged and there is a decrease in government saving (an increase in the government deficit), then, from this equation, the current account surplus must fall. This is roughly what appears to have happened during the 1980s. However, outside of this period, there were typically enough other factors at work generating comovements among savings, investment, and the current account that the twin deficits phenomenon does not appear. The conclusion is that we should not typically expect the government surplus and current account surplus to be closely related.

Production, Investment, and the Current Account

While the previous model yields some useful insights concerning the role of the current account in national consumption smoothing and some explanations for the behavior of the current account, we must understand more completely the relationship between the current account surplus and events in the domestic economy. In this section, we study a model based on the real intertemporal model in Chapter 10, which includes production and investment behavior.

In this model, just as in the previous one, the SOE faces a given world real interest rate. As in Chapter 10, output supply is given by the upward-sloping curve Y^s in Figure 14.12. Here, however, we assume that goods can be freely traded with foreign countries, and so from the income-expenditure identity $Y = C + I + G + NX$, the demand for goods also includes net exports, NX. In Figure 14.12, the world real interest rate is r^*, which then determines the domestic demand for consumption goods and investment goods. If total domestic demand, $C + I + G$, exceeds the domestic supply of goods at the world real interest rate, then goods are imported and net exports are negative; if domestic demand is less than the domestic supply of goods at the world real interest rate, then goods are exported and net exports are positive. The equilibrium quantity of net exports is the quantity NX, which yields a downward-sloping output demand curve Y_1^d that intersects the Y^s curve in Figure 14.12 at the world real interest rate r^*. We have depicted a case in Figure 14.12 where $NX > 0$, that is, if there were no trade in goods with the rest of the world, then the output demand curve would be Y_2^d, to the left of Y_1^d, and the domestic real interest rate would be r_c. In general, it could be the case that that $r^* < r_c$ or $r^* > r_c$. Given the world real interest rate r^*, the quantity of aggregate output produced in the SOE is Y_1, but in this case the domestic demand for goods, $C + I + G$, is less than Y_1. The domestic demand for goods,

Figure 14.12 A Small Open-Economy Model with Production and Investment

The world real interest rate, determined on world credit markets, is r^*. Net exports adjusts so that the Y^d curve intersects the Y^s curve at the world real interest rate. Here, $NX > 0$, and in the absence of trade, the domestic real interest rate would be r_c.

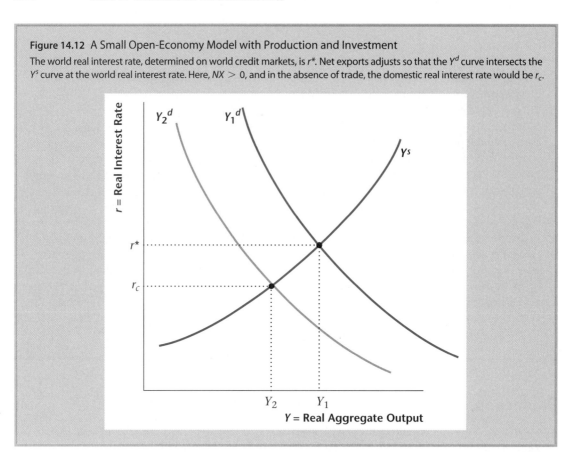

$C + I + G$, is sometimes referred to as **absorption**, as this is the quantity of aggregate output that is absorbed by the domestic economy. The quantity NX is then the current account surplus, or net exports. Recall that the current account surplus is net exports plus net factor payments from abroad, but net factor payments from abroad equal zero in this model. In Figure 14.12, the SOE has a positive current account surplus; that is, $NX > 0$, which implies that the SOE is accumulating assets from the rest of the world.

The Effects of an Increase in the World Real Interest Rate

Because the model here is essentially identical to the real intertemporal model with a real interest rate that is fixed on world credit markets, it is straightforward to use the model to analyze the effects of particular shocks to the domestic economy. The output demand curve and output supply curve shift in the same ways in response to shocks as in the real intertemporal model of Chapter 10, with the only modification in the analysis being that NX adjusts so that the output demand curve intersects the output supply curve at the world real interest rate r^*. The first experiment we carry out is to look at the effects in the model of an increase in the world real interest rate. Such a change could have many causes; it could result from, for example, a negative total factor productivity shock in other countries (recall our analysis of domestic total factor productivity shocks from Chapter 10).

Figure 14.13 An Increase in the World Real Interest Rate

An increase in the world real interest rate from r_1 to r_2 increases output and the current account surplus.

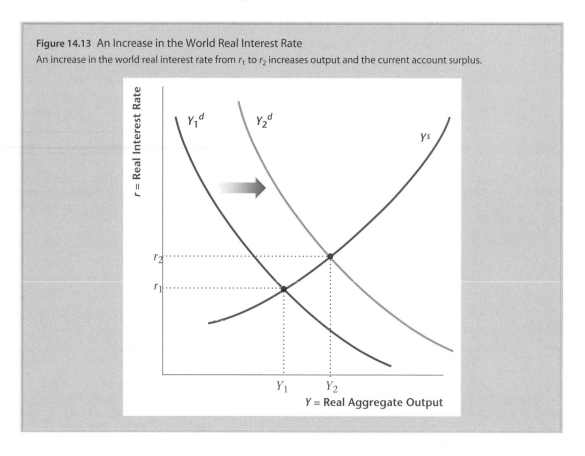

Suppose, in Figure 14.13, that the world real interest rate increases from r_1 to r_2. Then the current account surplus increases causing the output demand curve to shift to the right from Y_1^d to Y_2^d. Domestic investment must decrease, as the real interest rate increases, but domestic consumption may rise or fall as there is a negative effect from the increase in r and a positive effect from the increase in Y.

These results have the interesting implication that a negative total factor productivity shock abroad, which would *decrease* foreign output and cause the world real interest rate to rise, also causes an *increase* in domestic output. Therefore, a foreign shock of this sort, when transmitted to the domestic economy, does not cause output in the domestic economy and in the rest of the world to move together.

Government Expenditure and the Current Account

For our second experiment, we consider the effects of increases in domestic government expenditure. Although we considered some of these effects in the previous model, when we discussed the twin deficits phenomenon, this will give a more complete picture.

Consider the effects of an increase in G, a temporary increase in government spending. Just as in Chapter 10, there is a negative income effect on leisure for the representative consumer, because of the increase in the present value of taxes, and so labor supply increases, shifting the output supply curve rightward from Y_1^s to Y_2^s in

Figure 14.14. There is a shift to the right in the output demand curve resulting from the net increase in output demand caused by the increase in G. The current account surplus then adjusts so that the output demand curve ultimately shifts from Y_1^d to Y_2^d (see Figure 14.14). As in Chapter 10, the initial shift in the output supply curve is small relative to the shift in the output demand curve (because the increase in government spending is temporary, so that the effects on lifetime wealth are small). The current account surplus, therefore, must decrease.

It is useful to compare our results to what happened in the closed economy real interemporal model in Chapter 10. Here, note that the real interest rate does not increase, as the interest rate is determined on world markets. As a result, there is no crowding out of investment and consumption as a result of an interest rate increase. Further, consumption actually increases here (rather than decreasing, as in the real intertemporal model), since real income increases while the real interest rate stays constant. Crowding out does occur, but it is crowding out of net exports, since the current account surplus has gone down. We have thus seen one way in which results can change in important ways when we take account of open economy factors. While it is true in general that government spending crowds out private activity, this crowding out occurs in different ways in an open economy.

Figure 14.14 A Temporary Increase in Government Spending

An increase in current government spending shifts the output demand curve and the output supply curve to the right (the output demand curve shifts to a greater extent). Output increases and the current account surplus decreases.

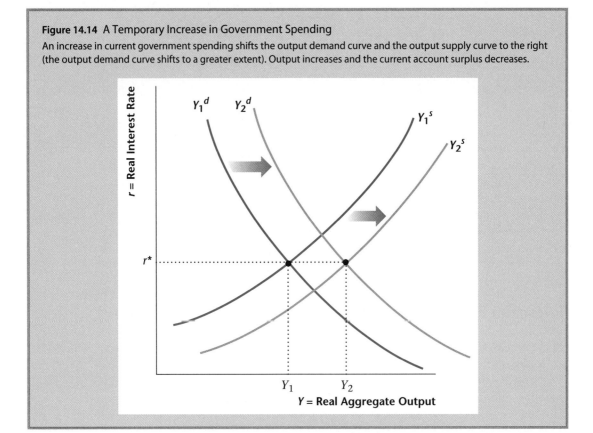

The Effects of Increases in Current and Future Total Factor Productivity

In Chapters 5 and 10, we showed how total factor productivity matters for domestic real aggregate activity. An increase in current total factor productivity in a closed economy increases labor demand, and it leads to increases in the real wage, employment, and output, as well as a decrease in the real interest rate. An anticipated increase in future total factor productivity increases the current demand for investment goods and consumption goods in a closed economy, and it increases current aggregate output and the real interest rate. In an SOE, some of these results are somewhat different, as the real interest rate is determined on the world credit market. We are also able to determine the effects of total factor productivity shocks on the current account.

Suppose first that current total factor productivity increases. Recall from Chapter 10 that this causes a shift to the right in the output supply curve. In Figure 14.15 the output supply curve shifts from Y_1^s to Y_2^s. Then, the current account surplus increases, shifting the output demand curve to the right from Y_1^d to Y_2^d. As a result, aggregate output increases from Y_1 to Y_2, and there is an increase in the current account surplus. Domestic consumption increases because of the increase in real income, but given that

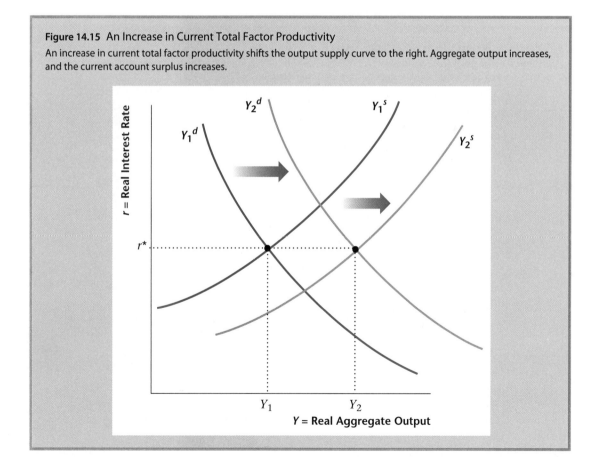

Figure 14.15 An Increase in Current Total Factor Productivity
An increase in current total factor productivity shifts the output supply curve to the right. Aggregate output increases, and the current account surplus increases.

the real interest rate is unchanged, there is no effect on investment. In a closed economy, the real interest rate falls when total factor productivity increases, causing increases in C and I. However, the real interest rate is determined on world markets here, and so an increase in total factor productivity in the domestic economy has no effect on the real interest rate. Typically, though, different countries simultaneously experience increases in total factor productivity at the same time, as changes in production technology tend to be transmitted across international borders. Therefore, an increase in total factor productivity domestically would also tend to be associated with a decrease in the world real interest rate and increases in domestic consumption and investment.

Next, suppose that an increase in future total factor productivity is anticipated. Recall from Chapter 10 that this implies the representative firm expects an increase in the future marginal product of capital, which causes an increase in the demand for investment goods. Further, the representative consumer anticipates higher future income as the result of the increase in future total factor productivity, and this causes an increase in the demand for current consumption goods. The increase in the demand for current consumption and investment goods shifts the output demand curve in Figure 14.16 rightward, but there is a corresponding decrease in the current account surplus so that

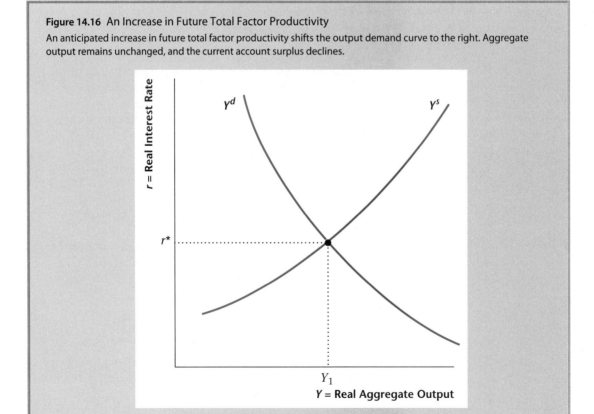

Figure 14.16 An Increase in Future Total Factor Productivity
An anticipated increase in future total factor productivity shifts the output demand curve to the right. Aggregate output remains unchanged, and the current account surplus declines.

Perspectives on the Financial Crisis
The World "Savings Glut"

The term "savings glut" appears to have been coined by Ben Bernanke, the current Chairman of the Federal Reserve Board, to refer to the pattern of current account surpluses and level of real interest rates that materialized in the world after 2000.[2] The decrease in the current account surplus in the United States that occurred from the early 1990s until 2005, as observed in Figure 14.11, had to have been matched by increases in the current account surpluses of other countries. This is because the world current account surplus must always be zero—for each borrower in the world credit market there must be a lender. It can be instructive, then, to think about the causes of a U.S. current account surplus in terms of the credit market behavior of other countries, rather than thinking solely in terms of what is happening in United States. This is the basic idea behind the "world savings glut" issue.

Why did net borrowing on world credit markets increase for the United States from the early 1990s until 2005? First, in terms of the determinants of the current account surplus we have studied in this chapter, it is clear that the U.S. government budget deficits after 2000 (Figure 14.11), and the high level of domestic investment (Figure 14.17) contributed to the increase in the U.S. current account deficit. In Figure 14.17, there was a dip in investment expenditures relative to GDP after 2000, but investment as a percentage of GDP subsequently increased, reaching a peak in 2005. Part of this increase in investment was related to a domestic housing boom, which we noted previously in Chapter 8, in terms of increases in housing prices. The boom was also reflected in an increase in residential investment. This housing boom was in part fueled by innovations in the housing market, including "subprime" lending to high-risk borrowers in the mortgage market.

Second, the increase in the U.S. current account deficit was in part due to more lending from other countries in world credit markets. These other countries were primarily developing countries, and of these, most were Asian developing countries. The reasons for the increase in lending by these countries are not entirely clear, but could include demographic factors (aging populations that save more) and the after-effects of the Asian Crisis in 1996–2007 (savers in East Asian countries were reluctant to lend to domestic financial institutions and moved their lending overseas). In the third model in this chapter, we can capture the effect of an increase in the desire of other countries to lend by a decrease in the world real interest rate, i.e., the reverse of what occurs in Figure 14.13. Thus, a decrease in the world real interest rate in our model acts to increase domestic investment, has an ambiguous effect on domestic consumption, and reduces the current account surplus.

The world savings glut that reduced world real interest rates, particularly after 2000, could in part be blamed for the financial crisis that began in the United States and spread worldwide. One of the principal causes of the financial crisis was incentive problems in the U.S. mortgage market and in the market for sophisticated financial instruments. These incentive problems were accentuated by low real interest rates, which increased the profit opportunities from financial misbehavior. Therefore, international borrowing and lending, as reflected in current account surpluses and deficits, can be an important factor in domestic financial developments and for domestic business cycles.

---

[2]See "The World Savings Glut and the U.S. Current Account Deficit," at www.federalreserve.gov/boarddocs/speeches/2005/200503102/

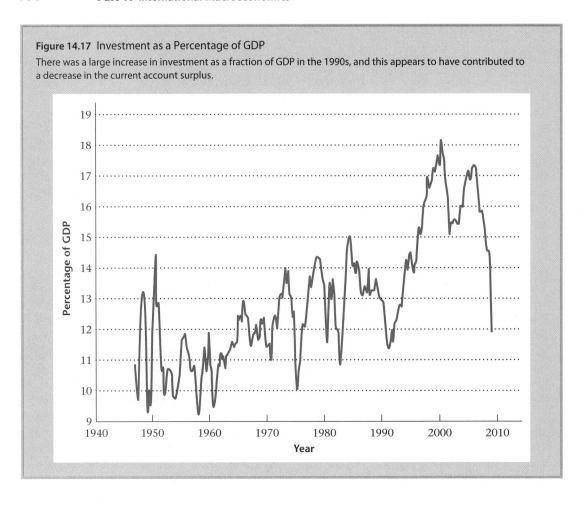

Figure 14.17 Investment as a Percentage of GDP

There was a large increase in investment as a fraction of GDP in the 1990s, and this appears to have contributed to a decrease in the current account surplus.

demand equals supply for domestically produced goods. In equilibrium, aggregate output remains fixed at Y_1, but the current account surplus falls.

The above provides a potential explanation for the reduction in the current account surplus that occurred in the 1990s, observed in Figure 14.11. In particular, in Figure 14.17, there was a large increase in investment expenditures during the 1990s to more than 19% of GDP in 1999 (before a rapid decrease and subsequent increase). This is consistent with anticipated increases in future total factor productivity causing increases in investment spending, which reduced the current account surplus, as in Figure 14.16. The increase in investment spending in the United States, particularly in the late 1990s, is typically attributed to optimism about the potential for new internet technologies. This period is sometimes referred to as the "dot com" boom.

This chapter explored the real macroeconomic implications of having trade in goods and assets among nations. In Chapter 15, we integrate money into the third model that we studied in this chapter so as to understand the determination of nominal exchange rates, the importance of flexible and fixed exchange rates, and why capital controls are important for macroeconomic activity.

Chapter Summary

- In this chapter we studied the implications of international trade in goods and assets for domestic welfare, output, consumption, investment, and the current account surplus. We constructed three small open-economy models and showed how these models can be used to understand the importance of openness for the domestic economy. In a small open economy (SOE), domestic residents are price-takers with respect to the rest of the world

- The first model is one where there are two goods, *a* and *b*, consumed and produced in an SOE. The relative price of good *a* in terms of good *b* is the terms of trade, or the real exchange rate, and this is the rate at which good *b* can be traded for good *a* on world markets.

- The representative consumer in the SOE is always better off by trading on world markets at the terms of trade than by not trading. In equilibrium, domestic production is determined by the condition that the marginal rate of transformation of good *a* for good *b* equals the terms of trade, and domestic consumption satisfies the property that the marginal rate of substitution of good *a* for good *b* equals the terms of trade.

- An increase in the terms of trade, which here means that good *a* becomes more expensive relative to good *b*, always implies that production in the SOE shifts away from production of good *b* and toward production of good *a*. However, whether the consumption of goods *a* or *b* increases or decreases depends on whether the SOE was an importer or exporter of good *a* before the change in the terms of trade and on income and substitution effects.

- The second model we considered was a two-period model of a SOE, where the representative consumer has exogenous income in the current and future periods, and the consumer pays taxes to the government in both periods. Government spending is exogenous in each period, and the government and the representative consumer can borrow and lend in the current period.

- In the model, the current account surplus increases whenever national saving increases. An increase in current income leads to an increase in the current account surplus in equilibrium, an increase in government spending leads to a decrease in the current account surplus, a change in taxes has no effect under Ricardian equivalence, and a change in the real interest rate has an indeterminate effect on the current account surplus.

- Current account deficits need not be a bad thing, as this implies borrowing abroad, which helps domestic consumers to smooth their consumption over time.

- In the third small open-economy model, we allowed for the determination of production and investment, with the domestic economy facing an interest rate determined on world markets. Here, the current account surplus is the difference between domestic output and absorption, where absorption is the domestic demand for goods, or consumption plus investment plus government spending.

- An increase in the world real interest rate increases domestic output, reduces absorption, and increases the current account surplus.

- A temporary increase in government spending increases domestic absorption and decreases the current account surplus.

- An increase in current total factor productivity increases domestic output and increases the current account surplus, whereas an anticipated increase in future total factor productivity causes no change in current aggregate output and reduces the current account surplus.

Key Terms

Absorption Consumption plus investment plus government expenditures; the quantity of domestically produced goods absorbed through domestic spending. (p. 524)

Comparative advantage How efficient a country is at producing one good relative to another, as compared with the rest of the world. Comparative advantage is determined by the slope of the production possibilities frontier. (p. 511)

Real exchange rate The terms of trade. (p. 506)

Small open economy (SOE) An economy that trades with the rest of the world, and for which the collective actions of domestic consumers and firms have negligible effects on prices on world markets. (p. 505)

Terms of trade The relative price at which imports trade for exports on world markets. (p. 506)

Twin deficits A current account deficit coupled with a government budget deficit. (p. 523)

Questions for Review

1. What is a small open economy?
2. Why is it appropriate to use a small open-economy model to explain events in the United States?
3. In the first model in this chapter, with two goods, what are the conditions that determine production and consumption in the SOE when there is no trade?
4. What are the conditions that determine production and consumption in the SOE when there is trade with the rest of the world?
5. Are the residents of the SOE better off or worse off when they can trade with the rest of the world? Why is this the case?
6. If the terms of trade increase and the SOE initially imports good a, what are the effects on consumption and production of goods a and b in the SOE?
7. If the terms of trade increase and the SOE initially imports good b, what are the effects on consumption and production of goods a and b in the SOE?
8. In the second model in this chapter, what are the four determinants of the current account surplus, and how does each of these determinants affect it?
9. Why could it be a good thing for a country to run a current account deficit?
10. What are the twin deficits and what causes them?
11. What are the effects of an increase in the world real interest rate on output, absorption, and the current account surplus?
12. What are the effects of a temporary increase in government expenditure on output, absorption, and the current account surplus?
13. What are the effects of an increase in current and future total factor productivity on output, absorption, and the current account balance?

Problems

1. Suppose that, in the model where two goods a and b are produced domestically and traded internationally, the representative consumer's preferences change so that the marginal rate of substitution of good a for good b increases for each consumption bundle. That is, the consumer is now less willing to give up good a in exchange for good b. Determine the effects of this change in preferences on the production of goods a and b in the SOE, on consumption of goods a and b, and on the

quantities of goods *a* and *b* imported and exported. Explain your results.

2. Suppose that there is an improvement in the technology for producing good *b* in the SOE. This implies that the marginal rate of transformation, MRT_{ab}, increases for each quantity of good *a*. Determine the effects of this technology change on the consumption of goods *a* and *b*, the production of goods *a* and *b*, and the quantities of goods *a* and *b* imported and exported. Explain your results in terms of income and substitution effects, and interpret.

3. The government imposes a quota on imports. Determine the effect of this on production and consumption of goods *a* and *b* in the first model in this chapter. Also determine the effect on the consumer's welfare. Explain your results.

4. Assume a two-period model where the representative consumer has income of 100 in the current period, income of 120 in the future period, and faces a world real interest rate of 10% per period. The consumer always wishes to set current consumption equal to future consumption, which implies perfect-complements preferences.
   (a) Suppose that current and future government expenditures are 15 and 20, respectively. Determine consumption in the current and future periods, and the current account surplus. Draw a diagram to illustrate your results.
   (b) Now, suppose that current government expenditures increases to 25, with everything else unchanged. Again, determine consumption in the current and future periods and the current account surplus and show these in your diagram.
   (c) Explain the difference in your results in parts (a) and (b).

5. Modify the second model in this chapter as follows: Suppose that real interest rates are determined on world markets. The government can borrow and lend on world markets at the interest rate *r*, but the representative consumer lends at the interest rate *r* and borrows at the interest rate *r**, which is also determined on world markets. Assume that $r^* > r$, perhaps because of the costs of operating international banks that make loans to consumers.
   (a) Suppose that *r** increases, with *r* unchanged. Determine the effects on consumption in the current and future periods, and on the

current account balance, and explain your results in terms of income and substitution effects.
   (b) Now, suppose that the government cuts current taxes and increases future taxes, holding constant government spending in the current and future periods. Assume, before the tax cut is put into effect, that the current account surplus is zero. Determine the effects of the tax cut in period 1 on consumption in the current and future periods, the trade balance, and the welfare of the representative consumer. Explain your results.

6. Use the third model in this chapter to answer this question. The government in a small open economy is concerned that the current account deficit is too high. One group of economic advisers to the government argues that high government deficits cause the current account deficit to be high and that the way to reduce the current account deficit is to increase taxes. A second group of economic advisers argues that the high current account deficit is caused by high domestic investment and proposes that domestic investment should be taxed, with these investment taxes returned to consumers as lump-sum transfers.
   (a) Which advice should the government take if its goal is to reduce the current account deficit? Explain.
   (b) Is the government's goal of reducing the current account deficit sensible? Why or why not? What will happen if the government takes the advice that achieves its goal, as in part (a)?

7. Suppose, as in Chapter 9, that in the second model in this chapter there is limited commitment in the credit relationships between the small open economy and the rest of the world. There is some portion of the nation's capital stock, denoted by K_c, which is collateralizable on world markets. This collateralizable capital is illiquid in the current period and is valued at price *p* on world markets in the future period. Assume that borrowing by the SOE on world markets is limited by the value of collateralizable wealth in the future period. Now, suppose that *p* falls. How does this affect consumption in the SOE in the present and the future and the current account surplus? Explain your results with the aid of diagrams.

8. In Chapter 11, we studied how persistent total factor productivity shocks in a closed economy can provide an explanation for business cycles. In the third model studied in this chapter, determine the effects of a persistent increase in total factor productivity on domestic output, consumption, investment, and the current account surplus. Are the predictions of the model consistent with what you observe in Figure 14.10? Explain why or why not.

9. An interpretation of events after 2000 in the United States is that the current account surplus was negative after 2000 so as to finance domestic investment spending. This investment spending was generated by optimism about future prospects. In 2008, people became much more pessimistic about the future, and investment spending and GDP began to fall. In response, the U.S. government decided to increase government spending in 2009, so as to reduce the negative effect of the decline in investment spending on aggregate economic activity.

   (a) Use the third model in this chapter to explain exactly how this story works.
   (b) Will the increase in government spending actually be "stimulative," in that it increases aggregate output by a large amount?
   (c) Will the increase in government spending have unintended consequences, in terms of effects on the current account surplus? Explain carefully, using diagrams.

Working with the Data

1. Answer the following:
   (a) Calculate consumption (C), investment (I), government spending (G), and net exports (NX), as percentages of GDP (Y) for the years 1947–2009.
   (b) Construct scatter plots of NX/Y vs. C/Y, NX/Y vs. I/Y, and NX/Y vs. G/Y for the years 1947–2009. What do you observe? What do these data tell us about the primary causes of fluctuations in the current account?

2. Calculate the real interest rate, measured as the quarterly treasury bill rate minus the inflation rate (measured as the percentage change in implicit GDP price deflator from 4 quarters previously). Then, plot the real interest rate and the ratio of net exports to GDP, for the years 1948–2009, in time series form and in a scatter plot. What do you observe? Is this consistent with the predictions of the third model in this chapter, if we treat the real interest rate as being determined on world credit markets?

chapter 15

Money in the Open Economy

Many issues in international macroeconomics can be well understood without the complication of monetary exchange in the picture, as we saw in Chapter 14. However, there are also many intriguing issues in international finance—particularly those involving the determination of nominal exchange rates, the effects of having flexible or fixed exchange rates, the transmission of nominal macroeconomic shocks among countries, the effects of capital controls, and the role of international financial institutions—that we need monetary models to understand. In this chapter, we build on the third small open-economy model we studied in Chapter 14 to integrate money into a monetary small open-economy model that can address some key issues in international monetary economics.

We will first consider the notion of purchasing power parity, or the law of one price, which is a cornerstone of the monetary small open-economy model in this chapter. Purchasing power parity would hold if the prices of all goods in the world economy were equal, corrected for nominal exchange rates, where a nominal exchange rate is the price of one currency in terms of another. While there are economic forces that result in a long-run tendency toward purchasing power parity, in reality there can be fairly large and persistent deviations from purchasing power parity, as we will show. However, although purchasing power parity may not be the best approximation to reality in the short run, it proves to be very useful in simplifying the model used in this chapter.

The monetary small open-economy model we construct and put to work in this chapter builds on the third small open-economy model from Chapter 14, in that the goods markets in the two models are identical. The model of this chapter also has much in common with the monetary intertemporal model in Chapter 11. In particular, the monetary small open-economy model features a classical dichotomy, in that nominal variables—in this case, the price level and the nominal exchange rate—are determined independently of real variables. Further, money is neutral. This is a useful starting point for international monetary economics, because adding some of the frictions that we considered in the business cycle models of Chapters 12 and 13—sticky prices, market segmentation, and coordination failures—involves straightforward extensions of this basic framework.

The first experiments we carry out with the model in this chapter emphasize the effects of shocks from abroad under flexible and fixed nominal exchange rates. A flexible exchange rate is free to move according to supply and demand in the market for foreign exchange, whereas under a fixed exchange rate the domestic government commits in some fashion to supporting the nominal exchange rate at a specified value. A flexible exchange rate has the property that monetary policy can be set independently in the domestic economy, and the domestic price level is not affected by changes in foreign prices. Under a fixed exchange rate, however, the domestic central bank cannot control its money supply independently, and price level changes originating abroad are essentially imported to the domestic economy. Flexible and fixed exchange rate regimes each have their own advantages and disadvantages, as we discuss.

Finally, we examine the effects of capital controls on the behavior of the domestic economy. Capital controls are restrictions on the international flow of assets, and these controls tend to dampen the fluctuations that result from some shocks to the economy. Capital controls are detrimental, however, in that they reduce economic efficiency.

The Nominal Exchange Rate, the Real Exchange Rate, and Purchasing Power Parity

The model we work with in this chapter is a monetary small open-economy model, which builds on the third small open-economy model of Chapter 14 and the monetary intertemporal model in Chapter 11. Key variables in this model are the nominal exchange rate and the real exchange rate, which are defined in this section. Further, in this section we derive the purchasing power parity relationship, which determines the value of the real exchange rate.

In the model in this chapter, just as in the monetary intertemporal model, all domestically produced goods sell at a price P, in terms of domestic currency. Foreign-produced goods sell at the price P^*, in terms of foreign currency. In the model, there is a market for foreign exchange, on which domestic currency can be traded for foreign currency, and we let e denote the price of one unit of foreign currency in terms of domestic currency. That is, e is the **nominal exchange rate.** Therefore, if a domestic resident holding domestic currency wished to buy goods abroad, assuming that foreign producers of goods accept only foreign currency in exchange for their goods, one unit of foreign goods costs eP^* in units of domestic currency. This is because the domestic resident must first buy foreign currency with domestic currency, at a price of e, and then buy foreign goods with foreign currency at a price of P^*. To give an example, suppose that a book in England costs five British pounds, and that the exchange rate between U.S. dollars and British Pounds is two U.S. dollars per British Pound, that is, $e = 2$. Then, the cost of the book in U.S. dollars is $2 \times 5 = 10$.

Because the price of domestic goods in domestic currency is P, and the price of foreign goods in terms of domestic currency is eP^*, the real exchange rate (or the terms of trade), which is the price of foreign goods in terms of domestic goods, is

$$\text{Real exchange rate} = \frac{eP^*}{P}.$$

Now, suppose that it is costless to transport goods between foreign countries and the domestic country and that there are no trade barriers, such as government-set import quotas and tariffs (import taxes). Then, if $eP^* > P$, it would be cheaper to buy goods domestically than abroad, so that foreign consumers would want to buy domestic goods rather than foreign goods, and this would tend to increase P. Alternatively, if $eP^* < P$, then foreign goods would be cheaper than domestic goods, and so domestic consumers would prefer to purchase foreign goods rather than domestic goods, in which case P would tend to fall. Thus, with no transportation costs and no trade barriers, we should expect to observe that

$$P = eP^*, \tag{15-1}$$

and this relationship is called **purchasing power parity (PPP)**. This relationship is also called the **law of one price**, because, if it holds, the price of goods is the same, in terms of domestic currency, at home and abroad. If PPP holds, then the real exchange rate is 1.

In the real world, we would not in general expect PPP to hold exactly if we measure P and P^* as the price levels in two different countries. Any measure of the price level, such as the consumer price index or the implicit GDP price deflator, includes the prices of a large set of goods produced and consumed in the economy. Some of these goods are traded on world markets, such as agricultural commodities and raw materials, while other goods are only traded domestically, such as local services like haircuts. While we would expect that there would be a tendency for the law of one price to hold for goods that are traded internationally, we would not expect it to hold for nontraded goods. For example, crude oil can be shipped at relatively low cost over large distances by pipeline and in large oil tankers, and there is a well-organized world market for crude oil, so that crude oil sells almost anywhere in the world at close to the same price (plus transport costs). However, there is not a world market in haircuts, as the cost of traveling to another country for a haircut is in most cases very large relative to the cost of the haircut. The law of one price should hold for crude oil but not for haircuts.

In general, there are strong economic forces that tend to make market prices and nominal exchange rates adjust so that PPP applies. For example, if PPP does not apply, then even if there are large costs of transporting goods across countries, consumers would want to move to where goods are relatively cheaper, and firms would want to move their production where goods are relatively more expensive, and ultimately we would expect PPP to hold over the long run. Unless it is very difficult to move goods, labor, and capital across international borders, purchasing power parity should hold, at least as a long-run relationship. Although PPP may be a poor description of short-run reality, as we show in the next section, and the adjustment to PPP may be quite slow, it simplifies our models considerably to make the PPP assumption, and this simplification helps us focus on the issues of this chapter.

Flexible and Fixed Exchange Rates

In addition to PPP, another important component of the monetary small open-economy model is the exchange rate regime. As we show, a key determinant of how the domestic economy responds to shocks, and an important factor for the conduct of domestic monetary and fiscal policy, is the set of rules for government intervention in foreign exchange markets. Roughly speaking, the polar extremes in foreign exchange market intervention are a **flexible exchange rate regime** and a **fixed exchange rate regime**. Currently, there are countries in the world that conform closely to an idealized flexible exchange rate regime, others that fix the exchange rate, and some countries that mix the two approaches.

The PPP Relationship for the United States and Canada

A case where we might expect relatively small deviations from PPP involves the relationship between the United States and Canada. Historically, there has been a high volume of trade between these two countries. The United States and Canada signed a free trade agreement in 1989, which was replaced in 1992 by the North American Free Trade Agreement (NAFTA), which included Mexico. An earlier trade agreement was the Canada–U.S. Auto Pact, signed in 1965, which permitted the shipment of autos and auto parts across the Canada–U.S. border by manufacturers. Given the close proximity of Canada and the United States, and natural north-south transportation links, transportation costs between the United States and Canada are quite low. Not only are goods easy to move between these two countries, but NAFTA now permits freer movement of labor across the Canada–U.S. border as well. Capital is also relatively free to move between these two countries. Therefore, there are especially strong forces in place in the U.S.–Canada case that would cause us to be surprised if PPP did not apply, at least approximately.

In Figure 15.1 we show the real exchange rate, $\frac{eP^*}{P}$, for Canada versus the United States for the years 1947–2009. Here, e is the price of Canadian dollars in terms of U.S. dollars, P^* is the Canadian consumer price index, and P is the CPI in the United States. The real exchange rate has been scaled for convenience, so that its value is 100 in January 1947. Purchasing power parity predicts that the real exchange rate in the figure should be constant, but it is certainly not. In the figure, the real exchange rate has fluctuated significantly. The fluctuations are not small short-run fluctuations around a constant value but are more persistent in nature. Indeed, there appears to be no tendency for the real exchange rate to fluctuate more closely around some long-run value after the free trade agreement in 1989. Between 1989 and 2002, the real exchange rate decreased by more than 40%, and then increased by about 30% between 2002 and 2006 before decreasing again. If there are such large deviations from PPP for Canada and the United States, we should expect PPP relationships to be even more loose in the short run between the United States and other countries of the world.

Under a flexible or floating exchange rate, there is no intervention by the domestic fiscal or monetary authorities to specifically target the nominal exchange rate e. If the nominal exchange rate is truly flexible, it is free to move in response to market forces. Some countries with flexible exchange rates[1] are India, South Korea, Brazil, Australia, New Zealand, Canada, and the United States. For reasons we discuss ahead, essentially all countries care about short-run movements in their nominal exchange rate, and they therefore intervene from time to time, through monetary and fiscal policy, to influence the value of the nominal exchange rate, even under a flexible exchange rate regime.

---

[1]See http://fx.sauder.ubc.ca/currency

Figure 15.1 The Real Exchange Rate for Canada vs. the United States

Purchasing power parity predicts that the real exchange rate should be a constant, but there have been large and persistent deviations from PPP in this case.

Source: Statistics Canada and Bureau of Labor Statistics.

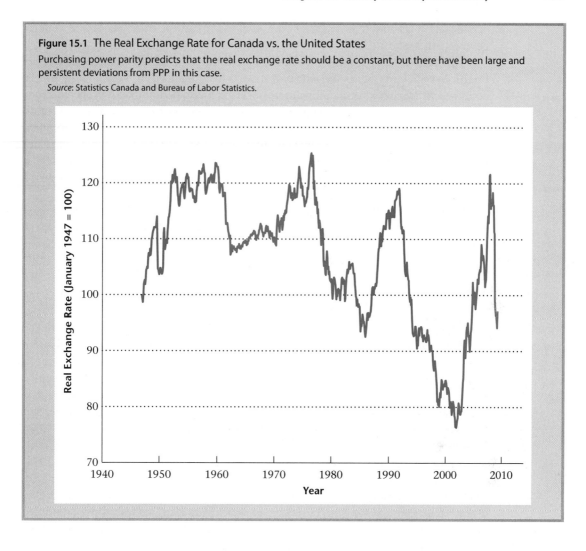

There are several different important fixed exchange rate systems, which can be roughly characterized as **hard pegs** and **soft pegs.** Under a hard peg, a country commits to a fixed nominal exchange rate relative to some other currency for the indefinite future. With a soft peg, there is no long-term commitment to a particular value for the exchange rate, but the exchange rate can be fixed relative to another currency for long periods of time, with periodic **devaluations** (increases in the nominal exchange rate e) and **revaluations** (decreases in e).

A hard peg can be implemented in basically three different ways. First, a country could abandon its national currency and **dollarize.** Dollarization essentially involves using the currency of another country as the national medium of exchange. For example, Ecuador currently uses the U.S. dollar as its national currency, although dollarization can refer to a situation in which a country uses a currency other than the U.S. dollar. A disadvantage of dollarizing is that a country relinquishes its ability to collect seigniorage (discussed in Chapter 11); that is, it cannot print money to finance government spending.

The second way to implement a hard peg is through the establishment of a **currency board.** With a currency board, there is a centralized institution, which could be the country's central bank, that holds interest-bearing assets denominated in the currency of the country against which the nominal exchange rate is being fixed. This institution then stands ready to exchange domestic currency for foreign currency at a specified fixed exchange rate, and it can buy and sell interest-bearing assets in order to carry out these exchanges. A country that currently uses a currency board is Hong Kong, which fixes its nominal exchange rate relative to the U.S. dollar. Under a currency board, a country maintains its ability to collect seigniorage.

Finally, a third approach to implementing a hard peg is through mutual agreement among countries to a common currency, as in the **European Monetary Union (EMU),** which was established in 1999. Most European countries are EMU members, with some notable exceptions such as the United Kingdom. The common currency of the EMU is the **Euro,** and the supply of Euros is managed by the **European Central Bank (ECB).** The rules governing the operation of the ECB specify how the seigniorage revenue from the printing of new Euros is to be split among the EMU members.

Soft pegs involve various degrees of commitment to a fixed exchange rate or to target bands for the exchange rate. For example, under the **European Monetary System (EMS),** which was established in 1979 and preceded the EMU, member European countries committed over the short run to target their exchange rates within specified ranges. In this arrangement, coordination was required among the EMS members, and there were periodic crises and changes in target bands for exchange rates. Another soft peg was the **Bretton Woods arrangement,** the rules for which were specified in an agreement negotiated at Bretton Woods, New Hampshire, in 1944. The Bretton Woods arrangement governed post–World War II international monetary relations until 1971. Under Bretton Woods, the United States fixed the value of the U.S. dollar relative to gold, by agreeing to exchange U.S. dollars for gold at a specified price. All other countries then agreed to fix their exchange rates relative to the U.S. dollar. This was, thus, a modified gold standard arrangement. For reasons we discuss later in this chapter, soft peg arrangements have tended to be unstable; the arrangements typically collapse and are replaced by alternative systems, as was the case with the EMS and the Bretton Woods arrangement.

A key international monetary institution that plays an important role in exchange rate determination is the **International Monetary Fund (IMF),** the framework for which was discussed at Bretton Woods in 1944, with the IMF established in 1946. The IMF currently has 186 member countries, and it performs a function that is in some ways similar to the one carried out by a central bank relative to the domestic banks under its supervision. Namely, the IMF plays the role of a **lender of last resort** for its member countries, just as a central bank is a lender of last resort for domestic financial institutions (as we discuss in Chapter 16). The IMF stands ready to lend to member countries in distress, although IMF lending comes with strings attached. Typically, IMF lending is conditional on a member country submitting to a program set up by the IMF, which typically specifies corrective policy actions.

A Monetary Small Open–Economy Model with a Flexible Exchange Rate

Now that we have discussed some of the institutional arrangements governing the determination of exchange rates, we can proceed to work with a monetary small open-economy model in which there is international monetary interaction. This model is in part based on the monetary intertemporal model in Chapter 11. This is a small open-economy model that essentially involves adding a money market to the third real small open-economy model in Chapter 14. In this model, we assume for now that the exchange rate is flexible, and we study the properties of a fixed exchange rate system in the next section.

In Figure 15.2 we show the goods market for the monetary small open-economy model, which is identical to the goods market for the third real small open-economy model of Chapter 14. The curve Y^d is the output demand curve, which is downward-sloping because of the negative effect of the real interest rate on the demand for consumption and investment goods, and Y^s is the output supply curve, which is upward sloping because of the intertemporal substitution effect of the real interest rate on labor

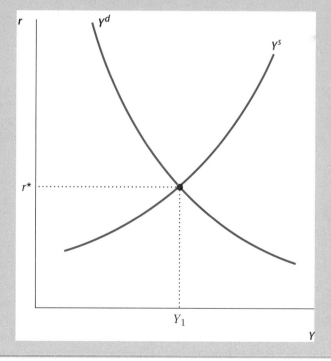

Figure 15.2 The Goods Market in the Monetary Small Open-Economy Model

The goods market in this model is identical to the goods market in the real small open-economy model with investment in Chapter 14. The world real interest rate is r^*, and equilibrium real output is Y_1. The current account surplus adjusts so that the Y^d curve intersects the Y^s curve at the world real interest rate r^*.

supply. The output supply and output demand curve shift as the result of factors discussed in detail in Chapter 14. Just as in Chapter 14, the small open-economy assumption implies that domestic firms and consumers are collectively price-takers on world markets. In equilibrium, the income-expenditure identity holds, so that $Y = C + I + G + NX$. Given that the domestic economy is, as a whole, a price-taker on world markets, any output not absorbed domestically as C, I, or G is exported (if net exports are positive) or any excess of domestic absorption over domestic output is purchased abroad (if net exports are negative).

We assume that PPP holds, so that

$$P = eP^*, \tag{15-2}$$

where P is the domestic price level, e is the price of foreign exchange in terms of domestic currency, and P^* is the foreign price level. Although we know from above that the PPP relationship typically does not hold in the short run, assuming PPP simplifies our model greatly and essentially implies that we are ignoring the effects of changes in the terms of trade (discussed in Chapter 14), which would cloud some of the issues we want to discuss here. Given the assumption of a small open economy, events in the domestic economy have no effect on the foreign price level P^*, and so we treat P^* as exogenous. However, the domestic price level P and the exchange rate e are endogenous variables. The exchange rate is flexible, in that it is determined by market forces, as we show below.

Next, we want to determine how the money market works in our equilibrium model. As in Chapter 11, money demand is given by

$$M^d = PL(Y, r^*), \tag{15-3}$$

where $L(Y, r^*)$ denotes the demand for real money balances, which depends positively on aggregate real income Y and negatively on the real interest rate. Here, recall that the domestic real interest rate is identical to the world real interest rate r^*, and we are assuming no long-run money growth, so that the domestic inflation rate is zero and the real interest rate is equal to the nominal interest rate given the Fisher relation (see Chapter 11). Now, given the PPP relation, equation (15-2), we can substitute in equation (15-3) for P to get

$$M^d = eP^*L(Y, r^*).$$

We take the nominal money supply to be exogenous, with $M^s = M$. In equilibrium, money supply equals money demand, so that $M^s = M^d$, or

$$M = eP^*L(Y, r^*). \tag{15-4}$$

In Figure 15.3, money demand and money supply are on the horizontal axis, while e, the exchange rate, is on the vertical axis. Then, given Y and r^*, money demand M^d is a straight line through the origin in the figure, while money supply M^s is a vertical line at $M^s = M$. The intersection of the supply and demand curves for money then determines the nominal exchange rate e, so that the equilibrium exchange rate in the figure

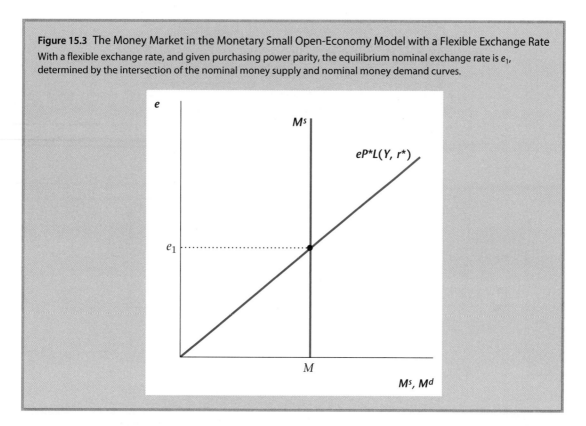

Figure 15.3 The Money Market in the Monetary Small Open-Economy Model with a Flexible Exchange Rate

With a flexible exchange rate, and given purchasing power parity, the equilibrium nominal exchange rate is e_1, determined by the intersection of the nominal money supply and nominal money demand curves.

is e_1. Once we have determined e, we have also determined the domestic price level P from the PPP equation, (15-2).

Thus, in this model, the nominal exchange rate is determined by the nominal demand for money relative to the nominal supply of money. Because the nominal exchange rate is a nominal variable, this seems natural. Movements in the exchange rate are caused either by a shift in money demand or a shift in money supply.

The Neutrality of Money with a Flexible Exchange Rate

Now that we have set up the model, we can proceed to study its properties. Just as in the monetary intertemporal model we studied in Chapter 11, this model features a classical dichotomy, in that real variables (the level of output, the current account surplus, consumption, and investment) are determined independently of nominal variables (the domestic price level P and the nominal exchange rate e). In Figure 15.3, the nominal exchange rate is determined by the supply and demand for money, and the level of the nominal exchange rate has no bearing on real variables.

If the central bank increases the money supply, say from M_1 to M_2 in Figure 15.4, this has the effect of shifting the money supply curve rightward from M_1^s to M_2^s. In equilibrium, the nominal exchange rate increases from e_1 to e_2, and there is no effect on the

Figure 15.4 An Increase in the Money Supply in the Monetary Small Open-Economy Model with a Flexible Exchange Rate

Money is neutral in the monetary small open-economy model with a flexible exchange rate. An increase in the money supply causes the nominal exchange rate and the price level to increase in proportion to the increase in the money supply, with no effect on real variables.

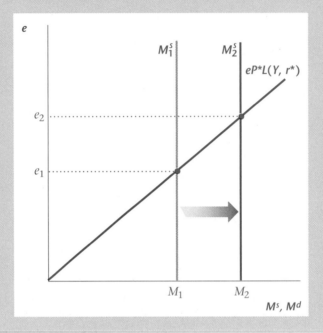

level of real output, the real interest rate (which is the real interest rate on world markets, r^*), consumption, investment, or the current account surplus. Because the price of foreign currency has risen in terms of domestic currency, we say that there is a **depreciation** of the domestic currency. Ultimately, because equation (15-4) implies that

$$\frac{M}{e} = P^*L(Y, r^*),$$

and because P^*, Y, and r^* remain unaffected by the change in the money supply, $\frac{M}{e}$ remains unchanged. Thus, the nominal exchange rate increases in proportion to the money supply; for example, if the money supply increased by 5%, the nominal exchange rate would also increase by 5%. Further, because PPP holds, or $P = eP^*$, and because P^* is fixed, the price level P also increases in proportion to the increase in the money supply.

Thus, money is neutral in this model economy with a flexible exchange rate. There are no real effects of an increase in the nominal money supply, but all money prices, including the nominal exchange rate, increase in proportion to the increase in the money supply. While most macroeconomists adopt the view that money is neutral in the long run in an open economy, there are differences of opinion about the short-run neutrality of money and the explanations for any nonneutralities of money, just as in closed-economy macroeconomics. As mentioned earlier, it is possible to extend this model to include frictions such as the money surprise mechanism or sticky wages from Chapters 12 and 13, under which money is not neutral in the open economy in the short run. In this chapter we cannot do everything, and we stick to the basic monetary small open-economy model.

A Nominal Shock to the Domestic Economy from Abroad: P^* Increases

We would like to use the monetary small open-economy model to investigate how the domestic economy is affected by events in the rest of the world. The first example we consider is the case of an increase in the price level in the rest of the world, which is essentially a nominal shock to the domestic economy. We see that a flexible exchange rate system has an insulating property with respect to increases in the foreign price level. That is, the nominal exchange rate adjusts to exactly offset the increase in the foreign price level, and there are no effects on the domestic price level or domestic real variables. In particular, the temporary foreign inflation resulting from the increase in the foreign price level is not imported to the domestic economy.

Suppose that P^* increases from P_1^* to P_2^*, perhaps because central banks in foreign countries increase the quantity of foreign money in circulation. Then, in Figure 15.5,

Figure 15.5 An Increase in the Foreign Price Level in the Monetary Small Open-Economy Model with a Flexible Exchange Rate

If the foreign price level increases, this shifts the nominal money demand curve to the right, with the nominal exchange rate falling from e_1 to e_2 in equilibrium. The decrease in the nominal exchange rate exactly offsets the increase in the foreign price level, and there is no effect on the domestic price level.

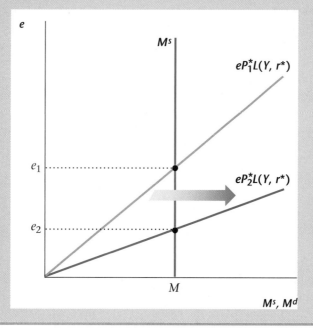

the money demand curve shifts rightward from $eP_1^*L(Y, r^*)$ to $eP_2^*L(Y, r^*)$. In equilibrium, there is no effect on real variables, but the nominal exchange rate falls from e_1 to e_2, so that there is an **appreciation** of the domestic currency. Because $P = eP^*$, from equation (15-4) we have

$$\frac{M}{P} = L(Y, r^*),$$

and because M, Y, and r^* remain unchanged, P is also unchanged. Therefore, no domestic variables were affected by the price level change in the rest of the world. In particular, the appreciation of the domestic currency was just sufficient to offset the effect of the increase in P^* on the domestic price level. That is, the flexible exchange rate insulated the domestic economy from the nominal shock from abroad. This is certainly a desirable property of a flexible exchange rate regime. Under flexible exchange rates, the domestic price level, and by implication the domestic inflation rate, is determined by the quantity of domestic money supplied by the domestic central bank, and it is not influenced by how monetary policy is conducted by foreign central banks.

A Real Shock to the Domestic Economy from Abroad

As an experiment to determine how real domestic variables, the nominal exchange rate, and the price level respond to a real disturbance transmitted from abroad, we examine the effects of an increase in the world real interest rate. Such a shock could result, for example, from a decrease in total factor productivity in the rest of the world (recall our analysis of the effects of total factor productivity shocks from Chapter 10). As we show, a flexible exchange rate cannot shield the domestic economy from the effects of a change in the world real interest rate; the nominal exchange rate appreciates (e falls), and the price level falls.

In Figure 15.6 the world real interest rate increases from r_1^* to r_2^*. The real effects of this are the same as we considered for the third real small open-economy model in Chapter 12. In Figure 15.6(a), the current account surplus increases, shifting the output demand curve to the right until it comes to rest at Y_2^d. Output increases from Y_1 to Y_2 because of the increase in labor supply that results from intertemporal substitution of leisure by the representative consumer. The increase in the real interest rate causes domestic consumption expenditures and investment expenditures to fall, though the increase in current income causes consumption to rise. On net, consumption may rise or fall. Total domestic absorption, $C + I + G$, may rise or fall, but any increase in absorption is smaller than the increase in domestic output, so that the current account surplus rises.

The nominal effects of the increase in the world real interest rate depend on how the demand for money changes. The increase in the real interest rate causes the demand for money to fall, while the increase in domestic output causes the demand for money to rise. It is not clear whether $L(Y_2, r_2^*) < L(Y_1, r_1^*)$ or $L(Y_2, r_2^*) > L(Y_1, r_1^*)$. However, if real money demand is much more responsive to real income than to the interest rate, then money demand will rise, and the money demand curve in Figure 15.6(b) shifts to the right. In equilibrium, the exchange rate appreciates, with the nominal exchange

Figure 15.6 An Increase in the World Real Interest Rate with a Flexible Exchange Rate

Under a flexible exchange rate, if the world real interest rate increases, this causes real output to rise, and the money demand curve shifts to the right, assuming money demand is much more responsive to real income than to the real interest rate. The nominal exchange rate decreases in equilibrium.

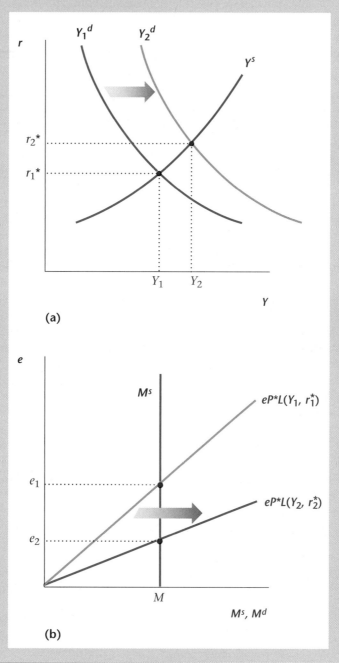

(a)

(b)

rate decreasing from e_1 to e_2. As purchasing power parity holds—that is, $P = eP^*-$, with P^* constant, P falls in proportion to the decrease in e. Thus, the increase in the world real interest rate leads to an exchange rate appreciation and a decrease in the price level. Clearly, the flexible exchange rate cannot automatically insulate the domestic economy from real shocks that occur abroad. For example, if the central bank wished to stabilize the price level in the face of the increase in the world real interest rate, it would have to increase the money supply in response to the increase in money demand resulting from the shock.

Macroeconomics in Action
The Asian Crisis

In 1997, there was a sharp depreciation in nominal exchange rates in East Asia, primarily in Indonesia, South Korea, Malaysia, and Thailand, and these exchange rate depreciations were the first symptoms of what became known as the Asian crisis. From 1996 until the fall of 1997, the nominal exchange rate (the price of a U.S. dollar in terms of domestic currency) increased by 98.5% in Indonesia, 110.7% in South Korea, 54.4% in Malaysia, and 86.5% in Thailand.[2] What could cause nominal exchange rates to depreciate so dramatically in East Asia over so short a time period? Some answers are provided in a National Bureau of Economic Research working paper, "What Caused the Asian Currency and Financial Crisis?" by Giancarlo Corsetti, Paolo Pesenti, and Nouriel Roubini, hereafter referred to as CPR.

At the time of the Asian crisis, Indonesia, South Korea, Malaysia, and Thailand were under flexible exchange rate regimes; thus, the model we worked with above should be useful in understanding the large exchange rate

depreciation that occurred. The model tells us that a large exchange rate depreciation (a large increase in e) would have to occur because the demand for money fell abruptly or because there was a large increase in the domestic money supply. In our model, money demand could fall because real GDP fell, and so let us first consider the possibility that money demand fell because of a reduction in real GDP in East Asia. This was certainly not the case. Economic growth had been quite strong in East Asia before and during the 1990s. Indeed, in Chapter 8, we discussed the miraculous growth performance of the "East Asian tigers," which included South Korea. From CPR, the growth rates in real GDP in 1996 for Indonesia, South Korea, Malaysia, and Thailand were 7.98%, 7.10%, 8.58%, and 5.52%, respectively. These rates of growth were very high relative to average growth rates in GDP in other countries, and growth continued to be high for most of these countries in 1997, although lower than in 1996. The exception is Thailand, which had negative real GDP growth in 1997. In general, though, for these countries money demand would have been increasing rather than decreasing because of growth in real GDP, and so this does not seem to explain the large nominal exchange rate depreciations.

[2]See G. Corsetti, P. Pesenti, and N. Roubini, 1998, "What Caused the Asian Currency and Financial Crisis?" working paper, National Bureau of Economic Research.

To consider a second possibility, the exchange rate depreciations could have been caused during the Asian crisis by rapid growth in the money supply. However, rapid growth in the money supply typically results in a high domestic inflation rate (recall our analysis from Chapter 9), and inflation rates in Indonesia, South Korea, Malaysia, and Thailand, in 1997, from CPR, were 11.62%, 4.45%, 2.66%, and 5.61%, respectively, which are certainly moderate relative to the size of the exchange rate depreciations. Thus, money supply growth does not seem to be a potential explanation.

The only other potential explanation could be a dramatic shift in the demand for the currencies of Indonesia, South Korea, Malaysia, and Thailand, and this explanation appears to be in agreement with the analysis of CPR. They argue that these four countries were running large current account deficits prior to the Asian crisis, and that these current account deficits were financing investment that would ultimately have poor returns. That is, the domestic financial institutions in these countries were badly regulated, and they were borrowing abroad to make loans to finance domestic investment projects that would ultimately have poor returns. In terms of our analysis of current account deficits from Chapter 12, international lenders became concerned that the large current account deficits in East Asia were not sustainable. That is, to ultimately pay off the foreign debt resulting from large current account deficits, these countries would have to generate large current account surpluses in the future. International lenders to these countries did not appear to believe that the capital stocks in these countries would increase sufficiently to produce high enough future current account surpluses.

The result was a loss in confidence in East Asia on the part of international lenders, who discontinued lending to these countries. Effectively, this loss in confidence works much like a loss in confidence in the domestic banking system. In a domestic banking panic, deposits are withdrawn from banks and converted into domestic currency. In the case of the Asian crisis, the deposits of foreign lenders were withdrawn from East Asian banks and converted into assets denominated in non-East Asian currencies. This is effectively a fall in the demand for East Asian currencies, and it results in an exchange rate depreciation, as in our model.

Why was the Asian crisis a crisis? The main risk from the large exchange rate depreciations was the possibility of a widespread failure of East Asian financial institutions. These institutions were having difficulty borrowing abroad to finance long-term lending, and the exchange rate depreciation implied that the real value of the liabilities of these institutions had increased a great deal relative to the real value of their assets. East Asian financial institutions could then become insolvent and fail. The Asian crisis had temporary and fairly small effects for countries outside of East Asia, in part because of the intervention of the IMF and the world's central banks.

A Monetary Small Open Economy with a Fixed Exchange Rate

Now that we have studied how the economy behaves under a flexible exchange rate regime, we explore how real and nominal variables are determined when the exchange rate is fixed. The type of fixed exchange rate regime we consider is a type of soft peg, where the government fixes the nominal exchange rate for extended periods of time, but might devalue or revalue the domestic currency at some times.

Perspectives on the Financial Crisis

Why Did the U.S. Currency Appreciate After the Onset of the Financial Crisis?

When a country or countries experience a financial crisis, problems in the domestic financial industry typically lead to a flight from the liabilities of domestic financial institutions and a flight from that country's currency. As for example during the Asian crisis, discussed in the previous "Macroeconomics in Action" box, a domestic financial crisis is often associated with an exchange rate depreciation.

In Figure 15.7, we show the trade-weighted exchange rate for the United States. This exchange rate measure is intended to capture the exchange rate of the U.S. currency against all the currencies of the world, with individual foreign exchange rates weighted in this index according to the importance of the respective countries as U.S. trading partners. The trade-weighted exchange rate is normalized to 100 in January 1973 in the figure.

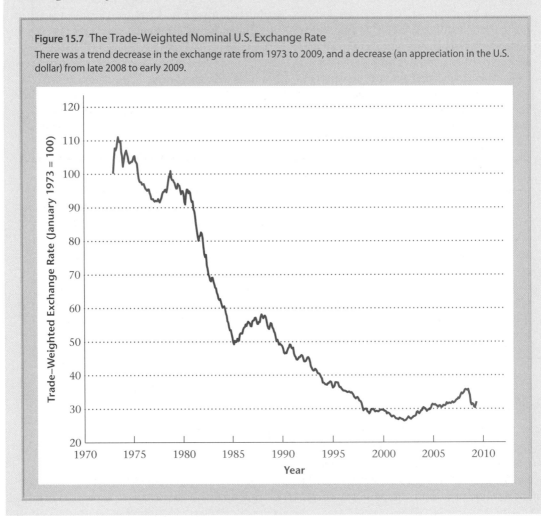

Figure 15.7 The Trade-Weighted Nominal U.S. Exchange Rate

There was a trend decrease in the exchange rate from 1973 to 2009, and a decrease (an appreciation in the U.S. dollar) from late 2008 to early 2009.

What we observe in Figure 15.7 is a trend decrease in the exchange rate—i.e., a U.S. exchange rate appreciation—through much of the period from 1973–2009. Particularly over the period from 1980–1985, this exchange rate depreciation was likely primarily due to a lower trend growth in money in the United States relative to the rest of the world.

A feature of note in Figure 15.7 is that the exchange rate decreased by about 15% from late 2008 to early 2009, at a time when the financial crisis was at its peak. The U.S. nominal exchange rate thus *appreciated* rather than depreciating during the financial crisis. What is even more puzzling is that this exchange rate depreciation occurred during a period of time when, as documented in Chapter 11, for example, the monetary base in the United States more than doubled. Given the results from the model in this chapter under a flexible exchange rate, we would expect a large U.S. exchange rate depreciation in response to such a large increase in the domestic money supply. What is going on here? An unusual feature of the United States relative to other countries is that its currency serves essentially as an international medium of exchange. Many transactions in the world, both at the consumer level and among financial institutions, are conducted using U.S. dollars. As well, large quantities of U.S. currency and other U.S. dollar–denominated assets are held outside the United States. Given that the U.S. dollar serves as an international medium of exchange, when there is a financial crisis, economic agents tend to shift their financial wealth from the liabilities of

financial institutions that have become more risky to U.S. dollars. This can occur even if, as in the case of the current financial crisis, the source of the problem was the behavior of U.S. financial market institutions. Then, for example in late 2008 and early 2009, the resulting increase in the demand for money could outweigh the increase in the supply of money in the United States, and the exchange rate could appreciate as a result.

The U.S. economy need not be immune indefinitely, however, from the effects of financial crises on the value of its exchange rate. World financial market participants are willing to use the U.S. dollar as an international medium of exchange principally because they trust the Federal Reserve System to manage U.S. monetary policy in a conservative fashion that assures that inflation in the United States will remain low. If the Fed chose to permanently increase the rate of growth in the U.S. money stock, generating a long-run exchange rate depreciation, then foreign residents holding U.S. dollar–denominated assets would suffer losses, and would therefore be reluctant to hold U.S. dollars in the future. Indeed, the Chinese government has been known to make explicit and implicit threats to reduce its holdings of U.S. dollar–denominated assets should the Fed not adequately control the U.S. dollar exchange rate and the inflation rate.[3]

---

[3]See "China Takes Aim at the U.S. Dollar," *Wall Street Journal*, March 24, 2009, at http://online.wsj.com/article/SB123780272456212885.html

Under the fixed exchange rate regime we model, the government chooses a level at which it wants to fix the nominal exchange rate, which is e_1 in Figure 15.8. The government must then, either through its central bank or some other authority, stand ready to support this exchange rate. For simplicity, we suppose that the fixed exchange rate is supported through the government standing ready to exchange foreign currency for domestic currency at the fixed exchange rate e_1. To see how this happens, consider the simplified government balance sheet in Table 15.1. This is a consolidated balance sheet for the central bank and the fiscal authority. To support a fixed exchange rate, the government must act to buy or sell its foreign exchange reserves (think of this as

Table 15.1   A Simplified Government Balance Sheet

Assets	Liabilities
Foreign Exchange Reserves	Outside Money
	Interest-Bearing Government Debt

foreign currency) for outside money (domestic currency) in foreign exchange markets, whenever there are market forces that would tend to push the exchange rate away from the fixed value the government wants it to have. For example, if there are forces tending to increase the exchange rate and, thus, cause a depreciation of the domestic currency, the government should sell foreign currency and buy domestic currency to offset those forces. If there are forces pushing down the exchange rate (appreciation), the government should buy foreign currency and sell domestic currency.

With a fixed exchange rate, the domestic central bank necessarily loses control over the domestic stock of money. To see this, consider Figure 15.8, where the nominal exchange rate is fixed at e_1. If the domestic central bank attempted to increase the money supply above M, its current value, the effect of this would be to put upward pressure on the exchange rate. Given the tendency for the price of foreign currency to

Figure 15.8 The Money Market in the Monetary Small Open-Economy Model with a Fixed Exchange Rate

With a fixed exchange rate, the money supply is endogenous. Given the fixed exchange rate e_1, the money supply M is determined so that the money supply curve M^s intersects the money demand curve for an exchange rate equal to e_1.

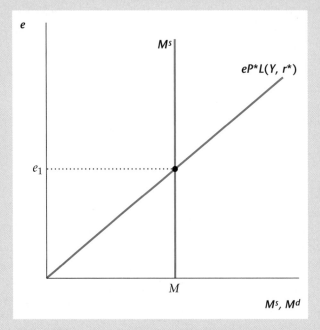

rise in terms of domestic currency, as a result, participants in foreign exchange markets would want to trade domestic currency for foreign currency, and the government would have to carry out these exchanges to support the fixed exchange rate. This would tend to reduce the stock of domestic money in circulation, and the attempt by the central bank to increase the money supply would be completely undone by actions in the foreign exchange market to support the fixed exchange rate. The money supply would remain at M, with the exchange rate and the domestic price level P unchanged. Similarly, if the domestic central bank attempted to engineer a reduction in the money supply below M, this would put downward pressure on the exchange rate, participants in the foreign exchange market would want to exchange foreign currency for domestic currency, and the government would be forced to exchange domestic currency for foreign currency, thus increasing the supply of money. The money supply could, therefore, not be reduced below M. The implication of this is that, under a fixed exchange rate regime, the supply of money cannot be determined independently by the central bank. Once the government fixes the exchange rate, this determines the domestic money supply.

A Nominal Foreign Shock Under a Fixed Exchange Rate

Suppose that the foreign price level increases when the domestic economy is under a fixed exchange rate. In Figure 15.9 P^* increases from P_1^* to P_2^*. As a result, the demand

Figure 15.9 An Increase in the Foreign Price Level in the Monetary Small Open-Economy Model with a Fixed Exchange Rate

With a fixed exchange rate, an increase in the foreign price level shifts the money demand curve to the right, which causes the domestic money supply to increase. The domestic price level increases in proportion to the increase in the foreign price level.

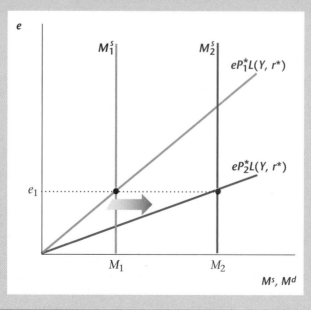

for money shifts rightward from $eP_1^*L(Y, r^*)$ to $eP_2^*L(Y, r^*)$. This increase in the demand for money results in downward pressure on the exchange rate, so that domestic currency becomes more attractive relative to foreign currency. On foreign exchange markets, the government must exchange domestic currency for foreign currency, and this leads to an increase in the domestic money supply from M_1 to M_2. Because $P = eP^*$, and the exchange rate is fixed, the domestic price level increases in proportion to the increase in the foreign price level. Thus, under a fixed exchange rate regime, in contrast to the flexible exchange rate regime, the domestic economy is not insulated from nominal shocks that occur abroad. When the foreign price level changes, this price level change is imported, and the domestic price level increases in proportion. Because domestic monetary policy is not independent under a fixed exchange rate, the domestic central bank is forced to adopt the world's inflation rate domestically.

A Real Foreign Shock Under a Fixed Exchange Rate

Now, we consider the effects of an increase in the world real interest rate from r_1^* to r_2^*, just as we did for the case of a flexible exchange rate. In Figure 15.10(a), as under the flexible exchange rate regime, the real effects of the interest rate increase are an increase in domestic output from Y_1 to Y_2, a decrease in investment, consumption may increase or decrease, and the current account surplus increases. Assuming that the effect of the increase in real income on money demand is much larger than that of the increase in the real interest rate, the demand for money shifts rightward in Figure 15.10(b), from $eP^*L(Y_1, r_1^*)$ to $eP^*L(Y_2, r_2^*)$. Then, with the exchange rate fixed at e_1, the domestic money supply must rise from M_1 to M_2. Because $P = eP^*$ and e and P^* do not change, the domestic price level does not change. Thus, a fixed exchange rate can insulate the domestic price level from real shocks that occur abroad. The same result could be achieved under a flexible exchange rate, but this would require discretionary action by the domestic central bank, rather than the automatic response that occurs under a fixed exchange rate.

Exchange Rate Devaluation

Under a fixed exchange rate regime, a devaluation of the domestic currency (an increase in the fixed exchange rate e) might be a course the government chooses in response to a shock to the economy. In this section, we show how a temporary reduction in domestic total factor productivity would lead to a reduction in foreign exchange reserves that the government may not desire. In this case, the decrease in foreign exchange reserves can be prevented by a devaluation of the domestic currency. The total factor productivity shock also causes a decrease in the current account surplus, but the devaluation has no effect in offsetting this current account change.

Suppose in Figure 15.11 that the domestic economy is initially in equilibrium with the output demand curve Y_1^d and the output supply curve Y_1^s determining domestic output Y_1 in panel (a), given the world real interest rate r^*. In Figure 15.11(b), the exchange rate is fixed at e_1 at first, nominal money demand is initially $eP^*L(Y_1, r^*)$, and the money supply is M_1. Now, suppose that there is a temporary negative shock to domestic total factor productivity. This shifts the output supply curve leftward from Y_1^s to Y_2^s in Figure 15.11(a), as in Chapter 10. The current account surplus falls, shifting the

Figure 15.10 An Increase in the World Real Interest Rate with a Fixed Exchange Rate

Under a fixed exchange rate, an increase in the world real interest rate causes an increase in real output and a shift to the right in nominal money demand. The money supply increases to accommodate the increase in money demand, and the domestic price level remains unchanged.

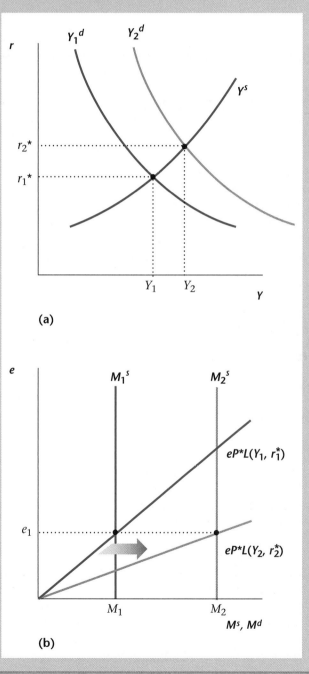

Figure 15.11 A Devaluation in Response to a Temporary Total Factor Productivity Shock

A temporary decrease in total factor productivity shifts the output supply curve to the left, reducing output and the current account surplus. The nominal money demand curve shifts to the left. If the government wants to avoid a loss in foreign exchange reserves, it can increase the fixed exchange rate from e_1 to e_2 and devalue the domestic currency.

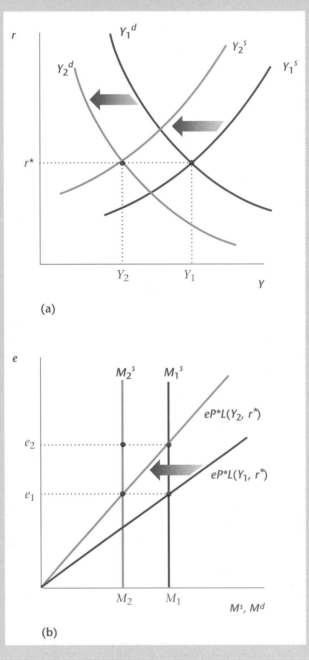

output demand curve to the left, until it comes to rest at Y_2^d. In equilibrium, output falls to Y_2, domestic absorption falls because of the decrease in consumption (as income falls), and the current account surplus falls. In Figure 15.11(b), the money demand curve shifts leftward to $eP^*L(Y_2, r^*)$ with the fall in real income. If the government were to continue to support the fixed nominal exchange rate at e_1, this would imply, given the fall in the demand for the domestic currency, that the government would have to sell foreign currency on the foreign exchange market and buy domestic currency. This implies that the money supply would contract from M_1 to M_2.

Suppose, however, that the government does not wish to sell any of its foreign exchange reserves or that it does not have the foreign exchange reserves to sell, when the demand for domestic money falls. The government can avoid selling foreign exchange by fixing the exchange rate at e_2 in Figure 15.11(b). This implies that the money supply remains fixed at M_1, and there is a devaluation in the exchange rate, as the price of foreign currency has risen relative to domestic currency.

An important point is that the devaluation of the domestic currency has no effect here on the current account deficit. We might think that a devaluation would make domestic goods cheaper relative to foreign goods, thus increasing the real exchange rate, and that this would cause imports to fall, exports to rise, and the current account deficit to fall. While this might be true in the short run in some types of Keynesian analysis with sticky prices (but there are income and substitution effects to be concerned with, in terms of the effect on the current account deficit), with purchasing power parity there is no effect on the real exchange rate. Ultimately, if the government determined that the current account deficit that results here is a problem—for example, if the current account deficit is caused by excessive government spending—then this is a real problem that should be corrected through real means. That is, the real current account deficit could be reduced through a reduction in government spending, which we know from Chapter 13 can reduce the current account deficit in Figure 15.11(a). Trying to reduce the current account deficit through a devaluation in the domestic currency essentially involves trying to make a real change through nominal means, which cannot work in the long run.

Flexible Versus Fixed Exchange Rates

Governments face important choices concerning exchange rate policy, and a key choice is whether a flexible or fixed exchange rate regime should be adopted. What are the arguments for the adoption of flexible versus fixed exchange rates? In the previous subsections, we have seen that the exchange rate regime affects how the domestic economy is insulated from shocks from abroad. If a country's central bank seeks to stabilize the price level, then our analysis tells us that if nominal shocks from abroad are important, then a flexible exchange rate is preferable to a fixed exchange rate, because a flexible exchange rate absorbs a shock to the foreign price level and stabilizes the domestic price level. Alternatively, if real shocks from abroad are important, then a fixed exchange rate is preferable to a flexible exchange rate, as this acts to prevent the domestic price level from moving in response to real shocks from abroad, because the domestic money supply acts as a shock absorber. Thus, in this respect, whether a particular country should choose a fixed or flexible exchange rate depends on its circumstances. It is possible that a particular country might want to move from a fixed to a flexible exchange rate over time and then back again.

It is sometimes argued that a flexible exchange rate allows the domestic central bank to implement a monetary policy independent of what happens in the rest of the world. In our model, with a flexible exchange rate the domestic government can set the domestic money supply independently, but with a fixed exchange rate, the money supply is not under the control of the domestic government. However, giving the domestic central bank the power to implement an independent monetary policy is useful only if the central bank can be trusted with this power. Some central banks, such as those in the United States, Canada, and parts of Europe, have excellent track records in controlling the rate of inflation after World War II. In other countries, the track record is not so good. For example, Argentina suffered very high rates of inflation until its nominal exchange rate was fixed relative to the U.S. dollar. If the central bank is weak, in that it has difficulty in controlling the domestic money supply, then a fixed exchange rate can be a very important commitment device. If the exchange rate is fixed against the currency of a country with a strong central bank, then this implies, given PPP, that the weak-central-bank country essentially adopts the monetary policy of the strong-central-bank country. With a fixed exchange rate, the price level of the domestic economy is tied to the foreign price level, which is essentially determined by foreign monetary policy.

In conclusion, there is no clear case for flexible versus fixed exchange rates in all circumstances. For the United States, where the central bank is relatively independent of political pressures and appears to be well focused on controlling inflation, a flexible exchange rate seems appropriate. The Federal Reserve System appears to be sufficiently trustworthy relative to foreign central banks that allowing the Fed to pursue a monetary policy geared to U.S. interests seems advisable. However, for other countries, particularly some in Latin America and Africa, a fixed exchange rate regime makes good sense.

There are many long-standing instances of fixed exchange rates that we take for granted. For example, rates of exchange between different denominations of Federal Reserve notes have always been fixed in the United States. Why should it necessarily be the case that five one-dollar bills trade for one five-dollar bill in all circumstances in the United States? This is because the Federal Reserve always stands ready to trade one five-dollar bill for five ones; essentially, the Fed maintains fixed exchange rates among notes of different denominations. Further, all of the regional Federal Reserve Banks in the United States issue different notes that are clearly marked according to the Federal Reserve Bank of issue (check your wallet, and you will see that this is true; for example, I9 denotes the ninth Federal Reserve district—a note issued by the Minneapolis Federal Reserve Bank). Why should a one-dollar bill issued by the Kansas City Federal Reserve Bank trade one-for-one for a one-dollar bill issued by the Richmond Federal Reserve Bank? The answer is that all Federal Reserve Banks stand ready to exchange all Federal Reserve notes at their face value for other Federal Reserve notes. Again, the Fed maintains fixed exchange rates in this respect.

Essentially, all countries maintain fixed exchange rates within their borders. There is a national currency that is accepted as legal tender, and typically this currency circulates nationally as a medium of exchange, although in some countries foreign currencies, in particular U.S. dollars, circulate widely. What then determines the natural region, or **common currency area**, over which a single currency dominates as a medium of exchange? Clearly, a common currency area need not be the area over which there is a single political or fiscal authority. In the United States, each state has the power to tax state residents, but the states cede monetary authority to the Federal Reserve System, for which the central decision-making unit resides with the Board of Governors in Washington, D.C. In the EMU, member countries maintain their fiscal independence, but monetary policy is in the hands of the ECB. An advantage of having a large trading area with a common currency is that this simplifies exchange; it is much easier to write contracts and trade across international borders without the complications of converting one currency into another or bearing the risk associated with fluctuating exchange rates. However, in joining a **currency union** such as the EMU, a country must give up its monetary independence to the group. The formation of the EMU clearly has created tensions among EMU members, concerning matters that include the choice of the leaders of the European Central Bank, and the monetary policy stance this central bank should take. Great Britain, which has the world's oldest central bank, the Bank of England, chose not to join the EMU so as to maintain its monetary independence.

Capital Controls

A useful application of the monetary small open-economy model is to the problem of the role of capital controls in the international economy. Capital controls refer broadly to any government restrictions on the trade of assets across international borders. We show here that capital controls can reduce movements in the nominal exchange rate in response to some shocks under a flexible exchange rate regime, and they can reduce fluctuations in foreign exchange reserves under a fixed exchange rate regime. We argue, however, that capital controls are in general undesirable, because they introduce welfare-decreasing economic inefficiencies.

The Capital Account and the Balance of Payments

To understand capital controls, we have to first understand the accounting practices behind the **capital account.** The capital account is part of the **balance of payments,** which includes the current account and the capital account. The capital account includes all transactions in assets, in which entries in the capital account where a foreign resident purchases a domestic asset are recorded as a positive amount—a **capital inflow**—and entries where a domestic resident purchases a foreign asset are recorded as a negative amount—a **capital outflow.** For example, if a British bank lends to a U.S. firm, this is a capital inflow, as the loan to the U.S. firm is an asset for the British bank. If a U.S. automobile manufacturer builds a new plant in Britain, this is a capital outflow for the United States, and it is part of **foreign direct investment** in Britain. Foreign direct investment is distinct from **portfolio inflows and outflows,** which are capital account transactions involving financial assets, including stocks and debt instruments. A helpful guideline in counting asset transactions in the capital account is that the transaction counts as a capital inflow if funds flow into the domestic country to purchase an asset, and as an outflow if funds flow out of the domestic country to purchase an asset.

The balance of payments is defined to be the current account surplus plus the capital account surplus. That is, letting BP denote the balance of payments, and KA the capital account surplus, we have

$$BP = KA + CA,$$

where CA is the current account surplus. A key element in balance of payments accounting is that the balance of payments is always zero (although it is not measured as such because of measurement error), so that

$$KA = -CA.$$

Therefore, the capital account surplus is always the negative of the current account surplus. If the current account is in deficit (surplus), then the capital account is in surplus (deficit). We have not discussed the capital account until now for this reason—the capital account surplus is just the flip side of the current account surplus, so that when we know the current account surplus, we know exactly what the capital account surplus is.

The balance of payments is always zero, because any transaction entering the balance of payments always has equal and opposite entries in the accounts. For example, suppose that a U.S. firm borrows the equivalent of $50 million in British pounds from a British bank so that it can purchase $50 million worth of auto parts in Britain to ship to the United States. The loan from the British bank enters as a capital inflow, because the British bank has accumulated a U.S. asset, and so there is an entry of $+\$50$ million in the capital account for the United States. Next, when the auto parts are purchased and imported into the United States, this enters as $-\$50$ million in the current account. Thus, in this as in all cases, the net effect on the balance of payments is zero. The offsetting entries associated with a given transaction need not be in the current account and the capital account, but in some cases could be all in the current account or all in the capital account.

The Effects of Capital Controls

In practice, capital controls can be imposed in terms of capital inflows or capital outflows, and they sometimes apply to foreign direct investment and sometimes to portfolio inflows and outflows. For example, restrictions on capital outflows were introduced in Malaysia in 1998 after the Asian crisis, and Chile used controls on capital inflows extensively from 1978 to 1982 and from 1991 to 1998. In both cases, the capital controls were in terms of portfolio inflows and outflows. Countries sometimes also restrict foreign direct investment, which is a control on capital inflows. Controls on foreign direct investment are sometimes put in place because of concern (perhaps misplaced) over the foreign ownership of the domestic capital stock.

What are the macroeconomic effects of capital controls? Essentially, capital controls alter the way in which the domestic economy responds to a shock. For example, suppose that there is a temporary negative shock to domestic total factor productivity under a flexible exchange rate. In Figure 15.12(a), suppose that the output demand curve is Y_1^d and the initial output supply curve is Y_1^s, and assume that initially the current account surplus is zero, with output equal to Y_1 at the world real interest rate r^*.

Figure 15.12 A Temporary Total Factor Productivity Shock, With and Without Capital Controls

With a temporary decrease in total factor productivity, under a flexible exchange rate there is a larger decrease in aggregate output and the current account surplus and a larger increase in the nominal exchange rate in the case without capital controls.

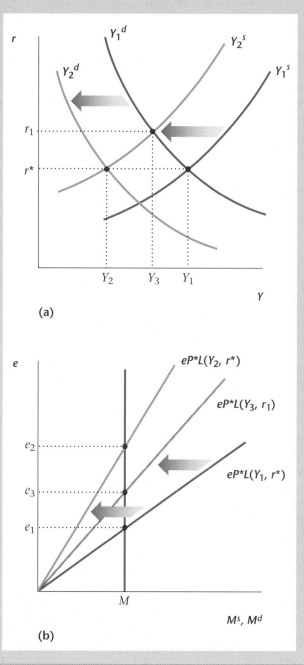

(a)

(b)

In Figure 15.12(b), the initial money demand curve is $eP^*L(Y_1, r^*)$, and the initial nominal exchange rate is e_1, given the nominal money supply M.

Now, suppose there is a temporary decrease in domestic total factor productivity, which shifts the output supply curve leftward to Y_2^s in Figure 15.12(a). With no capital controls in place, this implies that the current account surplus falls (with the current account then running a deficit), shifting the output demand curve to the left until it comes to rest at Y_2^d. Real output falls to Y_2 from Y_1, and consumption falls because of the decrease in income. In Figure 15.12(b), nominal money demand shifts leftward to $eP^*L(Y_2, r^*)$, and there is an exchange rate depreciation, with the nominal exchange rate increasing to e_2.

Now, assume an extreme form of capital controls where the government prohibits all capital inflows and outflows. This implies that the capital account surplus must be zero in equilibrium, and so the current account surplus must be zero as well. With a temporary decrease in domestic total factor productivity in Figure 15.12, the domestic real interest rate rises to r_1, which is above the world real interest rate r^*. In equilibrium, foreign investors would like to purchase domestic assets, as the return on domestic assets is greater than it is in the rest of the world, but they are prohibited from doing so. Thus, in this case, real output decreases to Y_3 in equilibrium. Assuming that money demand is much more responsive to real income than to the real interest rate, the money demand curve shifts to the left in Figure 15.12(b), although by less than it does in the case with no capital controls. The nominal exchange rate rises to e_3.

The results are that the nominal exchange rate increases by a smaller amount when capital controls are in place than when they are not, output falls by a smaller amount, and there is a smaller change in the current account deficit. Thus, capital controls tend to dampen aggregate fluctuations in output, the current account surplus, and the nominal exchange rate resulting from shocks of this type to the economy. If a country is concerned about the effects of fluctuations in the nominal exchange rate under a flexible exchange rate regime (for reasons that are not modeled here), capital controls tend to mitigate this problem, at least if the major source of shocks is temporary changes in total factor productivity. This solution is quite costly, however, as it produces an economic inefficiency. As in Chapter 5, the equilibrium allocation of resources is Pareto-optimal in this model in the absence of capital controls. With no capital controls, in this example, the domestic economy would face a lower real interest rate after the total factor productivity shock, and this means that lenders would be worse off and borrowers better off. Although some would win and some would lose from getting rid of capital controls, there would in general be an average gain in welfare.

Under a fixed exchange rate, Figure 15.12(a) still applies, but the money market works as in Figure 15.13. The nominal exchange rate is assumed to be fixed at e_1. Initially, the money supply is M_1, and in the absence of capital controls, the money supply declines to M_2, but with capital controls there is a decline in the money supply only to M_3. Here, fluctuations in the money supply are smaller with capital controls, which implies that foreign exchange reserves drop by a smaller amount with capital controls. Therefore, with capital controls in place a government can better support a fixed exchange rate, if exhausting the stock of foreign exchange reserves on hand is

Figure 15.13 A Total Factor Productivity Shock Under a Fixed Exchange Rate, With and Without Capital Controls

Under a fixed exchange rate, capital controls dampen the reduction in the money supply that occurs when there is a temporary decline in total factor productivity.

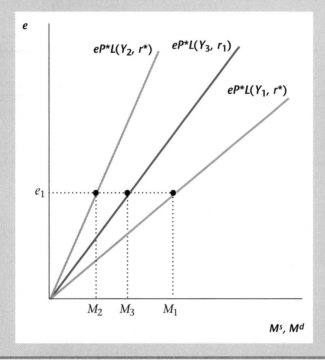

potentially a problem without controls. Again, though, capital controls come at a cost in lost economic efficiency.

While there are many more interesting issues to study in international macroeconomics, this chapter ends our discussion of this topic in this book. In Part VII, we move on to study topics in money and banking, unemployment, and inflation, which involve in-depth issues in closed-economy macroeconomics.

Chapter Summary

- We first studied purchasing power parity, or the law of one price, which predicts that prices are equated across countries in terms of the same currency. While there can be large and persistent deviations from purchasing power parity in practice, there are strong economic forces that move prices and exchange rates toward purchasing power parity over the long run. The purchasing power parity assumption is very useful in the model studied in this chapter.

- In the monetary small open-economy model the real interest rate and the foreign price level are determined on world markets.

MACROECONOMICS IN ACTION
Do Capital Controls Work in Practice?

With regard to how capital controls work in practice, we are primarily interested in two questions: (1) Can capital controls be effectively enforced, so that they have the intended effects? (2) How large are the economic inefficiencies that capital controls cause? In an article in the *Journal of Economic Perspectives*, Sebastian Edwards sets out to answer these questions, using the example of Chile.[4]

Edwards argues that there is little support by economists for restrictions on capital outflows, but that some economists have pointed to Chile as an example of how restrictions on capital inflows appeared to have worked well in practice. One aim of his article is to dismiss these latter arguments by studying the details of what happened in Chile, where controls on capital inflows were in place from 1978 to 1982 and from 1991 to 1998. These restrictions mainly applied to portfolio inflows of short-maturity securities, and they took the form of reserve requirements on these inflows. That is, if a foreigner purchased short-term, interest-bearing Chilean assets (a capital inflow), then a fraction of the value of these assets would have to be held as a non-interest-bearing deposit with the central bank of Chile. This had the same effect as would a tax on short-term capital inflows, as the non-interest-bearing deposits could otherwise be held in interest-bearing form.

What were the effects of the capital controls in Chile? Edwards finds that apparently many investors learned how to avoid the controls. While capital inflows appeared to have shifted somewhat toward longer-term inflows from shorter-term inflows, the shift was not that large, and investors seemed to have found many clever schemes for disguising short-term capital inflows as long-term ones. Edwards argues that the severe effects of the capital controls were on small and medium-sized Chilean firms, which faced much higher costs of borrowing.

Thus, the conclusion of Edwards's article is that the welfare costs of capital controls are small on average, mainly because the controls are ineffective, but the costs are large for some groups in the population. Edwards argues that capital controls should be phased out in countries where they still exist. However, he argues that in some cases this phaseout should be gradual. The inefficiencies caused by capital controls may in some cases be small relative to the potential inefficiencies arising from a poorly regulated banking system. If restrictions on capital inflows are relaxed quickly, then domestic banks can borrow more easily abroad so as to finance domestic lending. However, if domestic banks are improperly regulated (as we study in more depth in Chapter 16), then they take on too much risk, and this problem can be exacerbated in a wide-open international lending environment. The relaxation of capital controls sometimes needs to be coupled with improvements in the regulation of domestic financial institutions.

---

[4]S. Edwards, 1999, "How Effective Are Capital Controls?" *Journal of Economic Perspectives* 13, 65–84.

- Under a flexible exchange rate, money is neutral, and the domestic economy is insulated from nominal shocks from abroad, in that no real or nominal domestic variables are affected by a change in the foreign price level. The nominal exchange rate moves in equilibrium to absorb completely a shock to the foreign price level. However, the flexible exchange rate does not insulate the domestic price level against real shocks from abroad.

- A fixed exchange rate causes the domestic price level to increase in proportion to an increase in the foreign price level, but the fixed exchange rate regime insulates the domestic price level from foreign real shocks. Under a fixed exchange rate regime, a devaluation of the domestic currency might occur if the government's foreign exchange reserves are depleted. A devaluation raises the domestic price level.

- Whether a flexible exchange rate regime is preferred to a fixed exchange rate regime depends on a country's circumstances, but a flexible exchange rate regime implies that domestic monetary policy can be independent, whereas a fixed exchange rate regime implies that the domestic economy adopts the monetary policy of a foreign central bank.

- Capital controls involve restrictions on capital inflows and outflows, which are items in the capital account, where the asset transactions for a nation are added up. The balance of payments surplus is the sum of the capital account surplus and the current account surplus, and the balance of payments surplus is always zero.

- Capital controls can dampen fluctuations in output, the current account surplus, and the exchange rate (under a flexible exchange rate) or the money supply (under a fixed exchange rate), but these controls reduce economic efficiency. In practice, capital controls appear not to have been very effective, and in this sense they have not had large effects on efficiency.

Key Terms

Appreciation (of the exchange rate) A fall in the price of foreign currency in terms of domestic currency. (p. 546)

Balance of payments A system of accounts for a country for adding up all international transactions in goods and assets. (p. 559)

Bretton Woods arrangement A worldwide cooperative exchange rate system, in place from 1946 to 1971, under which the price of gold was fixed in terms of U.S. dollars, and there were fixed exchange rates for all other currencies in terms of the U.S. dollar. (p. 540)

Capital account The component of the balance of payments in which all international asset transactions between the domestic economy and foreign countries are added up. (p. 559)

Capital inflow The purchase of a domestic asset by a foreign resident, recorded as a positive entry in the capital account. (p. 559)

Capital outflow The purchase of a foreign asset by a domestic resident, recorded as a negative entry in the capital account. (p. 559)

Common currency area A region over which a single currency dominates as a medium of exchange. (p. 559)

Currency board An institution that fixes the exchange rate by holding foreign-currency-denominated interest-bearing assets and committing to buying and selling foreign exchange at a fixed rate of exchange. (p. 540)

Currency union A group of countries that agrees to become a common currency area. (p. 559)

Depreciation (of the exchange rate) A rise in the price of foreign currency in terms of domestic currency. (p. 544)

Devaluations Increases in the price of foreign exchange in terms of domestic currency. (p. 539)

Dollarize For a nation to abandon its own currency and adopt the currency of another country as its medium of exchange. (p. 539)

Euro The currency shared by the members of the EMU. (p. 540)

European Central Bank The central bank of the EMU countries. (p. 540)

European Monetary System (EMS) A cooperative exchange rate system in place among European countries from 1979 until 1999. (p. 540)

European Monetary Union (EMU) An organization of European countries, established in 1999, which shares a common currency, the Euro. (p. 540)

Fixed exchange rate regime A system under which the domestic government supports the value of the exchange rate at a specified level in terms of a foreign currency or currencies. (p. 537)

Flexible exchange rate regime A system under which a nation's nominal exchange rate is determined by market forces. (p. 537)

Foreign direct investment A capital inflow that involves the acquisition of a new physical asset by a foreign resident. (p. 559)

Hard pegs Exchange rate systems where there is a firm commitment to a fixed exchange rate, either through dollarization or a currency board. (p. 539)

International Monetary Fund An international monetary institution established in 1946, which was intended as a lender of last resort for its member countries, which now number 183. (p. 540)

Law of one price $P = eP^*$, where P is the domestic price, P^* is the foreign price, and e is the exchange rate. (p. 537)

Lender of last resort A centralized institution that lends to economic agents in distress; examples are central banks, which lend to domestic banks, and the IMF, which lends to its member countries. (p. 540)

Nominal exchange rate The price of foreign currency in terms of domestic currency, denoted by e in the model of this chapter. (p. 536)

Portfolio inflows and outflows Capital account transactions involving international transactions in financial assets. (p. 559)

Purchasing power parity (PPP) The same thing as the law of one price, except that P is the domestic price level and P^* is the foreign price level. (p. 537)

Revaluations Decreases in the price of foreign exchange in terms of domestic currency. (p. 539)

Soft pegs Exchange rate systems where the government commits to a fixed exchange rate for periods of time, but sometimes changes the value at which the exchange rate is fixed. (p. 539)

Questions for Review

1. Does purchasing power parity hold in practice in the short run? Why or why not? Does it hold in the long run? Why or why not?

2. What countries in the world have flexible exchange rates? Which have fixed exchange rates?

3. What are the different systems for fixing the exchange rate? Describe how each works.

4. Describe the role of the International Monetary Fund.

5. In the model constructed in this chapter, what are the effects on the domestic economy of an increase in the foreign price level under a flexible exchange rate and under a fixed exchange rate?

6. In the model, what are the effects on the domestic economy of an increase in the world real interest rate under a flexible exchange rate and under a fixed exchange rate?

7. In the model, is money neutral under a flexible exchange rate? Explain why or why not. Can we say that money is neutral under a fixed exchange rate? Explain.

8. Explain why domestic monetary policy is not independent under a fixed exchange rate.

9. What are the effects of a devaluation of the domestic currency under a fixed exchange rate?

10. List the key pros and cons of fixed versus flexible exchange rate regimes.

11. Give two examples of fixed exchange rates within the United States.

12. What are the advantages and disadvantages of a common currency area or currency union?

13. If the capital account surplus is positive, what can we say about the current account surplus?

14. Give two examples of countries where capital controls were imposed.

15. What do capital controls imply for the response of the economy to shocks?

16. Are capital controls a good idea? Why or why not?

17. Are capital controls effective in practice? Explain.

Problems

1. Suppose that there is a cost to carrying out transactions in the foreign exchange market. That is, to purchase one unit of foreign currency requires $e(1 + a)$ units of domestic currency, where e is the nominal exchange rate, and a is a proportional fee. Suppose that a decreases. What will be the equilibrium effects under a flexible exchange rate regime, and under a fixed exchange rate regime? Explain your results.

2. In the equilibrium small open-economy model, suppose that total factor productivity increases temporarily.
   (a) If the exchange rate is flexible, determine the effects on aggregate output, absorption, the current account surplus, the nominal exchange rate, and the price level.
   (b) Repeat part (a) for the case of a fixed exchange rate. If the goal of the domestic government is to stabilize the price level, would it be preferable to have a fixed exchange rate or a flexible exchange rate regime when there is a change in total factor productivity?
   (c) Now, suppose that under a flexible exchange rate regime, the domestic monetary authority controls the money supply so as to stabilize the price level when total factor productivity increases. Explain the differences between the outcome in this case and what happens in part (b) with a fixed exchange rate.

3. Suppose in the model that government expenditures increase temporarily. Determine the effects on aggregate output, absorption, the current account surplus, the nominal exchange rate, and the price level. What difference does it make if the exchange rate is flexible or fixed?

4. Suppose that better transaction technologies are developed that reduce the domestic demand for money. Use the monetary small open-economy model to answer the following:
   (a) Suppose that the exchange rate is flexible. What are the equilibrium effects on the price level and the exchange rate?
   (b) Suppose that the exchange rate is flexible, and the domestic monetary authority acts to stabilize the price level. Determine how the domestic money supply changes and the effect on the nominal exchange rate.
   (c) Suppose that the exchange rate is fixed. Determine the effects on the exchange rate and the price level, and determine the differences from your results in parts (a) and (b).

5. Consider a country with a flexible exchange rate, and which initially has a current account surplus of zero. Then, suppose there is an anticipated increase in future total factor productivity.
   (a) Determine the equilibrium effects on the domestic economy in the case where there are no capital controls. In particular, show that there will be a current account deficit when firms and consumers anticipate the increase in future total factor productivity.
   (b) Now, suppose that the government dislikes current account deficits, and that it imposes capital controls in an attempt to reduce the current account deficit. With the anticipated increase in future total factor productivity, what will be the equilibrium effects on the economy? Do the capital controls have the desired effect on the current account deficit? Do capital controls dampen the effects of the shock to the economy on output and the exchange rate? Are capital controls sound macroeconomic policy in this context? Why or why not?

6. Suppose a flexible exchange rate. There is an increase in the degree of uncertainty in credit

markets, which affects firms but not consumers, as considered in Chapter 9.

(a) Determine the effects on aggregate output, the price level, the exchange rate, and the real interest rate. Explain your results.

(b) Does this help to explain features of the financial crisis? Discuss.

7. The domestic central bank increases the supply of money under a flexible exchange rate regime, leading to a depreciation of the nominal exchange rate. If the government had imposed capital controls before the increase in the money supply, would this have had any effect on the exchange rate depreciation? Explain your results and comment on their significance.

8. Suppose that capital controls take the form of a total ban on capital inflows, but all capital outflows are permitted. Also suppose that initially the current account surplus is zero. Determine the effects of a temporary increase in total factor productivity and of a temporary decrease in total factor productivity under a flexible exchange rate. Carefully explain how and why your results differ in the two cases.

Working with the Data

1. Using the data from Figure 14.1, where e is the value of a Canadian dollar in terms of U.S. dollars, P is the U.S. consumer price index, and $P*$ is the Canadian consumer price index, construct a time series plot of e, $\frac{P*}{P}$, and $\frac{eP*}{P}$. What explains most of the variability in $\frac{eP*}{P}$ Is it variability in e or in $\frac{P*}{P}$? What does this tell us about the causes of changes in the real exchange rate in the short run?

2. Construct a time series plot of the German exchange rate relative to the U.S. dollar, the Japanese exchange rate relative to the dollar, and the Canadian exchange rate relative to the dollar. For comparability, scale these exchange rates so that they all are equal to 100 for the first data point. What do you observe in the time series plot? What does this tell us about how central banks in these countries control their exchange rates relative to the U.S. dollar?

3. Construct a scatter plot of the annual percentage changes (use December-to-December) in the U.S. trade-weighted exchange rate and the annual percentage changes in the monetary base. What do you observe? Is this consistent with the model constructed in this chapter?

PART VII

Topics in Macroeconomics

In this part, we deal with some in-depth topics. In Chapter 16, we study at a more detailed level the role of money in the economy, the forms that money has taken historically, the effects of long-run inflation on aggregate activity and economic welfare, and the role of banks and other financial intermediaries in the economy. Then, in Chapter 17 we study two models of unemployment, the search model and the efficiency wage model. Both models help explain why there are always unemployed people, even in a well-functioning economy, and they also help us understand the main determinants of the unemployment rate. Finally, in Chapter 18 we explain why central banks may cause inflation, even though it is well known that inflation is harmful. We use experience with inflation over the last 60 years in the United States as a backdrop in examining the role of central bank learning and commitment in inflation policy.

chapter 16

Money, Inflation, and Banking

In the monetary analysis we have done so far in this book, particularly in Chapters 11–13 and 15, we made some basic assumptions about how currency and credit cards are used in transactions to derive a demand for money function and proceeded from there. This allowed us to understand the effects of changes in the quantity of money, the role of money in the business cycle, and how money influences foreign exchange rates. In this chapter, we wish to gain a deeper understanding of the functions of money in the economy, to understand the long-run effects of inflation on aggregate economic activity and economic welfare, and to study the role of banks and other financial intermediaries in the economy.

In this chapter we first discuss how historical monetary systems worked, and we study the basic role of money in the economy in overcoming the difficulty of carrying out exchange using only commodities. Then, we return to the monetary intertemporal model developed in Chapter 11 and use this model to study the long-run effects of inflation. Empirically and in our model, long-run inflation is caused by growth in the money supply. We see that higher rates of money growth and inflation tend to reduce employment and output. This is because inflation erodes the purchasing power of money in the period between when labor income is earned and when it is spent. Thus, inflation tends to distort labor supply decisions. We show that an optimal long-run inflation policy for a central bank is to follow a **Friedman rule**, according to which the money supply grows at a rate that makes the rate of return on money identical to the rate of return on alternative assets and drives the nominal interest rate to zero. We discuss why real-world central banks do not appear to follow Friedman rules.

Finally, we examine the role of banks and other financial intermediaries in the economy. A **financial intermediary** is any financial institution that borrows from one large group of people and lends to another large group of people, transforms assets in some way, and processes information. Banks and other depository institutions are financial intermediaries that are of particular interest to macroeconomists for two reasons. First, some of the liabilities depository institutions issue are included in measures of the money supply and compete with currency as media of exchange. Second, depository institutions interact closely with the central bank and are typically on the receiving end of the first-round effects of monetary policy.

We study a simple model of a bank, which is the Diamond–Dybvig banking model. This model shows how banks supply a kind of insurance against the need to make transactions using liquid assets, why bank runs can occur (as happened in the Great Depression and before the existence of the Federal Reserve System), and why government-provided deposit insurance might prevent bank runs. We discuss the incentive problem that deposit insurance creates for banks. Finally, we examine the too-big-to-fail doctrine and its role in the financial crisis.

Alternative Forms of Money

In Chapter 11, we discussed how money functions as a medium of exchange, a store of value, and a unit of account, with the key distinguishing feature of money being its medium-of-exchange property. Although all money is a medium of exchange, historically there have been many different objects that have performed this role. The most important forms of money have been commodity money, circulating private bank notes, commodity-backed paper currency, fiat money, and transactions deposits at private banks. We discuss each of these in turn.

Commodity Money

This was the earliest money, in common use in Greek and Roman civilizations and in earlier times, and it was typically a precious metal, for example, gold, silver, or copper. In practice, commodity money systems involved having the government operate a mint to produce coins from precious metals, which then circulated as money. Control over the mint by the government was important, because the ability to issue money provided an important source of seigniorage revenue for the government. Commodity money systems, however, had several problems. First, the quality of any commodity is difficult to verify. For example, gold can be adulterated with other cheaper metals, so that there is an opportunity for fraud in the production of commodity money. Also, in the exchange of commodity monies, bits could be clipped off coins and melted down, with the hope that this would go undetected. Second, commodity money is costly to produce. For example, gold has to be dug out of the ground, minted, and then reminted when the coins wear out. Third, the use of a commodity as money diverts it from other uses. Gold and silver, for example, can also be used as jewelry and in industrial applications. In spite of these three problems, at the time commodity monies were used there were no good alternatives, mainly because any laws against the counterfeiting of paper currency would have been difficult or impossible to enforce. What may seem paradoxical is that the high cost of producing a commodity money was a virtue. To avoid inflation, the quantity of money must be in limited supply, and one characteristic of gold and silver that made them function well as commodity monies is their scarcity.

Circulating Private Bank Notes

In the **Free Banking Era** in the United States (1837–1863), and earlier, banks chartered by state governments issued pieces of paper that were exchanged hand-to-hand, much as currency is today. A system of note issue by private banks was also in place in Canada before 1935.[1] A problem during the Free Banking Era was that there were thousands of banks issuing notes, so that it was very difficult for a person offered a note in a particular location to evaluate its quality. For example, a storekeeper in Boston offered a note issued by a New Orleans bank may not have known whether this was an insolvent bank that might ultimately not redeem the note or if the New Orleans bank indeed even existed. Some characterize the Free Banking Era as chaotic, but the efficiency of free banking is an issue that is much debated by economic historians.[2]

Commodity-Backed Paper Currency

In this type of monetary system, there is government-issued paper currency, but the currency is backed by some commodity, as, for example, under the **gold standard.** The United States operated under the gold standard before 1933. Under the rules of the gold standard, the U.S. government stood ready to exchange currency for gold at some specified price, so that government currency was always redeemable in gold. Effectively, this was a commodity money system, but it saved on some of the costs of a commodity money, in that consumers did not have to carry large quantities of the commodity (in this case gold) around when they wanted to make large purchases.

Fiat Money

This is at least part of the monetary system in place in most modern economies. In the United States, fiat currency is the stock of Federal Reserve notes issued by the Fed. Fiat money consists of pieces of paper that are essentially worthless in that, for example, most people do not value U.S. Federal Reserve notes for their color or for the pictures on them. However, U.S. Federal Reserve notes are valued in that they can be exchanged for consumable goods. Why is fiat money accepted in exchange for goods? We accept fiat money because we believe that others will accept this money in exchange for goods in the future. This notion of the value of money supported by belief is intriguing, and it is part of what excites those who study monetary economics.

Transactions Deposits at Private Banks

In the United States, widespread deposit banking and the use of checks in transactions was mainly a post–Civil War phenomenon, and the U.S. financial system (and, similarly, the financial systems in most developed economies) has evolved to the point where much of the total volume of transactions is carried out through banks. With a bank deposit that can be transferred with a debit card or by writing a check, consumers can make purchases without the use of fiat money. A debit-card or checking transaction is

---

[1]See S. Williamson, 1989, "Restrictions on Financial Intermediaries and Implications for Aggregate Fluctuations: Canada and the United States 1870–1913," in *NBER Macroeconomics Annual 1989*, pp. 303–340, edited by Olivier Blanchard and Stanley Fischer, MIT Press, Cambridge MA; and B. Champ, B. Smith, and S. Williamson, 1996, "Currency Elasticity and Banking Panics: Theory and Evidence," *Canadian Journal of Economics* 29, 828–864.

[2]See, for example, B. Smith and W. Weber, 1999, "Private Money Creation and the Suffolk Banking System," *Journal of Money, Credit and Banking* 31, 624–659; and A. Rolnick and W. Weber, 1983, "New Evidence on the Free Banking Era," *American Economic Review* 73, 1080–1091.

a message that specifies that a given quantity of value is to be debited from the account of the person writing the check or using the debit card and credited to the account of the person on the other end of the transaction. If the accounts of the buyer and the seller are in different banks, then, for the correct accounts to be debited and credited, the transaction needs to be cleared through an interbank transaction. In the United States, most domestic transactions between financial institutions are cleared by means of **Fedwire**, a payments system operated by the Federal Reserve System.

Some readers may be concerned that we have not mentioned credit cards as a form of money. There is a good reason we have not done this—money and credit are fundamentally different. When a credit card purchase is made, the vendor of goods or services extends credit to the purchaser, and then this credit is transferred to the credit card issuer (Visa, Mastercard, or American Express, for example). The credit extended is not money in the sense that currency or a bank deposit is money, because the issuer of credit cannot use what is effectively an IOU of the purchaser as a medium of exchange. However, forms of credit, particularly credit cards, are a substitute for money in making transactions, and, therefore, they are important in terms of how we think about the monetary system. Indeed, in Chapter 11, we modeled the demand for credit card balances as an important component to explain the demand for money.

MACROECONOMICS IN ACTION
Commodity Money and Commodity-Backed Paper Money: Yap Stones and Playing Cards

A commodity money system that appears unusual on the surface but has several features common to other commodity money systems, is the exchange of so-called Yap stones on the island of Yap in Micronesia, as studied by the anthropologist William Henry Furness III in 1903.[3] On the island of Yap, there were large stones that served as money and measured from 1 foot to 12 feet in diameter.[4] These

---

[3]W. Furness, 1910, *The Island of Stone Money: Uap and the Carolines*, J. P. Lippincott Co., Philadelphia and London.

[4]You can see a picture and description of a Yap stone housed in the Federal Reserve Bank of Richmond's money museum at http://www.rich.frb.org/research/econed/museum/2.html.

stones were quarried from limestone deposits on another island about 400 miles from Yap and transported back by boat. What the Yap stones had in common with other commodity monies, such as gold and silver, was scarcity. It was quite costly in time and effort to create a new Yap stone, and the value of the stones increased with the difficulty in acquiring them, which might include weathering storms on the trip back to Yap. What seems different about the Yap stones as a commodity money is that they were extremely difficult to move around; an attractive feature of gold and silver as commodity monies was that the quantities required to make moderate-sized transactions were extremely portable. However, the Yap

(Continued)

islanders did not typically move the Yap stones when transactions were made. Yap stones were most often used to make large land transactions and to make large gifts, but the stones themselves usually stayed in a fixed location. It was well known to most of the small population of Yap who owned which stones, and a transaction involving a Yap stone was public knowledge, but there was no written record of ownership. Thus, it appears that exchange was actually carried out on the island of Yap using commodity-backed money. What changed hands in a transaction was the record of the ownership of the stone, which was stored in the collective memories of the islanders, and the stones were just the backing for the currency, which was not physical objects at all, but an entry in public memory.

Yap stones had much in common with the earliest known paper money used in North America, in New France, in 1685. There had been difficulties in keeping coins minted in France in circulation in New France (now the province of Quebec in Canada), as the coins were often used in payment for imports from France and, thus, left the colony. Therefore, the coins constantly had to be replenished by shipments from France in the form of payments to the troops in New France. In 1685, the shipment of coins was late in arriving from France, and De Meulles, the Intendant (governor of the colony) of New France authorized the issue of playing card money. De Meulles requisitioned the playing cards in the colony,

and the cards were issued, signed by him in different denominations, as payment to the troops. These playing cards were essentially IOUs, which promised payment in coin when the shipment arrived from France. The playing cards then circulated as a medium of exchange in New France, and they were subsequently retired, as promised. These cards were then issued repeatedly in later years, but ultimately the government of France lost interest in its colony in New France, and the shipments of coins did not arrive from France in the quantities promised, so that the IOUs that the playing cards represented could not be honored in full. There were problems with inflation, because of the temptation to issue the playing card money in excess of the promises that the Intendant could actually keep.[5]

Like the ownership rights to the Yap stones that circulated on the island of Yap, playing card money in New France was a commodity-backed money. However, the New France playing card monetary system seems to have been less successful than the Yap system, because the commodity backing of the playing card money was uncertain (due to the inability of public officials to keep their promises), whereas the existence of the Yap stones was well known to essentially everyone on the island of Yap.

---

[5]See http://collections.ic.gc.ca/bank/english/emar76 .htm for a description and photograph of card money in New France from the Bank of Canada currency museum.

Money and the Absence of Double Coincidence of Wants: The Role of Commodity Money and Fiat Money

Now that we know something about what objects have served as a medium of exchange, we consider in more detail what it means for some object to be a medium of exchange, which is the distinctive function of money. In this section, we consider a model that formalizes why money is useful as a medium of exchange. This model helps us understand the role of the two simplest types of money, commodity money and fiat money.

A fundamental question in monetary economics is why market exchange is typically an exchange of goods for money (monetary exchange) rather than of goods for goods (barter exchange). Jevons[6] argued that money helped to solve a problem of an **absence of double coincidence of wants** associated with barter exchange. To understand the double-coincidence-of-wants problem, imagine a world where there are many goods and people are specialized in what they wish to produce and consume. For example, suppose person *I* produces corn but wants to consume wheat. If person *I* meets another person *II* who has wheat, that would be a single coincidence of wants, because *II* has what *I* wants. However, *II* may not want corn in exchange for her wheat. If *II* wanted to consume corn, there would be a double coincidence of wants, because *I* wants what *II* has and *II* wants what *I* has. Barter exchange can only take place if there is a double coincidence. Now, searching for a trading partner is costly in time and resources (for example, hauling corn from place to place looking for a double coincidence of wants), particularly if there are many goods in the economy, so that there are many would-be sellers to search among. It would be much easier if, in selling corn, person *I* only needs to satisfy a single coincidence of wants, that is, find a person who wants corn. This would be the case if everyone accepted some object, called money. Then, in selling corn in exchange for wheat, all person *I* needs to do is to sell corn for money in a single-coincidence meeting, then sell money for wheat in another single-coincidence meeting.

To see how this might work, consider the following simple economy, depicted in Figure 16.1. This is an example from the work of Nobuhiro Kiyotaki and Randall Wright,[7] who formalized Jevons's notion of the role of money using modern dynamic methods. There are three types of people in this economy. Type *I* people consume good 1 and produce good 2, type *II* people consume good 2 and produce good 3, and type *III* people consume good 3 and produce good 1. There are many people of each type in the economy, and everyone lives forever, with people meeting each other pairwise and at random each period. That is, each person meets one other person each period, and that other person is someone he or she bumps into at random. If the people in this economy each produce their good, and then wait until they meet another person with whom they can engage in a barter exchange, everyone will wait forever to trade, because this economy has an absence of double coincidence of wants. This is the simplest type of example in which there are no possible pairwise meetings where a double coincidence of wants occurs.

How might trade be accomplished here? One solution would be for people to use a commodity money. Suppose, for example, that good 1 can be stored at a relatively low cost. Then good 1 might be used as a commodity money, in that type *II* people accept good 1 in exchange for good 3 when meeting type *III* people. Why does type *II* accept good 1 even though it is not something he or she consumes? This is because type *II* knows that type *I* accepts good 1 in exchange for good 2 (this is a double-coincidence

---

[6]See S. Jevons, 1910, *Money and the Mechanism of Exchange,* 23rd edition: Kegan Paul.

[7]N. Kiyotaki and R. Wright, 1989, "On Money as a Medium of Exchange," *Journal of Political Economy* 97, 927–954.

Figure 16.1 An Absence-of-Double-Coincidence Economy

In the model there are three types of people. A type *I* person consumes good 1 and produces good 2, a type *II* person consumes good 2 and produces good 3, and a type *III* person consumes good 3 and produces good 1.

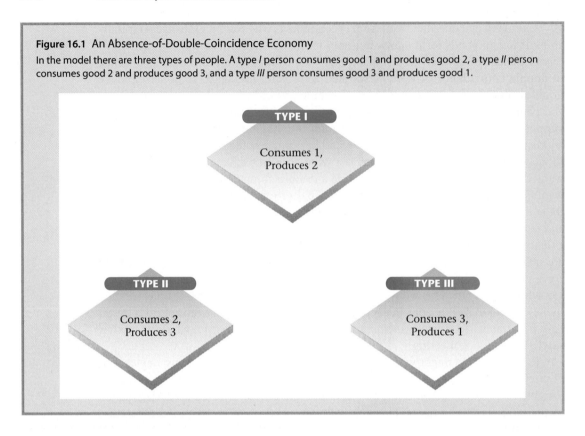

trade). Good 1 in this example is then a commodity money—a medium of exchange—as it is accepted in exchange by people who do not ultimately consume it. We show the equilibrium patterns of trade in Figure 16.2.

Another solution to the absence-of-double-coincidence problem would be the introduction of a fourth good, fiat money, which no one consumes but is acceptable to everyone in exchange for goods. A possible equilibrium pattern of exchange is shown in Figure 16.3. Here, when types *I* and *II* meet, *II* buys good 2 with money; when *I* and *III* meet, *I* buys good 1 with money; and when *III* and *II* meet, *III* buys good 3 with money. Thus, money circulates clockwise in Figure 16.3, and goods are passed counterclockwise.

For this model to say something interesting about the conditions under which commodity money would be useful, and when a fiat money system would be better than having commodity money, we would have to introduce costs of counterfeiting, the resource costs of producing commodity money, and so forth. This would be quite complicated to do. However, this simple model captures the essentials of the absence-of-double-coincidence problem and why this helps to make money socially useful in promoting exchange. Barter exchange is difficult, in fact impossible in this example, unless individuals accept in exchange objects that they do not consume. That is, a medium of exchange—money—is essential in allowing people to exchange

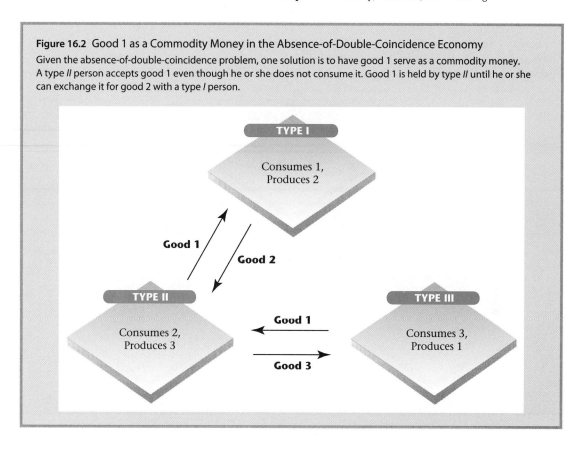

Figure 16.2 Good 1 as a Commodity Money in the Absence-of-Double-Coincidence Economy

Given the absence-of-double-coincidence problem, one solution is to have good 1 serve as a commodity money. A type *II* person accepts good 1 even though he or she does not consume it. Good 1 is held by type *II* until he or she can exchange it for good 2 with a type *I* person.

what they do not want for what they want, and it, therefore, increases welfare. In fact, in this example the institution of money is a Pareto improvement (recall our discussion from Chapter 5), because it increases welfare for everyone over what it would be otherwise.

Long–Run Inflation in the Monetary Intertemporal Model

The institution of monetary exchange matters for the determination of real macro-economic quantities and contributes in important ways to economic welfare in modern economies. Once this institution is in place, however, the money supply can change in ways that have no consequences at all for real macroeconomic variables or for welfare. Although short-run monetary nonneutralities might arise because of segmented markets (studied in Chapter 12) sticky prices (studied in Chapter 13), or money surprises (to be studied later, in Chapter 18), in the long run money is neutral (as we showed in Chapter 11), in that a one-time level increase in the stock of money only changes prices in proportion and has no long-run effects on real variables.

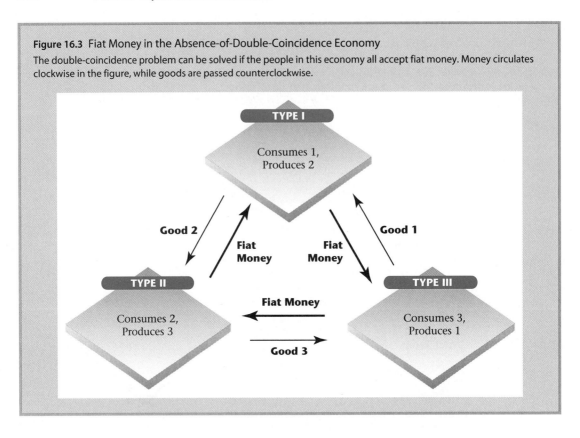

Figure 16.3 Fiat Money in the Absence-of-Double-Coincidence Economy

The double-coincidence problem can be solved if the people in this economy all accept fiat money. Money circulates clockwise in the figure, while goods are passed counterclockwise.

Although money is neutral in the long run, in that a change in the *level* of the money supply has no long-run real effects, changes in the *growth rate* of the money supply are not neutral. It should not be surprising, because an increase in the level of the money supply causes an increase in the price level, that an increase in the rate of growth in the money supply causes an increase in the rate of growth in the price level, that is, an increase in the inflation rate. Using the monetary intertemporal model we constructed in Chapter 11, we are able to show why money growth and inflation are costly in terms of lost aggregate output and misallocation of resources. Further, we determine an optimal prescription for monetary growth, often referred to as the Friedman rule for monetary policy, after Milton Friedman. The Friedman rule for optimal money growth is that money should grow at a rate that implies that the nominal interest rate is zero. It turns out that the optimal money growth rate and the implied optimal inflation rate are negative.

There are many factors that can cause changes in the price level, some of which we have explored in Chapters 11 to 13. For example, a change in total factor productivity changes equilibrium aggregate output Y and the equilibrium real interest rate r, and this shifts the money demand curve and causes a change in the price level. However, sustained inflations, where the price level continues to increase over a long period of time, are usually the result of sustained growth in the money supply. In Figure 16.4 we

Figure 16.4 Inflation Versus Money Growth: 1960–2007

The inflation rate is the percentage increase in the consumer price index from the same month in the previous year, while the money growth rate is the percentage increase in the monetary base, calculated in the same way. The two variables are positively correlated, as indicated by the positively sloped line that provides the best statistical fit, reflecting the long-run effects of money growth on inflation. The many short run non-monetary factors affecting inflation make the relationship noisy.

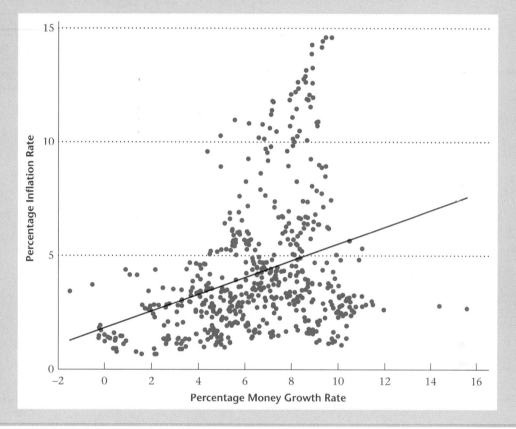

plot the rate of inflation in the United States (the percentage increase in the CPI over the previous 12 months) for the period 1960–2007 against the percentage rate of growth in the monetary base, M0, calculated in the same way. There is a positive relationship between the two, in that the positively sloped straight line in the figure is the best fit to the set of points, but the relationship is quite noisy, which reflects that there are factors in addition to money growth affecting the rate of inflation in the short run. The causal link between money growth and inflation was emphasized by Milton Friedman and Anna Schwartz in *A Monetary History of the United States 1867–1960*.[8]

---

[8]M. Friedman and A. Schwartz, 1960, *A Monetary History of the United States 1867–1960*, Princeton University Press, Princeton, NJ.

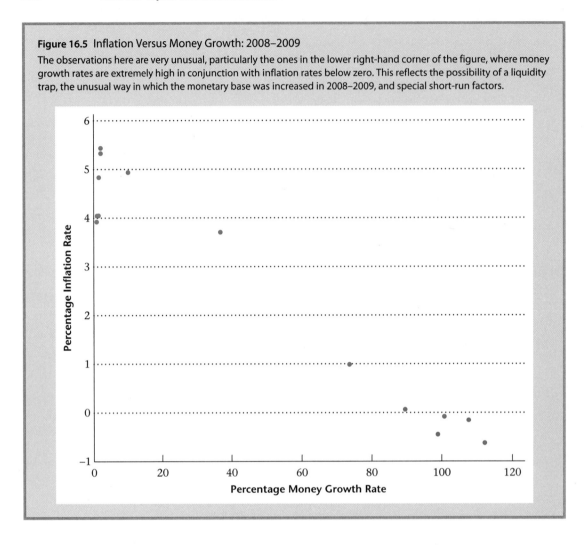

Figure 16.5 Inflation Versus Money Growth: 2008–2009

The observations here are very unusual, particularly the ones in the lower right-hand corner of the figure, where money growth rates are extremely high in conjunction with inflation rates below zero. This reflects the possibility of a liquidity trap, the unusual way in which the monetary base was increased in 2008–2009, and special short-run factors.

Figure 16.5 shows the same variables as in Figure 16.4, but for the months of January 2008 through April 2009. This figure is quite striking, as it shows a negative correlation between money growth and inflation. Indeed, the observations in the lower right-hand corner of the figure represent months in which the percentage increase in the monetary base was around 100% from the previous year (much greater than anything observed over the previous 50 years), but the inflation rate was at or below 0%. Here, the relationship between money growth and inflation does not look anything like what we would expect, from basic economic theory. Some of the reasons for the observations in Figure 16.5 were discussed in Chapters 11, 12, and 13—i.e., the possibility of a liquidity trap and the unusual way in which the Fed increased the monetary base in late 2008 and early 2009. Further, this could just reflect the fact that it takes time for a money supply increase, however large, to be reflected in price increases—money is neutral only in the long run.

To understand the effects of long-run inflation, we allow the money supply to grow forever at a constant rate in the monetary intertemporal model. We suppose that the government permits the money supply to grow by making lump-sum transfers to the representative household each period, with the money supply growing according to

$$M' = (1 + x)M \qquad (16\text{-}1)$$

where M' is the future money supply, M is the current money supply, and x is the growth rate of the money supply from the current period to the future period. For simplicity, we suppose that the economy looks exactly the same in every period, in that total factor productivity, real government spending, and consumer preferences are identical in every period. The only exogenous variable that changes over time is the money supply, which grows according to equation (16-1). This implies that all of the endogenous variables in the model, except the price level, remain the same for all time. That is, the real wage, employment, aggregate output, the real interest rate, and the inflation rate are constant for all time. In the current period, money supply is equal to money demand in equilibrium, and so from Chapter 11, we have

$$M = PL(Y, r + i). \qquad (16\text{-}2)$$

Recall from Chapter 12 that, on the left-hand side of equation (16-2), M is the nominal money supply and, on the right-hand side of equation (16-2), $PL(Y, r + i)$ is nominal money demand. From the Fisher relation, recall that $r + i$ (the real interest rate plus the inflation rate) is equal (approximately) to the nominal interest rate. It must also be the case in equilibrium that money supply is equal to money demand in the future period, so that

$$M' = P'L(Y', r' + i'), \qquad (16\text{-}3)$$

where P' is the price level in the future period, Y' is future aggregate output, r' is the future real interest rate, and i' is the future inflation rate. Then, from equations (16-2) and (16-3), we have

$$\frac{M'}{M} = \frac{P'L(Y', r' + i')}{PL(Y, r + i)} \qquad (16\text{-}4)$$

But in equilibrium, aggregate output, the real interest rate, and the inflation rate remain constant over time, which implies that $Y' = Y, r' = r$, and $i' = i$. This then gives $L(Y', r' + i') = L(Y, r + i)$, so that the real demand for money is the same in the future and current periods. Then, from equation (16-4), we get

$$\frac{M'}{M} = \frac{P'}{P},$$

so that the growth rates of the money supply and the price level are the same in equilibrium. This implies, from equation (16-1), that the inflation rate is given by

$$i = \frac{P'}{P} - 1 = \frac{M'}{M} - 1 = x,$$

so that the inflation rate is equal to the money growth rate. The equality of the money growth rate and the inflation rate is special to this situation in which real variables remain constant over time. From equation (16-4), if the real demand for money changes over time, so that $L(Y', r' + i') \neq L(Y, r + i)$, then the money growth rate is not equal to the inflation rate. However, it is still true that the inflation rate will increase as the money growth rate increases.

We wish to determine the effects of an increase in x on output, the real interest rate, employment, and the real wage in the monetary intertemporal model. To do this, we first need to understand how inflation affects labor supply and the demand for current consumption goods in this model. Recall from Chapter 11 that, in the monetary intertemporal model, consumption goods are purchased using currency acquired by the representative consumer before the goods market opens and that the consumer receives his or her wage income after goods are purchased, so that wage income must be held in the form of currency before it is spent in the future period. Just as in Chapter 8, when the representative consumer optimizes, he or she sets the marginal rate of substitution of current consumption goods for future consumption goods equal to $1 + r$, or

$$MRS_{C,C'} = 1 + r. \tag{16-5}$$

As well, because current wages cannot be spent on consumption goods until the future period, the effective real wage for the consumer is $\frac{Pw}{P'}$, which is the current nominal wage divided by the future price level. Therefore (recall Chapter 4), when the consumer optimizes, he or she sets the marginal rate of substitution of current leisure for future consumption equal to $\frac{Pw}{P'}$ or

$$MRS_{l,C'} = \frac{Pw}{P'} \tag{16-6}$$

Now, because equations (16-5) and (16-6) tell us how the consumer substitutes at the optimum between current and future consumption and between current leisure and future consumption, we can derive from these two equations a marginal condition for substitution at the optimum between current leisure and current consumption. That is, at the optimum it must be the case that

$$MRS_{l,C} = \frac{MRS_{l,C'}}{MRS_{C,C'}} = \frac{Pw}{P'(1 + r)},$$

from equations (16-5) and (16-6). Therefore, from the Fisher relation in Chapter 11, we have

$$MRS_{l,C} = \frac{w}{1 + R}, \tag{16-7}$$

where R is the nominal interest rate. To understand the marginal condition, equation (16-4), it helps to run through how the consumer would substitute between current consumption and current leisure, which is roundabout because of the cash-in-advance constraint. If the consumer wishes to supply one extra unit of time during the current period as labor, he or she earns additional real wages of w, which then must be held over to the future period, when their value in terms of future consumption goods is $\frac{Pw}{P'}$. To consume more current goods, the consumer can borrow against this amount in the credit market before he or she arrives in the goods market. The real quantity that can be borrowed is $\frac{Pw}{P'(1 + r)} = \frac{w}{1 + R}$, which then must be the relative price of current leisure for current consumption.

Given equation (16-7), a higher nominal interest rate R causes substitution away from consumption goods and toward leisure. Equation (16-4) then tells us that, from the approximate Fisher relation $R = r + i$, given the real interest rate r and the real wage w, and assuming that substitution effects dominate income effects, an increase in the inflation rate i causes substitution from consumption goods to leisure.

In Figure 16.6 we show the effects in the current period of an increase in the money growth rate from x_1 to x_2, which takes place for all periods, and is anticipated by everyone. In equilibrium the inflation rate in every period then increases from x_1 to x_2, given our analysis above where we showed that the money growth rate equals the inflation rate in equilibrium. The increase in the inflation rate causes substitution by the representative consumer from consumption goods to leisure. This causes the labor supply curve to shift to the left in Figure 16.6(a), which in turn shifts the output supply curve to the left in Figure 16.6(b). As well, because the consumer substitutes away from consumption goods, the output demand curve shifts to the left in Figure 16.6(b). Now, in

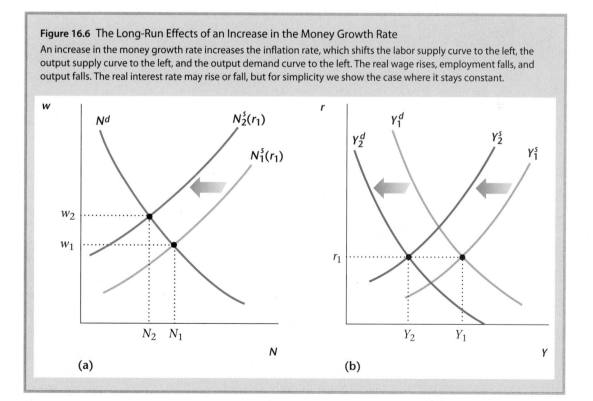

Figure 16.6 The Long-Run Effects of an Increase in the Money Growth Rate

An increase in the money growth rate increases the inflation rate, which shifts the labor supply curve to the left, the output supply curve to the left, and the output demand curve to the left. The real wage rises, employment falls, and output falls. The real interest rate may rise or fall, but for simplicity we show the case where it stays constant.

(a)

(b)

Figure 16.6(b), it is not clear whether the real interest rate rises or falls. For simplicity, we show the case where the output demand and output supply effects on the real interest rate just cancel, so that the real interest rate does not change. This also implies that investment and the capital stock are unaffected (assume that we are in a steady state where the capital stock is constant over time), which also greatly simplifies matters.

In Figure 16.6, in equilibrium output falls from Y_1 to Y_2, employment falls from N_1 to N_2, and the real wage rises from w_1 to w_2. In the figure the real interest rate remains constant, so that investment expenditures are unaffected, but consumption must fall as real income has decreased. From the approximate Fisher relation, we have $R = r + i$, where R is the nominal interest rate. Therefore, because r is constant, and i increases from x_1 to x_2, the nominal interest rate increases by the amount of the money growth rate increase (the **Fisher effect**; in the long run, an increase in the inflation rate is reflected one-for-one in an increase in the nominal interest rate). Also, given equilibrium in the money market,

$$\frac{M}{P} = L(Y, r + i), \tag{16-8}$$

real output Y has decreased, r is the same, and i has increased; therefore, real money demand on the right-hand side of equation (16-8) has decreased, so the current real money supply on the left-hand side of equation (16-8) must also decrease. Higher money growth and inflation causes the consumer to hold a smaller quantity of real cash balances in equilibrium.

Although money is neutral in this economy, in that a change in the level of the money supply has no real effects, a change in the growth rate of the money supply is not neutral. If a change in the money growth rate had no real effects, we would say that money was **superneutral.** However, money is not superneutral here, as an increase in the money growth rate leads to decreases in consumption, output, and employment. These effects occur because higher money growth leads to higher inflation, which affects the consumer's decisions concerning how much to work in the current period and how much and what to consume. Higher inflation increases the nominal interest rate, which is the opportunity cost of holding money for transactions purposes. As a result, the household economizes on money balances. The resulting costs of inflation are lost output and consumption.

Optimal Monetary Policy: The Friedman Rule

At this point, we would like to demonstrate the key economic inefficiencies that result from inflation, then show how these inefficiencies can be corrected by the appropriate long-run monetary policy. Recall from Chapter 5 that economic efficiency is achieved when the allocation of resources in an economy is Pareto-optimal, that is, when there is no way to rearrange production or the allocation of goods so that someone is better off and no one worse off. A key condition for Pareto-optimality that we derived in Chapter 5 was that the marginal rate of substitution of leisure for consumption must be equal to the marginal rate of transformation of leisure for consumption, that is,

$$MRS_{l,C} = MRT_{l,C}. \tag{16-9}$$

This condition applies at the Pareto-optimum because it is efficient for the rate at which the consumer is just willing to substitute leisure for consumption to be equal to the rate at which leisure can be converted into consumption goods using the production technology. Now in this model, as in the model of Chapter 5, the marginal rate of transformation of leisure for consumption is equal to the marginal product of labor, MP_N. In a competitive equilibrium, profit maximization by the representative firm implies that $MP_N = w$, so it is also true in a competitive equilibrium that

$$MRT_{l,C} = w. \tag{16-10}$$

Therefore, substituting for w in equation (16-7) using equation (16-10) gives

$$MRS_{l,C} = \frac{MRT_{l,C}}{1 + R}. \tag{16-11}$$

Therefore, because equation (16-11) holds in competitive equilibrium in this model, equation (16-9) does not hold, and so the competitive equilibrium is not Pareto-optimal, in general, as long as the nominal interest rate is positive, or $R > 0$. That is, a positive nominal interest rate drives a "wedge" between the marginal rate of substitution and the marginal rate of transformation, thus, creating an inefficiency. The fact that the nominal interest rate is positive implies that too much leisure is consumed, too little output is produced, consumption is too low, and real money balances are too low.

We know that an increase in the money growth rate x causes an increase in the nominal interest rate, so that higher money growth, which is associated with higher inflation, implies a larger wedge separating the marginal rate of substitution from the marginal rate of transformation. If the money growth rate and inflation were reduced, then it appears that this would promote economic efficiency, but what would be the best money growth rate for the government to set? Clearly, if the nominal interest rate were reduced to zero, then the marginal rate of substitution would be equal to the marginal rate of transformation in equation (16-11). What is the money growth rate x that would drive the nominal interest rate to zero? Because in equilibrium the nominal interest rate is $R = r + x$, if $R = 0$, then it is optimal for the money growth rate to be $x = -r$. Because the real interest rate is positive ($r > 0$), then at the optimum $x < 0$ and the money supply decreases over time. Further, if the money supply is decreasing over time, there is **deflation**, because the inflation rate is $i = x = -r < 0$. Thus, it is optimal for the government to generate a deflation that continues forever, implying that the nominal interest rate is zero in every period.

Another source of efficiency gains from reducing the nominal interest rate to zero is that this reduces the costs of supplying cash alternatives by the banking system. Recall from Chapter 11 that a decrease in the nominal interest rate will cause the representative consumer and the representative firm to reduce their use of credit balances in making transactions. This was why the demand for money rose with a decrease in the nominal interest rate. Now, if the nominal interest rate is reduced to zero, then in our model credit card balances go to zero, so that all transactions are conducted with currency. When credit card balances are zero, then the total costs absorbed by the banking system are zero. This result is perhaps implausible, as we would not think that the banking system would disappear if there were a deflation that caused the nominal interest rate to fall to zero. If we were to take account, for example, of the safekeeping services of banks, this would not happen. That is, people never want to conduct all of their transactions using currency, as this would require carrying around large quantities of cash and risking theft. The main ideas here would remain intact if we added the risk of theft to our model, but this would be much more complicated.

The fact that the optimal monetary policy drives the nominal interest rate to zero is of prime importance in understanding why this policy works to maximize welfare. A positive nominal interest rate on bonds implies that the representative consumer economizes too much on money balances in favor of holding bonds. The consumer also consumes too small a quantity of goods and too much leisure. If the nominal interest rate is driven to zero through deflation, giving money a higher real return, then the household becomes indifferent between holding bonds and money, and this is optimal.

This type of optimal deflationary monetary policy is called a Friedman rule, after Milton Friedman.[9] In practice, the Friedman rule means that the nominal interest rate on riskless securities should always be zero. This does not mean that all nominal interest rates should be zero (this would be impossible), but that the nominal interest rate on short-term government debt (for example, U.S. Treasury bills) should be zero. The Friedman rule is probably the most robust policy conclusion that comes from monetary economics, but it is a policy that essentially no central bank currently follows or ever has followed. No central bank pursues long-run deflation as a goal, and no central bank advocates pushing the nominal interest rate to zero permanently. The policies pursued by the Fed and other central banks in late 2008, continuing into 2009, are not Friedman rule policies. For example, the Fed clearly intends to target the short-term nominal interest rate at something above zero in the not-too-distant future. In not following a Friedman rule, central banks are doing something wrong; our model leaves out some important aspect(s) of the problem at hand, or inflation just does not matter much.

To pursue the last explanation, one possible reason central banks do not follow the Friedman rule is that, at low levels of inflation, say below 10% per annum, the gains from reducing inflation are very small. Indeed, Thomas Cooley and Gary Hansen[10] conclude that, in a monetary model similar to the one we have studied here, the welfare loss from an inflation rate of 10% per annum is about 0.5% of consumption for the average consumer, and the welfare loss from a monetary rule with 0% inflation versus the Friedman rule rate of deflation is about 0.14% of consumption for the average consumer.

Although most macroeconomic models tell us that the welfare losses from moderate inflations are quite small, the costs of extremely high rates of inflation—that is, **hyperinflations**—are clearly very large. Some prominent hyperinflations occurred in Austria, Hungary, Germany, and Poland in the early 1920s following World War I. For example, the inflation rate in Austria averaged 10,000% per annum between January 1921 and August 1922. Typically, hyperinflations occur because the government is unwilling

---

[9]See "The Optimum Quantity of Money," in M. Friedman, 1969, *The Optimum Quantity of Money and Other Essays*, pp. 1–50, Aldine Publishing, Hawthorne, NY.

[10]See T. Cooley and G. Hansen, 1989, "The Inflation Tax in a Real Business Cycle Model," *American Economic Review* 79, 733–748.

or unable to finance large government outlays through taxation or borrowing, and so it must resort to seigniorage. For example, the German hyperinflation following World War I occurred in part because the German government financed large war reparations to other European countries by printing money at a very high rate. The key to stopping a hyperinflation, as Thomas Sargent points out,[11] is gaining control over fiscal policy by reducing the government deficit.

Another reason that central bankers are wary of deflation and low nominal interest rates is that these have been characteristics of poorly performing economies. For example, there were deflation and low nominal interest rates in the United States during the Great Depression and more recently in Japan. The Japanese economy has performed poorly since the early 1990s, and short-term nominal interest rates there have been essentially zero. Keynes argued that, at a low nominal interest rate, there could be a **liquidity trap.** That is, if the nominal interest rate on government securities is zero, then money and government securities are essentially identical assets. If the central bank attempts to increase the money supply through an open market sale of government securities when the nominal interest rate is zero, this will have no effect, as the central bank is simply exchanging one type of asset for another identical asset. Perhaps central bankers fear a liquidity trap, but the logic of the Friedman rule tells us that a liquidity trap is a good place to be, and, in any event, an escape from the liquidity trap is possible if the government simply prints money and increases the money supply through transfers.

Financial Intermediation and Banking

The purpose of this section is to study the place of banks and other financial intermediaries in the monetary system. Earlier in this chapter we discussed the historical importance of currency issued by private banks and how in modern economies much of transactions activity takes place using bank deposits. The role that banks and other financial intermediaries play in the economy is intimately related to the properties that different assets have, and so in the following subsection we discuss the characteristics of assets and their economic importance.

Properties of Assets
The four most important properties of assets are rate of return, risk, maturity, and liquidity; we discuss each of these in turn.

Rate of Return   The rate of return on an asset is the payoff on the asset over some specified period of time divided by the initial investment in the asset, minus one. For example, the one-period rate of return on an asset that is bought at price q_t in period t, sold at price q_{t+1} in period $t + 1$, with a payout (say a dividend on a stock) of d in period $t + 1$, would be

$$r_t^a = \frac{q_{t+1} + d}{q_t} - 1.$$

Everything else held constant, consumers prefer assets that bear higher rates of return.

---

[11]See "The Ends of Four Big Inflations," in T. Sargent, 1993, *Rational Expectations and Inflation,* 2nd edition, pp. 43–116, Harper Collins, New York.

MACROECONOMICS IN ACTION
Should the Fed Reduce the Inflation Rate to Zero or Less?

Our monetary intertemporal model tells us that the optimal rate of inflation is negative, which implies that the Fed should engineer a rate of growth in the money supply that would give permanent deflation. However, as we pointed out, no central bank appears to have attempted to bring about a deflation. At most, some policymakers are willing to recommend that the inflation rate be reduced to zero, so that the price level will remain constant over time. For example, in 1989 a bill was introduced in the House of Representatives that would have directed the Fed to reduce the inflation rate to zero over a five-year period. Does this imply that there is something that the monetary intertemporal model is missing in terms of the costs and benefits of inflation? Could the optimal inflation rate be higher than zero? S. Rao Aiyagari, in "Deflating the Case for Zero Inflation,"[12] makes the case that the costs of reducing the inflation rate to zero would exceed the benefits. In making his argument, Aiyagari appeals to some of the costs of inflation that are contained in our monetary intertemporal model, but he considers other costs and benefits of inflation as well.

First, as in our model, Aiyagari argues that a cost of inflation arises because the nominal interest rate is positive, which causes people to economize too much on money balances. He points out that some of these costs could be eliminated if interest were paid on some components of the money stock. Indeed, the Fed

---

[12]See S. R. Aiyagari, 1990, "Deflating the Case for Zero Inflation," *Federal Reserve Bank of Minneapolis Quarterly Review*, Summer, 2–11.

began paying interest on bank reserves, at approximately the interest rate on short-term government debt, late in 2008. However, it is currently prohibited for depository institutions to pay interest on demand deposits, which are transactions deposits held by businesses. If interest were paid at the market interest rate on reserves and demand deposits, then only currency would be a non-interest-bearing asset. Currency is a fraction of the total money supply, and at that, much of the stock of U.S. currency is held by foreigners or held for illegal purposes. Inflation acts as a tax on currency holding, but if this tax falls mostly on foreigners and people engaged in illegal transactions, then inflation is not so costly for U.S. residents, and it might deter crime.

While the costs of inflation are very small, as Aiyagari argues, the short-run costs of reducing the inflation rate might potentially be large. Keynesian economists argue that price and wage stickiness can cause short-run decreases in aggregate output if the Fed were to reduce money supply growth to bring about a reduction in inflation, as we studied in Chapter 13. As well, if the private sector doubts the Fed's resolve to reduce inflation, this can cause a short-run drop in aggregate activity until the Fed proves that it is serious, an issue we address in Chapter 18. Given these potentially large short-run costs, Aiyagari concludes that a reduction in the inflation rate to zero would not be worthwhile, but that relaxing regulations on the banking sector—for example, by permitting the payment of interest on all transactions deposits—would certainly be beneficial.

Risk   In modern finance theory, the risk that matters for a consumer's behavior is the risk that an asset contributes to the consumer's entire portfolio, where a portfolio is the entire set of assets the consumer holds. For example, a set of stocks might be quite risky on an individual basis, in that their rates of return fluctuate a great deal over time. However, when all these stocks are held together in a well-diversified portfolio, the entire portfolio may not be very risky. For instance, holding all of one's wealth in shares of Joe's Restaurant might be quite risky, but holding shares in all the restaurants in town might not be very risky at all. Even though diversifying one's portfolio by holding many different assets reduces risk, because the rates of return on some assets can go up while other rates of return go down, there is a limit to the risk reduction that can be gained from diversification. Risk that cannot be diversified away is aggregate or macroeconomic risk, and it is the amount of this **nondiversifiable risk** present in a particular asset that matters for economic behavior. Here, we assume that consumers are **risk-averse**, so that, everything else held constant, a consumer prefers to hold assets with less nondiversifiable risk.

Maturity   Maturity refers to the time it takes for an asset to pay off. For some assets, maturity is a straightforward concept. For example, a 91-day U.S. Treasury bill is a security issued by the U.S. government that pays its face value 91 days from the date of issue, so maturity in this case is 91 days. For some other assets, however, this is not so clear, as in the case of a long-maturity bond. Many bonds provide for coupon payments, which are amounts the bearer receives at fixed intervals until the bond matures, when it pays its face value. Thus, a 30-year bond that provides for coupon payments at monthly intervals does not have a maturity of 30 years, but something less than that, because the payoffs on the asset take place during the 30-year period until all payoffs are received. All other things held constant, a consumer prefers a short-maturity asset to a long-maturity asset. Short-maturity assets imply more flexibility in meeting unanticipated needs for funds, and even if a consumer is certain that the funds will not be needed until far in the future (suppose the consumer is saving for a child's education, for example), it is possible to meet this need by holding a string of short-maturity assets rather than a long-maturity asset.

Liquidity   The final asset characteristic is liquidity, which is a measure of how long it takes to sell an asset for its market value, and of how high the costs are of selling the asset. Because money is widely acceptable in exchange and can, therefore, essentially be sold for its market value instantaneously, it is the most liquid asset. A good example of an illiquid asset is a house, which can often take weeks or longer to sell, with a high transaction fee paid to an intermediary—the real estate agent—to find a buyer. Liquidity is important to an asset holder, because investors face uncertainty about when they want to purchase goods or assets. For example, consumers may face unforeseen expenses such as medical bills, or they may want to take advantage of an unanticipated investment opportunity. All else held constant, consumers prefer more liquidity to less liquidity.

Financial Intermediation

Now that we know something about the properties of assets, we can examine the role of financial intermediaries in the monetary system.

A financial intermediary is defined by the following characteristics:

1. It borrows from one group of economic agents and lends to another.
2. The group of economic agents it borrows from is large, and so is the group it lends to. That is, a financial intermediary is well diversified.
3. It transforms assets. That is, the properties of its liabilities are different from the properties of its assets.
4. It processes information.

Examples of financial intermediaries are insurance companies, mutual funds, and depository institutions. The economic role that these intermediaries play is intimately related to their four defining characteristics. Suppose that we consider depository institutions as an example. Depository institutions include commercial banks, thrift institutions (savings and loan associations and mutual savings banks), and credit unions. These institutions exist in part because of difficulties in getting ultimate borrowers and ultimate lenders together. To see why this is so, consider how the borrowing and lending done by a depository institution would take place in the absence of this institution. An individual wanting to borrow to start up a business, for example, would have to first find a lender willing to loan him or her the funds. Even if the would-be borrower were well known to the would-be lender, the would-be lender may not have good information on the would-be borrower's ability to repay the loan, and some time and effort would have to be forgone to acquire this information. Further, given that the loan required is sizable, the would-be borrower might have to approach several would-be lenders to finance the business startup, and each of these would-be lenders would have to incur information costs to ascertain the riskiness of lending to the would-be borrower. Now, supposing the loan is made, each of the lenders would bear some risk, given that there is always some chance that the borrower will not repay the loan. Further, unless the lenders had the means to enforce the loan contract, the borrower might try to abscond with the loan without repaying, even though he or she could repay. Finally, after the loan is made, it would be difficult for the lender to sell the loan to someone else should he or she require funds at short notice. That is, the loan is illiquid, in part because it has a long maturity, supposing that it will take a long period of time for the borrower's business to become profitable. In fact, the funds required to start up the business might be very large relative to the monthly profit the business will yield. As a result, the maturity of the loan may be so long that few would-be lenders would want to tie up funds for this length of time. To summarize, there are six potential problems with direct lending from ultimate lenders to ultimate borrowers, without the benefit of a financial intermediary:

1. Matching borrowers with lenders is costly in time and effort.
2. The ultimate lenders may not be skilled at evaluating credit risks.
3. Because several lenders would often be required to fund any one borrower, there would be replication of the costs required to evaluate credit risk.
4. Because lenders economize on information costs by lending to few borrowers, lending is risky.

5. Loans tend to be illiquid.

6. Loans tend to have longer maturities than lenders would like.

Without financial intermediaries, few loans would be made, and the only lending would be to the least risky borrowers. However, in our running example, consider what a depository institution can do to alleviate the aforementioned six difficulties. First, the depository institution is a well-defined place of business and people know where to go if they wish to borrow or lend, so this eliminates the search costs involved in getting borrowers and lenders together. Second, the depository institution is specialized in evaluating credit risks, and so can do this at a lower cost per loan than would be the case for an unspecialized individual. That is, there are economies of scale in acquiring information. Third, because the financial intermediary pools the funds of many lenders, it can avoid the replication of costs that occurs when there is direct lending. Fourth, because the financial intermediary is well diversified with respect to both its assets and liabilities, it can transform risky, illiquid, long-maturity assets into relatively safe, liquid, short-maturity liabilities.

Taking a depository institution specializing in business lending as an example, each business loan may be risky, illiquid, and of long maturity. However, because the depository institution holds many business loans (it is well diversified on the asset side of its balance sheet), the payoff on the bank's entire asset portfolio is relatively predictable, because the fraction of business loans that default should be predictable. Further, even though all the assets of the depository institution are illiquid and of long maturity, the institution's liabilities can be liquid and of short maturity because of the diversification of its liabilities. That is, suppose that the depository institution has many depositors, all holding transactions accounts. An individual depositor could decide to make withdrawals and deposits or to make debit card transactions at random times, but taken as a group, the behavior of depositors is predictable. Thus, although a transactions deposit is highly liquid and has as short a maturity as the depositor might wish for, the institution can make highly illiquid and long-maturity loans based on its ability to predict the aggregate behavior of a large number of depositors.

The Diamond–Dybvig Banking Model

This banking model was developed in the early 1980s by Douglas Diamond and Philip Dybvig.[13] It is a simple model that captures some of the important features of banks and helps to explain why bank runs might occur (as they did historically) and what role the government might have in preventing bank runs.

In the model, there are three periods: 0, 1, and 2. There are N consumers, where N is very large, and each consumer is endowed with one unit of a good in period 0, which can serve as an input to production. The production technology takes one unit of the input good in period 0 and converts this into $1 + r$ units of the consumption good in period 2. However, this production technology can also be interrupted in period 1.

[13]D. Diamond and P. Dybvig, 1983, "Bank Runs, Liquidity, and Deposit Insurance," *Journal of Political Economy* 91, 401–419.

If interruption occurs in period 1, then one unit of consumption goods can be obtained for each unit of the good invested in period 0. If production is interrupted, then nothing is produced in period 2.

A given consumer might wish to consume early—in period 1—or to consume late—in period 2. However, in period 0, individual consumers do not know whether they are early or late consumers; they learn this in period 1. In period 0, each consumer knows that he or she has a probability t of being an early consumer and probability $1 - t$ of being a late consumer, and in period 1, tN consumers learn that they are early consumers and $(1 - t)N$ consumers learn that they are late consumers. We have $0 < t < 1$. For example, if $t = \frac{1}{2}$, then a consumer has equal probabilities of being an early or late consumer, as if consuming early or late were determined by the flip of a coin.

The production technology captures liquidity in a simple way. That is, using the production technology is much like investing in a long-maturity asset that could be sold with some loss before it matures. For a consumer, the possibility that he or she might consume early captures the idea that there exist random needs for liquid assets—that is, unforeseen circumstances when transactions need to be made. In practice we make many transactions over the course of a day or a week, and not all of these transactions are anticipated. For example, one might see a book in a store window and wish to purchase it, or one might be caught in an unexpected rainstorm and need to buy an umbrella.

Whether consumption takes place early or late, the utility (or pleasure) that the consumer receives is given by $U(c)$, where U is a utility function and c is consumption. The utility function is concave, as in Figure 16.7, because the marginal utility of consumption declines as consumption increases. The **marginal utility of consumption**, MU_c, is given by the slope of the utility function. For example, in Figure 16.7 the MU_c when $c = c^*$ is given by the slope of a tangent to the utility function at point A.

Given the world that an individual consumer lives in here, he or she needs to make decisions under uncertainty in period 0. In economics, a productive approach to modelling consumer choice under uncertainty is to assume that a consumer maximizes expected utility, which here is

$$\text{Expected Utility} = tU(c_1) + (1 - t)U(c_2),$$

where c_1 is consumption if the consumer needs to consume early and c_2 is consumption if the consumer is a late consumer. That is, expected utility is a weighted average of utilities that occur if the particular events happen (early or late consumption), where the weights are the probabilities that the particular events occur, which in this case are t and $1 - t$.

We can represent a consumer's expected utility preferences in terms of indifference curves, with c_1 (early consumption) on the horizontal axis and c_2 (late consumption) on the vertical axis in Figure 16.8. As in Chapters 4 and 8, these indifference curves are downward sloping and convex. The marginal rate of substitution of early consumption for late consumption for the consumer is given by

$$MRS_{c_1, c_2} = \frac{tMU_{c_1}}{(1 - t)MU_{c_2}}, \tag{16-12}$$

Figure 16.7 The Utility Function for a Consumer in the Diamond–Dybvig Model

The utility function is concave, and the slope of the function is the marginal utility of consumption, MU_c.

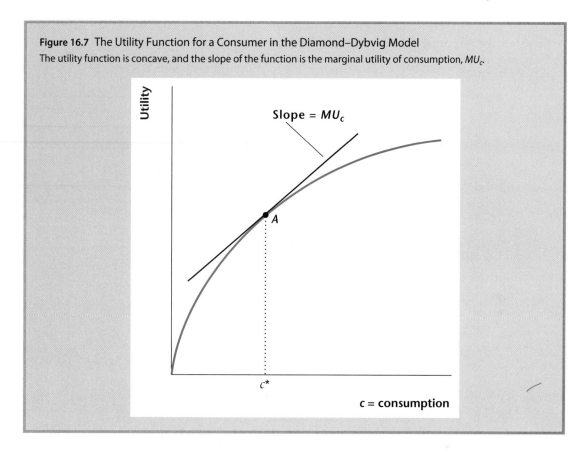

where MRS_{c_1,c_2} is minus the slope of an indifference curve in Figure 16.8. When $c_1 = c_2$, so that early consumption and late consumption are equal, we have $MU_{c_1} = MU_{c_2}$ (if consumption is the same, the marginal utility of consumption must also be the same). From equation (16-12) we have

$$MRS_{c_1,c_2} = \frac{t}{(1-t)},$$

when $c_1 = c_2$. Therefore, in Figure 16.8, an important property of the indifference curves is that, along the line $c_1 = c_2$, the slopes of each of the indifference curves is $\frac{-t}{1-t}$.

Now, suppose that each consumer must invest independently. On his or her own, what would a consumer do? Clearly, he or she invests all of his or her one unit of endowment in the technology in period 0. Then, in period 1, if he or she is an early consumer, then he or she interrupts the technology and is able to consume $c_1 = 1$. If he or she is a late consumer, then the technology is not interrupted and the consumer gets $c_2 = 1 + r$ in period 2 when the investment matures. What we would like to show is that a bank can form that allows all consumers to do better than this.

Figure 16.8 The Preferences of a Diamond–Dybvig Consumer

The figure shows the indifference curves for a Diamond–Dybvig consumer, who has preferences over early consumption and late consumption.

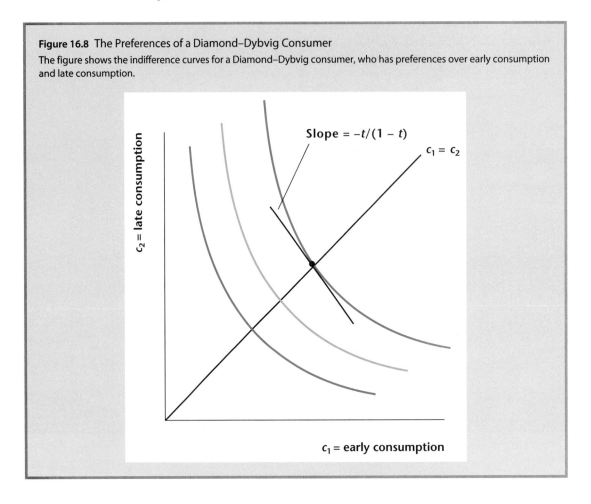

A Diamond–Dybvig Bank   In this model, a bank is an institution that offers deposit contracts to consumers. These deposit contracts allow consumers to withdraw c_1 units of goods from the bank in period 1 if they wish or to leave their deposit in the bank until period 2 and receive c_2 units of goods then. In period 1, consumers are served in sequence by the bank; that is, if a consumer wishes to withdraw his or her deposit in period 1, he or she is randomly allocated a place in line. We assume that the bank cannot tell the difference between early consumers and late consumers. While an early consumer would not want to pose as a late consumer by not withdrawing early, as this could only make him or her worse off, it is possible that there might be circumstances in which a late consumer might want to withdraw early. We suppose that a late consumer who withdraws in period 1 can store goods until period 2 and then consume them.

What determines the deposit contract (c_1, c_2) that the bank offers? We suppose that there is one bank in which all consumers make their deposits and that this bank behaves competitively. There is free entry into banking, implying that the bank earns zero profits in equilibrium. The bank makes each depositor as well off as possible, while earning zero profits in periods 1 and 2, because if it did not behave in this way, then some other bank could enter the market offering an alternative deposit contract and attract all consumers away from the first bank. Because all consumers deposit in the bank in period 0, the bank has N units of goods to invest in the technology in period 0. In period 1, the bank must choose the fraction x of the investment to interrupt so that it can pay c_1 to each depositor who wishes to withdraw at that time. Supposing that only early consumers show up at the bank to withdraw in period 1, we must have

$$Ntc_1 = xN \qquad (16\text{-}13)$$

or the total quantity of withdrawals equals the quantity of production interrupted. Then, in period 2, the quantity of uninterrupted production matures, and this quantity is used to make payments to those consumers who chose to wait, who we are supposing are only the late consumers. Then, we have

$$N(1 - t)c_2 = (1 - x)N(1 + r). \qquad (16\text{-}14)$$

That is, the total payout to the late consumers (on the left-hand side of equation (16-14)) is equal to the total return on uninterrupted production (on the right-hand side of equation (16-14)). If we substitute in equation (16-14) for x using equation (16-13) and simplify, we get

$$tc_1 + \frac{(1 - t)c_2}{1 + r} = 1, \qquad (16\text{-}15)$$

and equation (16-15) is like a lifetime budget constraint for the bank that governs how the deposit contract (c_1, c_2) can be set. We can rewrite the bank's lifetime budget constraint in slope-intercept form as

$$c_2 = -\frac{t(1 + r)}{1 - t}c_1 + \frac{1 + r}{1 - t}, \qquad (16\text{-}16)$$

and the bank's lifetime budget constraint is depicted in Figure 16.9; in the figure, points A, B, and D lie on the constraint. The constraint has a vertical intercept of $\frac{1 + r}{1 - t}$, which is the maximum payout to late consumers if the bank does not interrupt any of its production, and the horizontal intercept is $\frac{1}{t}$, which is the maximum amount that could be withdrawn by early consumers in the case where all production is interrupted by the bank. The slope of the bank's lifetime budget constraint is $\frac{-t(1 + r)}{1 - t}$. The equilibrium deposit contract offered by the bank is at point A in Figure 16.9, where an indifference curve for the consumer is tangent to the bank's lifetime budget constraint. The equilibrium deposit contract has two important properties, which are:

1. The equilibrium deposit contract, at point A in Figure 16.9, lies to the northwest of point B, which is the point on the bank's lifetime budget constraint where the bank's payouts to early and late consumers are the same. We know from above that at point B the marginal rate of substitution of early consumption for late consumption is $\frac{-t}{1 - t}$, and so an indifference curve running through point B is less

Figure 16.9 The Equilibrium Deposit Contract Offered by the Diamond–Dybvig Bank

Point A, where there is a tangency between the bank's lifetime budget constraint and the consumer's indifference curve, is the equilibrium deposit contract. Point B would have equal consumption for early and late consumers, and point D is what the consumer could achieve in the absence of the bank.

steep than the lifetime budget constraint of the bank. Therefore, A must lie to the northwest of B in the figure. The importance of this observation is that late consumers consume more than early consumers, given the equilibrium deposit contract; that is $c_2 > c_1$. Thus, if all other late consumers do not withdraw, any individual late consumer prefers not to withdraw in period 1. A late consumer is not tempted to pose as an early consumer if other late consumers do not do this.

2. The equilibrium deposit contract, at point A in Figure 16.9, lies to the southeast of point D, which is what the consumer would choose in the absence of the bank. By substituting in the bank's lifetime budget constraint, equation (16-15), the deposit contract $(1, 1 + r)$ (point D in the figure) satisfies this constraint, so that the consumption profile chosen by the consumer in the absence of the bank is a choice open to the bank as well. To guarantee that point D lies to the northwest of point A in the figure requires an extra assumption, essentially that there is enough curvature in the utility function depicted in Figure 16.7. Without getting into the technical details concerning why this makes sense, we simply assume here that D lies to the northwest of A in the figure. The reason this is important

is that it guarantees that $c_1 > 1$ and $c_2 < 1 + r$, so that there is a sense in which the bank provides insurance against the event that the consumer needs liquidity in period 1 to make a transaction (to consume). By accepting the banking contract, the consumer is able to consume more in period 1 than he or she could otherwise, at the expense of lower consumption in period 2.

The Diamond–Dybvig bank has some of the properties of financial intermediaries that we mentioned above. While it does not lend but instead holds assets directly, and it does not process information, the bank in this model borrows from a large number of depositors (it is well diversified), and it carries out an asset transformation. The fact that the bank is well diversified is important for its role in transforming assets. That is, because the bank holds the deposits of a large number of depositors, the number of depositors who wish to withdraw is predictable, and so the bank need only interrupt that fraction of production required to satisfy the withdrawal needs of the early consumers. The bank holds illiquid assets and is able to convert these assets into liquid deposits, providing depositors with a type of insurance against the need for liquid assets.

Bank Runs in the Diamond–Dybvig Model   The fact that the Diamond–Dybvig bank supplies consumers with insurance against the need for liquidity also leaves the bank open to bank runs. Given the banking contract at point A in Figure 16.9, where $c_1 > 1$ and $c_2 < 1 + r$, there is a *good equilibrium* where each early consumer lines up at the bank to withdraw his or her deposit in period 1, each late consumer waits to withdraw until period 2, and everyone is happy. Given these circumstances, no late consumer has the incentive to withdraw in period 1, as $c_1 < c_2$ at point A in Figure 16.9, so withdrawing early would only make a late consumer worse off. However, suppose that a late consumer believes that all other late consumers will go to the bank to withdraw in period 1. Because all early consumers withdraw in period 1, the individual late consumer then believes that everyone else will go to the bank in period 1. Because $c_1 > 1$ at point A in Figure 16.9, even if the bank liquidates all of its assets in period 1, which yields the quantity N in consumption goods, it cannot satisfy total withdrawal demand, which is $(N - 1)c_1$ (recall that N is large, so that $(N - 1)c_1 > N$ at point A in the figure). Thus, the individual late consumer is faced with two choices. He or she can run to the bank and hope to get a place close to the front of the line, in which case he or she gets c_1, while risking the chance of being too close to the rear of line, in which case he or she gets nothing. If he or she chooses to wait until period 2 to withdraw, there will definitely be nothing left. Therefore, the choice is clear; if a late consumer anticipates in period 1 that everyone else will run to the bank to withdraw his or her deposit, he or she will want to do it as well. Thus, there is a *bad equilibrium*, which is a **bank run.** Everyone runs to the bank in period 1; some consume c_1, but others consume nothing. This outcome is no better for some consumers (the early consumers who manage to get to the bank before it runs out of funds) and is worse for everyone else than the good equilibrium.

The Diamond–Dybvig model, thus, has multiple equilibria, much like the Keynesian coordination failure model we studied in Chapter 12. Multiple equilibria are used here to explain why bank runs have occurred historically. In the United States before the establishment of the Federal Reserve System in 1914, there were recurring **banking panics** during the **National Banking Era** (1863–1913). During these panic episodes, which were typically triggered by the failure of a large financial institution or institutions, there were large deposit withdrawals from banks that sometimes appeared to be contagious. As well, widespread bank runs occurred during the Great Depression in the United States. The Diamond–Dybvig model provides an explanation for why an otherwise sound bank could experience a bank run and fail. According to the logic of the model, because a bank provides a liquidity transformation service to consumers, this leaves it open to bank runs. Because bank deposits are liquid, if all depositors show up at the bank in the anticipation that the bank will fail, then their expectations are self-fulfilling, and the bank will indeed fail.

Deposit Insurance   A potential solution to the problem of bank runs is government-provided deposit insurance. In the Diamond–Dybvig model, if the government steps in and guarantees each depositor that they will receive the quantity c_2 given by the banking contract at point A in Figure 16.9, then no late consumer would have a reason to run to the bank. This leaves aside the question of who the government will tax if it has to make good on its deposit insurance guarantees. However, in the model the bad equilibrium will never occur with deposit insurance in place, so the government will never have to make any payouts related to its insurance program. The model tells us that promises by the government can serve to prevent a bad outcome.

In the United States, deposits in depository institutions are insured up to $100,000 by the Federal Deposit Insurance Corporation (FDIC). This means that, if a depository institution fails, the depositors are guaranteed that they will receive the value of their deposits up to $100,000. The FDIC was established in 1934, mainly in response to the failure of about one-third of all depository institutions during the Great Depression.

The main cost of deposit insurance is that it creates a **moral hazard** problem, and this problem is something that is not taken into account in the Diamond–Dybvig banking model. Moral hazard arises in essentially all insurance situations, because the insured individual tends to take less care in preventing the event against which he or she is insured. For example, if the owner of a car is completely insured against damages to his or her car, he or she takes less care in driving in parking lots, and, therefore, is more likely to have an accident. It is difficult for the insurance company to correct for this problem, because the amount of care taken by the driver of the car is hard to observe. Moral hazard can explain the existence of deductibles in insurance contracts, which require the insured party to bear the cost of small losses.

For a depository institution, moral hazard arises because deposit insurance encourages the depository institution to take on more risk. This happens because the riskiness of a bank's assets is difficult to observe and because with deposit insurance the depositors have no interest in whether the depository institution is risky or not. Therefore, although deposit insurance can prevent the failures of sound depository institutions that might occur because of self-fulfilling panics, it could produce more failures because of the increased riskiness of banks. Thus, the existence of deposit insurance requires that the regulators of depository institutions impose restrictions on depository institution activities to assure that these institutions do not take on too much risk.

Another element of moral hazard in the U.S. monetary system results from the **too-big-to-fail doctrine.** This represents the belief that the regulators of the U.S. financial system would not tolerate losses by depositors at any large depository institution in the country, because of the fear that such losses would lead to widespread financial panic. Given that large banks know that all or most of the holders of their liabilities are implicitly insured against loss, these large banks have an even greater incentive than small banks to take on too much risk.

Perspectives on the Financial Crisis

Banks, Non-Bank Financial Intermediaries, Too-Big-to-Fail, and Moral Hazard

The United States has a colorful history of financial crises and governmental responses to those crises. The repeated banking panic episodes of the National Banking Era, following the Civil War, resulted in the Federal Reserve Act (1913) and the establishment of the Federal Reserve System in 1914. The failure of about one-third of U.S. banks during the Great Depression led to legislation that introduced deposit insurance and the separation of banking and stock market activity in the United States. In the late 1980s, the savings and loan crisis (the failure of many savings and loan depository institutions due to excessive risk-taking) led to reforms of deposit insurance and bank regulation. These are only some examples of an at-times chaotic U.S. financial and banking history.

The intervention by the U.S. Treasury and the Fed in the financial system beginning in the fall of 2008 was unprecedented in scale. The two key interventions were (a) the Emergency Economic Stabilization Act of 2008 (EESA) and (b) a more-than-doubling of the monetary base by the Fed. The ESSA gave the Treasury considerable discretion to allocate up to $700 billion through the Troubled Asset Relief Program (TARP). Ultimately, intervention through this program amounted to an injection of funds to banks and other financial intermediaries in exchange for federal government equity participation in those financial institutions. The increase in the monetary base by the Fed was used to purchase large quantities of assets not typically found on the Fed's balance sheet, including loans to non-bank financial intermediaries and mortgage-backed securities.

What financial crisis were the U.S. Treasury and the Fed responding to, and what were its causes? The crisis had the following elements:

1. In most countries of the world where organized mortgage lending exists, mortgage loans are made by banks that hold and service the loans until they mature. The mortgage market in the United States is unusual. Currently, most mortgages in the United States are originated by brokers who negotiate the terms of the loan with the borrower, and who then sell the loan to another financial institution. This institution could be a government agency, such as FNMA or FHLMC ("Fannie Mae," the Federal National Mortgage Association and "Freddie Mac," the Federal Home Loan Mortgage Corporation, respectively), which finances purchases of mortgages by issuing debt, or a private financial intermediary that repackages these mortgages as *mortgage-backed securities*. A mortgage-backed security is an asset that is a claim to the payoffs (or some part of the payoffs) on an underlying portfolio of mortgages. Mortgage-backed securities are tradable on financial markets. With financial innovation, mainly after 2000, mortgage originators began lending to increasingly risky borrowers in the so-called *subprime mortgage market*. The financial institutions that purchased these mortgages and repackaged them as mortgage-backed securities, and the rating agencies that certified the quality of the mortgage-backed securities, seemed assured

(Continued)

that the underlying mortgages were sound, or at least that their payoffs were very predictable, given the diversification involved. However, the prices of houses began to fall widely across the United States in 2006, and this led to a large increase in the default rates on subprime mortgages. These mortgages appeared not to be so sound after all, and it became clear that there were severe incentive problems in the mortgage market—mortgage brokers were doing a poor job of screening borrowers, because they would be well paid for their work whether the mortgages ultimately paid off or not, and someone else would be left holding the bag.

2. Some investment banks that were heavy investors in mortgage-backed securities were carrying on activities that looked much like conventional banking. These investment banks would purchase mortgage-backed securities and finance these purchases through a sequence of short-term *repurchase agreements*, which are short-term collateralized loans. In these repurchase agreements, it was the mortgage-backed securities themselves that served as collateral for the loans. This type of financial intermediation looks somewhat like what a bank does, as the assets on the investment banks' balance sheets were long-maturity, while the liabilities were short-maturity. A difference from a conventional bank is that mortgage-backed securities are by nature liquid—they can be sold at any time on organized markets. However, the assets held by a traditional bank are illiquid.

3. An important recent financial innovation was the *credit default swap*, which is essentially insurance on a debt contract. Suppose, for example, that Lehman Brothers (a now-defunct investment bank) issued debt in order to purchase mortgage-backed securities. Someone, say the holder of this debt, could purchase a credit default swap at some price from American International Group (an insurance company), for example. If Lehman

Brothers were to default on its debt, then American International Group would guarantee the specified payoffs on the debt for the debtholder who had purchased the credit default swap. Holding the credit default swap in conjunction with the underlying debt essentially insures the debt-holder against the event that the debt-issuer defaults. However, someone could purchase a credit default swap and not hold the underlying debt, and thus be taking a bet on whether the debt-issuer would default.

4. Once it became clear (for most investors, mainly in 2008) that the ultimate payoffs on subprime mortgages were not going to be as high as expected, the mortgage-backed securities that represented packages of these mortgages fell in price. Investment banks such as Bear Stearns and Lehman Brothers found it increasing difficult to borrow short-term to finance their holdings of mortgage-backed securities, so that there was pressure to sell these securities. This further reduced the market prices of mortgage-backed securities and ultimately led to the failure of Lehman Brothers in the fall of 2008. Once Lehman Brothers had failed, financial market participants learned that American International Group (AIG) was the issuer of a large quantity of credit default swaps that would have to be paid out. At this point, there was the potential that AIG could fail, along with some other large financial institutions, including investment banks and the largest U.S. banks, principally Citigroup and Bank of America. It was in this context that the U.S. Treasury and the Fed intervened in such a massive way.

What was the rationale for this dramatic policy intervention, and what were the alternatives? It will be useful to frame the arguments in terms of (a) *the interventionist view* and (b) *the laissez-faire view*.

The interventionist view is perhaps best summarized in Fed Chairman Ben Bernanke's speech at the August 2009 Policy Conference at Jackson

Hole, Wyoming.[14] Bernanke argues that the financial intervention by the Treasury and the Fed was essentially staving off a repeat of the Great Depression. According to Bernanke, there were elements of the financial crisis that looked much like a Diamond–Dybvig bank run, although in this case a run on non-bank financial institutions that were not protected by deposit insurance. Indeed, the liabilities of these institutions were not deposits, but typically short-term repurchase agreements. However, the argument is that flight of lenders from short-term lending was much like a bank run or classic liquidity crisis. At risk, according to Bernanke, was the whole financial sector, through interrelationships of borrowing, lending, and elaborate financial arrangements that were difficult for anyone to understand in full. Should one large financial institution fail, the others would soon follow, according to the interventionist view. The correct response to the problem, in the Fed's view was (a) to intervene in conventional ways through open market operations, reducing the fed funds rate essentially to zero; (b) to lend generously by way of the Fed's discount window, not only to banks, but to other financial institutions; and (c) to have the Fed act essentially as a mortgage banker, issuing outside money and holding mortgage-backed securities.

The other piece of financial intervention, the TARP funds authorized through the ESSA, was another means to prevent the failure of large financial institutions. By "recapitalizing" banks and other financial institutions with government funds, it was thought that banks would begin lending more (lending in credit markets tightened dramatically in mid to late 2008), and the failure of these large financial institutions would be forestalled.

The laissez-faire view is that the Fed and the Treasury overdid their intervention. This appears to be the view held by several dissenters on the Federal Open Market Committee, including Jeffrey Lacker (President, Federal Reserve Bank of Richmond), Charles Plosser (President, Federal Reserve Bank of Philadelphia), and Thomas Hoenig (President, Federal Reserve Bank of Kansas City). In the laissez-faire view, some intervention in response to the crisis may have been called for, but the Fed should have restricted its activities to conventional types of central bank intervention—lending exclusively to banks and open market operations in short-term government securities. According to this view, activities such as the purchase of mortgage-backed securities by the Fed are at best ineffective and at worst misallocate credit in the economy. Laissez-faire economists would argue that large financial institutions should be allowed to fail. If not, serious moral hazard problems set in—these institutions come to expect that they can take on large amounts of risk, reap the benefits when times are good, and let taxpayers make up the difference when times are bad. Indeed, one could view the whole financial crisis as stemming from the too-big-to-fail doctrine. Large financial institutions engaged in some very risky activities knowing that, in the seemingly unlikely event that house prices should fall, setting off a chain reaction of defaults on credit arrangements, the government would intervene and bail out the losers. These large institutions were then ultimately correct in their assumptions about how the federal government and the Fed would behave.

Which view is correct, the interventionist view, or the laissez-faire view? It is impossible to know for sure, without rerunning history in the absence of the massive policy interventions. Currently, in mid-2009, it appears that the U.S. economy is on a path to recovery. Ben Bernanke insists that his astute intervention prevented a second Great Depression, and the Obama administration appears to agree, as Bernanke has been appointed (subject to approval by the Senate) to a second four-year term as Fed Chairman. Holders of the laissez-faire view do not agree. One could argue that, if financial intervention had been more modest and large financial institutions had been permitted to fail, the 2008–2009 recession may have been somewhat more severe, but the long-term costs of the too-big-to-fail doctrine and ensuing moral hazard problems easily outweigh this short-term cost in terms of severity.

---

[14]See http://www.federalreserve.gov/newsevents/speech/bernanke20090821a.htm

MACROECONOMICS IN ACTION
Bank Failures and Banking Panics in the United States and Canada

Canada and the United States are in many ways economically similar, but they have very different banking systems.[15] The two countries have also had very different historical experiences with banking panics and bank failures, and this represents a challenge to the Diamond–Dybvig banking model.

While the United States has a unit banking system, with thousands of small banks that typically serve small geographical areas, along with a few large banks, Canada has a branch banking system, with only a handful of commercial banks that branch nationally. On the one hand, the United States has had a network of regulations designed to keep banks small, and it is relatively easy to open a new bank. On the other hand, Canadian banks are typically not prevented from becoming large, and it requires federal legislation for a bank to obtain a charter and open for business.

U.S. banking history has many episodes of widespread bank failures and banking panics, as we have discussed. There were recurrent banking panics during the National Banking Era in the United States, from 1863 to 1913. The Federal Reserve System, established in 1914, was supposed to correct the institutional problems that caused banking panics, but missteps in monetary policy in the Great

Depression contributed to a situation in which about one-third of U.S. banks failed between 1929 and 1933.

Before the establishment of the Canadian central bank, the Bank of Canada, in 1935, there were no banking panics of note in Canada. Canada was a latecomer to deposit insurance, introducing it in 1967, but in spite of this, there were few bank failures before that time. No commercial banks failed in the Great Depression in Canada, and the most recent bank failure before 1985 was the failure of the Home Bank in 1923. The most recent commercial bank failures were those of the Northland Bank and the Canadian Commercial Bank in 1985. From January to August 2009, about 80 banks failed in the United States, while there were zero failures in Canada.

Why have the experiences with bank failures and panics been so different in Canada and the United States? This seems hard to explain using the Diamond–Dybvig banking model, where bank runs arise simply because banks are performing a useful intermediation service; in this sense U.S. banks and Canadian banks are no different. The evidence points to two factors (not included in the Diamond–Dybvig banking model) that appear to be important in explaining these differences between the United States and Canada. First, in the period before 1935, much of the circulating currency in Canada was issued by commercial banks (see the discussion earlier in this chapter). This private currency was viewed by the public as being quite safe. At times of the year when the demand for currency was particularly high (typically during the fall harvest) relative to bank deposits, it was easy for the chartered banks

---

[15]The material here relies heavily on S. Williamson, 1989, "Restrictions on Financial Intermediaries and Implications for Aggregate Fluctuations: Canada and the United States, 1870–1913," in O. Blanchard and S. Fischer, eds., *NBER Macroeconomics Annual 1989*, NBER, Cambridge, MA; and B. Champ, B. Smith, and S. Williamson, 1996, "Currency Elasticity and Banking Panics: Theory and Evidence," *Canadian Journal of Economics* 29, 828–864.

to convert deposit liabilities into notes in circulation by printing more notes to issue when depositors chose to withdraw. In periods of high demand for currency in the United States between 1863 and 1913, a panic could result, but this was averted in Canada because of the note-issuing ability of Canadian commercial banks. Bank failures are also averted in Canada by the fact that Canadian banks are relatively large and well-diversified geographically. One of the reasons for the failures of the Northland Bank and Canadian Commercial Bank in 1985 was that these banks did most of their lending in one western province of Canada, which exposed them to the risks associated with local shocks. In this case the local shock was a sharp drop in the prices of oil and natural gas that caused a reduction in local asset prices, resulting in borrowers at these banks defaulting on their loans. Small U.S. banks, which are typically not well diversified geographically, are exposed to the same kind of risk and, thus, are more likely to fail than a well-diversified Canadian branch bank.

One might think that the negative effects of the too-big-to-fail doctrine would be in evidence in Canada, with its large banks, but there appears to be no history in Canada of the government or the central bank propping up ailing banks. Indeed, Canada's banking system is viewed as one of the world's safest. Why is this so? In Canada, banks are regulated differently. First, Canada does not have the confusing, conflicting, and overlapping regulatory structure involving several different financial regulators, that the United States does. Second, Canadian banks are in some ways more tightly regulated (although they have more flexibility in terms of how they offer financial services). In particular, entry into the banking system is more difficult in Canada, and banks are required to hold higher levels of capital in Canada than in the United States. Canadian regulations, while they reduce competition among Canadian banks, give these banks a larger cushion against losses and make them fundamentally sounder.

This completes our study of money and banking in this book. In Chapter 17 we examine some issues in unemployment, and in Chapter 18 we return to the study of inflation to explain why central banks may resort to inflation in situations in which they know inflation is a bad thing.

Chapter Summary

- Money functions as a medium of exchange, a store of value, and a unit of account. Historically, the objects that have played the role of money are commodity money, circulating private bank notes, commodity-backed paper currency, fiat money, and transactions deposits at private banks.

- We considered a simple model capturing the absence-of-double-coincidence-of-wants problem that can exist in barter economies where people only have goods to trade. In the model, commodity money or fiat money can overcome the double-coincidence problem by providing a universally acceptable medium of exchange.

- The monetary intertemporal model from Chapter 10 was used to study the effects of long-run inflation. A higher money growth rate causes an increase in the rate of inflation, an increase in the nominal interest rate, and decreases in output, consumption, and employment.

- A positive nominal interest rate represents a distortion that drives a wedge between the marginal rate of substitution of leisure for consumption and the marginal rate of transformation of leisure for consumption.
- An optimal long-run monetary policy in the monetary intertemporal model is for the central bank to follow a Friedman rule, whereby the money growth rate and the inflation rate are equal to minus the real interest rate. This implies that the nominal interest rate is zero at the optimum.
- In the Diamond–Dybvig banking model, a bank provides its depositors with insurance against the event that they need liquid assets to make transactions. The bank converts illiquid assets into liquid deposits.
- In the Diamond–Dybvig model, there is a good equilibrium where all early consumers withdraw their deposits from the bank early and all late consumers withdraw late. There is also a bad equilibrium (a bank run) where all consumers choose to withdraw early, and the bank fails. The bank run equilibrium can be prevented through government-provided deposit insurance.
- There is a moral hazard problem associated with deposit insurance, in that an unregulated bank with insured deposits takes on too much risk. According to the too-big-to-fail doctrine, the implicit insurance of the deposits and other liabilities of large banks makes these banks especially prone to the moral hazard problem.

Key Terms

Absence of double coincidence of wants Situation in which there are two would-be trading partners, but it is not true that each has the good the other wants. (p. 575)

Banking panics Situations where bank runs are widespread. (p. 597)

Bank run A situation where a bank's depositors panic and simultaneously attempt to withdraw their deposits. (p. 597)

Deflation Decrease in the price level over time. (p. 585)

Fedwire A payments system operated by the Federal Reserve System through which transactions between financial institutions are cleared. (p. 573)

Financial intermediary Any financial institution that borrows from one large group of people and lends to another large group of people, transforms assets in some way, and processes information. (p. 570)

Fisher effect The increase in the nominal interest rate resulting from an increase in the rate of inflation. (p. 584)

Free Banking Era The period running from 1837–1863 in the United States characterized by the issuance of currency by many private banks. (p. 571)

Friedman rule An optimal rule for monetary policy, whereby the money supply grows at a rate that implies a zero nominal interest rate. (p. 570)

Gold standard An arrangement whereby a country stands ready to exchange its money for gold at a fixed price. (p. 572)

Hyperinflations Situations where the inflation rate is extremely high. (p. 586)

Liquidity trap A situation where, if the nominal interest rate is zero, then open market operations by the central bank have no effect. (p. 587)

Marginal utility of consumption The slope of the utility function, or the marginal increase in utility (happiness) resulting from a one-unit increase in consumption. (p. 592)

Moral hazard The tendency of insured individuals to take less care to prevent a loss against which they are insured. (p. 598)

National Banking Era The period in the United States between 1863 and 1913. (p. 597)

Nondiversifiable risk Risk that an individual cannot diversify away by holding a large portfolio of assets. (p. 589)

Risk-averse Describes an individual who does not like risk. (p. 589)

Superneutral Describes money in the situation where a change in the money supply growth rate has no real effects. (p. 584)

Too-big-to-fail doctrine The doctrine according to which U.S. regulatory agencies should intervene to prevent the failure of any large financial institution. (p. 598)

Questions for Review

1. What are five forms that money has taken historically?
2. What do Yap stones and the playing card money of New France have in common? What is different about these two forms of money?
3. How does an absence-of-double-coincidence-of-wants make money socially useful?
4. What are the effects of an increase in the money supply growth rate in the monetary intertemporal model?
5. What are the costs of inflation?
6. Should the monetary authority manipulate the money supply to hold the price level constant over time?
7. Why don't real-world central banks follow the Friedman rule?
8. List four properties of assets and explain why these properties are important.
9. What are the four defining characteristics of a financial intermediary?
10. What are three types of financial intermediaries?
11. What is unusual about depository institutions relative to other financial intermediaries?
12. In the Diamond–Dybvig banking model, why does a consumer do better by depositing in a bank rather than investing on his or her own?
13. What features of real-world banks does a Diamond–Dybvig bank have?
14. Why are there two equilibria in the Diamond–Dybvig banking model? How do the two equilibria compare?
15. How can bank runs be prevented?
16. Explain what moral hazard is and why and how deposit insurance and the too-big-to-fail doctrine induce a moral hazard problem.

Problems

1. Consider the absence-of-double-coincidence economy depicted in Figure 16.1. Determine who would trade what with whom if good 2 were used as a commodity money. Explain your results.

2. As an alternative to the economy depicted in Figure 16.1, suppose that there are three types of people, but now the person who consumes good 1 produces good 3, the person who consumes good 2 produces good 1, and the person who consumes good 3 produces good 2.
   (a) Determine who trades what with whom if good 1 is used as a commodity money, and compare this with what happens when good 1 is used as a commodity money in the economy in Figure 16.1. Explain.
   (b) Determine who trades what with whom if fiat money is used in exchange, and commodity money is not used. Explain.

3. In the monetary intertemporal model, suppose the central bank issues money in exchange for capital and rents this capital out to firms each period, thus earning the market real interest rate r on the capital. Over time, as the central bank earns interest on its capital holdings, it uses these returns to retire money from the private economy. What are the long run effects? Is the outcome economically efficient? Explain your results.

4. Suppose, in the monetary intertemporal model, that the government can pay interest on money, financing this interest with lump-sum taxes on consumers. If the nominal interest rate on money is the same as the nominal interest rate on bonds, determine the effects in the model, illustrating this in a diagram. Explain your results.

5. Suppose that consumers are concerned about theft, so they are willing to use banks for some of their transactions even if the nominal interest rate is zero. Further, suppose that, the more currency consumers hold, the more people are encouraged to steal, as theft is now more profitable. How would the Friedman rule for monetary policy be altered under these circumstances?

6. Consider the following assets: (i) a work of art, (ii) a United States Treasury bill, (iii) a share in Microsoft, (iv) a loan to a close relative, (v) a loan to General Motors. For each asset, answer the following questions:
   (a) Does the asset have a high rate of return or a low rate of return (on average)?
   (b) Is the asset high risk or low risk?
   (c) Is the asset a long-maturity asset or a short-maturity asset?
   (d) Is the asset highly liquid, less liquid, somewhat illiquid, or highly illiquid?
   (e) Explain why the asset has the above four properties.
   (f) Which of the properties of money (medium of exchange, store of value, unit of account) does the asset have? Would we consider it money and why or why not?

7. In the Diamond–Dybvig banking model, suppose that the banking contract includes a suspension of convertibility provision according to which the bank allows only the first tN depositors in line in period 1 to withdraw their deposits. Will there still be a bank run equilibrium? Carefully explain why or why not.

8. In the Diamond–Dybig banking model, suppose that, instead of a bank, consumers can trade shares in the production technology. That is, each consumer invests in the production technology in period 0. Then, if the consumer learns that he or she is an early consumer in period 1, he or she can either interrupt the technology or can sell their investment at a price p. A consumer who learns that he or she is a later consumer in period 1 can purchase shares in investment projects at a price p and can interrupt his or her production technology in order to acquire the goods required to buy shares.
   (a) Determine what p is in equilibrium, and what each consumer's quantity of early and late consumption is, in a diagram like Figure 16.9.

   (b) Do consumers do better or worse than they would with a banking system? Do they do better than they would with no banks and with no trading in shares?
   (c) Explain your results.

9. Alter the Diamond–Dybvig model in the following way. Suppose that there are two assets, an illiquid asset that returns $1 + r$ units of consumption goods in period 2 for each unit invested in period 0, and a liquid asset that returns one unit of consumption goods in period 1 for each unit invested in period 0. The illiquid asset production technology cannot be interrupted in period 1. The model is otherwise the same as outlined in this chapter.
   (a) Determine a consumer's lifetime budget constraint when there is no bank. Show this in a diagram and determine the consumer's optimal consumption when an early consumer and when a late consumer in the diagram.
   (b) Determine a bank's lifetime budget constraint, show this in your diagram, and determine the optimal deposit contract for the bank in the diagram. Are consumers who deposit in the bank better off than in part (a)? Explain why or why not.
   (c) Is there a bank run equilibrium? Explain why or why not.

10. Explain how moral hazard arises in each of the following situations:
    (a) A mother promises her daughter that she will help her with her homework during the coming school year but only if the daughter has difficulty with her homework.
    (b) An individual's house is insured against damage by fire for its full value.
    (c) An individual is appointed to manage an investment portfolio for a group of co-workers.
    (d) The same individual in part (c) is appointed to manage the investment portfolio, and the government guarantees that all investors in the group will receive a 5% return per year. That is, the government will make up the difference if the return on the portfolio falls below 5% in a given year.

Working with the Data

1. Answer the following questions:
   (a) Calculate the monthly percentage increases in the consumer price index and in M1 and display these in a scatter plot. What do you observe? Explain.
   (b) Now, calculate percentage increases in the consumer price index and in M1 over five-year periods and display these in a scatter plot. How does this scatter plot compare to the one you constructed in part (a)? Explain.

2. Display the 3-month Treasury bill interest rate, the interest rate on a 10-year Treasury note, and the interest rate on a 3-month certificate of deposit in a time series plot. What do you observe? How do the properties of assets explain the regularities in this interest rate data?

3. Plot the 3-month treasury bill interest rate and the rate of inflation over the previous year in a time series plot. To what extent does the nominal interest rate reflect the actual inflation rate? Is this consistent with the predictions of the monetary intertemporal model in this chapter? Explain.

chapter 17

Unemployment: Search and Efficiency Wages

To study the reasons for unemployment, we need to understand in more detail how people use their time. In the macroeconomic models we have used in previous chapters, consumers typically divide their time between leisure and market work, but in this chapter we would like to explore explanations for a third activity—unemployment— which, as measured by the Bureau of Labor Statistics in the United States, is neither leisure nor market work. There are two key features of unemployment that set it apart. One is that unemployment entails searching for work, which is costly. The reason the unemployed are willing to bear the costs of searching for work is that there is a chance that they will find a job and be better off. Thus, the fact that searching for work is painful implies the second key feature of unemployment, which is that the unemployed are worse off, in some sense, than the employed. Although unemployment is painful, and the unemployed would typically be better off working at some job, unemployment is a necessary evil in modern economies. Indeed, it would be impossible to eliminate all unemployment, and some government policies that could reduce unemployment would in fact be detrimental to overall economic welfare.

Our first goal in this chapter is to examine the behavior of the unemployment rate in the United States. As well, we study the behavior of another key labor market variable, the participation rate. We show how the unemployment rate and participation rate move over the business cycle and discuss some of the determinants of these two variables.

Next, we study two models that permit us to organize our thinking about the deter-minants of the unemployment rate. The first model is a search model of unemploy-ment, in which unemployed workers look for jobs and accept a job when the welfare they receive from working at the wage offered exceeds the welfare from turning down the job offer and continuing to search. The search model allows us to show how unem-ployment insurance benefits, taxation, and other government interventions affect the behavior of unemployed workers and the unemployment rate.

The second model we consider is the efficiency wage model, which builds on the idea that workers' effort on the job depends on the real wage they receive. This can imply that, in equilibrium, the real wage is higher than the market-clearing real wage, because the higher real wage allows the firm to elicit more effort from its workers. Thus, the real wage is "sticky," and there can be equilibrium unemployment. This model, thus, is related to the Keynesian ideas we studied in Chapter 13, in the New Keynesian sticky price model. Once we have constructed the efficiency wage model and have showed how it works, we will examine how well the efficiency wage model fits the business cycle facts discussed in Chapter 3.

The Behavior of the Unemployment Rate, the Participation Rate, and the Employment/Population Ratio in the United States

Before studying models of unemployment, we explore the empirical behavior of the unemployment rate, the participation rate, and the employment/population ratio in the United States. Recall from Chapter 2 that, if E is the number of working age persons who are employed, U is the number of unemployed, and NL denotes those who are not in the labor force, then the unemployment rate and participation rate are defined by

$$\text{unemployment rate} = \frac{U}{E + U},$$

$$\text{participation rate} = \frac{E + U}{E + U + NL},$$

where the total labor force is equal to $E + U$. As well, we will also be interested in the behavior of the employment/population ratio, defined by

$$\text{employment/population ratio} = \frac{E}{E + U + NL}$$

Figure 17.1 shows a plot of the monthly unemployment rate for the United States for the years 1948 to 2009. The unemployment rate is a countercyclical variable, in that it is high during recessions and low during booms. In particular, note in the figure that the unemployment rate spiked up during the recessions of 1974–1975, 1981–1982, 1991–1992, 2001, and 2008–2009, and decreased during the economic booms of the late 1970s, the late 1980s, and following the 1990–1991 and 2001 recessions. In addition to the cyclical behavior of the unemployment rate, there also appear to be longer-run movements in the unemployment rate in the figure. For example, from about 1970 until the mid-1980s, there was a trend increase in the unemployment rate and a trend decrease from the mid-1980s until 2008. We would like to understand the reasons for both the cyclical behavior and long-run behavior of the unemployment rate.

The key determinants of the unemployment rate are the following:

- *Aggregate Economic Activity:*   When aggregate real GDP is high relative to trend, the unemployment rate tends to be low. As mentioned above, the unemployment rate is a countercyclical variable. In Figure 17.2, which shows the deviations from trend in the unemployment rate and in real GDP (percentages in this case), we see that the unemployment rate tends to be below (above) trend when real GDP is above (below) trend.

- *Demographics:*   **Demography** is the study of population. The age structure of the population matters a great deal for the unemployment rate, as workers of different ages

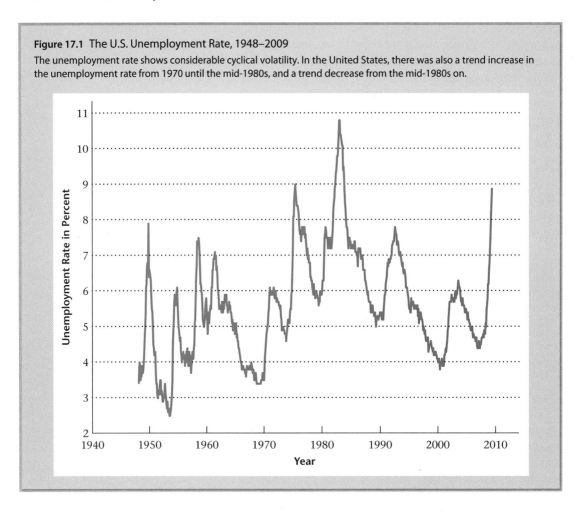

Figure 17.1 The U.S. Unemployment Rate, 1948–2009

The unemployment rate shows considerable cyclical volatility. In the United States, there was also a trend increase in the unemployment rate from 1970 until the mid-1980s, and a trend decrease from the mid-1980s on.

behave quite differently in the labor market. The unemployment rate for the young tends to be higher than that for the old, as younger workers have a weaker attachment to the labor force and switch jobs more frequently early in their careers, thus suffering more frequent spells of unemployment. In Figure 17.1, part of the increase in the average unemployment rate in the 1970s was because this was the period when many members of the post–World War II baby boom generation entered the labor force. Then, the average unemployment rate fell after 1980 as baby boomers aged.

- *Government intervention:* A key government program that affects the unemployment rate over the long run is government-provided unemployment insurance (UI). Workers who suffer a spell of unemployment typically experience a drop in their consumption. Why shouldn't this loss be insurable, just as is the loss from an automobile accident, a fire, or ill health? The problem is that UI is not supplied by private firms, and the government has taken on this insurance role in most developed countries. In the United States, UI programs are run by state governments, and the rules governing UI vary state by state. Typically, unemployed

Figure 17.2 Deviations from Trend in the Unemployment Rate and Percentage Deviations from Trend in Real GDP

The unemployment rate is countercyclical. It tends to be above (below) trend when real GDP is below (above) trend.

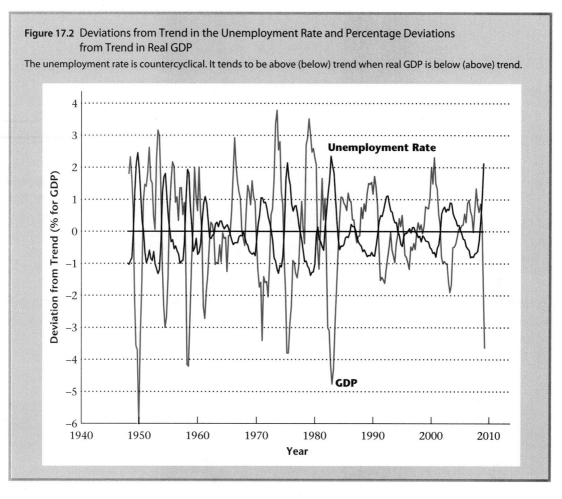

workers in the United States can draw UI benefits for about six months, and the **replacement ratio**, the ratio of UI benefits to the wage the unemployed worker was earning when employed, is about 0.5. Thus, the typical UI benefit in the United States is about one-half of the wage earned when employed. Just as happens with other types of insurance, there is moral hazard associated with UI. That is, the behavior of an insured person changes in a way that makes a loss more likely, as we discussed in connection with deposit insurance in Chapter 16. In the case of UI programs, more generous UI benefits tend to make unemployed workers more picky concerning the kinds of jobs they will take, and this tends to increase the duration of unemployment spells and increase the unemployment rate, as we show in a search model of unemployment later in this chapter. Also see "Macroeconomics in Action: Unemployment Insurance and Incentives."

• *Sectoral shifts*:   A sectoral shift is a change in the economy's aggregate structure of production. For example, in the United States, there has been a shift away from manufacturing (the production of tangible goods) and toward services (intangible goods). As a result, workers in manufacturing industries such as steel and textiles have been displaced. Displacement can imply a long period of unemployment, particularly for older workers, as displaced workers may have obsolete skills and may need to acquire new ones, and finding work in a different sector of the economy takes time. Given the level of aggregate economic activity, the greater the restructuring occurring among industries in the economy, the higher the unemployment rate will tend to be. For example, during the 2008–2009 recession, the unemployment rate was high primarily due to the drop in aggregate economic activity, but the sectoral decline in the U.S. automobile manufacturing industry also contributed to the rise in the unemployment rate.

Now that we have gained some understanding of the determinants of the unemployment rate, which are reinforced by our study of models of unemployment later in this chapter, we can turn to another key labor market variable, the participation rate, which is depicted in Figure 17.3 for the years 1948–2009. Here, the fraction of

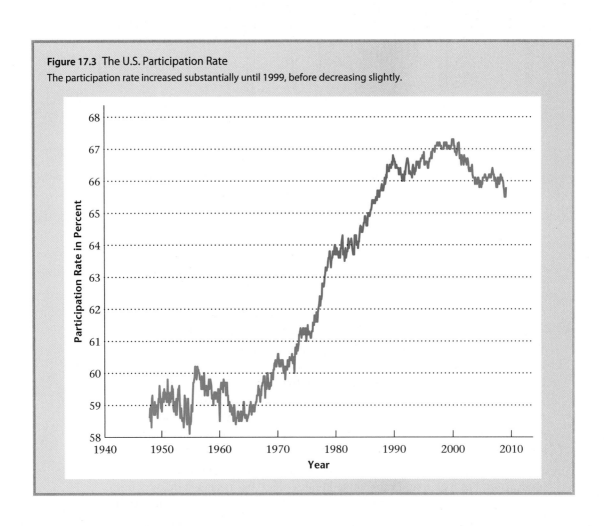

Figure 17.3 The U.S. Participation Rate
The participation rate increased substantially until 1999, before decreasing slightly.

the working age population in the labor force increased substantially, from less than 60% in the early 1950s to about 67% in 1999, before decreasing slightly. In Figure 17.4 we show the participation rates of men and women, which show a decline for men and a huge increase for women. Therefore, the increase in the total participation rate in Figure 17.3 until 1999 is accounted for solely by an increase in the labor force participation rate for women. Some point to sociological explanations for the increase in the participation rate of women, but economists do not find it surprising that more women would choose market work in the face of large increases in market real wages in the post–World War II period. The declining participation rate of men is closely connected to the increasing participation rate of women, because family decisions concerning labor market participation are made jointly. In 2009, the participation rate for women had leveled off at about 60%, but the participation rate for men was still declining.

The employment/population ratio, which is the fraction of people of working age who are employed full-time or part-time, is depicted in Figure 17.5 for the period

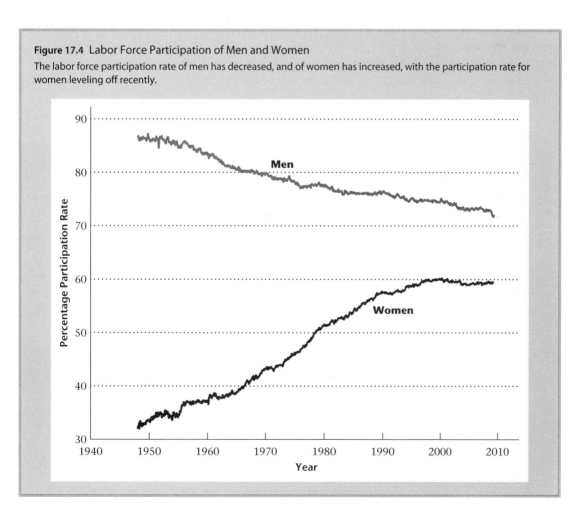

Figure 17.4 Labor Force Participation of Men and Women

The labor force participation rate of men has decreased, and of women has increased, with the participation rate for women leveling off recently.

1948–2009. This is one measure of the quantity of labor used as an input in aggregate production. There are two interesting features that can be observed in Figure 17.5. The first is that the increase in the participation rate since the 1960s that we observe is reflected in a trend increase in the employment/population ratio over the same period. The second is that the employment/population ratio in Figure 17.5 exhibits much more cyclical variation than does the participation rate in Figure 17.3 or Figure 17.4. That is, when there is a cyclical downturn, the size of the labor force does not decrease much in the short run; the important change is in the composition of the labor force between employment and unemployment. Note in particular that in the 2008–2009 recession there was a very large increase in the unemployment rate (Figure 17.1), a very large decrease in the employment/population ratio (Figure 17.5), and little change in the participation rate (Figure 17.3).

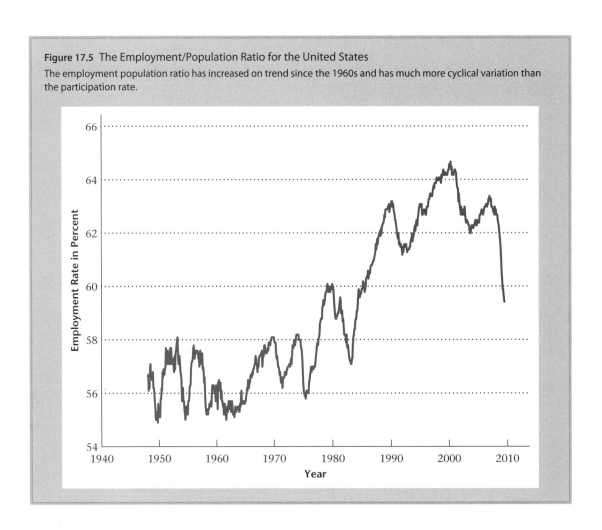

Figure 17.5 The Employment/Population Ratio for the United States

The employment population ratio has increased on trend since the 1960s and has much more cyclical variation than the participation rate.

MACROECONOMICS IN ACTION
Unemployment and Employment in the United States and Europe

Economists who study labor markets have long been interested in the differences between the United States and Europe in labor market outcomes. There has been much interest, for example, in explaining why, since the 1970s, unemployment rates have increased in European countries relative to the United States. Most research has focused on how labor market rigidities in Europe, including generous unemployment insurance, high minimum wages, high taxes, and tough restrictions on the hiring and firing of employees, act to increase European unemployment. The United States is generally characterized as being a country with a small amount of labor market rigidity, and so the question for many researchers has been only whether the greater rigidity in Europe can generate the observed quantitative difference in unemployment rates between Europe and the United States.

Richard Rogerson, in an article in the *Journal of the European Economic Association*,[1] comes up with a different characterization of European labor market problems that suggests some new directions for economic research. Rogerson examines the behavior of the employment/population ratios in Europe and the United States, as well as unemployment rates in the two places. For Europe, he focuses on three countries, France, Germany, and Italy. Rogerson documents an increase in the gap between the European unemployment rate

and the unemployment rate in the United States of about 6% between the 1970s and 2000, just as other authors have found. However, in terms of the employment/population ratio, Rogerson finds a relative deterioration in Europe that begins much earlier. He finds that a gap opened in the 1950s and that the size of this gap increased by about 18% between the 1950s and 2000. That is, the trend increase in the employment/population ratio that we observe in Figure 17.5 for the United States did not occur in Europe. This is perhaps a more startling finding than the relative deterioration in Europe in terms of unemployment rates, since it indicates a fundamental difference in growth in labor inputs in the United States and Europe.

What might explain this difference in labor market outcomes? Rogerson explores the labor market data further, but rather than seeking an explanation in terms of labor market rigidities, he studies the sectoral composition of output in Europe and the United States. Just as in the United States, Europe has experienced a sectoral shift from manufacturing to services since the 1950s. However, the nature of the sectoral shift was different in Europe. In the United States there was much more growth in the service sector than was the case in Europe. Thus, one explanation for the difference in labor market outcomes is the following. In both Europe and the United States, unemployment increased because of a sectoral shift from manufacturing to services, as workers were displaced from manufacturing jobs and experienced a spell of unemployment in transitioning to

[1] R. Rogerson, 2004, "Two Views on the Deterioration of European Labor Market Outcomes," *Journal of the European Economic Association* 2, 447–455.

(Continued)

employment in the service sector. However, in Europe this generated more long-term unemployment because the service sector was not growing to the extent it was in the United States, so that service sector growth could not absorb all of the workers who were displaced from manufacturing jobs. As well, it is possible that labor market rigidities in Europe exacerbated the transition, as protections for unemployed workers discouraged displaced workers from acquiring the new skills required for service-sector employment. In any event, these are only conjectures, which need to be carefully investigated in future research.

A Search Model of Unemployment

Now that we know some of the features of labor market data, we can proceed to study models that explain the behavior of the unemployment rate. In explaining the unemployment rate, we need to construct a more complicated model of how people use their time. In the models we have worked with to this point, consumers typically use their time for only two different purposes, market work and leisure. Unemployment, however, is an economic activity distinct from either work or leisure, being an activity that involves search. The first search models were developed in the late 1960s,[2] and they have since been refined and put into wide use in labor economics and macroeconomics. This model allows us to think about the factors that motivate the search behavior of unemployed workers, and it permits us to analyze the determinants of the unemployment rate.

The Welfare of Employed and Unemployed Workers

For simplicity, the workers in our model are all in the labor force; that is, they are either employed or unemployed, with U denoting the fraction of workers who are unemployed and $1 - U$ the fraction who are employed. The jobs of the employed differ according to the wages that they pay, where w denotes the real wage associated with a particular job. Let $V_e(w)$ denote the value of being employed. This is the welfare of a worker who is employed and earning a real wage w, and it takes into account the taxes that a worker pays and all possible future events, including the chances of the worker being separated from his or her job and what will happen to the worker in such an event. We let s denote the **separation rate;** that is, s is the fraction of workers who become randomly separated from their jobs every period. This is a simple way to capture job separations that occur in practice because of firings and quits arising from poor matches between workers and firms. We depict the function $V_e(w)$ in Figure 17.6. $V_e(w)$ increases with w, as the worker is better off with higher-paying jobs, and $V_e(w)$ is concave because the worker experiences diminishing marginal utility from higher-paying jobs. That is, the increase in welfare for the worker from an extra unit of real wage income becomes smaller as real wage income increases, reflected in the declining slope of $V_e(w)$.

---

[2]See J. McCall, 1970, "Economics of Information and Job Search," *Quarterly Journal of Economics* 84, 113–126.

Figure 17.6 The Welfare of an Employed Worker

The worker's welfare is increasing in the real wage w that he or she earns on the job, and the function is concave because the marginal benefit from a higher real wage declines as the real wage increases.

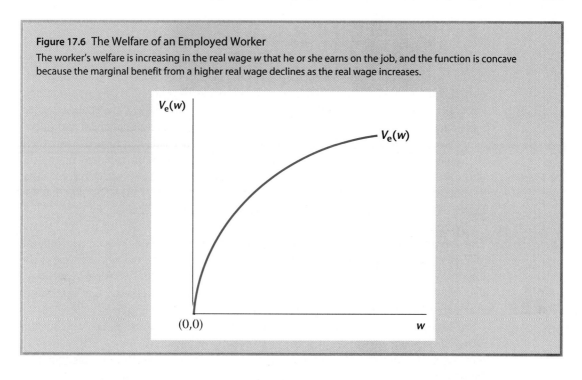

Shifts in the function $V_e(w)$ result as follows:

- The function $V_e(w)$ shifts down if the separation rate s increases. Given an increase in the separation rate, there is a greater chance of an employed worker losing his or her job and becoming unemployed. This makes employment less attractive, and the welfare from being employed at any wage must fall.

- The function $V_e(w)$ shifts down if taxes on wage income increase. Clearly, an increase in such taxes implies that effective wages are lower, which will decrease the welfare of an employed worker for each real wage.

Now, we want to consider the welfare of an unemployed worker, which we denote by V_u. The key determinant of V_u is the size of the UI benefit that an unemployed worker receives. For simplicity, we assume that the UI benefit is a constant real amount b that does not depend on the wage the unemployed worker earned when he or she was employed. Another important determinant of V_u is the frequency with which the unemployed worker receives job offers, and we denote this frequency by p. That is, each period a fraction p of all the unemployed workers receive job offers. Three important facts are the following:

- V_u increases when b increases. An increase in the unemployment benefit increases an unemployed worker's welfare.

- V_u increases when p increases. With a higher p, the chances are better for the unemployed worker of receiving a job offer he or she will take, and this will increase welfare.

- V_u decreases if taxes on unemployment benefits increase. This decreases the effective unemployment benefit and reduces the welfare of the unemployed.

The Reservation Wage

Now that we know how a worker's welfare is determined when employed and unemployed, we can work out how the unemployed worker makes choices. When an unemployed worker receives a job offer, it is a job offer at a particular wage, w. The key decision for the unemployed worker on receiving a job offer is whether to take the offer or to continue searching for work. If a low-wage job is turned down, there is some possibility of receiving a higher-wage offer in the future, but the worker must bear a period of unemployment and uncertainty before this higher-wage offer is received. Therefore, if a bad job is turned down, there is a trade-off in this decision between the short-run losses from unemployment and the uncertain long-run benefits from a good job. Clearly, some wage offer is sufficiently high that the unemployed worker accepts it, and he or she would also accept any wage offer that was higher than this amount. We call this the **reservation wage** and denote it by w^*.

When a wage offer w is received, this implies a level of welfare for the job, $V_e(w)$. The unemployed worker accepts the job if the welfare from taking it is higher than the welfare of being unemployed and declines it otherwise. That is, the worker accepts the job if $V_e(w) \geq V_u$ and turns it down if $V_e(w) < V_u$. In Figure 17.7 we have $V_e(w) \geq V_u$ if $w \geq w^*$ and $V_e(w) < V_u$ if $w < w^*$, and so w^* is the reservation wage that determines acceptance or rejection of job offers.

The reservation wage changes if there are shifts in either $V_e(w)$ or V_u. We consider two examples. First, suppose that the unemployment benefit increases. This causes an increase in V_u from V_u^1 to V_u^2 in Figure 17.8. As a result, the reservation wage increases from w_1^* to w_2^*. Therefore, with an increase in the unemployment benefit, there is a

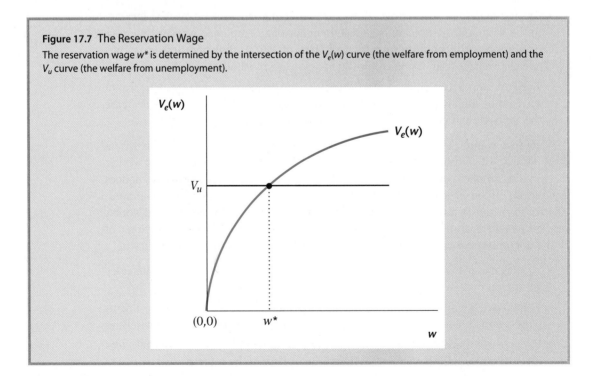

Figure 17.7 The Reservation Wage

The reservation wage w^* is determined by the intersection of the $V_e(w)$ curve (the welfare from employment) and the V_u curve (the welfare from unemployment).

Figure 17.8 An Increase in the Unemployment Insurance Benefit b
The increase in benefits increases the welfare from unemployment from V_u^1 to V_u^2. The reservation wage then increases from w_1^* to w_2^*.

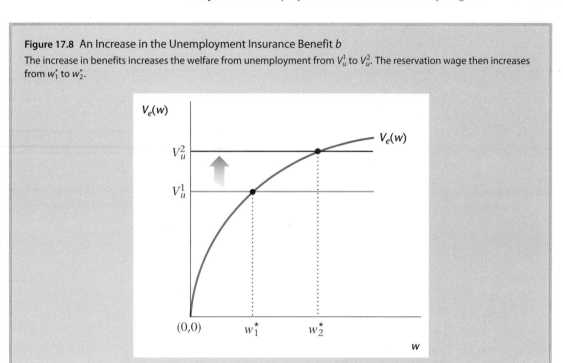

smaller cost to turning down a job to hold out for a higher wage offer, and an unemployed worker then becomes more picky concerning the jobs that he or she will take. Second, suppose that there is an increase in the tax on wage income, which in Figure 17.9 causes a shift down in the welfare of an employed worker from $V_e^1(w)$ to $V_e^2(w)$. As a result, the reservation wage increases from w_1^* to w_2^*. This occurs because, for a given wage offer w, there is now a smaller difference between welfare when employed and when unemployed, and so the net loss from turning down any job offer and waiting for a better one is now smaller. Unemployed workers are then more picky and, therefore, have a higher reservation wage.

The Determination of the Unemployment Rate

Having shown how an unemployed worker chooses his or her reservation wage, we can complete our search model of unemployment and show how it determines the long-run rate of unemployment. In the model, there are flows between the pool of employed workers and the pool of unemployed workers each period. Some employed workers are separated from their jobs and become unemployed, while some unemployed workers receive job offers that are sufficiently attractive to accept. If U is the unemployment rate—that is, the fraction of the labor force that is unemployed—then given that the separation rate is s, the flow of workers from employment to unemployment is $s(1 - U)$. Now, let $H(w)$ denote the fraction of unemployed workers receiving a wage offer whose offer is greater than w, where $H(w)$ is depicted in Figure 17.10. $H(w)$

Figure 17.9 An Increase in the Taxes on the Wage Income of the Employed

The tax increase reduces the welfare from employment, and increases the reservation wage from w_1^* to w_2^*.

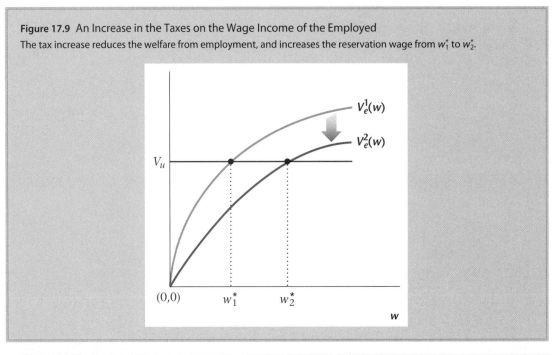

Figure 17.10 The Fraction of Unemployed Workers Receiving a Wage Offer Greater than w

As w increases, the fraction of unemployed workers, $H(w)$, who receive a wage offer greater than w falls.

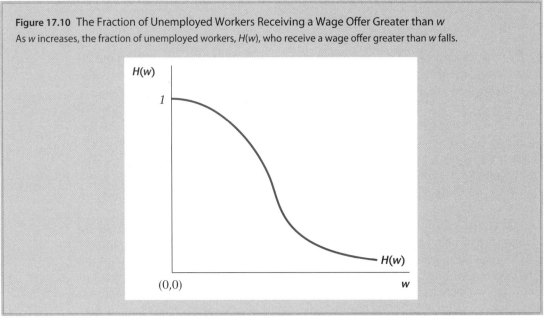

is decreasing in w. Now, if unemployed workers choose a reservation wage w^*, then given that a fraction p of the unemployed receive a job offer and a fraction $H(w^*)$ of those receiving an offer are offered a wage greater than w^*, the portion of the unemployed who will be employed next period is the fraction who receive a wage offer that is at their

Figure 17.11 The Determination of the Unemployment Rate U^* in the Search Model

In the figure, $s(1 - U)$ is the flow of workers from employment to unemployment, and $UpH(w^*)$ is the flow of workers from unemployment to employment. The long-run unemployment rate U^* is determined by the intersection of the two lines.

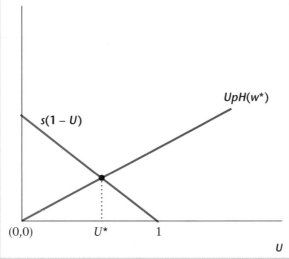

reservation wage or above. Therefore, the flow of workers from unemployment to employment is $UpH(w^*)$.

In a long-run equilibrium, the flow of workers from employment to unemployment must be equal to the flow of workers from unemployment to employment, and so we must have

$$s(1 - U) = UpH(w^*). \tag{17-1}$$

This is an equation that determines the unemployment rate U given s, p , and the reservation wage w^*. In Figure 17.11 we depict the left-hand and right-hand sides of equation (17-1), with the intersection of these two curves determining the long-run equilibrium unemployment rate, denoted by U^*.

Now, Figure 17.12 shows how the reservation wage and the unemployment rate are determined in equilibrium. In Figure 17.12(a), the reservation wage w^* is determined by the intersection of the V_u and $V_e(w)$ curves, while Figure 17.12(b) determines the unemployment rate given the reservation wage w^*.

Now that we have a complete model that determines the reservation wage and the long-run unemployment rate, we can use this model to analyze the effects on these two variables of changes in the economic environment.

An Increase in Unemployment Insurance Benefits   The first experiment we carry out is to look at the effects of a change in unemployment insurance benefits. In Figure 17.13(a) an increase in UI benefits b increases the welfare of the unemployed, V_u, from V_u^1 to V_u^2. The effect of this is to increase the reservation wage from w_1^* to

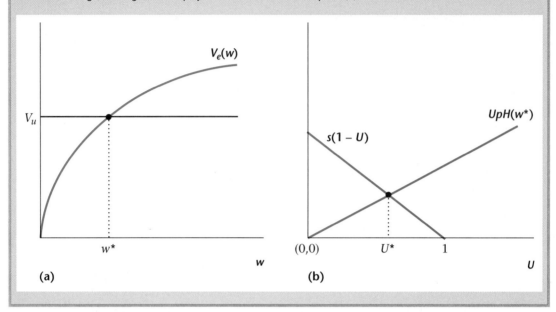

Figure 17.12 The Determination of the Reservation Wage and the Unemployment Rate in the Search Model

The reservation wage w^* is determined in panel (a) by the intersection of the curves $V_e(w)$ and V_u. Then, given the reservation wage, the long-run unemployment rate is determined in panel (b).

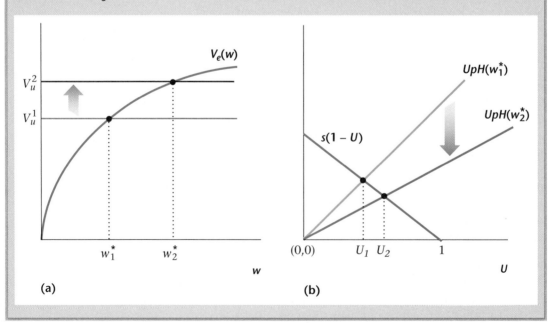

Figure 17.13 An Increase in the Unemployment Insurance Benefit b

The rise in UI benefit increases the value of unemployment from V_u^1 to V_u^2 in panel (a), causing the reservation wage to increase. This decreases the flow of workers from unemployment to employment in panel (b), and the unemployment rate rises in the long run.

w_2^*. This then implies that the fraction of unemployed workers receiving an acceptable wage offer is smaller. That is, because $H(w)$ is decreasing in w, we have $H(w_2^*) < H(w_1^*)$. In Figure 17.13(b), this implies that the line $UpH(w_1^*)$ shifts down to $UpH(w_2^*)$. As a result, the unemployment rate increases from U_1 to U_2 in the long run.

The intuition behind this result is that more generous UI benefits imply that unemployed workers can afford to be more picky about the jobs they accept. On average, then, spells of unemployment tend to be longer, and the long-run unemployment rate must increase. Relatively higher unemployment insurance benefits in part explain higher average unemployment rates in Europe and Canada than in the United States.

An Increase in the Job Offer Rate   A second experiment is to look at the effects of an increase in the job offer rate p on the reservation wage and the long-run unemployment rate. Suppose that the job offer rate p increases. Such a change would result from an increase in the efficiency with which firms and unemployed workers are matched. This could occur for two reasons. First, there might be technological change, such as better information technology, which could increase the likelihood of matches between unemployed workers and firms with vacancies. For example, the Internet greatly increases an unemployed worker's ability to find work at low cost. Second, p could increase because of government intervention. In many countries, the government plays an active role in finding work for unemployed workers, through government-run employment centers and the like.

In Figure 17.14 we show the long-run equilibrium effects of an increase in p. Here, when p increases, this raises the welfare of the unemployed from V_u^1 to V_u^2 in Figure 17.14(a). As a result, the reservation wage increases from w_1^* to w_2^*, because unemployed workers can now afford to be more picky, as they do not have to wait as long for another wage offer if the current offer is turned down. In Figure 17.14(b), there are two effects on the flow of workers from unemployment to employment. The direct effect is that an increase in p from p_1 to p_2 increases the flow of workers from unemployment to employment, because job offers are now received at a higher rate. This shifts up the line $UpH(w^*)$. The indirect effect is that the reservation wage rises, reducing $H(w^*)$, the fraction of workers receiving a job offer who accept the offer. On net, it is not clear whether $UpH(w^*)$ will rise or fall, but in Figure 17.14 we show it increasing from $Up_1H(w_1^*)$ to $Up_2H(w_2^*)$, which implies that the unemployment rate falls in long-run equilibrium from U_1 to U_2. However, if the indirect effect is greater than the direct effect, then the unemployment rate rises.

The implications of this for government policy are important. If the government uses resources to find work for unemployed workers, then this may be counterproductive if its goal is to decrease the unemployment rate. It may be the case that unemployed workers simply become picky enough concerning the jobs they will take that the unemployment rate rises. Also, workers may or may not be better off as a result. The welfare of the unemployed is affected positively, because unemployed workers have better choices, and the employed are in general working at higher-paying jobs, but there is a cost of the government's unemployment program, which

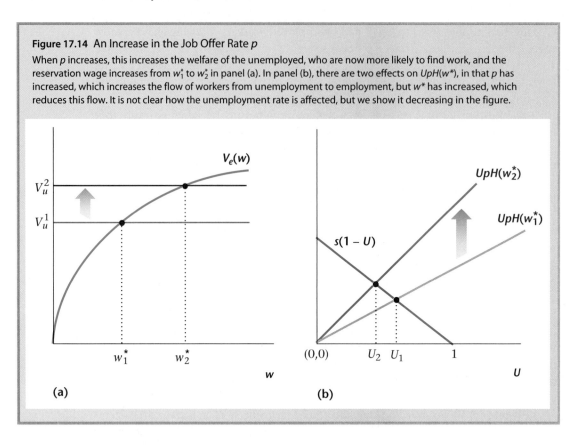

Figure 17.14 An Increase in the Job Offer Rate *p*

When *p* increases, this increases the welfare of the unemployed, who are now more likely to find work, and the reservation wage increases from w_1^* to w_2^* in panel (a). In panel (b), there are two effects on $UpH(w^*)$, in that p has increased, which increases the flow of workers from unemployment to employment, but w^* has increased, which reduces this flow. It is not clear how the unemployment rate is affected, but we show it decreasing in the figure.

ultimately is financed through taxation, and this reduces the welfare of those who are taxed. The net effect on economic welfare is, therefore, uncertain.

Taxes on Labor Income and Unemployment Insurance Benefits Our next set of experiments involves looking at the effects of taxing the labor income of the employed and the UI benefits of the unemployed. First, in Figure 17.15 we show the effects of a tax on labor income. This reduces the welfare of the employed in Figure 17.15(a), with $V_e^1(w)$ shifting down to $V_e^2(w)$. Therefore, the reservation wage increases from w_1^* to w_2^*. Then, the fraction of workers receiving wage offers who accept these offers falls from $H(w_1^*)$ to $H(w_2^*)$, which implies that, in Figure 17.15(b), the line $UpH(w_1^*)$ shifts down to $UpH(w_2^*)$. In equilibrium, the unemployment rate increases from U_1 to U_2.

The effect of the labor income tax is to discourage employment, so that in the long run the unemployment rate increases. This effect is neutralized if the income tax is levied on both labor income and UI benefits. In this case, $V_e(w)$ and V_u both shift down by the same amount, in Figure 17.16(a), so that the reservation wage remains unchanged at w^*. Then, in Figure 17.16(b), the long-run unemployment rate also stays constant at U^*. In the United States, UI benefits are taxed at the same rates as other income, so that employment is not discouraged.

Figure 17.15 An Increase in Taxes on Labor Income

This tax increase reduces the welfare of the employed, increasing the reservation wage from w_1^* to w_2^* in panel (a). In panel (b), the flow of workers from unemployment to employment goes down, which causes the unemployment rate to rise in the long run.

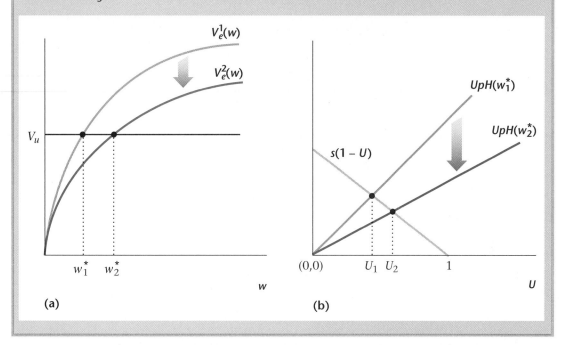

(a)

(b)

Figure 17.16 Taxes on Labor Income and Unemployment Benefits

If taxes fall equally on labor income and unemployment benefits, there is no effect on the reservation wage and no effect on the unemployment rate.

(a)

(b)

MACROECONOMICS IN ACTION
Unemployment Insurance and Incentives

The search model of unemployment illustrates one effect of UI, which is that higher UI benefits tend to make the unemployed more selective concerning the job offers they will accept. This increases the average duration of an unemployment spell and increases the unemployment rate. There are also other effects of UI that we have not included in our simple search model. A second effect has to do with the influence of UI on on-the-job performance. For those employed, effort is required to retain a job. If an employer feels that a worker does not meet some threshold level of effort, then the worker could be fired. Of course, it is difficult for the employer to observe a worker's effort level perfectly, so, in general, some errors might be made by the employer in that workers with good levels of effort might at times be fired and some workers with poor levels of effort might be retained. However, in general, if a worker increases his or her effort level on the job, the chance of being fired is reduced. With higher UI benefits, though, the cost of being fired from a job is lower, and workers, therefore, exert less effort on the job and stand a greater chance of losing their jobs. Higher UI benefits, therefore, act to increase the rate of transition from employment to unemployment through this effect, and this increases the unemployment rate.

A third effect of UI is its influence on the effort that the unemployed put into searching for work. Just as the unemployed become more choosy concerning the job offers they take with higher UI benefits, they also tend to search less intensively, because

higher UI benefits decrease the cost of being unemployed.

A key feature of the three effects of UI on behavior—the effect on job acceptances, the effect on on-the-job effort, and the effect on search effort—is that all of these effects are imperfectly observable. That is, there are moral hazard problems associated with UI, just as there are moral hazard problems for other forms of insurance (including deposit insurance, as discussed in Chapter 16), as we mentioned earlier in this chapter. It is difficult for the provider of UI to observe whether the unemployed are turning down good job offers, whether workers are being fired because their effort is too low, or whether long spells of unemployment are the result of low search effort. Indeed, the fact that UI is provided by the government in the United States may indicate that the moral hazard problems associated with UI are so severe that UI would not be provided by a private insurer in the absence of government provision.

UI systems need to be designed with moral hazard problems in mind, and the UI system in the United States certainly has features that, at least partially, correct for moral hazard. For example, the level of benefits does not imply full insurance, in that (as pointed out earlier in this chapter) the replacement rate (the ratio of benefits when unemployed to wages when employed) is about 0.5, and benefits are limited in duration for individuals, typically extending for only about six months of unemployment. An optimal UI system achieves an optimal tradeoff between the benefits of insurance and the costs of moral hazard. If there is too much insurance (for example, if the unemployed receive benefits equal to their wages on the job forever) then workers and the unemployed have poor incentives; but, if there is too little insurance, unemployment is too painful.

What would an optimal unemployment insurance system look like, and how close does the UI system in the United States come to such an optimal system? Several articles in the economics literature have attempted to address these questions. An approach that is useful in this context is a dynamic contracting model, which allows us to think about economic problems in a dynamic framework where information is not perfect, as is the case with unemployment insurance. An early article by S. Shavell and L. Weiss[3] shows that the optimal unemployment insurance benefit decreases over time. That is, in contrast to the UI system in the United States, where benefits are constant for six months of unemployment and then go to zero, optimally benefits should decrease over time continuously and extend indefinitely. The optimal benefit schedule looks like this because the longer a person has been unemployed, the more likely it is that they are not looking very hard for a job, and so a person should be penalized with lower benefits the longer they have been unemployed. However, a person may have been unemployed for a long time simply because he or she was unlucky, so it does not make sense to reduce benefits to zero for the long-term unemployed.

A more recent paper by Cheng Wang and Stephen Williamson[4] broadens the approach of Shavell and Weiss. Wang and Williamson show that an optimal unemployment insurance system should be more individual-specific, while having the Shavell–Weiss feature that UI benefits decline with the duration of unemployment. That is, the level of benefits for an unemployed person should depend not only on the length of time since the person became unemployed and the wage when employed but also on the whole history of employment and unemployment for that person. Such an optimal system would be implemented by having each U.S. citizen hold an account with the UI authority that would be credited during periods of employment and debited during periods of unemployment when the individual is drawing UI benefits. The level of the current UI benefit allowed would depend on the balance in the account at that time. While such a system looks far different from the UI system currently in place in the United States, the discouraging news is that the welfare gain from moving to an optimal system would be small. Wang and Williamson's estimate is that a welfare increase equivalent to about 1% of GDP, at most, would result from switching from the current UI system in the United States to an optimal system.

[3]S. Shavell and L. Weiss, 1979, "The Optimal Payment of Unemployment Insurance Benefits Over Time," *Journal of Political Economy* 87, 1347–1362.

[4]C. Wang and S. Williamson, 2002, "Moral Hazard, Optimal Unemployment Insurance, and Experience Rating," *Journal of Monetary Economics* 49, 1337–1371.

Perspectives on the Financial Crisis
The Natural Rate of Unemployment and the 2008–2009 Recession

The "natural rate of unemployment" is a term originally coined by Milton Friedman, who defined it as[5]

> ...the level that would be ground out by the Walrasian system of general equilibrium equations, provided there is imbedded in them the actual structural characteristics of the labor and commodity markets...

Friedman did not have modern search theory at hand to put some formal structure on what he meant, but it appears that Friedman's notion of a natural rate of unemployment could be captured in a search model, related to the one we have been studying. Friedman appeared to think that there were long-run factors in the economy determining the natural rate of unemployment, such as the generosity of unemployment insurance, the tax system, and demographic factors. Further, he argued that there could be short-run departures from the natural rate because of temporary shocks to the economy, such as changes in monetary policy or productivity shocks.

The natural rate of unemployment is closely related to the concept of an "output gap," which plays a central role in New Keynesian economics. The output gap has a specific theoretical meaning in a New Keynesian model, in that it is the difference between potential aggregate output and actual aggregate output, where potential aggregate output is the equilibrium level of output that would arise if prices were not sticky.

The language involving natural rates of unemployment and output gaps typically suggests that there is something wrong with a departure from the natural rate of unemployment

or the existence of a positive output gap. Keynesian economists, for example, believe that if the unemployment rate is above the natural rate, then there are idle resources that could be utilized through a policy intervention to " stimulate" the economy.

Suppose that we accept the Keynesian view that the unemployment rate fluctuates around some long-run natural rate and that fluctuations around this natural rate are due to the existence of sticky wages and prices. What problems could result? The first is the practical problem of measuring the natural rate of unemployment. Clearly, we should not measure the natural rate as some historical average unemployment rate. Over some periods of time this would have lead to significant policy errors. For example, from Figure 17.1, if the natural rate of unemployment in 1985 were measured as the average unemployment rate over the previous 20 years, policymakers over the next 15 years until 2000 would have thought that labor markets were too tight and would have been attempting to introduce more slack into the economy. This would have been inappropriate, as there was a downward trend in the unemployment rate after 1985.

Clearly, then, one would have to be more sophisticated about measuring the natural unemployment rate—for instance, by taking into account the relationship between the natural rate and the long-run factors determining it. Ultimately however, in using this approach, the policymaker must take a stand on what the natural unemployment rate is at any point in time—i.e., he or she must have some measure of what he or she thinks the unemployment rate should be. This is perhaps too much to ask.

Modern search theory, as it has been applied in macroeconomics, typically dispenses with the

---

[5]M. Friedman, 1968, "The Role of Monetary Policy," *American Economic Review* 58, p. 8.

notion of a natural rate of unemployment because, once one has a good model that can determine the unemployment rate at any point in time, the concept of a natural rate is useless. A good search model can tell us a great deal about the determinants of the unemployment rate, and can be useful for telling us what policy measures are appropriate in what contexts.

In the context of the 2008–2009 recession, a widespread view (particularly among Keynesians) appears to be that, because aggregate GDP fell so quickly and the unemployment rate rose so quickly (see Figure 17.1) in 2008 and 2009, that the level of GDP and the unemployment rate that existed in late 2007 are what is appropriate two years later. Further, a common view is that the

unemployment rate of late 2007 can be achieved in short order through a sufficiently large program of government spending increases, tax cuts, and accommodative monetary policy. However, the key problem is that there is nothing that can be done immediately to make world financial markets work in the same way that they did in late 2007, and even if this could be done, it is not clear that it should be. Belief in natural unemployment rates and output gaps can lead us to think that we can achieve something that is essentially impossible or ill-advised. While the concept of a natural rate of unemployment might have been useful for Milton Friedman in 1968, economic science has advanced to the point where we can now do better.

The Efficiency Wage Model

An alternative to search theory in modeling unemployment is the efficiency wage model, which takes seriously the notion that workers' wages affect their on-the-job performance.[6] In the efficiency wage model, a firm may be willing to pay its workers a real wage that is higher than the wage that would be competitively determined, because this induces the firm's employees to work harder. In equilibrium, more workers than are employed would like to work, but it is not efficient for firms to hire them; thus, there is unemployment. Efficiency wage considerations make the labor market work quite differently from the standard competitive labor market we studied in previous chapters, as we will see.

In the efficiency wage model, a worker's effort increases with the wage he or she receives. To capture this, we let $e(w)$ denote the effort of each worker on the job, where w is the real wage, and the function $e(w)$, an increasing function, is depicted in Figure 17.17. Then, if N denotes hours worked by all workers, the effective labor input for the firm is $e(w)N$, or effort per worker multiplied by total hours worked, which gives total effort.

There are two reasons that worker effort would tend to increase with the real wage, both of which are associated with information problems in the labor market. First, there can be problems of **adverse selection** in the labor market. Adverse selection problems generally occur in markets where there are different types of market participants, and it is difficult for other market participants to distinguish among these different types. In a labor market context, there can be workers of different abilities, but firms may have difficulty distinguishing high-ability workers from low-ability workers. Now, if

[6]For a survey, see L. Katz, 1986, "Efficiency Wage Theories: A Partial Evaluation," *NBER Macroeconomics Annual* 1, 235–276.

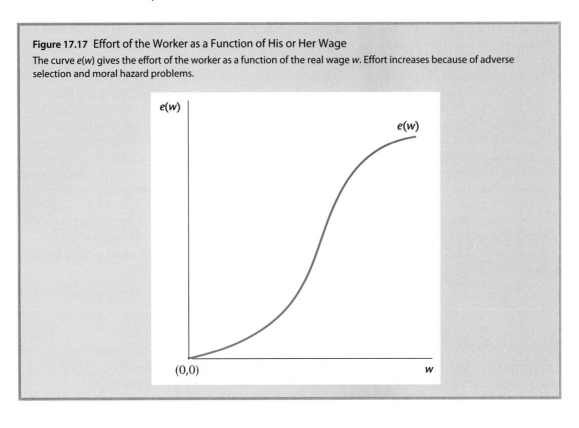

Figure 17.17 Effort of the Worker as a Function of His or Her Wage
The curve $e(w)$ gives the effort of the worker as a function of the real wage w. Effort increases because of adverse selection and moral hazard problems.

high-ability workers tend to have higher reservation wages than low-ability workers, because in general they have better options in the labor market, then a higher wage offered by a particular firm implies that the quality of the firm's job applicants will increase. Therefore, a higher real wage implies that average effort by workers is higher. Second, there may be a moral hazard problem in the relationship between a firm and its workers (recall our earlier discussion of moral hazard in this chapter and in Chapter 16). A moral hazard problem can arise if a firm has difficulty in monitoring the on-the-job effort of its workers. However, if the firm can threaten to fire a worker if it detects shirking, then the loss to the worker from being fired is larger the greater the gap between market real wages and the real wage offered by the firm. Therefore, effort by the worker increases with the real wage paid by the firm.

Optimization by the Firm: The Choice of Employment and the Efficiency Wage

Now, given that the effective quantity of labor hired by the firm is $e(w)N$, the production function for the firm is given by

$$Y = zF(K, e(w)N),$$

where Y is output, z is total factor productivity, and K is the capital stock, assumed fixed in the short run. The firm's goal is to maximize profits. In a competitive environment where a firm is a price-taker, typically the firm does not want to offer a real wage to its workers above the market real wage, as this would not be profit maximizing. In the efficiency wage model, however, it may be profit maximizing for the firm to pay a real wage higher than the market wage. Therefore, one of the choices for the firm here concerns what real wage it should pay. The firm then chooses the wage rate w and employment N to maximize profits, where profits are given by

$$\pi = F(K, e(w)N) - wN.$$

The firm hires labor N until the marginal product of labor is equal to the real wage. In this case, the marginal product of labor is

$$MP_N = e(w)MP_{e(w)N}.$$

That is, the marginal product of labor is the effort of the worker at the real wage offered by the firm multiplied by the marginal product of effective units of labor. Then, the firm hires labor until $MP_N = w$, or

$$e(w)MP_{e(w)N} = w. \tag{17-2}$$

Equation (17-2) describes a relationship between w and N that we can interpret as the firm's demand curve for labor. Under certain conditions, this demand curve does not slope downward everywhere, but we assume that $e(w)$ and the production function have properties that guarantee that the implied demand curve for labor N^d is downward sloping, as in Figure 17.18. The demand curve tells us how much labor N the firm wants to hire given any real wage w.

Now, in choosing the real wage, the firm wants to minimize the cost of inducing each worker to supply effort. If the firm offers its workers a higher wage, this induces more effort on the part of workers, but this is of course more costly for the firm. What the firm wants to do is to maximize $\frac{e(w)}{w}$, which is the effort received from the worker per unit of real wages paid to the worker. In Figure 17.19, if a worker receives a real wage w', then effort is $e(w')$. Then, $\frac{e(w')}{w'}$ is the slope of a line from the origin to point A in Figure 17.19. Now, given that the goal of the firm is to maximize $\frac{e(w)}{w}$, the firm chooses a wage such that a line from the origin to a point on the curve $e(w)$ is just tangent to the curve, as in Figure 17.20. Here, w^* is the optimal wage for the firm to choose, and we call this wage the **efficiency wage.** If the firm sets the real wage at the efficiency wage, then workers will supply the optimal amount of effort on the job.

Labor Market Equilibrium in the Efficiency Wage Model

The efficiency wage model implies that there can be unemployment in equilibrium. In Figure 17.21(a) the efficiency wage is w^*, which is above the market-clearing wage w^{**} that would imply equality between the supply and demand for labor. The representative firm does not reduce the real wage to w^{**} because this would decrease its profits, as workers would supply an inefficient quantity of effort. In equilibrium, the firm sets the real wage at the efficiency wage w^*, which implies that the equilibrium quantity of employment is N^*, and the quantity of unemployment is $N_1^s - N^*$, which is equal to the hours that workers want to supply at the efficiency wage minus the quantity of

Figure 17.18 The Demand for Labor in the Efficiency Wage Model
The demand curve for labor, N^d, is downward sloping in this model.

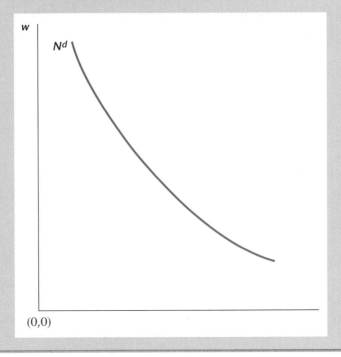

Figure 17.19 The Ratio of Effort to the Real Wage
Given the real wage w', the ratio of effort to the real wage is the slope of a line from the origin to point A.

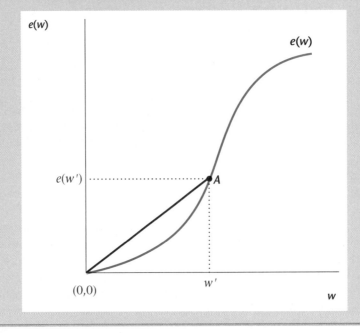

Figure 17.20 Determination of the Efficiency Wage

The efficiency wage w^* is chosen so as to maximize the ratio of effort to the real wage, $\frac{e(w)}{w}$. Point B is the point of tangency between the curve $e(w)$ and a line from the origin.

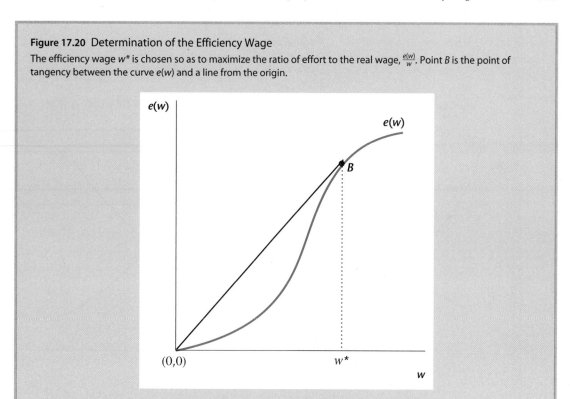

labor firms want to hire. This looks very similar to phenomena that occur in Keynesian macroeconomic models, although in the efficiency wage model we can have permanent real wage rigidity, as opposed to the temporary nominal rigidity that exists, for example, in the New Keynesian sticky price model in Chapter 13.

Alternatively, it is possible for the efficiency wage to be smaller than the market-clearing real wage, as in Figure 17.21(b). Here, the equilibrium quantity of employment is N^* and the equilibrium real wage is w^{**}. In this case, at the efficiency wage the firm cannot hire all the labor it would like, and, therefore, it is forced to bid up wages to the point at which the market real wage implies that the quantity of labor the firm wants to hire is equal to the quantity that workers want to supply.

The Efficiency Wage Model and Business Cycles

If there is unemployment in the efficiency wage model, then this implies that the quantity of employment is determined by the labor demand curve. Therefore, labor supply has no effect on employment and output. As a result, the output supply curve is vertical, as in Figure 17.22(c), because the real interest rate does not affect the labor demand curve. In the figure, the equilibrium real interest rate is r^*, aggregate output is Y^* [in panels (b) and (c)], employment is N^*, and the equilibrium real wage is the efficiency wage w^* [in panels (a) and (b)].

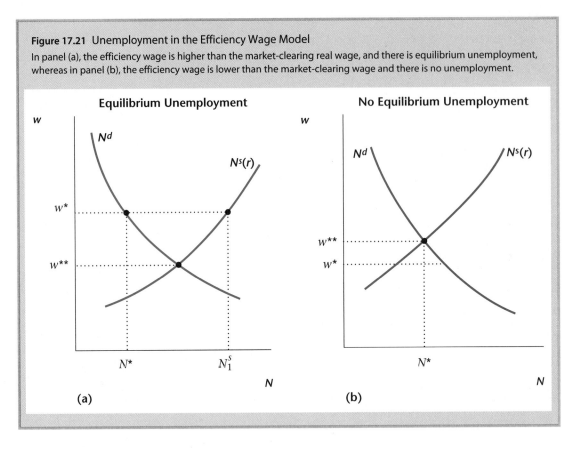

Figure 17.21 Unemployment in the Efficiency Wage Model

In panel (a), the efficiency wage is higher than the market-clearing real wage, and there is equilibrium unemployment, whereas in panel (b), the efficiency wage is lower than the market-clearing wage and there is no unemployment.

Given the vertical output supply curve, aggregate output changes only if there is a shift in the output supply curve. If there is a shock that increases some component of output demand—for example, if government spending G increases—then this shifts the output demand curve rightward in Figure 17.23(b) from Y_1^d to Y_2^d. The labor supply curve shifts rightward from $N_1^s(r_1)$ to $N_2^s(r_1)$ because of the negative wealth effect of an increase in government spending. In equilibrium, the real interest rate increases from r_1 to r_2, with output remaining unchanged at Y_1. In Figure 17.23(a), the labor supply curve shifts rightward from $N_2^s(r_1)$ to $N_2^s(r_2)$ given the increase in the real interest rate, as consumers substitute leisure in the future for leisure in the present. There is then an increase in unemployment with no change in employment.

The only shock to the economy that can cause aggregate output to fluctuate in the efficiency wage model is a shock that shifts the output supply curve. A candidate shock is a change in total factor productivity. Now, suppose that total factor productivity increases. In Figure 17.24(a) the labor demand curve then shifts rightward from N_1^d to N_2^d. However, there is no change in the efficiency wage w^*, because the efficiency wage is determined by the schedule $e(w)$, as in Figure 17.20. The output supply curve shifts rightward from Y_1^s to Y_2^s in Figure 17.24(b), which implies that the real interest rate falls from r_1 to r_2, causing a leftward shift in the labor supply curve from $N^s(r_1)$ to $N^s(r_2)$. In equilibrium, the level of employment rises from N_1 to N_2 and unemployment falls. Thus, the model is consistent

Figure 17.22 The Output Supply Curve in the Efficiency Wage Model

The output supply curve in panel (c) is vertical, because in panel (a) the quantity of employment is determined by the labor demand curve, which does not depend on the real interest rate.

Figure 17.23 An Increase in G in the Efficiency Wage Model

An increase in government spending shifts the output demand curve to the right in panel (b) of the figure. This increases the real interest rate but has no effect on aggregate output in equilibrium.

with most of the business cycle facts that are discussed in Chapter 3. That is, the model predicts that, under productivity shocks, consumption and investment are procyclical [because the decrease in r in Figure 17.24(b) causes C and I to increase], and employment is procyclical. However, the model does not predict the procyclicality of the real wage, because the efficiency wage does not respond to productivity shocks.

The only way that the efficiency wage model could be consistent with a procyclical real wage under total factor productivity shocks is if the change in total factor productivity somehow affects the efficiency wage. It would be useful to explore this possibility. If an increase in total factor productivity is the result of better management practices, this change might also imply that firms develop improved methods for monitoring workers in the firm and this could change $e(w)$. Effort then increases for each level of the real wage. In Figure 17.25 the effort function shifts up from $e_1(w)$ to $e_2(w)$, which implies that the efficiency wage decreases from w_1^* to w_2^*. Therefore, this would result in a decrease in the real wage in conjunction with an increase in aggregate output. Then, the model would predict that the real wage is countercyclical, which is inconsistent with the data.

To conclude, the efficiency wage model is not consistent with all of the business cycle regularities, although in this respect it is no worse than the Keynesian sticky price model studied in Chapter 13. A perhaps unexpected feature of the efficiency wage model is that it has a Keynesian-type sticky real wage, but the other properties of the model are actually quite different from those of Keynesian models. We typically think of Keynesian

Figure 17.24 An Increase in Total Factor Productivity in the Efficiency Wage Model

An increase in total factor productivity shifts the labor demand curve in panel (a) to the right, and the output supply curve in panel (b) to the right. The efficiency wage remains unchanged, and employment and output increase.

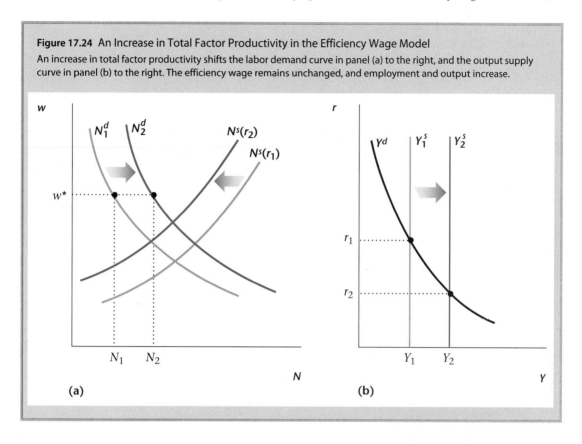

(a)

(b)

models as having the feature that shocks to the demand for output cause aggregate output to fluctuate. In the efficiency wage model, however, shocks that affect output demand have no effect on aggregate output, and changes in government spending are completely ineffective in changing the quantity of output produced.

This chapter ends our detailed study of the causes of unemployment. In Chapter 18, we examine why well-intentioned policymakers can generate inflation and the problems in obtaining commitment by a central bank to low inflation.

Chapter Summary

- The key determinants of the unemployment rate are aggregate economic activity, demographics, government intervention, and sectoral shifts.
- The participation rate is affected by demographics and by the different labor market behavior of men and women.
- The unemployment rate is a countercyclical variable, whereas the participation rate is procyclical.
- The employment/population ratio is more cyclically variable than is the participation rate.
- In the search model of unemployment, the welfare of an employed worker increases with the real wage the worker earns, decreases with the chances of separation from his or her current job, and decreases as taxes on wage income increase. The welfare of an unemployed worker

Figure 17.25 An Increase in the Effectiveness of Monitoring by the Firm

If firms more effectively monitor workers, this causes the effort function $e(w)$ to shift up and reduces the efficiency wage from w_1^* to w_2^*.

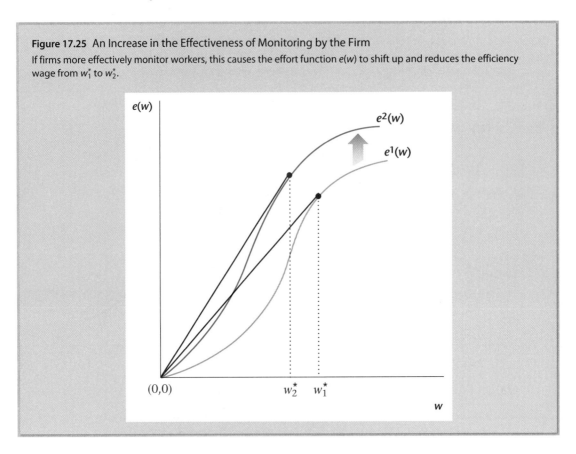

increases as unemployment insurance benefits increase, increases as the chances of receiving job offers increase, and decreases as taxes on unemployment benefits rise.

- The reservation wage is the wage at which an unemployed worker is indifferent between accepting a job offer and continuing to search for work. When an unemployed worker receives a wage offer, the wage offer is accepted if that wage offer is at or above the worker's reservation wage. The reservation wage increases as UI benefits increase and as taxes on wage income increase.

- In the search model, the long-run unemployment rate is determined by the condition that the flow of workers between unemployment and employment is equal to the flow in the opposite direction.

- An increase in UI benefits increases the unemployment rate, but an increase in the job offer rate has an indeterminate effect on the unemployment rate. Thus, government intervention designed to make it easier for unemployed workers to find jobs may not reduce the unemployment rate. Taxes on labor income increase the unemployment rate, but if labor income and unemployment benefits are taxed equally, then there is no effect on the unemployment rate.

- In the efficiency wage model, worker effort increases with the real wage as the result of adverse selection in the labor market and moral hazard on the job. The efficiency wage is the wage set by the firm that maximizes the ratio of worker effort to the real wage. In equilibrium, there may be unemployment, but the firm does not lower its wages, as this reduces worker effort and causes profits to fall.

- The efficiency wage model has the property that, if there is unemployment in equilibrium, then aggregate output is determined by the vertical output supply curve, and labor supply does not matter for employment.

- An increase in government spending has no effect on output and employment, and an increase in total factor productivity increases output and employment but has no effect on the efficiency wage or the equilibrium real wage. The efficiency wage model is not entirely consistent with the key business cycle facts.

Key Terms

Adverse selection Phenomenon that occurs in a market where there are different types of market participants, and other market participants have difficulty distinguishing among them. (p. 629)

Demography The study of population. (p. 609)

Efficiency wage In the efficiency wage model, this is the wage the firm sets to maximize the effort of workers relative to the wage they are paid. (p. 631)

Replacement ratio For an unemployed worker receiving unemployment insurance, this is unemployment benefits divided by the person's wages when he or she was working. (p. 611)

Reservation wage The wage such that an unemployed worker will accept any job offering this wage or more. (p. 618)

Separation rate The rate at which employed workers become separated from their jobs. (p. 616)

Questions for Review

1. What are the four key determinants of the unemployment rate?
2. Is the unemployment rate procyclical or countercyclical?
3. How do demographic factors affect the participation rate?
4. Is the participation rate procyclical or countercyclical?
5. What causes shifts in the welfare of the employed in the search model?
6. What causes shifts in the welfare of the unemployed in the search model?
7. What determines the reservation wage in the search model?
8. How does an increase in the UI benefit affect the reservation wage in the search model and why?
9. How does an increase in the tax on wage income affect the reservation wage in the search model and why?
10. How does an increase in the UI benefit affect the long-run unemployment rate in the search model and why?
11. How does an increase in the job offer rate affect the reservation wage and the long-run unemployment rate in the search model? What implications does this have for government policy?
12. Explain why it matters whether UI benefits are taxed.
13. Give two reasons that the effort of workers on the job can depend on the real wage workers are paid.
14. Why can there be unemployment in the efficiency wage model?
15. What are the effects of an increase in government spending in the efficiency wage model?
16. What are the effects of an increase in total factor productivity in the efficiency wage model?
17. Which business cycle facts does the efficiency wage model fit, and which does it not?

Problems

1. Determine the effects of an increase in the separation rate s on the reservation wage and on the long-run unemployment rate in the search model of unemployment. Explain your results.

2. Suppose that there is an increase in total factor productivity, which implies that all firms offer higher wages. In the search model of unemployment, determine the effects of this on the reservation wage and on the long-run unemployment rate. Explain your results.

3. Suppose that the government introduces an unemployment insurance program in which UI benefits are financed by taxes on employed workers. Determine the effects on the reservation wage and on the long-run unemployment rate in the search model of unemployment, and explain your results.

4. Suppose that the government makes it more difficult to qualify for unemployment insurance, for example, by increasing the duration of employment required before collecting UI benefits during an unemployment spell. Determine the effects of this change in government policy on the reservation wage and the long-run unemployment rate in the search model of unemployment.

5. Suppose that, in the efficiency wage model, it becomes more difficult for the firm to distinguish high-ability workers from low-ability workers in the labor market. What effects does this have on $e(w)$ and the efficiency wage? Explain your results.

6. Suppose in the efficiency wage model that some of the firm's capital stock is destroyed. Determine the effects on aggregate output, employment, unemployment, the real wage, and the real interest rate, and explain your results.

7. Because the real wage is sticky in the efficiency wage model, does this mean that efficiency wages imply that money is not neutral, as was the case in the Keynesian sticky wage model? Explain with the use of diagrams.

8. Suppose that future total factor productivity is expected to increase in the efficiency wage model. What are the effects on equilibrium output, employment, unemployment, the real wage, consumption, and investment? Explain your results.

Working with the Data

1. Construct a time series plot of the median duration of unemployment. What do you notice? How does the median duration of unemployment move over the business cycle? Can you make sense of these observations by appealing to the search model of unemployment? Why or why not?

2. Construct time series plots of the unemployment rates of white males 20 years old and over and white males 16–19. How do these compare? How would you explain the differences?

3. Construct time series plots of the unemployment rates of white males 20 years old and over, black males 20 and over, white females 20 and over, and black females 20 and over. What patterns do you notice here and how have they changed over time? Can a search model or an efficiency wage model explain the key features of this data?

chapter 18

Inflation, the Phillips Curve, and Central Bank Commitment

Since the mid-1980s, the inflation rate has been quite low in the United States. Using the rate of growth in the implicit GDP price deflator as a measure of inflation, the quarterly inflation rate in the United States, at annual rates, has been below 4% since 1991, and an inflation rate in excess of 10% was last seen in the United States in 1980. Further, the United States has never had a hyperinflationary episode on the order of the 10,000% inflation rate achieved in Austria in 1921–1922, or the 20,000% inflation rate in Argentina in 1989–1990. Inflation is of little public concern currently in the United States, and Americans have been able to avoid some of the truly calamitous experiences with inflation of other countries.

From Chapter 16, we know some of the economic costs of inflation, which arise from the distortions inflation causes in intertemporal rates of return. Inflation causes the public to hold an inefficiently low aggregate stock of real money balances, and it reduces aggregate output and employment below their efficient levels. The costs of inflation are certainly obvious to anyone who has lived through a hyperinflation. Significant public concern can even arise about inflation during relatively moderate inflations, such as what occurred in the United States during the 1970s when the average inflation rate was below 10%.

If it is widely recognized that inflation is undesirable, why then do governments let it happen? In some circumstances, inflation clearly results from problems associated with fiscal policy. Indeed, essentially all hyperinflations can be traced to the existence of large government budget deficits. A government may have high expenditures, perhaps because it must fight a war. However, the public may be unwilling to pay for these expenditures through taxation, or the government may be unwilling to increase taxes. As a result, the government may resort to printing money to finance the government deficit. Moderate inflations, though, need not result from high government budget deficits and the necessity of resorting to the inflation tax. For example, the moderate inflation in the United States in the 1970s was not associated with large government budget deficits and would not have generated much seigniorage, so what motivated the Fed to increase the money supply at a high rate so as to cause what appeared to be excessive inflation? In this chapter, we use a version of the Friedman–Lucas money surprise model to evaluate two potential explanations for the behavior of the Fed in the post–World War II period. In this model, an unanticipated increase in the rate of money supply growth (a money surprise) causes an unanticipated increase in the inflation rate and can cause the quantity of labor supplied and aggregate output to increase temporarily. We use the money surprise model and the post–World War II U.S. inflation experience as a convenient example to illustrate some general principles concerning the causes of inflation.

The Friedman–Lucas money surprise model provides an explanation for the Phillips curve, which is the sometimes-observed positive relationship between the inflation rate and real aggregate economic activity (as discussed in Chapter 3). In U.S. data, the Phillips curve is readily discernible during some time periods, while during other periods it is not. The Friedman–Lucas money surprise model is a useful aid in understanding why we should sometimes observe a Phillips curve, and sometimes not, in that the model tells us that the Phillips curve is an unstable relationship that shifts with the inflation rate that the private sector expects.

The Friedman–Lucas money surprise model is not the only theoretical framework predicting a Phillips curve relationship. In New Keynesian theory, a "New Keynesian Phillips Curve" results from the forward-looking behavior of price-setting firms. Although the mechanism by which the Phillips curve arises is similar in the two models, in that an output increase can be associated with unexpected inflation, the Friedman–Lucas money surprise model and the New Keynesian model have very different policy implications.

Two competing explanations for the behavior of the Fed over the post–World War II period are the *central bank learning story*, and the *central bank commitment story*. In the central bank learning story, high inflation in the 1970s was caused by a lack of knowledge on the part of the Fed concerning how the economy works. Once the Fed understood, by the early 1980s, that higher inflation could not permanently increase aggregate output, it acted quickly to reduce inflation. In the central bank commitment story, high inflation in the 1970s was caused by an inability of the Fed to commit to not using surprise inflation to increase output in the short run.

Ultimately, we conclude that central bank commitment was probably not an important element in recent U.S. inflation history. However, this does not mean that commitment is unimportant for central banks in all countries and under all circumstances. Indeed, as we discuss, central bank commitment appears to have been critical in controlling inflation in Hong Kong since 1983.

The Phillips Curve

In the 1950s, A. W. Phillips noticed, in data for the United Kingdom,[1] that there was a negative relationship between the rate of change in nominal wages and the unemployment rate. Other researchers found that such a relationship existed in data for other countries. Further, because the rate of change in nominal wages is highly positively correlated with the rate of change in other money prices, and the unemployment rate is highly negatively correlated with the deviation of aggregate economic activity from trend, it should not be surprising that if there is a negative correlation between the rate

---

[1]See A.W. Phillips, 1958, "The Relationship Between Unemployment and the Rate of Change of Money Wages in the United Kingdom, 1861–1957," *Economica* 25, 283–299.

of change in nominal wages and the unemployment rate, there is also a positive correlation between the inflation rate and the deviation of aggregate economic activity from trend. Indeed, the term *Phillips curve* has come to denote any positive correlation between aggregate economic activity and the inflation rate. For our purposes, we conveniently define the Phillips curve to be a positive relationship between the rate of inflation and the deviation of real aggregate output from trend. If we let Y^T denote trend real aggregate output and Y denote actual real aggregate output, then a Phillips curve is described by the relationship

$$i = H(Y - Y^T),$$

where i is the inflation rate and H is an increasing function. We depict this relationship in Figure 18.1.

Can we observe a Phillips curve in U.S. data? For this exercise, it is useful to look at data on inflation and the deviations of aggregate output from trend over different periods of time. The data we examine is for 1947–2009, and we divide this sample into three subperiods, 1947–1969, 1970–1984, and 1985–2009, which are periods of, respectively, low inflation, high inflation, and low inflation. In Figures 18.2 through 18.4, we graph the inflation rate, measured as the quarterly percentage change in the implicit GDP price deflator, against the percentage deviation of real GDP from trend. In each figure, the solid colored line represents the best statistical fit of a linear Phillips curve to the scatter plot.

A Phillips curve is most clearly discernible in the data for 1947–1969 in Figure 18.2. There is a statistically significant positive correlation between the inflation rate and the

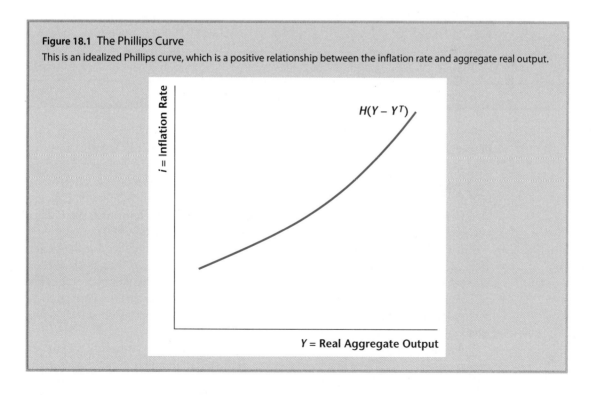

Figure 18.1 The Phillips Curve
This is an idealized Phillips curve, which is a positive relationship between the inflation rate and aggregate real output.

Figure 18.2 The Phillips Curve, 1947–1969

The Phillips curve is discernible, and there is a statistically significant positive correlation between the inflation rate and the percentage deviation in real GDP from trend. However, the Phillips curve relationship is noisy.

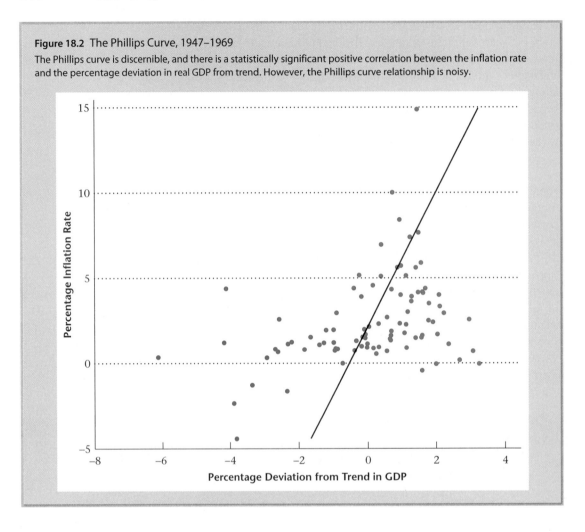

percentage deviation of real GDP from trend, but the relationship is fairly noisy. In Figures 18.3 and 18.4, a Phillips curve can be fitted to the data, and it has a positive slope, but the positive correlation between the inflation rate and the percentage deviation of real GDP from trend is not statistically significant. Further, there is a very wide scatter of points around the estimated Phillips curve in both Figures 18.3 and 18.4. Essentially, the Phillips curve more or less disappears from the pre-1969 period to the post-1969 period.

In Figure 18.5, we show a scatter plot that includes all of the data for the period 1947–2009, along with the Phillips curves fit for the sub-periods in Figures 18.2–18.4. There are two striking features of Figure 18.5. The first is that the Phillips curve is not visible in the data for the whole period 1947–2009. The second is that the Phillips curve shifted up during the period of high inflation from 1970–1984, and shifted back down when the inflation rate fell during the period 1985–2009.

Now, if we show the data in their time series form in Figures 18.6 and 18.7, we see in Figure 18.6 that there was a large increase in the inflation rate from low levels in the

Figure 18.3 The Phillips Curve, 1970–1984

A Phillips curve can be fitted to the data, but the positive correlation between the inflation rate and the percentage deviation in real GDP from trend is not statistically significant.

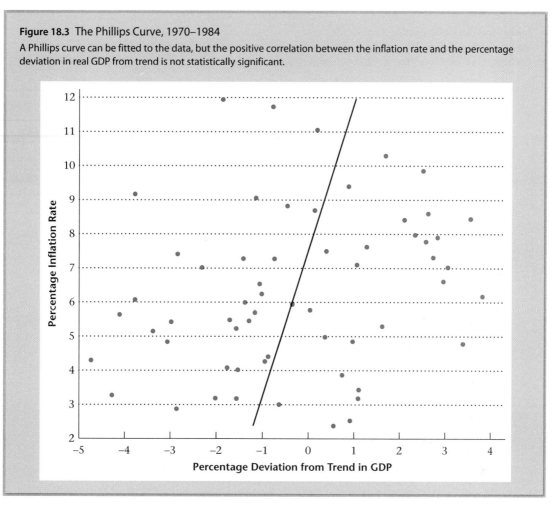

late 1940s and 1950s (except for the temporarily high inflations in the late 1940s and during the Korean War in the early 1950s) and 1960s to very high levels during the 1970s. In the early 1980s the inflation rate began to fall on trend until the late 1990s. This average behavior of inflation appears unrelated to the behavior of the deviations of GDP from trend in Figure 18.7. That is, the fact that inflation is high or low for an extended period of time does not seem to matter for how output moves about trend. Therefore, we can make two observations about empirical Phillips curve relations:

1. Clear Phillips curve relations do not exist in all data sets. In U.S. data, we can observe a Phillips curve before 1969, but not after.

2. The Phillips curve relation appears to shift over time. Over some extended periods the inflation rate is high, but it is low over other extended periods. However, this average behavior of the inflation rate seems unrelated to the behavior of deviations of real GDP from trend.

Figure 18.4 The Phillips Curve, 1985–2009

A Phillips curve can be fitted to the data, but the positive correlation between the inflation rate and the percentage deviation in real GDP from trend is not statistically significant.

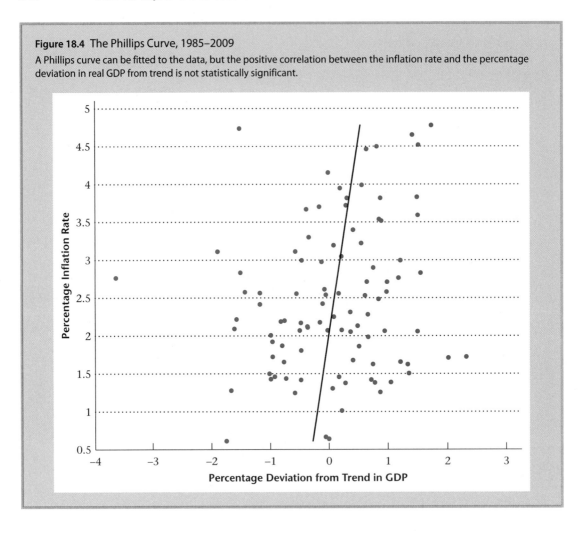

The Friedman–Lucas Money Surprise Model and the Phillips Curve

Now that we have studied empirical Phillips curve relations for the United States, and uncovered the important characteristics of the relationship between cyclical aggregate economic activity and inflation, our goal is to construct a version of the Friedman–Lucas money surprise model that we will use to understand this data. The idea behind the money surprise model was described by Milton Friedman in 1968, and later worked out explicitly by Robert Lucas.[2]

The money surprise model works as follows. We will suppose that, by controlling money supply growth, the central bank can control the inflation rate, so we will think

---

[2]See M. Friedman, 1968, "The Role of Monetary Policy," *American Economic Review* 58, 1–17; and R. Lucas, 1972, "Expectations and the Neutrality of Money," *Journal of Economic Theory* 4, 103–124.

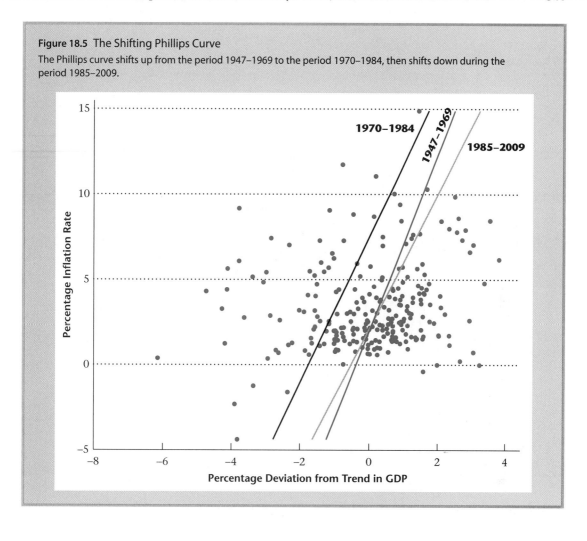

Figure 18.5 The Shifting Phillips Curve
The Phillips curve shifts up from the period 1947–1969 to the period 1970–1984, then shifts down during the period 1985–2009.

of the inflation rate as the central bank's policy variable. In the money-surprise world, workers have imperfect information about all of the prices in the economy, since there are goods that they buy infrequently (shoes and refrigerators, for example). Thus, any worker knows his or her own nominal wage, but can only make an inference about what his or her real wage is, because he or she does not know the price level with precision. If the central bank brings about a surprise increase in the inflation rate, then a given worker's nominal wage will also tend to increase at a higher rate. However, the worker only sees an increase in his or her nominal wage and does not realize in the short run that the inflation rate has also increased. Therefore, each worker mistakenly believes that he or she has experienced an increase in his or her real wage, and therefore (assuming the substitution effect on labor supplied dominates the income effect), increases the quantity of labor supplied. As a result, the surprise increase in the inflation rate will cause an increase in the aggregate quantity of labor supplied and in aggregate output.

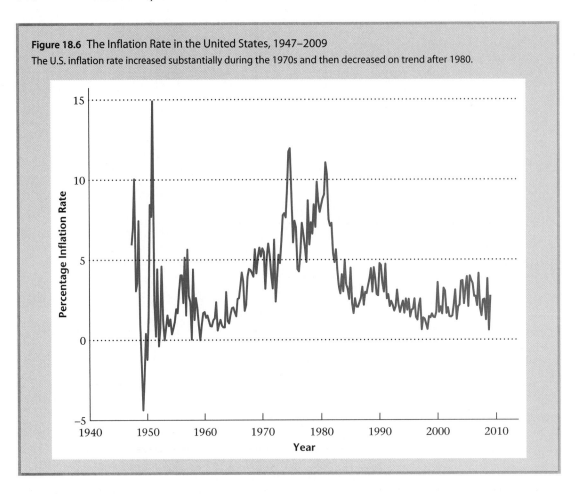

Figure 18.6 The Inflation Rate in the United States, 1947–2009
The U.S. inflation rate increased substantially during the 1970s and then decreased on trend after 1980.

According to the money surprise model, surprise increases in inflation cause increases in aggregate output above trend.

The Friedman–Lucas money surprise model can then be summarized by the simplified relationship

$$i - i^e = a(Y - Y^T), \tag{18-1}$$

where i is the actual inflation rate, i^e is the expected inflation rate, or the inflation rate perceived by the private sector, a is a positive constant, Y is aggregate output, and Y^T is trend aggregate output.[3] Equation (18-1) states that there is a positive relationship between the deviation of the inflation rate from what it is expected to be and the

---

[3]There are some dangers to representing the Friedman–Lucas money surprise model by equation (18-1). For example, the constant a, in general, depends, as Lucas pointed out, on particular features of central bank behavior. However, for what we wish to accomplish in this chapter, there is not much harm in using (18-1) as a reduced form for the Friedman–Lucas money surprise model.

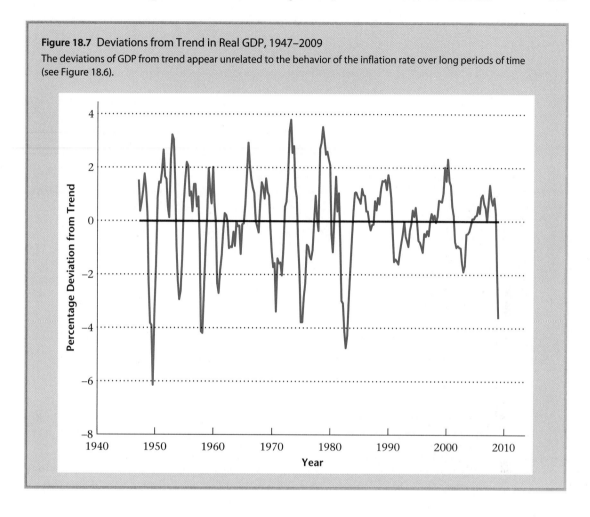

Figure 18.7 Deviations from Trend in Real GDP, 1947–2009

The deviations of GDP from trend appear unrelated to the behavior of the inflation rate over long periods of time (see Figure 18.6).

deviation of real output from trend. This relationship arises because real output only deviates from trend in the model if the central bank increases the growth rate of the money supply in a surprise way, causing a surprise increase in the inflation rate. We can rewrite equation (18-1) as

$$i = i^e + a(Y - Y^T), \tag{18-2}$$

which is a Phillips curve relationship graphed in Figure 18.8. When $i = i^e$, we have $Y = Y^T$. That is, if workers are not surprised by the current inflation rate, then output is equal to its trend value.

From equation (18-2), the position of the Phillips curve depends on i^e, the expected inflation rate. In Figure 18.9 we show the effects of an increase in the expected inflation rate from i_1^e to i_2^e. As a result, the Phillips curve shifts up by the change in the expected inflation rate, $i_2^e - i_1^e$. This provides an explanation for why the Phillips curve is difficult to find in the data over some periods of time, as we see in Figures 18.3, 18.4, and 18.5.

Figure 18.8 The Phillips Curve Relationship in the Friedman-Lucas Money Surprise Model

This is a linear Phillips curve relationship, from the version of the Friedman-Lucas money surprise model used in this chapter. When the inflation rate is equal to the expected inflation rate, then output is equal to trend output.

Understanding the Behavior of the Inflation Rate in the United States

The reduction in the inflation rate in the United States from the early 1980s through the late 1990s is viewed as an important success in the implementation of monetary policy by the Federal Reserve System. Indeed, two chairmen of the Board of Governors of the Federal Reserve System, Paul Volcker and Alan Greenspan, are often credited with this success. If it were so clear to the Fed early in the 1980s that the high inflation rate at that time was too costly and should be reduced through reduction in money growth, why was inflation not reduced earlier and why did the inflation rate increase in the 1970s? We consider two possible answers to these questions, the central bank learning story and the central bank commitment story.

The Central Bank Learning Story   In the late 1950s and the 1960s, the Fed became aware of the existence of the Phillips curve through the work of A. W. Phillips and others. The Fed may have become convinced, even though a good theory was not yet available to explain the existence of the Phillips curve, that the Phillips curve represented a stable relationship between the rate of inflation and the level of real aggregate output.

Now, to determine how the Fed would behave if it operated under the belief that the Phillips curve was stable, we need a device for representing the goals of the central bank. In general, a central bank should be concerned with the welfare of private citizens, although, of course, there is nothing to guarantee this because central bank

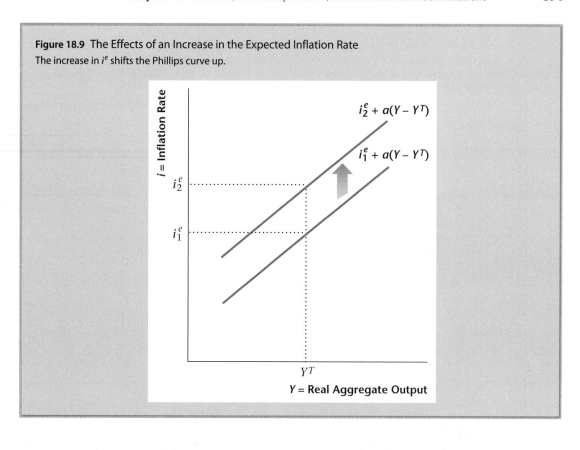

Figure 18.9 The Effects of an Increase in the Expected Inflation Rate
The increase in i^e shifts the Phillips curve up.

decisionmakers are guided by their own selfish motives, such as career advancement and the acquisition of more power. We assume, however, that the framers of the Federal Reserve Act and subsequent acts of Congress governing the Fed's behavior understood how to correctly align the selfish goals of Fed officials with the public good. Then, assuming that the Fed's goal is to maximize public welfare, it must decide how to further this goal indirectly by controlling some observable economic variables. For our purposes, we suppose that the Fed has indirect policy goals relating to inflation and aggregate output. First, there is some inflation rate i^* that is regarded as optimal by the Fed. Some economic models tell us that i^* should be the inflation rate that drives the nominal interest rate to zero (the Friedman rule; see Chapter 16), although in practice many central banks appear to behave as if $i^* = 0$ or $i^* > 0$ but small. If $i > i^*$, the Fed views more inflation as being more costly, so that less inflation is preferred to more. However, if $i < i^*$, then more inflation is preferred to less. In addition, the Fed always prefers more aggregate output to less, as higher GDP is assumed to be preferred by the public. We can then represent the Fed's preferences for inflation and aggregate output by indifference curves, as in Figure 18.10. When $i > i^*$, the Fed is happier if inflation falls and output increases, and when $i < i^*$, the Fed is happier when inflation rises and output increases. Further, the indifference curves capture a preference for diversity, in that they are concave when $i > i^*$ and convex when $i < i^*$. That is, as we move up

Figure 18.10 The Fed's Preferences Over Inflation Rates and Output

The figure shows the indifference curves for the Fed, capturing the Fed's preferences over output and inflation. The inflation rate $i*$ is optimal for the Fed, and the Fed always prefers more output to less. If $i < i*$, then the Fed prefers more inflation to less, and if $i > i*$ the Fed prefers less inflation to more.

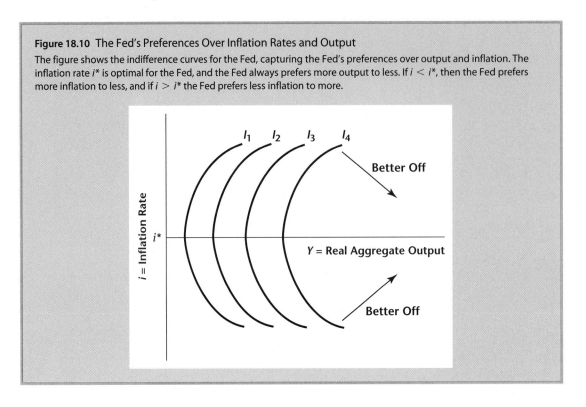

and to the right along a particular indifference curve where $i > i*$, output is rising and the inflation rate is rising. The slope of the indifference curve falls because the higher the inflation rate the smaller is the increase in the inflation rate that the Fed is willing to tolerate for a given increase in aggregate output. However, when $i < i*$, as we move down the indifference curve and the inflation rate falls, the Fed is willing to tolerate smaller decreases in the inflation rate for a given increase in output.

In Figure 18.11 we show the Phillips curve relationship, equation (18-2), along with the Fed's indifference curves. If the Fed treats the Phillips curve as a fixed relationship, then it thinks that it can simply choose the point on the Phillips curve that best suits it. Therefore, if we suppose that the indifference curve that passes through point A, where $i = i^e$ and $Y = Y^T$, is steeper than the Phillips curve at point A, then the Fed is willing to increase the money supply growth rate so as to surprise workers with a higher than expected inflation rate and generate a level of aggregate output above trend output Y^T. That is, the optimal choice for the Fed is point B, where an indifference curve is just tangent to the Phillips curve. At B, the inflation rate is i_1 and the level of aggregate output is Y_1. Note that $i_1 > i^e$, so that the actual inflation rate is greater than what is expected by the private sector and that $Y_1 > Y^T$, so that output is above trend.

This is not the end of the story, because the public is being fooled at point B in Figure 18.11. If the Fed attempts to hold output permanently at Y_1, then the public eventually learns that the actual inflation rate is higher than what they perceived, and they revise upward their expected inflation rate. In Figure 18.12, the Fed initially chooses point A on

Figure 18.11 The Fed Exploits the Phillips Curve

Facing a Phillips curve that it believes to be stable, the Fed optimizes by choosing point B, where an indifference curve is tangent to the Phillips curve.

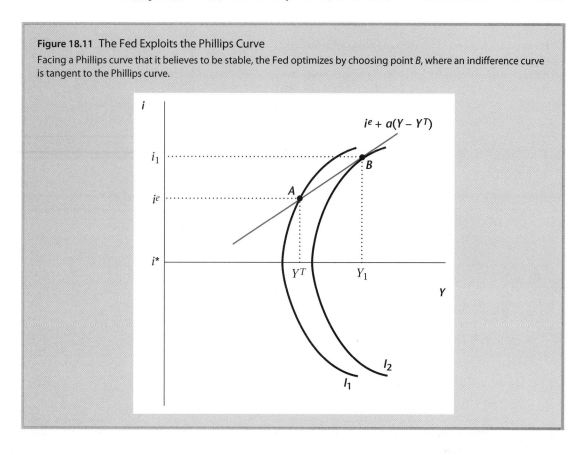

Phillips curve PC_1, but as the public observes that the actual inflation rate is higher than the expected inflation rate i_1^e, the expected inflation rate is revised upward, say to i_2^e. This then implies that the Phillips curve shifts up to PC_2, and the Fed now chooses point B, where again the public sector is fooled, because the actual inflation rate is still higher than the expected inflation rate i_2^e. Again, the public eventually catches on and revises upward the expected rate of inflation. Ultimately, the economy comes to rest at point D, where $i = i^e = i_3^e$, so that public expectations about inflation prove to be correct, and the Fed has no incentive at point D to change money growth so as to change the inflation rate.

After experiencing the movement from point A to point D in Figure 18.12 and after reading Friedman and Lucas's work,[4] the Fed now realizes that the Phillips curve is not a stable relationship and that it shifts with changes in expected inflation. This implies that there is no long-run trade-off between inflation and aggregate output; in the long run when the public is not fooled, output always settles down to its trend level, Y^T. Once the Fed realizes this, it does not optimize by choosing a point along the upward-sloping short-run Phillips curve, but it chooses the optimal inflation rate given that the

---

[4]See M. Friedman, 1968, "The Role of Monetary Policy," *American Economic Review* 58, 1–17; and R. Lucas, 1972, "Expectations and the Neutrality of Money," *Journal of Economic Theory* 4, 103–124.

Figure 18.12 The Fed Attempts to Increase Y Permanently

If the Fed attempts to increase Y above Y^T permanently, then initially it chooses A; but an upward revision in i^e shifts the Phillips curve up, so that the Fed chooses B on the Phillips curve PC_2. Ultimately, the economy comes to rest at D, where $i = i^e$ and $Y = Y^T$.

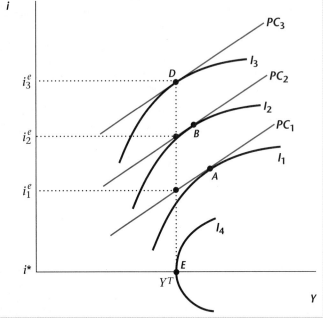

long-run level of output is Y^T. Therefore, once the Fed understands the theory correctly, it wants to set the money growth rate so that $i = i*$, and the economy is in the long run at point E, after expected inflation adjusts downward again.

This story fits the data on inflation in Figure 18.5, in that the period 1947–1969 could be thought of as a series of short-run changes in the inflation rate, with movements about trend in aggregate output along a more-or-less stable Phillips curve. The data for 1947–1969 are consistent with the view that the Fed was unaware of the existence of a potentially exploitable Phillips curve. Then in the 1970s, there is an increase in the inflation rate as the Fed attempts to exploit the Phillips curve and achieve greater output at the expense of higher inflation. During the 1970s, the Phillips curve shifts up in a manner related to the movement from point A to point D in Figure 18.12. By the early 1980s, the Fed has understood the problem, and it begins the move from point D to E in Figure 18.12.

This is a sanguine view of central banking in the United States, because it reflects the attitude that the Fed learns from its mistakes and acts fairly quickly to correct them. In this view, the inflation of the 1970s was an experiment gone wrong and an event that is not likely to be repeated. In the central bank learning story, the Federal Reserve System is fundamentally sound in that it has the ability to absorb new economic thinking, to efficiently make sense of the new data it is constantly receiving, and to use all of this information to make better decisions.

MACROECONOMICS IN ACTION
Learning to Control Inflation in New Zealand:
Inflation Targeting

Before reductions in the inflation rate occurred in New Zealand in the late 1970s, this country experienced inflation that was relatively high among developed countries. The average inflation rate in New Zealand between 1977 and 1986 was 13% per year—much higher than in the United States, for example (see Figure 18.6). However, the inflation rate was reduced in New Zealand to 3.3% per year in the 1990–1992 period and to 2.3% in the 1993–1996 period. In part, this reduction in inflation was brought about through changes in the legal structure within which the Reserve Bank of New Zealand (RBNZ)—the central bank of New Zealand—was constrained to operate, as discussed in a working paper by Michael Hutchison and Carl Walsh.[5]

The changes in the rules governing the operation of the RBNZ were enacted in the RBNZ Act in December 1989, which went into effect in February 1990. Under the Act, "the primary function of the Bank [the RBNZ] is to formulate and implement monetary policy directed to the economic objective of achieving and maintaining stability in the general level of prices." This statement of the goals of the central bank is quite restrictive, because left out are any Keynesian-type objectives, such as sustained growth, which are goals that often find their way into the language of central bankers. Given that the objective of the RBNZ as defined by the RBNZ Act is to achieve price stability, how should this be done? The Act also specifies that the finance minister (a cabinet member in the government of New Zealand) negotiate a Policy

[5]See M. Hutchison and C. Walsh, 1998, "Disinflation in New Zealand," working paper, University of California, Santa Cruz.

Target Agreement (PTA) with the governor of the RBNZ (the counterpart of the chairman of the Fed) at the beginning of the governor's term of office. This PTA specifies explicitly what price stability means, in terms of numerical objectives, for the governor's term. These objectives are then publicly announced. Should the governor be judged by the prime minister of New Zealand to have failed to meet the goals set out in the PTA, he or she can be removed from office.

In practice, the PTAs that have been negotiated consist of explicit inflation targets. For example, the first PTA agreed to under the RBNZ Act specified a target range for the inflation rate of 0–2% per annum to be achieved by December 1992. As mentioned above, the RBNZ Act appears to have been very successful in meeting its intended goal of reducing inflation in New Zealand. Inflation targeting in this instance seems to have been much more successful than was the targeting of monetary aggregates in some countries in the 1970s and 1980s.

The rules in the RBNZ Act governing the operation of New Zealand's central bank put an unusual amount of structure on monetary policy relative to what governs most central banks in the world. For example, in the United States, the Federal Reserve Act is quite vague about the policy objectives of the Federal Reserve System, and the chairman of the Fed can certainly not be fired by the President during his or her term of office because of monetary policy errors. New Zealand was highly innovative in central banking by setting up explicit objectives and penalties for its central bank. Other central banks, including the Bank of Canada and the Bank of England, have since introduced inflation targeting, although in a less restrictive structure than in New Zealand.

The Central Bank Commitment Story The second possible explanation for the reduction in inflation that occurred over the 1980s and 1990s in the United States is the central bank commitment story. The theory behind central bank commitment and inflation was first exposited by Kydland and Prescott,[6] who did the first work on the **time consistency problem** in macroeconomics. The fundamentals of the time consistency problem can be explained through a simple example. A teacher is giving a one-semester course in macroeconomics, and his or her goal is to make sure that the students in the class learn as much as possible. The students wish to get high grades but with as little effort as possible, because they have other things to do with their time than learning macroeconomics. If there is a final exam in the course, the students work hard to get good grades, they learn, and their teacher is happy. However, a problem is that the teacher does not like to grade exams. He or she can promise at the beginning of the semester to give a final exam, but by the end of the semester the students will have learned the course material anyway, in expectation of having to write an exam. Therefore, the teacher need not give the exam, as his or her goal has been accomplished, and he or she can avoid the work of grading exams. The plan made at the beginning of the semester to give a final exam is not time consistent. That is, when the time comes to have the exam, the teacher has no incentive to give it. However, the students are not stupid. They understand the teacher's motives and recognize that he or she has no incentive to give a final exam, even if he or she has promised to do so. They, therefore, do not learn anything. Thus, the outcome is that the students do not learn and the teacher does not give the final exam. The teacher would prefer to have to grade the exam and have the students learn than to not grade the exam and have no learning, and so the outcome is clearly bad.

Essentially, there is a commitment problem here. A better outcome would be achieved if the teacher could tie his or her hands at the beginning of the semester by somehow committing to giving the final exam. Of course, in practice such commitment is achieved through university rules that bind the teacher to carrying out the promises made in the course outline distributed at the beginning of the semester.

An analogous problem exists for the Fed if we make some modifications to our model. Suppose that each period there is a game being played between the private sector and the Fed. At the beginning of the period, the private sector chooses the expected rate of inflation, i^e. Then, the Fed chooses the rate of money growth, which effectively involves determining i. Thus, given i^e, the Fed chooses i satisfying the Phillips curve relationship

$$i - i^e = a(Y - Y^T),$$

so as to be as well off as possible. However, because the private sector is forward-looking and understands the motivation of the Fed, it must be true in equilibrium that the public cannot be fooled—that is, $i = i^e$. The assumption that $i = i^e$ is a version of the **rational expectations hypothesis,** which states that economic agents cannot make systematic errors; that is, they use all information efficiently. In this case, using information efficiently means that the public sector understands the Fed's preferences over output and inflation and uses this information efficiently to predict how the Fed will behave.

---

[6]See F. Kydland and E. Prescott, 1977, "Rules Rather than Discretion: The Inconsistency of Optimal Plans," *Journal of Political Economy* 87, 473–492.

Figure 18.13 The Commitment Problem

If the Fed could commit to an inflation rate, it would choose i^*, and the equilibrium would be at A. However, without commitment, the equilibrium is at B, where inflation is too high, and where an indifference curve is tangent to the Phillips curve at $i = i^e$ (rational expectations holds).

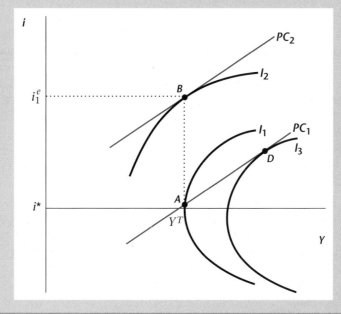

In Figure 18.13, because $i = i^e$ in equilibrium, this implies that $Y = Y^T$ in equilibrium. Therefore, if the Fed could commit in advance to an inflation rate, it would choose $i = i^*$, and the equilibrium would be at point A. However, if $i^e = i^*$, then the Phillips curve running through point A is PC_1, and the Fed then chooses point D, where $i > i^e = i^*$, and so point A is not an equilibrium. In equilibrium, the Fed's indifference curve must be tangent to the Phillips curve where $i = i_1^e$. That is, the equilibrium point is at B on Phillips curve PC_2. Point A is strictly preferred by the Fed to B, but A cannot be achieved because of the Fed's inability to commit.

Kydland and Prescott interpreted this exercise as indicating that central bank discretion is dangerous and that there is something inherently wrong with letting central banks make decisions on an ad hoc basis. The solution to the lack of commitment problem, in their view, is to tie the Fed's hands, for example, by imposing a rule that the Fed target the growth rate of the money supply. However, there may be problems in committing a central bank to some particular policy rule, as any rule could later be shown to be inappropriate. For example, many central banks, including the Fed, adopted money supply targeting in the 1970s, but money supply targets currently play a minor role in Fed policymaking. This is because of increasing instability in the relationships among monetary aggregates, prices, and real activity, which occurred in the 1980s and 1990s.

A problem with the central bank commitment story is that it does not explain the run-up in inflation in the 1970s or why inflation decreased after 1980. Did the Fed suddenly lose its ability to commit in the late 1960s and then find it again in the early 1980s? This seems unlikely. Further, as Robert Barro and David Gordon have argued,[7] if the Fed is playing a repeated game with the private sector, then the Fed's long-term reputation becomes important, and the long-run equilibrium can be point *A* in Figure 18.13. That is, the Fed understands that if it attempts to use surprise inflation to generate more aggregate output in the short run, then it destroys its reputation for producing low inflation. Therefore, a long-run equilibrium can exist at point *A* in Figure 18.13, because the Fed understands that if it loses its reputation, then the equilibrium will be at point *B* forever after. Of course, if we accept the importance of the Fed's concern for its reputation in determining its behavior, what was it about the 1970s that made the Fed willing to lose its reputation for low money growth and low inflation at that time?

In summary, several arguments cast doubt on the central bank commitment story as an explanation for U.S. inflation history. Commitment issues are probably not that important in the behavior of the Federal Reserve System. The central bank learning story seems to give a more plausible account of the run-up in inflation in the 1970s and the subsequent decline in the inflation rate after 1980.

MACROECONOMICS IN ACTION
Commitment to Low Inflation in Hong Kong

The world's central banks have resorted to several different means to show that they are committed to controlling inflation. During the 1970s and 1980s, many central banks announced explicit targets for the growth of monetary aggregates, and currently several central banks, including those of Canada, New Zealand, and Great Britain, have inflation targets. One device for tying the hands of the central bank is the introduction of a currency board. A prominent jurisdiction with a currency board is Hong Kong.

As was discussed in Chapter 14, a currency board is one way to operate a fixed exchange rate system. Under a currency board some governmental authority, which could be the central bank, stands ready to buy and sell domestic currency for some foreign currency at a fixed rate. All domestic currency is backed one-for-one by safe assets (including interest-earning assets) denominated in the foreign currency. If the currency board is run properly, there is no risk of the governmental authority running out of foreign exchange. Typically, a country adopting a currency board fixes its foreign exchange rate relative to the currency of a country with sound monetary policy. This is because, as we studied in Chapter 14, in the long run a country under a fixed exchange rate adopts the inflation rate of the country against which the currency is pegged.

In Hong Kong, the exchange rate was fixed at 7.8 Hong Kong Dollars per U.S. dollar in October 1983, and it has remained at that value

[7]See R. Barro and D. Gordon, 1983a, "A Positive Theory of Monetary Policy in a Natural Rate Model," *Journal of Political Economy* 91, 589–610; and R. Barro and D. Gordon, 1983b, "Rules, Discretion and Reputation in a Model of Monetary Policy," *Journal of Monetary Economics* 12, 101–121.

since then.[8] The currency board in Hong Kong is operated by the Hong Kong Monetary Authority (HKMA), although there is a sense in which the Hong Kong system is not a pure currency board. This is because the HKMA commits to sell U.S. dollars at a fixed rate against Hong Kong dollars, but there is no commitment to buy U.S. dollars at a particular rate. As well, the rules by which the HKMA operates are not written into law; there is only an implicit commitment to continue the currency board into the future.

The HKMA has been quite successful in controlling inflation. While the inflation experience of Hong Kong has not been identical to that of the United States since 1983, the difference between the Hong Kong inflation rate and the U.S. inflation rate from 1983–2003 has not been great. The HKMA was able to maintain its fixed exchange rate through the Asian Crisis of 1997, with some changes made in the system

in 1998. Recently, Hong Kong may have been too successful in reducing inflation, in that there was a deflation from 1998–2002, with the consumer price index falling by 12% over that period.[9] While this might be consistent with a Friedman rule (see Chapter 15), and thus be optimal, some would argue that deflation of this magnitude is excessive.

Hong Kong's success in controlling inflation under a currency board is not a story that was repeated in Argentina. In Argentina, the currency was pegged against the U.S. dollar in 1990 and supported by a currency board. Initially, there was success, with inflation reduced from triple-digit rates in the 1980s to single-digit rates in the 1990s. However, under the pressure of out-of-control fiscal policy, the currency board was abandoned in Argentina in January 2002. Thus, a currency board is not a simple recipe for establishing the commitment to control inflation.

[8]See S. Gerlach, 2003, "Monetary Operations of Hong Kong's Currency Board," working paper, Hong Kong Institute for Monetary Research.

[9]See "Tony Latter: Hong Kong's Currency Board Today—The Unexpected Challenge of Deflation," available at http://www.info.gov.hk/hkma/eng/public/qb20028/breakfa3.pdf.

Perspectives on the Financial Crisis
Monetary Policy, Inflation, and the Phillips Curve

In Chapters 11 through 13, we studied some recent features of monetary policy in the United States. Of particular note is that the Fed increased the monetary base by a factor of more than 2 in late 2008 and early 2009. From our analysis of the effects of money supply increases in Chapters 11 through 13, we know that a permanent increase in the money supply will, in the long run, result in a proportionate increase in the price level. Thus, our prediction would be that, if the increase in the monetary base that occurred in late 2008 and early 2009 were permanent, this would result in an

increase in the price level by a factor of more than 2. Ultimately we would expect at least a temporary period of inflation while the price level increases to its new higher level.

In Figure 18.6, we certainly do not see any significant increase in the inflation rate, in data up to the first quarter of 2009. Even in price data available up to mid-2009 (the consumer price index and producer price index for example), there appears to be no indication of a significant increase in the inflation rate. Are we at risk of a repeat of the inflation experience of the 1970s, or worse?

(Continued)

In our previous discussion in Chapters 11 through 13, we made clear that, in the circumstances of the financial crisis and 2008–2009 recession, there are reasons to believe that it may take a longer period of time than usual for the increase in the money supply to be reflected in an increase in the price level. For example, there is the possibility of a liquidity trap phenomenon, whereby the increase in the money stock is temporarily hoarded by financial institutions and consumers and not spent on goods, so that the price level does not increase in the short run. However, as the economy recovers, higher-return investment opportunities will materialize and, as economic agents attempt to exchange money for higher-return assets, inflation will result. The trick for the Fed is to reduce the money stock in a sufficiently timely manner that higher inflation does not materialize.

What does the Fed intend? In the FOMC statement of August 12, 2009,[10] there is the statement that "... the committee will maintain the target range for the federal funds rate at 0 to 1/4 percent and continues to anticipate that economic conditions are likely to warrant exceptionally low levels of the federal funds rate for an extended period." Thus, the Fed does not seem to intend to undo its dramatic monetary intervention any time soon.

Why is the Fed not more concerned about the possibility of higher inflation? An explanation is given in the August 12, 2009, FOMC statement, which is: "The prices of energy and other commodities have risen of late. However, substantial resource slack is likely to dampen cost pressures, and the Committee expects that inflation will remain subdued for some time." This statement reflects some concern of the FOMC with increases in the prices of raw materials, including crude oil, which in mid-2009 were not reflected in either wholesale or retail prices. However, this concern is then dismissed because the FOMC believes that "resource slack" will keep inflation "subdued" for a long time to come. This seems a clear reference to the Phillips curve and

appears to capture a belief by the FOMC that, because real output is well below trend, that the inflation rate cannot increase.

Belief by the Fed in a stable Phillips curve relationship may seem puzzling, in light of the inflation history of the United States since World War II, and advances in macroeconomic theory since 1970. However, the Fed's beliefs have in fact been propelled by New Keynesian thinking. In New Keynesian economics,[11] a Phillips curve relationship results because of the forward-looking behavior of price-setting firms. At any given date, firms set their prices expecting that they will not change these prices for some time. Then, if inflation is higher than expected, firms that have not changed their prices will experience higher-than-expected demand for their output. Firms increase their output to satisfy the forthcoming demand, and unanticipated inflation is associated with higher output—a Phillips curve. New Keynesian economists have encouraged monetary policymakers to view the Phillips curve as a relationship that is at least temporarily stable, due to sticky prices. Thus, the Fed believes that, because there is a large "output gap," that inflation cannot increase.

One view of the monetary policy problem, as of mid-2009, is that Fed policymakers have somehow "unlearned" what they learned in the 1970s. Just as in the 1960s and 1970s, they are acting as if they believe that the Phillips curve is stable. Because output is low, they believe they can dramatically increase the money supply without any increase in inflation, so long as the output gap is sufficiently large. There exists a significant risk that the Fed will repeat the policy errors of the 1970s, and that a large inflation will result. The key problem then is that it will be very difficult to reduce the rate of inflation once it increases. The US economy will have just recovered from the 2008–2009 recession, and Ben Bernanke and his fellow FOMC members will have little stomach for producing the type of recession that the Fed needed to generate in the early 1980s to reduce the inflation rate.

---

[10]See http://www.federalreserve.gov/newsevents/press/monetary/20090812a.htm

[11]See for example M. Woodford, 2003, *Interest and Prices*, Princeton University Press, Princeton NJ.

Chapter Summary

- The Phillips curve relationship studied here is a positive relationship between the inflation rate and the deviation of real aggregate output from trend.

- Between 1947 and 1969, a Phillips curve can be observed in U.S. data, but the relationship appears to disappear after 1969. We used a version of the Friedman–Lucas money surprise model to explain these facts.

- In the version of the Friedman–Lucas money surprise model we use, the deviation of real aggregate output from trend is positively related to the difference between the actual and expected inflation rates. If the Fed generates a surprise increase in money growth, leading to a surprise increase in inflation, this causes an increase in labor supply, employment, and real output. This happens because workers mistake an increase in their nominal wage for an increase in their real wage, and therefore work harder. The money surprise model predicts that the Phillips curve is unstable, as it shifts with changes in the expected rate of inflation.

- In the United States, the rate of inflation was moderate for most of the period 1947 to 1969, it increased substantially for the period 1970–1984, and decreased thereafter. We considered two possible explanations for this recent history of inflation rates in the United States.

- The first explanation for recent U.S. inflation experience was the central bank learning story, whereby the Fed discovered the existence of the Phillips curve in the 1960s and, assuming the Phillips curve was stable, attempted to exploit this relationship in the 1970s. However, the increased inflation in the 1970s did not generate permanently higher output, and it became clear to the Fed that there was no long-run trade-off between output and inflation. Higher inflation simply shifts up the Phillips curve relationship as expected inflation adjusts upward. Once the Fed discovered that there was no long-run trade-off between output and inflation, it could then, in the early 1980s, focus solely on the goal of reducing inflation.

- The second explanation for recent U.S. inflation history is the central bank commitment story. According to this story, high inflation is caused by the inability of the central bank to commit to a policy of not generating surprise inflation in an attempt to exploit the short-run Phillips curve.

- The central bank learning story provides a more plausible explanation than does the central bank commitment story for the path followed by the U.S. inflation rate, as it seems difficult to argue that the Fed found it difficult to commit in the 1970s, but easy to commit itself otherwise. However, for some countries, such as Hong Kong, a commitment mechanism appears to have been important in reducing inflation. In Hong Kong, this commitment mechanism was a fixed exchange rate enforced by a currency board.

Key Terms

Rational expectations hypothesis A hypothesis asserting that economic agents cannot make systematic errors; they use information efficiently. (p. 656)

Time consistency problem A situation that occurs when it proves optimal to abandon a previously announced plan. (p. 656)

Questions for Review

1. How did the Phillips curve get its name?
2. The Phillips curve relationship examined in this chapter is a positive relationship between what two variables?
3. During what periods in the post–World War II data for the United States can a Phillips curve be observed, and when is it not observed?

4. What are two observations about empirical Phillips curve relations?

5. Explain how the Friedman–Lucas money surprise model works.

6. What is the relationship that summarizes the Friedman–Lucas money surprise model in this chapter?

7. When real aggregate output is equal to trend output, what is the inflation rate equal to?

8. What is the effect of an increase in expected inflation on the Phillips curve?

9. Describe the course of the inflation rate in the United States from 1947 until 2009.

10. What are two explanations for the U.S. inflation rate history after 1947?

11. Why can the central bank have an incentive to increase the inflation rate if it believes that the Phillips curve is stable?

12. Can the Fed permanently increase the level of aggregate output? Explain why or why not.

13. What was different about the ways in which inflation was reduced in the United States and in New Zealand?

14. Why is the inflation rate high in the long run if the central bank cannot commit itself?

15. Explain why, if the central bank is concerned with its reputation, inflation can be low in the long run.

16. Which is a more satisfactory explanation of U.S. post–World War II inflation, the central bank learning story or the central bank commitment story? Why?

17. Explain why commitment was important in reducing inflation in Hong Kong.

Problems

1. Suppose that the private sector does not have rational expectations, but instead follows an adaptive expectations scheme. That is, the private sector's expected inflation rate is what the inflation rate was last period. Show in a diagram how the inflation rate and output move over time if the initial inflation rate is the optimal rate i^*, and then the central bank acts to exploit the Phillips curve. Explain your results.

2. Suppose that the economy is in a long-run equilibrium where the inflation rate is greater than the optimal rate i^*, and then the central bank acts to reduce the inflation rate to i^*.

   (a) Suppose that the central bank decides to take drastic action and reduces the inflation rate within one period to i^*. Also, suppose that the private sector has adaptive expectations, so that the current expected inflation rate is last period's actual inflation rate. Show in a diagram the path that real aggregate output and the inflation rate take over time.

   (b) Now, suppose that the central bank takes the drastic strategy in part (a), but that the private sector has rational expectations, so that $i = i^e$. Again, show in a diagram the path followed by output and the inflation rate over time.

   (c) Now, suppose that the central bank takes a gradual strategy of reducing the inflation rate in a number of steps to i^*. Under a gradual strategy, show what differences there are between adaptive and rational expectations for the path of output and the inflation rate over time.

   (d) Explain your results in parts (a) to (c), and comment on what light this sheds on Figures 18.6 and 18.7 for the early 1980s period.

3. Suppose that the inflation rate is higher than i^*, that the central bank announces it will reduce the inflation rate, and that it actually proceeds to do this. Answer the following:

   (a) Suppose that the private sector believes the central bank announcement. What are the effects on the inflation rate and real output? Show this in a diagram.

(b) Suppose that the private sector does not believe the central bank announcement. What are the effects on the inflation rate and real output now? Show this in a diagram.

(c) Explain your results in parts (a) and (b).

4. (Warning: This is challenging.) Suppose that the central bank is in a repeated relationship with the private sector. If the inflation rate is $i = i^*$ and output is $Y = Y^T$, then suppose the reward each period to the central bank is u_1. If consumers anticipate $i^e = i^*$, then the one-period reward the central bank receives from fooling consumers with $i > i^*$ is u_2 and we will have $i > i^e = i^*$. When the central bank cannot commit and there is rational expectations, then the reward the central bank gets is $u_3 < u_1$ with $i = i^e = i_1 > i^*$ and

$Y = Y^T$. Now, suppose that the government anticipates that if it deviates from $i = i^*$, then it will totally lose its reputation and consumers will anticipate $i = i_1$ forever after, so that the government will receive a reward of u_3 forever after. That is, suppose the central bank has two alternatives, which are (a) set $i = i^*$ forever receiving reward u_1, and (b) cheat for this period, receiving reward u_2 implying that the reward will be u_3 in every future period. Suppose that the central bank discounts the future at the rate r.

(a) Show that it is an equilibrium for the government to choose $i = i^*$ forever if

$$u_1(1 + r) - u_3 \geq ru_2.$$

(b) Interpret the condition in part (a).

(c) Show that, as r becomes small, that the condition in part (a) must hold, and explain this.

Working with the Data

1. Calculate the annual percentage rate of change in the consumer price index (December to December) and graph this in scatter plots against the unemployment rate for the 1950s, 1960s, 1970s, 1980s, 1990s, and 2000–2009. For which decades do you observe a Phillips curve relationship, and for which do you not? What reasons could there be for a shift in this Phillips curve relationship, other than shifts in inflationary expectations?

2. Use the quarterly increase in the GDP price deflator as a measure of the inflation rate and the inflation rate in the previous quarter as a measure of the current expected inflation rate. Construct a scatter plot of the inflation rate minus the expected inflation rate versus detrended GDP.

(a) What do you observe in the scatter plot?

(b) Is there a Phillips curve relationship evident in this data? Discuss.

Appendix

Mathematical Appendix

This appendix provides more formal treatments of some of the models in the book, and it is intended for students with a knowledge of calculus and more advanced algebraic techniques who wish to study some of the topics of this book in more depth. The appendix assumes an understanding of mathematical methods in economics at the level of Alpha C. Chiang and Kevin Wainwright's *Fundamental Methods of Mathematical Economics,* McGraw Hill/Irwin, New York, 2004. We proceed by working through results for selected models from selected chapters.

Chapter 4: Consumer and Firm Behavior

Chapter 4 dealt with the representative consumer's and representative firm's optimization problems in the closed-economy one-period model. We set up the consumer's and firm's problems and derive the main results of Chapter 4 formally.

The Representative Consumer

The representative consumer's preferences are defined by the utility function $U(C,l)$, where C is consumption and l is leisure, with $U(\cdot,\cdot)$ a function that is increasing in both arguments, strictly quasiconcave, and twice differentiable. These properties of the utility function imply that indifference curves are downward-sloping and convex and that the consumer strictly prefers more to less. The consumer's optimization problem is to choose C and l so as to maximize $U(C,l)$ subject to his or her budget constraint—that is,

$$\max_{C,\,l} U(C,l)$$

subject to

$$C = w(h - l) + \pi - T,$$

and $C \geq 0, 0 \leq l \leq h$, where w is the real wage, h is the quantity of time the consumer has available, π is dividend income, and T is the lump-sum tax. This problem is a constrained optimization problem, with the associated Lagrangian

$$L = U(C,l) + \lambda[w(h - l) + \pi - T - C],$$

where λ is the Lagrange multiplier.

We assume that there is an interior solution to the consumer's problem where $C > 0$ and $0 < l < h$. This can be guaranteed by assuming that $U_1(0,l) = \infty$ (i.e., the derivative of the utility function with respect to the first argument goes to infinity in the limit as consumption goes to zero) and $U_2(C,0) = \infty$. These assumptions imply that $C > 0$ and $l > 0$ at the optimum. In a competitive equilibrium we cannot have $l = h$, as this would imply that nothing would be produced and $C = 0$. Given an interior solution to the consumer's problem, we can characterize the solution by the first-order conditions from the problem of choosing C, l, and λ to maximize L. These first-order conditions are (differentiating L with respect to C, l, and λ, respectively, and setting each of these first derivatives equal to zero)

$$U_1(C,l) - \lambda = 0, \tag{A-1}$$

$$U_2(C,l) - \lambda w = 0, \tag{A-2}$$

$$w(h - l) + \pi - T - C = 0. \tag{A-3}$$

In equations (A-1) and (A-2), $U_i(C,l)$ denotes the first derivative with respect to the ith argument of $U(\cdot, \cdot)$, evaluated at (C,l). From equations (A-1) and (A-2), we can obtain the condition

$$\frac{U_2(C,l)}{U_1(C,l)} = w, \tag{A-4}$$

which is the optimization condition for the consumer that we showed graphically in Chapter 4, Figure 4.5. Equation (A-4) states that the marginal rate of substitution of leisure for consumption (on the left-hand side of the equation) is equal to the real wage (on the right-hand side) at the optimum. For our purposes, we can rewrite equation (A-4) as

$$U_2(C,l) - wU_1(C,l) = 0, \tag{A-5}$$

and then (A-3) and (A-5) are two equations determining the optimal choices of C and l given w, π, and T.

In general, we cannot obtain explicit closed-form solutions for C and l from equations (A-3) and (A-5) without assuming an explicit form for the utility function $U(\cdot, \cdot)$, but we can use comparative statics techniques to determine how C and l change when any of w, π, or T change. To do this, we totally differentiate equations (A-3) and (A-5), obtaining

$$- dC - w\,dl + (h - l)dw + d\pi - dT = 0, \tag{A-6}$$

$$[U_{12} - wU_{11}]dC + [U_{22} - wU_{12}]dl - U_1 dw = 0. \tag{A-7}$$

In equation (A-7), U_{ij} denotes the second derivative with respect to the ith and j^{th} arguments of $U(\cdot, \cdot)$. Now, it is useful to write (A-6) and (A-7) in matrix form, as

$$\begin{bmatrix} -1 & -w \\ U_{12} - wU_{11} & U_{22} - wU_{12} \end{bmatrix} \begin{bmatrix} dC \\ dl \end{bmatrix} = \begin{bmatrix} -(h - l)dw - d\pi + dT \\ U_1 dw \end{bmatrix} \tag{A-8}$$

Then, we can solve for the derivatives of interest by using Cramer's rule.

First, consider the effects of a change in dividend income π. Using Cramer's rule, from equation (A-8) we get

$$\frac{dC}{d\pi} = \frac{-U_{22} + wU_{12}}{\nabla}, \tag{A-9}$$

$$\frac{dl}{d\pi} = \frac{U_{12} - wU_{11}}{\nabla}, \tag{A-10}$$

where

$$\nabla = -U_{22} + 2wU_{12} - w^2U_{11}.$$

Now, ∇ is the determinant of the bordered Hessian associated with the constrained optimization problem for the consumer, and the quasiconcavity of the utility function implies that $\nabla > 0$. This, however, does not allow us to sign the derivatives in (A-9) and (A-10). Our assumption from Chapter 4 that consumption and leisure are normal goods is equivalent to the conditions $-U_{22} + wU_{12} > 0$ and $U_{12} - wU_{11} > 0$. Thus, given normal goods, we have $\frac{dC}{d\pi} > 0$ and $\frac{dl}{d\pi} > 0$, so that the quantities of consumption and leisure chosen by the consumer increase when dividend income increases. It is straightforward to show that $\frac{dC}{dT} = -\frac{dC}{d\pi}$ and $\frac{dl}{dT} = -\frac{dl}{d\pi}$, so that the effects of a decrease in taxes are equivalent to the effects of an increase in dividend income.

Next, we can derive the effects of a change in the real wage, again using Cramer's rule to obtain, from equation (A-8),

$$\frac{dC}{dw} = \frac{wU_1 + (h - l)(-U_{22} + wU_{12})}{\nabla}, \tag{A-11}$$

$$\frac{dl}{dw} = \frac{-U_1 + (h - l)(U_{12} - wU_{11})}{\nabla}. \tag{A-12}$$

Now, assuming that consumption is a normal good, we have $-U_{22} + wU_{12} > 0$, and because $\nabla > 0$ and $U_1 > 0$ (utility increases as consumption increases), we know from (A-11) that $\frac{dC}{dw} > 0$, so that consumption increases when the real wage increases. However, we cannot determine the sign of $\frac{dl}{dw}$ from (A-12) because of the opposing income and substitution effects of a change in the real wage on leisure. It is possible to separate algebraically the income and substitution effects in equation (A-12) by determining the response of leisure to a change in the real wage, holding utility constant. This gives a substitution effect, which can be expressed as

$$\frac{dl}{dw}(subst) = \frac{-U_1}{\nabla} < 0,$$

so that the substitution effect is for leisure to fall and hours worked to rise when the real wage increases. This implies that, from (A-12), the income effect is

$$\frac{dl}{dw}(inc) = \frac{dl}{dw} - \frac{dl}{dw}(subst) = \frac{(h - l)(U_{12} - wU_{11})}{\nabla} > 0,$$

assuming that leisure is a normal good, which implies that $U_{12} - wU_{11} > 0$. Therefore, the income effect is for leisure to increase when the real wage increases. In general, without putting additional restrictions on the utility function, we do not know the sign of $\frac{dl}{dw}$.

The Representative Firm

We assumed in Chapter 4 that the production function for the representative firm is described by

$$Y = zF(K,N^d),$$

where Y is output, z is total factor productivity, $F(\cdot, \cdot)$ is a function, K is the capital stock, and N^d is the firm's labor input. The function $F(\cdot, \cdot)$ is assumed to be quasiconcave, strictly increasing in both arguments, homogeneous of degree one or constant-returns-to-scale, and twice differentiable. We also assume that $F_2(K, 0) = \infty$ and $F_2(K, \infty) = 0$ to guarantee that there is always an interior solution to the firm's profit maximization problem, where $F_2(K,N^d)$ is the first derivative with respect to the second argument of the function $F(\cdot, \cdot)$. The firm's profit maximization problem is to choose the labor input N^d so as to maximize

$$\pi = zF(K,N^d) - wN^d,$$

subject to $N^d \geq 0$, where π is the difference between revenue and labor costs in terms of consumption goods. That is, the firm solves

$$\max_{N^d}(zF(K,N^d) - wN^d). \tag{A-13}$$

The restrictions on the function $F(\cdot, \cdot)$ imply that there is a unique interior solution to problem (A-13), characterized by the first-order condition

$$zF_2(K,N^d) = w, \tag{A-14}$$

which states that the firm hires labor until the marginal product of labor $zF_2(K,N^d)$ equals the real wage w.

We can determine the effects of changes in w, z, and K on labor demand N^d through comparative statics techniques. Totally differentiating equation (A-14), which determines N^d implicitly as a function of w, z, and K, we obtain

$$zF_{22}dN^d - dw + F_2dz + zF_{12}dK = 0.$$

Then, solving for the appropriate derivatives, we have

$$\frac{dN^d}{dw} = \frac{1}{zF_{22}} < 0,$$

$$\frac{dN^d}{dz} = \frac{-F_2}{zF_{22}} > 0,$$

$$\frac{dN^d}{dK} = \frac{-zF_{12}}{zF_{22}} > 0.$$

We can sign the above derivatives because $F_{22} < 0$ (the marginal product of labor decreases as the quantity of labor increases), $F_2 > 0$ (the marginal product of labor is positive), and $F_{12} > 0$ (the marginal product of labor increases as the capital input increases). These are restrictions on the production function discussed in Chapter 4. Because $\frac{dN^d}{dw} < 0$, the labor demand curve is downward sloping. Further, $\frac{dN^d}{dz} > 0$ and $\frac{dN^d}{dK} > 0$ imply that the labor demand curve shifts to the right when z or K increases.

Problems

1. Suppose that the consumer's preferences are given by the utility function $U(C,l) = \ln C + \alpha \ln l$, where $\alpha > 0$. Determine the consumer's choice of consumption and leisure and interpret your solutions.

2. In the consumer's choice problem, show that at least one good must be normal.

3. Suppose that the firm's production technology is given by $Y = zF(K,N) = zK^\alpha N^{1-\alpha}$, where $0 < \alpha < 1$. Determine the firm's demand for labor as a function of z, K, α, and w, and interpret.

4. Suppose that the firm's production technology is given by $Y = z\min(K,\alpha N)$, where $\alpha > 0$. As in problem 3, determine the firm's demand for labor as a function of z, K, α, and w, and interpret.

A Closed–Economy One-Period Macroeconomic Model

Here, we show formally the equivalence between the competitive equilibrium and the Pareto optimum in the one-period model and then determine, using comparative statics, the equilibrium effects of a change in government spending and in total factor productivity.

Competitive Equilibrium

In a competitive equilibrium, the representative consumer maximizes utility subject to his or her budget constraint, the representative firm maximizes profits, the government budget constraint holds, and the market on which labor is exchanged for consumption goods clears. From the previous section, the two equations describing consumer optimization are the budget constraint, equation (A-3), or

$$w(h - l) + \pi - T - C = 0, \tag{A-15}$$

and equation (A-5), or

$$U_2(C,l) - wU_1(C,l) = 0. \tag{A-16}$$

Optimization by the representative firm implies equation (A-14), or

$$zF_2(K,N^d) = w, \tag{A-17}$$

and profits for the firm are

$$\pi = zF(K,N^d) - wN^d. \tag{A-18}$$

The government budget constraint states that government spending is equal to taxes; that is,

$$G = T. \tag{A-19}$$

Finally, the market-clearing condition is

$$h - l = N^d, \tag{A-20}$$

or the supply of labor is equal to the demand for labor. Equations (A-15) to (A-20) are six equations that solve for the six endogenous variables C, l, N^d, T, π, and w, given the exogenous variables z and G. To make this system of equations more manageable, we can simplify as follows. First, using equations (A-18) to (A-20) to substitute for π, T, and N^d in equation (A-15), we obtain

$$C = zF(K,h - l) - G. \tag{A-21}$$

Then, substituting in equation (A-18) for N^d using equation (A-20), and then in turn for w in (A-16) using equation (A-18), we obtain

$$U_2(C,l) - zF_2(K,h - l)U_1(C,l) = 0. \tag{A-22}$$

Equations (A-21) and (A-22) then solve for equilibrium C and l. Then, the real wage w can be determined from (A-17), after substituting for N^d from (A-20), to get

$$w = zF_2(K,h - l). \tag{A-23}$$

Finally, aggregate output is given from the production function by

$$Y = zF(K,h - l).$$

Pareto Optimum

To determine the Pareto optimum, we need to ask how a fictitious social planner would choose consumption and leisure so as to maximize welfare for the representative consumer, given the production technology. The social planner solves

$$\max_{C,l} U(C,l)$$

subject to

$$C = zF(K,h - l) - G.$$

To solve the social planner's problem, set up the Lagrangian associated with the constrained optimization problem above, which is

$$L = U(C,l) + \lambda[zF(K,h - l) - G - C].$$

The first-order conditions for an optimum are then

$$U_1(C,l) - \lambda = 0, \tag{A-24}$$

$$U_2(C,l) - \lambda zF_2(K,h - l) = 0, \tag{A-25}$$

$$zF(K,h - l) - G - C = 0. \tag{A-26}$$

From equations (A-24) and (A-25), we obtain

$$U_2(C,l) - zF_2(K,h - l)U_1(C,l) = 0. \qquad \text{(A-27)}$$

Now, equations (A-26) and (A-27), which solve for the Pareto-optimal quantities of leisure l and consumption C, are identical to equations (A-21) and (A-22), so that the Pareto-optimal quantities of leisure and consumption are identical to the competitive equilibrium quantities of leisure and consumption. As a result, the competitive equilibrium and the Pareto optimum are the same thing in this model, so the first and second welfare theorems hold.

Equation (A-27) can be written (suppressing arguments for convenience) as

$$\frac{U_2}{U_1} = zF_2,$$

which states that the marginal rate of substitution of leisure for consumption is equal to the marginal product of labor (the marginal rate of transformation) at the optimum.

Comparative Statics

We would like to determine the effects of changes in G and z on equilibrium C, l, Y, and w. To do this, we totally differentiate equations (A-26) and (A-27), obtaining

$$-dC - zF_2dl + Fdz - dG = 0,$$

$$(U_{12} - zF_2U_{11})dC + (U_{22} + zF_{22}U_1 - zF_2U_{12})dl - F_2U_1dz = 0.$$

Then, putting these two equations in matrix form, we get

$$\begin{bmatrix} -1 & -zF_2 \\ U_{12} - zF_2U_{11} & U_{22} + zF_{22}U_1 - zF_2U_{12} \end{bmatrix} \begin{bmatrix} dC \\ dl \end{bmatrix} = \begin{bmatrix} -Fdz + dG \\ F_2U_1dz \end{bmatrix} \qquad \text{(A-28)}$$

Using Cramer's rule to determine the effects of a change in government spending G, from (A-28) we then get

$$\frac{dC}{dG} = \frac{U_{22} + zF_{22}U_1 - zF_2U_{12}}{\nabla},$$

$$\frac{dl}{dG} = \frac{-U_{12} + zF_2U_{11}}{\nabla},$$

where

$$\nabla = -z^2F_2^2U_{11} + 2zF_2U_{12} - U_{22} - zF_{22}U_1.$$

Here, ∇ is the determinant of the bordered Hessian associated with the social planner's constrained optimization problem, and the quasiconcavity of the utility function and the production function guarantees that $\nabla > 0$. To sign the derivatives above, in equilibrium $zF_2 = w$, from equation (A-17). This then implies, given our assumption that consumption and leisure are normal goods, that $U_{22} - zF_2U_{12} < 0$ and $-U_{12} + zF_2U_{11} < 0$ (recall our discussion from the previous section); because $F_{22} < 0$ (the marginal product of labor declines as the labor input increases), we have $\frac{dC}{dG} < 0$ and

$\frac{dl}{dG} < 0$, so that consumption and leisure decline when government purchases increase because of negative income effects. For the effect on the real wage w, because $w = zF_2(K,h - l)$, we have

$$\frac{dw}{dG} = -zF_{22}\frac{dl}{dG} < 0,$$

thus the real wage decreases. For the effect on aggregate output, because $Y = C + G$, we have

$$\frac{dY}{dG} = \frac{dC}{dG} + 1 = \frac{-z^2F_2^2U_{11} + zF_2U_{12}}{\nabla} > 0,$$

as leisure is assumed to be normal, implying $zF_2U_{11} - U_{12} < 0$.

Now, to determine the effects of a change in z, again we use Cramer's rule in conjunction with equation (A-28), obtaining

$$\frac{dC}{dz} = \frac{-F(U_{22} + zF_{22}U_1 - zF_2U_{12}) + F_2^2zU_1}{\nabla},$$

$$\frac{dl}{dz} = \frac{-F_2U_1 + F(U_{12} - zF_2U_{11})}{\nabla}.$$

Here, because consumption is a normal good, $U_{22} - zF_2U_{12} < 0$, and given $F_{22} < 0$, $F > 0$, and $U_1 > 0$, we have $\frac{dC}{dz} > 0$ and consumption increases with an increase in total factor productivity, as we showed diagrammatically in Chapter 5, Figure 5.9. However, we cannot sign $\frac{dl}{dz}$ because there are opposing income and substitution effects. We can separate out the income and substitution effects on leisure by determining the response of leisure to a change in z holding utility constant. This gives a substitution effect, which is

$$\frac{dl}{dz}(subst) = \frac{-F_2U_1}{\nabla},$$

so that the substitution effect is for leisure to decrease and employment ($= h - l$) to increase. The income effect of the change in z is then

$$\frac{dl}{dz}(inc) = \frac{dl}{dz} - \frac{dl}{dz}(subst) = \frac{F(U_{12} - zF_2U_{11})}{\nabla} > 0,$$

because leisure is a normal good. Therefore, an increase in z has a positive income effect on leisure.

Problems

1. For the closed-economy, one-period model, suppose that $U(C,l) = \ln C + \beta l$, and $F(K, N) = zK^\alpha N^{1-\alpha}$, where $\beta > 0$ and $0 < \alpha < 1$. Determine consumption, employment, output, leisure, and the real wage in a competitive equilibrium, and explain your solutions.

2. For the closed-economy, one-period model, suppose that $U(C,l) = \min(C,\beta l)$, and $F(K,N) = \alpha K + \delta N$, where $\beta > 0$, $\alpha > 0$, and $\delta > 0$. Determine consumption,

employment, output, leisure, and the real wage in a competitive equilibrium, and explain your solutions. Also draw a diagram with the consumer's preferences and the production possibilities frontier, and show the competitive equilibrium in this diagram.

Chapters 6 and 7: Economic Growth

In this section we work out explicitly the effects of changes in the savings rate, the labor force growth rate, and total factor productivity on the steady state quantity of capital per worker and output per worker in the Solow growth model. We omit an algebraic analysis of the Malthusian growth model, as this is very straightforward. We determine the golden rule for capital accumulation in the Solow model. Finally, we develop a growth model where consumption–savings decisions are made endogenously. In solving this model, we introduce dynamic programming techniques, which are useful later in this appendix.

Explicit Results for the Solow Growth Model

Recall from Chapter 6 that the aggregate quantity of capital in the Solow growth model evolves according to

$$K' = (1 - d)K + I, \tag{A-29}$$

where K' is future period capital, d is the depreciation rate, K is current period capital, and I is current period investment. In equilibrium, saving is equal to investment, and so $sY = I$, where s is the savings rate and Y is aggregate income. Further, the production function is given by $Y = zF(K,N)$, where z is total factor productivity and N is the labor force, so that substituting in equation (A-29), we have

$$K' = (1 - d)K + szF(K,N). \tag{A-30}$$

Then, dividing the right-hand and left-hand sides of equation (A-30) by N, using the relationship $N' = (1 + n)N$, which describes labor force growth, with N' denoting the future labor force and n the population growth rate, and rewriting in the form of lowercase variables that denote per-worker quantities, we have

$$k' = \frac{szf(k)}{1 + n} + \frac{(1 - d)k}{1 + n}. \tag{A-31}$$

Equation (A-31) then determines the evolution of the per-worker capital stock from the current period to the future period, where k is the current stock of capital per worker, k' is the stock of future capital per worker, and $f(k)$ is the per-worker production function.

In the steady state, $k' = k = k^*$, where k^* is the steady state quantity of capital per worker, which, from (A-31), satisfies

$$szf(k^*) - (n + d)k^* = 0 \tag{A-32}$$

Now, to determine the effects of changes in s, n, and z on the steady state quantity of capital per worker, we totally differentiate equation (A-32), getting

$$[szf'(k^*) - n - d]dk^* + szf(k^*)ds - k^*dn + sf(k^*)dz = 0 \qquad \text{(A-33)}$$

Then, solving for the appropriate derivatives, we obtain

$$\frac{dk^*}{ds} = \frac{-zf(k^*)}{szf'(k^*) - n - d} > 0,$$

$$\frac{dk^*}{dn} = \frac{k^*}{szf'(k^*) - n - d} < 0,$$

$$\frac{dk^*}{dz} = \frac{-sf(k^*)}{szf'(k^*) - n - d} > 0.$$

Here, capital per worker increases with increases in s and z, and decreases with an increase in n. We get these results because $szf'(k^*) - n - d < 0$ in the steady state. Because output per worker in the steady state is $y^* = zf(k^*)$, for each of these experiments, steady state output per worker moves in the same direction as steady state capital per worker.

In the steady state, the quantity of consumption per worker is

$$c^* = zf(k^*) - (n + d)k^*.$$

Now, when the savings rate changes, the response of consumption per worker in the steady state is given by

$$\frac{dc^*}{ds} = [zf'(k^*) - n - d]\frac{dk^*}{ds}.$$

Although $\frac{dk^*}{ds} > 0$, the sign of $zf'(k^*) - n - d$ is ambiguous, so that consumption per worker could increase or decrease with an increase in the savings rate. The golden rule savings rate is the savings rate s_{gr} that maximizes consumption per worker in the steady state. The golden rule steady state quantity of capital per worker solves the problem

$$\max_{k^*} [zf(k^*) - (n + d)k^*];$$

letting k^*_{gr} denote this quantity of capital per worker, k^*_{gr} solves

$$zf'(k^*_{gr}) - n - d = 0,$$

and then s_{gr} is determined from equation (A-32) by

$$s_{gr} = \frac{(n + d)k^*_{gr}}{zf(k^*_{gr})}.$$

For example, if $F(K,N) = K^\alpha N^{1-\alpha}$, where $0 < \alpha < 1$ (a Cobb–Douglas production function), then $f(k) = k^\alpha$, and we get

$$k^*_{gr} = \left(\frac{z\alpha}{n + d}\right)^{\frac{1}{1-\alpha}},$$

$$s_{gr} = \alpha.$$

Problem

1. Suppose in the Solow growth model that there is government spending financed by lump-sum taxes, with total government spending $G = gY$, where $0 < g < 1$. Solve for steady state capital per worker, consumption per worker, and output per worker, and determine how each depends on g. Can g be set so as to maximize steady state consumption per worker? If so, determine the optimal fraction of output purchased by the government, g^*, and explain your results.

Optimal Growth: Endogenous Consumption–Savings Decisions

In this model, we relax the assumption made in the Solow growth model that the savings rate is exogenous and allow consumption to be determined optimally over time. The model we develop here is a version of the optimal growth theory originally developed by David Cass and Tjalling Koopmans.[1] In this model, the second welfare theorem holds, and so we can solve the social planner's problem to determine the competitive equilibrium. We set the model up as simply as possible, leaving out population growth and changes in total factor productivity; but, these features are easy to add.

There is a representative infinitely lived consumer with preferences given by

$$\sum_{t=0}^{\infty} \beta^t U(C_t) \tag{A-34}$$

where β is the subjective discount factor of the representative consumer, with $0 < \beta < 1$, and C_t is consumption in period t. Throughout, t subscripts denote the time period. The period utility function $U(\cdot)$ is continuously differentiable, strictly increasing, strictly concave, and bounded. Assume that $\lim_{C \to 0} U'(C) = \infty$. Each period, the consumer is endowed with one unit of time, which can be supplied as labor.

The production function is given by

$$Y_t = F(K_t, N_t),$$

where Y_t is output, K_t is the capital input, and N_t is the labor input. The production function $F(\cdot, \cdot)$ is continuously differentiable, strictly increasing in both arguments, homogeneous of degree one, and strictly quasiconcave. Assume that $F(0, N) = 0$, $\lim_{K \to 0} F_1(K, 1) = \infty$, and $\lim_{K \to \infty} F_1(K, 1) = 0$.

The capital stock obeys the law of motion

$$K_{t+1} = (1 - d)K_t + I_t, \tag{A-35}$$

where I_t is investment and d is the depreciation rate, with $0 \le d \le 1$, and K_0 is the initial capital stock, which is given. In equilibrium, we have $N_t = 1$ for all t, and so it is convenient to define the function $H(K_t)$ by $H(K_t) = F(K_t, 1)$. The resource constraint for the economy is

$$C_t + I_t = H(K_t), \tag{A-36}$$

---

[1]See D. Cass, 1965, "Optimum Growth in an Aggregative Model of Capital Accumulation," *Review of Economic Studies* 32, 233–240; and T. Koopmans, 1965, "On the Concept of Optimal Growth," in *The Econometric Approach to Development Planning*, North Holland, Amsterdam.

or consumption plus investment is equal to the total quantity of output produced. It is convenient to substitute for I_t in equation (A-36) using (A-35) and to rearrange, obtaining a single constraint

$$C_t + K_{t+1} = H(K_t) + (1 - d)K_t. \qquad (A-37)$$

we can think of the resources available in period t to the social planner on the right-hand side of equation (A-37) as being period t output plus the undepreciated portion of the capital stock, which is then split up (on the left-hand side of the equation) between period t consumption and the capital stock for period $t + 1$.

The social planner's problem for this economy is to determine consumption and the capital stock in each period so as to maximize equation (A-34) subject to the constraint equation (A-37). Again, the solution to this problem is equivalent to the competitive equilibrium solution. The social planner solves

$$\max_{\{C_t, K_{t+1}\}^{\infty}_{t=0}} \sum_{t=0}^{\infty} U(C_t), \qquad (A-38)$$

given K_0 and (A-37) for $t = 0, 1, 2, \ldots \infty$.

Now, the problem of solving equation (A-38) subject to (A-37) may appear quite formidable, as we need to solve for an infinite sequence of choice variables. However, dynamic programming techniques essentially allow us to turn this infinite-dimensional problem into a two-dimensional problem.[2] To see how this works, note from the right-hand side of (A-37) that the current capital stock K_t determines the resources that are available to the social planner at the beginning of period t. Thus, K_t determines how much utility the social planner can give to the consumer from period t on. Suppose that the social planner knows $v(K_t)$, which is the maximum utility that the social planner could provide for the representative consumer from period t on. Then, the problem that the social planner would solve in any period t would be

$$\max_{C_t, K_{t+1}} [U(C_t) + \beta v(K_{t+1})]$$

subject to

$$C_t + K_{t+1} = H(K_t) + (1 - d)K_t.$$

That is, the social planner chooses current period consumption and the capital stock for the following period so as to maximize the sum of current period utility and the discounted value of utility from the next period on, subject to the resource constraint. Now, because the problem of the social planner looks the same in every period, it is true that

$$v(K_t) = \max_{C_t, K_{t+1}} [U(C_t) + \beta v(K_{t+1})] \qquad (A-39)$$

---

[2]For more detail on dynamic programming methods in economics, see N. Stokey, R. Lucas, and E. Prescott, 1989, *Recursive Methods in Economic Dynamics,* Harvard University Press, Cambridge, MA.

subject to

$$C_t + K_{t+1} = H(K_t) + (1 - d)K_t. \qquad (A\text{-}40)$$

Then, equation (A-39) is called a Bellman equation, or functional equation, and it determines what $v(\cdot)$ is. We call $v(K_t)$ the value function as this tells us the value of the problem at time t to the social planner as a function of the state variable K_t. Given the assumptions we have made, there is a unique function $v(\cdot)$ that solves the Bellman equation. There are some circumstances where we can obtain an explicit solution for $v(\cdot)$ (see the problem at the end of this section), but in any case the dynamic programming formulation of the social planner's problem, equation (A-39) subject to (A-40), can be convenient for characterizing solutions, if we assume that $v(\cdot)$ is differentiable and strictly concave (which it is here, given our assumptions).

We can simplify the problem above by substituting for C_t in the objective function (A-39) using the constraint (A-40), getting

$$v(K_t) = \max_{K_{t+1}} \{U[H(K_t) + (1 - d)K_t - K_{t+1}] + \beta v(K_{t+1})\} \qquad (A\text{-}41)$$

Then, given that the value function $v(\cdot)$ is concave and differentiable, we can differentiate on the right-hand side of (A-41) to get the first-order condition for an optimum, which is

$$U'[H(K_t) + (1 - d)K_t - K_{t+1}] + \beta v'(K_{t+1}) = 0. \qquad (A\text{-}42)$$

Now, to determine $v'(K_{t+1})$, we apply the envelope theorem in differentiating equation (A-41), obtaining

$$v'(K_t) = [H'(K_t) + 1 - d]U'[H(K_t) + (1 - d)K_t - K_{t+1}].$$

then, we update one period, and substitute for $v'(K_{t+1})$ in (A-42), getting

$$- U'[H(K_t) + (1 - d)K_t - K_{t+1}] + \beta[H'(K_{t+1}) + 1 - d] \times U'[H(K_{t+1})$$
$$+ (1 - d)K_{t+1} - K_{t+2}] = 0. \qquad (A\text{-}43)$$

Now, we know that, in this the model, the quantity of capital converges to a constant steady state value, K^*. Equation (A-43) can be used to solve for K^* by substituting $K_{t+1} = K_t = K^*$ in (A-43), which gives, after simplifying,

$$- 1 + \beta[H'(K^*) + 1 - d] = 0, \qquad (A\text{-}44)$$

or

$$H'(K^*) - d = \frac{1}{\beta} - 1$$

in the optimal steady state. That is, in the optimal steady state, the net marginal product of capital is equal to the subjective discount rate of the representative consumer.

In the model, the savings rate is given by

$$s_t = \frac{I_t}{Y_t} = \frac{K_{t+1} - (1 - d)K_t}{H(K_t)},$$

and so in the steady state the savings rate is

$$s^* = \frac{dK^*}{H(K^*)}.$$

In this model, because the savings rate is optimally chosen over time, choosing a "golden rule savings rate" makes no sense. Indeed, the steady state optimal savings rate in this model does not maximize steady state consumption. Steady state consumption would be maximized for a value of the steady state capital stock K^* such that $H'(K^*) = d$, but this is different from the optimal steady state capital stock determined by equation (A-44).

Problem

1. In the optimal growth model, suppose that $U(C_t) = \ln C_t$ and $F(K_t, N_t) = K_t^\alpha N_t^{1-\alpha}$, with $d = 1$ (100% depreciation).
    (a) Guess that the value function takes the form $v(K_t) = A + B\ln K_t$, where A and B are undetermined constants.
    (b) Substitute your guess for the value function on the right-hand side of equation (A-41), solve the optimization problem, and verify that your guess was correct.
    (c) Solve for A and B by substituting your optimal solution from part (b) on the right-hand side of equation (A-41) and equating coefficients on the left and right-hand sides of the equation.
    (d) Determine the solutions for K_{t+1} and C_t as functions of K_t, and interpret these solutions.

Chapter 8: Two–Period Model

In this section we formally derive the results for individual consumer behavior, showing how a consumer optimizes by choosing consumption and savings over two periods and how the consumer responds to changes in income and the market real interest rate.

The Consumer's Optimization Problem

The consumer has preferences defined by a utility function $U(c, c')$, where c is current period consumption, c' is future consumption, and $U(\cdot, \cdot)$ is strictly quasiconcave, increasing in both arguments, and twice differentiable. To guarantee an interior solution to the consumer's problem, we assume that the marginal utilities of current and future consumption each go to infinity in the limit as current and future consumption go to zero, respectively. The consumer chooses c and c' to maximize $U(c, c')$ subject to the consumer's lifetime budget constraint, that is,

$$\max_{c,c'} U(c,c')$$

subject to

$$c + \frac{c'}{1 + r} = y + \frac{y'}{1 + r} - t - \frac{t'}{1 + r},$$

where y is current income, y' is future income, t is the current tax, and t' is the future tax. The Lagrangian associated with this constrained optimization problem is

$$L = U(c,c') + \lambda\left(y + \frac{y'}{1 + r} - t - \frac{t'}{1 + r} - c - \frac{c'}{1 + r}\right),$$

where λ is the Lagrange multiplier. Therefore, the first-order conditions for an optimum are

$$U_1(c,c') - \lambda = 0, \tag{A-45}$$

$$U_2(c,c') - \frac{\lambda}{1 + r} = 0, \tag{A-46}$$

$$y + \frac{y'}{1 + r} - t - \frac{t'}{1 + r} - c - \frac{c'}{1 + r} = 0. \tag{A-47}$$

Then, in equations (A-45) and (A-46), we can eliminate λ to obtain

$$U_1(c,c') - (1 + r)U_2(c,c') = 0, \tag{A-48}$$

or rewriting (A-48),

$$\frac{U_1(c,c')}{U_2(c,c')} = 1 + r,$$

which states that the intertemporal marginal rate of substitution (the marginal rate of substitution of current consumption for future consumption) is equal to one plus the real interest rate at the optimum.

For convenience, we can rewrite (A-47) as

$$y(1 + r) + y' - t(1 + r) - t' - c(1 + r) - c' = 0. \tag{A-49}$$

Then, equations (A-48) and (A-49) determine the quantities of c and c' the consumer chooses given current and future incomes y and y', current and future taxes t and t', and the real interest rate r.

Comparative Statics

To determine the effects of changes in current and future income and the real interest rate on current and future consumption and savings, we totally differentiate equations (A-48) and (A-49), obtaining

$$[U_{11} - (1 + r)U_{12}]dc + [U_{12} - (1 + r)U_{22}]dc' - U_2dr = 0,$$
$$- (1 + r)dc - dc' + (y - t - c)dr + (1 + r)dy + dy' - (1 + r)dt - dt' = 0;$$

these two equations can be written in matrix form as

$$\begin{bmatrix} U_{11} - (1 + r)U_{12} & U_{12} - (1 + r)U_{22} \\ -(1 + r) & - 1 \end{bmatrix}\begin{bmatrix} dc \\ dc' \end{bmatrix}$$

$$= \begin{bmatrix} U_2dr \\ -(y - t - c)dr - (1 + r)dy - dy' - (1 + r)dt - dt' \end{bmatrix} \tag{A-50}$$

First, we determine the effects of a change in current income y. Applying Cramer's rule to (A-50), we obtain

$$\frac{dc}{dy} = \frac{(1 + r)[U_{12} - (1 + r)U_{22}]}{\nabla},$$

$$\frac{dc'}{dy} = \frac{(1 + r)[-U_{11} + (1 + r)U_{12}]}{\nabla},$$

where

$$\nabla = -U_{11} + 2(1 + r)U_{12} - (1 + r)^2 U_{22}.$$

Given our restrictions on the utility function, ∇, which is the determinant of the bordered Hessian associated with the consumer's constrained optimization problem, is strictly positive. Further, assuming current and future consumption are normal goods, we have $U_{12} - (1 + r)U_{22} > 0$ and $-U_{11} + (1 + r)U_{12} > 0$, and so $\frac{dc}{dy} > 0$ and $\frac{dc'}{dy} > 0$. Thus, an increase in current income causes increases in both current and future consumption. Saving in the current period is given by $s = y - c - t$, so that

$$\frac{ds}{dy} = 1 - \frac{dc}{dy} = \frac{-U_{11} + (1 + r)U_{12}}{\nabla} > 0,$$

because the assumption that goods are normal gives $-U_{11} + (1 + r)U_{12} > 0$. Therefore, saving increases in the current period when y increases.

To determine the effects of a change in future income y', we again apply Cramer's rule to (A-50), getting

$$\frac{dc}{dy'} = \frac{1}{1 + r}\frac{dc}{dy} > 0,$$

$$\frac{dc'}{dy'} = \frac{1}{1 + r}\frac{dc'}{dy} > 0,$$

so that the effects of a change in y' are identical qualitatively to the effects of a change in y, except that the derivatives are discounted, using the one-period discount factor $\frac{1}{1+r}$. The effect on saving is given by

$$\frac{ds}{dy'} = -\frac{dc}{dy'} < 0,$$

thus saving decreases when future income increases.

Finally, to determine the effects of a change in the real interest rate r on current and future consumption, we again apply Cramer's rule to (A-50), getting

$$\frac{dc}{dr} = \frac{-U_2 + [U_{12} - (1 + r)U_{22}](y - t - c)}{\nabla},$$

$$\frac{dc'}{dr} = \frac{(1 + r)U_2 - [U_{11} - (1 + r)U_{12}](y - t - c)}{\nabla}.$$

The signs of both of these derivatives are indeterminate, because the income and substitution effects may be opposing. As above, we can separate the income and substitution effects by determining the responses of c and c' to a change in r holding utility constant. The substitution effects are

$$\frac{dc}{dr}(subst) = \frac{-U_2}{\nabla} < 0,$$

$$\frac{dc'}{dr}(subst) = \frac{(1 + r)U_2}{\nabla} > 0,$$

so that the substitution effect is for current consumption to decrease and future consumption to increase when the real interest rate increases. The income effects are

$$\frac{dc}{dr}(inc) = \frac{dc}{dr} - \frac{dc}{dr}(subst) = \frac{[U_{12} - (1 + r)U_{22}](y - t - c)}{\nabla},$$

$$\frac{dc'}{dr}(inc) = \frac{dc'}{dr} - \frac{dc'}{dr}(subst) = \frac{[U_{11} - (1 + r)U_{12}](y - t - c)}{\nabla}.$$

Here, the assumption that goods are normal gives $U_{12} - (1 + r)U_{22} > 0$ and $U_{11} - (1 + r)U_{12} < 0$, thus given this assumption the signs of the income effects are determined by whether the consumer is a lender or a borrower, that is, by the sign of $y - t - c$. If the consumer is a lender, so that $y - t - c > 0$, then the income effects are for current consumption to increase and future consumption to increase. However, if $y - t - c < 0$, so that consumer is a borrower, then the income effect is for current consumption to decrease and future consumption to decrease.

Because savings is $s = y - c - t$, the effect on savings of a change in the real interest rate is determined by the effect on current consumption, namely,

$$\frac{ds}{dr} = -\frac{dc}{dr}.$$

Problems

1. Suppose that $U(c, c') = \ln c + \beta \ln c$, where $\beta > 0$. Determine consumption in the current and future periods for the consumer, and interpret your solutions in terms of income and substitution effects.

2. Suppose that $U(c, c') = \ln c + \beta \ln c$, where $\beta > 0$, and assume that the consumer lends at the real interest rate r_1 and borrows at the interest rate r_2, where $r_1 < r_2$. Under what conditions is the consumer (a) a borrower, (b) a lender, and (c) neither a borrower nor a lender? Explain your results.

Chapter 10: A Real Intertemporal Model with Investment

There is not much to be gained from analyzing the model developed in this chapter algebraically. It is possible to linearize the model so as to make it amenable to an explicit solution, but to do analysis with this linearized model requires a good deal of tedious algebra. For this chapter, we confine attention to a formal treatment of the representative firm's investment problem.

The current and future production functions for the firm are given, respectively, by

$$Y = zF(K, N) \tag{A-51}$$

and

$$Y' = z'F(K', N'), \tag{A-52}$$

where Y and Y' are current and future outputs, respectively, z and z' are current and future total factor productivities, K and K' are current and future capital stocks, and N and N' are current and future labor inputs. The capital stock evolves according to

$$K' = (1 - d)K + I, \tag{A-53}$$

where d is the depreciation rate and I is investment in capital in period 1. The present value of profits for the firm is

$$V = Y - I - wN + \frac{Y' - w'N' + (1 - d)K}{1 + r} \tag{A-54}$$

where w is the current real wage, w' is the future real wage, and r is the real interest rate. We can substitute in equation (A-54) for Y, Y', and K' using (A-51) to (A-53) to obtain

$$V = zF(K, N) - I - wN$$
$$+ \frac{z'F[(1 - d)K + I', N'] - w'N' + (1 - d)[(1 - d)K + I]}{1 + r} \tag{A-55}$$

The objective of the firm is to choose N, N', and I to maximize V. The first-order conditions for an optimum, obtained by differentiating equation (A-55) with respect to N, N', and I are

$$\frac{\partial V}{\partial N} = zF_2(K, N) - w = 0, \tag{A-56}$$

$$\frac{\partial V}{\partial N'} = \frac{z'F_2[(1 - d)K + I, N'] - w'}{1 + r} = 0, \tag{A-57}$$

$$\frac{\partial V}{\partial I} = -1 + \frac{z'F_1[(1 - d)K + I, N'] + 1 - d}{1 + r} = 0. \tag{A-58}$$

Equations (A-56) and (A-57) state, respectively, that the firm optimizes by setting the marginal product of labor equal to the real wage in the current period and in the future period. We can simplify equation (A-58) by writing it as

$$z'F_1[(1 - d)K + I, N'] - d = r, \tag{A-59}$$

or the firm chooses investment optimally by setting the future net marginal product of capital equal to the real interest rate, given N'. To determine how changes in z', K, d, and r affect the investment decision, given future employment N', we totally differentiate equation (A-59), getting

$$z'F_{11}dI + z'(1 - d)F_{11}dK + F_1dz - (z'KF_{11} + 1)dd - dr = 0.$$

Then, we have

$$\frac{dI}{dr} = \frac{1}{z'F_{11}} < 0,$$

so that investment declines when the real interest rate increases;

$$\frac{dI}{dK} = d - 1 < 0$$

so that investment is lower the higher is the initial capital stock K;

$$\frac{dI}{dz'} = \frac{-F_1}{z'F_{11}} > 0,$$

so that investment increases when future total factor productivity increases; and

$$\frac{dI}{dd} = \frac{z'KF_{11} + 1}{z'F_{11}},$$

which has an indeterminate sign, so that the effect of a change in the depreciation rate on investment is ambiguous.

Problem

1. Suppose that the firm produces output only from capital. Current output is given by $Y = zK^{\alpha}$, and future output is given by $Y' = z'(K')^{\alpha}$, where $0 < \alpha < 1$. Determine investment for the firm, and show how investment depends on the real interest rate, future total factor productivity, the depreciation rate, and α. Explain your results.

Chapter 11: A Monetary Intertemporal Model

Here, we develop an explicit cash-in-advance model, which is a simplified version of the model in Chapter 11. In particular, in this model there is no investment or capital, and all consumption goods are purchased with cash. There are no credit purchases. However, the model has most of the same implications as those discussed in Chapters 11 and 16.

In the cash-in-advance model there is a representative consumer, who lives forever and has preferences given by the utility function

$$\sum_{t=0}^{\infty} \beta^t [U(C_t) - V(N_t)], \tag{A-60}$$

where β is the subjective discount factor, with $0 < \beta < 1$, C_t is consumption in period t, N_t is labor supply in period t, $U(\cdot)$ is a strictly increasing and strictly concave function with $U'(0) = \infty$, and $V(\cdot)$ is a strictly increasing and strictly convex function with $V'(0) = 0$. Assume that $U(\cdot)$ and $V(\cdot)$ are twice continuously differentiable.

For simplicity we do not have capital or investment in the model, to focus on the key results, and the production function is given by

$$Y_t = zN_t, \tag{A-61}$$

where Y_t is output in period t and z is the marginal product of labor. The linear production function has the constant-returns-to scale property.

Within any period t, timing works as follows. At the beginning of the period, the representative consumer has M_t units of money carried over from the previous period, B_t nominal bonds, and X_t real bonds. Each nominal bond issued in period t is a promise to pay one unit of money in period $t + 1$, and each real bond issued in period t is a promise to pay one unit of the consumption good in period $t + 1$. With nominal and real bonds in the model, we can determine explicitly the nominal and real interest rates. A nominal bond issued in period t sells for q_t units of money, while a real bond sells for s_t units of period t consumption goods.

At the beginning of the period, the asset market opens, the consumer receives the payoffs on the bonds held over from the previous period, and the consumer can exchange money for nominal and real bonds that come due in period $t + 1$. The consumer must also pay a real lump-sum tax of T_t at this time. After the asset market closes, the consumer supplies N_t units of labor to the firm and buys consumption goods on the goods market, but he or she must purchase these consumption goods with money held over after the asset market closes. Consumption goods are sold at the money price P_t in period t. Therefore, the representative consumer must abide by the cash-in-advance constraint

$$P_t C_t + q_t B_{t+1} + P_t s_t X_{t+1} + P_t T_t = M_t + B_t + P_t X_t. \qquad \text{(A-62)}$$

When the goods market closes, the consumer receives his or her labor earnings from the representative firm in cash. The consumer then faces the budget constraint

$$P_t C_t + q_t B_{t+1} + P_t s_t X_{t+1} + P_t T_t + M_{t+1} = M_t + B_t + P_t X_t + P_t z N_t, \qquad \text{(A-63)}$$

where M_{t+1} is the quantity of money held by the consumer at the end of the period and z is the real wage in period t, which must be equal to the constant marginal product of labor in equilibrium.

Letting $\overline{M}_t$ denote the supply of money at the beginning of period t, the government budget constraint is given by

$$\overline{M}_{t+1} - \overline{M}_t = -P_t T_t, \qquad \text{(A-64)}$$

and the government sets taxes so that the money supply grows at a constant rate α. That is, we have $\overline{M}_{t+1} = (1 + \alpha)\overline{M}_t$ for all t. This then implies, from equation (A-64), that

$$\alpha \overline{M}_t = -P_t T_t. \qquad \text{(A-65)}$$

Now, it is convenient to scale the constraints (A-62) and (A-63) by multiplying through by $\frac{1}{\overline{M}_t}$ and letting lowercase letters denote scaled nominal variables, for example, $p_t = \frac{P_t}{\overline{M}_t}$. Then, we can rewrite (A-62) and (A-63) as

$$p_t C_t + q_t b_{t+1}(1 + \alpha) + p_t s_t X_{t+1} + p_t T_t = m_t + b_t + p_t X_t \qquad \text{(A-66)}$$

and

$$p_t C_t + q_t b_{t+1}(1 + \alpha) + p_t s_t X_{t+1} + p_t T_t + m_{t+1}(1 + \alpha)$$
$$= m_t + b_t + p_t X_t + p_t z N_t. \qquad \text{(A-67)}$$

The representative consumer's problem is to choose C_t, N_t, b_{t+1}, X_{t+1}, and m_{t+1} in each period $t = 0, 1, 2, \ldots, \infty$, to maximize (A-60) subject to the constraints (A-66) and (A-67). We can simplify the problem by formulating it as a dynamic program. Letting $v(m_t, b_t, X_t; p_t, q_t, s_t)$ denote the value function, the Bellman equation associated with the consumer's problem is

$$v(m_t, b_t, X_t; p_t, q_t, s_t) = \max_{C_t, N_t, b_{t+1}, X_{t+1}, m_{t+1}} [U(C_t) - V(N_t)$$

$$+ \beta v(m_{t+1}, b_{t+1}, X_{t+1}; p_{t+1}, q_{t+1}, s_{t+1})],$$

subject to (A-66) and (A-67). Letting λ_t and μ_t denote the Lagrange multipliers associated with the constraints (A-66) and (A-67), the first-order conditions for an optimum are

$$U'(C_t) - (\lambda_t + \mu_t)p_t = 0, \tag{A-68}$$

$$- V'(N_t) + \mu_t p_t z = 0, \tag{A-69}$$

$$- q_{t+1}(1 + \alpha)(\lambda_t + \mu_t) + \beta \frac{\partial v}{\partial b_{t+1}} = 0, \tag{A-70}$$

$$- p_t s_t(\lambda_t + \mu_t) + \beta \frac{\partial v}{\partial X_{t+1}} = 0, \tag{A-71}$$

$$- (1 + \alpha)\mu_t + \beta \frac{\partial v}{\partial m_{t+1}} = 0. \tag{A-72}$$

We can also derive the following envelope conditions by differentiating the Bellman equation and applying the envelope theorem:

$$\frac{\partial v}{\partial b_t} = \lambda_t + \mu_t; \tag{A-73}$$

$$\frac{\partial v}{\partial X_t} = p_t(\lambda_t + \mu_t); \tag{A-74}$$

$$\frac{\partial v}{\partial m_t} = \lambda_t + \mu_t. \tag{A-75}$$

Now, we can use the envelope conditions, equations (A-73) to (A-75), updated one period, to substitute for the derivatives of the value function in (A-70) to (A-72), and then use (A-68) and (A-69) to substitute for the Lagrange multipliers in (A-70) to (A-72), obtaining

$$\frac{-q_t(1 + \alpha)U'(C_t)}{p_t} + \beta \frac{U'(C_{t+1})}{p_{t+1}} = 0, \tag{A-76}$$

$$-s_t U'(C_t) + \beta U'(C_{t+1}) = 0, \tag{A-77}$$

$$\frac{-(1 + \alpha)V'(N_t)}{p_t z} + \beta \frac{U'(C_{t+1})}{p_{t+1}} = 0. \tag{A-78}$$

Next, the market-clearing conditions are

$$m_t = 1, \quad b_t = 0, \quad X_t = 0,$$

for all t; that is, money demand equals money supply, the demand for nominal bonds equals the zero net supply of nominal bonds, and the demand for real bonds equals the zero net supply of these bonds as well, in each period. Substituting the market-clearing conditions in equations (A-66) and (A-67) and using equation (A-65) to substitute for T_t, we obtain

$$p_t C_t = 1 + \alpha, \tag{A-79}$$

$$C_t = zN_t. \tag{A-80}$$

Equations (A-69) and (A-80) state, respectively, that all money is held in equilibrium at the beginning of the period by the representative consumer and is used to purchase consumption goods and that in equilibrium all output produced is consumed.

Now, there is an equilibrium where $C_t = C$, $N_t = N$, $p_t = p$, $q_t = q$, and $s_t = s$, for all t, and we can use equations (A-76) to (A-80) to solve for C, N, p, q, and s. We obtain

$$q = \frac{\beta}{1 + \alpha}, \tag{A-81}$$

$$s = \beta, \tag{A-82}$$

$$(1 + \alpha)V'(N) - \beta z U'(zN) = 0, \tag{A-83}$$

$$C = zN, \tag{A-84}$$

$$p = \frac{1 + \alpha}{C} \tag{A-85}$$

Here, equations (A-81) and (A-82) give solutions for q and s, respectively, while equation (A-83) solves implicitly for N. Then, given the solution for N, we can solve recursively for C and p from (A-84) and (A-85). We can solve for the Lagrange multiplier λ using Equations (A-68), (A-69), (A-79), (A-80), and (A-83), to get

$$\lambda = \frac{CU'(C)}{1 + \alpha}\left(1 - \frac{\beta}{1 + \alpha}\right) = \frac{CU'(C)}{1 + \alpha}(1 - q) \tag{A-86}$$

Now, note that the nominal interest rate is determined by the price of the nominal bond q, as $R = \frac{1}{q} - 1$, so that the nominal interest rate is positive as long as $q < 1$. From (A-81), the nominal interest rate is positive when $\alpha > \beta - 1$, that is, as long as the money growth rate is sufficiently large. The Lagrange multiplier associated with the cash-in-advance constraint is positive, that is, $\lambda > 0$ if and only if $q < 1$. Thus, a positive nominal interest rate is associated with a binding cash-in-advance constraint.

From equation (A-81), the nominal interest rate is

$$R = \frac{1 + \alpha}{\beta} - 1.$$

The real interest rate is $\frac{1}{s} - 1$; from equation (A-82) this is

$$r = \frac{1}{\beta} - 1,$$

which is the representative consumer's subjective rate of time preference. Further, the inflation rate is

$$i = \frac{P_{t+1}}{P_t} - 1 = \frac{p_{t+1}\overline{M}_{t+1}}{P_t\overline{M}_t} - 1 = \alpha,$$

so that the inflation rate is equal to the money growth rate. Now, from the above, it is clear that the Fisher relation holds, as

$$1 + r = \frac{1 + R}{1 + i}$$

The effects of money growth on real variables can be obtained by totally differentiating equation (A-83) with respect to N and α and solving to obtain

$$\frac{dN}{d\alpha} = \frac{-V'}{(1 + \alpha)V'' - \beta z^2 U''} < 0;$$

thus, employment declines with an increase in the money growth rate, and because $Y = C = zN$ in equilibrium, output and consumption also decline. This effect arises because inflation distorts intertemporal decisions. Period t labor income is held as cash and not spent on consumption until period $t + 1$, and it is, therefore, eroded by inflation. Higher inflation then reduces labor supply, output, and consumption.

What is the optimal rate of inflation? To determine a Pareto optimum, we solve the social planner's problem, which is to solve

$$\max_{\{C_t, N_t\}_{t=0}^{\infty}} \sum_{t=0}^{\infty} \beta^t [U(C_t) - V(N_t)]$$

subject to $C_t = zN_t$ for all t. The solution to this problem is characterized by the first-order condition

$$zU'(zN^*) - V'(N^*) = 0,$$

where N^* is optimal employment in each period t. In equilibrium, employment N is determined by equation (A-83), and equilibrium employment is equal to N^* for the case where $\alpha = \beta - 1$. The optimal money growth rate $\beta - 1$ characterizes a Friedman rule, as this implies from (A-81) that the nominal interest rate is zero and that the inflation rate is $\beta - 1$, so that the rate of return on money is $\frac{1}{\beta} - 1$, which is identical to the real interest rate r. From (A-86), the cash-in-advance constraint does not bind when $\alpha = \beta - 1$, because $\lambda = 0$. Thus, a Friedman rule relaxes the cash-in-advance constraint and causes the rates of return on all assets to be equated in equilibrium.

Problem

1. Suppose in the monetary intertemporal model that $U(C) = 2C^{\frac{1}{2}}$ and $V(N) = (\frac{1}{2})N^2$. Determine closed-form solutions for consumption, employment, output, the nominal interest rate, and the real interest rate. What are the effects of changes in z and α in equilibrium? Explain your results.

Chapter 16: Money Inflation, and Banking

We work through formal results for two models here, which are a Kiyotaki–Wright monetary search model and the Diamond–Dybvig banking model. The results on money growth using the monetary intertemporal model are derived in the previous section.

A Kiyotaki–Wright Monetary Search Model

Here, we develop a version of the Kiyotaki–Wright random matching model to show how fiat money can overcome an absence-of-double-coincidence-of-wants problem. This model is closely related to the one constructed by Alberto Trejos and Randall Wright in an article in the *Journal of Political Economy,*[3] and it generalizes the model of Chapter 15 to a case where there are n different goods rather than three. To work through this model requires an elementary knowledge of probability.

In the model, there are n different types of consumers and n different goods, where $n \geq 3$. Each consumer is infinite-lived and maximizes

$$E_0 \sum_{t=0}^{\infty} \left(\frac{1}{1+r} \right)^t U_t,$$

where E_0 is the expectations operator conditional on information at $t = 0$, r is the consumer's subjective discount rate, and U_t is the utility from consuming in period t, where $U_t = 0$ if nothing is consumed. Given that the consumer faces uncertainty, we have assumed that he or she is an expected-utility maximizer. A consumer of type i produces good i and consumes good $i + 1$, for $i = 1, 2, 3, \ldots, n - 1$, and a type n consumer produces good n and consumes good 1. If $n = 3$, then this is the same setup we considered in Chapter 15. In this n-good model, there is an absence-of-double-coincidence problem, as no two consumers produce what each other wants.

Goods are indivisible, so that when a good is produced, the consumer produces only one unit. At $t = 0$, a fraction M of the population is endowed with one unit of fiat money each, and fiat money is also indivisible. Further, a consumer can hold at most one unit of some object at a time, so that at the end of any period a consumer is holding one unit of a good, one unit of money, or nothing. It is costless to produce a good and costless to hold one unit of a good or money as inventory.

At the end of period 0, each consumer not holding money produces a good, and then he or she holds this in inventory until period 1. In period 1, consumers are matched

[3]See A. Trejos and R. Wright, 1995, "Search, Bargaining, Money, and Prices," *Journal of Political Economy* 103, 118–141.

two-by-two and at random, so that a given consumer meets only one other consumer during period 1. Two consumers who meet inspect each other's goods and announce whether they are willing to trade. If both are willing, they trade, and any consumer receiving his or her consumption good in a trade consumes it (this is optimal), receives utility $u > 0$ from consumption, and produces another good. Then consumers move on to period 2, and so on. No two consumers meet more than once, because there are infinitely many consumers in the population. We assume that there are equal numbers of each type of consumer, so that the fraction of the population who are of a given type is $\frac{1}{n}$. Then, in any period, the probability that a consumer meets another consumer of a particular type is $\frac{1}{n}$.

What can be an equilibrium in this model? One equilibrium is where money is not valued. That is, if no one accepts money, then no one wants to hold it and, because of the absence-of-double-coincidence problem, there is no exchange and everyone's utility is zero. If no one has faith that money has value in exchange, then this expectation is self-fulfilling. A more interesting equilibrium is one where everyone accepts money. Here, we let μ denote the fraction of the population that holds money in equilibrium, V_g denotes the value of holding a good in equilibrium, and V_m is the value of holding money. Although there are n different goods, the optimization problems of all consumers are identical in equilibrium, so the value of holding any good is the same for each consumer. The Bellman equations associated with a consumer's optimization problem are

$$V_g = \frac{1}{1+r}\left[(1 - \mu)V_g + \mu\left(1 - \frac{1}{n}\right)V_g + \mu\frac{1}{n}(V_m - V_g)\right], \qquad \text{(A-87)}$$

$$V_m = \frac{1}{1+r}\left[(1 - \mu)\left(1 - \frac{1}{n}\right)V_m + (1 - \mu)\frac{1}{n}(u + V_g) + \mu V_m\right]. \quad \text{(A-88)}$$

In equation (A-87), the value of holding a good at the end of the current period is equal to the discounted sum of the expected payoff in the following period. In the following period, the consumer meets another agent with a good with probability $1 - \mu$, in which case trade does not take place, and the consumer is holding a good at the end of the next period and receives value V_g. With probability $\mu(1 - \frac{1}{n})$, the consumer meets another consumer with money who does not wish to purchase the consumer's good, and again trade does not take place. With probability $\mu\frac{1}{n}$, the consumer meets a consumer with money who wants his or her good, trade takes place, and the consumer is holding money at the end of the next period. In equation (A-88), a consumer with money does not trade with another consumer who has money or with another consumer who has a good that he or she does not consume. However, with probability $(1 - \mu)\frac{1}{n}$ the consumer meets another consumer with his or her consumption good, in which case trade takes place, the consumer gets utility u from consuming the good, and then he or she produces another good.

We can solve for V_g and V_m from equations (A-87) and (A-88), which give

$$V_g = \frac{\mu(1 - \mu)u}{rn(1 + rn)},$$

$$V_m = \frac{(rn + \mu)(1 - \mu)u}{rn(1 + rn)},$$

so that

$$V_m - V_g = \frac{(1 - \mu)u}{1 + rn} > 0.$$

Therefore, the value of holding money is greater than the value of holding a good, so that everyone accepts money (as conjectured) in equilibrium. Further, consumers who have money in any period prefer to hold it rather than producing a good, and so we have $\mu = M$ in equilibrium.

The values of V_g and V_m are the utilities that consumers receive from holding goods and money, respectively. As $V_g > 0$ and $V_m > 0$, everyone is better off in an economy where money is used than in one where it is not used.

Problem

1. Suppose a search economy with the possibility of double coincidences; that is, assume that when an agent produces a good, she cannot consume it herself. In a random match where two agents meet and each has the good that they produced, the first agent has what the second consumes with probability x, the second has what the first consumes with probability x, and each has what the other consumes with probability x^2.

   (a) In this economy, show that there are three equilibria; a barter equilibrium where money is not accepted, an equilibrium where an agent with a good is indifferent between accepting and not accepting money, and an equilibrium where agents with goods always accept money.

   (b) Show that x needs to be sufficiently small before having money in this economy actually increases welfare over having barter, and explain this result.

The Diamond–Dybvig Banking Model

There are three periods, 0, 1, and 2, and an intertemporal technology that allows one unit of the period 0 good to be converted into $1 + r$ units of the period 2 good. The intertemporal technology can be interrupted in period 1, with a yield of one unit in period 1 for each unit of input in period 0. If production is interrupted in period 1, there is no return in period 2. Goods can be stored from period 1 to period 2 with no depreciation. There is a continuum of consumers with unit mass, and each consumer maximizes expected utility

$$W = tU(c_1) + (1 - t)U(c_2),$$

where c_i is the consumer's consumption if he or she consumes in period i, for $i = 1, 2$, and t is the probability that the consumer consumes early. Here, t is also the fraction of agents who are early consumers. We assume that t is known in period 0, but consumers do not know their type (early or late consumer) until period 1. Each consumer is endowed with one unit of goods in period 0.

Suppose that there are no banks, but consumers can trade investment projects in period 1, with one project selling for the price p in terms of consumption goods. Then, each consumer chooses to invest all of his or her goods in the technology in period 0, and in period 1 a consumer must decide how much of the investment to interrupt and how many investment projects to buy and sell. In period 1 an early consumer wants to sell the investment project if $p > 1$ and will want to interrupt the investment project and consume the proceeds if $p < 1$. The early consumer is indifferent if $p = 1$. A late consumer in period 1 wants to interrupt the investment project and purchase investment projects if $p < 1$, chooses to hold the investment project if $p > 1$, and is indifferent if $p = 1$. The equilibrium price is, therefore, $p = 1$, and in equilibrium fraction t of all projects is interrupted in period 1, early consumers each consume $c_1 = 1$, and late consumers consume $c_2 = 1 + r$. Expected utility for each consumer in period 0 is

$$W_1 = tU(1) + (1 - t)U(1 + r).$$

Now, suppose that there is a bank that takes deposits from consumers in period 0, serves depositors sequentially in period 1 (places in line are drawn at random), and offers a deposit contract (d_1, d_2), where d_1 is the amount that can be withdrawn in period 1 for each unit deposited, and d_2 is the amount that can be withdrawn in period 2 for each unit deposited. Assume that all consumers deposit in the bank in period 0. Then, the bank chooses d_1, d_2, and x, the quantity of production to interrupt, to solve:

$$\max[tU(d_1) + (1 - t)U(d_2)] \qquad \text{(A-89)}$$

subject to

$$td_1 = x, \qquad \text{(A-90)}$$

$$(1 - t)d_2 = (1 - x)(1 + r), \qquad \text{(A-91)}$$

$$d_1 \leq d_2 \qquad \text{(A-92)}$$

Here, equation (A-90) is the bank's resource constraint in period 1, (A-91) is the resource constraint in period 2, and (A-92) is an incentive constraint, which states that it must be in the interest of late consumers to withdraw late rather than posing as early consumers and withdrawing early.

Ignoring the constraint (A-92), substituting for d_1 and d_2 using the constraints (A-90) and (A-91) in the objective function (A-89), the first-order condition for an optimum is

$$U'\left(\frac{x}{t}\right) = (1 + r)U'\left(\frac{(1 - x)(1 + r)}{1 - t}\right) \qquad \text{(A-93)}$$

with $d_1 = \frac{x}{t}$ and $d_2 = \frac{(1 - x)(1 + r)}{1 - t}$. Equation (A-93) then implies that $d_1 < d_2$ so that (A-92) is satisfied. Further, if we assume that $\frac{-cU''(c)}{U'(c)} > 1$, then (A-93) implies that $d_1 > 1$ and $d_2 < 1 + r$. Thus, under this condition, the bank provides consumers with insurance against the need for liquid assets in period 1, and the bank gives consumers higher expected utility than when there was no bank ($d_1 = 1$ and $d_2 = 1 + r$ if the bank chooses $x = t$).

However, there also exists a bank-run equilibrium. That is, if a late consumer expects all other consumers to run to the bank in period 1, he or she will want to do it as well.

Problems

1. Suppose that consumers can meet and trade in period 1 instead of going to the bank in sequence. Show that, given the banking contract (d_1, d_2), there could be Pareto-improving trades that early and late consumers could make in period 1 that would undo the banking contract, so that this would not constitute an equilibrium. Discuss your results.

2. Show that, if $U(c) = \ln c$, then there is no need for a bank in the Diamond–Dybvig economy, and explain this result.

Chapter 17: Unemployment: Search and Efficiency Wages

In this section we formally set up the search model of unemployment from Chapter 16, derive some of the results for that model, and construct an illustrative example. For this model, an elementary knowledge of probability is useful.

In the search model, the infinite-lived worker has preferences given by

$$E_0 \sum_{t=0}^{\infty} \left(\frac{1}{1+r}\right)^t U(C_t),$$

where E_0 is the expectation operator conditional on information known in period 0, r is the subjective discount rate, C_t is consumption, and $U(\cdot)$ is the period utility function, which is strictly increasing, continuous, and strictly concave. Here, because the worker faces uncertainty, we have assumed that he or she is an expected-utility maximizer.

A worker who is employed at a job paying the real wage w supplies one unit of labor during the period and consumes his or her labor earnings (we assume no savings). There is a probability s, where $0 < s < 1$, that the worker will be separated from his or her job and become unemployed at the end of the period. We let $V_e(w)$ denote the value of being employed at the real wage w, and V_u the value of being unemployed, where both values are calculated as of the end of the current period. Then, the Bellman equation for an employed worker is

$$V_e(w) = \frac{1}{1+r}[U(w) + sV_u + (1-s)V_e(w)]. \tag{A-94}$$

that is, the value of being employed at the end of the current period is the present discounted value of the utility from employment next period plus the expected value at the end of the period, given the separation rate s.

Next, a worker who is unemployed receives the unemployment insurance benefit b at the beginning of the period, and then with probability p receives a wage offer, which is a random draw from the probability distribution $F(w)$, which has the associated probability density function $f(w)$. Assume that $w \in [0, \overline{w}]$, where $\overline{w} > 0$. The unemployed worker must decide whether to accept a given wage offer or turn it down. Thus, the value of unemployment is given by

$$V_u = \frac{1}{1+r}\left\{U(b) + (1-p)V_u + p\int_0^{\overline{w}} \max[V_u, V_e(w)]f(w)dw\right\}, \tag{A-95}$$

so that the value of being unemployed at the end of the current period is equal to the discounted value of the utility from consuming the unemployment benefit plus the probability of remaining unemployed times the value of remaining unemployed plus the probability of receiving a job offer times the expected value of the job offer.

Equations (A-94) and (A-95) can be simplified, respectively, as follows:

$$rV_e(w) = U(w) + s[V_u - V_e(w)] \tag{A-96}$$

$$rV_u = U(b) + p \int_0^{\bar{w}} \max[0, V_e(w) - V_u] f(w) dw \tag{A-97}$$

From equation (A-96), we can solve for $V_e(w)$ to get

$$V_e(w) = \frac{U(w) + sV_u}{r + s},$$

so that $V_e(w)$ inherits the properties of $U(w)$—that is, it is strictly increasing, continuous, and strictly concave. This implies that the worker accepts any wage offer greater than or equal to w^* and rejects any offer less than w^*, where w^* solves

$$V_e(w^*) = V_u.$$

That is, w^* is the reservation wage, at which the worker is just indifferent between accepting the job offer and remaining unemployed.

To determine the unemployment rate, the flow of workers from employment to unemployment must be equal to the flow from unemployment to employment in the steady state, or

$$s(1 - U) = p[1 - F(w^*)]U;$$

solving for the unemployment rate U, we obtain

$$U = \frac{s}{p[1 - F(w^*)] + s}.$$

An example shows how the model works. Suppose that, conditional on receiving a wage offer, an unemployed worker receives a wage offer w_1 with probability π and a wage offer of zero with probability $1 - \pi$, where $0 < \pi < 1$. Then, conjecturing that a wage offer of w_1 is always accepted and a wage offer of zero is always turned down, equations (A-96) and (A-97) in this case give

$$rV_e = U(w_1) + s(V_u - V_e),$$

$$rV_u = U(b) + p\pi(V_e - V_u),$$

where V_e is the value of being employed at the real wage w_1. Then, solving the above two equations for V_e and V_u, we get

$$V_e = \frac{(p\pi + r)U(w_1) + sU(b)}{r(s + p\pi + r)},$$

$$V_u = \frac{(s + r)U(b) + p\pi U(w_1)}{r(s + p\pi + r)},$$

with

$$Ve - Vu = \frac{U(w_1) - U(b)}{s + p\pi + r}.$$

Therefore, we have $V_u > 0$, so that a wage offer of zero will be turned down as conjectured, even if the unemployment insurance benefit b is zero. Further, the wage offer of w_1 will be accepted if and only if $w_1 \geq b$, that is, if the wage on the job is higher than the unemployment insurance benefit. The unemployment rate is

$$U = \frac{s}{p\pi + s},$$

but if $b > w_1$, then no one would accept jobs, and we would have $U = 1$ and everyone would be unemployed. This is an extreme example of how an increase in the unemployment insurance benefit can increase the unemployment rate.

Problem

1. Suppose in the search model that an unemployed worker receives a wage offer with probability π. Then, conditional on receiving a wage offer, the offer is w_1 with probability α_1, w_2 with probability α_2, and zero with probability $1 - \alpha_1 - \alpha_2$, where $0 < w_1 < w_2$. Determine under what conditions an unemployed worker would turn down a wage offer of w_1, accepting a wage offer of w_2, and under what conditions an unemployed worker would accept any wage offer greater than zero. Interpret these conditions.

Chapter 18: Inflation, the Phillips Curve, and Central Bank Commitment

In this section we construct a somewhat more explicit version of the model we worked with in Chapter 17 to show some of the results of that chapter more formally.

The first component of the model is the Phillips curve relationship, which captures the key idea in the Friedman-Lucas money surprise model of Chapter 11. That is,

$$i - i^e = a(Y - Y^T), \tag{A-98}$$

where i is the inflation rate, i^e is the private sector's anticipated inflation rate, $a > 0$, Y is aggregate output, and Y^T is trend output. The second component of the model is the preferences of the central bank, which we represent by supposing that the central bank maximizes $f(Y, i)$, where $f(\cdot, \cdot)$ is a function. That is, the central bank cares about the level of output and the inflation rate. It is convenient to express $f(Y, i)$ as a quadratic function, that is,

$$f(Y, i) = \alpha(i - i^*)^2 + \beta(Y - Y^*)^2, \tag{A-99}$$

where α and β are negative constants, i^* is the target inflation rate for the central bank, and Y^* is the target level of aggregate output for the central bank.

Now, suppose, according to the central bank learning story, that the central bank treats the anticipated inflation rate i^e as being given and chooses i and Y to maximize equation (A-99) given (A-98). Solving this optimization problem, the central bank then chooses

$$i = \frac{\alpha a^2 i^* + \beta i^e - \beta a(Y^T - Y^*)}{\alpha a^2 + \beta}. \tag{A-100}$$

We then have

$$i - i^e = \frac{\alpha a^2 (i^* - i^e) - \beta a(Y^T - Y^*)}{\alpha a^2 + \beta}.$$

In this circumstance, if the central bank had a target level of output that was higher than trend output—that is, $Y^T - Y^* < 0$—then even if $i^e > i^*$, in which case anticipated inflation is higher than the target inflation rate, the central bank may want to have $i > i^e$ so that the private sector is fooled by positive surprise inflation. Ultimately, though, the private sector is not fooled in the long run, so that $i = i^e$, and if the central bank learns this, then it realizes that, from (A-98), it cannot engineer a level of output other than Y^T, and the best strategy for the central bank is to set $i = i^*$.

Under the central bank commitment story, the central bank cannot commit to an inflation rate, and it is playing a game with the private sector. The private sector first chooses i^e, then the central bank chooses i, and in equilibrium $i = i^e$. In this case equation (A-100) is the central bank's reaction function, and we can solve for the equilibrium inflation rate by substituting $i = i^e$ in (A-100) getting

$$i = i^* + \frac{\beta}{\alpha a}(Y^* - Y^T);$$

hence, if $Y^* > Y^T$, in equilibrium the inflation rate is higher than i^*, which is the inflation rate the central bank would choose if it could tie its hands and commit itself to an inflation policy.

Problem

1. Suppose that, instead of expectations being rational, expectations are adaptive. That is, each period the private sector expects that the inflation rate will be what it was the previous period. That is, $i^e = i_{-1}$, where i_{-1} is the actual inflation rate last period. Under these circumstances, determine what the actual inflation rate and the level of output will be, given i_{-1}. How will the inflation rate and output evolve over time? What will the inflation rate and the level of output be in the long run? Explain your results.

Index

Page numbers with *f* indicate figures; those with *t* indicate tables.